W9-BDL-670

THE WINES
OF
FRANCE

THE WINES
OF
FRANCE

CLIVE COATES M.W.

WINE APPRECIATION GUILD

First Published in the United States by
The Wine Appreciation Guild Ltd.
South San Francisco, CA 94080
(650) 866–3020
FAX (650) 866–3532

Reprinted 1992
Revised Edition 1999

Originally published in Great Britain by
Century Editions, an imprint of the
Random Century Group Ltd.

Clive Coates's right to be identified as the author
of this work has been asserted by him in accordance
with the Copyright, Designs and Patents Acts, 1988.

ISBN 1–891267–14–0

Original Editor Fiona Holman
Original Designer Behram Kapadia
Maps by José Stocker
Illustrations from La Vigne by Bertall, Paris 1878

CONTENTS

MAPS

Preface

Good wine is never too dear – the bad always is.
– *Patrick de Ladoucette*

Vinous France can be separated as Caesar divided Gaul into three parts. There is the north – the departments which front the English Channel – which the French, with an atypical lack of chauvinism, call La Manche. Here there are no vines. Next there is the bulk of France – from the point of view of area – where the vine is occasionally the supreme fruit, but where in the main the vineyards are interspersed with woodland and meadow, fruit trees, cereal crops and market gardens. And finally there is the south, paradoxically called the Midi, the land of the olive as well as the vine. Here, between the seaside resorts and the rocky *garrigues* in the foothills of the Alps, the Cévennes and the Pyrenees the vine is supreme, the land monocultural, producing millions and millions of hectolitres of largely indifferent, insipid, barely legitimate wine. Yet here can also be found some of the most exciting, value-for-money bottles in the whole of France.

My object in writing this book is to cover *all* the wines of France – or at least all that are worthy of note. Too many books covering the whole of France spend a disproportionate amount of text on the great areas – Bordeaux, Burgundy and Champagne – already well covered separately, and neglect the remainder. I have tried to redress this imbalance.

Fine wine, good wine, wine that is worth drinking – call it what you will – comes from all over France, from the Minervois as well as the Médoc, from Bandol as well as Beaune, from Cahors as well as Champagne. The country is prolific; prolific in its number of different soils, grape varieties and methods of making wine. There is a wealth – perhaps unrivalled throughout the world – of good wine; some, obviously, is classic, rare, expensive; more, perhaps more than some people realize, is remarkable value, within the means of anyone who cares to drink wine regularly. I have attempted to note all the best growers in every single *appellation*.

It is the variety of French wine which fascinates me. For most of the twenty years that I spent as a wine merchant before 'retiring' to become a full-time wine writer at the end of 1984 I specialized in the wines of France. Every year I would spend weeks if not months touring round the highways and byways of France rootling out good growers in unexpected areas, importing their wines and – with a reasonable degree of success – introducing them into the English market. It would be rash to be too positive, but I *think* that I may have been the first to ship the wines of Fronton and the Côtes Roannaises, Bellet, Bugey and Vins d'Orléanais to Britain. I hope I also did something to give the wines of Bandol the full recognition that they deserve.

Unearthing the best sources was sometimes difficult, often frustrating and inevitably tiring; but always – and there is no other word for it - fun. I remember the first time I seriously investigated the wines of Cahors. Armed with a list from the local Syndicat d'Initiative I arrived in the town on a bleak and crisp February afternoon, and, as was my custom, descended to the local one-star restaurant for a meal in the evening. I had discovered that you could rely on the indigenous gastronomic centres to list at least most of the good local growers in their wine lists. A little preliminary tasting would prepare me – by setting a few yardsticks – for what I would uncover during the next couple of days.

The restaurant (I have not supped there these last ten years and it has since disappeared from the guides) was a long, thin, dark cavern in the old town of Cahors. Trade was calm in February, and apart from a quartet of local businessmen I was the sole client. On the wine list they offered nine Cahors, but at a combined price of a bottle of decent Meursault (which they didn't have) or a flagon of Champagne. I ordered all nine. '*Grandes bouteilles?*' asked the incredulous Madame (there were no halves). '*Oui*', I nodded.

I proceeded to take my notes on all nine to the accompaniment of some home-made *foie gras* and a *confit de canard*. The best part of the meal as I remember was an absolutely delicious *gratin* of chicory.

Madame stopped occasionally to check that I was not drinking myself insensible and eventually her husband, the chef, ambled by. I had already explained my purpose was degustatory rather than inebriation and I didn't have to push him too hard before he began telling me who was who in the Cahors *vignoble*. The local quartet soon joined us, finished up my nine bottles, and before too long my list of sixty-odd growers to visit had been whittled down to a nucleus of eight. In return I was fed countless different twenty-year-old vintage armagnacs – down the side of the dining-room was a low shelf ranked with large bottles the size of *impériales* in which it is customary to imprison this nectar – and given the run-down on the local political situation, the world and the universe as it appeared to the inhabitants of south-west France. The next day I swiftly snapped up the best available grower in the area, and, having saved a day on my schedule, celebrated by touring the magnificent Gorges du Tarn and some of its extraordinary grottoes. An evening well spent.

While it never occurred to me in those far-off days that one day I would attempt to write a book on the whole of France's wines, it was nevertheless a private ambition to visit and taste extensively in every single *appellation contrôlée* and VDQS (*Vins Delimités de Qualité Supérieure*). Finally in the autumn of 1982 I arrived at Irouléguy at the Basque end of the Pyrenees. I had made it! (Not that the journey was worth it, as it happens.)

I have made many other vinous excursions: to the vineyard on top of the battlements of the Château at Angers, to that in Montmartre in Paris (on the Rue Gordon Bennett, would you believe), to several vineyards in the Savoie which proclaim themselves as the highest vineyard in the country and to another near Collioure which lies both in France and in Spain. This pilgrimage has been the result of a love of France, its people, its food, its wines, its countryside and its climate. Long may this love affair continue!

The French vineyard scene and the standard and styles of its wines develop and change at a pace with which no one individual can keep up. Though I have spent a great deal of time in France in the last three and a half decades no single person can cover everyone, every region even, every year: every rising star, every change of management, every declining reputation. It would be like attempting a one-man Michelin Guide. I have followed up the suggestions of my friends, consulted the wine lists of merchants I trust and restaurants I approve and attempted to examine each district in as much depth as possible. Everyone discussed or recommended in the pages which follow is personally known to me and their wines I have known very well in the 1980s and 1990s. But there is bound to be the odd important producer who has been unwittingly excluded. My apologies to them in advance. The mistakes will, I trust, be rectified in a new edition of *The Wines of France*.

Clive Coates
London, January 1999

ACKNOWLEDGMENTS
A very large number of people have helped me to write this book. Indeed almost every grower or merchant I have met in the last twenty-five years or more has contributed in some way.

My chief acknowledgments must therefore be extended to the hospitality of the wine producers of France. Particular thanks though are due to several friends who read the first drafts of some of the chapters: to William Bolter in Bordeaux; to Becky Wasserman and Russell Hone in Burgundy; to Robin Yapp; to Tom Stevenson; to Rosemary George MW; to John Bertaut and Martin Sookias. Any errors which might remain, I hasten to add, are all mine.

I must also thank Food and Wine from France, the London office of the Champagne Bureau and the local offices of the various French wine regions for background information, statistics and other suggestions. Lastly I extend my deepest gratitude to my wife Juliet and my secretary Alison Bean for their support, their enthusiasm and their unfailing good humour during the gestation of this book. What would I have done without them?

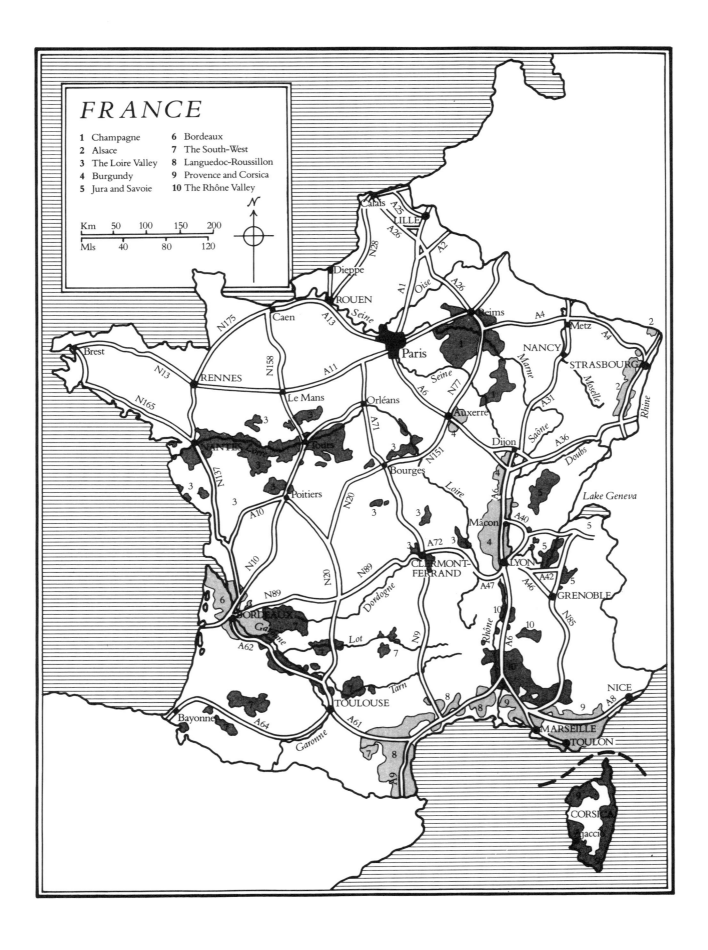

FRANCE

1 Champagne
2 Alsace
3 The Loire Valley
4 Burgundy
5 Jura and Savoie
6 Bordeaux
7 The South-West
8 Languedoc-Roussillon
9 Provence and Corsica
10 The Rhône Valley

N

Km   50   100   150   200
Mls   40   80   120

FRANCE

France is the greatest wine-producing country in the world. This is no idle boast. No other country produces a larger volume of quality wine; no other country produces it in such diversity. There are just under a million hectares of vineyard in France, creating an annual volume of some 70 million hectolitres of wine. Forty-seven per cent of this surface area is authorized for wine of *appellation contrôlee* or VDQS standard. Thirty per cent of the total volume produced is of this quality. This is the equivalent of some 240 million cases of quality wine. No other country can claim this amount of top standard wine.

There are said to be as many as a thousand different varieties of grape planted in Italy. France has fewer, but it has many more that produce wine of yardstick quality; many more that winemakers in the 'New World' — the United States, Australasia and South America — want to import and try out for themselves. What other country can rival the glorious variegation of Cabernet Sauvignon, Pinot Noir, Syrah, Merlot, Cabernet Franc, Mourvèdre and Grenache for red wines; of Chardonnay, Sauvignon, Sémillon, Chenin, Marsanne, Viognier, Gewürztraminer and Riesling for whites? Only Germany, with its own version of Riesling, and Italy with its Sangiovese Grosso and Nebbiolo can offer serious additions to this list of first-division grape varieties.

The first country to implement a system of legislation codifying viticultural and horticultural practices and protecting geographical names of origin, France today has some 450 different *appellations d'origine*. In many regions there is an additional hierarchical system, isolating the best vineyard and domaines from the rest. The fact that a wine comes from a *premier* or *grand cru* vineyard or a classed growth estate does not in itself ensure that it is of top quality, but it must be of considerable help to the consumer in making his choice of what to buy and what to avoid. The diversity of different *appellations* is complex, but the range of styles and tastes is unrivalled.

Moreover — and this may indeed be the explanation for France's pre-eminence — she has been growing and exporting fine wine far longer than most. Once again only the Rhineland, one or two isolated pockets in Italy, and the fortified wine centres of Jerez, Oporto and Madeira have as long a history of quality wine production as Bordeaux and Burgundy, the Rhône and Champagne.

The history of wine in France is inextricably bound up with the political and socio-economic evolution of the country. The vine was introduced by Phoenician and Greek traders. From about 600 BC onwards they formed settlements along the Mediterranean coast. Wine was certainly imported. Whether and indeed when the vine was introduced is less certain, but amphorae, coins and other artifacts dating from the pre-Roman period have been found as far north as Burgundy.

The subjugation of the northern part of the country by Julius Caesar in the middle of the first century BC — Roman power had already been long-established in the Midi — followed by the colonization of this country in the time of Augustus and his great general, Agrippa, brought the technique of vine cultivation and wine production to France; and the impetus was swift. At the time of the birth of Christ there is no clear evidence of wines in France outside the Midi; beyond Vienne to the north, or Gaillac to the west. But by AD 71 Pliny records that there were wines in Bordeaux; there were vineyards in the vicinity of Augustodunum (present-day Autun in Burgundy), capital of the Aedui, the Romans' first allies in Gaul; and the vine had reached Paris (Lutetia) and Trier (Augusta Treverorum) by the turn of the century.

It is customary to consider the decline and fall of the Roman Empire and the replacement of its civilization in France by the ravaging incursions of barbarian tribes such as the Alamans, the Goths, the Visigoths and the Franks as one of the world's all time great disasters. This is not wholly true. These tribes were not just old enemies, waiting impatiently on the Empire's borders for authority to crumble, but customers as well. When the Roman legions departed the vineyards were not completely destroyed, nor were all their magnificent constructions put to the torch. The barbarians, for the most part, simply moved in to fill the vacuum. Moreover, one great Roman institution remained in Gaul, the established Christian church. With typical efficiency the Romans had created a system of dioceses throughout the country, a hierarchical system of bishops and priests. Parallel to this was an embryonic monastical order, its heyday still to come. One of the greatest achievements of the early Christian church was the maintenance of organized agriculture, of which the traditions of viticulture and viniculture were a vital part, throughout the Dark Ages.

By the time of the re-emergence of 'civilization' around the time of Charles Martel and his grandson Charlemagne and the establishment of the Holy Roman (and Christian) Empire in AD 800, the focus of Western Europe had moved to Aachen, and it was the Rhineland that experienced the first expansion of viticulture since Roman times. That in France followed somewhat later. In northern and eastern France the driving force was the church. The great abbey at Cluny in the Mâconnais was founded in AD 910 and its tentacles rapidly spread as it spawned a multitude of sister, subsidiary establishments through Europe. Two centuries later the rival Cistercian order was formed at Citeaux near Dijon. The church was financed by a system of tithes. In theory the laity had to pay a tenth of their agricultural income, in cash or in goods, to the ecclesiastical authorities. In practice the percentage was less, and there were other ways of meeting one's obligations — or of avoiding them.

The church soon grew fat. As their economic influence grew, so did their political clout. And their land-holdings increased likewise, swelled by donations from the aristocracy, anxious to ensure their favourable reception in the life to come. Wine was a valuable commodity, together with cloth the mainstay of the French economy at the time, and the church gave every encouragement to the establishment of vineyards. Its influence, particularly in Burgundy, was paramount.

Meanwhile Bordeaux, in the South-West, slumbered in the backwaters. Bordeaux had begun as an *emporium*, a depot through which the wines of the *Haut Pays* further inland (Cahors, Gaillac, the Dordogne) were exported. The vines of the Gironde around

Bordeaux itself were few. Even by the time of the famous union between Henry Plantagenet and Eleanor of Aquitaine in 1152 the position had little changed. There were vineyards in the Saint-Émilion area and in the Entre-Deux-Mers, but few in the Graves except to the south near Langon and none in the marshy Médoc. It was the arrival of the English which produced the decisive change. Exports expanded, not just to the British Isles but to the Netherlands and the Hanseatic ports, and the vineyard area soon increased to meet the demand. Twice a year a vast fleet – 900 ships in AD 1300 – sailed from Bordeaux with the latest vintage. By the middle of the fourteenth century, as much land was under vine in the Gironde as exists today. The Bordelais were soon imposing taxes and other restrictions on the inland wines in order to maintain premier position for their local produce. The position did not radically change even when the English lost the South-West at the end of the Hundred Years War.

For the next two hundred years, despite the decline in the influence of the church, changing fashions on the export market – most of England and northern Europe turned to the richer but not yet fortified wines of Iberia – and the arrival of distilled wines, Cognac and other brandies, the pattern of life of the French *vigneron* and his *patron* and the way he made his wine hardly changed. Wine was made in a fairly artisanal way, shipped or otherwise transported in wooden casks and consumed as early as possible, before it went off. The produce was anonymous, identified only by the area of origin. The rise of individual estates, the emergence of a hierarchy separating the best from the mundane, and the concept of wine as a product of quality which could last, indeed could improve with keeping, had to wait until the reinvention of the glass bottle and the rediscovery of the sealing properties of cork around 1650. From this period on, in the economic glory of the Sun King and his successors, the concept of fine wine grew apace. In the more leisured pursuits of the aristocracy the appreciation of wine and food – gastronomy – began to take its place in the art of good living. The rising merchant classes were not slow to join in. The eighteenth century saw an enormous expansion of monocultural vineyard estates in the recently drained Médoc, the emergence of named domaines in the Rhône, the development of Champagne as the drink we know today and the creation of a number of aristocratic, as opposed to ecclesiastical, domaines in Burgundy.

Then came Revolution. The old order crumbled. Church land, and that of the old aristocracy who had emigrated, was sequestered and sold as *biens nationaux*. A new moneyed class, soon ennobled, swiftly moved in to take the place of the old. Little changed: much less than we are given to believe. In Bordeaux the effects were barely noticeable. A few proprietors went to the guillotine, but rather more properties changed hands in the economic depression of the 1830s than during Napoleonic times. In Burgundy where the ecclesiastical land-holding was a small proportion of what it had been at its zenith, but nevertheless the equivalent of some 10,000 hectares, perhaps a third of the vineyard, changed hands. Most was sold in significant pieces to the *nouveau riche*, the *haute bourgeoisie*. The socializing, the democratization of land, if that had been an object of the Revolution, did not come about. What the new order did introduce, its effect to be insidious, a canker which was ultimately to disrupt almost the whole of the French *vignoble*, was the *Code Napoléon*, a change in the laws of inheritance. Primogeniture was abolished. Henceforth estates would have to be equally divided among the heirs. The consequences were to be far-reaching. They still are today.

The nineteenth century saw a rise in the power of the wine merchant and his increasing involvement as vineyard proprietor, the gradual implementation of more scientific and mechanized techniques of viticulture and vinification, the elimination of lesser strains and the concentration on particular noble grape varieties in each major *vignoble*, and a vast expansion of communication, particularly with the arrival of the railway. The first half of the century saw not so much an expansion of the area of vineyard under cultivation but of consolidation, vineyards being rationalized and set apart from other crops in a more efficient manner. Population and prosperity grew, and with it the demand for wine. Each vineyard area, finally, began to produce wines with their own individual characters.

Nemesis was to follow. Three great scourges, the cryptogramic diseases of oidium and mildew bracketing the more catastrophic phylloxera epidemic, followed by the Franco-Prussian war of 1870–1871 and the economic depression which it left in its wake, changed the face, the prosperity and the socio-economic parameters of French viticulture. The last thirty years of the century reduced the French vineyard to a state of abject crisis from which it was not fully to recover until the 1960s.

The convulsions caused by phylloxera were the most far-reaching. Phylloxera is an aphid, an insect with a very complicated life cycle. In both the nymph and the adult states the insect sucks the sap out of the roots of the vine, forming galls on these roots which eventually kill the plant. Once it has arrived in the vineyard it is ineradicable. The only solution, it was eventually found, was to graft the noble *Vitis vinifera* cutting into a more resistant non-*vinifera* (American) rootstock. The solution, like the origin of the insect itself, was American.

The effect of this climactic event, the sheer cost of reconstructing vineyards which had ceased to produce, especially in the unfortunate economic situation which prevailed, was to produce a major contraction of the French *vignoble*. Many of the lesser, more northerly French vineyards had found life tough going since the time the wines of the Midi could be rapidly brought up to Paris and the other major conurbations of the north by the railway. They were never reconstituted. In the 1840s vineyards extended uninterruptedly from Sens to Dijon. Today only Chablis and a few neighbouring hectares are left. Even Chablis almost ceased to exist. The same can be said of Cahors, Madiran and other important, but only latterly fashionable, vineyard areas.

Elsewhere the consequences were equally monumental. While in Bordeaux the large estates, owned by the new aristocracy or the wealthy merchant classes, managed to survive more or less unscathed, the large estates in Burgundy were sold up. This began a process of fragmentation which has resulted in, to take a single example, the fact that the 50-odd hectares of Clos Vougeot have no less than eighty owners today.

For seventy years, until the late 1950s, the life of the French vineyard proprietor and merchant, wherever he existed in the social scale, was an unhappy one. Making and selling wine was barely profitable. More and more vineyards fell into disuse, particularly those which were impossible to work mechanically such as the steep slopes of Côte-Rôtie in the Rhône, as the younger generation emigrated into the factories of the nearby cities. There was a mass evacuation of the country in favour of the town throughout France. With the flower of French manhood slaughtered on the Western Front between 1914 and 1918 economic privation became yet more acute. Even in Bordeaux, hitherto largely immune, protected by the importance of its export market, the wolf was at the gate. By 1945 a quarter of the sixty classed growths of the 1855 Classification existed in name only. The vineyards and *chais* suffered from a lack of investment, the quality of the wine being further diminished by a run of unsuccessful vintages in the 1930s.

Meanwhile, beginning in Champagne before the First World War, altruistically encouraged by the Baron le Roy de Boiseaumarié in Châteauneuf-du-Pape in the 1920s, and finally promulgated in the mid-1930s, the French had codified their viticultural and vinicultural practices, established the right to legally protected regional and communal wine names, and introduced the *Comité National des Appellations d'Origine*. The *Loi Capus*, named after its godfather Joseph Capus, was passed in 1935. After the Second World War the *Comité* became an *Institut* (often abbreviated to INAO), and it continues today as the governing body of French wine and the model for similar developments in wine-producing countries throughout the world.

The last thirty years have seen changes as far-reaching as any of the previous two hundred and fifty. Most fundamental of all has been in the understanding of what precisely happens when the juice of the grape is fermented into wine, the increasing control over the processes of nature, the implementation of new technology and the realization that *élevage* – which one can roughly translate as what goes on during the period between wine-making and wine-bottling – is as important as vinification itself. Financed by increasing prosperity and profitability, the result has been an enormous increase in wine quality. In 1959 it was hard to find drinkable French wine outside the better wines of the mainstream areas, and many of *them* were rustic and sulphury. Today, from Muscadet to Bellet, from Irouléguy to Alsace, and especially in the lesser areas in between, there is a wealth of good, honest, carefully made wine. The change has been dramatic.

Fashions have changed. Beaujolais and Muscadet, to take two examples, were rarely seen outside their areas of origin in the 1940s. They were sold by the glass, direct from the cask, in the bistros of Lyon and Nantes. They were rarely exported. Today 55 per cent of Beaujolais is sold abroad, most of it as Nouveau. Sancerre and Pouilly-Fumé, unheard of thirty years ago, are today widely distributed, both within and without metropolitan France. There is increasing interest in the wines of the Midi, the South-West and other hitherto 'lesser' areas.

The pattern of drinking has changed both in France and elsewhere. The French man (and woman) drinks less than he used to – but still rather more than everybody except his counterpart in Italy – but he drinks better. Consumption of *vin ordinaire* is on the decline: of *appellation* wines on the increase. In the non-wine-making countries of northern Europe, in the Americas, in Australasia and the Far East, the market base has expanded. In Britain – and we lag behind the Netherlands and other countries with a less puritanical attitude to wine taxation – the consumption of table wine is today 15 bottles a year, and 68 per cent of the population drink wine at least once a month. This is an increase in sales of nearly 300 per cent since 1970. Once again the selection has evolved: less *vin ordinaire*, more *vins d'appellation*. And despite the increasing competition of better and better wines from other countries France continues to hold its own. Thirty-nine per cent of British wine consumption is of French wine.

The way French wines are marketed by those who make it has also changed, and radically. Domaine bottling is on the increase, merchant bottling on the decline. More and more wines are marketed direct by the producer. More and more estates in more and more areas now have their own personality and individuality unsubmerged with the wine of their neighbours. The pride that comes with domaine bottling has encouraged perfectionism. It has widened the diversity. It has increased the quality. And prices have risen. This is a prosperous time for the French *vigneron*. The pace of these developments is both exhilarating and breathtaking. What is encouraging is that the profits have been ploughed back into a continuing search after higher standards and the implementation of all the resources of modern science and technology to achieve them. Today the French winemaker is expertly trained, insatiably curious and often surprisingly knowledgeable about wines made elsewhere. He is increasingly dedicated, and rightly confident in his ability to compete in the world markets. The future looks rosy.

A Year in the Vineyard

Good wine is produced from ripe, healthy, concentrated grapes. The object of viticulture is to produce fruit in as optimum a condition as possible at the time of the harvest, to produce as much as is compatible with the highest quality – but not too much, for quality is inversely proportional to quantity – and to mitigate the vagaries of the climate and the depredations of pests and diseases.

The first element to consider is the soil. The vine will thrive on a wide range of geological structures and compositions, but some varieties do better on some soils than on others. Cabernet Sauvignon, for instance, while it has a tolerance for limestone and marl (limestone–clay mixtures) and even for loam (sand–clay mixtures), provided the soils are not too cool, performs to its most elegant capacity on well-drained gravel. Hence its preponderance in the Médoc and the Graves areas of Bordeaux. Gamay is found in the marly soils of the Loire and Ardèche and in the undulating limestone hills of the Mâconnais and the lower Beaujolais; but it produces its greatest definition on the granite slopes of the Beaujolais-Villages area. Syrah thrives on the granite debris of the northern Rhône Valley, Pinot Noir on a subtle mixture of limestone scree, marl and older alluvial deposits which you can only find in Burgundy. Where the soil is purer limestone Chardonnay will perform better, as it will in the chalk of Champagne or the marly Kimmeridge clay of Chablis.

In general the soil needs to be poor in nitrogenous matter. Above all it must be well-drained, particularly in the north of the country and in other pockets where the rainfall is higher. Aspect is important. An orientation towards the east or south-east is ideal. The first rays of the morning will warm up the ground, drive away the mist and ensure that maximum use is made of the heat of the sun. Moreover the vineyard must be protected from wind, and the prevailing wind, in general in France, approaches from the west. It is therefore no coincidence that many of the greatest vineyards lie halfway down the south-eastern-facing slopes of river valleys. The slope aids drainage, trees at the top of the slope protect against the prevailing wind, and the nearby water protects equally against frost in winter and spring and drought in the later part of the summer.

Having chosen his site and prepared his land, if necessary by manuring and adjusting the chemical composition and certainly by ensuring that it is free of disease, the grower's next task is the choice of grape variety and clone or strain of that particular variety, and the selection of a rootstock to go with it. The former choice will, of course, be determined by the local *appellation contrôlée* laws. A permanent result of the phylloxera epidemic is that all vine varieties in France (except in one or two isolated pockets, particularly where the soil is predominantly sandy, for the aphid cannot thrive here) are today grafted on to American, phylloxera-resistant rootstocks.

While it is fair to say that over the last thirty years the developments in viniculture have outstripped the evolution of viticulture, there has nevertheless been considerable research into the production of disease-resistant clones which can produce quantity without sacrificing quality, and the propagation of suitable rootstocks which are compatible, both with the clone and with the chemical and physical composition of the soil. Grafting normally takes place at the horticulturalist's greenhouse, not in the vineyard.

With considerations of mechanical tending of the vineyard, and, indeed, increasingly today, mechanical harvesting of the vintage, determining the space between the vines and the space between the rows, the vineyard is then planted. The amount of vines per given area varies greatly. Half as many vines can exploit the same amount of soil and produce as much wine as double the quantity. But in the better areas the density tends to be greater. The closer together, the more the vine is encouraged to develop a deeply penetrating root system. It will then extract the maximum complexity from soil and subsoil and be more resistant to temporary drought and floods.

Over the next few years, as the vine slowly develops into a mature plant, it is carefully pruned and trained into a particular shape. There are, in essence, two basic pruning methods: long- or cane-pruning, and short- or spur-pruning; and two basic shapes. Cane-pruning lends itself to the ultimate formation of a hedge shape, the canes – one or two with about six buds on each – being tied to a series of horizontal wires stretched along the row of vines. This is known as the Guyot system. Spur-pruning or the Gobelet method produces a free-standing bush shape. There are six or so short spurs, each with two or so buds. A compromise between the two, giving short spurs on horizontal branches which can be trained on wires, is the Cordon de Royat system.

The vine flowers, and therefore will ultimately fruit, on the previous year's wood. The object of pruning is to select the best of this wood, to cut it back, eliminating all the rest, and to reduce the eventual crop to a potential of six to a dozen bunches of grapes per vine.

The yearly cycle of the vine begins after the harvest. With the onset of the cold weather of winter the vine has become dormant, the sap has descended into the roots of the vine and the process of tidying up, cutting away the dead wood and preparing the vineyard for next year's harvest can begin. The roots will be earthed up to protect them against frost, manure and other fertilizers can be ploughed in, and stakes and wires can be renewed if necessary. This is the time to rip up old vines which are dead or beyond their useful life and to begin to prepare sections of the vineyard for replanting in the spring after a year or two's rest. It is also the time to replace soil which may have been washed down the slopes by the rain of the previous season. Throughout the winter pruning takes place. It must be finished before the warmer weather returns again in the spring and the sap of the vine begins to rise anew.

In March the vine begins to wake up from its winter dormancy. A further ploughing is undertaken, this time to weed and aerate the soil and to uncover the base of the vine. The buds begin to swell, and will eventually burst in late April to reveal a small cluster of tiny leaves. This is when the danger of frost is at its greatest. The vine itself can withstand winter temperatures as low as minus 20°C. The embryonic leaf-cluster is susceptible to just the slightest descent below zero.

From the emergence of the leaves the vineyard is regularly sprayed: with sulphur against oidium, with copper sulphate (Bordeaux mixture) against mildew, and with other chemicals against red spider, moths and other insects. Later on the fruit may be sprayed to harden its skin and prevent the emergence of rot. Increasingly nowadays, particularly in the South of France where the risk of insect depradation is less and the climate drier, vineyards – and indeed the wine-making which follows – are run on organic and ecological principles.

In June the vine flowers, and this is one of the most critical times in the yearly cycle. Warm, dry weather is required to ensure that the fruit setting, which follows the flowering, takes place swiftly and successfully. If the weather is cold and humid the flowers may not set into fruit (*coulure*) or the fruit may remain as small, green, bullet-hard berries and not develop (*millerandage*). Moreover, should the flowering be prolonged the result will be bunches of uneven ripeness at the time of the harvest.

Throughout the summer spraying continues, particularly if the weather is inclement; the vineyard is ploughed to aerate the soil and eliminate weeds; the shoots are trained on to the wires, so that they do not break off in the wind, and the vegetation is trimmed back so that the vine can concentrate its resources into producing fruit. Increasingly in the best vineyards today there is a 'green harvest', an elimination of excess bunches before they develop and change colour, in order to reduce the final crop and so concentrate the eventual wine.

This colour change (*véraison*) takes place in August. Grapes as green as Granny Smith apples turn red and eventually black, or else soften into a greeny gold. From then it is seven weeks or so to the harvest (100 to 110 days after the flowering). Spraying must soon cease. The work in the vineyard is now over. All one can do is to pray for fine weather. Whatever might have happened earlier in the season the result will only have affected the quantity to be harvested. The weather from the *véraison* onwards is critical for the quality. What is required during these weeks is an abundance of sunshine, to ripen the fruit, an absence of excessive rain, which would only expand the grapes and dilute the wine, and an absence of humidity, which would encourage rot.

In about the third week of September the harvest starts. Preliminary tests to establish the sugar and acidity contents of the grapes will have taken place to ensure that ripeness and concentration are at their optimum at the time of collection. The weather forecast is anxiously studied. A preliminary passage through the vineyard to eliminate the diseased or otherwise inadequate bunches or part of bunches, and therefore make the life of the picker easier, is often undertaken. And when the time is ripe the vintage begins. The result of a year's hard labour is soon evident.

Today the majority of French vineyards, like the majority elsewhere, is harvested by machine. Only in the top estates of Bordeaux and Burgundy and elsewhere, or where the land is inappropriate – and of course in places which produce individual bunch-selected sweet wines such as Sauternes – does harvesting continue by hand. And even here, for instance among the classed growths of the Haut-Médoc, mechanical harvesters are increasingly seen.

The advantage of mechanical harvesting is its convenience and its speed. One machine can do the work of twenty-five manual pickers and removes the stems from the bunches of grapes too. It can work 24 hours a day, if desired; and the new, second generation of machines, if correctly driven, does little harm to the vines. Mechanical harvesting can mean a later start to the harvest and a quicker conclusion, concentrating collection at the optimum state of the fruit's ripeness. This is the future.

How Wine is Made

Wine is produced by fermenting the juice of freshly gathered grapes. It sounds simple. But in fact it is extremely complicated. Yeasts excrete enzymes which cause the sugar in the grape juice (or must) to turn into alcohol. The chemical process is very complicated. The reaction is exo-thermic, producing heat, so needs to be controlled. Carbon dioxide is also produced and there is an additional 3 per cent of other chemical by-products.

It is this 3 per cent of 'other' which is crucial. Alcohol has no flavour, nor does water – and the grape juice and therefore the wine is 85 per cent or so water. It is in the 3 per cent of other that you will find the colour and the flavour. The reason the fermentation process needs to be controlled is not only that at too high temperatures the process will 'stick' and the danger of acetifaction (the production of vinegar) will arise but that the flavour elements are very volatile. They need to be prevented from evaporating into the air. They need to be preserved in the wine. Moreover the extraction of colour, tannins and flavour from the skins of the grape varies with both the temperature, pressure and availability of oxygen and with the length of maceration of these skins with the fermenting must.

There is a further problem. The effect of oxygen on wine will cause further chemical reactions to take place. Wine (alcohol) is only a halfway house between sugar and vinegar. While a little oxygenation is necessary for maturation, at all times in the vinification process, and during the time the wine is retained in bulk thereafter, evolving and undergoing the various treatments which take place before it is put in bottle, the winemaker must ensure that the wine is uncontaminated by too much oxygen. He must not unduly expose the wine to air. Control, and the equipment with which to control, as well as a thorough knowledge of the process, is crucial.

MAKING RED WINE

Vinification
On arrival at the *cuverie* or vinification centre, the grape bunches are dumped into a V-shaped trough and churned by means of a revolving vice through a *fouloir-égrappoir*. This pulls off the stalks and gently breaks the skin of the grape berry. Only rarely outside

Burgundy is the must (or grape juice) vinified with the stalks. There is enough tannin in the skins already.

The produce of different grapes, different sections of the vineyard, and, particularly, vines of different age, will be vinified separately. For red wines, there are two concurrent aspects to vinification: the fermentation itself – the grape sugar being converted to alcohol – and maceration, the length of time the must is in contact with the skins, extracting tannin, colour and extract from the pulp. The temperature is important, for the reasons outlined above.

Today the finer red wines are usually vinified at about 30°C, allowing the temperature to rise no higher than 33°C before cooling. Some estates prefer to ferment between 26°C and 28°C. The lighter red wines, where excessive tannin is to be avoided, are vinified at a lower temperature of 25°C or less. The need for control of temperature, as well as the ability to fully clean and sterilize the fermenting receptacle, has led to a movement away from the more traditional oak to the adoption of stainless-steel fermentation vats, which are easily cooled by running cold water down the outside, or by means of an enveloping, thermostatically controlled 'cummerbund'.

Periodically during fermentation the juice is pumped over the floating mass of skins, pips and stalks, if any, or this cap or *chapeau* is pushed down into the must and broken up, a process called *pigeage*. This is to combine the colour-releasing components with the must, equalize the temperature and assist the release of colour, tannin and extract from the skins. The current trend is to 'pump over' more frequently, but to macerate in total for a shorter time before running the liquid off the skins. The length of maceration (or *cuvaison*) will vary from three or four days for a light red wine such as Beaujolais or *vins de pays* from the South of France to as much as four weeks in the case of a top red Bordeaux.

When fermentation is over, the juice is then run off into a clean, empty vat or barrel. This juice is the *vin de goutte*. The residue of skins is then pressed. The *vin de presse* that results is important. It will be firmer, more tannic and more acidic than the free-run juice, and a proportion will normally be blended back in varying quantities, or added periodically when the wine is later racked. No addition of *vin de presse* may result in a rather weak, ephemeral wine, however enjoyable and supple it may be in its youth.

CARBONIC MACERATION

Carbonic maceration or *macération carbonique*, though a technique which is hardly used for the finest wines, particularly those intended to be wines for ageing, is now increasingly employed where the object is to produce fruity, soft, red wines for early drinking. This technique is discussed in more detail in the chapter on Beaujolais (*see page 181*).

In brief, on arrival at the *cuverie* the bunches of grapes are not crushed, but poured into the vats whole. These vats are normally closed to the air, allowing the carbon dioxide produced by the fermentation process to escape, but not the oxygen in the air to come into contact with the fruit.

The first part of the fermentation takes place within the skins of the grapes, in an atmosphere of carbon dioxide. This produces colour and extract but not much tannin. After a few days the free-flow juice is decanted off, the residue is pressed, and the fermentation process proceeds as normal. Often *macération carbonique* fermented wine is later blended with wine vinified in the natural way at the time of the *égalisage* or blending.

COLD MACERATION

A further technique, employed particularly in Burgundy, is cold maceration or *macération à froid*, the maceration taking place before fermentation. The principle is to maximize extraction of colour and aroma before the fermentation process takes place and without producing an excess of tannin at the same time. It is normally cool in Burgundy at the time of the harvest, and the lightly crushed grapes or whole bunches, or a proportion of the two, are left for a few days to macerate with the free-run juice, no deliberate steps being taken to start the fermentation process early. Some Burgundian growers, following the counsels of a local *oenologue* Guy Accad, deliberately prolong this maceration, and ensure that it takes place at an even colder temperature.

CHAPTALIZATION

Chaptalization is the addition of sugar to a fermenting must and is a practice permitted for white and rosé wines as well as for red. The process is not intended to make sweet wine but to make one with a higher level of alcohol. In vintages unblessed by a sunny autumn there is not enough natural sugar in the fruit to produce a wine with a sufficiently stable level of alcohol, say 12 degrees or so. It is now customary everywhere in France except in parts of the Midi to add sugar to the must, to the equivalent of a degree of alcohol or so or more, even in years when the grapes are fully ripe. It is said to knit the wine together. Moreover, if the sugar is added, not at the beginning of the fermentation but towards the end, it will extend the process, thus helping to extract more tannin (because the temperature will increase) and give both added density and added suppleness (eventually) to the wine.

ÉLEVAGE

Once the fermentation process is complete the must is now wine and it must be looked after with meticulous care until it is ready for bottling, a process that must be done at the right time and with correct attention to detail. I am convinced that as much potentially good wine is ruined by incorrect or simply sloppy cellarwork or *élevage* as by poor vinification before or inferior storage afterwards.

After fermentation the first thing is to ensure that the wine is clean, in the sense of free of potential chemical or bacteriological contamination, and that it has completed its malolactic fermentation. This 'second' or malolactic fermentation, which also gives off carbon dioxide, often takes place immediately following the sugar-to-alcohol fermentation, and can be encouraged by warming the must or the surrounding environment to between 18°C and 20°C, and the addition of an artificial malolactic bacterium to get the fermentation going. The result is to lower the apparent acidity by a degree or two; so rounding off the wine and softening it up. In many white wines, particularly those of the South with an already low acidity level, this would be a mistake, but with reds the malolactic fermentation is generally encouraged.

The next step is the *égalisage* or blending. This takes place normally during the winter a few months after the harvest. This is the moment of truth – the creation of the château or domaine wine, the blending together of the constituent parts from different grape varieties (if there are more than one), vine ages and sections of the vineyard. A large property might have as many as thirty vats-worth of wine to choose from, and not all of these may be suitable. If the weather has not been perfect, or if much of the vineyard consists of immature vines – less than ten or even fifteen years old in a top growth – many will not be of the required standard for the *grand vin* or top wine.

Having made the blend (and we are assuming wine of some pretension here: lesser wines are stored in bulk), the wine is transferred to oak barrels – in which it may well have been lying before the *égalisage* – and allowed to mature and settle out its sediment, or lees. The barrels will need constant topping up, to make up for evaporation, particularly in the first few months, and for this reason they are first stored with the bung-hole upright, loosely covered by a glass stopper or rubber bung. Later, a wooden, more permanent bung will be driven into this hole, and the casks moved over so the bung is on the side.

One of the questions continually asked of a proprietor or his cellar manager is the proportion of new oak hogsheads he uses each year. As a new cask now costs upwards of 2300 *francs* or £250 (1990 price), the provision of a large proportion of new oak is a major financial undertaking. Nevertheless, the extra muscle and tannin, coupled with the flavour the oak gives to a wine, is an essential ingredient in the taste of a fine red wine. A few of the very top estates invariably put their top wine entirely into new oak. For most producers, a proportion of between a quarter and a half, depending on the quality and style of the vintage, is normal. More would impart too much of a *boisé* (woody) smell to the wine. This view would be echoed by many in Burgundy and elsewhere. Nevertheless, there has been a trend toward the use of more new wood. On the other hand, together with more new wood has come a reduction in the time the wine spends there. Ageing used to be for a minimum of two years. Today it is frequently as much as six months less before bottling, and the wine may well have been run off into older casks or into vat after only a year to avoid taking up too much taste of the oak. The major French oak forests lie in the centre of the country. Limousin imparts a very marked oak flavour and is not used for fine wine. Tronçais, Nevers and Allier are widely found, the latter being the most delicate and is largely used for white wines. Elsewhere in France Burgundian oak and oak from the Vosges are used.

During the first year of a wine's life, it will be racked to separate the wine from its lees, and also to transfer it from new to old oak and vice versa, so that all the wine spends an equal amount of time in wood of different ages. Big full wines such as Bordeaux throw more sediment than lighter wines such as Burgundy. In Bordeaux the wine will be racked every three months in the first year, in Burgundy every six months. In principle the less you move or manipulate the wine the better. During the second year, the racking is less frequent, but additionally the wine is 'fined', traditionally with beaten white of egg for fine wines, to coagulate and deposit further unstable elements. Lesser wines are fined with isinglass, casein (milk powder), bentonite and other natural or proprietary substances.

BOTTLING

The date of bottling is an important matter which has only received sufficient attention relatively recently. I still do not consider that it is flexible enough to allow for variations between one vintage and the next. A wine matures much quicker in cask than in bottle, and a variation of six or even three months in the date of bottling can hence have a decisive effect on the eventual date of maturity and on the balance of the wine.

A big, concentrated, tannic wine from a Bordeaux vintage such as 1982 may need a full two years or even more in cask before it is ready for bottling, but equally a light vintage, particularly one that is feeble in acidity – a Côte Chalonnaise from 1986, for example – needs early bottling; and Beaujolais is bottled almost as soon as it is stable. Currently, most top Bordeaux châteaux and their Côte d'Or equivalents in Burgundy bottle during the summer or early autumn of the second year, when the wine is between eighteen and which dries out and becomes astringent, having lost some of its fruit before it is ready for drinking.

WHEN TO DRINK THE WINE

Once a wine has been bottled, when will it be ready for drinking? And perhaps more important, how long will it be at peak after that? It has for long been the general rule that a wine such as a good Second or Third Growth Médoc from a fine vintage like 1983, '78 or '70 requires ten years from the date of harvest to mature; a First Growth fifteen or more; and lesser Médocs, Saint-Émilions and Pomerols from five to ten years. *Petits châteaux* are at their best between three and six years after the harvest. These figures would be less in a softer, less tannic vintage such as 1981, '79 or '76, and proportionately more in a big, hard vintage such as 1982 or '75. These figures would similarly apply to wine from the northern Rhône. For Burgundy they should be reduced by a third. Thereafter, a well-made, well-stored wine will last for at least as long as it has taken to mature. The proportion between the time a wine will live once mature and the time it has taken to reach maturity increases with the quality of the wine and the vintage, so that a top wine from an excellent claret vintage, 1961, ready in 1981, instead of having thereafter a twenty-year life at peak, may have as much as forty, or twice the length of time it took to mature, before beginning to go downhill.

When you prefer to drink your wine is a matter of personal taste. While I personally incline more to the French taste – which to some in England and elsewhere seems a predilection for infanticide – I normally stick to the Bordeaux ten-year rule, and its equivalent elsewhere. Given the choice, however, I would prefer to drink a wine at the beginning of its 'at peak' plateau, rather than at the very end.

MAKING ROSÉ WINE

The normal rosé process begins as for red wine: the must is racked off the skins after only a matter of hours (somewhere between 6 and 24 hours). Thereafter the juice is run off and the vinification proceeds as for a dry white wine. Most rosés are produced for early consumption and few age with any dignity.

MAKING DRY WHITE WINE

VINIFICATION
The grapes which will produce dry white wine normally reach maturity a few days before the red varieties, and the precise date for top quality is even more crucial in order that the exact balance between sugar and acidity can be obtained.

With the trend in the 1960s towards drier, crisper wines came an unfortunate move in the Loire, Bordeaux and elsewhere towards picking a few days in advance of the optimum moment in order to make wines with a good refreshing acidity. This was sadly carried a bit too far and the results, too often, were wines with a rasping, malic acidity and a consequent lack of ripe fruit. The wines were too green. As the grape ripens the malic acidity changes into tartaric acidity. Now, with the help of mechanical harvesting, the grower can wait longer without the risk of prolonging the collection of the crop beyond the desired period. It is now appreciated that once the correct maturity in the grapes has been reached, provided the climatic conditions are favourable, the acidity, now essentially tartaric rather than malic, will not continue to diminish and may even concentrate further to give a wine with both ripeness and balance.

White wines are vinified without their skins, and the first procedure is to press them as soon as possible after arrival from the vineyard, normally in some form of horizontal cylindrical apparatus. The juice is then run off and allowed to settle (a process called *débourbage*) for twenty-four hours so that the solid matter falls to the bottom before being vinified. Except in the top estates where fermentation takes place in oak barrels, vinification takes place in vat or tank, often in anaerobic conditions and for white wines must proceed at a reduced temperature in order to prolong the process as long as possible, thus preventing loss of the volatile elements which impart flavour and aroma, and maximizing the intensity of the fruit. The common temperature for the controlled fermentation of most white wines is between 18°C and 20°C. For a long time it has been accepted that the lower the temperature of fermentation the more the volatile, flavour-enhancing chemicals in the fruit are preserved in the resulting wine. It is not the lower temperature *per se*, however, but the prolongation of the fermentation which is important. The longer the fermentation, the more complex the flavour. Today 'artificial' yeasts are widely employed, for they make the fermentation easier to control and produce wines of greater fruit definition and finesse.

Today in order to maintain a crisper acidity in the finished wine the second, malolactic fermentation is discouraged for many fine white wines in Bordeaux, Alsace, the Rhône and the Midi, even in the Mâconnais and the Côte d'Or in some vintages, though it is necessary for more northern wines such as Sancerre and Chablis. Whether the wine is matured in cask or in tank, bottling takes place much earlier than for reds, often as early as the following spring. The object is to preserve the freshness and fruit and to minimize oxidation. Only the best, oak-vinified and oak-aged examples will develop in bottle.

Macération préfermentaire or skin contact before fermentation is a white-wine technique new to France. The principle which lies behind this idea of allowing white grape juice to remain in contact with the grape skins for a few hours before pressing is that it has been realized that most of the flavour-producing elements in the pulp of the grape lie near or within the skin. It is a process which needs to be handled with great care, for bruised or rotten berries will taint the whole wine. The results though are most rewarding: wines of greater complexity and depth of flavour, and it is a procedure which is spreading. So is the idea of leaving the new white wine on its fine lees (*sur lie*) for as long as possible before the first racking. The wine feeds off this sediment, mainly dead yeast cells, and becomes richer and fuller in flavour. In Bordeaux, Burgundy and elsewhere the wine might be kept on its lees until midsummer.

Another development after leaving the wine for several months on its fine lees is to bottle without racking first. The result, once again, is an enhancement of the complexity. Muscadet has long been bottled *sur lie* in March or so six months after the vintage.

The bane of white wine has been the over-use of sulphur. Sulphur is a necessary ingredient in the preservation of wine. It protects it against oxidation and bacterial infection, but too heavy a hand with it will kill the wine. The sulphur will bind in with the wine, destroying the freshness, the nuances of the fruit, and producing a sickly, heavy 'wet-wool' flavour. This used to be particularly prevalent in Bordeaux. Thankfully, after years of maltreating their white wines, the Bordeaux winemakers are beginning to realize – as their counterparts in the Loire and southern Burgundy did years ago – that, well-handled, dry and sweet white wine does not require as much sulphur to protect it as they thought. More careful wine-making, in anaerobic conditions and with a cleaner must, enables the winemaker to reduce his recourse to sulphur dioxide during the fermentation. Healthy wine, correctly balanced, requires less sulphur thereafter. Modern equipment and sensitive *élevage* reduces its necessity even more. If the Loire and Burgundian winemakers can do it, why can't the Bordelais? The penny is beginning to drop. Fewer and fewer dry white Graves – though there are still far too many depressing examples – taste of nothing but sulphur dioxide.

ÉLEVAGE

The use of oak, new or newish, is another relatively recent development in white-wine production. Prior to the 1960s, wood – old barrels for the most part – was the most common receptacle for *élevage* and transport. The fashion then swung to the tank, enamelled or stainless steel, and the concrete vat. All the old, diseased, bug-infected barrels were burned, and probably a good thing too. Only the very top wine estates persisted with oak for their dry white wines.

But oak, new oak, adds weight, complexity of flavour, depth and class. Happily today, not only across the board of the nine white Bordeaux classed growths but more widely elsewhere a proportion of new oak is *de rigueur*. Wines are even being fermented in new wood. This is yet more preferable. The wood flavours derived thereby are more delicate and complex and exist in greater harmony with the rest of the flavour ingredients of the wine. Oak should be *de rigueur* for any white wine aspiring to quality status.

BOTTLING

White wines are generally bottled much earlier than reds: the vast majority, those not matured in oak, within six months of vinification. Most of the rest of the fine dry wines are bottled the following autumn. Only the richest sweet wines such as those of Sauternes are given more than twelve months in cask.

WHEN TO DRINK THE WINE

When should you drink white wine? The lesser wines, like 'small' white wines all over the world, are essentially made one year for drinking the next. Within twelve months after bottling, i.e. eighteen months after the harvest, they will begin to lose their youthful fruity freshness. This applies to most Sauvignon wines, to Muscadet and Mâcon, to the whites of Bergerac, Gaillac and the Midi, and to the standard Alsace *cuvées*.

Grander white wines, those that have been fermented and matured in oak, can, and must, be kept. Often they enter a rather dumb phase after bottling, and for two or three years they will appear rather clumsy, particularly if they have been bottled with a little too much sulphur, as is still, sadly, often the case. Lesser vintages will be at their best between three and eight years after the harvest. The best white wines need longer before they are fully ready, and will keep for a decade or more after that.

MAKING SWEET WHITE WINE

The world's greatest sweet wines are rare in number, highly prized, expensive to produce and infrequent in occurrence. That they appear at all is a tribute to the dedication and patience of the few wine growers who make a speciality of them, and is a consequence of a particular microclimate acting on a small number of specific grape varieties, the result of an Indian summer of misty mornings and warm balmy afternoons continuing long after the rest of the *vignerons* have cleared their vines and are busy in the cellars nurturing the birth of their new vintage.

The great sweet wines are not merely sweet. If this were all, the addition of sugar syrup to a finished dry wine would be all that was necessary. Indeed, this is how cheap sweet wines are made. But these the consumer will soon find bland and cloying.

Noble Rot
The finest dessert wines are the result of a particular phenomenon, the attack on the ripe, late-harvested fruit by a fungus known as *Botrytis cinerea*. It produces what is known in France as *pourriture noble* and in Germany as *Edelfäule*, both of which can be translated as 'noble rot'. Leave any fruit on the tree after it has ripened and eventually it will rot. This rot (*pourriture grise*), however, will not be 'noble'; the fruit will be ruined and the taste disgusting. In certain parts of the vineyard areas of the world though, in the right climatic conditions, the noble rot will occur and this in Bordeaux will produce the great Sauternes, in the Loire Valley will produce the sweet wines of the Layon and Vouvray and in Alsace will produce Sélections de Grains Nobles.

What is required is a particular microclimate. The grapes are left on the vine after the normal harvesting time for the production of dry white wine. The conditions thereafter need to combine both warmth and humidity. It must continue fine and sunny long into the autumn but not be too dry. Most high-quality vineyard areas, however, are near the extremes of viable grape production; in poor years the fruit does not ripen sufficiently and the later the harvest the greater the risk that summer will have finished and autumn rains and chilly winter weather will have set in. This further complicates matters for the quality sweet wine producer. He needs not just a fine late summer but a prolonged and clement autumn. These occur rarely. Two years out of three, or even three out of four, are good years for red and dry white wines. For great sweet wines, the regularity is hardly one in three or even one in four.

When the noble rot attacks the ripe grapes, they will first darken in colour. From golden, they will turn a burnished, almost purple brown. Then the surface will appear to get cloudy, the skin will begin to wither and get mouldy as the spores of the fungus multiply, feeding on the sugar and the berry. Finally, the grape will become shrivelled like a raisin and completely decomposed. The noble rot does not have a very prepossessing appearance!

It, unfortunately, does not strike with equal regularity and precision over the whole vineyard or even over the whole of a single bunch of grapes. This necessitates picking over the vineyard a number of times in order to select each bunch, part bunch or even, at Château d'Yquem, each individual berry, separately. A prolonged harvest is therefore implicit in the production of noble rot wines. In some cases it will continue not just into November but even into December.

The effect of this noble rot attack is to alter the chemical and physical composition of the grape and therefore, obviously, the taste of the wine. First, the water content of the berries is considerably reduced. Second, the acidities are changed and, third, the quantity of higher sugars such as glycerine is increased. The net effect is to create a very small quantity of juice with a sugar content equivalent to an alcohol level which in a top Sauternes will be well above 20 degrees. This produces a wine with an actual alcohol level of 14 or 15 degrees or so and 4 or 5 degrees (higher in the most successful vintages) of unfermented sugar. This is the sweetness. The other effect of the noble rot is to combine this sweetness with a luscious, spicy, complex, individual flavour and a high, naturally ripe acidity level.

There is much talk in Sauternes today of a new technique called cryo-extraction. Briefly the principle is that juice heavy in sugars and glycerine freezes at a lower temperature than water. Thus, should you have a situation where it rains during the harvest, if you are able to freeze the grapes to a certain temperature and then press them carefully you should be able to capture the concentrated Sauternes-producing juice without it being diluted by the rain, for this rain will be frozen into ice-crystals and will not flow off during the pressing: a sort of artificial *Eiswein*, in fact.

Sauternes by its very nature is an aberration. Contrary to all normal agricultural principles and practices the grower deliberately allows his harvest to rot. He has to wait until he is at the mercy of the elements as autumn evolves into winter: 'We are all playing poker with God', as one grower once told me. All too often a state of rot which was incipiently noble can be turned by bad weather into ignoble. This is where cryo-extraction comes on. It is not intended to replace normal harvesting and pressing in fine weather, but it will enable a grower to rescue his harvest if the climatic conditions turn against him. Of course, the majority of sweet and semi-sweet wines are made from grapes which, while ripe, are not affected by noble rot. They are sweet because the fermentation process is arrested before all the sugar is converted into alcohol. This can be done by increasing the sulphur content and/or filtering out the active yeasts.

The fermentation of sweet white wine proceeds in general along the same lines as that for dry white wines. Crushing has to be slow, repeated and gentle – often, paradoxically, the best juice does not come from the first pressing – and the wine is often chilled or centrifuged to eliminate the gross lees rather than being allowed to settle of its own accord. This is in order to prevent oxidation. The fermentation is slow, often difficult. It is important to preserve the correct balance between alcohol and sugar. A Coteaux du Layon with, say, 12.5 degrees of alcohol can support only a maximum 35 grams of sugar per litre. This wine would be called *moelleux* (medium-sweet) but not *doux* (very sweet).

A *doux* Vouvray, such as was produced in 1989, with say 50 grams of sugar per litre, will need to be more alcoholic. A Sauternes with 14 to 15 degrees of alcohol needs to be really luscious or it will appear oily and heavy.

Once the sweet wine has been made it will take longer than a dry one to settle down and stabilize. Moreover the wine will be susceptible to further fermentation as, by its very nature, it will have a large amount of unfermented sugar in it. It needs therefore to be carefully nurtured, its sulphur level maintained at a relatively high level to preserve it. Exposure to the air must be avoided at all costs.

Nevertheless maturation in (at least partially) new oak, and often for a year and a half or more, does wonders for the richest and most concentrated of these sweet wines. No classy Sauternes should be matured without oak. The lighter sweet wines of the Loire see less oak, if any, and are bottled sooner.

Sweet white wines need maturing. Though often delicious young they mature so well and can reach such levels of complexity that it is a tragedy to pull the cork too soon. A medium-sweet Loire wine may be mature at five years. Ten is the minimum for a *doux*, for a good Sauternes and for a top Alsace selected late-harvest wine. And they will last. A twenty-year-old Sauternes of a top vintage like 1988, '86 or '83 will still be a virile teenager.

MAKING SPARKLING WINE

A sparkling wine is produced by adding further yeasts and sugar to a young finished still wine, thus causing a second fermentation. The carbon dioxide so produced is not allowed to escape until the final bottle is opened by the consumer. The gas then rises up in the form of a mousse of tiny bubbles.

There are essentially two ways of making sparkling wine. In the first, the Champagne method, the second fermentation takes place in individual bottles (*see page 303*). In the second, the second fermentation takes place in bulk, in a sealed tank, and the wine is eventually transferred to bottle under pressure. This cheaper method is known as the *cuve close* or Charmat method. Most *appellation contrôlée* sparkling wines, including the Crémants of the Loire, Burgundy and Alsace and Blanquette de Limoux and of course Champagne, must be made by the first method.

Grape Varieties

The grape variety – or mix of grape varieties – is the single most important contributor to both the flavour and the character of a wine. The soil is important, as is the expertise and techniques of vine-growing (viticulture) and wine-making (vinification). The weather is paramount in determining the quality of the vintage. But the grape variety contributes most to the style of the wine. These are the main quality varieties planted in France.

RED VARIETIES

CABERNET SAUVIGNON

Location: Bordeaux, particularly in the Médoc and Graves areas; Bordeaux satellites such as Bergerac and Buzet; widely used in Provence and the Languedoc-Roussillon as a *cépage améliorateur* or on its own for *vin de pays* wines.

Though not the most widely planted grape in the Gironde, Cabernet Sauvignon is accepted as the classic claret grape. It is a vigorous but small producer, which develops late in the season – thus an advantage against spring frosts – and ripens late. It flourishes on most types of soil, consistently showing its style and quality, as evidenced by the wide adoption of this grape outside the Bordeaux area, as a *cépage améliorateur* in the Midi, and in Australia and California. It is less susceptible to *coulure* (failure of the flower to set into fruit) or to *pourriture grise* (grey rot) than Merlot, but more so to powdery mildew. The grape cluster is cylindrical-conical, made up of small round berries, very black in colour. The vine is cane pruned.

This is the grape which gives claret its particular blackcurrant taste. It provides the firmness, the tannin and the backbone. It gives the colour and the acidity, from whence comes the longevity, the depth, the finesse and the complexity of top Bordeaux wine.

CABERNET FRANC

Location: Bordeaux; Bordeaux satellites; Madiran; Touraine (Chinon and Bourgueil); Anjou (Saumur-Champigny, Anjou-Villages and also for Cabernet Rosé d'Anjou).

This vine is the 'poor country cousin' of Cabernet Sauvignon, and shares many of its characteristics, though wine made from it is less positive and less distinctive. Though losing ground in the Médoc, it is widely preferred to Cabernet Sauvignon in Saint-Émilion and Pomerol (where it is called Bouchet), where it thrives better on the more limestone and clay-based soils. Wine made from it is softer, more subtle, more aromatic than from Cabernet Sauvignon. It is for this reason, as well as its shorter growing cycle, that Cabernet Franc is the grape used for Chinon and Bourgueil in the Touraine. The bunch is looser, the grapes still small, but larger than Cabernet Sauvignon, and the resultant wine is more fragrant but less coloured, less full and less tannic. The vine is cane pruned.

MERLOT

Location: Bordeaux, particularly in Saint-Émilion, Pomerol and the rest of the Libournais; Bordeaux satellites; Cahors; Languedoc-Roussillon (as a *cépage améliorateur* or on its own for *vin de pays* wines).

The Merlot is the leading grape of the Dordogne side of the Bordeaux region and the most widely planted across the area as a whole. It is a vigorous, productive vine, which buds early – thus rendering it liable to spring frost damage – and ripens earlier than both the Cabernets. It is susceptible to *coulure*, downy mildew and botrytis (rot) which can cause considerable damage if there is rain at the time of harvest. It is less adaptable to different soils. The grape cluster is cylindrical, but looser than the Cabernets, and the berries are round, but larger, and less intensely coloured. The vine is cane pruned. A Merlot wine is generally a degree or two higher in alcohol than the Cabernets, less acidic, less tannic and less muscular. It is softer, fatter and more aromatic in character, and it matures faster.

MALBEC

Location: Cahors; Loire; Bordeaux; Bordeaux satellites.

This is the principal grape of Cahors, where it is called the Auxerrois, and is grown in the Loire, where it is known as the Cot. In Bordeaux it is also authorized but it is little grown in the top properties, particularly in the Médoc, though it can be found in small proportions, in the top estates of Saint-Émilion and Pomerol where it is known as the Pressac. The berries are large and the cluster loose. Merlot is prone to *coulure*, downy mildew and rot. The vine is cane pruned. The quantity of wine which results is large, compared to other Bordeaux varieties. Malbec is quite rich in tannin and colour, but with less intensity of aroma and with much less finesse. In the Loire and Bordeaux the wine is only medium in body. In the best part of Cahors, on the baked limestone flanks or *causses* the grape makes wine that is rather more beefy.

PETIT VERDOT

Location: Bordeaux (Médoc only).

This variety is of minor importance, but is inserted here in order that all the five Bordeaux red varieties are listed together. The Petit Verdot is a sort of super-concentrated Cabernet Sauvignon, which has all but disappeared except in some of the top Médoc estates. It is difficult to grow, prone to disease, and ripens last of all, often not completely successfully. The vine is cane pruned. Some growers swear by it, saying it brings finesse, acidity, alcoholic concentration and backbone. Others, like Monsieur Charmolüe at Château Montrose or Robert Dousson at Château de Pez, who have each carried out tests to discern the development of blends with or without wine from this grape, have decided it is not for them. As Peter Sichel of Château Palmer ruefully points out, in the good vintages when everything ripens successfully, Petit Verdot is superfluous; in the poor years, when you need it, it does not ripen at all. Nevertheless, he adds, a mixture of grape varieties, each budding, flowering and ripening at a different time, acts as a kind of insurance against sudden attacks of frost, hail and other climate hazards.

PINOT NOIR

Location: Burgundy; Champagne; Sancerre and other communes of the Central Loire; Alsace; Jura.

Pinot Noir is said to be an old variety, close to the types the Romans brought with them when Burgundy was first planted with vines. It can be traced back in records to the early Middle Ages when there were a number of ducal edicts promoting the Pinot and outlawing the ignoble Gamay in the Côte d'Or. The variety is sensitive to cold, both during the winter and during the flowering. It buds early, making spring frost a potential hazard, and ripens early. Pinot Noir produces a small, cylindrical cluster of densely packed, slightly oval berries. As a result of being close together, and particularly as many of the newer strains have thinner skins than hitherto, grey rot can be a serious problem if the weather turns humid towards harvest-time.

As important are two other traits. Wine made from Pinot Noir is much more susceptible than most other varieties to over-production. The concentration and character dissolve rapidly if the yield is excessive. The introduction of high-yielding clones – particularly the infamous Pinot Droit – has been one of the banes of post-war Burgundy. Moreover Pinot Noir is very susceptible to the temperature as it nears the end of its ripening cycle. As with other varieties the wine can be mean and unripe if the sun fails to shine, but if the weather is too hot and roasted a Pinot Noir wine is prone to becoming coarse and leaden-footed. For this reason it is rarely successful outside the Burgundy region. The vine is cane pruned.

A Pinot Noir wine is rarely a blockbuster. Finesse rather than muscle is the keynote. The flavour of young Pinot Noir wine is of slightly sweet, freshly crushed, soft summer fruits; a fragrant, silky, multi-faceted and delicately elegant combination of raspberries, strawberries, mulberries and plums. Burgundy is feminine while claret and Hermitage are masculine. Concentrated young burgundy often offers up a hint of coffee. The elusive character can often, though, be swamped by excessive maceration or by too much new oak. As a Pinot Noir wine matures it takes on a totally different character. An animal, gamy almost vegetal aspect will evolve. The fruit flavours deepen, incorporating hints of damson and blackberry. The whole thing becomes much more sensuous. Pinot Noir also makes an attractive rosé wine.

PINOT MEUNIER

Location: Champagne.

Readers may be surprised to read (I certainly was when I was first told) that it is the Meunier or hairy Pinot and not the Pinot Noir or the Chardonnay which is the most widely planted grape variety in Champagne. It buds later, so suiting sites vulnerable to frost and thriving in years when *coulure* has been a problem, and ensuring a larger and more consistent crop than the Pinot Noir. The variety shares many of the characteristics of its noble cousin but matures slower in the vineyard, so producing a wine of lower alcohol and higher acidity. This makes it rather more aromatic, though less long-tasting. Fine for a non-vintage blend, but its comparative lack of finesse as well as staying power render it unsuitable for fine vintage wines. It is cane pruned.

GAMAY

Location: Beaujolais; Mâconnais; Lyonnais; Savoie; Ardèche (*vin de pays*); Languedoc-Roussillon (*vin de pays*); Loire; Gaillac and Poitou.

If the Pinot Noir is aristocratic, however much it may hint at having been born as the result of a dalliance with a member of a visiting circus, the Gamay is a solid, expansive and reliable member of the *bourgeoisie*. There are a number of Gamay varieties. The best and that grown in Burgundy is the Gamay Noir à Jus Blanc.

It is a vigorous, productive variety which ripens early. It is susceptible to spring frost, but is able to produce a second generation of buds to replace those which have been lost, so a serious deterioration in yield after poor weather is hardly ever a problem. It produces a medium-sized, compact cluster of berries, somewhat cylindrical, which makes a lightish wine of highish acidity, an abundant, crisp, cherry-like fruit, and very low tannin, which is at its best very young, often as soon as it has settled down after bottling. Gamay should be ripe but never sweet.

The Gamay is grown throughout France except in Alsace and Bordeaux, but comes into its own on the granitic soils of the northern Beaujolais and when vinified by carbonic maceration methods. It is also grown widely in the Mâconnais and to an extent on the lesser soils further north in Burgundy. In the Côte d'Or and the Côte Chalonnaise wines from Gamay are often blended with Pinot Noir (two-thirds of Gamay to one-third Pinot Noir) to make Bourgogne Passetoutgrains. This is one of the mismatches of the wine world, in my view, but it may be that the constituent parts — the grapes for the wines by implication of its name coming from the worst-exposed vineyards — were just as poor. Unlike the other Burgundian varieties the Gamay is spur pruned.

SYRAH

Location: Rhône Valley, particularly in the northern section; Provence and the Languedoc-Roussillon; Gaillac.

The Syrah is one of the three great black grapes of France, similar in quality and depth of character to the Pinot Noir and Cabernet Sauvignon. It is the classic variety of all the *appellations* of the northern Rhône and is now increasingly used as a *cépage améliorateur* in the southern Rhône, Languedoc-Roussillon and Provence. It is said to have originated in either Syracuse in Sicily or Shiraz in Persia (or even both), but has certainly been established in the Rhône Valley for many centuries, if not since Roman times. Prior to the phylloxera epidemic it was distributed even more widely in France.

The Syrah is not a productive variety and indeed loses much of its character when grown on more fertile, alluvial or gravel soils rather than on the essentially granite-based rock of the northern Rhône. It is susceptible to *coulure* but resistant to mildew and oidium. The berries are small and densely purple in colour and give a wine which is solid, tannic, full-bodied and long-tasting. When young, the wines have a youthful, even raw, slightly 'green' damson or blackberry aroma. On ageing the flavour mellows, softens and becomes more obviously rich as the wine takes on the extra complexity of age. Syrah wines need a long time to mature but their character is noble and aristocratic and worth the patience. The Syrah is spur (Gobelet) pruned, or trained to the Cordon de Royat.

GRENACHE

Location: Southern Rhône; Provence; Languedoc-Roussillon.

Though the Grenache originated in Spain, where under the name Garnacha it is one of that country's most popular red wine varieties, it has conquered southern France. This is the staple quality grape not only of Châteauneuf-du-Pape and Côtes du Rhône but of Côtes de Provence and the entire Languedoc-Roussillon.

Spur-pruned and trained to the Gobelet (bush) shape, Grenache is a fairly early developer though a late ripener. It is hardy, vigorous and adaptable, its major disadvantage being its lack of resistance to *coulure* and a tendency to rot if the weather changes to wet and humid in the run-up to the harvest.

A Grenache wine – and this is the reason why it is invariably blended with other varieties – has a wild, spicy, almost burned, slightly sweet character; very alcoholic on the one hand but blowsy because of a lack of acidity on the other and not particularly tannic.

CINSAULT

Location: Southern Rhône; Provence; Languedoc-Roussillon.

Cinsault – some authorities prefer to spell Cinsaut without the 'l' – is, with the superior Syrah and Mourvèdre, the variety most planted in the southern Rhône as an accessory to the Grenache. Like the Grenache but unlike the other two, the wine it produces is low in tannin, but it is less affected by *coulure* and rot. It produces a wine with a better acidity and colour and rather more stylish fruit. The wine has rather an innocuous character and does not age well. The vine is spur pruned.

MOURVÈDRE

Location: Southern Rhône; Provence, especially in Bandol; Languedoc-Roussillon.

Mourvèdre is a variety of Spanish origin and is a difficult plant to rear. Trained by either Gobelet or Cordon de Royat, it buds late but also ripens late. Even in the magnificent Bandol sun it does not often reach full maturity before the last week of September. It is a fussy plant, susceptible to mildew and oidium, though less to *coulure*, preferring a sheltered spot and a deep, well-drained stony soil, but being sensitive to prolonged drought in the summer. The wine is full, quite alcoholic and rather bitter and dense at first. Underneath it is rich and classy, but patience is required before the full glories are evident.

BRAUCOL AND DURAS

Location: Gaillac; other vineyards in the South-West.

I list these two varieties together because they are the mainstay of Gaillac. Braucol, known as the Fer Servadou, is seen in Marcillac, Madiran and Béarn in the South-West and is generally regarded as the superior of the two. It produces the bigger wine. Wine made from Duras (not to be confused with AC Côtes de Duras) is medium-bodied and fruity. Neither grape makes wine of great distinction. Both vines are cane pruned.

NEGRETTE

Location: Fronton; also found in Cahors, Gaillac and elsewhere in the South-West.

The Negrette is similar to the Gamay in that it produces the same style of wine. The wine is without tannin, soft and fruity, but also without a very pronounced acidity and so is incapable of ageing well. When young, crisp and intelligently made, the wine can be a delicious *petit vin*. The Negrette is cane (single-Guyot) pruned.

TANNAT

Location: Madiran, Béarn; elsewhere in the South-West.

The Tannat is the classic red wine variety of the extreme South-West of France. It buds and ripens late, in cool vintages not entirely successfully, but when it does the leaves turn completely red, a fiery russet, and seem to shimmer in the late afternoon sun of a glorious autumn day. Tannat produces a deeply coloured, astringently tannic wine, with high acidity and alcohol. Potentially, if fully ripe, this can be of excellent quality when mellow, if always somewhat larger than life; a bit too much of a blockbuster. As a result it is invariably blended with other varieties. When young, the primary fruit of raspberry is hopelessly overwhelmed by a harsh, tannic bitterness, so much so that the wine almost appears metallic. The Tannat is cane pruned.

POULSARD, TROUSSEAU AND MONDEUSE

Location: Jura; Savoie.

These three grapes are the indigenous varieties of the red wines of the Jura and the Savoie. None is particularly distinguished. The first two are found in the Jura and the Mondeuse in Savoie. The Poulsard is prone to frost because it buds early, to *coulure* and to rot, because the skin is thin. The wine is reasonably perfumed, light in body but oxidizes quickly. It makes a pretty but essentially uninspiring red which is more akin to a rosé.

Trousseau is a moderately producing variety with a thicker skin, producing fullish, well-coloured wine which needs time to soften. The wine is rustic though, and it does not age well, losing colour and also oxidizing fast. In the Jura both these varieties are losing out to the Pinot Noir; and a good thing too. Both are cane pruned.

The Mondeuse is confined to the Savoie, though appears under the name of Refosco in northern Italy. It is a vigorous variety, and can produce wine with good body, colour and fruit, though rarely in the cool alpine climates of the Savoie. Here the wine is all too often weak, tart and attenuated, and without any potential for ageing. The vine is spur pruned.

WHITE VARIETIES

SAUVIGNON BLANC

Location: Bordeaux, Bergerac, Duras and other Bordeaux satellites; Touraine; Central Loire; Auxerre (Sauvignon de Saint-Bris); Provence and Languedoc-Roussillon as a *cépage améliorateur* or as *vin de pays*.

The Sauvignon Blanc, to differentiate it from other Sauvignons, is a vigorous variety which matures early, forming a compact, conical cluster of small round berries. According to leading ampelographers it is subject to *coulure*, but in my experience the size of the crop in Bordeaux does not seem to vary nearly as much as a result of poor flowering as does the Merlot, for example, and in the Loire crops suffer more as a result of frost, so no doubt more *coulure*-resistant strains have been developed. Oidium is more of a problem. It is also prone to botrytis, though not so much as Sémillon. Sauvignon is cane pruned.

The Sauvignon grape produces a wine with a very individual flavour: steely, grassy, high in acidity, very flinty and aromatic. Words like gooseberry, blackcurrant leaf, even cat's pee are employed. As such the dry, stainless-steel-aged, youthfully bottled Sauvignon is a wine now widely seen, though the Bordeaux version is somewhat fuller and less racy than that of the Touraine and Central Loire, and in Bordeaux many seemingly pure Sauvignons have a little Sémillon in the blend to round the wine off. Strange as it may seem for a white wine, this variety produces a wine with a certain amount of tannin, and as a result of this, *élevage* (initial maturing) of pure Sauvignon in new oak is a procedure which needs to be handled with care. Combined with Sémillon in various proportions and aged in oak, Sauvignon produces the great white Graves.

Sémillon

Location: Bordeaux; Bergerac and other Bordeaux satellites.

Sémillon is the base for all Bordeaux's great sweet wines, though its value for dry wine production is only just beginning to be appreciated once again. This is the most widely planted white grape in the Bordeaux area. Sémillon is a vigorous, productive variety. It is spur pruned; and pruned very hard in Sauternes to reduce the crop to a minimum. It produces a cylindrical bunch of round berries, noticeably larger than the Sauvignon Blanc. These tend to develop a pinkish shade at full maturity, turning to browny-purple with over-ripeness. It is a hardy variety but susceptible to rot, both *pourriture grise* and *pourriture noble*, as it has a thin skin.

Poorly vinified, dry Sémillon wines can lack freshness and bouquet, character, breed and acidity. The result is heavy, neutral and dull. Correctly vinified, as increasingly this variety is in the Graves, particularly at places such as Château Rahoul and in enterprising hands elsewhere in the region, the results are totally different. The wines, though dry, are rich, fat and aromatic, with almost tropical, nutty fruit flavours and quite sufficient acidity. Good dry Sémillon is very classy, a far more interesting wine in my view than dry Sauvignon, and it has been under-rated in Bordeaux. It has taken the Australians, where for many years the variety has been grown in the Hunter Valley, to show the Bordeaux wine producers the potential for this grape.

Muscadelle

Location: Bordeaux; Bergerac and other Bordeaux satellites.

I insert Muscadelle here, though it is of less importance than some of the following grape varieties, in order to list the three main Bordeaux varieties together. The Muscadelle has nothing in common, despite the similarity of spelling, with either the Muscadet of the Pays Nantais or the various varieties of Muscat. It is moderately vigorous but very productive, develops late, and produces a large, loose, conical cluster of sizeable round berries. It is susceptible to *coulure*, powdery mildew, *pourriture grise* and botrytis (*pourriture noble*) while being less prone to downy mildew. You will rarely come across the Muscadelle except in small proportions in the sweet white wine areas of Bordeaux. Even here it is frowned upon at the highest level, for it is considered to produce coarse wine, very perfumed, but lacking finesse. The variety is cane pruned.

CHARDONNAY

Location: Burgundy; Champagne; Jura; Savoie; Ardèche (*vin de pays*); Loire (*vin de pays*); South of France (*vin de pays*); increasingly elsewhere.

The first thing to get straight about Chardonnay is that it has nothing to do with the Pinot family. The phrase Pinot-Chardonnay is a misnomer. Chardonnay is currently the most fashionable white wine variety in the world. It is probably now grown in every single wine-making region in France save for Bordeaux and parts of the South-West (it is now even allowed in Bergerac for *vin de pays*) as well as almost everywhere else.

Chardonnay is a fairly vigorous variety. It starts and finishes its growing season just a little after the Pinot Noir but is nevertheless also susceptible to spring frost, particularly in the cooler climate of Chablis, but is more hardy to extreme winter temperatures. *Coulure* is also a problem. It forms a small, relatively compact, winged-cylindrical cluster of small berries, not as densely closed as that of the Pinot Noir, and so is less susceptible to grey rot, though in the Mâconnais excessive heat in the run-up to the vintage has occasionally produced *pourriture noble*.

Chardonnay grows well on all calcareous-chalky soils and is in general a much more adaptable variety than Pinot Noir, performing equally well in Champagne and Chablis as in California, though there is a danger of excessively high degrees of alcohol in hotter conditions, as much in Pouilly-Fuissé as in the Napa Valley. Chardonnay is cane pruned. The best Chardonnay wines are both fermented and matured in wood, a percentage of which is new. It is the blend of subtle, ripe, opulent, nutty-buttery fruit and oak which is the true taste of fine Chardonnay and one of the great flavours of the world. It ages very well in bottle.

ALIGOTÉ

Location: Burgundy.

Aligoté is an old Burgundian variety of very secondary importance, producing only generic wine. It has diminished in favour in recent years. Aligoté is a resistant grape which crops well, ripening early to produce a light, *primeur*-style wine with a slightly herbal flavour and rather higher levels of acidity than the Chardonnay. The variety needs good pre-harvest weather lest the wine be somewhat tart.

There is a certain amount of Aligoté in odd parcels throughout the region. Only in the Auxerrois and in Bouzeron in the northern Côte Chalonnaise is it a speciality; Pernand-Vergelesses in the Côte de Beaune used to be another commune boasting a fine Aligoté, but in recent years, as elsewhere, the variety has tended to be replaced with Chardonnay. Aligoté is spur pruned. Aligoté is the traditional wine for mixing with a little Crème de Cassis to make Kir.

CHENIN BLANC

Location: Loire, particularly Touraine and Anjou.

Though there is a great deal more Sauvignon and Muscadet under cultivation than Chenin Blanc, it is Chenin which immediately springs to mind when one thinks of the

Loire. It is the quality white wine grape of Anjou and Touraine, exclusively producing the wines of Vouvray and Montlouis, Coteaux du Layon and Savennières, as well as the other quality white wines of the area. It is a vigorous, reasonably high-yielding variety that buds early, rendering it susceptible to spring frost. It is sensitive to both mildews though resistant to *coulure* and, most importantly, prone to rot. This is both its greatest advantage and its chief drawback. If the autumn weather is benign the grower can wait for an attack of *pourriture noble*. If not, and in the Loire we are almost at the northernmost limit of viable viticulture – so the risk is even higher than in Bordeaux – the rot will be grey, ignoble, and the Vouvray or Coteaux du Layon producer is wisest to avoid the risk and make a wine which is merely sweet or even only *demi-sec*.

Chenin wines have another failing. For some reason the flavour absorbs sulphur, becoming hard, neutral and somewhat sickly if the winemaker has over-protected his wine. The flavour is essentially fuller, richer and sweeter-smelling than Sauvignon, even if the wine is dry. It reminds me of a mixture of Victoria plums, greengages and something herbal and flowery such as camomile. There is a tart acidity in Chenin wines which admirably balances the more peachy, nectarine fruit of the sweeter versions, but can be somewhat lean in the drier wines if the autumn weather has not provided enough sun. It is spur pruned.

MUSCADET

Location: Muscadet.

Muscadet is the name of a wine and a vineyard area as well as a grape. It is an interloper in the Pays Nantais at the western end of the Loire Valley, having arrived from Burgundy in the early eighteenth century. The variety is, in fact, the white Gamay or Melon de Bourgogne.

Muscadet is resistant to frost, moderately vigorous and buds and ripens early. It is susceptible to both mildews and to rot, but does not suffer unduly from *coulure*. Muscadet wine has a flavour which is somewhat neutral, but fresh and soft, not overly acidic. It needs drinking early. The vine is spur pruned.

SYLVANER

Location: Alsace.

Sylvaner is a variety which is less popular than it was a decade or so ago but it is still, if only just, the most widely cultivated grape variety in Alsace, particularly in the northern section of the vineyards in the Bas-Rhin, where it is responsible for over half of the production. Its origin is said to be Austria or Transylvania, and it only arrived in Alsace in force in 1870. Without being a hardy plant, it is a grape which gives a high yield, even in cool conditions, and it is also resistant to rot. It ripens later than most of the rest of the Alsace grapes. It is usually cane pruned.

Sylvaner wine has a low alcohol but a refreshing acidity, making it an excellent carafe wine. Occasionally, some really fine Sylvaners can be found, which are appropriate for maturing in bottle, but these are rare. Most Sylvaner, soft, fruity and easy to drink, is best drunk young.

PINOT BLANC AND PINOT AUXERROIS

Location: Alsace; Burgundy.

Clevner, or Klevner, is the Alsace name for wine which can come from a number of members of the Pinot family. Normally it is made from the Pinot Blanc which originated in Burgundy or from its slightly spicier cousin, the Pinot Auxerrois. Clevner can also be made from the Pinot Noir vinified as a white wine, or from the Pinot Gris. Whatever the blend, the wine can be called either Clevner or Pinot Blanc, and normally the latter for the export markets. Pinot Blanc is more productive than Pinot Auxerrois but Auxerrois gives a slightly higher alcohol degree and marginally lower acidity, though in neither variety is the acidity level of the resultant wine very high. Clevner wine has the typical, rather four-square Alsace character, fuller and more interesting than the Sylvaner, and also used for carafe wine. It is soft, fruity, supple and fairly low in acidity. It is best consumed young while still preserving its youthful freshness. Production of Pinot Blanc has increased considerably in the last twenty years as the variety can be planted on soils generally unfavourable to other varieties and it has a good resistance to frost, though it is susceptible to a number of fungoid diseases. Pinot Blanc forms the base for most Crémant d'Alsace, the local sparkling wine. Both varieties are cane pruned.

PINOT GRIS

Location: Alsace; Burgundy.

That the wine from the Pinot Gris should be called Tokay d'Alsace in Alsace is explained by local tradition that the variety was brought back by Baron Lazari de Schwendi who led an expedition of French mercenaries which captured the town of Tokay from the Turkish invaders in 1565. Sadly for the story, Pinot Gris has no connection at all with the Furmint, the real Tokay grape, it being the same as the Szükebarat of Lake Balaton, the Ruländer of Germany and the Malvoisie of the Loire. Despite recent EC directives, endeavouring to prohibit the use of the title Tokay d'Alsace, the locals seem determined to persist, so Tokay d'Alsace it will stay. Pinot Gris ripens early but produces feebly and is prone to disease. Pinot Gris wine is full, fat, rich and spicy with a sort of barley sugar after-taste, and quite a high level of alcohol. Its lack of acidity prevents Tokay d'Alsace from being as interesting and as satisfying as the wines made from Riesling and Gewürztraminer. Nevertheless, it is a 'first division' Alsace variety, and though not widely planted, one of three which are regularly made into Vendange Tardive and Sélection de Grains Nobles wines and will develop in bottle. In Burgundy it is known as Pinot Beurot, but is not very widely planted. It is cane pruned.

MUSCAT

Location: Alsace; southern Rhône and Languedoc-Roussillon for *vin doux naturel*.

There is a phrase in the Song of Solomon, 'a fountain of gardens', which to me summarizes the flavour of dry Muscat wines. Muscat makes the most grapey of all wines, for wines do not normally taste of grapes. Normally, in the Midi and elsewhere around the Mediterranean, it is found as a sweet wine. In these regions – Beaumes-de-Venise,

Rivesaltes, Frontignan and Lunel — the fermentation of the must is arrested by fortification with brandy, producing a naturally sweet wine with an alcohol level of just over 15 degrees. These are called *vins doux naturels*.

There are many, many different varieties of Muscat grape. In Alsace there are two, the Muscat à Petit Grains, which is also grown in Beaumes-de-Venise and Frontignan, and the Muscat Ottonel. The resulting wine is always dry. Neither variety is easy to grow in the Alsace climate. Both are rather particular about the soil they prefer and are very prone to *coulure*, mildew and rot, sometimes failing to produce at all. The Muscat à Petits Grains, perhaps the oldest variety in the region, ripens late, a further disadvantage, and so has been largely replaced since the late nineteenth century by the Ottonel, a variety developed from the Chasselas, which develops earlier and produces more regularly. I find the Ottonel wine less fine, less distinctive, coarser, and it is sad that more hardy strains of the true Muscat d'Alsace have not so far been developed. A good Muscat from Alsace will have a wonderfully fresh, flowery, sweet grapey nose — there are elements of honeysuckle — and yet be dry on the palate. It makes a perfect apéritif, and is best drunk young. Both varieties are spur pruned.

Gewürztraminer

Location: Alsace.

Nowhere else in the world does the Gewürztraminer reach such an apogee of quality than in Alsace. With its easily enjoyed, memorable, spicy flavour, Gewürztraminer is the ambassador of Alsace; as the late Jean Hugel wrote, 'everyman's *Grand Vin*'.

The flavour is attractive and the wine, when well made, a delight. The Gewürztraminer is said to be a form — a sort of particularly spicy cousin — of the Traminer grape, a variety which has been indigenous to Alsace since the Middle Ages. The Traminer may possibly originally have come from the village of Tramin or Termano in the Italian Alto-Adige — it is certainly still widely planted there — or this may be pure coincidence. As Gewürztraminer, the grape has had its own individuality for at least a century or more, when it first appeared on wine lists as a superior and more expensive alternative to Traminer. For years the names Traminer and Gewürztraminer were interchangeable in Alsace, the latter name — for *Gewürze* is German for 'spice' — being the spicier example. Since 1973 all wine has been labelled as Gewürztraminer.

It is not an easy variety to cultivate. Though vigorous and thriving on most soils, particularly those heavy with clay, it is prone to frost in the spring because the buds break early, and also to powdery mildew. More importantly it is also more susceptible than most to *coulure*. In 1977, and again in 1978 and 1980, there was a tiny Gewürztraminer crop in Alsace as a result of poor weather in June. Gewürztraminer requires a particularly good autumn in order fully to ripen. When this happens, the small, rather loose bunch of small, thick-skinned grapes will turn salmon pink in colour, leading some to mistake them for unripe red grapes. Because of this late ripening, I often find merchants' basic Gewürztraminer to be a little insufficient in fruit, thus sometimes a little bitter. The 'reserve' qualities are invariably better value for money and will keep. The better examples still will develop for five years or more, and last for twenty.

Gewürztraminer varies widely in style, largely because of the soil on which it is grown.

Some *négociants*, having allowed a malolactic fermentation to occur, produce a soft, scented wine. Others make a more masculine example, firmer and with higher acidity, longer-tasting. Others still produce a very aromatic Gewürztraminer; some, even the rather over-perfumed wine the locals call *pommadé*. Above all Gewürztraminer is unmistakeable. It is fat, scented, aromatic and spicy. It is mouth-filling, strong and flamboyant. There is nothing particularly subtle or elegant about a Gewürztraminer wine but there is plenty which is irresistible, even seductive. The variety is cane pruned.

RIESLING

Location: Alsace.

The noble Riesling, producer of nearly all the really fine wines of Germany, is equally at home in Alsace. While, to the outsider, Gewürztraminer may be the most 'typical' Alsace grape, the locals are normally proudest of their Riesling wines. Though it has been grown in Alsace since 1477, and widely since the mid-eighteenth century, the development of Riesling as a major force in Alsace dates from the 1920s.

The Riesling prefers a well-drained slope, generally of a limestone nature. Yet it will thrive on the volcanic soil of the famous Rangen vineyard at Thann, on the granitic soil of the Brand vineyard at Turckheim, on the gravelly alluvial soil of the Herrenweg in Turckheim, on the chalky clay of the Clos Hauserer, as well as the limestone of the Hengst vineyard, both in Wintzenheim. The Wintzenheim producer Zind-Humbrecht has vineyards planted with Riesling on all these sites. A comparative tasting of all their different Rieslings, each made in the same way, but each with its own particular characteristics and nuances, is a fascinating experience.

The Riesling vine is hardy and resistant to disease, and though a relatively shy cropper compared with the Sylvaner or Pinot Gris, it is regular. It ripens late, but – a great advantage in a northern climate – it continues to develop even in fairly cool autumns. When allowed to come to full maturity it will give a wine of extraordinary finesse and complexity of fruit, with a complex nose, and a rich, full flavour balanced with a high level of acidity, giving an excellent length on the palate. In Alsace, unlike on the Rhine and the Mosel, the must is allowed to ferment completely, any residual sugar, in the case of Vendange Tardive or Sélection de Grains Nobles wines, being natural, the sugar of perfect ripeness.

An Alsace Riesling can be anything from a classy but essentially rather four-square wine, albeit with the characteristic clean, slightly austere fruit of the Riesling grape, to a wine of superlative quality, one of the really great wines of the world. Even in poor years like 1977 and '84, a Riesling from a good site such as Trimbach's Clos Ste Hune can be remarkably fine, while the wines of the other Alsace grapes remain no better than undistinguished. The Riesling is cane pruned.

ROUSSANNE AND MARSANNE

Location: Rhône; Savoie; Languedoc-Roussillon.

It is convenient to take these two varieties together for, outside Condrieu and Château-Grillet where the Viognier is grown, they produce all the white wine *appellations* of the northern Rhône. Roussanne is the classy variety but very susceptible to oidium, and even now that more resistant clones have been developed, a poor cropper. Its wine is delicate and fragrant, with a crisp mountain herbs flavour, a refreshing acidity and a depth of character which means that not only can it be delicious young, but it will age; though it seems to go through a curious adolescent phase in the middle. Today it is almost entirely confined to the Hermitage hill.

Elsewhere in the northern Rhône the Marsanne has taken over. More vigorous and more productive than the Roussanne, the Marsanne ripens almost too easily. There is a tendency to produce wines with a little too much alcohol and not enough acidity. Blended half with Roussanne and correctly vinified as in the top wines like Jaboulet's Hermitage, Le Chevalier de Stérimberg, its threatening coarseness can be contained. Elsewhere the wine needs to be bottled and consumed early before it maderizes.

In the Savoie, where the Roussanne is known as the Roussette, the wines, of whichever origin, are lighter, more ephemeral, and have a mountain herbs flavour. In the Languedoc-Roussillon only the Marsanne is found, and this rarely, though some enterprising producers of *vins de pays* make some interesting examples. Both Roussanne and Marsanne are cane pruned.

VIOGNIER

Location: Condrieu and Château Grillet; southern Rhône; Provence; Languedoc-Roussillon.

This is an intriguing variety. The Viognier produces one of the most deliciously fragrant and complex wines in the whole world (in Condrieu and Château Grillet), but with such a grudging attitude towards quantity that even the most altruistic millionaire must view it with suspicion. Viognier is difficult to establish, though once it has settled in it is capable of living to a grand old age. It is susceptible to both *coulure* and *millerandage*, and even when the flowering takes place successfully the variety only ripens with difficulty, and the yield is consequently very low.

The wine, though, is of the highest quality, full-bodied, quite alcoholic and rich, yet at the same time delicate, flowery and with a touch of citrus. It has a flavour of great individuality and elegance. I am pleased to see that estates in the southern Rhône and in the Midi such as Mas de Daumas Gassac at Aniane and Château Sainte-Anne at Saint-Gervais are now encouraging this variety. The Viognier is cane pruned.

SAVIGNIN

Location: Jura.

The Savignin Blanc is said by ampelographical experts to be the same as the Traminer of Alsace. (Do not confuse it with the Savignin Rosé or the Klevner of Heiligenstein which makes a particular, rather uncommon wine in Alsace. This is said not to be a true relation.) The legend has it that Savignin was brought from Hungary to France by Benedictine monks in the tenth century. The variety is a late developer and a poor cropper but produces a wine powerful in both alcohol and flavour. I find it has little in common with the Traminer, but that is not to say that it does not have either quality or individuality.

The wine is full and has a peculiar spicy nuttiness that reminds me of green walnuts. You will rarely see it on its own as what I might term a table wine for it is normally the minor partner in a Chardonnay/Savagnin blend. As the 'onlie begetter' of the Jura *vins jaunes* it is uncomparable. The Savignin is cane pruned.

MAUZAC

Location: Limoux; Gaillac; elsewhere in the South-West.

Mauzac is a vigorous variety which ripens late and produces a crisp, somewhat neutral, lightish wine with quite a high acidity. The flavour is herbal and appley; and the wines are best drunk young while they are fresh. As a wine with high acidity Mauzac is the ideal base for the sparkling wines of Limoux. In the Tarn the wine is often slightly *pétillant* or *perlé*. The variety is spur pruned.

GROS MANSENG AND PETIT MANSENG

Location: Jurançon; elsewhere in the South-West.

The Petit Manseng is the one with the smaller berries, as you might expect, and it is also the superior variety. Unfortunately it is the more difficult of the two to grow and much the lower yielder. The skins, particularly of Petit Manseng, are thick, but nevertheless will attract *pourriture noble* in the finest of vintages, though most commonly the wines are merely sweet and concentrated, not botrytis-affected. Both varieties produce wines with a good level of flavour and quality. The character is herbal and gently spicy, with good levels of both alcohol and acidity. Both Mansengs are cane pruned.

The French Laws of Wine

Progressively since the beginning of the twentieth century – gathering momentum in the early 1930s and finally being enacted in its present form in 1935 – the government of France, together with the local representatives of the growers and the wine merchants, developed a system of wine laws. While *inter alia* these regulations *do* affect the standard of the wines, their concept was *not* to offer a guarantee of quality. The purpose was to endeavour to protect the geographical origin of the wines against fraud and to determine the often time-honoured ways in which the wines were made and the grape varieties used.

   The French authorities have decreed four standards of wine.

1. The best are those with the designation *Appellation d'Origine Contrôlée* or AOC, often shortened simply to AC or *Appellation Contrôlée*. This has covered all the mainstream areas of France since 1935 and is slowly but surely being extended to the lesser regions. Twenty-eight per cent of the total wine production of France is now AC. The total area delimited is some 387,000 hectares (390 separate *appellations*) and the total production (1988) is some 21 million hectolitres per annum.

2. The second category after AC wines is that of the *Vins Delimités de Qualité Supérieure* or VDQS. These are the wines of the lesser areas of France. As standards rise more and more VDQS are being promoted to AC. The latest is Marcillac in the Aveyron. Only 1.3 per cent of France's production is now VDQS: 60 *appellations* and 13,000 hectares.

3. *Vins de pays*, the third category, are a superior form of *vins ordinaires*. Higher yields and a more liberal choice of grape varieties are allowed than for VDQS and AC wines but each wine must pass a tasting test. Enterprising growers in Provence, the Midi and the South-West, where most of these wines are to be found, often find they can produce some very interesting wines in this category, largely because they can be made with a higher percentage of non-indigenous quality grape varieties than the local AC and VDQS regulations allow. Thirteen per cent of French wine falls into this category.

The concept of *vins de pays* was devised in 1973. There are now 132, which I feel is so large a number as to be almost self-defeating, particularly as it is hard to differentiate between the styles of a great number of them. They fall into three categories: regional (from a large wine area, covering more than one *département*); departmental (covering the wines of a whole *département*), and zonal (limited to a small district, perhaps even just one commune). (*See page 404 for a full list.*)

Vins de pays vary in style, quality, pretension and price. Most of the examples from the South of France are red wines intended for early drinking; those from the Loire are similar white wines; good quaffing bottles with nothing more to say for themselves. Here and there you will find better examples: pure Cabernet Sauvignons such as that of Bandol's Bunan brothers, a Vin de Pays de Mont Caume, or those of Pierre Bezinet at Vias in the Languedoc. I list a few favourites on pages 375–7. At a more expensive level, a *vin de pays* which has a pretension of a *cru classé* is Mas de Daumas Gassac. Here the parallel is with the new breed of Tuscan *vini da tavola* such as Tignanello and Sassicaia.

4. *Vins de Table*, *Vins Ordinaires* and *Vins de Consummation Courante*. This category covers the remainder and includes wine destined for distilling into brandy – Cognac from the Charentes, Armagnac from Gascony and a little Fine elsewhere. Thirty-four million hectolitres are produced. Most is produced in the Midi and consumed in France rather than exported. The domestic market for this sort of wine has declined. The French consumer now drinks less in total, but more wines of better quality, like his counterpart in other wine-producing countries.

The specifications for AC and VDQS wine cover the following categories.

[a] *Area of production*. This defines the area entitled to a particular *appellation*, in principle restricting the land only to suitable vineyard sites.

[b] *Grape varieties*. This lists which grape varieties may be planted in order to qualify for the *appellation*. In practice this means a list of 'recommended' varieties together with, in some cases, an additional list of varieties 'permitted' in small proportions. Often these 'permitted' varieties are to be slowly phased out by a given date.

[c] *Viticultural regulations*. This lays down the density of the vines per given area and determines how they should be planted, pruned and treated during the viticultural season.

[d] *Ripeness of the fruit*. This determines the minimum alcohol level of the wine before chaptalization. The grape juice must have enough natural sugar to produce a wine which

will reach the minimum alcohol level before chaptalization. In some areas in the South of France chaptalization is not permitted. The legal amount by which a wine can be chaptalized is also regulated.

[e] *Quantity*. This sets maximum yields per given area. It is expressed in hectolitres of juice per hectare. This is explained more fully below.

[f] *Wine-making*. This determines what is and is not allowed during the vinification and maturation process for each *appellation*.

[g] *Age of commercialization*. This regulates, in some instances, the minimum age at which a wine can be put on the market.

[h] *Tasting and chemical analysis*. All wines must pass both a tasting test – in practice this seems more to be directed towards typicity, i.e. that it demonstrates the style of the grape or grapes from which it originates, than (high) quality – and satisfy the authorities by its chemical analysis. This was introduced in 1974.

[i] *Declaration of stocks and yields*. This requires growers to make a declaration of their production each vintage and of their unsold stocks at 31 August each year.

The authorized maximum yield per given area has always been the most thorny of the legislative problems and the one most open to abuse. Prior to 1974 the 'Cascade' system was in operation. A grower producing more than the permitted quantity of a top *appellation* could declare the maximum for that *appellation* and the remainder under a lower category where the restrictions on the yield were not quite so strict – and if there was still some wine over, that would be declared as a generic wine.

Thus, to take a Burgundian example, let us suppose a grower in Chambertin-Clos de Bèze, a *grand cru* in Gevrey-Chambertin, produced 50 hectolitres from his one hectare of vines. A maximum of 30 hectolitres would be declared as Clos de Bèze, a further 5 (because the legislation allowed 35 hectolitres per hectare) as village Gevrey, and 15 as Bourgogne Rouge, for the allowable limit for the generic wine was 50 hectolitres per hectare. In theory it was, or could have been, all the same wine. In practice the Cascade system was rampant with fraud, thousands of casks or cases being exported to such countries as Britain as 'Bourgogne No 9', with a nod and a wink that it was 'surplus production'. This was labelled and eventually sold as Nuits-Saint-Georges or some other name.

Today an alternative, marginally more satisfactory system is in practice. (What prevents it from being more satisfactory still is that the yields are too lenient.) In essence there is more flexibility. The basic permitted yield (*rendement de base*) remains. Each year the local growers' syndicate will propose an annual yield (*rendement annuel*) to the INAO (*Institut National des Appellations d'Origine*). This figure will take into account the actual climatic conditions of the year. The figure can indeed in theory be less than the basic yield. But in practice it is invariably higher. On top of this a grower is permitted to produce a fixed percentage more, usually 20 per cent. If the grower decides to apply for this *plafond limite de classement* (PLC), all his wine must pass a tasting test. If it is rejected it must be distilled.

The main criticism to be made of the AC laws is that they protect the grower rather than the consumer. There are a number of improvements that would help to redress the balance.

The first and most important improvement would be to bring on to the various legislative bodies, controlling syndicates and tasting committees qualified representatives who can speak and argue from the point of view of the consumer and who have no commercial axes to grind. Tasting certificates of approval should be based on quality as well as on typicity rather than on an absence of obvious flaws. Wines should be sampled after bottling, when all the cellarwork has been completed, not merely at the end of the vinification process. The authorities should have the power to demote a wine, though its origins and style may be totally authentic, solely on the basis of quality.

We live in a time when, with the help of modern science, yields are plentiful; but often they are excessive. Whatever the growers and their oenologists may argue, there is a point where quantity becomes inversely proportional to quality – when the heavily laden vines have to struggle to achieve a reasonable level of alcohol and are then chaptalized up to the limit to reach the point where the wine is stable. When additionally they do not have a natural balancing level of acidity, no wine of real quality and concentration can result. Maximum allowable yields need to be reduced, the 20 per cent PLC should be abolished for 'quality', i.e. classed growth wine and more rigorous pruning and obligatory crop thinning after a successful flowering must be introduced. Anyone who produces over the allowable limit should be threatened with automatic rejection of the entire crop.

A further improvement would be the introduction of compulsory estate bottling of all classified, *premier cru* (in Burgundian terms) or other wines which are to be dignified with a single domaine or site-name label. All other wines of *appellation* or VDQS quality should be bottled in the area of their origin (as already is decreed for Alsace). This will not in itself guarantee quality but it should guarantee origin and authenticity. It will also concentrate the mind of both grower and *négociant*, and that might not be a bad thing. The designations *domaine* (which can mean almost anything and is therefore valueless and meaningless) and *mise en bouteille à la propriété* need to be tightened up. The use of *sous marques* (second labels) needs to be examined, and the practice of some organizations and co-operatives using other 'invented' names, which might make the consumer think that it is an individual grower's wine, must be prohibited.

The information on the wine label could also be improved to the benefit of the consumer. We already have informative back labels on many wines from California and Australia which the French could do well to copy.

All this might sound as if I consider that the intention of those in the wine business is to mislead the consumer and foist him or herself off with inferior or fraudulent wine. And that the consumers are themselves being fooled. This is in no way so. The wine trade in my experience is a very honourable one. The vast majority of the producers are doing their very best to make as good a wine as they possibly can. The buyers select with care and their marketeers – for we live in a competitive world – must make sure they can sell it at a reasonable price or they will go out of business. Nor are the consumers such fools. Most of them can tell good from bad and will recognize quality and reject the inferior. As a result of modern methods, a widening of the market and increasing knowledge on both sides the standard of wine has increased out of all proportion in the three decades since I started regularly drinking wine. But it can go higher. And today if we are, as we are, being asked to pay very high prices for the best, we are surely entitled to demand that we do get commensurate quality in the bottle.

Chapter 1

BORDEAUX

Bordeaux is by far the largest fine wine region in France. It is also, arguably, the greatest, and as such, again a matter for dispute, the finest in the world. Bordeaux produces all the three main types of wine, red, dry white and luscious sweet white wine. At the top levels these are the most aristocratic, the most profound and the most sumptuous of all wines. Here the word 'breed', used to describe wines of the highest finesse and elegance, can be applied in the greatest numbers and with the most consistent regularity.

It is the number and variety of its finest wines that, for me, makes Bordeaux the most fascinating wine area of all. Burgundy has as many quality wine growers and top domaines, but production is on a very much smaller scale: a few casks rather than several dozen *tonneaux*. One single vineyard, itself much less extensive than a Bordeaux estate, may in Burgundy be divided among a couple of dozen owners. In Bordeaux the vineyard will be in a single hand and the economies of scale make it much easier for the top growers to be as rigorous as possible in their selection of which *cuvées* will go into the *grand vin* and which will be rejected.

There are some 175 classed growths in Bordeaux; 60 Médocs, 28 Sauternes, 75 Saint-Émilions and a dozen Graves. Add to this the top wines of Pomerol – which has never been classified – and the best of the *bourgeois* estates, many of whom produce wine of similar quality, and you have perhaps 250 single wine names producing at the highest level. Multiply that figure by the number of vintages drinkable or not yet mature that may be on the market, and you will have upwards of 5000 different wines. Each will be constantly changing as it gradually ages; and of all wines Bordeaux, whether red or sweet white – and indeed the top dry whites as well – has the greatest capacity to age, acquiring

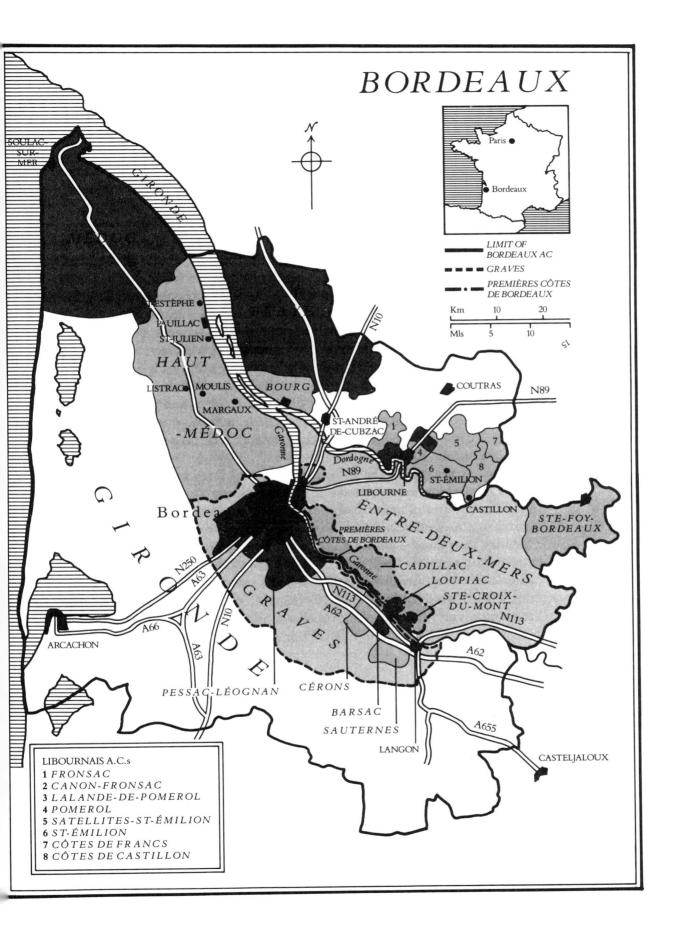

BORDEAUX

Paris ●
Bordeaux ●

LIMIT OF
BORDEAUX AC
━ ━ GRAVES
━ · ━ PREMIÈRES CÔTES
DE BORDEAUX

Km   10   20
Mls   5   10

N

SOULAC-
SUR-
MER

GIRONDE

MÉDOC

ST-ESTÈPHE ●
PAUILLAC ●
ST-JULIEN ●

HAUT

LISTRAC ● MOULIS ●
MARGAUX ●

-MÉDOC

BOURG

Garonne

ST-ANDRÉ-
DE-CUBZAC

Dordogne
N89

LIBOURNE

COUTRAS   N89

1
4   5   7
        8
6   ST-ÉMILION ●

CASTILLON

STE-FOY-
BORDEAUX

ENTRE-DEUX-MERS

Bordea

PREMIÈRES
CÔTES DE BORDEAUX

CADILLAC
LOUPIAC
STE-CROIX-
DU-MONT

Garonne

N113   N113

GIRONDE

GRAVES

N250
A63

N10

A63

A66

ARCACHON

PESSAC-LÉOGNAN

CÉRONS

A62

BARSAC
SAUTERNES

LANGON

A62

A655

CASTELJALOUX

LIBOURNAIS A.C.s
1 FRONSAC
2 CANON-FRONSAC
3 LALANDE-DE-POMEROL
4 POMEROL
5 SATELLITES-ST-ÉMILION
6 ST-ÉMILION
7 CÔTES DE FRANCS
8 CÔTES DE CASTILLON

further profundity, complexity and uniqueness of character as it does so. Every year a new crop will unleash another substantial batch to be appreciated.

But this is only the tip of the iceberg. This cream will represent perhaps 5 per cent – but as much as 26 million bottles in total – of the annual harvest. Underneath that lies the unsung Bordeaux – good, if not fine, but still worthy of recognition. Not perhaps the sort of wines to which wine writers will devote pages of purple prose, nor drinkers any abject ceremony, but bottle after bottle of the most part solidly dependable wine at prices we can all afford to dispense regularly.

Bordeaux is both a city and the name of wine. The city, eighth largest in France, and until recently one of its major ports, lies on a bend of the river Garonne in south-west France. The Garonne flows north-westwards from the middle of the Pyrenees into the Atlantic Ocean. Some ten kilometres north of Bordeaux it is joined by the last of its great tributaries, the river Dordogne. Together these form the estuary of the Gironde, from which comes the name of the *département* of which Bordeaux is the capital.

The Gironde *département* (with the exception of the coastal area) corresponds with the wine-growing region of Bordeaux. Roughly 100,000 hectares of land are planted with vines, producing, during the last decade, an average of over 4 million hectolitres of AC wine per annum, about 22 per cent of the total AC production of France. This is approximately twice as much as that of Burgundy (including Beaujolais) and half as much again as the Rhône Valley. For example, Château Brane-Cantenac, one of the largest of the classed growths, produces over 40,000 cases of wine, as much as the total production of Hermitage in the Rhône Valley.

Almost 75 per cent of the AC Gironde harvest is red wine. This makes the Bordeaux area by far the largest quality red wine area of France. The Gironde's production of over 3 million hectolitres of *appellation contrôlée* red wine dwarfs that of Burgundy's mere one quarter of a million hectolitres of red (Pinot Noir) *appellation contrôlée* wine.

Unlike Burgundy – indeed unlike much of the rest of France – Bordeaux is an area of largely proprietorial rather than peasant ownership and hence is one of relatively large estates, often long-established, self-sufficient in wine terms and which market their wines under their own 'château' names. Cocks and Féret, the 'Bible of Bordeaux', lists some 4200 single vineyards and the proprietors thereof, and this itself is only the cream of around 21,000 growers who officially declare a crop each vintage.

History

In books devoted solely to the wines of Bordeaux, such as Edmund Penning-Rowsell's *The Wines of Bordeaux* and Pamela Vandyke Price's *The Wines of the Graves*, the history of the region and its produce has been covered with great depth and authority. I shall not attempt to emulate them. I refer readers to both these lucid accounts and acknowledge my debt to them in preparing the résumé which follows.

It seems likely, says Penning-Rowsell, that Bordeaux was a wine-trading centre before it was a vine-growing region. The western side of the region is very flat, and in early

Roman times it would have been marshy, covered in forest and infested with mosquitoes. The soil was poor and the climate less propitious for the cultivation of the vine than the higher ground, the *Haut Pays* further to the south and west. At the start Bordeaux was an *emporium*, important primarily as a port. It is therefore probable that it was not until the third century AD that the vine began to be widely planted in the locality. Ausonius, poet, consul and tutor to Roman emperors, owned vineyards in the area in the fourth century, though whether this was at Château Ausone is a matter for dispute. In one of his poems he refers not to the Dordogne but to the Garonne flowing gently at the bottom of his garden. Yet the most impressive Roman ruins outside Bordeaux are to be found in the grounds of Château La Gaffelière, at the foot of the Château Ausone escarpment.

Historical details during the next several hundred years, as elsewhere in the Europe of the Dark Ages, are sparse. There was an expansion of the vineyard in the eleventh century, but it was the arrival of the English after the marriage of the redoubtable Eleanor of Aquitaine to Henry Plantagenet in 1152 that had the profoundest effect. For three centuries the Bordeaux vineyards came under the jurisdiction of the English crown. England became the Gironde's most important export market, and each year, shortly after the harvest, before the winter had set in, a vast fleet would transport the cream of the crop, first chiefly to Bristol and Southampton, later to London. During the thirteenth, fourteenth and fifteenth centuries the vine gradually replaced all other forms of agriculture in the area, and though at first most of the wine shipped to England seems to have come from further north, from the Poitou and the Charente, Bordeaux soon became the major point of departure. For many hundreds of years, long after the departure of the English in 1453, wine was France's leading export, Britain its most important customer and Bordeaux the chief exporter.

Not all the wine exported was strictly 'Bordeaux', however; much was the produce of the *Haut Pays* – wine of the Dordogne, the Lot, the Tarn and the upper Garonne. These had to pay a tax, higher if from the French side of whatever was the border between the French and the English at the time, and faced other restrictions, such as being embargoed from shipment until after the Gironde harvest had left. Nevertheless, the whole of the South-West looked to England, and later to the Low Countries, Hamburg and the Baltic ports, for its market. Communications overland were cumbersome, hazardous and prolonged, and the French crown bought its wine from nearer at hand, from the upper Loire, Champagne and Burgundy.

Sensibly, even after the expulsion of the English after the battle of Castillon in 1453, the French kings took care not to disrupt the Bordeaux trade. The local inhabitants had never considered themselves anything other than Gascon, neither English nor French. The privileges the Bordeaux merchants had enjoyed under the English were confirmed, and after an initial bout of petty commercial warfare the French were forced to realize that they were now competing on their most important export market with wines from the Iberian peninsula and elsewhere.

The English remained customers for the finest Bordeaux wines even after the rise of the Dutch as an economic power in the seventeenth century and the various economic treaties discriminating against the French and in favour of Portugal which culminated in the Methuen Treaty in 1703. The Dutch became Bordeaux's major customer, but their requirements were for cheap wines, largely white, much of which was re-exported to

Scandinavia and the Hanseatic ports.

The last quarter of the seventeenth and the first half of the eighteenth centuries was the period of the establishment of most of the great estates, what were to become the *crus classés* in 1855. Prior to this period the quality red wines had come from the upper Graves, surrounding the town of Bordeaux. Dutch engineers, with their experience in the Low Countries, drained the Médoc, formerly a land of marshes liable to widespread flooding at the time of neap tides, thus exposing the mounds of almost pure gravel, excellent for the vine, on which the great properties are centred to this day.

Château Haut-Brion in the Graves and then owned by the influential Pontac family, was the first of the Bordeaux estates to achieve renown and the first in English literature to be specifically named, Samuel Pepys enjoying the wine at the Royal Oak Tavern in 1663. Forty years later the *London Gazette* advertised the sale of Lafite, Margaux and Latour wines, as well as 'Pontac', looted from ships captured in the War of Spanish Succession. These estates were all owned by a new aristocracy, the *noblesse de la robe*. As the seventeenth century had progressed, a new breed of moneyed class had replaced the old *noblesse d'épée*. These families, of largely merchant origin, owed their power to their place in the Bordeaux *parlement*, their wealth to their land. Increasingly during the eighteenth century, suitable terrain in the Médoc was converted into monocultural vineyards, and after the French Revolution this expansion continued in Saint-Émilion, Pomerol and the Léognan part of the Graves.

The Revolution and the Napoleonic wars which followed, though serious for the wine trade, left the top growths relatively unscathed. A few proprietors were guillotined, others emigrated and had their estates sequestered, as were those vineyards in ecclesiastical ownership. Though business suffered, there was little social upheaval. The great estates preserved their unity and remained the property of the moneyed classes. Bordeaux is a region of large domaines, vinously self-sufficient, bourgeois in ownership; Burgundy is a region of much fragmented vineyards in largely peasant possession. It is this which has caused the great difference between Bordeaux and Burgundy which continues to this day.

The nineteenth century saw three major scourges in the vineyard, the arrival of a new generation of proprietors, industrialists or those who had made their money out of the wine trade itself, and the beginning of the adoption of modern mechanical and scientific methods of tilling the land and making the wine.

The first of the great natural disasters was the arrival of oidium in the early 1850s. Oidium, or powdery mildew, is a cryptogamic disease which affects both leaves and grapes. The leaves shrivel and drop off; the fruit is split and dries up. Though the solution, the application of sulphur, was soon discovered, production was decimated and prices rose steeply, never to return to their previous levels.

Though phylloxera, a member of the aphid family, was first discovered in France in 1863, it did not make its appearance in the Gironde until 1869, and did not really begin to cause serious damage in the Médoc until a decade later. Phylloxera is the greatest pest of them all, for, unlike oidium and mildew, which, like a spring frost attack, bad weather during the flowering or hail in late summer, only affect a single year's harvest, the phylloxera kills the plant itself. Potentially its ravages are catastrophic. It is not for nothing that its cognomen is *Vastastrix*. Phylloxera arrived in Europe from America, and it was in America that the imagination of the Bordeaux viticulturalist Leo Laliman found the solution to the problem, astonishingly as early as 1871. This was to graft the noble European varieties of the *vinifera* vine on to American non-*vinifera* rootstocks. Opposition to this radical proposal seemed solid until, despairing of finding an alternative solution, the growers had to face the inevitable. By 1882 97.5 per cent of the Gironde had been over-run by the louse, but it was only gradually, far more gradually in the top states than most people realize, that grafted vines began to be introduced. As late as the 1890s *vignes françaises* were still being planted. Château Latour did not begin to plant grafted vines seriously until 1901 and it took a couple of decades completely to replace the non-grafted old French vines.

Meanwhile Bordeaux had been hit by the third of its plagues. Downy mildew or peronospera arrived in the South of France in 1882, and seems to have spread rapidly west to the Gironde. Like oidium it is a cryptogamic disease, but affecting mainly the leaves. An antidote, copper sulphate solution, was soon discovered, and by 1888 the outbreak was under control.

As important as this succession of natural disasters were the economic consequences. Bordeaux, indeed the whole of France south of Paris, had many more hectares of land under vine in the 1850s than in 1900, even today. In hard-nosed financial terms the arrival of phylloxera could be termed salutary. Uneconomic vineyards were allowed to decay; their owners and their workers forced to seek alternative employment. The human corollary compounded by the Franco-Prussian War and by a recession in wine prices which remained until the mid-1950s, is incalculable. This cloud of misery which hung over the peasant *vigneron* for three successive generations, still continues as a folk memory.

It was not just the smallholder who was affected by this lack of prosperity. Though Bordeaux was not in general as badly off as elsewhere in France, owing to the reputation of its wines and the fact that the majority of its reds could be held to mature in bottle, nevertheless it was more dependent than other areas on its export markets. Demand from Germany, a major customer for the cheaper wines, collapsed after the First World War, the British market was moribund before the war and declined afterwards, and sales to pre-Prohibition America were negligible. The world recession of the 1930s, followed by the Second World War, forced even well-known classed growths almost out of business.

All this seems hardly credible today. Rising standards of living, appreciation of wine as part of the art of good living, a widening of the consumer base and the emergence of countries such as the United States as customers for the top growths have transformed the scene. At the bottom level of the pyramid a minor change in the ratio of the price of Bordeaux Rouge to Côtes du Rhône or Beaujolais, coupled with a plentiful harvest, can still cause problems. At the top end, a handful of proprietors seem to think they can get away with anything. Prices of First Growths and the best of the rest have been rising at an alarming rate alongside a succession of very good but also highly plentiful vintages. It is now apparent that even the 'second best' Bordeaux are wines which most of us can only afford to drink rarely. And with prices of new wines almost as expensive as those now reaching maturity it hardly seems worthwhile to bother to buy them *en primeur*.

One benefit, though, has been that the whole of Bordeaux, from First Growth to the regional co-operative, is making better wine. Scientific progress in vineyard and *chai*, the arrival of the trained *oenologue* (wine chemist), the financial means and the moral duty to make a rigorous selection of the *grand vin* have led to fewer poor vintages, more wine and a higher quality product. Some of those proprietors who price the best wines may believe they can get away with murder. At least those who market them are fully aware of the competition from elsewhere.

The Wines

RED WINES

There are two quite separate wine-making districts in Bordeaux as far as the top red wines are concerned. West of the Garonne and Gironde, on a low-lying, gravel-covered peninsula, stretch the vineyards of the Graves and the Médoc, on either side of Bordeaux. The best wines of the Médoc come from six communes, each of which has its own particular character, described in detail in the following pages. The coastal parishes of Margaux, Saint-Julien, Pauillac and Saint-Estèphe contain the majority of the most respected growths. In the Graves, the best wines are found in Léognan, and closer to Bordeaux in Pessac and Talence.

Fifty kilometres away, north of the Dordogne river, lies a quite separate region covering the wines of Saint-Émilion and Pomerol which, in their own but different ways, are the equal of the Médoc and the Graves. Saint-Émilion itself is divided into an easterly section, known as the Côtes Saint-Émilion, on the slopes around the town of Saint-Émilion itself, and the Graves Saint-Émilion, four kilometres to the west on the border of Pomerol. Pomerol, north of the port of Libourne, has only recently received its due recognition for the quality of its wines.

Médoc and Graves wines, based on Cabernet Sauvignon, are full, firm and tannic when young, even austere. Saint-Émilion wines may be equally abundant and rich, but lack the muscle and backbone of their westerly neighbours. Based on the Merlot, their wines are fruitcakey rather than blackcurrant in flavour, more aromatic in character. They mature faster and do not last as long. Pomerol wines, from a clay rather than limestone soil, are fuller than those of Saint-Émilion. They can be rich and fat, heavier than Graves or Margaux (the two lightest regions of the west bank) and as long-lasting.

Adjacent to Saint-Émilion and Pomerol are the Libournais satellites. Lalande-de-Pomerol, Néac, Fronsac and Côtes-Canon-Fronsac produce lesser wines in the style of Pomerol. Surrounding Saint-Émilion are Montagne-Saint-Émilion, which absorbed Saint-Georges-Saint-Émilion and Parsac-Saint-Émilion in 1972 (though they still exist as *appellations* in their own right), Lussac-Saint-Émilion and Puisseguin-Saint-Émilion. Some of these wines are as good as ordinary Saint-Émilion themselves, but in the main those with a simple Saint-Émilion AC are more consistently reliable.

North-west of the Libournais, on the right bank of the Gironde estuary, lie the districts of Bourg and Blaye. East of Saint-Émilion in the direction of Bergerac are the Côtes de Castillon and the Côtes de Francs. All these are now thriving areas, providing *petit château* wines of great interest at prices hardly far removed from that of Bordeaux Supérieur. These are wines which can be bought and drunk regularly, rather than being preserved for special occasions. Land in these areas is cheap compared with the astronomical prices now being paid for classed growths in the Médoc. Able young men and women, suitably trained, have moved in, or taken over from their less expert parents.

The remainder of the Gironde region, with the exception of the coastal area, is authorized for the production of Bordeaux and Bordeaux Supérieur. Entre-Deux-Mers is a white wine *appellation* only and any red wines produced there will be simply Bordeaux or Bordeaux Supérieur.

White Wines

The Graves, stretching south from the suburbs of Bordeaux down the west side of the Garonne as far as Langon, produces the best dry white wines of Bordeaux as well as red wines; though to many people's surprise more red wine is made than white. For many years the dry white wines continued to be made by rustic, old-fashioned methods. Quite deservedly, they fell out of fashion. Recently there has been a dramatic improvement in the wine, and a revival of the region's fortunes.

Within the Graves, towards the southern end, is the enclave of Sauternes and Barsac, origin of the world's richest and most sumptuous sweet white wines. Lesser, medium-sweet white wines are made nearby at Cérons, and on the opposite bank of the Garonne at Sainte-Croix-du-Mont, Loupiac and the Premières Côtes de Bordeaux.

The peninsular between the Dordogne and Garonne rivers is known as the Entre-Deux-Mers. This generic *appellation*, like that of Graves and Graves Supérieures, is used solely for white wines. Yet this is another source of good *petit château* red wine. Within the Entre-Deux-Mers are four more districts: Graves de Vayres, opposite Fronsac and the town of Libourne; Sainte-Foy-Bordeaux, at the extreme east below Montravel in the *département* of Dordogne; Côtes de Bordeaux Sainte-Macaire in the south, taking over where the Premières Côtes de Bordeaux ends; and Haut-Benauge, a sub-division of the Entre-Deux-Mers. In all, there are forty-six *appellations* within the Gironde.

Production and Surface Area

The largest harvest since the Second World War took place in 1995. Of a total of 6.54 million hectolitres 84 per cent was red wine (including a little rosé), still. Of a total of 5.6 million hectolitres 80.4 per cent was red wine (including a little rosé), the highest proportion ever. The majority of this wine is sold as Bordeaux or Bordeaux Supérieur. The combined production of the 'quality' areas (the Médoc, Graves, Saint-Émilion and Pomerol, Sauternes and Barsac) was only some 1.84 million hectolitres, 28 per cent of the grand total – and it is arguable how much generic Graves, Saint-Émilion and Médoc is 'quality' wine.

The decades since the end of the Second World War have seen a number of parallel trends in the Bordeaux area. The total surface area under vines has decreased from nearly 140,000 hectares – the peak was in 1950 – to under 100,000 in the last 1970s, though it has climbed back to 116,000 hectares since then. But the area producing AC wine has steadily climbed and now stands at 97 per cent of this amount. As well as increased surface area clonal section and better vineyard husbandry have meant that the production of AC wine has more than doubled – the average yearly yield in the five years from 1945 to 1949 was just over 2 million hectolitres. In the five years between 1992 and 1996 it was 6.14 million. At the same time there has been a dramatic shift away from white to red wine – from one third of the harvest being Bordeaux Rouge to over 80 per cent. In the five years from 1992 to 1996 almost as much AC wine was produced in the Bordeaux area as in the thirty vintages from 1945 to 1974.

It is the change from white to red, despite the increased fashion for white wine-drinking in the 1980s, which is the most curious and significant of these trends. Prior to the Second World War, oceans of generic Graves, Entre-Deux-Mers and Bordeaux Blanc, produced with various levels of sweetness from dry to almost luscious, provided France and its export markets with most of its staple white wine-drinking at a level of quality that was just above *ordinaire*. The fashion then changed to something a bit lighter and cleaner. The French lost their export market to Germany and Yugoslavia and the French domestic preference moved to Muscadet and Mâcon Blanc. White Bordeaux became almost unsaleable, fetching, at its cheapest level, no more than *vin ordinaire*. The growers began to switch to making red wines, and 1962 remains the only vintage when over 2 million hectolitres of white Bordeaux was harvested in the Gironde.

BORDEAUX

PRODUCTION AND SURFACE AREA (1996 HARVEST)

	Surface area in hectares		Production in '000 hectolitres	
	RED	WHITE	RED & ROSÉ	WHITE
Regional Wines				
BORDEAUX	38,064	10,220	2308	599
BORDEAUX CLAIRET	1716	—	103	—
BORDEAUX MOUSSEUX	—	78	(79 hl)	5
BORDEAUX SUPÉRIEUR	8467	—	477	2
CÔTES DE BORDEAUX				
SAINT-MACAIRE	—	60	—	3
ENTRE-DEUX-MER	—	2394	—	148
SAINTE-FOU-BORDEAUX	101	39	8	2
Côtes				
BLAYE, CÔTES DE BLAYE,				
PREMIÈRES CÔTES DE BLAYE	4310	337	248	24
CÔTES DE CASTILLION	2832	—	168	—

	Surface area in hectares		Production in '000 hectolitres	
	RED	WHITE	RED & ROSÉ	WHITE
CÔTES DE FRANCS	458	29	30	1
BOURG	3560	30	211	1
GRAVES DE VAYRES	360	165	21	9
PREMIÈRES CÔTES DE BORDEAUX	2868	410	164	16

Médoc, Graves

GRAVES	2128	—	121	45
GRAVES SUPÉRIEURES	—	699	—	31
PESSAC-LÉOGNAN	991	—	53	15
MÉDOC	4741	—	280	—
HAUT-MÉDOC	4269	—	246	—
MARGAUX	1358	—	72	—
SAINT-JULIEN	900	—	49	—
PAUILLAC	1185	—	66	—
SAINT-ESTÈPHE	1245	—	71	—
LISTRAC	646	—	38	—
MOULIS	548	—	32	—

Libournais

CANON-FRONSAC	301	—	17	—
FRONSAC	818	—	46	—
POMEROL	784	—	38	—
LALANDE-DE-POMEROL	1106	—	57	—
SAINT-ÉMILION	2196	—	127	—
SAINT-ÉMILION GRAND CRU	3244	—	161	—
LUSSAC-SAINT-ÉMILION	1404	—	83	—
MONTAGNE-SAINT-ÉMILION	1540	—	91	—
PUISSEGUIN-SAINT-ÉMILION	742	—	44	—
SAINT-GEORGES-SAINT-ÉMILION	188	—	10	—

White Wines (Dessert)

SAUTERNES	—	1637	—	37
BARSAC	—	610	—	15
CÉRONS	—	84	—	3
SAINTE-CROIX-DU-MONT	—	462	—	18
LOUPIAC	—	385	—	15
CADILLAC	—	275	—	1

| Total Bordeaux | 93,049 | 19,168 | 5434 | 980 |
| Total of Red and White Wines | 112,217 | | 6414 | |

The Style of the Wine

The name claret means any red Bordeaux wine. The word is derived from the French *clairet*, indicating a lightish red wine as opposed to the fuller, more robust wines formerly produced in the hinterland beyond the Bordeaux area, but shipped through the same port. Bordeaux, unlike many other top red French wines – Burgundy and Hermitage, for example – is made from a mixture of grapes. The red wines are produced from Cabernet Sauvignon, Cabernet Franc and Merlot, with Petit Verdot used in small proportions in many of the top Médoc estates, and Malbec found in some of the lesser properties of the Saint-Émilion and Pomerol and the Libournais. Some years, such as 1985, favour the Merlot; others, such as '86, the Cabernet. In general the wines of the Médoc are largely produced from Cabernet Sauvignon with some Cabernet Franc and Merlot. The Libournais wines are mainly made from the Merlot, with Cabernet Franc as the additional variety in Saint-Émilion and Pomerol, but little Cabernet Sauvignon except in rare cases.

The quality of the final wine depends on the quality of these grapes at harvest time. The purpose of all viticultural procedures is to produce as much fruit as is consistent with quality – for, to a very large extent, quality is inversely proportional to quantity – in as perfect a condition as possible on the date that they are picked.

The character of a wine depends on a number of other things, most importantly the soil and, as vital in viticulture, the subsoil. Soils in the Bordeaux area combine, in one form and proportion or another, the following ingredients: gravel (of various types), sand, clay and limestone. The Médoc and the Graves are based on the first two, on a subsoil of gravel, *alios* (a hard, iron-rich sandstone), marl, clay or sand; Saint-Émilion and Pomerol soils contain more limestone, especially round the town of Saint-Émilion itself, and there is also more clay. Gravel and sand are present to a lesser extent. The subsoil consists of limestone, though in the Graves-Saint-Émilion and Pomerol there is gravel and clay.

Of equal importance to the chemical constituents of the soil is its aspect: the relation of the vineyard to the rays of the sun, and its protection from wind, hail and particularly frost; and the efficiency of its drainage. Unlike many other vineyards in France and Germany, most of the top Bordeaux vineyards lie on flat ground, not on a slope so much as a small mound, rarely more than a few metres above the surrounding countryside. Thus there is no natural protection from the prevailing weather, and severe frost can damage large tracts of vineyard, as it did spectacularly in Saint-Émilion and Pomerol in 1956 and throughout the region in '77 and '85. The Médoc is well drained and can withstand heavy rain better in wet years such as 1973 or '69 than can the heavier clay or limestone soil of Pomerol and Saint-Émilion. On the contrary, these latter areas can cope with severe drought, as in 1964 (prior to the rain of October) and in '85, better than the Médoc.

The climate in Bordeaux is conditioned by the nearby Atlantic Ocean, and is, in general, less extreme than in Burgundy, and better both in terms of a higher average temperature and less severe bouts of rainfall. Unlike in Burgundy, where the white wine harvest often runs concurrently with that of the red, and occasionally even afterwards, the harvest in Bordeaux always begins with the dry white wines. When the red wine vintage begins a week or so later, the Merlots are picked before the Cabernets, the Libournais area usually beginning a few days before the Médoc and the Graves. The sweet wine harvest commences last of all.

Compared with Burgundy, wine-making in Bordeaux is on a much larger scale: a domaine of 20 (or greatly more) hectares may make only two wines, the *grand vin* and a second wine; while in Burgundy an estate half the size or even smaller may have as many as ten different wines to offer. In general in Bordeaux the vats are closed rather than open during fermentation, as is often the case in Burgundy, the fruit for red wines is almost invariably entirely destalked and vinification temperatures are high (30°C or so) for the top red wines. The malolactic fermentation seems to follow more easily, permitting an early *égalisage*, or blending of the vats of different grape varieties.

A relatively recent development in the leading estates has been the expansion of second wines. With increased prosperity and perfectionism only the very best vats are today assembled into the *grand vin*. The rejected wine, from younger vines or less successful parts of the vineyard, is bottled under another name. The best of these second wines are mentioned in the château descriptions within each *appellation*.

WHEN TO DRINK THE WINES

Fine red Bordeaux is a much fuller, more tannic wine than red Burgundy. It has a deeper colour, the best wines remaining purple-hued for many years. It needs time to mature. Lesser red Bordeaux, the generic wines and the lightest *petits châteaux*, will be ready for drinking a couple of years or so after the harvest. The *bourgeois* wines will be mature at three to six years, the classed growths after five to ten years. The wines of lighter vintages, of course, will mature sooner than those of fuller years.

While there is a smaller proportion of top dry whites than there is in Burgundy these too need time (a minimum of five years), though most of Bordeaux's dry white wine harvest is bottled early, having not been vinified or matured in oak, and is intended for early drinking. A good Sauternes has the capacity for long ageing. The best, like the best red wines, need to be kept for a minimum of a decade.

BORDEAUX VINTAGES

1997: A very early harvest, but the most extended one in recent memory. After a very early bud-break the flowering commenced in mid-May, but the fruit-setting was prolonged by adverse weather, and this was reflected in state of ripeness at vintage time. A variable result therefore for both red and dry whites, with the top properties proportionately more successful than the lesser estates. Some fine wines. A very good Sauternes year.

1996: A large harvest: only just below the record 1995. After fine weather during the flowering the summer was cool and wet, and the harvest was saved by a largely dry, sunny but cool September. Rain at the end of the month affected the Libournais. A fine October enabled the later-developing Cabernets in the Médoc to mature to an excellent ripe and healthy condition. The results therfore are variable: largely disappointing in Pomerol and Saint-Emilion, average in the Graves and southern Médoc, very fine in Pauillac, Saint-Estèphe and Saint-Julien: where the wines will keep well. A fine vintage for Sauternes. An average vintage for dry wines. Prices were unprecedentedly high.

1995: A record vintage: for the first time the total crop exceeded 6.5 million hectolitres. The summer was largely dry, but, for the fifth year in succession, rain in September dashed hopes of a really spectacular quality harvest. Overall the results are more even than in 1996: good to very good in the Libournais, especially in Pomerol, good in the Graves for both red and dry white, good to very good in the Médoc, particularly in Saint-Julien, Pauillac and Saint-Estèphe. A quite good vintage in

Sauternes. The red wines will evolve in the medium to long term, well in advance of the best 1996s. Prices were high.

1994: A splendid, hot, dry summer led everyone to hope for a high quality vintage. Sadly it was not to be. It began raining on September 9th and hardly ceased until the end of the month. Modern methods, however, can ensure at least acceptable wine, provided, as in 1994, there is no rot. The results are heterogenous. Acidity levels are low; some of tannins are not really properly ripe. But the wines, if lacking real character, are at least clean. They will evolve in the medium term. The dry whites are adequate. The Sauternes disappointing. The yield was large.

1993: Another large vintage, and another where summer expectations were dashed by a rainy September. Indeed there was even more rain than in 1994, though less than in 1992. At first the wines were lean and skinny. A year on they had taken up a bit more new oak from the cask than young Bordeaux usually does, and were pleasantly juicy if one dimensional. By 1997, though, a lot of the fruit had dried out. An unexciting vintage, though with a little more substance than the 1992s. Again the dry whites were adequate. Again not a vintage for Sauternes. The wines are as good as ever they will be and should be drunk soon.

1992: This year saw the rainiest September of the 1991-1996 period: indeed a record 279mm. The result is a poor vintage of hollow, watery wines which are already showing age. So are the dry whites, which were better. No Sauternes of note either. It was a large crop.

1991: Following April frosts, a small vintage. After this disaster the summer was fine, raising hopes of a small-but-beautiful vintage like 1961. But there was rain in the second half of September right through the harvest, which was late. Many Saint-Emilion and Pomerol estates did not produce a *grand vin*. The best wines – more interesting than those produced in 1992 and 1993 – come from those estates in the Médoc nearest to the estuary of the Gironde and least affected by the frost. These are now ready, and worth investigating. The remainder are dull and now old. Some reasonable dry whites, now showing age. No Sauternes of consequence.

1990: A harvest which was very large, early and of consistently very fine quality - for dry white wines and Sauternes as well as for red wines. It was a hot summer, but the wines were not as stressed as in 1989, and the more mature tannins as a result are one of the reasons this vintage generally has the edge on 1989. The reds are big, rich and classy, and will be slow to mature, but will last well. Though not as expensive as the 1989s at the outset, prices are now rather higher, indeed the highest of recent years apart from the 1982s.

1989: A very large vintage again, an early one, and a succesful one, though a little uneven, and for the most part eclipsed by 1990. A hot dry summer produced fruit at the time of the time of the vintage which was physiologically ripe (the sugar/acidity ratio) but was not completely phenollically ripe (i.e the quality of the tannins). As a result, though the Saint-Emilions and Pomerols are fine, as are most Graves, some Médoc wines exhibit rather hard dry tannins. Acidity levels are marginally lower than in the 1990 vintage too. A fine red wine vintage nevertheless, which is only now beginning to mature. The dry whites, though rich, lacked a bit of zip and have aged fast. Very fine Sauternes. Prices at the outset were high.

1988: A large harvest. After a very rainy first half of the year the Cabernets struggled to achieve full maturity, and there was some rain towards the end of September and again in October. Medium to medium-full red wines which were rather austere at the outset. This higher than normal acidity has preserved the fruit and finesse, and at 10 years old the best wines now show a lot of interest, though the lesser wines are proportionately more boring. These best wines are only just ready and will keep well. Very good dry white wines. Fine Sauternes. Unjustly ignored at present, the best wines are now excellent value.

1987: A medium-sized vintage, spoiled by rain. In their prime the reds provided light, pleasant "lunchtime" wines. Most are now too old. Not of note in dry white or Sauternes either.

1986: A huge crop: in terms of yield per hectare the largest ever. There was a thunderstorm towards the end of September, just as the red wine harvest was due to start. This posed problems in the Graves and in the Libournais, where the rain was at its heaviest. The northern Médoc escaped unscathed. Excellently concentrated, long lasting wines in Saint-Julien and Paulliac, as good, if different, as 1982. This is where the 1986 harvest is at its best. These have been slow to come round. Good quality elsewhere in the Médoc, though there is inconsistency. In general the Graves and the Libournais wines are somewhat diluted and not as good as those of 1985. Fine elegant quality too in the dry white wines. Excellent sauternes. Prices were lower than the 1985s at the outset. Now the better Médocs make considerably more at auction.

1985: A very big crop, and an exceptional dry end to the ripening season. In contrast to 1986, the Merlots were more successful than the Cabernets. Very good quality in Saint-Émilion and Pomerol. Also very good in the Graves and Margaux, though in Saint-Julien and Paulliac the 1986 vintage is much better. In general the wines evolved in the medium term and are now in their prime. This is not a heavyweight year but the wines have balance and elegance. Very good, dry white wines, fuller and richer than those of 1986. Ripe Sauternes, though without nearly as much botrytis character as those of the 1986 vintage. Opening prices of the vintage were high.

Earlier Vintages

Red Wines: 1983 is very good in the southern Médoc and the Graves, but disappointing elsewhere. 1982 is superb, but the Saint-Emilion and Pomerol wines lack grip. 1981 has held up surprisingly well. The best years prior to 1981 are 1978, '70, '66, '62, '61 (outstanding) and '59. The 1978s still need keeping. Most wines from before 1966 need drinking. Good but

EARLIER VINTAGES

not great years are 1981, '79, '76, '75, '71, '67 and '64 (but fine in Saint-Émilion and Pomerol) – 1976 and vintages prior to '71 need drinking. The 1975s are hard: the Libournais wines have more charm and are now ready. Avoid therest.

Dry white Wines: In recent vintages you can divide the dry white wine crop into those châteaux which picked very early – even in August and were not caught by rain in the 1991-1996 period (these are fine and will keep), and the rest. The former are scarce, fine and expensive. The rest have been disappointing. 1986 and 1990 are the best vintages. The rest, apart from the 1996 and 1997, will probably be already getting tired.

Sauternes: After the magnificent 1990, 1989, 1988 trio, and then the 1986, the good years are '83, '76, 75, '71 (patchy), '62 and '59. The rest are best avoided.

Classifications

Since the creation of primarily monocultural, wine-making estates in the last years of the seventeenth and the first half of the eighteenth centuries, the wines of these properties have been categorized and classified by the Bordeaux brokers and *négociants*. These lists were based on the prices the wines would fetch and were no doubt of use in the continual battle between the proprietor or his bailiff and the *négoce* in Bordeaux. Once the price had been fixed for one wine, prices for the rest would fall into place according to the unofficial lists circulating at the time. This was the price at which the haggling would commence. These lists were fluid and they altered with the times. The names of properties come and go, reputations are made and lost, and the effects of neglect and dedication can be clearly seen.

The first 'official' classification is that of 1855. In this year, the new French Second Empire sent to Bordeaux for a 'representative selection of the wines of the *département* of the Gironde' for display at the Paris Exhibition, the *Exposition Universelle*. The selection was to include not only examples of the commune wines, but also a list of the *crus classés*. At the behest of the Chamber of Commerce, the Bordeaux brokers produced a list of the top red and top sweet white wines, the dry wines not being considered of *cru classé* standard. In the red wine list, reproduced in an updated form below, there are five categories, and, counting the divided Rauzan and Léoville vineyards as single estates, there are sixty-one properties. It is by accident – and the prices the wines fetched – that all but one of the wines come from the Médoc. It was never intended to be a classification of Médoc wines only, as many people now believe.

At the same time the top sweet white wines were classified. These were all wines of Sauternes and Barsac. Château d'Yquem was put into a class of its own: *grand premier cru*. Then followed what are today, allowing for changes, twenty-four more properties, eleven *premiers crus* and thirteen *deuxièmes crus*, one of which is currently dormant though has recently been resurrected.

For some reason, the 1855 Classification has assumed permanent status. Some châteaux mention their position on their label, and all wine books and wine lists refer to it. The reputation of some wines is unduly enhanced by having been chosen as a Second or Fifth Growth in 1855, while others now producing better wine were excluded. Various authorities have long called for a reclassification, but with the sole exception of Mouton-

Rothschild's elevation to First Growth status in 1973, and despite various abortive attempts in the 1960s and 1970s initiated by the INAO (*Institut National des Appellations d'Origine*), nothing has yet resulted.

Meanwhile, in 1954 (revised in 1969, 1984 and in 1996) the INAO classified the wines of Saint-Émilion; the Graves was classified in 1953 and 1959 and is now overdue for reclassification; and in 1932, 1966, 1978 and again in 1984 attempts were made to classify the lesser growths of the Médoc. Pomerol has never had an official classification.

THE 1855 CLASSIFICATION OF THE RED WINES OF BORDEAUX

This is the original list of 1855, with the incorporation of Château Mouton-Rothschild. It takes into account divisions and other changes since 1855.

Premiers Crus	*Commune*
LAFITE-ROTHSCHILD	Pauillac
MARGAUX	Margaux
LATOUR	Pauillac
HAUT-BRION	Pessac (Graves)
MOUTON-ROTHSCHILD (1973)	Pauillac

Deuxièmes Crus	
RAUSAN-SÉGLA	Margaux
RAUZAN-GASSIES	Margaux
LÉOVILLE-LAS-CASES	Saint-Julien
LÉOVILLE-POYFERRÉ	Saint-Julien
LÉOVILLE-BARTON	Saint-Julien
DURFORT-VIVENS	Margaux
GRUAUD-LAROSE	Saint-Julien
LASCOMBES	Margaux
BRANE-CANTENAC	Cantenac
PICHON-LONGUEVILLE-BARON	Pauillac
PICHON-LONGUEVILLE, COMTESSE DE LALANDE	Pauillac
DUCRU-BEAUCAILLOU	Saint-Julien
COS D'ESTOURNEL	Saint-Estèphe
MONTROSE	Saint-Estèphe

Troisièmes Crus	
KIRWAN	Cantenac
D'ISSAN	Cantenac
LAGRANGE	Saint-Julien
LANGOA-BARTON	Saint-Julien
GISCOURS	Labarde

Troisièmes Crus	Commune
MALESCOT-SAINT-EXUPÉRY	Margaux
BOYD-CANTENAC	Cantenac
CANTENAC-BROWN	Cantenac
PALMER	Cantenac
LA LAGUNE	Ludon
DESMIRAIL	Margaux
CALON-SÉGUR	Saint-Estèphe
FERRIÈRE	Margaux
MARQUIS-D'ALESME-BECKER	Margaux

Quatrièmes Crus	
SAINT-PIERRE	Saint-Julien
TALBOT	Saint-Julien
BRANAIRE-DUCRU	Saint-Julien
DUHART-MILON-ROTHSCHILD	Pauillac
POUGET	Cantenac
LA TOUR-CARNET	Saint-Laurent
LAFON-ROCHET	Saint-Estèphe
BEYCHEVELLE	Saint-Julien
PRIEURÉ-LICHINE	Cantenac
MARQUIS-DE-TERME	Margaux

Cinquièmes Crus	
PONTET-CANET	Pauillac
BATAILLEY	Pauillac
HAUT-BATAILLEY	Pauillac
GRAND-PUY-LACOSTE	Pauillac
GRAND-PUY-DUCASSE	Pauillac
LYNCH-BAGES	Pauillac
LYNCH-MOUSSAS	Pauillac
DAUZAC	Labarde
MOUTON-BARONNE-PHILIPPE	Pauillac
DU TERTRE	Arsac
HAUT-BAGES-LIBÉRAL	Pauillac
PÉDESCLAUX	Pauillac
BELGRAVE	Saint-Laurent
DE CAMENSAC	Saint-Laurent
COS-LABORY	Saint-Estèphe
CLERC-MILON	Pauillac
CROIZET-BAGES	Pauillac
CANTEMERLE	Macau

This is the original list, but brought up to date to take account of divisions and other changes.

Grand Premier Cru	Commune	Deuxièmes Crus	Commune
D'YQUEM	Sauternes	DE MYRAT	Barsac
		DOISY-DAËNE	Barsac
Premiers Crus		DOISY-DUBROCA	Barsac
		DOISY-VÉDRINES	Barsac
LA TOUR-BLANCHE	Bommes	D'ARCHE	Sauternes
LAFAURIE-PEYRAGUEY	Bommes	FILHOT	Sauternes
CLOS HAUT-PEYRAGUEY	Bommes	BROUSTET	Barsac
DE RAYNE-VIGNEAU	Bommes	NAIRAC	Barsac
SUDUIRAUT	Preignac	CAILLOU	Barsac
COUTET	Barsac	SUAU	Barsac
CLIMENS	Barsac	DE MALLE	Preignac
GUIRAUD	Sauternes	ROMER-DU-HAYOT	Fargues
RIEUSSEC	Fargues	LAMOTHE-DESPUJOLS	Sauternes
RABAUD-PROMIS	Bommes	LAMOTHE-GUIGNARD	Sauternes
SIGALAS-RABAUD	Bommes		

THE 1959 CLASSIFICATION OF THE GRAVES

Haut-Brion did not originally wish to be included for its white wine as production was too tiny. It was added to the list in 1960.

Red Wines	Commune	White Wines	Commune
BOUSCAUT	Cadaujac	BOUSCAUT	Cadaujac
HAUT-BAILLY	Léognan	CARBONNIEUX	Léognan
CARBONNIEUX	Léognan	DOMAINE DE	Léognan
DOMAINE DE	Léognan	CHEVALIER	
CHEVALIER		OLIVIER	Léognan
DE FIEUZAL	Léognan	MALARTIC-LAGRAVIÈRE	Léognan
OLIVIER	Léognan	LA TOUR-MARTILLAC	Martillac
MALARTIC-LAGRAVIÈRE	Léognan	LAVILLE-HAUT-BRION	Talence
LA TOUR-MARTILLAC	Martillac	COUHINS-LURTON	Villenave
SMITH-HAUT-LAFITTE	Martillac		d'Ornon
HAUT-BRION	Pessac	COUHINS	Villenave
LA MISSION-HAUT-	Talence		d'Ornon
BRION			
PAPE-CLÉMENT	Pessac		
LATOUR-HAUT-BRION	Talence		

The wines of Saint-Émilion were first classified in 1959, and this classification was revised in 1967, 1985 and again in 1996. The *Premiers Grands Cru Classés* are divided into two section, A and B. This is the current version.

Premiers Grands Crus Classés

A
AUSONE
CHEVAL-BLANC

B
L'ANGÉLUS
BEAU-SÉJOUR-BÉCOT
BEAUSÉJOUR-DUFFAU-
LAGAROSSE
BELAIR
CANON
CLOS FOURTET
LA GAFFELIÈRE
MAGDELAINE
PAVIE
TROTTEVIEILLE

Grandes Crus Classés
L'ARROSÉE
BALESTARD LE TONNELLE
BERGAT
BERLIQUET
CADET-BON
CADET-PIOLA

CANON-LA-GAFFELIÈRE
CAP DE MOURLIN
CHAUVIN
CLOS DES JACOBINS
CLOS DE L'ORATOIRE
CLOS SAINT-MARTIN
LA CLOTTE
LA CLUSIÉRE
CORBIN LE
CORBIN MICHOTTE
COUVET DES
     JACOBINS
CURÉ-BON
DASSAULT
LA DOMINIQUE
FAURIE DE SOUCHARD
FONPLÉGADE
FONROQUE
FRANC-MAYNE
GRAND-MAYNE
GRAND-PONTET
GUADET-SAINT-JULIEN
HAUT-CORBIN

HAUT-CORBIN
HAUT-SARPE
LANOITE
LAMARZELLE
LARCIS-DUCASSE
LARMANDE
LAROQUE
LAROZE
MATRAS
LE PRIEURÉ
RIPEAU
SAINT-GEORGES-CÔTE-FIGEAC
     PAVIE
LA SERRE
SOUTARD
TERTRE-DAUGAY
LA TOUR-DU-PIN-FIGEAC
     (GIRAUD-BÉLIVIER)
LA TOUR-DU-PIN-FIGEAC
     (MOUEIX)
LA TOUR-FIGEAC
TROPLONG-MONDOT
VILLEMAURINE

THE 1978 CLASSIFICATION OF CRUS BOURGEOIS OF
THE MÉDOC AND HAUT-MÉDOC

In 1932 six properties in the Haut-Médoc were classified as *crus bourgeois exceptionnels*, and others in both the Haut-Médoc and the Bas-Médoc into *crus bourgeois* and *crus bourgeois supérieurs*. In the 1960s this list was expanded, and in 1978 was replaced by a division into the categories of *cru bourgeois*, *cru grand bourgeois* and *cru grand bourgeois exceptionnel*. Only properties in the Haut-Médoc can be considered for the latter category, and these wines must be château-bottled. A number of the better growths declined to be considered for the 1978 classification, fearing that inclusion on this list would preclude consideration in a revision of the *crus classés*.

Grands Bourgeois
  Exceptionnels

AGASSAC
ANDRON-BLANQUET
BEAUSITE
CAPBERN
CARONNE-SAINTE-
  GEMME
CHASSE-SPLEEN
CISSAC
CITRAN
LE CROCK
DUTRUCH-GRAND-
  POUJEAUX
FOURCAS-DUPRÉ
FOURCAS-HOSTEN
DU GLANA
HAUT-MARBUZET
MARBUZET
MEYNEY
PHÉLAN-SÉGUR
POUJEAUX

Grands Bourgeois

BEAUMONT
BEL-ORME-TRONQUOY-
  DE-LALANDE
BRILLETTE
LA CARDONNE
COLOMBIER-MONPELOU
COUFRAN
COUTELIN-MERVILLE
DUPLESSIS
  (HAUCHECORNE)
FONTESTEAU

LA-FLEUR-MILON
GREYSAC
HANTEILLAN
LAFON
DE LAMARQUE
LAMOTHE
LAUJAC
LIVERSAN
LOUDENNE
MACCARTHY
DE MALLERET
MARTINENS
MORIN
MOULIN-À-VENT
LE MEYNIEU
LES ORMES-DE-PEZ
LES ORMES-SORBET
PATACHE D'AUX
PAVEIL-DE-LUZE
PEYRABON
PONTOISE-CABARRUS
POTENSAC
REYSSON
LA ROSE-TRINTAUDON
SÉGUR
SIGOGNAC
SOCIANDO-MALLET
DU TAILLAN
LA TOUR-DE-BY
LA TOUR-DU-HAUT-
  MOULIN
TRONQUOY-LALANDE
VERDIGNAN

Bourgeois

ANEY
BALAC
LA BÉCADE
BELLERIVE
BELLEROSE
BONNEAU-LIVRAN
LE BOSCQ
LE BREUIL
LA BRIDANE
DE BY
CAP-LEON-VEYRIN
CARCANIEUX
CASTÉRA
CHAMBERT-MARBUZET
LA CLARE
LA CLOSERIE
DUPLESSIS-FABRE
FONRÉAUD
FONPIQUEYRE
FORT VAUBAN
LA FRANCE
GALLAIS BELLEVUE
GRAND-DUROC-MILON
GRAND-MOULIN
HAUT-BAGES-
  MONPELOU
HAUT-CANTELOUP
HAUT-GARIN
HAUT-PADARNAC
HOUBANON
HOURTIN-DUCASSE
DE LABAT
LAMOTHE-DE-
  BERGERON

Bourgeois (continued)

	PANIGON	TAYAC
	PIBRAN	LA TOUR-BLANCHE
LE LANDAT	PLANTEY-DE-LA-CROIX	LA TOUR-DU-MIRAIL
LANDON	PONTET	LA TOUR-HAUT-
LARTIGUE-DE-BROCHON	RAMAGE-LA-BÂTISSE	CAUSSAN
CRU LASSALLE	LA ROQUE-DE-BY	LA TOUR-SAINT-BONNET
LESTAGE	DE LA ROSE-MARÉCHALE	LA TOUR-SAINT-JOSEPH
MAcCARTHY-MOULA	SAINT-BONNET	DES TOURELLES
MONTHIL	SARANSOT	VIEUX ROBIN
MOULIN ROUGE	SOUDARS	

AUTHOR'S CLASSIFICATION

I produced a comprehensive list of the top red wines of the whole Bordeaux area in my book *Grands Vins* published in 1995. I confined myself to the top sixty or so wines, the same number as the brokers in 1855, and I divided them into four categories: First Growths, Outstanding Growths, Exceptional Growths and Very Fine Growths. Here is my ammended 1999 revision. The wines are listed in alphabetical order within each category. Second wines have not been included.

Since then, seven more vintages have arrived and we can see more clearly just how good the wines of the late 1970s are as they have matured in bottle. It is time I revised and extended this 1982 list. Here is this revision based on the quality, reputation and prices of the properties concerned over the last decade or so and with particular reference to the performance in the five years between 1982 and 1986. The wines are listed in alphabetical order within each category. Second wines have not been included.

First Growths

The Undisputed Top Wines of Bordeaux

Médoc	*Graves*	*Saint-Émilion*	*Pomerol*
LAFITE	HAUT-BRION	CHEVAL BLANC	PÉTRUS
LATOUR			
LEOVILLE-LAS-CASES			
MARGAUX			
MOUTON-ROTHSCHILD			

Outstanding Growths

These are the super seconds, wines which, more than occasionally, produce wine of First-Growth quality. One could argue very forcibly that in terms of absolute quality (if there is such a thing), some at least should be included in the category above. Prices, however, push the First Growths into a category apart.

Médoc	*Graves*	*Pomerol*
DUCRU-BEAUCAILLOU	DOMAINE DE CHEVALIER	CERTAN DE MAY
L'ÓVILLE-BARTON	LA MISSION HAUT-BRION	LA CONSEILLANTE
LYCH-BAGES		CLINET
PALMER	*Saint-Émilion*	L'ÉVANGILE
PICHON-LONGUEVILLE-	AUSONE	LAFLEUR
BARON	CANON	TROTANOY
PICHON-LONGUEVILLE-	FIGEAC	VIEUX-CHÂTEAU-
COMTESSE DE LALANDE	MAGDELAINE	CERTAN
RAUSAN-SÉGLA		

Exceptional Growths

These wines are often as fine as those in the category above and many are clearly of equal standing as a general rule if not as prestigious or as expensive.

Médoc	*Graves*	*Pomerol*
BEYCHEVELLE	DE FIEUZAL	BEAUREGARD
BRANAIRE	HAUT-BAILLY	L'EGLISE-CLINET
CLERC-MILON	MALARTIC-LAGRAVIÈRE	LA FLEUR DU GAY
GRAND-PUY-LACOSTE	PAPE-CLÉMENT	LA FLEUR-PÉTRUS
GRUAUD-LAROSE		LATOUR-À-POMEROL
LA LAGUNE		PETIT VILLAGE
LÉOVILLE-POYFERRÉ	*Saint-Émilion*	LE PIN
MALESCOT	BELAIR	
SAINT-PIERRE	L'ANGELUS	
	L'ARROSÉE	
	PAVIE	
	TROPLONG MONDOT	

Very Fine Growths

Many of these regularly produce wine in the 'Exceptional' category and some, I am sure, will join the ranks before too long.

Médoc

D'ANGLUDET
BATAILLEY
BOYD-CANTENAC
BRANE-CANTENAC
CALON-SÉGUR
CANTENERLE
CHASSE-SPLEEN
COS-LABORY
DESMIRAIL
DUHART-MILON
DURFORT-VIVENS
FONBADET
GISCOURS
GLORIA
GRAND-PUY-DUCASSE
HAUT-BAGES-LIBÉRAL
HAUT-BATAILLEY
HAUT-MARBUZET
ISSAN
KIRWAN
LABÉGORCE-ZÉDÉ
LAFON-ROCHET
LAGRANGE
LALANDE-BOIRE
LANGOA-BARTON
LASCOMBES
LILAN LOUYS
MARQUIS-D'ALESME-
  BECKER
MARQUIS-DE-TERME

MOUTON-BARONNE-
  PHILIPPE
MONTROSE
DE PEZ
PONTET CANET
POUGET
POUJEAUX
PRIEURÉ-LICHINE
SOCIANDO-MALLET
TALBOT
DU TERTRE
LA TOUR-DE-MONS

Graves

BOUSCAUT
CARBONNIEUX
LARRIVET-HAUT-BRION
LA LOUVIÈRE
LA TOUR-HAUT-BRION
LA TOUR-MATTILLAC

Saint-Émilion

BEAU-SÉJOUR-BÉCOT
BEAUSÉJOUR-DUFFAU-
  LAGAROSSE
CADET-PIOLA
CANON-LA-GAFFELIÈRE
DASSAULT
LA DOMINIQUE

FONROQUE
CLOS FOURTET
LA GARRELIERE
LARCIS DUCASE
LARMANDE
PAVIE-DECESSE
LA SERRE
SOUTARD
TERTRE-DAUGAY
LE TETRE ROTENBOEUF
LA TOUR-FIGEAC
TROTTEVIEILLE

Fronsac

CANON (MOUEIX)
CANON-DE-BREM

Pomerol

LE BON-PASTEUR
CERTAN-GUIRAUD
CLOS DU CLOUCHER
CLOS L'EGLISE
LA CROIX DE GAY
LE GAY
GAZIN
LA GRAVE-TRIGANT-DE
  BOISSET
LAGRANGE
LA POINTE
CLOS RENÉ

The Wine Regions

MÉDOC

The Médoc (also called Médoc Maritime or Bas-Médoc to differentiate it from the Haut-Médoc) begins where the Haut-Médoc leaves off, north of Saint-Estèphe, and runs from Saint-Yzans and Saint-Germain d'Esteins all the way up to Soulac at the tip of the peninsula. Viticulturally, as well as in terms of prestige, it is a minor area compared with its more famous neighbour to the south. There are fourteen wine-producing communes, with a total area under vine of some 4700 hectares, producing some 280,00 hectolitres a year. The *appellation* covers red wines only. It is a part of the world which few outsiders — tourists or foreign wine merchants — ever visit. The countryside is low-lying, flat and open to the skies. Even more than the Haut-Médoc the atmosphere often resembles that of Holland. Fields of pasture cover the land more than vines, interspersed with copses, hamlets and the occasional wine-producing farmhouse surrounded by its dependent buildings. It is peaceful but bleak, rural and remote.

Nevertheless, the wines are well worth investigating, for they are inexpensive, and no serious list of Bordeaux *petits châteaux* will be without one or two of the better examples. Like the more famous estates to the south Cabernet Sauvignon and Cabernet Franc form the bulk of the plantings, together with Merlot and a little Malbec, and this mixture of varieties gives the wine body and backbone, albeit at a lower level of breed and concentration than in Pauillac or Margaux. The wines will have a similar blackcurrany taste, but without the oak element found in the better wines from further south.

While there are no classed growths, nor indeed *grands bourgeois exceptionnels*, for these are confined to the Haut-Médoc, there are nine *grands bourgeois* estates. These include Gilbey's Château Loudenne in Saint-Yzans, Château La Cardonne, owned by the Rothschilds of Lafite in Blaignan and Château Patache-d'Aux, La Tour-de-By and Greysac, all in Bégadan, the most important viticultural commune of the north Médoc. I must add Château Sigognac and Château Potensac, the latter owned by the family of Michel Delon of Léoville-Las-Cases. Other well-known wines include Château Plagnac, owned by Cordier, Château du Castéra, owned by Alexis Lichine and Company, and Châteaux La Tour-Saint-Bonnet, Christoly, Les Ormes-Sorbet, La Tour-Haut-Caussan and Livran. There are a number of important co-operatives, at Bégadan, Ordonnac, Saint-Yzans, Queyrac, Drignac and Gaillan.

HAUT-MÉDOC

The Haut-Médoc begins at the Jalle de Blanquefort, north of Bordeaux, and continues to Saint-Seurin-de-Cadourne, a distance of some fifty kilometres as the crow flies. The vineyards stretch back from the Gironde estuary on a series of rippling mounds or *croupes* of gravel banks as far as the D1/N215, the main road from Bordeaux to Le Verdon and the ferry across the mouth of the estuary over into the Charente country.

This is the largest, greatest and most concentrated red wine area on earth. Once the traveller from Bordeaux reaches the first of the classed growths, Château La Lagune in the commune of Ludon some half an hour's drive away from the city centre, the vines and the great names continue almost uninterruptedly until you pass Château Coufran and Soudars in the hamlet of Cadourne and cross into the Bas-Médoc. To the right, particularly from Saint-Julien onwards, the great vineyards lie close to the water. The brown, sluggish, shallow estuary, within which lie long sandbanks or marshy islands, covered with tangled undergrowth, can clearly be seen. Behind, to the left, the vineyards continue until the gravel gives way to sand and pines. 'The best vines are those which can view the water' is a much repeated quotation and in general this is so. Those properties whose land lies on the first *croupe* facing the Gironde, produce the wines with the greatest complexity of character and depth of flavour. Those from the plateau behind often have more body, but have less finesse. In principle those from the five parishes which make up the *appellation* Margaux and those from Macau and Ludon in the south of the Haut-Médoc are more delicate than those further north.

This is a countryside dominated by fine wine. The estates are large, can boast long histories. There are many fine parks and elegant buildings. It was in the Médoc that the *noblesse de robe*, the wealthy Bordelais in the eighteenth century, established their country estates. During the nineteenth century a new breed of the moneyed classes, whose wealth was based in finance and industry or in wine, replaced those who had died out or disappeared. These in their turn have been superseded by multinationals, insurance companies and other conglomerates in the post-Second World War era.

The Haut-Médoc is not only more homogenous but more alive, more vigorous than the sleepy, more desolate countryside further north. The villages are larger and those who do not work in the *chais* and vineyards of the great estates commute to Bordeaux. There is an element of creeping suburbia, particularly close to the great city and the industrial developments that lie on its outskirts. The Haut-Médoc consists of twenty-nine communes; over 10,000 hectares of vineyard produce a total of about 570,000 hectolitres of wine. Some 2800 hectares, just under a third of the land under vine, is classed growth. The majority of these estates lie in the four great communes of Margaux, Saint-Julien, Pauillac and Saint-Estèphe. Each of these has a separate superior *appellation* to that of Haut-Médoc, as additionally do the communes of Moulis and Listrac. The Haut-Médoc AC is described on *page 83*.

The Haut-Médoc is the Bordeaux heartland of the Cabernet Sauvignon grape. Together with the Cabernet Franc, balanced with a proportion of Merlot, and, in the best properties, combined with the flavour of new oak, this produces the blackcurrant–blackberry fruit, and the austere, firm, tannic, full-bodied character which is associated with the word 'claret' or the words 'Red Bordeaux' the world over.

SAINT-ESTÈPHE

Saint-Estèphe is the largest and most northerly of the four great Haut-Médoc communes, within which you will find all but five of the local classed growths. Yet it has long suffered by comparison with the others. Writers extol the magnificence of Pauillac, the breed of

Saint-Julien, the subtlety and fragrance of Margaux. Yet they do not warm to the wines of Saint-Estèphe. Saint-Estèphe can only boast five classed growths (two Seconds, a Third, a Fourth and Fifth) and I do not consider would manage to scrape many more if there were to be a reclassification. The commune is dominated by a large cluster of good-but-never-great *bourgeois* growths, many extensive in area, regularly exported and deservedly popular. But these are middle-class wines rather than aristocrats.

The soil in Saint-Estèphe is varied. In the south-east corner of the *appellation* it is heavy gravel on the hard sandstone base rich in iron known as *alios*, similar to that in Pauillac. Progressively west and north it contains more clay, less gravel, becomes heavier and more fertile. In parts there is limestone. Naturally the style of the wines varies too. Although in general there is more Merlot here than elsewhere in the Haut-Médoc, there are nevertheless many properties with 70 per cent or more Cabernet Sauvignon and Cabernet Franc.

Compared with Pauillacs the wines are in general tougher and denser, though not necessarily fuller. They are more aromatic and less elegant. They are solid rather than austere: firm, full and tannic but in a less distinguished way; less obviously richly blackcurranty in flavour, and more robust and spicy – even sweeter – in character. Some Saint-Estèphes do not age too gracefully. That said, the best wines – Cos d'Estournel clearly, and Montrose also – both from the south-eastern end of the parish, are as good, and can last as well, as the very greatest of their peers elsewhere. Overall in the commune there has been an encouraging change for the better in recent years. Saint-Estèphe produces an average of 70,000 hectolitres a year from 1245 hectares of vines.

Cross over the Jalle de Breuil (*jalle* means an artificial drainage ditch or stream) after you have passed by the old *manoir* of Château Lafite in Pauillac and admired its weeping willows and neat kitchen garden and you will find that the land rises abruptly. You are in the commune of Saint-Estèphe, and a sign will indicate the hamlet of Cos. 'Cos' is a Gascon telescoping of the words *Colline de Cailloux* (hill of stones) and the 's' is pronounced, not silent. Soon you will see the exotic Chinese pagoda turrets of Cos d'Estournel. This is not the château, mind you, only the *chai*. There is no château. If you stop, go and have a look at the cellar door. This intricately carved piece of hardwood with its exotic plants and animals once formed the entrance to the harem of the Sultan of Zanzibar. The wine behind the doors today is almost as lush and seductive as must have been the sultan's concubines. The proprietor is Bruno Prats, a tall, rather scholarly-looking man, who is not as mild as he seems at first. His is a free-ranging, flexible mind. And the pursuit of quality is carried out with a determination which if he were less intelligent and less hospitable I could only describe as grim. This is quite clearly the best wine of the commune, a super second as good as Ducru and Las-Cases and others further south. Cos' second wine is blended in with the neighbouring Château de Marbuzet, also owned by Monsieur Prats.

Nearer the estuary of the Gironde is Saint-Estèphe's other Second Growth, Château Montrose. The name has no Scottish connotations and the 't' is silent. Montrose is owned by the small and dapper Jean-Louis Charmolüe and guarded by a family of squawking peacocks. The vineyard contains more Cabernet Sauvignon than most Saint-Estèphes. Most of Saint-Estèphe has a richer soil containing more clay compared with the other three great communes. As a result – for otherwise the wines would be too dense – the proportion of Merlot tends to be higher than, say, in Pauillac or Saint-Julien. But at Montrose the soil is more gravelly and a more regular Haut-Médoc planting can be employed. Nevertheless, Montrose produces a big, firm, tannic, muscular wine which often needs years to mature. Some vintages – 1970, '61 – have been magnificently brutal in potential (for those who enjoy being savaged rather than caressed) but have remained impossibly inky for decades or more. In recent years they have softened and polished up the style of Montrose, in one or two vintages to excess in my view. But the 1986 and '88 are very good indeed. The second wine is called La Dame de Montrose.

Saint-Estèphe's Third Growth is one of the oldest in the Médoc and lies behind a partially crumbling brick wall just outside the eponymous village itself. Calon-Ségur takes its name partly from the old flat-bottomed boats (*calones*) used to transport men and cargo around in older times when much of the low-lying Médoc was marsh, and partly from the name of the most powerful viticultural families in eighteenth-century Bordeaux. The Marquis de Ségur owned Lafite and Latour as well as Calon, and even, briefly, Mouton. He was known, I doubt it not, as the Prince of Vines. But his heart was in Calon, hence the heart on the estate's wine label. The wine is puzzling. It shows well in cask but never seems quite to live up to its early promise when you taste it in bottle. Yet the potential is there in the soil. The wines in the post-Second World War decade were splendid. The second wine is Château Capbern-Gasqueton.

The château of Lafon-Rochet is spurious, a modern reproduction of an elegant Directoire *chartreuse*. It is under the same ownership as Château Pontet-Canet in Pauillac. As at Pontet-Canet the standard has improved considerably since the mid-1980s. With 80 per cent Cabernet Sauvignon Lafon tends to be a firm, unyielding and charmless wine. But watch this space. Alfred Tesseron is going places. There is a second wine called, simply, No 2 de Lafon Rochet.

Château Cos-Labory lies near Cos d'Estournel and is presided over by Madame Cécile Audoy and her son Bernard. These are gentle, charming, unassuming people and their efforts are so far going unrewarded. Cos-Labory is quite a small vineyard, only 15 hectares, and it produces a lighter wine than the other four Saint-Estèphe classed growths. But there is no lack of fruit, harmony and balance. I found their 1988 very seductive: one of the top three wines in the commune. And the wine is reasonably priced. The Audoy family also own the Saint-Estèphe *bourgeois* growth, Andron Blanquet into which the second wine of Cos Labory is blended.

Top of the *bourgeois* growths is Château Haut-Marbuzet (not to be confused with Château de Marbuzet of Cos d'Estournel). I rate this estate's wine higher than all other Saint-Estèphe wines except for Cos d'Estournel and Montrose. Henri Duboscq is in his mid-forties, bald, voluble and exuberant. He describes himself and his wines as *caressant et virile* (caressing and virile). The wine is made with half Merlot, half Cabernet Sauvignon and is matured entirely in new oak. There is something Californian or Australian about its honeyed, toasted, exotic flavour. The impact is immediate, but the wine lasts in bottle. Monsieur Duboscq owns a number of other small properties in the area, including Chambert-Marbuzet and MacCarthy-Moula.

Château Phélan-Ségur has had a troubled history recently. It changed hands in July 1985, being bought by Xavier Gardinier who had up to then been running Champagne Lanson. Hardly had he arrived when customers began to return their 1983 wine as it had acquired a rather metallic, plastic taste. This was allegedly traced to a chemical which had been sprayed on the vines. Monsieur Gardinier had to reimburse all his 1983 clients and pour the 1984 and '85 wine down the drain. A long legal action ensued which was eventually settled out of court. Phélan-Ségur had produced good wines before, particularly in the 1950s and early 1960s. It is producing even better wines now.

Château de Pez is a wine well known in Britain, as up until recently it was exclusively marketed by Gilbey of Loudenne, the Bordeaux end of IDV (Peter Dominic chain). Monsieur Robert Dausson had the idea of bottling a separate hogshead of the 1970 vintage of all his four main grape varieties, Cabernet Sauvignon, Cabernet Franc, Merlot and Petit Verdot, in order to see how they evolved on their own. I tasted these, together with the château blend on several occasions, and always the blend was greater than the sum of its parts, proving once again that Cabernet Sauvignon needs the addition of a little something to produce its maximum potential. Dausson eliminated his Petit Verdot, and since 1970 has refused to add any *vin de presse* to his wine, as, in his opinion, it is structured enough. This is a reliable and consistent property producing surprisingly good wine.

Château Les Ormes-de-Pez is nearby and belongs to the Cazes family, proprietors of the excellent Château Lynch-Bages in Pauillac. Jean-Michel Cazes is one of Bordeaux's best-known ambassadors, an able, ambitious man who is now also in charge of Pichon-Longueville-Baron, another of Pauillac's illustrious estates. There have been improvements at Ormes in recent years, more elegance, less rusticity, a better expression of the fruit. Sadly a fire in autumn 1989 destroyed most of the 1988 crop.

Château Meyney is a large estate, an ancient priory, and the buildings are organized like a cloister around four sides of a lawn. It belongs to the Cordier family, whose domaine includes Gruaud-Larose and Talbot, both in Saint-Julien. Dependable rather than inspired is how I describe the wine: a typical, slightly tough *bourgeois* Saint-Estèphe.

There are a number of other good *bourgeois* wines in the commune, including Le Crock, run by the Cuvelier family of Léoville-Poyferré, Tronquoy-Lalande, Beau-Site-Haut-Vignoble, Beau-Site, Houissant, Pomys, MacCarthy and Le Boscq. The co-operative ennobles its wines with the name Marquis de Saint-Estèphe.

Leading Saint-Estèphe estates	*Surface area in hectares*	*Composition of vineyards (%)*			
		CABERNET SAUVIGNON	MERLOT	CABERNET FRANC	PETIT VERDOT
COS D'ESTOURNEL	54	60	40	—	—
MONTROSE	67	65	25	10	—
CALON-SÉGUR	48	60	20	20	—
LAFON-ROCHET	45	80	20	—	—
COS LABORY	12	40	35	20	5
HAUT-MARBUZET	38	40	50	10	—
PHÉLAN-SÉGUR	52	60	30	10	—
DE PEZ	23	70	15	15	—
LES ORMES-DE-PEZ	30	50	35	10	5
MEYNEY	50	70	24	4	2

PAUILLAC

The commune of Pauillac lies between Saint-Julien and Saint-Estèphe some forty-five kilometres north of Bordeaux. The vineyards of the three parishes are in fact contiguous, the vines of Léoville-Las-Cases in Saint-Julien marching with those of Latour, separated only by a narrow gully; those of Lafite facing those of Cos d'Estournel in Saint-Estèphe across a stream, the Jalle de Breuil. Pauillac is not the largest of the main communes – that honour falls to Margaux in size but Saint-Estèphe in volume of production; but it is the most important. Pauillac contains three of the four First Growths and no fewer than fifteen other classified châteaux, almost a third of the 1855 Classification. It also boasts a number of good *bourgeois* properties. Pauillac possess 1185 hectares of vines and produces an average of 65,000 hectolites of wine a year.

The commune is split in two by a stream, the Pibran, which flows diagonally across the parish in a north-easterly direction, debouching into the Gironde at the northern end of the town of Pauillac itself. North and west of this stream the land rises steeply (in Médocain terms) to some 27 metres above sea level, and includes the vineyards of both the Rothschilds and Pontet-Canet. South and east lie the Bages and Grand-Puy-Lacoste plateau, the Batailleys, the Pichons and Château Latour. The Pauillac soil is heavy gravel, thicker to the north than to the south, based on a subsoil of larger stones, and iron-based sand. The wines of Pauillac are the archetype of Bordeaux and the taste of Cabernet Sauvignon, which in some cases – as at Château Mouton-Rothschild and Château Latour – form the vast part of the *encépagement*. The wines are full-bodied, dense and tannic; austere when young, rich and distinguished when mature; and the longest-lived of all Bordeaux wines. At their best they are incomparable, the fullest, most concentrated, and most profound of all red wines.

Pauillac's three First Growths are Lafite-Rothschild, Latour and Mouton-Rothschild. Which is the best? It is invidious to make a choice and perhaps it is best to say that it is a question of personal taste. All three have made the occasional disappointing vintage; some have gone through longer periods of being in the doldrums. All three have the ability to produce wine of such inspiring magnificence that tears would be brought to the eyes of even the most hardened wine cynic. These are the yardsticks of claret indeed!

Château Lafite has perhaps prior claim to superiority. It is one of the oldest wine-making estates in the Médoc and its wine has for a long time achieved the highest prices of all when older vintages come under the auctioneer's hammer. It is the largest of the First Growths; it is owned by one branch of the Rothschild family – that associated with the Rothschild bank in Paris – and its character can be simply described as the perfection of elegance. Lafite at its best has a supreme balance, a persistence of flavour and a breed of which the only adequate descriptive adjective is regal. But having more Merlot in its *encépagement* than the other two First Growths it is neither as full nor as powerful.

During the 1960s and early 1970s Lafite was not as brilliant as it should have been, and after 1962 there was a string of vintages where the wine was not of First Growth quality. Since 1976 it has been back on song and in '79, '81, '83 and again in '85 it produced the best wine in the commune. Pre-1961 vintages may be beginning to fade a little – it depends on storage – but the '53 is utterly beautiful, the '49 sheer delight and the '45 quite splendid.

Château Latour is the wine professional's favourite claret, triumphant in its austerity and in its totally untrammelled expression of gravelly *terroir* and the Cabernet grape. Undoubtedly the finest tasting in which I have ever participated was a vertical succession of Latour vintages back to 1920, with the 1893 thrown in for good measure. This was in 1988. Not a single bottle was over the hill and the consistency of quality breathtaking. The wine needs a decade or two to soften up and acquire all the complexity of maturity, and it can often seem unnecessarily reserved and ungenerous when you sample it young. Prior to 1975 there has hardly been a single disappointing Latour vintage, and the wine has a particular knack of succeeding in minor vintages. In the 1980s, I regret to report, the standard has fallen somewhat. Since 1990 it has been back on form.

While both Latour and Lafite are run, somewhat at arm's length, from Paris and elsewhere, Mouton was personally controlled with an obsessive attention to detail by that flamboyant and multi-talented genius, the late Baron Philippe de Rothschild. For more than a century, indeed since the 1855 Classification itself, Mouton fetched prices comparable with those of the First Growths. Yet it was only the top wine of the Second Growths. Baron Philippe finally succeeded in getting this injustice rectified in 1973 and Mouton-Rothschild became a First Growth. The style of Mouton-Rothschild is like the personality and lifestyle of the late Baron: opulent, flamboyant, rich and full. Though, like Latour, made almost entirely from Cabernet Sauvignon, this wine could not be more different. It has a cedary, lead-pencilly flavour which is quite distinctive. In 1982 and again in '86 the wine is magnificent, but the '78 and '75 are a shade disappointing, and the '83 is not as lovely as either Lafite or Margaux. My favourite of all the earlier vintages is the 1949: simply one of the three best wines made since the Second World War. (Latour 1945 and Lafite '53 are the others, should you ask!)

No mention of Mouton-Rothschild would be complete without a brief reference to the museum, built up by the late Baron and his wife during the 1950s and 1960s. The range is eclectic, but the pieces all have a vinous connotation; and each is a work of art in its own right. No visitor to Bordeaux should miss it.

The two Pichons, divided into the larger Comtesse de Lalande and the smaller Baron de Longueville in the 1850s, lie near Latour at the southern end of the commune. These are the only Second Growths in Pauillac. Since 1978 the wine of the Comtesse, a suitably softer, sumptuous, more feminine Pauillac than its opposite neighbour, has been of a standard that is practically of First Growth quality. Madame May-Elaine de Lencquesaing needs a team which combines both energy and a ruthless commitment to perfection.

Pichon-Longueville-Baron, on the other hand, has suffered from a lack of investment. The property was *en indivision*, owned by numerous members of the Bouteiller family, and the wine in bottle never seemed to match the quality it had shown in cask. In character it is a firmer, more Cabernet-based wine; a true Pauillac. In 1987 the property was sold to AXA, a large insurance group, and is now managed by Jean-Michel Cazes of Château Lynch-Bages. Resources have been poured into Pichon-Baron and an improvement in quality has been clearly discernible.

Château Duhart-Milon is Pauillac's sole Fourth Growth (there are no Thirds) and the vineyard lies in the extreme north-west of the commune, though the *chais* is in the town itself. Since 1962 it has been owned by the Rothschilds of Château Lafite. At the time the vineyard had contracted, and the consequence of the major scheme of replanting was to

leave the vineyard for many years with an average age of vines which was less than desirable. Only in the 1980s has the wine of Duhart regained its true stature. It has been criticized for producing a hard wine, quite unlike that of its stablemate, Château Lafite. The character is now somewhat softer, as well as more elegant.

The rivals for the title 'Best of the Fifth Growths' in Pauillac are Lynch-Bages and Grand-Puy-Lacoste. Lynch-Bages, owned by the able and ambitious Jean-Michel Cazes, is a large estate, whose wine is justly popular throughout the world. The wine has sometimes been described as the poor man's Mouton (not exactly a back-handed compliment). Grand-Puy-Lacoste has been the property of the Borie family of Saint-Julien's Château Ducru-Beaucaillou since 1978 but has consistently made excellent wine for at least sixty years (my tasting notes do not extend back beyond 1928 and '29). The character of Grand-Puy-Lacoste is less opulent than that of Lynch-Bages: a typical full, rich, concentrated long-tasting Pauillac.

It would be hard today, taking one's assessment on the performance of the 1980s, to separate the best of the rest among Pauillac's other Fifth Growths. Clerc-Milon, owned by the Rothschilds of Mouton, is a particular favourite of mine, and is in my view unjustly ignored. Mouton-Baronne-Philippe, in the same stable, is a slightly more feminine wine. Pontet-Canet has shown great strides since the mid-1980s. Haut-Batailley, another Borie wine, is firmer than Château Batailley; the two estates were divided as recently as 1942. Châteaux Grand-Puy-Ducasse and Haut-Bages-Libéral are ultimately owned by the same large group. There is quality and good value in both of these Pauillac Fifth Growths.

This brings us to the remaining classed growths: Lynch-Moussas, Croizet-Bages and Pédesclaux. The latter is rarely seen on the export market, the other two are under-achievers, surpassed in quality by the best of the *crus bourgeois* wines. Among the best of the unclassified estates the following should be noted: Fonbadet, La Couronne, Haut-Bages-Monpelou, La Fleur-Milon, Pibran and La Tour-Pibran. The second wines of the top properties – Les Forts-de-Latour, Moulin des Carruades of Lafite and Reserve de la Comtesse of Pichon-Lalande – are also fine wines in their own right. The co-operative, La Rose-Pauillac, has a good reputation.

Leading Pauillac estates	Surface area in hectares	Composition of vineyards (%)			
		CABERNET SAUVIGNON	MERLOT	CABERNET FRANC	PETIT VERDOT
LAFITE-ROTHSCHILD	90	70	15	13	2
LATOUR	60	80	10	10	—
MOUTON-ROTHSCHILD	72	85	8	7	—
PICHON-LONGUEVILLE, COMTESSE DE LALANDE	60	46	34	12	8
PICHON-LONGUEVILLE-BARON	50	75	24	—	5
DUHART-MILON	50	57	21	20	2

Leading Pauillac estates (continued)	Surface area in hectares	Composition of vineyards (%)			
		CABERNET SAUVIGNON	MERLOT	CABERNET FRANC	PETIT VERDOT
LYNCH-BAGES	80	70	18	10	2
GRAND-PUY-LACOSTE	45	70	25	5	—
CLERC-MILON	30	70	20	10	—
MOUTON-BARONNE-PHILIPPE	50	65	20	15	—
PONTET-CANET	75	68	20	12	—
HAUT-BATAILLEY	20	65	25	10	—
BATAILLEY	50	73	20	5	2
GRAND-PUY-DUCASSE	36	70	25	—	5
HAUT-BAGES-LIBÉRAL	26	70	25	—	5
CROIZET-BAGES	22	37	30	30	(includes Malbec)
LYNCH-MOUSSAS	25	70	30	—	—
PÉDESCLAUX	18	70	20	5	5

SAINT-JULIEN

Saint-Julien lies immediately to the south of Pauillac and is the smallest of the four main Haut-Médoc communes in terms of its production. The commune is compact and dominated by its eleven classed growths, all of which produce excellent wine and many of which produce wine above their 1855 Classification level. There are five Second Growths, two Thirds and four Fourths. There are 900 hectares under vine in the commune. The average annual production is 50,000 hectolitres.

At the northern end of the commune lie the three Léoville estates, at the southern end Beychevelle, Ducru-Beaucaillou and Gruaud-Larose. Langoa is in the middle, between the villages of Saint-Julien and Château Beychevelle; set back from the river are Châteaux Talbot and Lagrange. The Saint-Julien soil is predominantly gravel, particularly in those vineyards nearest to the Gironde, where it is based on a subsoil of the iron-based sandstone known as *alios* and clay. Further inland the soil has less gravel and more sand, and beneath this is a richer subsoil containing clay, *alios*, and occasionally marl.

Saint-Julien wines are the closest to those of Pauillac in character, and like Pauillac they contain high proportions of Cabernet Sauvignon. Indeed, with the exception of such First Growths as Mouton-Rothschild, Latour and Lafite, there is not a great deal of difference in weight or style between the wines of the two communes. Properties such as Léoville-Las-Cases and Léoville-Barton can produce wine every bit as full-bodied and slow-maturing as Lynch-Bages and Grand-Puy-Lacoste in Pauillac.

The quintessence of a wine from Saint-Julien is its balance and its finesse. The wines are well-coloured, have plenty of body, are full of fruit, rich and elegant. It is harmony rather than power which gives longevity; so Saint-Juliens, if without the firmness and reserve of a great Pauillac, nevertheless keep exceptionally well.

My two favourites – rivals and justly prized (and priced) above all others – are Châteaux Ducru-Beaucaillou and Léoville-Las-Cases, both Second Growths. Ducru is owned by Jean-Eugène Borie, one of the most modest but capable owners in Bordeaux. Borie and his charming wife Monique live literally over the shop, at Ducru all the year round, and above their *chai* and cellars. This is rarer than you might think. His other Saint-Julien property is the unclassified Château Lalande-Borie whose wine normally sells for about 40 per cent of the price of Ducru. It is better than many a classed growth at double the price.

Monsieur Delon of Léoville-Las-Cases is a reserved man, a workaholic widower who lives in Bordeaux and is not seen much on the social scene. Behind the cool exterior is a burning pride for his property and wines, and a perfectionism that has few rivals. Delon produces not one, but two, second wines – or to be precise, a second and a third wine. The second wine, Clos du Marquis, sells for the same price as Monsieur Borie's Lalande. Even the third wine, Domaine de Bigarnon, is well worth buying. Las-Cases is a fuller, more masculine wine than Ducru. Rarely has there been a dull vintage of either in recent years. Though Ducru had a celler problem which caused much of the 1988, 1989 and 1990 to be tainted. Las-Cases is the largest of the three Léoville châteaux, half as much again as Poyferré and three times the size of Barton.

Léoville-Poyferré, in the past widely considered the best property in the Médoc outside the First Growths, went through a bad patch in the 1960s and 1970s, but has since been rescued by the energies of young Didier Cuvelier, who took charge in 1980. Under Didier's aegis the cellar has been extensively modernized, the wine-making equipment brought up to date, and the percentage of new oak for maturing the wine increased. The improvement in the quality of the wine has been dramatic.

Léoville-Barton is run from the elegant Château of Langoa by Anthony, nephew of Ronald Barton who died aged eighty-three in 1975 and who had been in charge of Langoa since the 1920s. Léoville and Langoa-Barton have been the property of the Anglo-Irish Barton family since the 1820s, the longest period of consecutive ownership among all the classed growths. While the two properties are run in harness the produce of each is kept entirely separate, and the Léoville, a Second Growth, is invariably just that little bit superior to the Langoa, a Third Growth. The Bartons have never been greedy about their prices. Leaving delusions of grandeur to the French they concentrate on making marvellous long-tasting wine and selling it at sensible prices. While I felt standards had slipped just a little in the last years of Ronald Barton, the improvement since Antony has been in charge has been dramatic. Las-Cases can now no longer claim to make indisputably the best Léoville wine.

Gruaud-Larose, a Second Growth, and Talbot, a Fourth, used to be another pair of Saint-Julien estates linked in common ownership, this time the *négociants* Cordier who came originally from Lorraine. Monsieur Cordier set up in Bordeaux just before the First World War and quickly embarked on a process of vineyard acquisition, finally reuniting Gruaud-Larose, which had been divided in the nineteenth century, in 1933. Both estates are large and impeccably run, and pioneered the concept of second wines in Saint-Julien by releasing their Le Sarget de Gruaud-Larose and Le Connétable de Talbot in 1979. Both Gruaud-Larose and Talbot are big, rich wines but do not have, in my view, the finesse of the Saint-Juliens already mentioned. They need time to mature. Gruaud is materially more complex and more concentrated that Talbot, as befits its higher standing. Gruaud has not been sold. Talbot remains the personal property of the Cordier family.

Lagrange, like Langoa-Barton, is a Third Growth but unlike it, it is little known. Until recently this ignorance was not undeserved. Since 1984 the property and its cellars have been the subject of a major reconstruction programme. The Japanese whisky firm of Suntory are now the proprietors. Michel Delon of Léoville-Las-Cases is the consultant. Since the takeover there has been a considerable improvement.

Saint-Pierre, a Fourth Growth, is, like Gruaud-Larose, another property which was divided in the nineteenth century and has since been reunited. The estate was the passion and culmination of a lifetime's ambition of the late Henri Martin, once manager of Château Latour and selfless propagandist for the wines of Bordeaux. Martin built up an estate called Château Gloria during the 1950s and rapidly established it as one of the best *crus bourgeois* in the commune. In 1982, having failed to persuade the authorities to reclassify the wines of the Médoc (and therefore promote Gloria to classed growth) he bought Saint-Pierre. This is today run by his son in law Jean-Louis Triand. The wine is a classic full Saint-Julien.

At the southern end of the commune the elegant Directoire-style, single-storey *chartreuse* which is the château of Branaire faces the venerable cedar tree, planted in 1757, which fronts the impressive château of Beychevelle. Branaire-Ducru, a Fourth Growth, produces excellent wine, full, firm and long-tasting, rather neglected by those who only buy the well-known names – with the result that the rest of us can buy it for a reasonable price. Beychevelle, another Fourth Growth, has deservedly always been popular; but the wine in recent years has failed to excite me.

Saint-Julien is such a compact commune that there is hardly any room for other unclassified, *bourgeois* growths. I have already mentioned Châteaux Gloria and Lalande-Borie. The Cuvelier family, who own Léoville-Poyferré, also own Moulin-Riche and use its name for Léoville-Poyferré's second wine. Château du Glana enjoys a high reputation. Perhaps the best of the unclassified châteaux, however, are Châteaux Terry-Gros-Caillou and Hortevic. Hortevie, marketed exclusively by the excellent wine merchants Nathaniel Johnston et Fils, is effectively a selection of the Terry-Gros-Caillou production and is one of the best-value wines in the commune.

Leading Saint-Julien estates	*Surface area in hectares*	*Composition of vineyards (%)*			
		CABERNET SAUVIGNON	MERLOT	CABERNET FRANC	PETIT VERDOT
DUCRU-BEAUCAILLOU	49	65	25	5	5
LÉOVILLE-LAS-CASES	85	65	18	14	3
LÉOVILLE-POYFERRÉ	63	65	35	—	—
LÉOVILLE-BARTON	39	70	15	7	8
GRUAUD-LAROSE	82	62	25	10	3
LANGOA-BARTON	20	70	15	7	8
LAGRANGE	110	70	30	—	—
BEYCHEVELLE	72	60	28	8	4
BRANAIRE-DUCRU	48	60	20	15	5
SAINT-PIERRE	20	70	20	10	—
TALBOT	103	71	20	5	4
GLORIA	45	65	25	5	5

MARGAUX

While the other three great communes of the Haut-Médoc form a continuous chain of vineyards – from Beychevelle in Saint-Julien north to Calon-Ségur in Saint-Estèphe – Margaux lies separately to the south. In between much of the land is too marshy for vines, the gravel *croupes* less well defined, and no great properties are to be found. The *appellation* Margaux covers not one but five communes. As well as Margaux itself, Labarde, Arsac and Cantenac, the communes to the south, and Soussans, Margaux's neighbour to the north, all have the right, in whole or in part, to call their wines Margaux. This conglomeration of parishes boasts no fewer than twenty classed growths: one First (Château Margaux), five Seconds, no fewer than nine Thirds, three Fourths and two Fifths. Some of these, like some of Pauillac's Fifth Growths, are relatively obscure, small in production terms, and little seen on the market or at auction. Others are very large, like Château Brane-Cantenac, or, like Château Palmer, deservedly extremely fashionable. In total there are 1358 hectares of AC Margaux vineyards spread over the five communes. The average annual production is 72,000 hectolitres.

The soil varies within Margaux but is generally a sandy gravel, thinner than in Saint-Julien and Pauillac, and lighter in colour. This lies on a base which in Margaux itself is partly marl, partly clay. Elsewhere the subsoil is sometimes gravel, sometimes iron-rich sandstone *alios*, and in Labarde is sand and *graviers* (grit).

I find it difficult to generalize about the style of Margaux wines, for they vary greatly. While on the whole they are softer, have less backbone, and develop sooner than Saint-Juliens, and also have less of the pronounced Cabernet Sauvignon-oak flavour (one is supposed to find a scent of violets in a Margaux), there are some Margaux wines – Lascombes for example – which are every bit as 'big' as wines from further north in the Haut-Médoc. The classic character of the commune, however, which many call feminine, can be found at Château Margaux itself, Château Palmer, and in wines like Issan. These have an inherent delicacy and elegance right from the start, which is not to say they do not have plenty of body and potential for ageing well.

On the whole the vineyards in the five Margaux communes are planted with more Merlot and less Cabernet than further north, and this gives a 'soft fruits' flavour, also found in wines of the Graves. In general, Margaux wines are less successful than those of Pauillac and Saint-Julien in lighter, poorer years.

The glory of the Margaux *appellation* is Château Margaux itself. At its best its wine is the most fragrant, the most elegant and the most delicate (which should not for a minute be understood to imply anything feeble) of all the First Growths: for sheer breed the wine is comparable with Lafite. The château itself, which is approached up a long avenue of plane trees, is an imposing First Empire building with a colonnaded portico dating from 1804 and will be familiar to anyone who has seen a label of Château Margaux. The heart of the vineyard is a gravel plateau which rises up to the north and west, behind the château and its park, in the direction of Soussans. Château Margaux had a long aristocratic history until the 1920s when Fernand Ginestet, a Bordeaux wine merchant and already at the time the owner of Cos d'Estournel in Saint-Estèphe and Clos Fourtet in Saint-Émilion, acquired a share in the estate. His son Pierre completed the purchase in 1949.

As at Lafite, the period from 1962 to 1976 was an unhappy time for Château Margaux and these wines are not of First Growth standard. At the end of 1976 the estate was acquired by Monsieur André Mentzelopoulos of the French grocery and supermarket chain Felix Potin, and the improvement thereafter was swift and comprehensive. Mentzelopoulos died in 1980, and the estate is now run by his widow and daughter. Château Margaux 1981 is the best wine of the vintage; so is the exquisite '83. Even in 1982 and '86, vintages said not to favour the wines of Margaux as much as those of Saint-Julien and Pauillac, the château's wine is one of the top examples. The second wine is called Pavillon Rouge. There is, unusually for the Médoc, a white wine called Pavillon Blanc. Both are excellent.

Second to Château Margaux in quality is not one of the many Second Growths, but Château Palmer. Named after a British general who fought in the Peninsular War, the property is now owned by a consortium whose nationalities embrace three countries: the Netherlands, Britain and France, and the flags of all three nations fly from the château's turreted rooftops. Palmer's high place in the Margaux hierarchy is long-established and consistent, its wine only surpassed in its velvetness, complexity and finesse by Margaux itself. The 1961 is fabulous, though needing to be consumed, the '66 nearly as good, the '70 also very fine indeed. In recent years the 1986, the '85 and the '78 stand out.

Rauzan-Ségla is one part of an estate divided early in the nineteenth century and it is indisputably the better half. Sadly Rauzan-Gassies, the other half produces a wine which is not even up to the standard of a Fifth Growth. The Ségla half was bought by the John Holt group in 1959, at which time it was somewhat run-down and management was entrusted to the *négociants* Eschenauer, also acquired at the same time by Holt. At first the wines, though elegant, were somewhat light and ephemeral. In 1983 a change of management at Eschenauer resulted in a major scheme of reconstruction at Rauzan-Ségla and the celebrated Professor Peynaud was broght in as consultant. A dramatic improvement in the quality was the immediate result. In recent years the quality at Rauzan-Ségla has clearly justified this growth's position as the top of the Second Growths. The property is now owned by the Chanel Group.

I would today put the elegantly castellated, moated Château d'Issan in fourth place after Château Margaux itself. Issan, a Third Growth, is owned by the Cruse family, once a more powerful force in the Médoc than they are today. Like many neighbouring properties the estate was allowed to run down during the inter-war years. Since 1961 at least – my experience of older vintages is scant – Issan has produced a wine with a real delicate, soft-fruits-and-violets style, and in the 1980s the quality has been very high.

Château Lascombes is the largest property in the Margaux *appellation*. It was acquired by the late Alexis Lichine and a group of American businessmen in the early 1950s, rapidly expanded, and then sold, together with Lichine's own *négociant* company, to the British brewers Bass Charrington in 1971. There has been considerable investment in the last decade, though the quality has been consistently second division since the 1950's. The wine is bigger and sturdier than other Margaux wines.

Château Brane-Cantenac, a Second Growth, may have one of the smallest buildings but boasts one of the largest vineyards in the Médoc. It is owned by Lucien Lurton who is also the proprietor of Château Durfort-Vivens and the recently reconstituted Château Desmirail, both in Margaux. The three wines have something in common, as one might expect, though Durfort is a bigger wine than Brane. Quality is good, but not up to the standard of the very top classified châteaux in the commune.

The château of Malescot Saint-Exupéry lies in the heart of the village of Margaux and is owned by the charming Roger Zuger, whose brother is the proprietor of the neighbouring Château Marquis d' Alesme-Becker. Since Roger's son Jean-Luc has been in charge of Malescot there has been a considerable improvement in quality: from good to super-second.

Château Prieuré-Lichine, a Fourth Growth, was an extremely run-down property when acquired by the late Alexis Lichine in the early 1950s. Despite his formidable energies, it was only in recent years that the quality of the wine has been of great consequence and today it is one of the best value wines in the Bordeaux area. Since 1978 this Cantenac estate has produced a succession of very good vintages.

Nearby, and still in Cantenac, lies Château Kirwan, a Third Growth owned by the Bordeaux *négociants* Schröder et Schÿler. After many years in the doldrums I have noticed distinct improvements in the wine since 1983. Back in Margaux behind the Rauzans you will find Château Marquis-de-Terme, a Fourth Growth. This property produced inky, solid wines until 1983, since when there have once again been great strides.

Château Giscours, a Second Growth, lies in Labarde. It is a large château with a large vineyard (81 hectares), and is owned by the energetic Pierre Tari. The quality can be very good, there has been a lack of concentration here in recent vintages. Chaleau Femère, formerly in buisness with Les Combes is now independent, and producing very good wine. The estate is tiny but the wine is worth seeking out.

Château Boyd-Cantenac, a Third Growth, and Château Pouget, a Fourth Growth, are run in harness by the engaging Pierre Guillemet and his son until 1983 Pouget was Boyd-Cantenac's second wine, but each is now made independently. Both wines are rather firm and solid, lacking in generosity and what one might term sex-appeal. Across the Brane-Cantenac plateau lies the imposing mid-nineteenth-century construction of Cantenac-Brown, once part of Boyd. Here again after many years of undistinguished wine from this Fourth Growth estate, improvements can be discerned. It now belongs, as does Pichon-Baron to axis Millésimèl.

Last, in the list of the best Margaux classed growths, but by no means least, is Château du Tertre, situated out in the backwoods near the village of Arsac. This is owned by the Gasqueton family of Calon-Ségur in Saint-Estèphe. The château is an elegant building, though uninhabited; the wine full but rich. Since 1975 there have been good wines here.

Château Dauzac is Margaux's only other classed growth. Once again there have been improvements here with a change of management in recent years. The best of a fine bunch of non-classed growths, such as Château d' Angludet, owned by Peter Sichel who is also the largest shareholder in Palmer, or Château Labégorce-Zédé, owned by Luc Thienpont, and Château Monbrizon are often superior. I also recommend the following châteaux: Labégorce, la Gurgue, Bel-Air-Marquis d' Aligre, Paveil-de-Luze, La Tour de Mont, Siran and Martinens.

Leading Margaux estates	*Surface area in hectares*	*Composition of vineyards (%)*			
		CABERNET SAUVIGNON	MERLOT	CABERNET FRANC	PETIT VERDOT
MARGAUX	85	75	20	—	—
PALMER	45	55	40	3	2
RAUZAN-GASSIES	30	40	20	39	1
RAUSAN-SÉGLA	42	55	28	4	1

Leading Margaux estates (continued)	Surface area in hectares	Composition of vineyards (%)			
		CABERNET SAUVIGNON	MERLOT	CABERNET FRANC	PETIT VERDOT
D'ISSAN	32	75	25	—	—
LASCOMBES	94	65	30	3	2
BRANE-CANTENAC	85	70	15	13	2
DURFORT-VIVENS	20	80	8	12	—
DESMIRAIL	18	80	10	9	1
FERRIERE	10	75	20	—	5
MALESCOT-SAINT-EXUPÉRY	34	50	35	10	5
MARQUID D'ALESME-BECKER	9	40	30	20	10
PRIEURÉ-LICHINE	40	55	33	6	6
KIRWAN	31	40	30	20	10
MARQUIS-DE-TERME	35	45	35	15	5
GISCOURS	81	75	20	3	2
BOYD-CANTENAC	18	67	20	7	6
POUGET	10	60	30	—	4
CANTENAC-BROWN	32	75	8	15	2
DU TERTRE	48	80	10	10	—
DAUZAC	50	60	30	5	5
ANGLUDET	30	45	35	15	5
LABÉGORCE-ZÉDÉ	26	50	35	10	5
SIRAN	35	50	25	10	15
LA TOUR-DE-MONS	30	45	40	10	5

MOULIS AND LISTRAC

Moulis and Listrac lie inland in the Haut-Médoc and together produce about 70,000 hectolitres annually from 1200 hectares of vines.

sturdy wines though those of Moulis are finer – the explanation that being nearer to the estuary this commune's soil is a purer gravel – and it possesses at least two good growths both classified at present as *grand bourgeois exceptionnel*.

The first of these is Château Chasse-Spleen owned by a consortium of wine companies and banks, run by Claire Villars. Mademoiselle (Madame Gonzag Lurton) Villars also manages Haut-Bages-Libéral in Pauillac Château Femère the *bourgeois* Château La Gurgue in Margaux and Château Citran in Avensan. Chasse-Spleen's wine has an element of richness and breed lacking in most of the other Moulis wines. Château Poujeaux is owned by the Theil family and is another very fine estate which has made great strides in the last fifteen years. The wine is similar to that of Chasse-Spleen, equally concentrated as well as firm and full. Other Moulis estates of note are Gressier-Grand-Poujeaux, Dutruch-Grand-Poujeaux, Maucaillou and Brillette. Listrac's top growths are headed by Fourcas-Hosten and Fourcas-Dupré. Fonréaud and its associate Château Lestage and Château Ducluzeau also produce good wine.

Leading estates	Surface area in hectares	Composition of vineyards (%)			
Moulis		CABERNET SAUVIGNON	MERLOT	CABERNET FRANC	PETIT VERDOT
CHASSE-SPLEEN	62	50	45	2	3
POUJEAUX-THEIL	50	35	35	15	15
Listrac					
FOURCAS-HOSTEN	40	55	40	5	—
FOURCAS-DUPRÉ	42	50	38	10	2

THE REST OF THE HAUT-MÉDOC

Outside the six communes which are entitled to their own individual *appellation*, there are a further twenty-three communes whose *appellation* is simply Haut-Médoc. Most of these form a line behind the more famous parishes, lying on what one might term the third and fourth ridge of gravel mounds as they ripple away from the Gironde estuary. Two lie south of Margaux (Macau and Ludon); others (Cussac, Lamarque, Arcins) lie between Margaux and Saint-Julien. Excluding the six communes with their own separate *appellations*, the Haut-Médoc produces annually nearly 250,000 hectolitres of wine.

There are five classed growths. Château La Lagune in Ludon is a Third Growth and is justly popular. Derelict after the Second World War, the estate was resurrected and replanted by Georges Brunet in the mid-1950s, but then sold to Monsieur Chayoux of the Champagne house Ayala in 1962, at which time Monsieur Brunet went off to create Château Vignelaure in Provence. One hundred per cent new oak, a perfectionistic but unflamboyant approach to wine-making, and a realistic attitude to prices rapidly ensured success for the new owners. The wine is medium-full, ripe and generous; and also very consistent. In character the flavour has much in common with a Graves wine.

Château Cantemerle in Macau is a neighbour of Château La Lagune and these are the first famous properties encountered when driving north out of Bordeaux. It is a Fifth Growth, but for long produced a medium-bodied, very elegant, Margaux-style wine of a quality much above Fifth Growth status. During the later 1960s and 1970s quality declined, until in 1980 Cantemerle was acquired by a consortium in which Domainis Cordier minor shareholders. Today Cordier both manage the estate and make the wine.

Further north, inland from Saint-Julien, lies the commune of Saint-Laurent. Here there are three presently somewhat unfashionable classed growths: Château La Tour-Carnet, which is a Fourth Growth and Châteaux Belgrave and de Camensac, which are Fifth Growths. All three estates produce medium- to full-bodied wines, based on the Cabernet grapes. In character they are similar to Saint-Julien wines but they are not as fine for the soil is richer. The quality at de Camensac has risen recently, as the vines, largely replanted in the 1960s, have attained full maturity. But, in general, these châteaux are no better than the best of Haut-Médoc *crus bourgeois*. Among these I would single out one I consider worthy of promotion to classed growth status. This is Château Sociondo-Mallet which lies north of Saint-Estèphe in Saint-Seurin. Elsewhere in the Haut-Médoc, the following properties are among the best. I list them roughly from north to south.

Château	Commune
PONTOISE-CABARRUS	Saint-Seurin-de-Cadourne
VERDIGNAN	Saint-Seurin-de-Cadourne
COUFRAN	Saint-Seurin-de-Cadourne
SOUDARS	Saint-Seurin-de-Cadourne
BEL-ORME-TRONQUOY-DE-LALANDE	Saint-Seurin-de-Cadourne
LE BOURDIEU	Vertheuil
VICTORIA	Vertheuil
CISSAC	Cissac
HANTEILLAN	Cissac
RAMAGE-LA-BÂTISSE	Saint-Saveur
LANESSAN	Cussac
LIVERSAN	Saint-Saveur
LA TOUR-DU-HAUT-MOULIN	Cussac
BEAUMONT	Cussac
MOULIN-ROUGE	Cussac
LAMOTHE-BERGERON	Cussac
LAMARQUE	Lamarque
MALESCASSE	Lamarque
ARNAULD	Arcins
DE VILLEGEORGE	Avensan
CITRAN	Avensan
SÉNÉJAC	le Pian
DE MALLERET	le Pian

Leading Haut-Médoc estates	Surface area in hectares	Composition of vineyards (%)			
		CABERNET SAUVIGNON	MERLOT	CABERNET FRANC	PETIT VERDOT
LA TOUR-CARNET	55	55	20	20	5
CANTEMERLE	53	40	40	15	5
LA TOUR-CARNET	31	33	33	33	1
DE CAMENSAC	60	60	20	20	—
BELGRAVE	55	60	35	—	5
SOCIONDO-MALLET	30	60	30	10	—

GRAVES and PESSAC-LÉOGNAN

The Graves region produces annually about 265,000 hectolitres of red wine. This is about as much as the combined total of Margaux, Saint-Julien, Saint-Estèphe and Pauillac and rather less than half that of Saint-Émilion. Of this, some 68,000 hectolitres come under the new Pessac-Léognan *appellation*, about as much as in Margany ot Pauillac. and far richer in history. There is more for the tourist to see – the ancient fortress at Roquetaillade, castles at Villandraut and Budos, the cathedral at Bazas and the early Gothic church at Uzeste, where Clement V, the Gascon Pope, lies buried. And of course there is the lovely moated Château de La Brède, home of the seventeenth-century French statesman and philosopher, Montesquieu, and perhaps the greatest tourist attraction in the entire Gironde.

The Graves is both hillier and more wooded than the Médoc. The countryside becomes gradually more undulating as you travel south, oak progressively giving way to pine as you approach the pine forests of the Landes, whose sandy soils form a natural limit to the vineyard area. The soil within Graves is similar to that of the Médoc. As might be expected from its name, the area is composed of ridges of gravel rippling away from the river Garonne. This is for the most part combined with and based on sand or sandstone although there is also clay. The soil to the south nearer Langon contains more limestone and is perhaps more suitable for white wines than red, though both are made in the area.

The vine shares the cleared landscape with pasture and arable land. There are fields of maize and market gardens. In the northern part of the Graves, immediately outside the motorway *Rocade* which encircles Bordeaux and extending down to Léognan and Cadaujac the region is heavily populated. In the south away from Bordeaux the atmosphere is more pastoral. This is a larger area than the Haut-Médoc – 55 kilometres from north to south and 20 kilometres at its widest east–west point. But there are fewer vines. Much of the best vineyard area close to Bordeaux has disappeared in the expansion of the city and the creation of the airport at Mérignac. At the turn of the century there were 168 properties or individual growers recorded in the Mérignac-Pessac-Talence-Gradignan sector in what are now the suburbs of the city. Today there are only nine. Production in the Graves is less than half that of the Haut-Médoc.

The Graves is commonly thought to be a white wine region even though more red wine is actually produced. Certainly the generic wine, hugely popular a generation or two ago before the rise of Liebfraumilch and the vogue for Muscadet and Mâcon, was, and still is, a white wine – though there is nothing to stop red wines being labelled simply as Graves. Today if a white wine is labelled 'Graves', the wine will be dry, and probably in a dark green glass bottle. If labelled 'Graves Supérieures' it can only be a medium, almost medium-sweet wine, and will be in a clear bottle.

Château Haut-Brion was included in the Bordeaux red wine classification of 1855, at a time when the rest of what are now the leading estates further south, with the exception of Château Carbonnieux, had only recently been formed. After the Second World War, like those of Saint-Émilion the Graves proprietors lobbied for a separate classification, and this was granted in 1953 and revised in 1959, adding a white wine section. There is one category only, that of *cru classé*. Sadly, unlike in Saint-Émilion, no periodic revision clause was incorporated in the legislation. The classification should have been revised twenty-five years on, in 1984. It is now long overdue: there are not only one or two red wine *bourgeois* Graves estates such as Château La Louvière which deserve promotion to *cru classé* status, but, more importantly, many white wines which deserve recognition.

In 1984 the INAO issued a decree permitting the classed growths in the communes of Pessac and Léognan to add the name of their commune to that of Graves on the labels of their wines. (For some time there had been an insistence by the growers in the 'Graves du Nord' that their wine was superior to that of their neighbours to the south, and they lobbied for an official distinction between the two parts of the region similar to that between the Haut and Bas-Médoc.) This 1984 decree has now been replaced from the 1987 vintage onwards. Instead of two separate sub-appellations only relative to the communes in question, there is now a single denomination, that of Pessac-Léognan. The *appellation* covers ten communes – Pessac and Léognan, plus Talence, Gradignan, Villenave d'Ornon, Cadaujac, Martillac, Mérignac, Canéjan and Saint-Médard-d'Eyrans. The Graves has been cut in two, and all the classed growths of the Graves are found in Pessac-Léognan.

RED WINES

The Graves region produces annually about 120,000 hectolitres of red wine. This is about as much as the combined total of Saint-Estèphe and Pauillac and rather less than half that of Saint-Émilion. Of this, some 36,000 hectolitres come under the new Pessac-Léognan *appellation*, about as much as in Saint-Julien or Pomerol.

Among the thirteen classed growths there is a wide variation in style but built around a central characteristic of medium-full aromatic wines which often mature to produce what is sometimes called a 'warm brick' flavour. For me, the wine is redolent of soft summer fruits – mulberry, raspberry and blackberry – mixed with roast chestnut and autumn brushwood.

With the exception of Château Smith-Haut-Lafitte (which has only 16 per cent Merlot), the classed growths are made from between 25 and 40 per cent Merlot and between 50 and 65 per cent Cabernet Sauvignon, the balance being made up of Cabernet Franc, Petit Verdot and Malbec. In general, the wines are not as full as the sturdiest classed growth Médocs made with more or less the same *encépagement*. The wines are similar in weight to those of Margaux and mature within the same timescale.

The senior estate in the Graves is Château Haut-Brion. Indeed, it can claim to be the oldest of all the Bordeaux First Growths. Owned by the American Dillon family, and now enclosed by the sprawling Bordeaux suburbs, Haut-Brion has had a long and consistent history of producing fine, very elegant wine whose essence, like that of Château Margaux at its best, is in delicacy and finesse rather than in power. This is one of the most harmonious and subtle of all wines. The tiny production of white wine is also among the world's finest examples.

Château La Mission-Haut-Brion lies opposite, on the other side of the busy thoroughfare which is the main road south-west out of the city towards Arcachon. The estate was separated from that of Haut-Brion a long time ago, and was once under the order of St Vincent-de-Paul, the Lazarites. La Mission-Haut-Brion's present reputation was created by Henri Woltner, who died shortly after making his fiftieth vintage in 1974. The quality of the wine then lapsed somewhat. In 1983 the estate was put up for sale, and acquired by its illustrious neighbour. The wine is fuller, firmer and more masculine than that of Haut-Brion itself. The white wine, called Laville-Haut-Brion, is also very fine and keeps well.

Château Pape-Clément is the third important growth, and almost the only other still remaining in the Bordeaux suburbs. Though the white wine vineyard has recently been extended (1989 and 1990) the production up until the present has been only a few hogsheads a year, and the property is only *cru classé* for its red wine. The red wine has enjoyed a high reputation, but in the late 1960s and throughout the 1970s the quality was unimpressive. Since 1984 it has improved. Pape-Clément produces a fullish wine. In Margaux terms it resembles Lascombes rather than Palmer.

In recent years Domaine de Chevalier has produced the second best wine, both red and white, in the Graves – or in Pessac-Léognan, as we should now say. The unpretentious château is more a simple country home, and is located out in the backwoods at the south-western corner of the commune of Léognan. The Chevalier red wine is medium-bodied, very elegant and harmonious: the epitome of subtlety and finesse. The white wine, like most of those in the Graves which are made for keeping, seems rather unpleasantly sulphury when tasted in bottle during its youth. Patience is required.

These four properties seem to be on a level of quality above the remaining classed growths. Château de Fieuzal has made great strides in the 1980s and threatens to rival the top estates. There is a little, but very stylish (but as yet unclassed, for production on a serious scale is recent) white wine. Château Haut-Bailly only produces red wine: soft, plump, elegant and delicious, very good indeed in recent years. Château Malartic-Lagravrière's wine is firmer; somewhat hard, historically, but more ample in recent years and not without depth. The white wine can be good, but like many white Graves has in the past suffered from too much sulphur.

Châteaux Carbonnieux, Olivier, Bouscaut, La Tour-Martillac and Smith-Haut-Lafitte are good medium-bodied wines but never desperately exciting. They all also make white wine, though that of the latter is not *cru classé*. Château La Tour-Haut-Brion, neighbour and stablemate of La Mission, was for many years its second wine. Post-1983, under the new Dillon regime, it has its own identity. The wine is fullish, somewhat hard and it seems to lack roundness.

There are three properties which stand out as being of classed growth standard but are as yet unclassified. These are Châteaux La Louvière, Larrivet-Haut-Brion and Les Carmes-Haut-Brion. The first two lie in Léognan and the latter is one of the few estates left in the city suburbs.

But there is plenty of wine outside the classed growth area (not that the north, the Pessac-Léognan, is officially this – one just gets the feeling that in practice this will be so). What are these wines like? In style, these *bourgeois* Graves wines have much in common with the lesser wines of the Médoc. They are not so dominated by Cabernet Sauvignon as the more illustrious growths but are, nevertheless, Cabernet-based. This is the basic taste of a lesser Graves. However, there are some wines, to the south, which are rather softer, with more Merlot in the *encépagement*, and which mature rather sooner. These are almost a halfway house between a lesser Médoc and a minor Libournais wine. Other good red wine estates in the Graves include Châteaux Brown, Cabannieux, du Cruzeau, de France, Ferrande, La Garde, Haut-Gardère, Millet, Picque-Caillou, de Rochemorin and Domaine de Grandmaison.

Leading red wine estates	Surface area in hectares	Composition of vineyards (%)			
		CABERNET SAUVIGNON	MERLOT	CABERNET FRANC	PETIT VERDOT AND MALBEC
HAUT-BRION	41	55	30	15	—
LA MISSION-HAUT-BRION	21	60	35	5	—
LA TOUR-HAUT-BRION	4	65	30	5	—
DOMAINE DE CHEVALIER	15	65	30	5	—
BOUSCAUT	32	55	35	5	5 (Malbec only)
CARBONNIEUX	35	50	30	10	10
DE FIEUZAL	23	65	30	—	5 (Petit Verdot only)
HAUT-BAILLY	25	60	30	10	—
MALARTIC-LAGRAVIÈRE	14	44	25	31	—
OLIVIER	18	65	35	—	—
PAPE-CLÉMENT	29	60	40	—	—
SMITH-HAUT-LAFITTE	45	72	16	11	—
LA-TOUR-MARTILLAC	20	60	25	6	9
LA LOUVIÈRE	37	70	20	10	—
LARRIVET-HAUT-BRION	16	60	35	—	5
LES CARMES-HAUT-BRION	3.5	—	50	50	—

WHITE WINES

Just over 45 per cent of the annual Graves production of 220,000 hectolitres is white wine. The trend here, as elsewhere in Bordeaux, is from white to red, though it has not been as marked as in the lesser outlying areas. Much of this white wine is uncomplicated generic stuff, Graves or Graves Supérieures. In the northern part of the region, in what is now the Pessac-Léognan *appellation*, only some 22 per cent of the production is white wine but here you will find all the nine classed growths. With the exception of Château Carbonnieux and Château Olivier, most of the classed growths and other leading estates only toy with white wine production, few making more than 20 *tonneaux*. Only one of the classed growths, the divided Château Couhins, solely produces white wine. Some, like Château Haut-Bailly, do not produce any white wine at all.

In this part of the Graves, the dominant white wine grape is Sauvignon Blanc. Château Malartic-Lagravière and Château Smith-Haut-Lafitte, as well as the part of Château Couhins owned by the Lurtons of Château La Louvière (Couhins-Lurton), produce their Graves whites exclusively from this variety. Only at Château Olivier is Sémillon in the ascendant. The 1987 decree outlining the new regulations for the Pessac-Léognan AC stipulated a minimum quantity of 25 per cent Sauvignon Blanc in the vineyards of those properties within the new AC. Personally, I consider this an unnecessary restriction. Sémillon is a higher quality grape variety than Sauvignon. Correctly vinified, the flavours of Sémillon are more subtle and complex, the feel of the wine is richer, more ample and generous and the wine has a greater capacity for ageing. The combination of Sauvignon and new or newish oak has to be handled with great care lest the oak dominates and the tannins are too blatant. The Sémillon marries better with new wood as all of us who have enjoyed fine Sauternes can substantiate.

Further south in Graves, Sémillon is more widely planted. At Château Rahoul, run by Peter Vinding-Diers until 1988 (he has now moved to Château de Landiras) a white wine is made exclusively from Sémillon. At Château de Roquetaillade-La-Grange, at the various estates owned by members of the Dubourdieu family and at those owned or whose wines are sold by Pierre Coste, and elsewhere, the percentage of Sémillon is 70 per cent or more.

Up to relatively recently, white Graves was for the most part anonymous, heavy, sulphury, coarse and deservedly suffering in reputation. And this criticism applied to the majority of classed growth wines as well as to those from the lesser estates. In the late 1980s, particularly since 1985 the change has been dramatic. There used to be no fermentation expected in 1984?), the change has been dramatic. There used to be no fermentation or *élevage* in new oak outside Haut-Brion, La Mission-Haut-Brion and Domaine de Chevalier. Even there the winemakers often oversulphured the wine.

Today a revolution is taking place. There is a new determination to achieve something clean, elegant and gently underpinned with oak; but above all letting the delicious combination of Sauvignon and Sémillon shine through. Even at *bourgeois* level where perhaps the new wood cannot be afforded – or so the accountants might say – the owners are prepared to invest. There is some way to go yet, but the days when one can order a bottle of white Graves with the same confidence as a Muscadet or a Mâcon-Blanc-Villages cannot be far off. I am pleased and relieved to see the change.

To summarize, non-classed growth Graves estates worth recommending for white wines are Châteaux Archambeau, Clos Floridène, du Cruzeau, Montalivet, Rahoul, Rochemorin, Roquetaillade-La-Grange and Peter Vinding-Diers' Domaine de la Grave (and, potentially, his recently extended Château de Landiras). Pierre Coste, *négociant* in Langon, is a splendid source for inexpensive, well-made, dry white Graves.

Leading white wine estates	*Surface area in hectares*	*Composition of vineyards (%)*		
		SÉMILLON	SAUVIGNON BLANC	MUSCADELLE
HAUT-BRION	3	55	45	—
LAVILLE HAUT-BRION	6	60	40	—
DOMAINE DE CHEVALIER	3	30	70	—
BOUSCAUT	10	52	8	—
CARBONNIEUX	35	30	65	5
LA TOUR-MARTILLAC	4.75	55	30	—
MALARTIC-LAGRAVIÈRE	1.5	—	100	—
OLIVIER	17	65	30	5
COUHINS	6	50	50	—
COUHINS-LURTON	6	—	100	—
DE FIEUZAL	1.5	40	60	—

Leading white wine estates (continued)	Surface area in hectares	Composition of vineyards (%)		
		SÉMILLON	SAUVIGNON BLANC	MUSCADELLE
SMITH-HAUT-LAFITTE	5.6	—	100	—
PAPE-CLÉMENT*	I	33	33	33
LA LOUVIÈRE	18	15	85	—
LARRIVET-HAUT-BRION	0.5	40	60	—
HAUT-GARDÈRE	2	40	60	—

*Pape-Clément's white wine vineyard is currently being enlarged to 2½ hectares and this curious *encépagement* will be changed to something more traditional.

SAUTERNES AND BARSAC

In the south of the Graves, on the left bank of the river Garonne just above the town of Langon, lies the Sauternes district, home of the greatest, richest and most luscious sweet wines of the world. Surrounding Sauternes on either side of the river are the other, lesser sweet wine areas of Bordeaux: Cérons, Loupiac and Sainte-Croix-du-Mont. Here the wines are less intensely sweet, less concentrated, less honeyed, but they can nevertheless be fine wines in their own right.

Sauternes consists of five communes covering some 2250 hectares and produces an annual average of 52,000 hectolitres. Of these the largest, and an *appellation* in its own become affected by noble rot. What produces the microclimate necessary for its production is a little river, hardly more than a stream, called the Ciron. The Ciron arises out of a spring deep in the Landes and flows into the Garonne between the villages of Barsac and Preignac. The waters are cold; when they meet the warmer Garonne the atmosphere becomes suffused in mist, particularly in the early morning. This creates the humidity necessary for the production of the *Botrytis cinerea* fungus.

There are three grape varieties used for Sauternes: Sémillon, Sauvignon Blanc and Muscadelle, but it is Sémillon which is the basis of the wine, for it is this grape which is the most susceptible to rot. It is very rigorously pruned to reduce the yield, more so than the Sauvignon (Muscadelle is present to only a very small extent, and disapproved of by the leading châteaux), and so while the average *encépagement* in the vineyard might be 85 per cent Sémillon to 15 per cent Sauvignon the blend in the wine might be 75 to 25 per cent.

Sauternes consists of five communes covering some 2100 hectares and produces an annual average of 49,000 hectolitres. Of these the largest, and an *appellation* in its own right, is Barsac. Barsac lies to the north, on the bank of the Garonne, its vineyards stretching back to the motorway. To the south is Preignac, also on the river bank, but with its best vineyards inland from the autoroute where it marches with the commune of Sauternes. On the other sides of Sauternes are the communes of Fargues and Bommes.

The Sauternes is a laid-back, idle, bucolic region, seemingly one of the backwaters of Bordeaux, despite the worldwide fame of its wines. The region is attractive, undulating and well-wooded. Each of the important classed growths occupies its own little hillock, the less well-exposed valleys being left to pasture or planted with maize and wheat rather than with vines. The roads in between the fields and vineyards are narrow and winding and it is easy to lose one's way.

Until recently the fortunes of the Sauternes region were in the doldrums. After a fine run of vintages between the end of the Second World War and the early 1960s, successful years became sparse. The market for sweet wines evaporated. Life became increasingly uneconomic. One Second Growth, Château de Myrat, grubbed up its vines and gave up entirely (though it has been recently resurrected). Others gave up even the pretence of producing serious wine. Many changed hands – four classed growths in 1971 alone. Not only was production unprofitable, but the owners seemed to have lost faith in their product. There was no combined marketing effort, indeed little communication between one owner and another. I remember as late as 1982 introducing one château proprietor to his neighbour. In the ten years one had lived in the region (he was one of the 1971 arrivals – the other had been resident far longer) they had never actually met!

Today the position is different. There is a new mood of buoyancy, profitability and confidence in the air. In part this is a question of new blood and new brooms, the arrival of a new generation and outsiders such as the Canadian Hamilton Narby late of Château Guiraud. They have been helped by one good (1985) and four excellent (1983, '86, '88, '89) vintages in six years for which they asked and readily obtained economically realistic prices. These prices enabled investment in new oak and refrigerated stabilization equipment, made it a commercial possibility to wait for the arrival of an abundance of *pourriture noble* and to pick over each row of vines a number of times, and allowed for a severe selection of only the best *cuvées* for the *grand vin*. There has been a revolution in Sauternes since the mid-1980s, equivalent to that which has taken place in the Graves with the dry white wines. For the first time for a generation most of the classed growths – indeed nearly every single one of them – are making fine wine. The future looks exciting.

Sauternes will always be expensive. If in the Médoc and the Graves a yield of one bottle of wine per vine is the norm in the top properties, in the Sauternes the yield will be only a third or less. One glass of wine per vine, they will tell you at Château d'Yquem. In Sauternes collection costs are higher and successful vintages rarer. For these reasons we must be prepared to pay high prices for good Sauternes or the wine will cease to exist.

There are significant differences between the style of wines produced in the five Sauternes communes. Sauternes itself is the fullest, the richest, the most concentrated, especially at Château d'Yquem, but potentially, at least, also in the other top estates. Fargues, nearby, as characterized by Château Rieussec, Yquem's immediate neighbour, produces wines the closest in character. Those of Bommes (Lafaurie-Peyraguey, Rayne-Vigneau, Sigalas-Rabaud and Rabaud-Promis) and Preignac (Suduiraut) are ample and plump, marginally less honeyed, a little more flowery. Barsac's wines (Climens, Coutet, Doisy-Daëne and Nairac) are the most racy of them all, the least luscious. But it is in fact difficult, as well as dangerous, to generalize. Because of the prolonged harvest, where one grower may wait and have his patience rewarded, or his neighbour pick early and avoid the terrible consequences of a change in climate, Sauternes is not only much less consistent from vintage to vintage but also between one château and his neighbour. Among the First Growths, apart from Yquem, I would single out Climens and Rieussec as being exceptional, and Guiraud, Lafaurie-Peyraguey, Rayne-Vigneau, Rabaud-Promis and Sigalas-Rabaud as almost as fine in the last few successful vintages. Doisy-Védrines, Doisy-Daëne, Nairac, Broustet and Lamothe-Guignard are the best of the Second Growths. Leading the non-classified châteaux are de Fargues, owned by the Lur-Saluces

family of Yquem, Raymond-Lafon, Bastor-Lamontagne and Saint-Armand, part of whose production is labelled as La Chartreuse.

When should you drink your fine Sauternes? The wines are full-bodied, alcoholic, high in sugar and high in balancing acidity. They are big wines, in short. It is infanticide to drink the richest, best-balanced vintages too early; before ten years old in fact. Château d'Yquem, however, is an exception. The wines are twice as concentrated as the rest of Sauternes and so the time-scales need to be doubled. On the other hand, I consider lesser vintages are at their best young. The wines may be sweet but they will not be as honeyed and luscious, the harmony may not be what it should be. As a result, wines from these years may get coarse as they age. Drink them young, at the age of five years or so, and you will enjoy their youthful freshness and fragrance.

Following the lead of Château d'Yquem, which rather surprised everybody by producing a dry wine called Ygrec in 1960, many of the estates now earmark part of their crop, often the Sauvignon element where it has produced prolifically, for early harvesting and the production of a dry white wine. For most châteaux, this was a form of insurance in case the sweet crop should turn out to be a disaster. For many it was also a compensation in the days when the area was beleaguered by a lack of demand.

Most of these dry whites I find rather heavy and sulphury. I can't say I am even a great fan of Ygrec. Pierre Dubourdieu's dry wines from Doisy-Daëne are the best made, the most supple, fruity and interesting (Doisy-Daëne Sec and Doisy-Daëne-Saint-Martin). Rayne Sec, from Château de Rayne-Vigneau, can also be recommended. Like lesser Graves, these dry white wines are best drunk young. Curiously, they carry a mere Bordeaux *appellation*, as do the few red wines which are produced in the area.

Leading Sauternes estates	Surface area in hectares	Composition of vineyards (%)		
		SÉMILLON	SAUVIGNON BLANC	MUSCADELLE
D'YQUEM	81	80	20	—
LA TOUR-BLANCHE	30	70	27.5	2.5
LAFAURIE-PEYRAGUEY	32	90	5	5
CLOS-HAUT-PEYRAGUEY	15	83	15	2
DE RAYNE-VIGNEAU	68	50	50	—
SUDUIRAUT	70	80	20	—
COUTET	36	80	20	—
CLIMENS	30	98	2	—
GUIRAUD	118	54	45	1
RIEUSSEC	66	80	18	2
RABAUD-PROMIS	32	80	18	2
SIGALAS-RABAUD	14	90	10	—
DOISY-VÉDRINES	20	80	20	—
DOISY-DUBROCA	3	90	10	—
DOISY-DAËNE	36	80	15	5
D'ARCHE	14	100	—	—

Leading Sauternes estates (continued)	Surface area in hectares	Composition of vineyards (%)		
		SÉMILLON	SAUVIGNON BLANC	MUSCADELLE
FILHOT	60	60	37	3
BROUSTET	16	63	25	12
NAIRAC	15	90	37	4
CAILLOU	15	90	10	—
SUAU	7	80	10	10
DE MALLE	26	75	22	3
ROMER-DU-HAYOT	15	70	25	5
LAMOTHE-GUIGNARD	11	85	5	10
LAMOTHE-DESPUJOLS	8	70	20	10
DE FARGUES	10	80	20	—
RAYMOND-LAFON	20	80	20	—
SAINT AMAND/LA CHARTREUSE	18	75	20	5
BASTOR-LAMONTAGNE	40	70	20	10

CÉRONS

North of Barsac lies Cérons, both a village and an *appellation*. The wine can be made in the communes of Illats and Podensac as well as Cérons itself. All three villages can also produce dry white and red Graves and Graves Supérieures. Little Cérons is produced – barely 3000 hectolitres annually, one twentieth that of Sauternes. Demand and prices being what they are, the proprietors cannot afford several visits to the vineyard nor new oak. Cérons wine is therefore sweet but lacks a noticeable flavour of *pourriture noble*. It is best drunk young, chilled, as an apéritif. Most of the leading estates, particularly those in Illats and Podensac such as Châteaux d'Archambeau and Chantegrive, choose to produce dry Graves rather than sweet Cérons. Grand Enclos du Château de Cérons is the leading estate for sweet wines.

SAINTE-CROIX-DU-MONT and LOUPIAC

Rather larger, rather better and altogether more vigorous than Cérons are the neighbouring *appellations* of Sainte-Croix-du-Mont and Loupiac on the other side of the river Garonne. The communes lie adjacent to one another on the top of a steep bank above a bend in the river opposite Barsac and Preignac. From the top of the hill there is a superb view over the Sauternes area and out towards the pine forests of the Landes.

There is little to distinguish between the wines of one commune and the other, and in style, quality and lusciousness they come between the sweet wines of Cérons and Sauternes. Indeed, many of the best properties produce wine of equal quality to the *bourgeois* Sauternes châteaux, including Château de Ricaud in Loupiac and the tiny

Château de Tastes in Sainte-Croix. Château Loubens, also in Sainte-Croix, can also be recommended. These sweet wines should be drunk soon, like those of Cérons.

CADILLAC

North of Loupiac, opposite Cérons, lies the village of Cadillac. This is a curious, and recent (1973) *appellation*. Cadillac, like most of the right bank of the Garonne between Bordeaux and Langon (with the exception of Loupiac and Sainte-Croix-du-Mont) was, and continues to be, part of the Premières Côtes de Bordeaux AC. Effectively, since 1973, the southern half of this area, some twenty-one communes, is now allowed to produce a Cérons-type sweet wine under the *appellation* of Cadillac. Few growers seem to be interested. The annual harvest is a mere 10,000 hectolitres. Château du Juge, which is in the commune of Cadillac itself, is the only property which is well-known.

ENTRE-DEUX-MERS

Between the seas, or more correctly between the rivers, Garonne and Dordogne, lies the Entre-Deux-Mers. This is a large, heterogeneous attractive part of the world; a prosperous landscape of farms and orchards and vineyards, of spinneys, copses and large forests, of running rivers and sudden hidden valleys. It is undulating, even hilly in parts. There are pleasant country farmsteads, elegant manors, imposing ruins and medieval churches. It is a rich land of mixed agriculture and it is where I would like to live if I were to settle in Bordeaux.

Yet it was not always as benign and prosperous an area as it seems today. The area, and the *appellation*, is a white wine region but the demand for white Bordeaux wines has contracted. Much of the Bordeaux change-over in the vineyards from white vines to red in the last generation or so has occurred in the Entre-Deux-Mers. For some time it has been more profitable to produce either red wine, simply labelled as Bordeaux or Bordeaux Supérieur, or even larger quantities of non-*appellation* white wine, than Entre-Deux-Mers AC, which must be a dry white wine. The co-operative at Rauzan in the middle of the area and one of the largest and most up to date in the Gironde, produces nearly 70,000 hectolitres of Bordeaux Rouge but only 14,000 of Entre-Deux-Mers.

Happily in recent years, with the arrival of the trained oenologist, increasing use of the mechanical harvester and controlled vinification methods in modern equipment (paid for by subsidies from the EC), both yields and quality have been increased while unit costs have been reduced. Moreover, albeit slowly, Entre-Deux-Mers is now beginning to recapture a wider market. It is once again an economic proposition for the *vigneron* to concentrate on quality rather than quantity. The region is beginning to thrive.

The Entre-Deux-Mers is triangular in shape, occupying most of the land between the two rivers with the departmental border with the Lot-et-Garonne as its base in the south-east corner. There are various sub-regions such as the Haut-Benauge, Saint-Macaire, Sainte-Foy-Bordeaux and the Graves de Vayres, as well as the sweet wine areas of Sainte-Croix-du-Mont, Loupiac and Cadillac. On the right bank of the Garonne, opposite the

Graves, lies the *appellation* of the Premières Côtes de Bordeaux. Sainte-Foy-Bordeaux, at the extreme east of the region, and the Graves de Vayres opposite Libourne, are *appellations* for both red and white wines, though rarely seen. Haut-Benauge lies behind the Premières Côtes at its southern end and continues into Saint-Macaire. These *appellations* are for white wines only. Production of Saint-Macaire and Sainte-Foy is miniscule.

There is a total of nearly 2400 hectares under vine in 125 communes which produce an average of almost 150,000 hectolitres of Entre-Deux-Mers annually. In addition, a large proportion of the 2 million hectolitres of plain Bordeaux or Bordeaux Supérieur comes from the Entre-Deux-Mers. The soil structure is complex, essentially loam or marl with patches of gravel; occasionally *boulbènes*, a sort of sand-clay mixture which can compact almost to a concrete-like substance and is hence very difficult to work. The vines are trained high, spaced far apart to assist mechanical cultivation, and grass is allowed to grow in between the rows of vines. It makes altogether quite a different picture from the immaculate, flat, intensively cultivated but essentially arid-looking Médoc.

Entre-Deux-Mers wine, while largely made from Sauvignon Blanc and Sémillon, plus Muscadelle, can include some Merlot Blanc, Colombard, Mauzac and Ugni Blanc, albeit in small proportions only. In practice, Sauvignon is in the ascendant, producing crisp, dry, sometimes grassy-flavoured, racy wines, suitable for early drinking and today these are increasingly well made. Châteaux Bonnet, Goumin, Peyrebon, de Toutigeac, Thieuley, Launay and Moulin-de-Launay (both of which have a number of alternative labels) are estates to note. Some of the estates are quite extensive.

PREMIÈRES CÔTES DE BORDEAUX

Along the right bank of the Garonne, all the way from Saint-Maixant opposite the town of Langon to Bassens north of Bordeaux, a distance of some sixty kilometres, the land rises steeply away from the river and, at the top of the slope, stretches inland for a few kilometres. This narrow strip is the region of the Premières Côtes de Bordeaux, interrupted only by the indentations of Sainte-Croix-du-Mont and Loupiac. Twenty-one communes in the southern half of the region can use the Cadillac *appellation* for their sweet white wines.

This is an interesting region, not only because of the attractive scenery, similar to that of the Entre-Deux-Mers, but also because of the wines. A significant proportion of gravel in the soil gives the reds more definition and character than most of the *petits châteaux* of Bordeaux. There are white wines too, but these must be off-dry, and can often be quite sweet, a style which finds little market these days. Those producers who do produce a dry white wine, such as Denis Dubourdieu at the excellent Château Reynon at Béguey, can only call it Bordeaux Blanc. There are nearly 3300 hectares of vineyards, spread over sixteen communes in the northern part of the region and including the twenty-one in the southern part which can also make Cadillac. Annual production amounts to approximately 160,000 hectolitres of red and 16,000 hectolitres of white wine.

There are many useful, enterprising estates in the Premières Côtes de Bordeaux, as well as a good co-operative at Quinsac, which separately vinifies the produce of a number of domaines. Château Birotú and Château Carsins, neighbours of Château Reynon, Château Lezongars, at Villenave-de-Rions, the Cordier-owned Châteaux Laurétan, Tanesse and Le Gardéra, and Châteaux du Peyrat and Peconnet are some of the best-known individual estates.

SAINT-ÉMILION

Some forty kilometres east of Bordeaux, across the peninsula of the Entre-Deux-Mers, can be found the sizeable, bustling but architecturally nondescript town of Libourne, centre both geographically and economically of the 'Right Bank'. The portmanteau phrase Dordogne or Libournais wines means the wines of Saint-Émilion, Pomerol, Fronsac and their satellites. For centuries this region was, literally, a backwater. The wines were the poor 'country cousins' of those of the Graves and the Médoc. Holdings were small and ownership in the hands of the peasants or local *petite bourgeoisie*. Communications with Bordeaux were tedious – there was neither a bridge across the Dordogne at Libourne nor one across the Garonne at Bordeaux until 1820 or so. And the wines had little impact on the Bordeaux marketplace as a result. While the extensive, aristocrat-owned châteaux of the Médoc, monocultural estates from the 1740s, found equally well-to-do customers in Britain and Ireland, the artisanal produce of the Libournais was shipped as generic wine to the burghers of Holland, Bremen and the Hanseatic ports. The area remained one of mixed farming until much later than the Médoc and the Graves, few domaines having any individual reputation until the 1830s or 1840s.

Not surprisingly, when the Bordeaux brokers drew up the 1855 Classification, the wines of the Libournais were ignored. It was not until post-phylloxera times towards the end of the nineteenth century that prices began to match those of even the lesser Médoc classed growths, and only since the Second World War that there has been parity. The Libournais remains a wine region of small estates, of charming but largely unsophisticated and architecturally undistinguished dwellings, but one with often surprisingly lengthy family histories of ownership.

Some six kilometres north-east of Libourne lies the ancient walled town of Saint-Émilion. In contrast with Libourne Saint-Émilion is almost too self-consciously picturesque. Wine has been made here since Gallo-Roman times. Whether the poet and statesman Ausonius, after whom one of the area's most prestigious estates is named, ever had a vineyard in Saint-Émilion is a matter for dispute, but there is plenty of archaeological evidence to support a history of almost two millennia of continuous vine cultivation. Above Château Ausone on the plateau you can see ancient trenches excavated out of the limestone bedrock. These were filled with earth and planted with fruit trees – apples, pears, cherries and peaches. Vines were then trained up the trees and on to overhanging trellises in a sort of pergola system. Not long ago, not at Ausone but in the vineyard of Château La Gaffelière, another Saint-Émilion First Growth, an impressive mosaic showing a vineyard scene, was partially uncovered. This is no longer on view to the tourist, sadly, having been earthed up to await a more comprehensive dig in twenty-five years' time or so when techniques are yet more advanced.

The town itself is named after the hermit, Aemilianus, who lived in the eighth century.

CHATEAU AUSONE
SAINT-ÉMILION
1er GRAND CRU CLASSÉ
APPELLATION SAINT-ÉMILION 1er GRAND CRU CLASSÉ CONTROLÉE
1982
Mme J. DUBOIS-CHALLON & Héritiers C. VAUTHIER
PROPRIÉTAIRES A SAINT-ÉMILION (GIRONDE) FRANCE
MIS EN BOUTEILLES AU CHATEAU
PRODUCE OF FRANCE

Deciding to retire from life completely he sought a quiet spot where he could calmly meditate on the cares of the world. He found his site, a grotto in a limestone bluff above the valley of the Dordogne. Today this is Saint-Émilion. Above the hermit's cell, excavated deep into the rock, is a vast, underground monolithic church, the largest in Europe. Surrounding this the steep, cobbled streets and houses cling to the sides of a defile in the slope. The narrow alleys are filled with shops selling the celebrated local macaroons as well as wine and cans of *confit d'oie, cèpes* and *pâté de foie gras*.

From the Église Collègiale and Place Pioceau at the top of the town the view south is spectacular: the celebrated classed growths on the plateau and the slopes, lesser vineyards on the valley floor and finally the Dordogne, glinting away in the distance. You can also look directly down to the Place du Marché. Here, outside the Église Monolithique, the Jurade of Saint-Émilion congregate four times a year in their red ceremonial robes to proclaim the commencement of the harvest in September and command the ritual burning of an old wooden barrel, commemorating the old days when the Jurade (and not some bureaucrat in Paris or Bordeaux) held power over the legislation of the local wines.

Saint-Émilion, though by no means the largest in overall surface area, is the most compact and the most intensely cultivated *appellation* in Bordeaux. There is hardly a spare field which is not covered in neat rows of vines. The area forms a rough rectangle only ten kilometres by five, yet there are as many as 5000 hectares of vines. By comparison, the entire Haut-Médoc (measuring fifty kilometres from Blanquefort to Saint-Estèphe) has only just over half as much again under cultivation, about 8600 hectares of vines.

Moreover, in contrast to the rolling gravel plateaux of the Médoc, where the château holdings are large and the atmosphere is aristocratic, Saint-Émilion is a region of the small peasant proprietor. The 5300 hectares are divided among a thousand or more different owners, some 25 per cent of whom are members of the thriving local co-operative. Annual production of Saint-Émilion wine is around 280,000 hectolitres.

Geographically and also in terms of the style of its wines, Saint-Émilion can be divided into three main areas. South of the town itself, the land falls away abruptly towards the river Dordogne. The best vineyards lie either on these slopes or occupy the plateau on the other three sides of the town. This is the area known as the Côtes-Saint-Émilion. Here the soil consists of a thin layer of limestone debris on a solid limestone rock base, into which many a quarry has been hewn and is now used for cellaring the wine. Mixed with the limestone is a certain amount of clay. There is more sand as you descend down the slope into the valley. All but two of Saint-Émilion's First Growths lie in the Côtes. To the west of the Côtes, adjacent to Pomerol, is the smaller area of Graves-Saint-Émilion. As the name suggests, there is gravel in the soil. There is less limestone and clay than in the best sites of the Côtes but more sand. The subsoil is of the same composition. This area is almost entirely occupied by two First Growths, Châteaux Cheval Blanc and Figeac.

Between these two areas, but largely north and west of the town itself, lies an area of old weathered sand known as the *sables anciennes*, similar to that found in the Graves-Saint-Émilion, but without the gravel and on a base of limestone. The sand here is distinct from the more alluvial soil to the south of Saint-Émilion. Wines from here are good, if not of the very highest quality. There are no First Growths.

The wines of Saint-Émilion – and indeed the whole of the Libournais – are made from the three great red varieties of the Bordeaux area, but in a different proportion to that used in the Médoc. In the Médoc the Cabernet Sauvignon is king, occupying between 60 and 90 per cent of the vineyards; Merlot is an important subsidiary; Cabernet Franc is out of favour. In Saint-Émilion the Merlot is the most widely planted variety, with Cabernet Franc the main additional grape, whilst Cabernet Sauvignon is hardly used at all. The reason for the choice of Cabernet is the difference in soil structure. Cabernet Sauvignon thrives in the gravelly soils of the Médoc but Cabernet Franc performs far better in the predominantly limestone soils of the Saint-Émilion area, where it is known locally as the Bouchet.

The two main areas of Saint-Émilion, the Côtes and the Graves, produce quite different wines; though with the exception of Château Cheval-Blanc (made from 66 per cent Cabernet Franc and 33 per cent Merlot) and Château Figeac (which because of its gravel soil contains one-third Cabernet Sauvignon) the top growths have similar *encépagements*, roughly 50 to 70 per cent Merlot and 30 to 50 per cent Cabernet Franc or Bouchet.

The Côtes wines can vary depending whether the vineyard is largely or indeed entirely on the plateau or mostly on the slope. Some of the plateau wines can be very full and sturdy like Château Canon and Clos Fourtet. Mostly, though, all these Côtes wines start off well-coloured, quite full, without being particularly densely structured, and develop quickly, being ready for drinking a few years earlier than a Médoc or Graves of similar standing. In character they are loose-knit, somewhat warmer and sweeter than in the Médoc, with a spicy, fruitcaky flavour which derives from the predominant Merlot grape. A good First Growth from a successful vintage needs to be kept eight years or so before it is ready for drinking. It will keep well for at least a decade after that if properly stored. The wines of the *sables anciennes* are similar but both less intense and less stylish.

The Graves-Saint-Émilion really needs to be considered as a quite separate area. The wines have more power and are fuller and more concentrated, richer and firmer than those of the Côtes; they still have the predominant Merlot grape flavour, though it is less marked. These Saint-Émilions are more similar to Pomerols, their nearest neighbours. They tend to require a couple of years longer to mature and last better.

The lesser wines of the Saint-Émilion area, and this applies to the satellites as well as to Saint-Émilion itself, are predominantly Merlot-based, loose-knit, gentle wines without a great deal of grip. In weaker years they can rapidly become attenuated – but, at least, unlike a lesser Médoc in a poor year, they do not have unpleasant unripe tannins. Personally I find Fronsacs and lesser Pomerols have more interest than these wines.

It is commonly but erroneously believed that the famous 1855 Classification of Bordeaux was of the Médoc only, with Château Haut-Brion being smuggled in on the old-boy network because it was too important to be left out. In fact, the classification was of all the red wines of Bordeaux. It was simply that the Libournais wines were not then considered fashionable and fetched low prices at that time. Indeed, at the time it was the wines of Fronsac which fared better.

Anxious not to be left out for ever, the local growers lobbied for their own separate classification in the 1950s. This is under the ultimate control of the INAO and is supposed to be revised every ten years. In fact the original classification of 1954 was revisited in 1969 again in 1985, and again in 1996. The wines and growths of Saint-Émilion are divided into three categories: *grands crus classés* (itself subdivided into categories A and B), *grands crus* and plain or generic Saint-Émilion. (*See page 63.*)

The two Category As are Château Ausone in the Côtes and Château Cheval-Blanc in the Graves-Saint-Émilion. These are (or at least Cheval-Blanc is) clearly the two best wines of the area and sell for almost double the price of the others. Prices are equivalent to those of Château Haut-Brion and the First Growths in the Médoc.

Of the *premiers grands crus classés* I would class Canon, Figeac and Magdelaine in a class above the rest and equivalent to the 'super-seconds' of the Médoc, wines such as Châteaux Ducru-Beaucaillou, Léoville-Las-Cases, Palmer and Pichon-Longueville, Comtesse de Lalande. La Gaffelière and Pavie are very good, Belair is elegant if somewhat unconcentrated and Clos Fourtet is fuller and improving. L'angelus deserves its recent promotion. In my view the remaining two should be demoted and replaced with one or two châteaux from the next category.

This list of *grands crus classés* is far too cumbersome, not least because many of the properties are very small and their wines rarely encountered. The highfliers ought to be separated out into a superior classification (and into which Châteaux Trottevieille and Beauséjour-Duffau-Lagarosse should be demoted from *premiers grands crus classés*). These châteaux are, in alphabetical order: L'Arrosée, Beau-Séjour-Bécot, Berliquet, Cadet-Piola, Canon-La-Gaffelière, Dassault, La Dominique, Fonplégade, Fonroque, Larcis-Ducasse, Larmande, Laroze, Pavie-Decesse, La Serre, Soutard, Tertre-Daugay, La Tour-du-Pin-Figeac (Moueix), La Tour-Figeac and Troplong-Mondot. Châteaux L'Arrosée, Larmande and Soutard should be promoted to the First Growth B category.

The next category below *grands crus classés* is *grands crus*. This is a misleading title, for there is little *grand* about these wines. The wines are ordinary, equivalent to the *petits châteaux* found in the northern part of the Médoc, in Bourg and Blaye and the other lesser areas of the Médoc. To be classified *grand cru* the wines have to attain a requisite level of alcohol, pass a chemical analysis and be approved by a tasting panel. There are some 200 *grands crus*. Château Le Tertre-Rôteboeuf is a small but shining example.

Finally there is the simple Saint-Émilion classification. This is simple generic wine, without a property name, and normally appears under the label of a local merchant or co-operative. Good daily drinking, but nothing more pretentious than that.

The last updating of the Saint-Émilion classification took place in 1984. There was great consternation when this 1984 revision, to take effect from 1 January 1985, was first published. Some estates had actually been demoted! In particular one of the First Growths, Château Beau-Séjour-Bécot. Instead, though, of basing this demotion solely on quality grounds, the INAO reinforced their decision by pointing out that Monsieur Bécot had incorporated into Beau-Séjour some of the land or some of the *cuvées* of wine therefrom of two neighbouring properties in his ownership: Trois-Moulins and Grand-Pontet.

The reason for this is in the nature of the original Saint-Émilion classification. Unlike that of 1855, it has the force of law. Moreover, each category, and therefore by implication the precise land of the properties therein, has a specific *appellation contrôlée*. By 'diluting' his First Growth wine with that of *grand cru classé* wine, Monsieur Bécot was in effect blending the wines of two different *appellations*. He could no longer claim the classification of First Growth. Ironically, while many could have made a case at the end of the 1970s for demoting Beau-Séjour-Bécot on quality grounds, as I would argue should be done with two other First Growths, the quality of Beau-Séjour-Bécot has *improved* in the 1980s. Indeed, the wine is today better than that of its neighbour, Beauséjour-Duffau-Lagarosse.

Monsieur Bécot, naturally, was furious. He inundated the authorities with depositions and affidavits, as well as voluminous press articles and reports of tastings where his wine had done well. He has been trying to get the decision reversed ever since.

To further the irony, in the Médoc, because the 1855 Classification is *not* part of the *appellation contrôlée* laws there would be nothing illegal in doing what Monsieur Bécot had done. A wine of Pauillac, whether Château Lafite or a simple local village wine, has the same *appellation*, simply that of Pauillac. If Château Lafite wanted to enlarge its vineyard, as many other classed growths have indeed done, it could if it so wished incorporate the wine therefrom into the Lafite blend – and still label it as First Growth. The name Lafite is in effect a brand. But in Saint-Émilion the *premiers grands crus classés* existed under a different *appellation* from the rest of Saint-Émilion. I say 'existed', because to compound the irony further, in 1984 the INAO reduced the number of Saint-Émilion *appellations* from four to two. Now there is simply Saint-Émilion and Saint-Émilion Grand Cru, the latter incorporating all the previously higher categories. Today all the Saint-Émilion classed growths are in *appellation* terms classed as *grand cru*.

Leading Saint-Émilion estates	Surface area in hectares	Composition of vineyards (%)			
		MERLOT	CABERNET FRANC	CABERNET SAUVIGNON	MALBEC
Premiers Grands Crus Classés					
A					
AUSONE	7	50	50	—	—
CHEVAL-BLANC	35	40	60	—	—
B					
ANGÉLUS	24	45	50	5	—
BEAU-SÉJOUR-BÉCOT	18.5	70	15	15	—
BEAUSÉJOUR-DUFFAU-LAGAROSSE	7	50	25	25	—
BELAIR	13	60	40	—	—
CANON	18	55	40	5	—
CHEVAL-BLANC	Cussac				
CLOS FOURTET	17	60	20	20	—
FIGEAC	40	40	35	35	—
LA GAFFELIÈRE	22	65	25	10	—
MAGDELAINE	11	80	20	—	—
PAVIE	38	55	25	20	—
TROTTEVIEILLE	10	55	40	5	—
Leading Grands Crus Classés					
L'ARROSÉE	10	50	15	35	—
BERLIQUET	7.5	75	25 (combined)		—
CADET-PIOLA	7	51	18	28	3
CANON-LA-GASSELIÈRE	19	60	35	5	—
DASSAULT	23	70	20	10	—

Leading Saint-Émilion estates (continued)	Surface area in hectares	Composition of vineyards (%)			
		MERLOT	CABERNET FRANC	CABERNET SAUVIGNON	MALBEC
LA DOMINIQUE	18.5	76	8	8	8
FONPLÉGADE	18	60	35	5	—
FONROQUE	20	70	30	—	—
LARCIS-DUCASSE	10	65	35 (combined)		—
LARMANDE	18.5	65	30	5	—
LAROZE	28	50	40	10	—
PAVIE-DECESSE	9	65	20	15	—
LA SERRE	7	80	20	—	—
SOUTARD	28	60	35	5	—
TERTRE-DAUGAY	16	60	30	10	—
LE TERTRE-ROTEBOEUF	5.7	80	20	—	—
LA TOUR-DU-PIN-FIGEAC (MOUEIX)	9	60	30	10 (combined)	
LA TOUR-FIGEAC	13.5	60	40	—	—
TROPLONG-MONDOT	30	70	30 (combined)—		—

THE SAINT-ÉMILION SATELLITES

Above and behind Saint-Émilion are the Saint-Émilion satellites: Montagne, Lussac, Puisseguin, and Saint-Georges. All these communes can add the name Saint-Émilion to their own. Here there are some large estates, for this area was only developed more recently, and by the moneyed classes of the late nineteenth century. There are some fine buildings and some good wine, often better than that from the more alluvial, peripheral soils of Saint-Émilion itself. In general the *encépagement* contains more Merlot and less Cabernet than in the heart of Saint-Émilion. The wines are round and generous, though sometimes both rather diffuse and lacking finesse. They are best drunk young, within three to six years after the vintage.

There are now only four separate *appellations*, Montagne-Saint-Émilion having absorbed the smaller neighbouring commune of Parsac in 1972. In total these *appellations* cover some 3850 hectares of vines and produce around 225,000 hectolitres per annum, two-thirds the production of Saint-Émilion itself. The leading growths include Châteaux Calon, Lyonnat, Rodier and Saint-Georges.

POMEROL

Pomerol is a strange area. If one excludes the vineyard of its greatest domaine, Château Pétrus, it has no focus. Travelling north out of Libourne along the road which leads to Montagne-Saint-Émilion you pass a few vineyards and then come to the village of Catusseau. At this point the road forks. Between these two roads, about half a kilometre away on the highest ground of the area, lies Château Pétrus surrounded by most of the rest

of the top Pomerol domaines. This is the nucleus of the area. A little further on, to the left, there is a church and a few houses. This is all there is of Pomerol as a village.

The Pomerol *vignoble* is by far the smallest of the top-quality wine regions of Bordeaux. It is a compact commune of relatively small estates, many of which are now owned, managed or marketed by the excellent firm of Jean-Pierre Moueix in Libourne. The heart of the area is a gravel and clay plateau which lies on a hard, iron-rich base known as *crasse de fer* or *machefer* and which slopes down to the more alluvial sandy soils of the Dordogne, Isle and Barbanne rivers on three sides, and adjoins the Graves-Saint-Émilion vineyards on the east. The area measures barely three kilometres by four and consists of some 784 hectares of vines. This is hardly one seventh of the whole of Saint-Émilion, and roughly comparable with the smallest of the great Médoc communes, Saint-Julien. Annual production is around 38,580 hectolitres.

Pomerol's fame is recent. While a number of the leading growths can trace their history back to before the French Revolution, the vineyards were neglected until very recently indeed. Pomerol was only recognized as an area in its own right in 1923 and as late as 1943, when a list of comparative prices was produced for the Vichy Government, Pétrus could only command the price of a Second Growth Médoc and the next category of top Pomerols below Pétrus, Vieux-Château-Certan and La Conseillante, for example, were rated the equivalent of Giscours and La Lagune. It took two people – Madame Loubat, proprietor of Château Pétrus, and her ally Jean-Pierre Moueix, plus two enthusiastic disciples, Ronald Avery and Harry Waugh, to transform the situation. Yet Pomerol still remains a small, sleepy, *bourgeois* backwater, with few imposing estates.

Despite its size, Pomerol is today renowned the world over. If forty years ago the wines were barely recognized as being part of the Bordeaux pantheon, today they are much in demand. The name of Pétrus, the prodigious prices of its wines at auction, and the quality of the other top wines of the area hardly need pointing out any longer. On the other hand, as the vast majority of the individual properties are so tiny, barely a dozen hectares in surface at their largest, some wines are rarely encountered and difficult to acquire. Look at any list of old wines: plenty of Médocs, few Pomerols. The main grape is the Merlot, the principal subsidiary variety the Cabernet Franc (here as in Saint-Émilion called the Bouchet). You may also find a few rows of Malbec (here known as the Pressac). One or two properties such as Vieux-Château-Certan even have Cabernet Sauvignon, but in general this variety does not do as well on this side of the Gironde as the Cabernet Franc.

Pomerol wines are subtly different from those across the border in Saint-Émilion, particularly those from the limestone rock and *sables anciennes* (weathered sandstone) around the town of Saint-Émilion itself. Saint-Émilions are in general soft, aromatic, plump, fleshy and slightly spicy. Compared with the deeper-coloured, intense, firm, blackcurranty Médocs they are looser-knit, quicker to mature and do not last as long. Pomerols in many respects are a sort of half-way house. They are fresher and more solid than Saint-Émilions, richer, more plummy and less fruitcaky in flavour. Compared with the Médocs on the other hand, they are more obviously velvety but have less austerity and backbone. The concentration of fruit is more apparent, particularly when the wines are young, because it is less hidden by the tannin. I find the style delicious and the wines of increasingly high quality. The following table is my own personal classification of the leading Pomerol estates. I have divided them into two categories.

Leading Pomerol estates	Surface area in hectares	Composition of vineyards (%)			
		MERLOT	CABERNET FRANC	MALBEC	CABERNET SAUVIGNON

Outstanding Growths

PÉTRUS	11	95	5	—	—

Great Growths

CERTAN-DE-MAY	5	65	25	10 (combined)	
LA CONSEILLANTE	13	45	45	10	—
L'ÉGLISE-CLINET	4.5	60	30	10	—
L'ÉVANGILE	13	65	35	—	—
LAFLEUR-PÉTRUS	7.5	75	25	—	—
LAFLEUR	4	50	50	—	—
LATOUR-À-POMEROL	8	80	20	—	—
PETIT-VILLAGE	11	80	10	—	10
LE PIN	2.5	100	—	—	—
TROTANOY	7.5	85	15	—	—
VIEUX-CHÂTEAU-CERTAN	14	50	25	5	20

Good Growths

LE BON-PASTEUR	7	80	20	—	—
BOURGNEUF-VAYRON	10	80	20	—	—
LA CABANNE	10	70	30	—	—
CERTAN-GIRAUD/CERTAN-MARZELLE	6	70	30	—	—
CLINET	7	60	15	—	25
CLOS DU CLOCHER	6	70	30	—	—
CLOS L'ÉGLISE	6	55	20	—	25
CLOS RENÉ/MOULINET LASSERRE	11	60	30	10	—
LA CROIX	14	60	20	—	20
DE SALES	47.5	66	17	—	17
DOMAINE DE L'ÉGLISE	7	85	10	—	10
L'ENCLOS	10.5	80	20	—	—
FEYTIT-CLINET	7	85	15	—	—
LE GAY	8	50	50 (both Cabernets)		
GAZIN	20	80	15	—	5
LA GRAVE-TRIGANT-DE-BOISSET	8	90	10	—	—
LAGRANGE	8	90	10	—	—
NENIN	27	50	30	—	20
LA POINTE	25	80	15	5	—
ROUGET	18	90	10	—	—
LA VIOLETTE	4	95	50	—	—
VRAIE CROIX-DE-GAY	3.7	55	40	—	5

THE POMEROL SATELLITES

Across the river Barbanne to the north of Pomerol are two areas which are now incorporated into one, Néac having been increasingly absorbed into Lalande-de-Pomerol (an easier name to sell, no doubt) in the 1980s, though it still exists as an *appellation* in its own right. There are 1100 hectares in total, producing 57,00 hectolitres in an average year, and the wines have a character and a definition which I rate higher than those of the other Libournais satellites. The wines, naturally, are like lesser Pomerols, plump and fruity, without seeming to be too Merlot-based and loose-knit in character. They are attractive and stylish, at their best between three and eight years old, and we shall see a lot more of them. Leading properties include Châteaux Annereaux, Bel-Air, Bertineau-Saint-Vincent, Haut-Chaigneau and Siaurac.

FRONSAC

Of all the non-classic areas of Bordeaux – outside the districts of Haut-Médoc, Pessac-Léognan, Saint-Émilion and Pomerol – Fronsac wines have the most definition, the most personality. The wines have fruit, character and charm and are increasingly well made. A good Fronsac wine will usually cost less than a Médoc *cru bourgeois* or a Saint-Émilion *grand cru* and is normally a better wine. So the area has value for money too on its side. This is an exciting part of Bordeaux. There has been considerable investment in the area of late and the wines deserve to be better known.

Fronsac lies west of Pomerol, across the river Isle, a tributary of the Dordogne which it joins at Libourne. Viewed from the river or from the opposite bank in the Entre-Deux-Mers, you can see the land rising sharply. On this limestone bluff, the Tertre de Fronsac, and on the land behind it descending gradually towards the village of Galgon, are the Fronsac vineyards. The Fronsac plateau dominates a bend in the Dordogne and the surrounding countryside. Over twelve centuries ago, the Emperor Charlemagne commanded a fortress to be built to control the neighbouring area and to defend the Libournais against marauding pirates. The site was known as Fransiacus.

In 1623 the fortified castle which had evolved from Charlemagne's stockade was razed to the ground. Ten years later the great Cardinal de Richelieu bought the land – and the title of Duke of Fronsac – for the children of his younger sister. In the Fronsac area there are many elegant eighteenth- and early nineteenth-century buildings. The countryside is also attractive, with carefully tended vineyards interspersed with woodland and smaller, more formal parks surrounding the larger mansions. The views from the higher ground across to the Entre-Deux-Mers and along the Dordogne in both directions are well worth a detour.

Two centuries ago Fronsac's leading wines were the stars of the Libournais. References to Canon meant Fronsac's most famous wine owned by the Fontémoing family and not the Saint-Émilion *premier cru*. Indeed, the very first Bordeaux wine to appear in a Christie's catalogue refers to 'a hogshead of Canon Claret'. This can only be the Fronsac wine, for what is now Eric Fournier's estate in Saint-Émilion was known as the Domaine de Saint-Martin until 1857.

The rise in fame of Saint-Émilion wines in the mid-nineteenth century and those of Pomerol somewhat later was paralleled by a decline in the prestige of Fronsac. By the end of the century, a good Fronsac wine could fetch between 500 and 1000 francs a *tonneau*, roughly equivalent to a Pomerol satellite or Saint-Émilion *grand cru*, but by the 1950s the price was little more than that of Bordeaux Supérieur. Most wines were sold in bulk to the *négociants*, standards were poor and the wine rustic. It was not until after the frost disaster of 1956 when Fronsac, because of its elevated position, was affected least of all the Libournais wine areas — but still severely enough — that an organized effort to improve standards and promote the wines was made.

The real progress has begun more recently and is still accelerating. Comparisons of comprehensive tastings I have made over the last fifteen years since the mid-1970s show more and more establishments vinifying under controlled conditions, investing in new oak casks and producing wine to be reckoned with. Fronsac has also begun to attract the investor in real estate. The excellent company of Jean-Pierre Moueix, established in Libourne, has long been a source of good Fronsac wines. They are now the owners of several estates, as are the d'Arfeuilles, *négociants* and owners of Château La Pointe in Pomerol. As well as Moueix other Libournais merchants such as Horeau-Beylot, Janoueix, Armand Moueix and René Germain are also owners or *fermiers* of wine estates in the Fronsac area.

Fronsac is about the same size as Pomerol and consists of two *appellations* spread over six communes. The total area is some 1100 hectares and the annual yield produces some 63,000 hectolitres. The better of the two *appellations*, in theory if not necessarily in practice, is Canon-Fronsac, formerly known as Côtes Canon-Fronsac, and comes from the two communes of Saint-Michel-de-Fronsac and Fronsac itself. Surrounding Canon-Fronsac and producing about two-and-a-half times as much wine (33,000 hectolitres from 780 hectares) is plain Fronsac AC which, until 1976, was known as Côtes de Fronsac. This *appellation* covers part of the commune of Fronsac plus La Rivière, Saint-Germain-La-Rivière, Saint-Aignan, Saillans and part of Galgon.

The soil is clayey-limestone, with some sand on the lower-lying land nearest to the Dordogne, on a limestone base, the *Molasses de Frondasais*. Like Saint-Émilion, the area is honeycombed with quarries and man-made caves, many of which are now used for the cultivation of mushrooms.

Where Fronsac differs from the rest of the lesser Libournais wines is in its *encépagement*. While the remainder of the region concentrates on the Merlot, with the Cabernet Franc or Bouchet as an important subsidiary grape and Malbec or Pressac as it is known locally as a minor partner, Fronsac wines have less Merlot and plenty of Cabernet Franc in their mix and many have Cabernet Sauvignon too; though growers, as in Saint-Émilion, consider the former superior for their terrain. This blend of grapes gives the wine more backbone and a better acidity than the satellite Saint-Émilions, a more masculine richness and longer life. I find the wine most attractive.

The leading Fronsac estates include (in Canon-Fronsac): Châteaux Canon, of which there are two, Canon-de-Brem, Coustolle, du Gaby, Jumayne, Mazeris and Mazeris-Bellevue, Moulin-Pey-Labrie, Tourmalin and Vrai-Canon-Bouché and (in Fronsac) Châteaux Dalem, de la Dauphine, Fontenil, Mayne-Vieil, Moulin-Haut-Laroque, Richelieu, la Rivière, Vieille-Cure and Villars.

CÔTES DE CASTILLON and CÔTES DE FRANCS

East of Saint-Émilion, further upstream towards the boundary with the *département* of Dordogne, where the Bergerac area begins, is the Côtes de Castillon, an up-and-coming region. North of the Côtes de Castillon is the more recently developed Côtes de Francs.

Castillon itself, an attractive outpost at the eastern extremity of the Bordeaux vineyards, is the site of the famous battle of 1453, commemorated in Shakespeare's *Henry VI Part One*, when after three centuries of hegemony the English were finally driven out of Bordeaux. The date, 17 July 1453, should be commemorated by claret lovers every year! The French can celebrate, English-speaking people can hold a wake.

The Castillon wines are interesting, increasingly well made and some of the best value for money among the myriad *petits châteaux*. The soil consists of gravel, sand and marl nearer the river, and becomes progressively more calcareous as the land rises to the north. There are some 2800 hectares of vines spread over eight communes. Production averages 165,000 hectolitres per annum. From the 1989 vintage this *appellation* has been known as Côtes de Castillon, instead of previously as either Bordeaux Supérieur Côtes de Castillon or Bordeaux Côtes de Castillon. The leading estates are Château Pitray and Château Bardoulet. The area has doubled in size since the mid-1970s.

Côtes de Francs was created as a separate *appellation* in 1967 and is a continuation to the east of the Saint-Émilion satellites of Puisseguin and Lussac. There are three communes, that of Montbadon having been moved from Côtes de Francs to Côtes de Castillon in 1976. There are upwards of 450 hectares of vines producing an annual average of 30,050 hectolitres. This is a new and expanding *appellation*, one of whose leading entrepreneurs has been the Thienpont family of Le Pin and Vieux-Château-Certan in Pomerol. Their properties include Châteaux La Claverie and Puygueraud. Château de Francs, jointly owned by Messieurs Hébrard and de Bouard, is the leading estate.

BOURG and BLAYE

The up-and-coming districts of Bourg and Blaye lie on the right bank of the Gironde estuary and the river Dordogne and are the first Bordeaux vineyards the traveller will see as he drives down the motorway from the Loire Valley past Cognac. There is only one Bourg *appellation*, Côtes de Bourg (though it can be described in three ways: Côtes de Bourg, Bourg or Bourgeais), but a number for the wines of Blaye of which Premières Côtes de Blaye is the most important. Though white wines are allowed the wines are predominantly red.

This is a thriving, attractive region of little villages, gently undulating countryside and neat little wine estates. There is a lot of good wine at the *petits châteaux* level: a good hunting-ground for those seeking wine with somewhat more personality than a simple Bordeaux but at not too exaggerated a price.

Blaye is the larger of the two geographically, yet produces only a marginally greater quantity of wine (272,000 hectolitres from 4647 hectares as opposed to 212,000 hectolitres from 3580 hectares). The town itself, an active fishing port, especially for *alose* or shad during its restricted spring season, and for sturgeon from which the local caviar is extracted, lies alongside a vast Gallo-Roman *castrum*, re-fortified in the seventeenth century by Vauban, the French military architect.

The wines of Blaye are said to be inferior to the best of the Côtes de Bourg, but the leading estates, most of which are in the southern part of the region – much of the north is forest – are in my view the equal of the best of the Bourg. Among these I would include Châteaux L'Escadre, Haut-Sociondo, Peyredoulle and Segonzac.

Côtes de Bourg is a more compact area and forms a semi-circle round the town of Bourg itself. The countryside is quite hilly, and there are even one or two grottoes and prehistoric caves. It is much more extensively planted than the Blaye. There are a large number of estates whose wines make excellent value for money. Leading estates include Châteaux de Barbe, Bousquet, Guerry, Gionne, Mendoce, Rousset and Sauman. This is an active and improving area, perhaps destined to take the place of Fronsacs, when the Fronsacs are fully discovered and exploited, as the 'best value' in Bordeaux. In general, like most *petits châteaux*, they are at their best between three and six years of the harvest.

VINS DE PAYS

VIN DE PAYS DE LA GIRONDE
I have never encountered Vin de Pays de la Gironde, and was unaware it existed until I started researching all the *vins de pays* for this book. The wine can be red, rosé and white, and comes from vineyards in the *département* not classified for all the production of AC Bordeaux.

VIN DE PAYS CHARENTAIS
Another *vin de pays* is produced in the Charente (Cognac country), just to the north of the Gironde. Like its Armagnac equivalent in Gascony, this *vin de pays* is the base white wine, before distillation, and likewise the grape is the Ugni Blanc, locally called the Saint-Émilion. The local co-operatives are the chief sources of this wine. I find the Gascon wine rather more interesting; Vin de Pays Charentais in my experience is shallow and acid. Red and rosé wines are also authorized. They are thin and rustic.

Chapter 2

BURGUNDY

Burgundy is in many ways the most confusing, the most frustrating, the most inconsistent and the most individual of all the world's great wine-making areas. The wines can be sublime; so often they are disappointing. The best are difficult to obtain and they are certainly expensive. The region is complex, as is the structure of its wine economy. There is no easy classification of the best hundred or so wines or properties towards which to point the newcomer; indeed there is a plethora of *appellations*, villages, vineyards and producers. Yet the consumer should not allow himself to be put off. Great bottles of red Burgundy may seem far rarer than claret, but when they come they are nectar. They are worth searching for.

The individuality and the inconsistency of red Burgundy arises from the Pinot Noir grape and the wine it produces. When the season is fine, the yield is restricted and the wine-maturing is expert, the wine can be exquisite. When the reverse is the case, to a greater extent than in Bordeaux, the result is drear. Good Pinot Noirs now hail from elsewhere in the world; from California and the Pacific North-West in the United States, from Australia and New Zealand, from Sancerre and Alsace in France, even from Eastern Europe. But they are good rather than great. So far Burgundy seems to be the only region which can produce great Pinot Noir.

The frustration and confusion of Burgundy lies in its size and diversity. It is a small area, smaller than we realize. The whole region, including Beaujolais, which should really be regarded as a separate vineyard area, produces less than half the wine of Bordeaux; excluding Beaujolais the fraction is more like one-fifth. Moreover, Burgundy is a fragmented region. In Bordeaux and elsewhere in France there is generally one *appellation* per district with a large number of sizeable estates, most of which are self-sufficient in wine terms. Each estate will produce only one or two wines and under a clearly recognizable château or domaine name. In Burgundy, each village – and indeed some of the best individual *climats* or vineyards – may have its own *appellation*. These vineyards are themselves tiny, and will be divided among dozens of different owners. One domaine of no more than a few hectares may have its holdings spread over a number of different villages and vineyards. The result is a multitude of different wines, whose production figures are numbered in dozens rather than in thousands of cases. The consequence of this lack of economy of scale is a further reduction in the possibility of great wine. If a domaine only makes three casks of Chambertin what does it use for topping up? Can it afford to isolate the yield of the younger vines? How can it properly control the fermentation of such a small quantity of must?

Historically, the solution to this problem has lain in the hands of the local merchant or *négociant*. The merchant will buy up small parcels of wine and blend them together, or increasingly these days enter into a contract with a grower to purchase his grapes and vinify them together with others. Thus this complex fragmentation is transformed into quantities of uniform wine of a more sensible commercial size which he will market under his own name. A large merchant such as Louis Jadot may have contracts with a dozen or more growers in Meursault or Gevrey-Chambertin. He will produce just one village wine from each of these communes, but there will be enough for all his potential customers. How very sensible, you might think.

Yet there are a number of disadvantages. There are firstly good *négociants* and bad *négociants* just as there are good growers and bad growers. There are those who are prepared to pay up to a quality and those who insist on buying down to a price. Sadly there are some who are not above a bit of sly manipulation, promoting a village wine to a higher *premier cru*, or even blending in a bit of wine from outside the region, though this is rarer these days than it used to be. It is true to say that there is more genuine Burgundy on the market than there was a decade or more ago. What is not true is that the standard of quality – the sheer palatability – of ordinary merchant Burgundy wine has improved. Regrettably most is very disappointing.

There are further drawbacks to merchant Burgundy wine. The individuality of the grower's wine is submerged into the melting-pot of the blend. It will take on the house style of that particular merchant. If I buy a wine from, say, two neighbouring châteaux in Saint-Julien, each will express its own character, influenced by its soil, the personality and skill of the winemaker (and, in this case, the *encépagement*). Each will be different. But both will be recognizably Saint-Julien. In Burgundy on the other hand, it is usually far easier to pick out the same *négociant* in a range of wines than to pick out the village from whence the wines have come. Too often the house style obliterates the communal character. Finally there is yet another important deterrent to buying merchant wine, however easier it may be so to do. The best are even more expensive than the best grower's wines – and they are expensive enough.

Yet for all its exasperation Burgundy is a delightful area, and the rewards for those who travel there and are prepared to devote a little time to uncovering its secrets and to seeking out the best growers are great. It is, for a start, a much more attractive part of the world than Bordeaux. The food is better and the region abounds in friendly little *auberges* and bistros where you can eat not only stylishly and abundantly, but inexpensively. The growers themselves, once you have broken down the traditional French suspicion of foreigners and outsiders, are genuinely welcoming. There is little of the *de haut en bas* stand-offish reception one occasionally meets in the grand châteaux of Bordeaux.

Geographically there is nothing homogenous about Burgundy. The region extends from Sens in the north to Lyon in the south; from the shores of the upper Loire to the foothills of the Jura. It includes the forests, the valleys and the escarpments of the Morvan as well as the rolling pastures of the Charollais and the marshy *étangs* of the Bresse. It is an area rich in history and in ecclesiastical architecture; of the abbey of Cluny, the basilica of Sainte-Madelaine at Vézelay, the Hôtel-Dieu in Beaune and the palace of the Dukes of Burgundy in Dijon. And of the more humble and charming but no less impressive Romanesque churches of the Brionnais and southern Mâconnais. Gastronomically Burgundy is a plentiful and rich part of France. There are the plump, sleek, coffee-coloured Charollais cattle, the *appellation contrôlée* corn-fed chickens of the Bresse, the smoked Morvan hams, *jambons persillés* and *escargots*, and a multitude of cheeses and freshwater fish. In the north among the vineyards of the Auxerrois you will see cherry trees and in the south in the Beaujolais you will find walnut and almond trees. Throughout Burgundy the locals will devote a substantial portion of their garden to the cultivation of fresh vegetables, and the most gastronomic will have their favourite place in the woods for wild mushrooms and toadstools, *chanterelles*, *morilles* and *cèpes*.

And of course there is the wine. These are superlative reds and incomparable whites: Chambertin and Romanée-Conti, Le Montrachet and Corton-Charlemagne. But there are also plenty of increasingly good bottles at a more affordable price: reds from the Hautes-Côtes and the Côte Chalonnaise; whites from less fashionable villages such as Saint-Aubin and Auxey-Duresses. Bear in mind also that you may well get a much better wine under a simple '*Bourgogne*' label from a high-class domaine than something supposedly more distinguished but at an inflated price from a less reputable source. These top domaines are meticulous about separating the not-quite-so-good from the best; but the lesser *cuvées* can nevertheless prove excellent value for money. You need to buy from a specialist though, someone who has done his homework and has built up a personal relationship with a grower and his family over a number of years. In Burgundy, rather more than elsewhere in France, small is beautiful. Good growers' wines are better and cheaper than the equivalent from a *négociant*. The difficulty is running them to earth.

History

The origins of Burgundian viticulture lie buried in history but there is little in the way of actual evidence. Wine enjoyment by the locals obviously preceded actual cultivation, but it is difficult to pinpoint precisely when the first vines were planted on the slopes of the Côte d'Or. It was not until after Caesar's great victory at Alesia in 52 BC and the imposition of Roman subjugation in Gaul, that conditions became ripe for such a long-term project as the cultivation of the vine. Phoenician traders had brought wine to France some five centuries previously, setting up a trading station at Marseille from which they travelled up through France and even across the Channel in search of tin from Cornwall. It seems clear that the Phoenicians also introduced the vine and viticultural techniques to southern France. But how long did it take for this culture to spread up the Rhône Valley and into Burgundy? It is not until the second century AD that there is firm evidence of local viticulture in Burgundy.

But there is another theory – a seductive local tradition which still continues today – that the vine was brought back from northern Italy by a returning Celtic tribe, the Aedui, in about 200 BC. The ancestors of the Aedui, seduced by the wine they had enjoyed at the hands of itinerant travellers, had invaded the rich plains of Lombardy some two hundred years previously. Forced north later by the expanding Roman Empire, some returned to their homeland. And, having abandoned their nomadic instincts in the meanwhile and learned about viticulture, it was natural that they should return bringing with them the vine.

Whatever the origins, the vine was certainly firmly established by AD 150. A panegyric thanking the Emperor Constantine for reducing taxes in the locality in AD 312 gives a convincing illustration of not only long-established but well-regarded vineyards.

Burgundy seems to have survived the fall of the Roman Empire and subsequent barbarian invasion with comparative ease. Indeed it was one of these tribes, in the interregnum between the Romans and the arrival of the Frankish King Clovis in the early sixth century, which has given the area its name. The Burgondes were an obscure people who settled in the region in the second half of the fifth century. They had arrived via Germany and the Rhône Valley and remained until AD 534 when they were defeated in battle and absorbed into the Frankish kingdom. From Clovis onwards the story has two themes: the evolution of Burgundy as a political entity – first an independent kingdom until the early eighth century, and then an autonomous duchy, considerably enlarged by dynastic marriages in the later Middle Ages – and the rise of the influence of the church. In no other region of France was the church to play such an important role. Its power was immense, its viticultural holdings huge, and its hegemony, alongside the equally significant estates of the local nobility, was to continue until the French Revolution.

The first records of gifts of land including vines to a local Burgundian abbey date from AD 587, when Gontran, king of Burgundy, made a donation to the Abbey of Saint-Bénigne in Dijon. From then on the gifts came thick and fast. The Emperor Charlemagne donated part of the hillside between Pernand and Aloxe to the Abbey of Saulieu in AD 775, and with the rise of Cluny, founded by the Benedictines in AD 910 in the Mâconnais and the breakaway Cistercian abbey near Nuits-Saint-Georges at Citeaux, founded in AD 1098, the development of the vineyards increased as did the fame of their wines.

Burgundy reached its apogee under the successive reigns of the four royal Valois Dukes, Philip the Bold (Le Hardi) (1364–1404), John the Fearless (Sans Peur) (1404–1419), Philip the Good (1419–1467) and Charles the Bold (Le Téméraire) (1467–1477). The four built up an empire which stretched from Holland to Savoy. Their power was immense, greater in influence, in land and in wealth than their nominal liege-lords, the kings of France themselves, with whom they were normally at loggerheads, if not actually at war. It was Philip the Good who appointed an Autun minor nobleman, Nicolas Rolin, as his chancellor, the controller of his court and its exchequer, and the most influential official post in Burgundy. In 1443 Rolin endowed a religious foundation and hospital, the Hôtel-

Dieu, in Beaune. This was the origin of what is now the famous Hospices. While Rolin did not in fact donate any vineyards (though both he and his wife Guigone de Salins are commemorated in two of the wines sold by the Hospices), this charitable institution soon began to receive gifts of land and now possesses 55 hectares, all except one in the Côte de Beaune. The auction of the wines made from the Hospices' vineyard holdings is traditionally held during the weekend of the Trois Glorieuses in November and is normally regarded as setting the trend for the price of the Burgundian vintage as a whole.

Valois Burgundy collapsed with the death of Charles the Bold before the walls of Nancy in 1477. His infant daughter was already betrothed to the Hapsburg Emperor Maximilian of Austria. The duke had no other heirs, and in the vacuum Burgundy was rapidly annexed into the kingdom of France. Nevertheless it was some time before the wines of Burgundy were more appreciated in Paris than in their traditional export markets of the Low Countries and Flanders – markets which are still vigorous today. There had been a significant Protestant population in Burgundy, and the expulsion of the Huguenots from France after the Revocation of the Edict of Nantes in 1685 only served to increase the opportunity of sales abroad. It was not until the eighteenth century, following the success of the surgeon Fagon in curing Louis XIV of a fistula by dosing him with Romanée-Saint-Vivant, coupled with the improvement in communications between Burgundy and the capital, that the wines began to be preferred in Paris to those of the Loire.

The consequences of the French Revolution were decisive and far-reaching, not only in the ownership and structure of the Burgundian vineyards but on the market for its wines. Both the church and the aristocracy were dispossessed of their land. The great estates were broken up and sold off, though at first the best individual vineyards were not fragmented. This happened later as a result of the Code Napoléon, the change in the French laws of inheritance promulgated in 1790. Primogeniture was abolished. Henceforth a man's estate must be divided equally among his children.

The result, two centuries on, is that the Burgundian vineyard is the biggest and most complicated jigsaw in the world. Vineyards, parts of vineyards, even individual rows of vines have been divided and sub-divided over the generations as the effect of the Code Napoléon has remorselessly surged on. Today some of the holdings are so small that it is inevitable that fraud must occur and that the yield of one *climat* (vineyard) must be vinified with the crop of another. The most notorious example of the Code Napoléon is Clos Vougeot. This vineyard, the largest of Burgundy's *grands crus*, was not broken up until 1889, when it was sold off to fifteen different owners. The 50 or so hectares are now divided into over a hundred different plots, shared between some eighty different owners.

Having lost one market, the church and nobility, Burgundy was soon to gain another. Napoleon was said to drink only Chambertin, and this helped to promote the wines of this commune. With the rise in population and the arrival of nineteenth-century *bourgeois* prosperity the demand for Burgundy grew: so much so that abuse became rife. Blending with inferior wine became widespread. With the fragmentation of the vineyards came the rise of the *négociant*, the activities of the most nefarious of which, in the days before the *appellation contrôlée* laws, could not be controlled.

As elsewhere in France, the triple scourges of oidium, phylloxera and mildew dealt a devastating blow to Burgundy. In Burgundy the effect was yet more severe as a result of the opening up of the Paris-Lyon-Marseille railway line in 1856, bringing cheap Midi wines within easy reach of the capital. The result was a contraction of the Burgundian vineyard. Hitherto vines had continued uninterruptedly from Chablis as far south as Dijon. Before phylloxera there had been 31,000 hectares of vineyards in the Côte d'Or and 40,000 in the Yonne, most of them, it is fair to say, planted with inferior varieties producing *vin ordinaire*, not with Pinot Noir or Chardonnay. In the harsh economic conditions which were to follow and continue until the 1950s even the vineyards in Chablis itself almost disappeared. Even today in the Côte d'Or there are only some 8000 hectares of *appellation contrôlée* vineyards. Phylloxera, however, had one positive consequence. It reduced the area under vine to only the most suitable sites.

The 1980s have seen some dramatic changes in Burgundy. Led by growers such as Henri Gouges and the Marquis d'Angerville in the 1930s and encouraged by buyers such as Frank Schoonmaker and Alexis Lichine, the best estates were encouraged to forsake their traditional customer, the Beaune *négociant*, and to mature, bottle and sell their wine direct. Since 1975 this movement has accelerated. It is now estimated that 40 per cent of the Côte d'Or crop is estate-bottled and the percentage of the better wines is even greater.

There has been a dramatic improvement in the quality of the wine-making and a lessening of the traditional Burgundian suspicion of outsiders and petty jealousies among neighbours. The new generation of winemakers have all been to wine school together and friendships have been made between former rival families. They have formed unofficial tasting groups, they exchange information among themselves and even travel abroad to other wine-making regions to see how the Pinot Noir is grown elsewhere.

The Wines

Burgundy consists of five main regions – or four if you regard the Beaujolais as a separate area as many do. These are Chablis, the Côte d'Or, the Côte Chalonnaise, the Mâconnais and finally the Beaujolais. Chablis and its satellites, the red wines of the Auxerrois and the VDQS white Sauvignon wines of Saint-Bris lie isolated from the rest of Burgundy some 130 kilometres north-west of Dijon, almost half-way to Paris. The remaining four regions merge into one another in a line between Dijon and Lyon on the western side of the valley of the river Saône.

Unlike Bordeaux and the southern Rhône Burgundy is not a very intensive vineyard area, however. Only 2 per cent of the *département* of the Côte d'Or is vineyard, and not much more in either the Saône-et-Loire (covering the Chalonnais and Mâconnais regions) or in the Rhône (confusingly the Beaujolais vineyards are in the Rhône *département*). Looking at a wine map, the area seems to be one continual vineyard south of Dijon but it is only in the best sites that the vine has been left to flourish. Largely these exist on the slopes where the uplands to the west fall down into the flatter plains of the east. Up in the hills it is too exposed and too cold for vines and in the lowlands it is too marshy and too alluvial.

The heart of Burgundy is the Côte d'Or, the Golden Slope. The Côte d'Or is not so much a ridge of hills as the eastern perimeter of the hilly plateau known as the Morvan. It extends south of Dijon, through Nuits-Saint-Georges and Beaune, and finally peters out just below Santenay, west of Chagny, a distance as the crow flies of fifty-five kilometres. The vines lie on the eastern or south-eastern-facing slopes of this ridge, facing towards the flat lands of the Saône. At the top of the slope the soil is too barren and exposed, at the bottom it is too rich and alluvial. Only in a narrow band – hardly a kilometre or two wide – between the two extremes is the vine planted. Only in an even more confined position on mid-slope at about 275 metres above sea level do all the ingredients of soil, drainage, aspect, protection and microclimate unite to provide the perfect environment needed for wines of quality.

The soil structure of the Côte d'Or is limestone, but limestone of a wide number of different origins, consistencies and admixtures. It is a complex mixture of elements of different rocks which have outcropped and decomposed, been washed down the slope and been carried back up again. This scree has been mixed with marl, clay, sand and pebbles. Broadly speaking at the top of the slope is the most calcareous and the surface layer above the bedrock is at its thinnest; at the bottom there is more silt and clay and the soil is deeper. In general white wines will do best where the limestone is dominant or even chalky; red wines are more suitable where there is more clay or marl.

The Côte d'Or is divided in two by a marble quarry at Comblanchien to form the Côte de Nuits in the north and the Côte de Beaune in the south. The Côte de Nuits is narrower and steeper and faces predominantly east, the Côte de Beaune is wider, more gently sloping and faces more to the south. This is predominantly a red wine-making region. Excluding generic wine, 85 per cent of the production is red. Almost all the white wine comes from the four Côte de Beaune communes of Meursault, Puligny-Montrachet, Chassagne-Montrachet and Aloxe-Corton. But only Meursault and Puligny-Montrachet are predominantly white wine communes.

Up in the hills behind the towns of Nuits-Saint-Georges and Beaune are the Hautes-Côtes, logically divided into the Hautes-Côtes de Nuits and the Hautes-Côtes de Beaune. This is a relatively new wine-making area, the *appellations* dating only from 1961. Modern techniques, particularly those of using clones more resistant to the cooler microclimates in these uplands and of mechanical harvesting, have made production in the Hautes-Côtes more viable. The wine made is almost entirely red.

Where the Côte de Beaune ends the Côte Chalonnaise begins. Across the river Dheune and the Canal du Centre from Santenay lies the commune of Bouzeron. The soil structure is similar but this is a much smaller vineyard area. There are only another four Chalonnais communes which produce wine, yet the distance from Bouzeron in the north to Montagny in the south is as much as from Santenay to Beaune. The vineyards are restricted to the best sites which lie mainly on the west side of the road which runs down from Chagny towards Cluny, the D981. Paradoxically it is marginally colder in the Côte Chalonnaise than further north, so the harvest begins later. The wines have less definition, less body and less concentration. They are predominantly red, even though this has traditionally been the centre for the sparkling wines of Burgundy.

As the Chalonnais hills lie separate from the Côte d'Or, so the Mâconnais hills are themselves distinct from those of the Chalonnais, across the valley of the river Grosne.

BURGUNDY

PRODUCTION AND SURFACE AREA (1996 HARVEST)

	Surface area in hectares	Production '000 hectolitres	
		RED & ROSÉ	WHITE
Generic Wines			
BOURGOGNE	2255 (R) PLUS 826 (W)	133	58
BOURGOGNE ALIGOTÉ	1384	—	96
BOURGOGNE ALIGOTÉ BOUZERON	59	—	3
BOURGOGNE CÔTE CHALONNAISE	384	27	8
BOURGOGNE GRAND ORDINAIRE	188	9	(3)
BOURGOGNE IRANCY	125	7	—
BOURGOGNE PASSETOUTGRAINS	1219	77	—
HAUTES CÔTES DE BEAUNE	598	32	6
HAUTES CÔTES DE NUITS	567	25	5
CRÉMANT DE BOURGOGNE	587	31	1
Total Generic	8192	341	172
Chablis	4006	—	201
SAUVIGNON DE SAINT-BRIS VDQS	99	—	6
Côte d'Or			
CÔTE DE NUITS			
VILLAGE & PREMIERS CRUS	1549	75	2
GRANDS *CRUS*	266	11	(21)
CÔTE DE BEAUNE			
VILLAGE & *PREMIERS CRUS*	3502	118	55
GRANDS CRUS	185	4	4
Total Côte d'Or	5502	208	82
CÔTE CHALONNAISE	1408	43	31
MACONNAIS	5287	49	276
Beaujolais			
BEAUJOLAIS, BEAUJOLAIS SUPÉRIEUR	10244	635	9
BEAUJOLAIS VILLAGES	5500	362	4
BEAUJOLAIS *CRUS*	6656	362	—
Total Beaujolais	22,400	1359	13
Coteaux du Lyonnais	323	20	2
Total Burgundy	47118	2020	777
Total of Red & White Wines		2997	

The Mâconnais soil is limestone again but the wines are largely white, particularly in the south around Pouilly-Fuissé. The area begins to the west of Tournus and effectively ends when the limestone gives way to the granite of the Beaujolais just below Mâcon on the borders of the Saône-et-Loire and Rhône *départements*.

Finally we come to the Beaujolais. On a map the area seems to be no larger than the Mâconnais, yet this is a much more intensively cultivated vineyard area. Beaujolais, particularly Nouveau, is one of the world's most successful and popular wines.

Wine-Making in Burgundy

On pages 19–26 I have outlined the general principles for the vinification and maturation of red and white wines. Throughout Burgundy you will find much less conformity between one cellar and the next. It is a region of passionate individualists, each with his own views on how the wine should be made. This is one of its fascinations. The structure of the Burgundian vineyard does not lend itself to anything on a large scale. Thus not only are there few harvesting machines, but neither are there batteries of large stainless-steel fermentation vats except in those establishments belonging to either major *négociants* who buy in grapes or to the larger co-operatives. Wine-making is much more artisanal, more modest.

Both hail and the incidence of rot are more prevalent in Burgundy than in Bordeaux, and the necessity of picking through the fruit, either in the vineyard or on arrival at the winery, is therefore of crucial importance. This process is known as *triage*. In some years as much as a third of the crop might be rejected in this way.

Red wines are normally vinified in small wooden *foudres* with removable tops, metal vats or large casks. Leaving a proportion of the stalks in the macerating wine, in order to extract more body and tannin, is also a more usual occurrence in Burgundy than in Bordeaux. The breaking-up of the *chapeau* or cap of grape skins which floats up to the top of the vat during fermentation (called *pigeage*) is achieved by the use of poles or even by feet, the men balancing themselves on the top of the fermenting must and treading down the *chapeau* for half an hour to an hour two or three times a day.

In order to increase the ratio of pulp to juice and to concentrate the eventual wine in abundant vintages, a process called *saigner* (to bleed) is also performed. Before fermentation a certain proportion, between 5 and 15 per cent of the free-run juice, is tapped off. This is separately fermented and will result in a rather weak rosé wine, but it means that the remainder of the wine will be more concentrated. While it is a useful, indeed admirable technique the process is criticized in some quarters for being no substitute for severe pruning, followed by crop-thinning when necessary during the summer before the harvest.

The use of 100 per cent new oak is less prevalent in Burgundy than in Bordeaux. While some estates such as the Domaine de la Romanée-Conti and Henri Jayer, both in Vosne-Romanée, swear by it, others will cite the delicacy of the Pinot Noir and the care required not to dominate its flavour with the taste of new wood as a reason for not using it. In most estates only the *grands crus* are totally matured in new wood. There are some winemakers who abjure it entirely. For the same reason, that the Pinot Noir is a less tannic, less substantial wine, bottling takes place a few months earlier, twelve to eighteen months after the vintage being the norm rather than eighteen to twenty-four months as in Bordeaux.

White wines are vinified very much in a conventional way: pressing, *débourbage*, fermentation in wood for the top wines, in tank for the lesser wines, and earlier bottling than for the reds. Nearly all the top, even village, white wines of the Côte de Beaune are fermented and/or matured in wood, and the practice is spreading south to the Côte Chalonnaise. Unlike in Bordeaux, where the malolactic fermentation of the top white wines is often avoided this often takes place in Burgundy in order to ensure the correct acidity level. There are some growers who make the error of excessively warming the cellar in order to induce this to occur soon after the first fermentation. This often produces a rather cooked, oaky flavour and results in a wine which is a bit flabby.

The Style of Burgundy

Red Burgundy is made exclusively from the Pinot Noir grape. There are one or two minor exceptions – in the Yonne some rare local grapes can be incorporated into the blend; in the Beaujolais for some obscure reason the wines of the *cru* villages (made from the Gamay) can be termed Bourgogne Rouge; elsewhere the Pinot Liebault and Pinot Beurot (the Pinot Gris or Tokay d'Alsace) are admitted – but essentially the Pinot Noir makes red Burgundy and red Burgundy tastes of the Pinot Noir. Red Burgundy is a wine of finesse, subtlety, delicacy, fragrance and complexity: not, essentially, a wine of power and substance. Yes, it is a wine of concentration and intensity of flavour, but this comes in terms of a precious stone rather than a lump of granite.

Despite the difficulties of production and the susceptibilities of the Pinot Noir to over-production, vagaries of climate and poor vinification, there is one important feature that saves the day: the fact that mature, low-yielding vines in the best *climat* in Burgundy will always produce wine of subtlety and depth, even if the climatic conditions are inauspicious – provided of course the fruit does not rot. In this respect Burgundy is helped by the fact that it is not as tannic a wine as Bordeaux. Burgundy is essentially a wine of elegance, and this elegance is not swamped by unripe tannins in unripe vintages. In contrast with Bordeaux I would rather drink a wine of a top *climat* in a poor vintage than a village or communal wine of a great vintage. Even in the worst years good wine-making, old vines and prestigious land will produce wine of individuality and finesse. For this reason vintage charts in Burgundy are even more misleading than they are elsewhere.

While the lesser white wines of Burgundy are vinified in stainless steel or concrete vats and bottled early without ever coming into contact with oak, the best wines are both fermented and matured in wood, a percentage of which is new. It is the blend of subtle, ripe, opulent, nutty–buttery fruit and oak which is the true taste of fine white Burgundy, one of the great wines of the world. It ages very well in bottle.

The flavours of different white Burgundies obviously vary according to where the grapes are grown as well as to how the wine is made. Chablis will be crisper and more racy; the acidity level will be higher – though the Chardonnay does not produce excessively acidic-tasting wine – and the wine will be less fat. Classic Côte de Beaune will be the most complex and perfectly balanced of all white Burgundy, and the wines of the Côte Chalonnaise and Mâconnais will have less depth and will mature faster. Côte Chalonnaise is leaner and less easy to drink than the latter.

There is also a little Burgundy rosé made mainly from Pinot Noir. Most of it comes from Marsannay at the northern end of the Côte de Nuits and the wine is raspberry–strawberry flavoured, racy and elegant. I find it delicious. It is for early drinking.

Crémant de Bourgogne is the regional sparkling wine (there are lesser, branded sparkling wines made in the region but not with wine *from* the region). Crémant de Bourgogne is made by the Champagne method, as are Crémant de la Loire and Crémant d'Alsace, and like Champagne, the second fermentation takes place in the bottle. All the Burgundian white grape varieties can be used, but often a mixture is used, the higher acidity of the Aligoté and other grapes blending with the fatness of the Chardonnay.

WHEN TO DRINK THE WINES

Red Burgundy matures faster than red Bordeaux but this is not to say that it does not last as long. Moreover, though it never has the intensity of colour of a claret, the colour seems to be more stable and, indeed, even to deepen, at least initially, as the wine ages. Côte de Beaunes are less full than Côte de Nuits, and mature faster. *Premier cru* wines are normally more advanced than *grand cru*, and village wines are ready for drinking earlier still, as you would expect.

Burgundy is such a complex area, with so many different styles of wine, that it is almost impossible to generalize about how long to suggest a wine should be kept. I would start drinking a red village wine from a lighter Côte de Beaune commune such as Volnay but from a good vintage five years after the harvest. The fullest *grands crus* of the Côte de Nuits – say Chambertin – would keep for twelve years. In lesser vintages the wines will mature more quickly. The top white wines will also develop in bottle: a *premier cru* Chablis for four years, a *grand cru* for seven or eight before fully mature. White wines from the Côte de Beaune should be kept for six years for a *premier cru* and ten years for a *grand cru*.

Beaujolais and Mâconnais (both red and white) are made for drinking early – as early as a month after the harvest in the case of Beaujolais Nouveau. Exceptionally, the weighter Beaujolais *crus* such as Moulin-à-Vent will keep for several years. But it is best to consume them, and most of the white wines except the very finest Pouilly-Fuissés, within eighteen months or two years of the harvest. Crémant de Bourgogne is normally produced as a non-vintage wine and is intended to be drunk within a year or two of bottling.

BURGUNDY VINTAGES

1997: An early harvest, and not an excessive one. The spring was fine, but the weather was poor during the flowering of the Pinot Noir, though better later when the Chardonnay flowered. The vintage weather was excellent however, offering the prospect of the third fine vintage in a row. The red wines started out with low acidities – and a more uneven state of ripeness – and are more variable than the white wines. A fine vintage in Chablis, smaller in volume than 1996. A very good vintage in the Beaujolais.

1996: A large vintage, and a highly successful one. The run up to the harvest was characterised by warm, very sunny days and cool nights. This produced very healthy fruit, concentrated in both sugar and acidity. Fine red wines of medium-full weight, very pure fruit and the capacity to age well. Very good fresh peachy-appley white wines, though some show the size of the harvest and lack backbone. A very good year indeed for generic wines and the Côte Chalonnaise. An excellent, though large, vintage in Chablis. A very good Beaujolais vintage.

1995: A small crop as a result of poor weather during the flowering. The white wines are excellent, the best since 1985; firm and concentrated, with the ability to age. The reds are of medium-full weight with abundant plump fruit: generous and seductive. Rain at the end of the picking diluted some of the last-to-be-cleared plots in the Côte de Nuits: the village wines from Vosne-Romanée northwards. A very good vintage in Chablis and the Beaujolais.

1994: An average-sized crop and of average quality, rain infering with the harvest and causing premature botrytis. The white wines are ripe but lack depth and definition. Most are now ready or will be by the year 2000. The reds are variable, but better in the Côte de Nuits than the Côte de Beaune, where in many cases they are to be preferred to the 1992s. These are soft, medium-bodied wines which will prove to be pleasant bottles for drinking from 1999 or so. Similarly average quality in the Beaujolais and Chablis.

1993: A crop of normal size, but of exciting quality in Pinot Noir. The white wine harvest, except for those *climats* on the Meursault-Puligny border, which suffered hail damage, was rather more abundant, and the wines proportionately more dilute. The red wines are structured, have good tannins, abundant ripe fruit and firm acidity. This is a consistently fine vintage from Maranges to Marsannay which still needs keeping and will last very well. Start drinking the village wines from 1999, the better wines from 2001. There are some unexpectedly good white wines, with concentration as well as grip, from Meursault Perrières and neighbouring *climats*. Though lean at first, they have put on weight in bottle. These will keep well. The remainder are ready now and should be drunk soon. A good year in Beaujolais. An average vintage in Chablis.

1992: A large crop of red wine, but not quite so prolific in white. Ten days of great heat before an early harvest benefited the Chardonnays, which are rich and ample, even concentrated, though without quite the acidity level of a great vintage. There was then rain, and this affected the Pinots Noirs. These are of medium weight, round and plump, pleasant but with less *terroir* definition than usual. They are now for the most part fully ready. The very best white wines can still be held. An above average vintage in Beaujolais, average in Chablis.

1991: Born under the shadow of the great 1990 harvest, it was perhaps inevitable that the 1991s would be unjustly scorned. It was a small vintage, and the climatic conditions were not perfect, with hail in Chambolle in midsummer and rain at the beginning and at the end of the harvest. The red wines have good colour and structure, some of the tannins are a little hard, but there is good fruit and grip to give underlying support. They are just beginning to come round. They should last well. Certainly a very good vintage. The white wines are less interesting: they lack ripeness and real concentration. Drink them soon. An average vintage in Chablis. A very good vintage in the Beaujolais.

1990: A large vintage. Magnificent in red; fine in white. Though the flowering weather was mixed, the rest of the summer was dry and hot, and despite the eventual quantity produced the berries were small and concentrated, giving a low juice to solid ratio in the fermenting must. As a result the wines were densely coloured, full-bodied, rich and concentrated, with, because of the heat, an almost cooked-fruit flavour. Highly successful both hierarchically and geographically, 1990 is better than any of the rest of the red Burgundian vintages produced in the previous 30 years, and it has not been surpassed since. The white wines also are fine, though most growers now marginally prefer their 1989s; full, balanced, rich and classy. Both red and white wines are for the long term. Even in 1998, only a few village wines are yet at their peak. A fine vintage in Chablis. A very good vintage in Beaujolais, but now getting old.

1989: A large vintage, though not as abundant as 1990. Very good indeed in red, even better in white (the best between 1985 and 1995) where, at least in Meursault and Chassagne, the quantity produced was less excessive than in the Pinots Noirs. It was a largely dry and hot summer, and it was very warm at vintage time. The skins of the Pinots Noirs were thin, and the acidities were on the low side. Nevertheless the best growers made wines with no lack of colour or staying power, and, after nine years these are only just beginning to come into their own. The white wines have grip and concentration and are real keepers: more so than 1990 and 1992. In both colours quality increases more than proportionately as one climbs up the hierarchy. Good Chablis. Beaujolais now old.

1988: An average sized red wine crop but a large white wine crop. After a successful flowering the summer was mixed, but the vintage weather was largely clement. The red wines have high acidities, seemed a bit austere to begin with, and have taken their time to come round. They are only just ready, 10 years on. But now one can see the balance and finesse one always suspected. These red wines are better than 1989 and 1985, as good as 1993, so only just below the 1990, the best in recent memory. The character however is more classic. There are some fine white wines, but generally one can see the size of the crop. Most are correct, but dull, and will not improve. A very good vintage in Chablis. Beaujolais now old.

A SUMMARY OF OLDER VINTAGES

Both the 1987 and 1986 vintages were affected by indifferent weather in September and are now old in both colours. Initially the white 1986s promised much, but they have not aged gracefully.

The 1985 whites are fine, and still vigorous. The best reds are very good, but few promise much life beyond 2000. These are ample fruity wines, but in many cases lack vigour as they were low in acidity. 1984 was the last really poor Burgundian vintage. The 1983 reds are tannic and muscular, in some cases disagreably so, for there is a prevailing hint of rot and in some cases hail. The whites are alcoholic and overblown: now past their best. 1982 was abundant. Only a few reds still hold up, but there are some surprisingly good white wines.

The following are fine vintages: 1978, 1976 (tannins a bit hard), 1971 (uneven, now weakening), 1969, 1966, 1964, 1962, 1961, 1959, 1952, 1949.

Classifications

The layman, recently introduced to the intricacies of Burgundy, may find the *appellations* of the region rather daunting. Many more seasoned wine lovers still do. There are two main reasons for this. Most of the villages have adopted the name of their most celebrated vineyard as a suffix (for example Aloxe-Corton) and in Burgundy vineyards rather than individual estates are classified as *grand* and *premier cru*. An additional but less important complication is that there is frequently a choice of alternative spellings for names of individual vineyards.

It was a wily Burgundian mayor who first decided to aggrandize the reputation of the wines of his village by tagging on the name of its most famous growth to that of the commune. Gevrey was the first and it was rechristened Gevrey-Chambertin in 1847. Soon nearly all the others were following suit. Vosne became Vosne-Romanée; Aloxe, Aloxe-Corton, and both Puligny and Chassagne claimed Montrachet. This may be smart marketing, but is confusing for the consumer, doubly so when there are hyphenated *grand cru* names as in the commune of Gevrey. Thus Gevrey-Chambertin is a village wine, Charmes-Chambertin is a *grand cru*.

GENERAL REGIONAL *APPELLATIONS*

At the bottom of the Burgundian AC hierarchy lie the generic wines. First comes Bourgogne Grand Ordinaire or Bourgogne Ordinaire. These names are synonyms. There is little grand about the wine and it is little seen. It can come in red, white and rosé, the red and rosé made largely from Gamay, the white from a mixture of varieties, mainly Aligoté. Production is declining as the more noble Pinot Noir and Chardonnay replace the minor grape varieties in the region. This is the cheapest wine in Burgundy and my advice is to pay a little more for the next category, AC Bourgogne, which is distinctly superior. The majority of Burgundy's generic wines fall into this category. With minor variations, Bourgogne Rouge comes mainly from Pinot Noir and Bourgogne Blanc has to come from Chardonnay and/or Pinot Blanc. Bourgogne Aligoté comes from Aligoté. Roughly 60 per cent of Bourgogne comes from the Saône-et-Loire *département*, 30 per cent from the Côte d'Or and 10 per cent from the Yonne.

Simple Bourgogne Rouge or Blanc *can* be an extremely good wine. All the top domaines produce a little generic wine, from their younger vines or less good vats, but it is vinified and matured with the same care as that bestowed on their grander *cuvées*. These wines can seem expensive but often offer a much better glass of wine than a more pretentious label from a lesser grower or less reputable merchant. They should be regarded in the same light as the second wines of the top Bordeaux châteaux.

Less expensive but equally commendable can be the generic wines of the better merchants and those of co-operatives such as that of Buxy in the Côte Chalonnaise. Like the top generic wines of the leading domaines these wines can also be aged in oak to give them a sheen of extra class. Bourgogne Passetoutgrains is a mixture of Gamay and Pinot Noir, normally in the ratio of two-thirds Gamay to one-third Pinot Noir. Whether because the vines are located in less favourable sites or because they are young, I have always found the wines disappointing.

SPECIFIC REGIONAL *APPELLATIONS*

These generic wines can come with a specific note of their origin. Bourgogne Hautes-Côtes de Nuits and Bourgogne Hautes-Côtes de Beaune come from the hills behind the main Côte d'Or vineyards and are for both red and white wines. Bourgogne Aligoté de Bouzeron (for white wine) comes from Bouzeron in the Côte Chalonnaise. From the Yonne *département* comes Bourgogne Irancy, a red wine. Until Marsannay, at the north of the Côte de Nuits, was promoted to a full village *appellation* in 1986, there was additionally the *appellation* of Bourgogne Rosé de Marsannay. These wines using the name Bourgogne with a region of origin are roughly analogous to the regional wines of Chablis, Mâcon Rouge, Mâcon Blanc and Beaujolais. As from 1990 there has been a separate *appellation* of Bourgogne-Côte Chalonnaise.

There is no regional *appellation* for the Côte d'Or, though there is the tiny *appellation* of Côte de Beaune for the wine from a small parcel of land on the east side of the town of Beaune itself. Instead, for the wines of the lesser villages of the Côte d'Or, there are the two *appellations*, Côte de Beaune-Villages and Côte de Nuits-Villages. These cover wines coming either from a single specified village or from a blend of several villages.

VILLAGE *APPELLATIONS*

The hierarchy then ascends to the wines made from the grapes of a single village; for example, Gevrey-Chambertin, Nuits-Saint-Georges, Volnay and Meursault.

PREMIERS CRUS

Within these villages or communes, certain vineyards or *climats* are classified as *premier cru*. The name of a specific *premier cru* will appear on the label after the village name. If the wine is a blend of several *premier cru* vineyards, the label will state simply *premier cru* after the village name. Many villages have a large number of these vineyards. In total there are 350 in the Côte d'Or (127 in the Côte de Nuits and 223 in the Côte de Beaune). Gevrey-Chambertin and Meursault have twenty-three each and Beaune thirty-four. However, to confuse matters, some of the *climats* are classified as partly *premier cru* and partly AC village wine. Uniquely in Montagny in the Côte Chalonnaise all the wine can be labelled *premier cru* if it attains the requisite level of alcohol.

There are also *premier cru* vineyards in Chablis and elsewhere in the Côte Chalonnaise, as well as in the Côte d'Or. The classification of both *premier cru* and *grand cru* is part of the *appellation contrôlée* regulations. This means that, for example, a wine labelled Beaune Grèves will be, in fact, 'appellation Beaune Premier Cru Grèves contrôlée', and will state this somewhere on the label, even if in smaller print.

GRANDS CRUS

At the top of the classification are the *grand cru* vineyards, found only in Chablis and the Côte d'Or. These are *not* – except for Chablis – labelled with the name of the village, the vineyard name is sufficient. There are now thirty *grands crus* in the Côte d'Or, of which two (Musigny and Corton) produce both red and white wine. The rest are for either red or white wine only. Most *grands crus* are in the Côte de Nuits and their total surface area is 350 hectares (roughly equivalent to that of the five First Growths of the Médoc and the Graves). In Chablis there are seven *grands crus*.

Grand cru	Red or white wine	Commune
Côte de Nuits		
BONNES-MARES	R	Chambolle-Musigny and Morey-Saint-Denis
CHAMBERTIN	R	Gevrey-Chambertin
CHAMBERTIN-CLOS DE BÈZE	R	Gevrey-Chambertin
CHAPELLE-CHAMBERTIN	R	Gevrey-Chambertin
CHARMES-CHAMBERTIN	R	Gevrey-Chambertin
CLOS DE LA ROCHE	R	Morey-Saint-Denis
CLOS DU TART	R	Morey Saint Denis
CLOS DES LAMBRAYS	R	Morey-Saint-Denis
CLOS SAINT-DENIS	R	Morey-Saint-Denis
CLOS VOUGEOT	R	Vougeot
ÉCHÉZEAUX	R	Flagey-Echézeaux
LE GRANDE RUE	R	Vosne-Romanée
GRANDS-ÉCHÉZEAUX	R	Flagey-Echézeaux
GRIOTTE-CHAMBERTIN	R	Gevrey-Chambertin
LATRICIÈRES-CHAMBERTIN	R	Gevrey-Chambertin
MAZIS-CHAMBERTIN	R	Gevrey-Chambertin
MUSIGNY	R, W	Chambolle-Musigny
RICHEBOURG	R	Vosne-Romanée
LA ROMANÉE	R	Vosne-Romanée
LA ROMANÉE-CONTI	R	Vosne-Romanée
ROMANÉE-SAINT-VIVANT	R	Vosne-Romanée
RUCHOTTES-CHAMBERTIN	R	Gevrey-Chambertin
LA TÂCHE	R	Vosne-Romanée
Côte de Beaune		
BÂTARD-MONTRACHET	W	Puligny-Montrachet and Chassagne-Montrachet
BIENVENUES-BÂTARD-MONTRACHET	W	Puligny-Montrachet
CHEVALIER-MONTRACHET	W	Puligny-Montrachet

Grand cru (continued)	Red or white wine	Commune
CORTON	R, W	Aloxe-Corton, Ladoix and Pernand-Vergelesses
CORTON-CHARLEMAGNE (OR CHARLEMAGNE)	W	Aloxe-Corton and Pernand-Vergelesses
CRIOTS-BÂTARD-MONTRACHET	W	Chassagne-Montrachet
LE MONTRACHET	W	Puligny-Montrachet and Chassagne-Montrachet

Chablis

BOUGROS		
PREUSES		
VAUDÉSIR		
GRENOUILLES	W	Chablis
VALMUR		
LES CLOS		
BLANCHOT		

The Burgundy Négociants

Négociant means merchant in French and, traditionally in Burgundy, the merchant not only deals in the wine, he is responsible for its maturation (*élevage*) and eventual bottling, so you may see the words *négociant-éleveur* on the label. Today many merchants are important vineyard owners as well and also vinify the grapes of those suppliers contracted to them. As the fragmentation of the Burgundian vineyards increased and the size of the domaines declined, the importance of the merchant rose. He was the middleman. He would buy the wines from a large range of small domaines, and blend them into *cuvées* of economic size for the mass market. The role of the *négociant* here, in fine wines as well as in basic Burgundy, is of far greater importance than anywhere else in France outside Champagne and Alsace. Most of the major Burgundian merchants have their head-quarters in the centre of the Côte d'Or in the towns of Beaune or Nuits-Saint-Georges.

In the first division I would include the following (in alphabetical order): Bouchard Père et Fils, Champy Drouhin, Faiveley, Jadot, Latour, Leroy (now an important domaine as well), Moillard (particularly for their domaine wines), Albert Morot (who, though technically *négociants*, only seem to sell their own domaine wines) Remoissenet and Antonin Rodet. Among those specializing in white wines I recommend Olivier Leflaive Frèzres.

My second division would include La Compagnie de Vins d'Autrefois (an enterprising concern which sells some good-value, individual domaine wines, which they have matured and bottled themselves), Bourrée, Joseph de Buce, Chanson, Raoul Clerget,

Jaffelin, Labouré-Roi (who sells the wines of René Manuel and Chantal Lescure), Naigeon-Chauveau and Prosper-Maufoux. A large number of growers now act as merchants in a small way, bringing in grapes to increase what they have to offer. I can recommend Jean-Mare Boillot in Pommard, Etienne Savzet in Puligney and Pierre Morey (Morey Blanc) in Meusante.

The following *négociants* need to be approached with more caution. You *can* find good wines, but by no means always or even regularly. *Caveat emptor!* The wines of Albert Bichot who are partners in the Chablis firm of Long-Depaquit and own the Domaine du Clos Frantin in Vosne-Romanée, J. C. Boisset (who now owns a number of other well-known names such as Charles Vienot and Pierre Ponnelle), Champy, Coron, Doudet-Naudin, Jaboulet-Vercherre, Patriarche Père et Fils, Poulet, Reine-Pédauque and Henri de Villamont.

There are a number of firms who specialize in the wines of the Côte Chalonnaise. These include Émile Chandesais, André Delorme, Picard Père et Fils and François Protheau. Antonin Rodet, already mentioned, is also based in Mercurey.

The Wine Regions

CHABLIS

Equidistant between Champagne, Sancerre at the eastern end of the Loire Valley and the Côte d'Or, the isolated region of Chablis lies on the banks of the small river Serein in the Yonne *département*. A dozen kilometres away, the Paris–Lyon autoroute cuts a great concrete swathe across the fields of wheat, maize and pasture. Across the autoroute you come to the busy city of Auxerre, dominated by its cathedral of Saint-Étienne.

But Chablis lies in a backwater, on the road to nowhere of any importance. The town of the same name is sleepy and rural – hardly more, indeed, than a large village. There are no buildings of any note and nothing really to distinguish it from a hundred other small towns in arable France, nothing except for what is produced from a single noble grape which has found here an ideal soil in which to thrive. This grape is the Chardonnay. The soil is a peculiar and highly individual mixture of chalky limestone and clay and the resulting wine is one of the world's best-known dry white wines, but one quite different from other Chardonnays produced 150 kilometres further south in the Côte de Beaune.

A century or more ago, before the arrival of phylloxera, the Burgundian vineyard began at Sens and continued, uninterrupted, through the Auxerrois and down to Monbard and Dijon. There were then in the Yonne as many as 40,000 hectares under vine. Much of the resulting wine, no doubt, was thin and very ordinary, destined to be consumed direct from the cask in the *comptoirs* of Paris and the other conurbations of northern France. Chablis and the other local vineyards benefited greatly from this close proximity to the capital, but, with the arrival of the phylloxera louse – rather later than in the Côte d'Or, for it did not seriously begin to affect the Chablis vines until 1893 – coupled with increasing competition from the Midi once the railway system connecting Paris with the Midi had been completed, most of the Yonne vineyards disappeared. This decline was further accentuated by the First World War and the resulting economic stagnation and rural depopulation. By 1945, when a particularly savage frost totally destroyed the potential harvest – not a single bottle of Chablis was produced in this vintage – the total area under vine was down to less than 500 hectares. As late as the severe winter of 1956 the locals were skiing down what is now the *grand cru* of Les Clos in February.

Since then, however, there has been a gradual but accelerating increase in the total area of vineyards to 4000 hectares in 1996. As more efficient methods of combating the ever-present threat of frost damage have been devised, as greater control of other potential depredations of the yield has been introduced and as more prolific strains of Chardonnay have been planted, production has risen disproportionately from an average of 23,673 hectolitres per annum in the 1960s to 180,000 hectolitres in the late 1990s.

The heartland of the Chablis region is the south-west-facing slope north of the town. Here all the *grands crus* are situated in a continuous line, adjacent to some of the best of the *premier cru* vineyards. These famous vineyards lie on a soil of crumbly limestone, grey or even white in colour, which is named after a small village in Dorset, Kimmeridge. Elsewhere, particularly at Beines to the east and the communes of Maligny, Villy and Lignorettes to the north, the soil has a different appearance, being more sandy in colour and is marginally different – Portlandian limestone as opposed to Kimmeridgian. There has been much argument over whether the wines from Portlandian soils are as good as those from Kimmeridgian. At times there has been heated opposition, even lawsuits, between those who favour a strict delimitation of Chablis and those who favour expanding the vineyards. The first camp stresses the overriding importance of Kimmeridgian soil, the second believes that an extension of the Chablis vineyards over further suitable slopes of Portlandian soil will relieve pressure on the existing vineyards and better enable the whole community to exploit and benefit from the world-wide renown of its wine. Each grower has his own opinion and will probably be a member of one or other of the two rival *syndicats* or producer groups. Le Syndicat de la Défense de l'Appellation Chablis, as its name implies, is in favour of the strict delimitation of Chablis and is led by William Fèvre of Domaine de la Maladière. The second group, La Fédération des Viticulteurs Chablisiens, is led by Jean Durup of Domaine de l'Églantière in Maligny.

Following a decision by the INAO in 1978 which effectively diminished the importance of the soil in favour of microclimate and aspect when considering a further revision of the area, the expansionists are in the ascendant. Since then the total vineyard area has increased by 58 per cent. New *premiers crus* have appeared on the scene. No one who has tasted the new *premier cru* Vaudevey alongside other *premiers crus*, such as Vaillons or Montmains from the same grower, can be in any doubt that it is at least as good. Whether this extension of vineyard area will help to avoid some of the extreme fluctuations in the price of Chablis we have seen recently remains to be seen. Greater stability, in my view, is crucial to the continuing commercial success of the wine.

The Chablis vineyards lie very close to the northernmost limit for rearing the vine successfully. The vine will not start to develop in the early spring until the average temperature reaches 10°C and the fruit must ripen before the leaves begin to fall in the autumn. More important is the incidence of frost. Chablis, particularly the lower slopes adjacent to the river Serein, lies in a frost pocket. The *grand cru* vineyards are the most susceptible but even on the higher plateaux used for the generic wine or plain Chablis, the young shoots are vulnerable from the time they break out of the buds in late March through until the middle of May. The exposure and angle of the slope is critical and there are a number of techniques the grower can use in order to protect his vines from being harmed.

The most primitive method is simply to instal a little fuel burner or a paraffin *chaufferette* in the vineyard. The grower must be in the vineyard, usually at three o'clock in the morning (the coldest part of the night is normally just before sunrise), to light his burners and these must then be refilled in readiness for the following night. More recently automatic fuel-heating systems connected to a nearby tank, and infra-red devices have been installed in some vineyards. These are expensive both in fuel and in labour but are effective. Another technique is the aspersion method. First, a system of water sprinklers must be set up in the vineyard and connected to a supply of water. (There is a large reservoir outside Beines which serves over 80 hectares of vines, chiefly in the *premier cru* Fourchaume.) When the temperature descends to 0°C, the system is switched on, spraying the vines with a continual fine stream of water, just as you might do if you were sprinkling your garden. Water freezes at 0°C but the vine buds will not suffer until the temperature sinks below minus 5°C by which time the bud is protected by a snug coating of ice.

There are some Chablis producers who argue that regularly imprisoning the embryonic leaf cluster in ice for five or six hours a day, perhaps for a month or more, will do it no good. Nevertheless, and despite the difficulties of keeping the nozzles unblocked, this is a technique which has spread rapidly since it was first introduced in the late 1970s. Installation costs are high and maintenance is crucial but operating expenses are minimal.

There are currently over 4000 hectares of vineyard in production in the Chablis area. Just over a hundred of these are the *grand cru* vineyards, a continuous slope of undulating vines facing south-west and directly overlooking the town itself.

Looking up at the slope from the town these *grands crus* are, from left to right: Bougros (16 hectares), Preuses (11 hectares), Vaudésir (16 hectares), Grenouilles (10 hectares), Valmur (13 hectares), Les Clos (26 hectares) and Blanchot (12 hectares). It is generally agreed that Les Clos is the best *grand cru*, producing the most powerful and long-lasting wines, the ones with the most intensity and richest flavour. Valmur and Vaudésir are also highly regarded (Valmur, in particular, also needs time to age). Preuses and Grenouilles produce more floral and delicate wines. Bougros and Blanchot are the least fine.

Opinions on these *grands crus* vary and, quite naturally, it is difficult to find a grower who can be totally objective. Michel Remon of the *négociant* Albert Pic, who can afford to be more dispassionate than most as this *négociant* does not own any vineyards at all, holds the following views: he describes wine from Blanchot as the most rustic and he condemns Grenouilles for its lack of class; in his opinion, it is only a *grand cru* because it lies alongside the rest. He says that Les Clos is racy and the most *nerveux*; Vaudésir is the roundest and richest but occasionally is a bit heavy; Preuses is similar but with less style; Bougros produces wine somewhat like it on its upper slopes but is more like Grenouilles on the lower land. Monsieur Remon gives first prize to Valmur – a feminine wine, the most elegant and full of depth.

The important grower William Fèvre sees three different categories. Leading the list he puts Les Clos, which he describes as intense and long on the palate, with a toasted, gamy flavour. Bougros is *tendre* and *douceâtre* (soft and sweetish) with elements of chocolate. The wine is less steely and more obviously fruity than Preuses. Grenouilles and Vaudésir come somewhere between the two in style – less powerful than Les Clos, with more delicate and floral perfumes and a touch of violets. Christian Moreau of the *négociant* J. Moreau simply says that Les Clos, Valmur and Vaudésir are the three finest *climats* and the remainder do not merit *grand cru* prices. Jean-Pierre Simonnet, an important *négociant-éleveur*, finds the quality–price ratio for *all* the *grands crus* to have ceased to be useful. These wines are difficult to buy, finance or sell, he will tell you. He concentrates now on *premiers crus*.

In 1996 there are nearly 750 hectares of *premier* cru vineyards, almost two and a half times the amount in 1978. In 1967, the first group of *premiers crus* were classified at the same time. To facilitate their commercialization, what was then a total of twenty-six original *lieux-dits* (site names) was reduced to eleven *premiers crus*. The grower now has a choice before him. He can either use the main *premier cru* name on the label – and blend the wine from several subsidiary vineyards under this title – or he can continue to use the old *lieu-dit*.

These are the eleven *premiers crus* created in 1967 and their subsidiary vineyards.

Premier cru	*Vineyards*
FOURCHAUME	Fourchaume, Vaupulent, Côte de Fontenay, Vaulorent, L'Homme Mort
MONTÉE DE TONNERRE	Montée de Tonnerre, Chapelot, Pied d'Aloup
MONTS DE MILIEU	
VAUCOUPIN (OR VAUCOUPAIN)	
LES FOURNEAUX	Les Fourneaux, Morein, Côte des Prés-Girots
BEAUROY	Beauroy, Troesmes (or Troême)
CÔTE DE LÉCHET	
VAILLONS	Vaillons, Châtains, Séchet (or Séché), Beugnon, Les Lys
MÉLINOTS	Mélinots, Roncières, Les Épinottes
MONTMAINS	Montmains, Forêts, Butteaux
VOSGROS	Vosgros and Vaugiraut

In 1986 this list of *premiers crus* was extended to include seven other sites, some of which incorporate several *lieux-dits*: Vau Ligneau; VaudeVey and Vaux Ragons; Côte de Vaubarousse; Berdiot; Chaume de Talvat; Les Landes and Verjuts; and Les Beauregards and Côte de Cuissey; while Mélinots was absorbed into Vaillons.

Of these, the longest established – and still considered the best today – are Fourchaume, Montée de Tonnerre and Monts de Milieu. It is no coincidence that these three *premiers crus* all lie on the right bank of the Serein above and below the *grands crus*, facing south-west like the *grands crus*. The largest and most important of the rest, Beauroy, VaudeVey, Côte de Léchet, Vaillons and Montmains, are all in side valleys on the left bank and face south-east. The wines from Vaillons and Montmains are better than the rest though the first results from VaudeVey are promising. These wines are shorter in flavour, less powerful, more floral than those on the right bank of the Serein. When made from ripe grapes, they have a peachy, Granny-Smith appley flavour while a Fourchaume wine is rich and plump and Montée de Tonnerre and Monts de Milieu are firm, nutty and steely, and are the closest in style to Les Clos, the best *grand cru*.

Not surprisingly, the largest increase in surface area has been in those vineyards which are merely generic Chablis. Between the 1970s and the 1990s there has been a ten fold rise to 2678 hectares. The area delimited as Petit Chablis, the lowest ranking of the Chablis *appellations*, has tended to fluctuate greatly. New vineyards have come into production while others have been upgraded to Chablis or declassified entirely. There were 184 hectares in 1976, decreasing to only 113 in 1981 and we were lead to believe that the authorities were going to eliminate this *appellation* entirely. However, as the result of new vineyards being authorized the figure has risen to 475 hectares today. Good intentions have found it hard to compete with local politics. Petit Chablis wine is dry and crisp, but not as intensely flavoured as Chablis and should be drunk young.

As well as the feud in Chablis between the restrictionists and the expansionists there has been a vehement debate about whether the wine should or should not be vinified and matured in whole or in part in wood. William Fèvre of Domaine de la Maladière leads the oak faction as he does the restrictionists. As a grower and largest proprietor of *grand cru* vineyards, he is able to control the vinification of his wine from the start as well as the *élevage* (most of the *négociants* buy must, not grapes) and he ferments all his own *grands crus* in wood. All his wines are partly matured in oak as well.

The non-oak faction has many supporters, including most of the top *négociants* (Moreau, Michel Rémon of Albert Pic who also trade as A. Régnard et Fils, Michel Laroche, Jean Durup and, until recently, the La Chablisienne co-operative). Other supporters include respected growers such as Louis Michel. Their general belief is that Chablis should not try to ape the Côte de Beaune. Chablis should be as natural a wine as possible; its flavours are subtle and delicate and its essential gun-flinty, steely character should not be swamped by the supplementary aromas which result from vinifying or maturing the wine in oak.

There are arguments in favour of both sides. I have had many a well-matured, non-oak-aged Chablis which have proved that tank-matured wine need not be ephemeral. Ageing potential is as much a result of the correct balance between fruit and acidity (plenty of each and plenty of concentration) as of maturation and fermentation in wood *per se*. On the other hand, the extra weight and tannins added by the wood do help, especially in the weaker vintages. Fèvre's wines and those of Joseph Drouhin in Beaune – an important Chablis proprietor and also a believer in new wood – *do* keep extremely well. Moreover, their capacity for ageing is not so dependent on the vagaries of the vintage.

Chablis, at its best, is a magnificent wine and is quite unique. The colour should be a full, in the sense of quite viscous, greeny-gold. The aromas should combine steeliness and richness, gun-flint, grilled nuts and crisp toast. The flavour should be long, individual and complex. Above all, the wine should be totally dry but without greenness. The after-taste must be rich rather than mean, ample rather than hard, generous rather than soulless. Chablis is an understated wine, so it should be subtle rather than obvious, reserved rather than too obviously charming.

Many wine writers have been too diffident or too polite to come out into the open with a hierarchy of the top Chablis growers and *négociants*. The position is complicated for various reasons; first, the controversy over whether the wine should be matured in wood or not; second, the arm's-length presence of the *négociants* in Beaune and Nuits-Saint-Georges, all of whom sell Chablis but few of whom, except Drouhin, own any Chablis vineyards; and third, the presence of a very powerful local co-operative, La Chablisienne, which accounts for a third of the Chablis crop. Not unnaturally, this latter concern has a major influence on the annual price of the wine. La Chablisienne was my major Chablis supplier throughout most of my professional life and I never found anything in the quality of its best wines – obviously with such a large business you have to pick and choose – which was not of the very highest standard. You may criticize the co-operative for its policy of allowing commercial buyers to choose the name of one of the co-operative's members to put on its label: for example Fèvre Freres for Fourchaume which, together with *mise en bouteille à la propriété*, is certainly misleading, but you cannot deny that the wine inside the bottle can be as good as anything the *appellation* can produce.

Among the *négociants* Joseph Drouhin of Beaune is an impeccable source, and the local firms of Moreau and Albert Pic (who also sell under the label of A. Régnard) are reliable. Simonnet-Febvre, Henri Laroche and Lamblin follow in the second division. Among the growers, William Fèvre at the Domaine de la Maladière (in a small way also a *négociant* and also selling under the name of Fillippi), Louis Michel, Jean-Marie Raveneau and René Dauvissat stand out as the top four, with competition from Jean-Paul Droin & Fils, Robert Vocoret, Adhémar Boudin (GAEC La Chantemerle), Billaud-Simon, Philippe Testut and the Domaine A. Long-Depaquit (associated with the Beaune *négociants* Bichot). Marcel Servin, Louis Pinson, Jean-Claude Dauvissat, Pascal Bouchard, Alain Geoffroy, Jean Durup, Jean Collet, Gerard Tremblay and Jean-Paul Tricon (Domaine de Vauroux) are in the next tier. I can also recommend the wines of Claude Laroche (no relation of Henri Laroche), the Grossot family in Fleys and Jean-Bernard and Lynne Marchive of the Domaine des Malandes.

OTHER WINES OF THE YONNE

After Chablis the other wines of the Yonne can be divided into two groups. By far the largest and most important are the Auxerrois wines, to the west of Chablis and south of Auxerre, from the villages of Saint-Bris, Chitry, Irancy and Coulanges-La-Vineuse. From the east of Chablis come the wines of Epineuil, near Tonnerre. Elsewhere, in one or two isolated spots such as at Joigny and Saint-Père, near Vézelay, a few brave growers continue to plant a few vines. Provided these are approved varieties and the wines pass a tasting test, the growers can use the AC Bourgogne. The total *appellation contrôlée* area under vine in the Yonne is some 770 hectares, producing 50,000 hectolitres per annum (about one-tenth of the generic wine of Burgundy). In addition there is Burgundy's sole VDQS wine, the Sauvignon de Saint-Bris, which I shall discuss separately.

With one exception these lesser Yonne wines are little seen, and seldom exported outside the region. There is a certain amount of light, red wine, the best exclusively from the Pinot Noir, but also from Pinot Noir blended with the Tressot, the César and the

Gamay. Rather more of the local production is white wine, not so much from the Chardonnay as from Aligoté and Sacy. These last two grapes, both producing wines of low alcohol and high acidity, are useful base varieties for the sparkling Crémant de Bourgogne, a Champagne-method AC created in 1975. The flagship of the Auxerrois is currently the Crémant of the Cave de Bailly, produced by an organization of growers known as SICAVA. This is one of Burgundy's best sparkling wines.

The best of the red Auxerrois wines come from Irancy and Coulanges-La-Vineuse. These villages lie on either side of the river Yonne south of Auxerre. Irancy has its own separate *appellation*, Bourgogne (Rouge) Irancy, and produces about 3600 hectolitres per annum. The wine is normally made from Pinot Noir but César is also permitted. The wine from Coulanges is lighter and is made exclusively from Pinot Noir. The village name will appear on the label though the wine is, rather confusingly, not entitled to a separate *appellation*. Sergé Hugot and Raymond Dupuis in Coulanges and Léon Bienvenu, Jean Renaud, Roger Delaloge and his cousin Gabriel in Irancy are the best-known growers.

The villages of Chitry and Saint-Bris produce mainly white wine and are the centres for the local Crémant. Aligoté wine is another speciality here, and can be one of the best of Burgundy, for unlike elsewhere it is not relegated to inferior vineyard sites. Louis Bersan et Fils, Jean Brocard, Robert Defrance, Michel Esclary, André Sorin, Jean-Paul Tabit and Claude Verret are the best growers in Saint-Bris and better than anyone in Chitry.

Sauvignon de Saint-Bris VDQS is a curious *appellation*. The grape variety, Sauvignon Blanc, must have originally come from the Loire – it is only eighty kilometres west to Sancerre, after all – but it is not permitted anywhere else in Burgundy. Locally it is now in decline in favour of the Aligoté, not just because it cannot be used in the Crémant, but also because the growers do not regard it as highly. Sauvignon de Saint-Bris is more expensive than a generic Touraine Sauvignon, but no better, and so it is difficult to sell. No more Sauvignon is being planted. Production of Sauvignon de Saint-Bris averages about 5000 hectolitres from 99 hectares of vineyards.

Epineuil lies a kilometre or so to the north of Tonnerre and has been rescued from oblivion in the past few years by the local mayor André Durand, together with one of his disciples, a Chablisien named Jean-Claude Michaut. Like Coulanges-La-Vineuse this is not a separate *appellation*, but the village name will appear on the label. The wine is red, solely from Pinot Noir, and there are about 25 hectares in cultivation, largely of young vines. So far the wine is unremarkable, but it is early days.

The Côte de Nuits

The Côte de Nuits begins at Marsannay, just south of Dijon, and continues for some 22 kilometres to Corgoloin, about half-way between Nuits-Saint-Georges and Beaune. The heart of the Côte de Nuits is one of the greatest red wine-making areas in the world. From Nuits-Saint-Georges northwards, the famous village names ring out: Vosne-Romanée, Flagey-Échézeaux, Vougeot, Chambolle-Musigny, Morey-Saint-Denis and, finally, Gevrey-Chambertin. Above and behind these villages, neatly parcelled behind

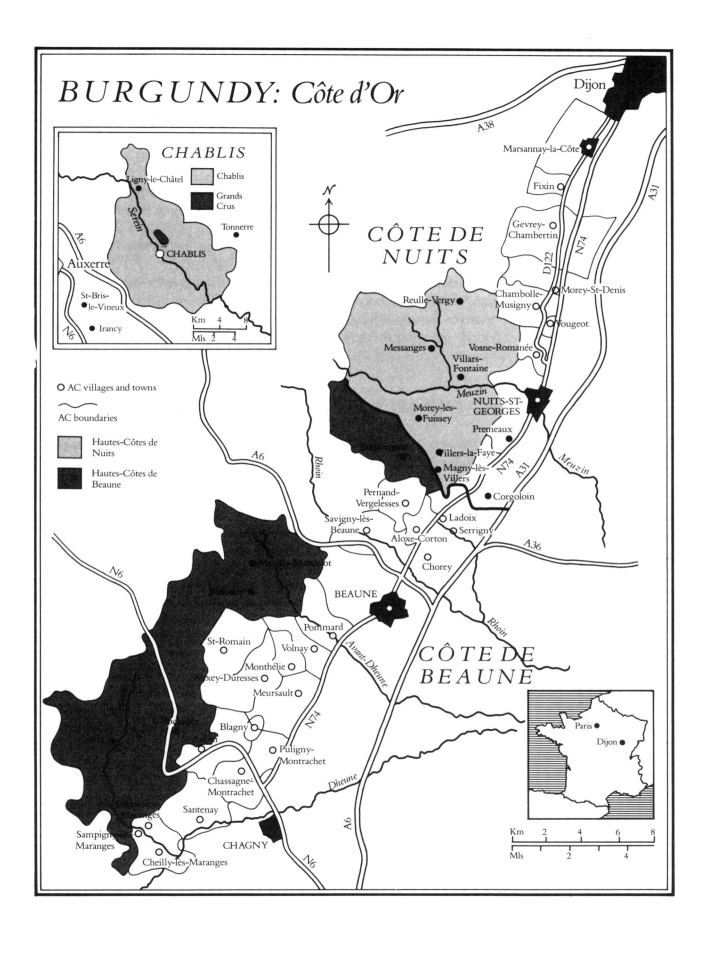

BURGUNDY: *Côte d'Or*

CHABLIS

Chablis
Grands Crus

Ligny-le-Châtel
Serein
Tonnerre
CHABLIS
Auxerre
St-Bris-le-Vineux
Irancy

Km   4   8
Mls 2   4

○ AC villages and towns

〜 AC boundaries

Hautes-Côtes de Nuits

Hautes-Côtes de Beaune

Dijon
A38
Marsannay-la-Côte
Fixin
Gevrey-Chambertin
D122
N74
A31

CÔTE DE NUITS

Reulle-Vergy
Chambolle-Musigny
Morey-St-Denis
Vougeot
Messanges
Vosne-Romanée
Villars-Fontaine
Meuzin
NUITS-ST-GEORGES
Morey-les-Fuissey
Premeaux
Villers-la-Faye
Magny-lès-Villers
Corgoloin
Rhoin
A6
Pernand-Vergelesses
Savigny-lès-Beaune
Ladoix
Serrigny
Aloxe-Corton
A36
N6
Chorey
BEAUNE

CÔTE DE BEAUNE

Rhoin
Pommard
St-Romain
Volnay
Avant-Dheune
Monthélie
Auxey-Duresses
Meursault
N74
Blagny
Puligny-Montrachet
Dheune
Chassagne-Montrachet
A6
Santenay
Sampigny-Maranges
CHAGNY
Cheilly-lès-Maranges
N6

Paris
Dijon

Km   2   4   6   8
Mls   2   4

crumbling dry-stone walls, every available scrap of land is planted with vines. In winter, the land is bare and bleak, the fields broken up by little bonfires of prunings as the plants are ruthlessly close-cropped to stunted stumps. In high summer, the green vines rustle gently in the breeze. In late autumn, the wine now actually bubbling away in the growers' cellars, the vineyards are stripped and savaged but the colours are flame and russet in the low cool sun.

The *climats* which give the best wines lie on mid-slope, sheltered from the prevailing winds from the west by the forest which crowns the topmost ridges. From La Tâche at the southern end of Vosne-Romanée on to Mazis on the doorsteps of the village of Gevrey-Chambertin is an almost unbroken line of *grands crus*. Only in Corton, further south, is there another *grand cru* for red wine.

The Côte de Nuits is half the size of the Côte de Beaune, consisting of some 1500 hectares of vines. The vineyards are not only narrower, from east to west, but also steeper, and directed more to the east rather than to the south-east. Production is almost entirely of red wine. There is some rosé in Marsannay, and the odd few hundred cases of white, but this latter is more of a curiosity than a commercial proposition.

CÔTE DE NUITS-VILLAGES

This useful local *appellation* is used for the peripheral, minor villages of the Côte. Though not as well known as its equivalent, Côte de Beaune-Villages, Côte de Nuits-Villages provides an inexpensive introduction to the greater wines of the Côte, and is often as good as a village wine from a more important commune at half the price. The wines can come from Fixin and Brochon in the north and from Prissey, Comblanchien and Corgoloin in the south. Fixin wines can also be sold under their own name. There are some 162 hectares under vines producing around 8000 hectolitres per annum. The wine can be somewhat four-square, even a bit rustic, but is fuller than wine from the Hautes-Côtes. The best, such as that from Philippe Rossignol in Gevrey, comes from the northern villages. In theory there is a tiny amount of white wine as well as the red but I have never seen it offered, let alone sampled it.

MARSANNAY

The Côte d'Or officially begins in the suburbs of Dijon, but continuing south, the first commune of importance is Marsannay. Marsannay vineyards total about 188 hectares and produce an average of 7000 hectolitres per annum. Up until 1986 Marsannay could only use the simple Bourgogne *appellation* for its wines. In that year, as a result of some successful lobbying by the local growers, it was decided not to promote the village wines to Côte de Nuits-Villages which would have been logical and merited, but to award them an *appellation* in their own right. This applies to red, rosé and white wines.

The village has long been renowned for its rosé, one of the most delicious in France. The Pinot Noir produces a delightful rosé, dry but full of fruit and fragrance and for drinking within a couple of years of the vintage, like all rosés. Marsannay had made a speciality of this wine, for which it had had a separate *appellation*, Bourgogne-Marsannay Rosé. Sadly production has been in decline for some years, and even before the promotion of the village to its own AC in 1987 only some 15 per cent of the harvest was made into pink wine. Let us hope that as Marsannay now has its own village *appellation* the fortunes of the rosé will be revived.

The most prestigious domaine in the village used to be that of Clair-Daü, now owned by Louis Jadot in Beaune. Bruno Clair now owns some of the family vineyards, and works closely with André Geoffroy. I consider this an excellent domaine. Bruno's father, Bernard Clair, also makes wine, in association with Jean-Louis Fougeray (Domaine Fougeray-Beauclair). André Bart is another domaine to watch, as are Régis Bouvier and Lucien and Alain Guyard. This might be an appropriate place to mention, and recommend, Philippe Naddef who is based in the neighbouring village of Couchey.

FIXIN

Fixin – pronounced 'Fissin' – is the next commune south on the Côte. Its wines can claim either the village *appellation* or that of Côte de Nuits-Villages. There is a total of 150 hectares of vines under cultivation, producing annually around 4000 hectolitres of mainly red AC Fixin or Fixin *premier cru* and perhaps half as much again of Côte de Nuits-Villages. There is a tiny amount of white wine.

The village has Napoleonic connections. Some one hundred and fifty years ago Claude Noisot, a local aristocrat who fought alongside the Emperor Napoleon in many a battle and even accompanied him in exile to Elba, arrived back in the village. He proceeded to rechristen the name of one of his vineyards Clos Napoléon, install a small museum of memorabilia and commission a statue for the local village square. All this did much to help the esteem of the local wine. Clos Napoléon is probably not quite Fixin's best wine, though it is one of its five *premiers crus*. That honour can be bestowed on Clos du Chapitre. The leading domaine in the village, Domaine Pierre Gelin, has a monopoly of both. Another prime *premier cru* vineyard is La Perrière, the monopoly of Philippe Joliet. A third domaine to note is that of Vincent and Denis Berthaut.

The locals refer to the style of Fixin as *sauvage*: robust, full, gamy, somewhat four-square, and these three top vineyards, lying above the village on a fairly steep slope, all produce wine that is very strong. The village wines come from vineyards which are lower down, on more clayey soil and are meaty in texture; similar to those of Marsannay, but with less concentration and finesse.

GEVREY-CHAMBERTIN

With Gevrey we arrive at the beginning of the finest sector of Burgundy vineyards. Gevrey-Chambertin is the largest of the great communes of the Côte de Nuits, and it possesses eight out of the twenty-three Côte de Nuits *grands crus*. Gevrey vies with Vosne as being the most important commune of them all. The *appellation* covers red wine only.

The name Gevrey comes from Gabriacus, a name dating from Gallo-Roman times and first recorded in AD 640. About this time, the Abbey of Bèze was given land by Duke Amalgaire of Burgundy which the monks then planted with vines. Shortly after, so the tale runs, a peasant named Bertin decided that he, too, would plant vines on his neighbouring plot of land. From the Campus or Champ Bertin comes the title of Gevrey's greatest vineyard.

In 894, the Abbey of Sainte-Bénigne was donated land by another Burgundian Duke, Richard le Justicier. This abbey soon came under the jurisdiction of the great ecclesiastical establishment at Cluny. A castle built at the behest of Yves de Poissy, Abbot of Cluny, was begun in 1257 and part of it still stands. In the Middle Ages the Abbey of Bèze sold their vineyards to the Cathedral chapter of Saint Mammes at Langres, who remained the nominal proprietors until the French Revolution. During the seventeenth century, the chapter leased out these and other vineyards in their possession and, in 1731 the bulk of the Clos de Bèze passed to Claude Jobert. Jobert was an important official in the royal court at Versailles and soon became its Burgundian supplier. Under his forceful promotion, the reputation of the local wines increased by leaps and bounds. Exceptionally, the Jobert domaine survived the French Revolution intact while most of the remaining estates, more directly in ecclesiastical hands prior to the Terror in 1793, were sequestered and broken up.

Napoleon's predilection for the wines of Chambertin is well known. He is reputed to have drunk little else. It would seem that the Emperor drank his Chambertin – five or six years old and bottled with an embossed 'N' – much diluted with water. On the retreat from Moscow, though, his 'cellar' was stolen by Cossacks, so his stewards alleged. The French market was soon flooded with fake Chambertin 'returned from Russia', enough to have been the total production of a number of vintages!

During the nineteenth century, as a result of the Code Napoléon and the laws of inheritance, the vineyards of Gevrey were divided and sub-divided among more and more owners. By 1850, there were nine owners in the 28 hectares of Le Chambertin and Clos de Bèze. By 1900, the number had grown to nineteen. Today, the figure is twenty-five.

The wine of Chambertin and Clos de Bèze, not least as a result of its Napoleonic patronage, has a great reputation. Understandably, the neighbouring wines have sought to share its glory. In 1847, by a decree of Louis-Philippe, the village of Gevrey was allowed to add Chambertin to its name. Subsequently, a number of neighbouring *grands crus* were, similarly, allowed to add the magic name of the top vineyard onto their own. Only Clos de Bèze, equal to Le Chambertin in prestige, is allowed to place the name of Chambertin before its own and, indeed, its wines can be sold as Chambertin without the Clos de Bèze. The other *grands crus* may only add the name Chambertin after their own.

Together the 87 hectares of *grand cru* vineyards produce 3300 hectolitres, the equivalent of some 36,000 cases, in a reasonably prolific year. This is 25 per cent of the total yield of red *grand cru* Burgundy but compared with Bordeaux it is a drop in the ocean – Château Lafite on its own can produce as much. These eight vineyards stretch in a line south of the village along the little road which connects Gevrey with Morey. Ruchottes, Mazis, Clos de Bèze, Chambertin itself and Latricières lie upward of this road. Chapelle, Griotte, Charmes and Mazoyères are on the downward side.

GEVREY-CHAMBERTIN *GRANDS CRUS*

	Surface area in hectares	1996 harvest in hectolitres
CHAMBERTIN	13	517
CHAMBERTIN-CLOS DE BÈZE	15	555
CHAPELLE-CHAMBERTIN	35	198
CHARMES-CHAMBERTIN/ MAZOYÈRES-CHAMBERTIN	31	1316
GRIOTTE-CHAMBERTIN	3	118
LATRICIÈRES-CHAMBERTIN	7	306
MAZIS-CHAMBERTIN	9	345
RUCHOTTES-CHAMBERTIN	3	134

What is the difference between the various *grands crus*? While the answer is made more complex by the myriad different owners, ages of vineyard and vinification methods, any explanation is essentially due to variations in exposure and altitude of the vineyards and subtle alterations in soil structure. The soil is a Bajocian limestone covered by a thin layer of earth comprised of a mixture of pebbles, flint, chalk, clay and limestone debris; the higher up the slope the lower the clay content.

Few would deny that Chambertin and Clos de Bèze are the best *grands crus*. I would rate Latricières and Ruchottes next. A section of Mazis-Chambertin is owned by the Hospices de Beaune and this is normally the finest red wine in the Hospices range. Charmes, if not Chapelle, produces a more feminine wine, less powerful, less intensely flavoured and, in my experience, less full-bodied. I do not quite agree with Monsieur Trapet that all those lower down the slope are 'more full'.

Apart from the *grands crus* the remainder of Gevrey consists of 455 hectares of vines and produced over 20,000 hectolitres in 1996. This includes 86 hectares of *premier cru* vineyards which are divided up among twenty-four *climats*, in whole or in part. Much of the village wine, in contrast to the rest of the Côte de Nuits, comes from the east of the main Dijon to Nuits-Saint-Georges road. Gevrey's vineyards also extend north into the commune of Brochon.

The best section of these *premiers crus* lies on the north-west side of the village up in the valley of the Combe aux Moines. The slope here is steep but sheltered, and many of these vineyards – Clos Saint-Jacques, Varoilles, Estournelles and Cazetières – produce wine every bit as good as the lesser *grands crus*. Most of those who own vines in Clos Saint-Jacques as well as in Charmes or Chapelle consider the Clos Saint-Jacques to be superior, will give its wine the benefit of 100 per cent new oak and consider it an error that it was not given *grand cru* status when the legislation was drawn up in the 1930s.

You would expect a village like Gevrey to have an abundance of top estates, and this is precisely the case. Encouragingly, a significant proportion are now directed by young

men of energy and talent. This new breed of Burgundians have often built up their domaines from scratch, but while they do not enjoy the riches of those such as Camus, Damoy, Drouhin-Laroze, Pernot-Fourrier, Rebourseau and Tortochot – all large properties but under-achieving at present in my view – they can frequently produce something quite startlingly good, and good value. In this category I would include Denis Bachelet, Alain Burguet, Bemand Dugat-Py, Claude Dugat, Frederick Esmonin, Michel Esmonin et Fille, and Denis Mortet. The two greatest Gevrey domaines are those of Joseph Roty and Charles Rousseau. The wines of Lucien et Fils, Philippe Charlspin, the Domaine des Varoilles, Dorwnigne Gallois, Vincent Feantet, Philippe Leclerc, Réne Leclerc, Henri Magnien, the Domaine Marchand-Grillot, Bernard Maume, Christian Serafin and Jean Trapet can also be recommended.

Stephen Gelin of Fixin and Jean-Marie Ponsot of Morey, while the Roumier domaine in Chambolle has a splendid wine from Clos de Ruchottes. Among the *négociants*, Faiveley of Nuits-Saint-Georges and Louis Jadot, with the benefit of the vineyards they bought from Clair-Daü, can compete with the very best of the local domaines, as can Joseph Drouhin, while Madame Bize of Leroy has always had an excellent Mazis and acquired part of the domaine of the Rémy family in 1989 which has given her vines in Chambertin, Latricières and other top *climats*. There is plenty of good Gevrey, and every time I go there to taste the latest vintage I come across another good producer. I wish I could say the same for every commune in France.

MOREY-SAINT-DENIS

Sandwiched between Gevrey and Chambolle, Morey has never received the recognition it deserves. This is curious, for the village has four *grands crus* plus a small section of the Bonnes-Mares *grand cru*, most of which lies in Chambolle, and it produces very good red wine of a style which, when in the hands of the best producers, can combine the concentration and the delicacy of both of its neighbours. There is a tiny amount of white wine. The origins of Morey are closely connected with the Cistercian abbey of Citeaux and with their benefactors, the Seigneurs of Vergy. Between the two of them they held authority over the village and its land until the French Revolution. This ecclesiastical heritage is echoed in the many 'Clos', walled vineyards with their attendant buildings, which still exist today.

Only the excellent Gevrey-Chambertin *premier cru* Combottes separates the Latricières-Chambertin *grand cru* from Clos de La Roche, after which the *grands crus* follow in a line above the Route des Vins which runs through the village, until the *climat* of Bonnes-Mares spreads over into Chambolle-Musigny. In general Clos de La Roche, not Clos Saint-Denis from which the village has prized its suffix, is considered the best wine. Both these *grands crus* are in the hands of a number of proprietors, while Clos des Lambrays and Clos du Tart are, rarely for Burgundy, *monopoles* or in the exclusive control of the Domaine Saier and the Mâcon *négociants* of Mommessin respectively. Domaine Saier acquired Clos des Lambrays in 1979 at which time it was in an extremely dilapidated condition, and succeeded in getting it promoted to *grand cru* in 1981, an achievement which I feel was in advance of the wine having improved to the requisite quality. The Clos du Tart, too, has been disappointing, though it has improved considerably of late.

MOREY-SAINT-DENIS *GRANDS CRUS*

	Surface area in hectares	1996 harvest in hectolitres
BONNES-MARES	1.5 in Morey 13.5 in Chambolle	557
CLOS DE LA ROCHE	16	640
CLOS DU TART	8	290
CLOS DES LAMBRAYS	8	366
CLOS SAINT-DENIS	6	250

VINS FINS DE BOURGOGNE
Mis en bouteille à la propriété
MOREY-SAINT-DENIS
"En la rue de Vergy"
APPELLATION MOREY-SAINT-DENIS CONTRÔLÉE
DOMAINE BRUNO CLAIR
Viticulteur à Marsannay-la-Côte, Côte-d'Or-France
Produit de France

The remainder of Morey-Saint-Denis consists of 109 hectares, of which 28 hectares are *premiers crus*, and produced 4610 hectolitres in 1996. There are no fewer than twenty-five different *premiers crus*, which seems rather a large number given the surface area. Morey *premier cru* wine from a single *climat* is rarely found, though Pierre Amiot can offer several such wines. Monts Luisants, Les Millandes, Les Ruchots, Clos des Ormes and Clos de La Bussière (of which Domaine Roumier in Chambolle have the monopoly) are the best known. In the main the *premiers crus* lie further down the slope from the *grands crus* and the wines display the same characteristics of their neighbours – firmer to the north and more fragrant to the south.

The leading domaine in Morey is that of Jean-Marie Ponsot, and from the terrace in front of his house, above the village, is a splendid view across the plain of the Saône towards the Jura. Domaine Dujac, owned by the meticulous and imaginative Jacques Seysses, vies with Ponsot for quality. Other good sources are Pierre Amiot, Georges Lignier, Hubert Lignier, Claude Marchand, Renot-Minot, Bernard Serveau, J. Truchot-Martin, Vadey-Castagnier, and the thoroughly brilliant Robert Groffier. Groffier is indeed one of the best growers in the whole of the Côte d'Or, but while he lives in Morey his domaine is mainly in Chambolle. Charles Rousseau of Gevrey has a fine wine from Clos de La Roche.

CHAMBOLLE-MUSIGNY

Geographically Chambolle is a large commune, but is split in two by a narrow valley which seeps out of the upland plateau, thus turning a substantial part of the hillside round to face north, making it unsuitable for the production of high quality wine. This is mainly a red wine *appellation*. The village name comes from *Campus Ebulliens* or *Champ Bouillant*: not so much boiling as bubbling, indicating that after a violent storm the little river Grosne would burst its banks and flood the surrounding fields. Like Morey much of the land was under the control of the monks of Citeaux until sequestered at the time of the

French Revolution. There are two large, important *grands crus*, Bonnes-Mares to the north and Le Musigny to the south, lying above Clos Vougeot.

CHAMBOLLE-MUSIGNY *GRANDS CRUS*

	Surface area in hectares	1996 harvest in hectolitres
BONNES-MARES	13.5 in Chambolle	557
	1.5 in Morey	
LE MUSIGNY	10	370 (plus 21 hl white wine)

Bonnes-Mares wine is the fuller of the two *grands crus*, and the more reserved when young, though it is less substantial than the wine of Clos de La Roche or the *grands crus* of Gevrey. At its best Le Musigny is one of the most ravishing wines of Burgundy: delicate, feminine and fragrant, all silk and lace, the epitome of finesse. The soil in Chambolle contains more limestone, less clay than most of the other communes of the Côte de Nuits, and as a result all the wines of the village should be exemplified by their subtlety rather than their power. Chambolle is the Côte de Nuits equivalent to Volnay in the Côte de Beaune. There is a little white Musigny made from Chardonnay. It is rare, extremely expensive and in my view overpriced.

There are 190 hectares under vines in Chambolle, of which 62 are divided up among twenty-two *premiers crus*, altogether producing 7110 hectolitres in 1996. Best of the *premiers crus* are Les Amoureuses, which lies just below the northern end of Le Musigny, and Les Charmes, which is across the little road leading up from Vougeot. As the names suggest, wines from these two *climats* are similarly soft and feminine, though less intensely flavoured than Le Musigny. The important *premiers crus* on the Bonnes-Mares side, and equally similar, are Cras, Fuées, Baudes and Sentiers.

There are a number of very fine estates based in Chambolle, the leading two being the Domaine Comte Georges de Vogüé and the Domaine Georges Roumier. The styles of the domaines' wines are quite different, though until 1985 they were directed by two brothers, Alain Roumier having deserted the family domaine to work across the road. The Vogüé wines are soft, round and fragrant, cedary and occasionally at the almost-too-insubstantial end of delicate. Those of the Domaine Roumier are sturdy, even masculine for Chambolle, a bit raw and aggressive in their youth, but they age beautifully.

Other good domaines include those of Bernard Amiot, Ghislaine Barthod-Noëllat, Pierre Bertheau, Henri Felletig, Daniel Moine-Hudelot and Maurice and Hervé Sigaut. The Château de Chambolle-Musigny, a rather gaunt, early eighteenth-century building at the top of the village, belonging to Freddy Mugnier, currently lets out some of its vineyards on long-term leases to various landowners and merchants in the area. The Nuits-Saint-Georges *climat* Clos de La Maréchale, for instance, belongs to the firm of Faiveley until 2002. So production under the château's own label is tiny. But Freddy Mugnier's wine is worth investigating.

VOUGEOT

While the village of Chambolle is at the top of the slope, the hamlet of Vougeot, hardly more than a main street off which there are a couple of alleyways, lies down on the main Dijon to Nuits-Saint-Georges road, though thankfully for the peace of mind of its few dozen inhabitants, the through traffic now by-passes the village. The commune is dominated by its *grand cru*, Clos Vougeot, which accounts for four-fifths of the commune's production of red wine. There is a tiny amount of white wine, sold under the village name. *Premiers crus* account for the rest and there is little if any village wine. To most people Vougeot's name is synonymous with Clos Vougeot.

VOUGEOT *GRAND CRU*

	Surface area in hectares	1988 harvest in hectolitres
CLOS-DE-VOUGEOT	50	1988

By the beginning of the twelfth century, the centre of the western world was neither London, nor Paris, nor even Rome but the Abbey of Cluny in the southern Mâconnais. Founded by the followers of Saint Benedict in AD 910, Cluny was the wealthiest and most powerful religious settlement in Christendom.

Elsewhere in France, however, there were Benedictines who felt that with such power had come a relaxation in the strict monastic virtues laid down by their founder Saint. Humility, obedience, silence, even chastity, had been forgotten, replaced by rich living, sumptuous eating and drinking and a worldliness far removed from the original objective. One such was Robert, Abbot of Molesmes, a monastery north of Dijon between Langres and Les Riceys. Robert had attempted unsuccessfully to reform the way of life at Molesmes but he found that only a few of his fellow monks wished to return to the simple life. In 1098, with some twenty companions, he left Molesmes and established a new monastery, a reformed commune, on the flat plains of eastern Burgundy, in a clearing within forests of oaks and marshy reedlands. From the ancient French word for reed, *cistel*, the name evolved to the Latin *cistercium*. The new order became known as the Cistercians and the new abbey renamed Citeaux.

But at Citeaux the land was unsuitable for the vine. No matter how hard they tried, the monks could not persuade the vine to thrive in the marshy bogs surrounding the abbey. Following the Vouge river upstream, the monks explored the higher ground to the west. Eventually they settled on some uncultivated slopes, bartered with four Burgundian landowners and acquired a few hectares of land. This was the nucleus of Clos Vougeot.

The monastery soon started receiving gifts of adjoining land suitable for the vine. The poverty, industry, austerity and saintliness of the Cistercians contrasted well with the opulent high life of the other religious orders. Donors shrewdly decided that the appropriate gesture in this world would be recompensed when it might be needed later and the vineyard grew. Around 1160, a press house was constructed but it was not until

1336 that the vineyard took the form we know today and, later still, that the famous wall, forming the Clos, was eventually completed. Finally, in Renaissance times, the château was constructed, affording guest rooms for the abbot and distinguished visitors. The château has been modified several times since, finally being completed in 1891 and restored after the Second World War. It is now the headquarters of the Chevaliers de Tastevin, Burgundy's leading wine promotion fraternity.

Clos Vougeot, by now a vineyard of some 50 hectares, remained in the ownership of the Cistercians until the French Revolution in 1789 when it was sequestered and put up for sale as a *bien national*. It was decided to sell the Clos as one lot and, on 17 January 1791, ahead of six adversaries, it was acquired by a Parisian banker, one Jean Foquard, for the huge sum of 1,140,600 livres, payable in *assignats* (paper money). Foquard, it appears, never settled his debt and the authorities turned to Lambert Goblet, the monk cellarist or *Magister Celarii*, to continue to administer the estate. A year later the vineyard passed to the brothers Ravel but after the Restoration in 1815, Clos Vougeot changed hands yet again, the Ravels and their associates having been continually in dispute over their relative shares and responsibilities over a period of twenty-five years.

This time Clos Vougeot's proprietor was a man of financial substance. Jules Ouvrard took the ownership of his important vineyard with the seriousness that it deserved. He was the local *député* (Member of Parliament) for much of his career. He was a conscientious proprietor, with land in Corton, Chambertin and Volnay as well as being the owner of La Romanée-Conti which he vinified at Clos Vougeot.

After Ouvrard's death in 1860, there was the usual difficulty about inheritance and this was not finally resolved until 1889. For the first time the land was divided. Originally there were six purchasers, five Burgundian wine merchants and one other; but these six soon became fifteen and now there are eighty: an average of 0.6 hectares or 200 cases per proprietor.

Clos Vougeot is the largest *grand cru* in Burgundy and the only one whose land runs from the slope right down to the main road running between Nuits-Saint-Georges and Dijon. Not surprisingly over such a large area, the soil structure is complex and there are differences in aspect and drainage. Add to these the many different owners, each making an individual wine, and you can see why there are variations from one grower's Clos Vougeot to another's.

At the top and best part of the Clos, where the vineyard borders the *grands crus* of Grands-Échézeaux to the south and Le Musigny to the north, the soil is a pebbly, oolitic limestone of Bathonian origin. There is little clay. Halfway down the slope, the soil becomes marl, that is a mixture of limestone and clay but of a different origin – Bajocian; however, there are still pebbles here so the land drains well. Further down the slope still the soil is less good; it becomes more alluvial and drains less well.

Understandably, Clos Vougeot wines from this lower part of the vineyard are criticized. The critics argue that this land is not worthy of its *grand cru* status, pointing out that over the wall to the south the vineyards are only entitled to the plain village Vosne-Romanée *appellation*. If the Clos had not been one large vineyard, contained within its retaining walls, it would never have been decreed *grand cru* in its entirety.

Tradition has it that the original ecclesiastical proprietors produced three wines: from the top or best land came the Cuvée des Papes, from the middle the Cuvée des Rois and from the lower slopes the Cuvée des Moines and only this one was sold commercially. Some people suggest the division was, in fact, vertical, as you face up the slope, not horizontal. Is the wine from the lower, flatter slope, inferior? In practice as well as in principle, yes; but it nevertheless remains more important to choose your grower rather than the geography within the vineyard. Jean and Etienne Grivot own a large area of Clos Vougeot, by which I mean almost 2 hectares; but on the lower levels of the *climat*. Yet with old vines – at least half date from 1920 – and with meticulous vinification, this is by no means one of the lesser Clos Vougeot wines. In fact, I would certainly place it in the top ten. Jean Grivot explains that in dry vintages the upper slopes can become a little parched though he fairly admits that the lower land can get somewhat humid if the weather turns wet.

Currently, no fewer than twenty-three of the Clos owners possess holdings which are smaller than a quarter of a hectare. One third of a hectare will produce, before evaporation, racking and other losses, just a little over three small barrels or *barriques* of wine. What do you do if you are one of these owners and some of your land is under young vines? Sacrifice a third of your crop? Is it too cynical to suggest that only a few Burgundians are saintly enough to be as perfectionist as this?

At its best, Clos Vougeot wine can rank among the greatest Burgundies, alongside Chambertin and the best of Vosne-Romanée. But it rarely does so. Normally though, I would consider it in the second division of *grands crus*, comparable with those of Morey and Corton, or indeed its neighbours Échézeaux and Grands-Échézeaux. In style, the wine is plumper and lusher than Chambertin or La Tâche, less firm, less intensely flavoured and with less definition. It also does not possess the cumulative complexity and fragrance of Musigny. Yet when rich, fullish and generous, with a fruit which is half redolent of soft, red, summer berries and half that of blackberries and chocolate, plus undertones of liquorice, burnt nuts and even coffee (a promising sign in a young Burgundy), the wine can be immensely enjoyable. Sadly, because of the vineyard's size and renown and the multiplicity of owners, it is one of the most abused names in the area.

The largest owners in Clos Vougeot are the sisters, Jacqueline Labet and Nicole Dechelette, whose wine is sold under the label Château de La Tour de Clos Vougeot. Engel, Grivot, various members of the Gros family, Méo-Camuzet, Prieur and Rebourseau are other important proprietors, as are the long-established *négociants* Champy, Albert Bichot (under their Clos Frantin domaine label), Joseph Drouhin, Drouhin-Laroze, Faiveley, Lamarche, Mongeard-Mugneret, L'Héritier-Guyot and the Domaine Paul Misset, co-owner of the Domaine des Varoilles in Gevrey-Chambertin, also possess land in this *grand cru*. The purchase of the Domaine Charles Noëllat has given Maison Leroy of Auxey-Duresses a more substantial parcel to add to the currently newly planted plot this excellent, if expensive, merchant already possesses in Clos Vougeot. I have had recent experience of wines from other important Clos Vougeot producers: Robert Arnoux, Bertagna, Alain Hudelot-Noëllat, Charles Mortet, Dr Georges Mugneret, Georges Roumier and Tortochot as well as the *négociant* wines of Jadot who now manage the Clair-Daü parcel, Labouré-Roi (under the Domaine Chantal Lescure label), Moillard (who own two parcels) and Remoissenet.

Using the vintages of 1988 to 1985 as a guide ('83 was a more irregular and difficult vintage and '84 less exciting), I would place the following growers in my first division of producers: Domaine Jean Gros (whose vines were grubbed up in 1986, so I am talking about his '85 in this instance), Domaine Grivot, Engel, Hudelot-Noëllat, Mongeard-Mugneret, the late Dr Georges Mugneret (Mugneret-Gibourg), Gros Frère et Soeur, Méo-Camuzet and the Château de La Tour. Equal with these are the wines from the following *négociants*: Maison Leroy, Drouhin, Jadot, Faiveley and Moillard. Patrice Rion and Charles Mortet's wines are also impressive, the latter despite coming from the lower half of the Clos. Without tasting them all side by side under blind conditions, it is impossible to suggest which would be *the* best, though I suspect Jean Gros's '85 would take the gold medal in any tasting of this excellent vintage; but you will not go wrong with any example from these producers. Beware, though, of other Clos Vougeot wines, particularly from one of the less reputable Beaune *négociants*. They may be marginally cheaper but you will be wasting your money. Buy from an impeccable source, though, and you *will* get a Clos Vougeot which will live up to its status of *grand cru*.

The *premiers crus* of Vougeot, lying to the north of Clos Vougeot, occupy 12 hectares. There is also a further 1.5 hectares of village wine, and together these two produced 723 hectolitres in 1996. Of this total some 167 hectolitres is white wine. White wine is rare to find in the Côte de Nuits and most of it comes from a *lieu-dit* in Vougeot suitably called La Vigne Blanche solely owned by l'Héritier-Guyot. Like that of Le Musigny, I find this white wine overpriced for what it is.

Leaving aside the Clos Vougeot owners already mentioned, most of whom do not reside in Vougeot itself, the best domaine in Vougeot is that of Alain Hudelot-Noëllat. Alain Hudelot is one of my favourite Burgundian growers, and a visit to his large, modern two-storey winery and cellar is always a high spot of my annual three-week sally to taste the year's red wines. Georges Clerget is another useful source, though at a lower level. The Bertagna estate, now German owned, is an important domaine, but I have not found their wines to be any better than competent.

FLAGEY-ÉCHÉZEAUX

If Vougeot is governed by its Clos, Flagey is even more curiously laid out. The village itself lies in flatlands on the wrong side (east side) of the railway and is surrounded by maize fields and orchards, not vineyards. Flagey's vineyards lie back on the west side of the railway, the right side, and consist solely of two *grands crus* which lie south-west of Clos Vougeot, further up the slope, completely isolated from the village. The village wine is sold as Vosne-Romanée, the next village to the south.

FLAGEY-ÉCHÉZEAUX *GRANDS CRUS*

	Surface area in hectares	1996 harvest in hectolitres
ÉCHÉZEAUX	37	1327
GRANDS-ÉCHÉZEAUX	9	335

Grands-Échézeaux lies halfway up the slope, immediately above Clos Vougeot and Échézeaux is even higher up. Wine from Grands-Échézeaux is considered to be the better of the two and fetches higher prices. It could well be argued that many an Échézeaux wine is as good as a Grands-Échézeaux, that the best sections of its vineyard are as capable of producing wines as fine as those from Grands-Échézeaux, but in general, Grands-Échézeaux is worth the extra money.

I find both wines sturdier and more robust – even *sauvage* – than their immediate neighbours; there is more clay in the stony soil. And the result is a wine of less finesse, sometimes hardly worth the *grand cru* designation. In fairness, these are the cheapest of all Côte de Nuits *grand cru* wines and they are often no more expensive than a good Vosne-Romanée *premier cru*. In good hands these wines can represent excellent value.

Most Vosne-Romanée growers own land in one or other of the Échézeaux vineyards. Of the few growers in Flagey itself I can safely recommend Emmanuel Rouget, inheritor of the vines of Henri Jayes and his brothers.

VOSNE-ROMANÉE

Vosne-Romanée is the last of the six great communes of the Côte de Nuits – in the sense that it possesses *grand cru* vineyards – as one travels south towards Nuits-Saint-Georges. The village itself is small and tranquil, set back a few hundred metres from the main road. On either side of the village lie the *premiers crus*; above and behind the houses are the celebrated *grands crus*, which produce some of the finest wines of the Côte de Nuits.

Vosne is mentioned in documents as early as the seventh century, and, like much of the surrounding area, came under the control of the Abbey of Citeaux during the Cistercian heyday. More recently it suffered badly at the hands of both Austrian troops in Napoleonic times and German troops in 1870. Little remains of the original medieval village. Chambolle, with its steep streets and narrow *culs de sac* has more charm. Morey, with its wide main street, off which are many substantial medieval and Renaissance courtyards, is more imposing.

The Abbe Courtepée, in the late eighteenth century, said of Vosne-Romanée *il n'y a pas de vin commun*: there are no common wines in the village. The wines were famous then – Louis XV's cousin, the Prince de Conti, owned a large area of La Romanée – and they are highly regarded now. The village possesses a large number of excellent growers but growers, however, cannot produce fine wine without having prime land. The Vosne mixture is as good as you can get: a well-drained slope with the right exposure, facing east or south-east, and lying approximately 250 to 300 metres above sea level, and soil which is essentially an oolitic, iron-rich limestone on a base of marl, rock and pebbles. The vineyards are sheltered from the west and north by the trees on the top of the slope and the *grands crus* vineyards, plumb in the middle of the slope, are in the best position of all.

Nearest to the village is Romanée-Saint-Vivant, the largest *grand cru*. Further up the slope is the tiny, gently sloping La Romanée-Conti and the even smaller La Romanée, at less than one hectare the smallest individual *appellation* in France. As the hill curves round to the right to face more north-east than south-east lies the steeper Richebourg. To the left, across the narrow row of vines which make up the *premier cru* vineyard, La Grand'

Rue, runs the slope of La Tâche, which is again steep at the top. On either side of this memorable roll-call of names are two of Vosne's top *premiers crus*: Les Malconsorts, which borders one of Nuits-Saint-Georges's best *premiers crus*, Les Boudots, and to the north Les Suchots, which borders the *grand cru* Échézeaux.

VOSNE-ROMANÉE *GRANDS CRUS*

	Surface area in hectares	1996 harvest in hectolitres
LA GRANDE RUE	1.3	57
RICHEBOURG	8	274
LA ROMANÉE	0.8	31
LA ROMANÉE-CONTI	1.8	50
ROMANÉE-SAINT-VIVANT	10	339
LA TÂCHE	6	225

Four of the six *grands crus* are under single ownership. La Romanée-Conti and La Tâche are solely owned by the Domaine de La Romanée-Conti. La Romanée belongs to the Comte Liger-Belair's Domaine de Vosne-Romanée whose wine is sold by the *négociant*, Bouchard Père et Fils. La Grand' Rue is owned by the Lamarche family.

Romanée-Conti is the best and most expensive *grand cru*, selling for more than twice that of La Tâche and three times that of the Domaine de La Romanée-Conti's Richebourg or Romanée-Saint-Vivant wines. At a price which is four times that of Lafite it is probably the most expensive wine on earth, and therefore *should* be sublime. It often is: the most intensely and subtly perfumed, the richest and most concentrated, the most explosively flavoured and the most persistently long on the palate of all Burgundy. The very best vintages take fifteen years to mature.

La Tâche runs at a very close second, and is significantly superior to the other Domaine de La Romanée-Conti wines, good as they are: Richebourg, whether from the hands of the Domaine de La Romanée-Conti or others, is opulent and velvety; Romanée-Saint-Vivant is lighter and more feminine, akin to Le Musigny. All have a finesse missing in either the Domaine's or other growers' two Échézeaux *grands crus* and a definition lacking in all but the very best Clos Vougeots.

Apart from the *grands crus* the remainder of the Vosne-Romanée vineyards occupy 162 hectares, of which 57 are premiers crus. There together produced a total of 7306 hectolitres in 1996. Among the thirteen premiers crus, Les Malconsorts, already mentioned as being one of the Vosne's best, has as its neighbours the *premiers crus* of Chaumes and Clos de Réas, the latter solely owned by the excellent Domaine Michel Gros. Above Les Suchots, the other top *premier cru*, are the *premiers crus* of Les Beaumonts – technically partly in the commune of Flagey – but selling its wine as Vosne – and Les Brûlées. La Grande Rue was recently elevated from *premier cru* to *grand cru*. Currently the quality of the wines does not merit this higher distinction.

There are a large number of good producers based in Vosne-Romanée. As well as the celebrated Domaine de La Romanée-Conti and Domaine Jean Gros, other good producers are: Robert Arnoux, Sylvan Cathiard, Jacky Confuron-Cotétidot, Philippe Engel, Forey Père et Fils, Jean Grivot/Anne Gros, Gros Frère et Soeur, Henri Jayer/Emmanuel Rouget, Georges Jayer, Lucien Jayer, Méo-Camuzet, Mongeard-Mugneret, Mugneret-Gibourg, Pernin-Rossin, Bernard Rion, and Jean Tardy. Madame Lalou-Bize, owner of Maison Leroy in Auxey and co-owner of the Domaine de La Romanée-Conti, bought the large but moribund Domaine Charles Noëllat in 1988. The wines since then have been splendid.

NUITS-SAINT-GEORGES

Nuits-Saint-Georges is an industrial conglomeration rather than a wine-making village and is the commercial centre of the Côte de Nuits. It is a bustling, busy, friendly town, less self-conscious than Beaune. Nuits-Saint-Georges' vineyards stretch on either side of a gap in the Côte, and on the southern side of the town continue into the commune of Prémeaux, whose wines are also entitled to the Nuits *appellation*.

The original Nuits was a Gallo-Roman villa further out in the plain. The name though has no nocturnal connections and is more likely to be either a corruption of the Celtic *Un Win*, a stream in a valley, or else to have something to do with nuts from the French word, *noix*. In the early Middle Ages the area was the fief of Hugues, sire of Vergy, who donated much of the land to the local monastery of Saint-Denis and the priory of Saint-Vivant, and a village slowly began to expand further up the valley of the river Meuzin in the site it occupies today. Though Nuits was originally fortified, it lost its strategic importance when the Duchy of Franche-Comté was absorbed into the kingdom of France in 1678. It was no longer a frontier outpost and the walls surrounding it were slowly dismantled over the next few hundred years. As a result of this, and the fact that the main road thunders right through its centre, Nuits has little of the medieval attraction of Beaune.

Like Beaune, though, it has its own Hospices, a charitable foundation, which dates from 1692 and is similarly endowed with vineyards. The wines are also sold by auction, and this takes place on the Sunday before Palm Sunday, preceded by a tasting at the château of Clos Vougeot. The Hospices has 13 hectares of vines, mainly *premiers crus*.

Nuits-Saint-Georges has no *grands crus* but, instead, an impressive list of twenty-seven *premiers crus*, plus another ten in Prémeaux. On the northern Vosne side, the vineyards cover a wide area from east to west. The *premiers crus* here lie at the top of the slope. The best known include Boudots, Richemone, Murgers, Damodes and Chaignots. South of the town the vineyards begin again and the slope is narrower. Here are the *premiers crus* of Pruliers, Roncières, Poirets, Vaucrains, Cailles and Les Saint-Georges itself, the most renowned. Across the commune boundary into Prémeaux the slope becomes steeper at first and the vineyards are more confined. Here you will find the *premiers crus* of Les Forêts, Perdrix, Corvées, Argillières and two which have single owners: Clos Arlot and Clos de La Maréchale. Clos de La Maréchale faces south-east rather than east like the others, and the slope is once again quite gentle.

The soil structure of the Nuits–Saint-Georges vineyards is as complex as any in Burgundy, for the distance from Les Boudots on the boundary with Vosne in the north to Clos de La Maréchale in the south of Prémeaux is six kilometres as the crow flies. North of the town the subsoil, like that of Vosne, is essentially Bajocian in origin, covered with a mixture of pebbles, silt, limestone debris and clay. Here the wines have a lot in common with those from neighbouring vineyards across the commune boundary, but the further south you go the level of clay in the soil increases, and the soil becomes richer and heavier. As a result the wines have a tendency to be four-square.

On the south of Nuits–Saint-Georges the limestone is either Bathonian or the harder Comblanchien type. Here and there the surface soil contains sand which moderates the effect of the clay. Across into Prémeaux the soil is thin on the higher slopes as the vineyards lie on rock. Lower down on the gentler slopes the soil has more clay and marl.

The authorities were quite correct not to make any vineyard in Nuits–Saint-Georges a *grand cru*. At their best, wines from the top *premiers crus*, from Les Saint-Georges, Vaucrains and Pruliers in the centre, for instance, or from Boudots in the north, can have concentration and finesse as well as richness and structure, but there is always a certain minerally, gamy robustness about a Nuits *premier cru*, an aspect of leaden-footedness that detracts from the class, the definition, the flair. It would be fair to point out though that as a consequence of the huge popularity of the name, there has been much abuse. More sin has been committed in the name of Nuits–Saint-Georges than in the name of all the other villages in Burgundy put together. Not everything is the fault of the genuine wines themselves, and there are an increasing number of good individual properties.

Among these estates are Jean Chauvenet Georges and Michel Chevillon, Robert Chevillon, Georges Chicotot, Henri Gouges, Bernard Machard de Gramont, Alain Michelot and Henri Remoriquet in Nuits–Saint-Georges itself, and the Domaine L'Arlot Chopin-Groffier, Jean-Jacques Confuron, Arnaud Machard de Gramont and Patrice Rion in Prémeaux, the neighbouring hamlet of Prissey and in Comblanchien. The Domaine de L'Arlot in Prémeaux changed hands in 1987 and a new winemaker, Jean-Pierre de Smet, produced excellent wines in 1987 and 1988. This is an estate to watch.

The merchant houses of Faiveley, Moillard and Labouré-Roi are based in Nuits–Saint-Georges. Faiveley's wines concentrate on their own grapes and their Côte de Nuits wines are of a particularly high standard. Moillard have 19 hectares of their own or under contract almost entirely in the Côte de Nuits, sold under the name of Domaine Thomas-Moillard, while Labouré-Roi manage the estate of Chantal Lescure in Nuits and René Manuel in Meursault.

There are a total of 317 hectares under vine in Nuits–Saint-Georges and Prémeaux of which 143 are *premiers crus*. Production in the 1996 totalled 14,723 hectolitres. To my knowledge, three estates make a little white wine, Robert Chevillon, Henri Gouges and the Domaine de L'Arlot. Gouges' wine comes from some Pinot Noir which mutated into giving white grapes. The Clos de L'Arlot white comes from Chardonnay and Pinot Beurot. All are excellent but difficult to come by. With Prémeaux we come to the end of not only the Côte de Nuits *premiers crus* but also of the villages which are entitled to their own individual *appellation*. Much of the best land of the Côte here is now given over to marble quarrying and such wines as are produced in the villages of Prissey, Comblanchien and Corgoloin are only entitled to the *appellation* of Côte de Nuits-Villages.

HAUTES-CÔTES DE NUITS
and HAUTES-CÔTES DE BEAUNE

Above and behind the Côte d'Or in the Hautes-Côtes the countryside is peaceful and pastoral. There are valleys and plateaux, pastures and woodlands, rocky outcrops and gently sloping fields. Up here it is cooler, often more exposed, and the soils are less fine, less complex. Only in carefully selected sites is the aspect suitable for the vine. This is the area known as Hautes-Côtes.

There have always been vines in the Hautes-Côtes. Before phylloxera there were as many as 4500 hectares in cultivation, though much was planted with non-'noble' grapes. But then, as elsewhere, the vineyards declined and as recently as 1968 there were barely 500 hectares of vines.

This was the nadir, but resurrection was already at hand. *Appellation contrôlée*, with the prefix Bourgogne, had been bestowed on the Hautes-Côtes in 1961, and in 1968 a co-operative cellar called Les Caves des Hautes-Côtes – not up in the back of beyond but sensibly on the main road outside Beaune where no passer-by could fail to notice it – was established. This now vinifies and sells 25 per cent of the combined *appellation*. Meanwhile, on the research station at Echevronne above Pernand-Vergelesses suitable clones of the Pinot Noir were being developed, and, following a visit to Bordeaux, trials were being carried out with high-trained vines, thus avoiding the worst of the frost and, because they would be planted further apart for mechanical cultivation, thus economizing on the expense of planting and maintaining new vineyards. Since then the fortunes of the Hautes-Côtes have blossomed. There are now well over 1000 hectares under vine and production in 1996 reached a total of 57,305 hectolitres (25,784 in the Hautes-Côtes de Nuits and 31,521 in the Hautes-Côtes de Beaune).

From a geographical point of view the two parts of the Hautes-Côtes do not quite correspond with the division between the Côte de Nuits and the Côte de Beaune. The northern section, the Hautes-Côtes de Nuits, begins at Ruelle-Vergy above Chambolle and continues to Echevronne and Magny-Lès-Villers. Echevronne is in the Hautes-Côtes de Beaune while the land at Magny is divided between the two. There is then a separate section of the Hautes-Côtes de Beaune which begins at Mavilly-Mandelot above Beaune and extends south to Sampigny-Lès-Maranges and Cheilly-Lès-Maranges near Santenay.

There is a little white Hautes-Côtes wine and it is less successful than the red wine. But it is the red wine, exclusively from the Pinot Noir, which is the cornerstone of the *appellation* and the key to its deserved recent success. This is a wine to buy in a warm, ripe year like 1988 or '85 – the wines are then delicious, and some of the best value in Burgundy. Avoid the wines of a cold, rainy vintage.

The best wines of Les Caves des Hautes-Côtes, who supply much of the *négociant* wine, can be very good value for money in these best vintages. Elsewhere in the Hautes-Côtes there are a number of enterprising growers, some of whom sell Côte d'Or wines as well. Robert Jayer-Gilles and Claude Cornu live opposite one another at Magny-Lès-Villers. Thierry Vigot lives in Messanges. Domaine Thevenot-Le-Brun is a large estate in Morey-Les-Fussy. Lucien Jacob is in Echevronne. The Mazilly family in Meloisey, Jean Joilot and François Charles in Nantoux and Michel Serveau at La Rochepot also make good wines.

Côte de Beaune

The Côte de Beaune begins with a bang at Ladoix with the hill of Corton and continues down beyond Santenay until the hills peter out at Cheilly-Lès-Maranges, a distance of 26 kilometres as the crow flies. This is a region making richly fruity, elegant, but essentially soft-centred red wines, neither as full and concentrated nor as long-lasting as those of the Côte de Nuits.

In the north part of the Côte de Beaune, on the hill of Corton and in the surrounding *premiers crus* in the village of Aloxe, the wines are firmer, a transition between those of the Côte de Beaune and the Côte de Nuits. From Savigny onwards, interrupted only by the motorway which surges out of the Morvan hills, the Côte continues through Beaune and Pommard to beyond Volnay, producing almost entirely red wines. We then come to the magnificent trio of Meursault, Puligny and Chassagne, source of the Chardonnay grape at its finest and the greatest dry white wines in the world.

Such is the renown of the Côte de Beaune white wines – and with the exception of Corton all the *grands crus* in the Côte de Beaune are white rather than red – it is easy to forget that three-quarters of Côte de Beaune wine is red. The Côte de Beaune is still part of the Pinot Noir's noble fief, even if on this occasion it has a mighty consort.

The Côte de Beaune is twice as large as the Côte de Nuits: it is both wider and more gently sloping, and the orientation is more to the south-east than the east. In the Côte de Beaune more of the vineyards are not only on the flat land at the bottom of the slope but also up in little gorges in the Côte, and in the lesser tucked-away communes such as Saint-Aubin and Saint-Romain, Auxey-Duresses, Monthélie and Pernand-Vergelesses, there is some excellent good-value wine to be found.

CÔTE DE BEAUNE

There is also a Côte de Beaune *appellation*. This is very rare and justly obscure. The vineyards – there are only some 30 hectares – lie up in the hills above Beaune itself. Most of the wines I have seen are unremarkable and should really be downgraded into Hautes-Côtes. In 1996 1401 hectolitres were produced, of which 566 were white. Maurice Jolliette of Domaine de Pierres Blanches makes a respectable white wine.

CÔTE DE BEAUNE-VILLAGES

Côte de Beaune-Villages is a much more important *appellation* than its counterpart in the Côte de Nuits. It covers the red wine of the following sixteen villages: Auxey-Duresses, Blagny, Chassagne-Montrachet, Cheilly-Lès-Maranges, Chorey-Lès-Beaune, Dézize-Lès-Maranges, Ladoix-Serrigny, Meursault, Monthéile, Pernand-Vergelesses, Puligny-Montrachet, Saint-Aubin, Saint-Romain, Sampigny-LèsMaranges, Santenay and Savigny-Lès-Beaune. All of these can also sell their red wine under their individual village name and indeed many do. This is an *appellation* which you will more likely come across under a *négociant's* or co-operative's name than under that of a private grower. It is generally a soft, unpretentious wine from Pinot Noir for early drinking, and fills a gap between Hautes-Côtes and the cheapest of the village wines. Local statistics, which only reveal what is annually declared as Côte de Beaune-Villages, do not bear any relation to the much greater amount eventually sold under this appellation.

LADOIX-SERRIGNY

Unlike the other village names of the Côte d'Or, Ladoix, the most northerly commune of the Côte de Beaune, has adopted the name of Serrigny, a neighbouring hamlet, not that of its most important vineyard. Ladoix lies on the main road between Nuits-Saint-Georges and Beaune and Serrigny is down in the plain, surrounding an attractive, small Louis XIV château belonging to the Prince Florent de Mérode, an important grower in Corton.

Ladoix itself lies immediately under the Corton hill, and the Rognet, Vergennes and Maréchaudes sections of the Corton *grand cru* rise up directly behind the village. Although within the Ladoix communal boundaries the lower sections of this slope are, confusingly, *appellation premier cru* Aloxe rather than Ladoix. Ladoix does have seven *premiers crus* but they lie to the north, on either side of a road which leads up into the Hautes-Côtes. You will rarely come across them, for the surface area currently in production only comprises some 14 hectares. And unless you stop to buy wine in the village you will not often be offered Ladoix itself. Most of the yield of the 121 hectares of village wine is sold as Côte de Beaune-Villages. In 1996 4885 hectolitres of village and *premier cru* wine were produced, 780 hectoliters of this was white wine.

The best growers in Ladoix-Serrigny can all boast vines on the Corton hill. As well as the Prince de Mérode, already mentioned, I can recommend Georges Chevalier et Fils, Edmond Cornu, René Durand, Jean-Pierre Maldant, André and Jean-René Nudant and Gaston and Pierre Ravaux.

ALOXE-CORTON

Six kilometres to the north of Beaune, clearly visible by anybody descending the slope on the motorway, the lone buttress of the hill of Corton marks the north end of the Côte de Beaune. Densely wooded at its summit, oval in shape, with the sharp ends facing southwest and north-east, the steeply inclined surfaces of the Corton hill form the largest *grand cru* in the whole of Burgundy, a total of some 178 hectares.

Corton is a confusing *appellation*. The *grand cru* is spread over three communes, Ladoix, Aloxe and Pernand, and covers both red and white wines. The white wine can be occasionally found labelled simply as Corton, usually as Corton-Charlemagne or, rarely but theoretically, as plain Charlemagne. The red wine, though technically *appellation* Corton, can also appear under a number of names: as Le Corton, a particular *lieu-dit*, as Corton followed by the name of a *lieu-dit* such as Corton-Clos du Roi, or as Corton without the definite article, a blend of several *grand cru lieux-dits*. To further complicate matters, Maison Louis Latour, an important landowner in Aloxe, produces a branded wine called Corton, named after their domaine headquarters, Château Corton-Grancey.

CORTON AND CORTON-CHARLEMAGNE *GRANDS CRUS*

1996 harvest in hectolitres

CORTON	3949
CORTON-BLANC	84
CORTON-CHARLEMAGNE	2295

Surface area in hectares (by commune)

LADOIX-SERRIGNY	22	(Corton and Corton-Charlemagne)
ALOXE-CORTON	100	(Corton)
	46	(Corton-Charlemagne)
PERNAND-VERGELESSES	17	(Corton and Corton-Charlemagne)

Charlemagne, Charles the First and the Great, as was befitting for a man who was Holy Roman Emperor and effectively the ruler of the western civilized world, was a giant of a man. He towered over his subjects, dominating them as much physically as by the force of his personality. One of his many domaines and the one producing one of his favourite wines was at Corton, itself named, one interpretation suggests, after an obscure first-century Roman emperor named Orthon: Curtis (domaine) d'Orthon becoming contracted to Corton. The story is related that, as with certain vineyards in Germany, noticing the snows were always the first to melt on this particular slope, Charlemagne ordered vines to be planted there, and lo, these produced excellent wine.

At the time the wine produced was red, but, as Charlemagne grew older, and his beard whiter, his wife Liutgarde, ever watchful over the dignity of her spouse, objected to the majesty of her emperor being degraded by red wine stains on his beard and suggested that he switched to consuming white wine. White grapes were commanded to be planted on a section of the hill, Corton-Charlemagne was born, and it continues still.

White wine production from the Chardonnay grape on the hill of Corton is a recent development. Jullien, in his *Topographie de Tous les Vignobles Connus* in 1816, makes no mention of white Corton. By the mid-nineteenth century, however, Chardonnay had arrived. Dr Lavalle, in his *Histoire et Statistique de la Vigne et des Grands Vins de la Côte d'Or*, published in 1855, speaks of Pinot Noir on the mid-slope and lower ground and what he terms Pinot Blanc on the upper parts. In the 16-hectare section of Corton-Charlemagne lying in the commune of Aloxe Messieurs Gouveau, de Grancey, Chantrier, Jules Pautet and the Hospices de Beaune are listed as the main proprietors, while in the 19 hectares of land across the border in Pernand only Monsieur Bonneau-Véry (now the Bonneau du Martray family) is worthy of note. By the end of the nineteenth century the owners included Louis Latour, who had acquired the Grancey domaine, and Jules Senard, two families who are still important proprietors in the area.

The Chardonnay is planted on the upper slopes in a whitish coloured marly soil with a high calcareous content on a hard limestone rock base. Further down the slope there is more iron and clay in the soil, and the colour of the earth is redder. Here the Pinot Noir produces better wine, particularly on the more easterly-facing slopes above Aloxe and

Ladoix. Today, however, growers in Le Corton and elsewhere can get a better price for white wine than for red, and there is a gradual changeover to Chardonnay in the vineyards at the top of the slope. On the Pernand side of the Corton hill the soil is flinty, and the wine will have more austerity and be steelier than that coming from above Aloxe. The whites from Aloxe *climats* are softer in their youth and develop faster.

Nevertheless, Corton-Charlemagne, whoever makes it and wherever he has his vines, is, or should be, a firm, full, masculine wine, perhaps even slower to mature than Le Montrachet; more closed and less accessible, but opening out after five years or so to give a wine of marvellous richness, albeit always with a certain amount of steely reserve behind the opulence. The best wines need at least ten years to mature, and it is a shame to waste them by drinking them any sooner.

Red Corton is the biggest, the firmest, the most masculine of all the Côte de Beaune reds. It is an austere wine, and you can taste the iron in the soil, but at the same time it is rich and will eventually become opulent. There are some twenty separate *lieux-dits*, the best of which are Clos du Roi, Bressandes, Renardes and Pougets rather than Le Corton itself.

Compared with the amount of *grand cru* wine the production of *premier cru* Aloxe wine is tiny. There are 40 hectares of vines, a quarter of which lie in the commune of Ladoix. A further 112 hectares produce village Aloxe wine, anf together these yielded 6132 hectolitres in 1996. Most of this is red wine.

Not surprisingly with such a large *grand cru*, there are many proprietors in Corton and Corton-Charlemagne who are not based in either Aloxe, nor in neighbouring Pernand or Serrigny. Of those in Aloxe the name of the *négociant* Louis Latour is the most important. Château Corton-Grancey is the headquarters for the firm's 50-hectare domaine, of which no less than 26 hectares are *grand cru* Corton or Corton-Charlemagne. Philippe Senard, André Masson, Michel Voarick and Maurice Chapuis are the other leading names in the village. Other important landowners on the Corton hill whose wines can be recommended include the Domaine Chandon de Briailles, Pierre Bitouzet and Antonin Guyon in Savigny, Miollard and Faiveley in Nuits-Saint Georges, Roumies in Chambolle, Coche-Dury in Meursouelt, Michel Juillot in Mercurey, Louis Jadot and previous section in Ladoix-Serrigny and Claude Cornu up in the Hautes-Côtes de Nuits at Magny-Lès-Villers. Those based in Pernand and Chorey-Lès-Beaune will be discussed in the next two sections.

PERNAND-VERGELESSES

Pernand is a pretty little village full of sharp corners and steep alleys which clings to the side of a hill on the western side of the Bois de Corton. The village overlooks the Charlemagne part of the Corton *vignoble*, which looms up on the other side of a little valley. Pernand also commands a fine view back over the flatter land towards Beaune.

Apart from Corton and Corton-Charlemagne, the main part of Pernand's vineyard is on the east-facing slopes of the Bois Noël which separates the village from Savigny. Here are the five *premiers crus*, of which the best is the Île des Vergelesses. There is rather more communal land up and behind the village than one realizes, where the vines of Pernand flow imperceptibly into those of the Hautes-Côtes. Here there are also the remaining

vines of Aligoté, for which Pernand used to have a fine reputation. Most of this Aligoté has now been replaced by Chardonnay, for which the growers can demand a higher price.

Village Pernand wine, whether white or red – the former represents about a fifth of the production – can be somewhat lean in lesser years, but is usually good value. The *premiers crus*, particularly the Île des Vergelesses, are a different matter, and are very similar to Corton in flavour, with hints of damson and black cherry on the palate. These wines can be very fine, and can represent excellent value.

The leading Pernand domaines are headed by Bonneau du Martray, producer of an excellent Corton-Charlemagne (though a disappointing red Corton) and an important landowner in the combined Corton grand cru. Manius Delarche, Pierre Dubreuil-Fontaine, Laleure-Piot and Roland Rapet are other good names. Production of *premier cru* and village Pernand wine totalled 5337 hectolitres (1592 of which was white) in 1996. Apart from the hill of Corton there are 193 hectares of vines of which 56 are *premier cru*.

CHOREY-LÈS-BEAUNE

Chorey-Lès-Beaune – the Lès with the accent denoting 'near' – is another village with most of its wine finding its way into *négociant* Côte de Beaune-Villages. There are 150 hectares of vines, lying on flat, fairly alluvial soil mainly on the 'wrong' side of the Beaune–Nuits-Saint-Georges highway. There are no *premier cru* vineyards but there is a fine château which is the headquarters of Domain Germain, as well as two other leading domaines: Tollot-Beaut, and Maillard Père et Fils, all of whom also make Corton and Aloxe wines. Chorey itself is a soft, inexpensive, easy-to-drink red wine. In 1996 there were 6709 hectolitres, almost entirely red wine.

SAVIGNY-LÈS-BEAUNE

Up at the beginning of the valley of the river Rhoin, six kilometres north-west of Beaune, lies Savigny, one of the larger of the Côte de Beaune communes with 379 hectares of vines. Savigny is a modest little village but is flanked by a rather impressive castle dating partly from the fourteenth century. Savigny's main claim to fame is that it was here in the mid-nineteenth century that the first viticultural tractor was invented, and as a consequence of this that vines were first planted in rows in the surrounding vineyards.

The main vineyards of the Savigny *appellation* lie on either side of the village. To the north they continue on from the Pernand vineyards on the south-eastern or south-facing slopes of the Bois Noël. On the other side of the village the vineyards adjoin those of Beaune and face north-east. Here the soil tends to be more sandy and less pebbly. Above the vineyards, halfway up the Mont Battois, the motorway thunders down from the Morvan to the plain of Beaune. There is, incidentally, a rest-site up here called the Aire de Savigny les Galloises, from which there is a splendid panorama towards the hill of Corton. If you stop here you will find yourself exactly halfway between Lille and Marseille.

About 140 hectares are *premier cru*, of which there are 19, in whole or in part of the Savigny *vignoble*. Those lying below the Bois Noël – Vergelesses, Lavières, Serpentières and Guettes are the most important – produce lighter and more elegant wines than those under Mont Battois – Marconnets, Les Dominodes, Narbontons, Peuillets. These can be firm and hard, even a little *sauvage*, with a marked *goût de terroir*. In general Savigny's wines are not as fine as those of Beaune, Pommard and Volnay, but they are also cheaper. They mature in the medium term, similar to the wines of Beaune.

The main estates based in the village include the Domaine Chandon de Brialles, an important Corton producer, and those of Simon Bize, Maurice Ecard, Girard-Vollot, Jean-Marc Pavelot, Capron-Manieux and Antonin Guyon. One of the best Savigny wines comes from ninety-year-old vines in Les Dominodes, produced by Bruno Clair of faraway Marsannay. In 1996 164,458 hectolitres of Savigny and Savigny *premier cru* were produced, including a little white wine, made from both Pinot Blanc and Chardonnay. These wines have a slightly spicy flavour and resemble the white wine of Beaune.

BEAUNE

Though Dijon is the departmental capital of the Côte d'Or, Beaune is the wine capital of Burgundy. Inside the old walled town the atmosphere is still largely medieval. Outside market days, and away from the Place Carnot and the few shopping streets that surround it, Beaune is a sleepy, shuttered town, full of hidden alleys, quiet Renaissance courtyards and ecclesiastical reminders of its glorious religious and aristocratic past. There is a fine church, the Collégiale Notre-Dame, dating from the twelfth century. There is a Musée du Vin, housed in a mansion formerly owned by the Dukes of Burgundy in the fifteenth and sixteenth centuries. The Hôtel de Ville was once a convent and another, the Couvent des Cordeliers, houses one of Beaune's wine firms, and is a trap for the unwary tourist. And of course there is the Hôtel-Dieu, heart of the Hospices de Beaune, one of the most magnificent wine monuments in the world.

Each year Beaune explodes to life during the weekend of the *Trois Glorieuses*, three extravagant feasts which surround the Hospices de Beaune charity auction on the third Sunday in November. The town teems with people: local growers who have come to show their wines to the massed throngs in the Hôtel de Ville or in the rather more sedate surroundings of the Salle des Jeunes Professionels; and also tourists, agents, buyers and friends of the local *négociants*, most of whom have their headquarters in the centre of Beaune, though today their actual cellars are housed in modern warehouses on the outskirts of town. Everybody is there. For one hectic week countless gallons of wine are drunk or sampled and spat, it is impossible to find a parking space for your car, let alone a bed for the night. And then life returns to normal.

Beaune lies on a natural crossroads. It was where the old east–west road from Besançon to Autun met the north–south road from Champagne and Dijon to Lyon and Marseille; there was the added benefit of two natural springs which had their sources in the hills nearby. Colonized by the Romans as Belna or Belno Castrium in AD 40, the influence of Beaune grew as the importance of Autun, the capital of Burgundy in Gallo-Roman days, fell, particularly after Autun's destruction by the sons of Clovis in the sixth century. Even then the vine was already important in the region.

Until the Dukes of Burgundy moved to Dijon in the fourteenth century, Beaune was in all senses the capital of Burgundy. In 1395 Philippe Le Hardi published an ordinance prohibiting the plantation of the ignoble Gamay in favour of the noble Pinot, and from then on the best sites of the Côte d'Or were exclusively planted with members of the Pinot or Chardonnay family and the wines accordingly grew in fame.

Beaune is the Côte d'Or's third largest commune after Gevrey and Meursault, with 538 hectares of vines, producing almost 19,751 hectolitres of wine in 1996 of which 1987 was white. The slope of *premier cru* vineyards extends from the boundary with Savigny-Lès-Beaune at the northern end towards the border with Pommard at the southern end and is divided in half by the D970 which leads up to Bouze in the Hautes-Côtes and on to Bligny-sur-Ouche. The soil structure, based on limestone, is complex. In general it is thin to the north (in the Marconnets, Clos du Roi, Fèves and Bressandes *premiers crus*), especially on the steeper, upper part of the slope, and the vine roots have to search deep in the soil to find their nutrient. Wines from these slopes are full, firm, even solid at the outset, and need time to mature. In the middle section of *premiers crus* (Toussaints, Grèves, Teurons), there is some gravel (as the name Grèves indicates) and the wine is of medium weight, plump and succulent. Bouchard Père's Vigne de l'Enfant Jésus wine comes from an enclave in the Grèves vineyard. South of the D970 there is some sand in the sloping *climat* of Montée Rouge, and also in Aigrots, Pertuisots and the upper part of Vignes-Franches. Mid-slope (in the *premiers crus* of Clos des Mouches, Vignes-Franches, Sizies, Avaux) the soil is very stony and hard to work; while at the southern end and lower down the slope (the *premiers crus* of Boucherottes, Epenottes, Chouacheux), there is more clay and less gravel. Here the soil is deep, and production can be excessive if not restricted. This section of the vineyards is known as *le puit* (the well) *de Beaune*, and produces soft wines which mature rapidly.

Though the colour of the soil is mainly a reddish brown, there are parts where it is a whitish marl, more suitable for the Chardonnay grape than the Pinot Noir. On the upper part of the Clos des Mouches Drouhin have vines which produce their celebrated white Beaune wine whose flavour is somewhat more spicy than that of a Meursault. It also tends to mature more quickly. Bouchard Père have white wine vines in the vineyards of Tulivans. The production of white Beaune was a mere 400 hectolitres or so in 1988.

Which are the best *climats*? Beaune can boast thirty-four which, in whole or in part, are classed as *premier cru* (there are no *grands crus*) and no one seems to agree which are the best. Dr Morelot in 1831 cited Clos de la Mousse (a small vineyard now solely owned by Bouchard Père et Fils), Teurons, Cras, Grèves, Fèves, Perrières, Cent-Vignes, Clos du Roi and Marconnets, all of which 'have the capacity to produce exquisite wines'. Dr Lavalle in 1855 lists Fèves, Grèves, Crais (now Cras) and Champs-Pimonts as the leading wines.

Camille Rodier, writing in 1920, says that the best is Fèves, with its finesse and delicate aroma; Grèves produces a very complete wine, with more body but not without finesse and velvet (*velouté*); Marconnets, on the Savigny border, is closed and solid, full but *bouqueté*. Clos des Mouches, at the southern end adjoining Pommard, is full-bodied, fruity and very elegant. Others (Cras, Champimonts, Clos du Roi, Avaux, Aigrots) are supple and perfumed, and 'easy to drink' – a familiar phrase for damning with faint praise, I have always thought. He adds Marconnets, Bressandes and Clos des Mouches to Dr Lavalle's list of top wines. Poupon and Forgeot in their book, *The Wines of Burgundy*, list Marconnets, Fèves, Bressandes, Grèves and Teurons as the best.

I would certainly agree with this final five, and would add Vignes-Franches, Clos du Roi and Clos des Mouches, with the rider that, as always in Burgundy, the grower or *négociant* is of equal importance as the actual source. The *négociant* Leroy has always had a good range of Beaune *premiers crus*, as does the *négociant* Albert Morot, whose Beaune wines come from the 7-hectare family domaine and include Cent-Vignes, Grèves, Toussaints, Bressandes, Marconnets and Teurons. Bouchard Père et Fils is the largest landowner in the commune of Beaune, with 48 hectares of *premiers crus*. The *négociant* Chanson comes next with 26, including the majority of Fèves which they sell as Clos de Fèves. The Hospices de Beaune have eight *cuvées* of Beaune and possess 19 hectares of vineyards. Drouhin have 15½ hectares, Patriarche 12, Jadot 9, Louis Latour just over 4 and Remoissenet a couple of hectares: most of the best land is owned by the *négociants*.

How do the wines of Beaune compare with other wines of the Côte d'Or? I find that in style they come midway between those of Pommard and those of Volnay, both communes to the south of Beaune. Pommard wines, particularly those of Rugiens, but equally from the upper part of Épenots and elsewhere, are rich and sturdy. They can be somewhat four-square, but there should always be muscle. Volnay wines, on the other hand, are elegance personified: fragrance, delicacy, subtlety and finesse are the keynotes. The wines of Beaune are varied but they lie somewhere between these two. Only rarely do they reach the quality of the best of these other two communes.

HOSPICES DE BEAUNE

The Hospices de Beaune comprises two charitable institutions, the Hôtel-Dieu, founded in 1443 by Nicolas Rolin, chancellor of Philippe Le Hardi, Duke of Burgundy, and his wife Guigone de Salins, and the Hospice de la Charité, endowed by Antoine Rousseau and his wife Barbe Deslandes in the seventeenth century. The Hôtel-Dieu is a remarkable building in the centre of Beaune and is one of the world's great vinous tourist attractions. It is no longer used as a charitable institution for the sick and poor but is preserved as a museum. The central feature of the building is a huge dormitory, the Grande Salle or Chambre des Pauvres, its walls lined with curiously wide yet short beds – the inmates slept two to a bed – each with a sight of the altar in the chapel at the far end so that, though bedridden, they could participate in the services.

Over the years both these institutions were the fortunate recipients of vineyards, and the holdings now total some 60 hectares, nearly all of it in *premier cru*, making the Hospices of one of the largest domaines in Burgundy. These 60 hectares are split up into thiry-seven different wines most of which are blends of a number of different vineyards within the same commune. They are sold each year under the name of major benefactors to the Hospices, by auction on the Sunday afternoon (and well into the evening: this is a lengthy, tedious auction *à la chandelle*) on the third weekend of November. In 1997 617 casks were auctioned. This is not the entirety of the production as the produce of the younger vines is disposed of in bulk to the local *négociants*. The auction is the central event of the weekend of the *Trois Glorieuses* and traditionally sets the trend of prices for the vintage in Burgundy, though the actual levels paid are always grossly inflated.

The wines are sold when they are barely a month old, and as crucial as their initial quality is the competence of the firm who will look after it subsequently. It is wise to choose a merchant whose name you can trust.

THE HOSPICES DE BEAUNE WINES

Wine name	Commune
Red wines	
CHARLOTTE DUMAY	Corton
DR PESTE	Corton
RAMEAU–LAMAROSSE	Pernand-Vergelesses
FORNERET	Savigny-Lès-Beaune
FONQUERAND	Savigny-Lès-Beaune
ARTHUR GIRARD	Savigny-Lès-Beaune
NICOLAS ROLIN	Beaune
GUIGONE DE SALINS	Beaune
CLOS DES AVAUX	Beaune
CYROT CHAUDRON	Beaune
BRUNET	Beaune
MAURICE DROUHIN	Beaune
HUGUES ET LOUIS BÉTAULT	Beaune
ROUSSEAU–DESLANDES	Beaune
DAMES HOSPITALIÈRES	Beaune
DAMES DE LA CHARITÉ	Pommard
CYROT CHAUDRON	Pommard
BILLARDET	Pommard
BLONDEAU	Volnay
GÉNÉRAL MUTEAU	Volnay
JEHAN DE MASSOL	Volnay (Santenots)
GAUVAIN	Volnay (Santenots)
LEBELIN	Monthélie
BOILLOT	Auxey-Duresses
MADELAINE COLLINGON	Mazis-Chambertin
CYROT CHAUDRON ET GEORFES URSTER	Clos-de-la-Roche
White wines	
FRANÇOIS DE SALINAS	Corton-Charlemagne
PAUL CHANSON	Corton (vergennes)
BAUDOT	Meursault (Genevrières)
PHILIPPE LE BON	Meursault (Genevrières)
DE BAHÈZRE DE LANLAY	Meursault (Charmes)
ALBERT GRIVAULT	Meursault (Charmes)
JEHAN HUMBOLT	Meursault
LOPPIN	Meursault
GOUREAU	Meursault
DAMES DE FLANDRES	Bâtard-Montrachet
FRANCOIS POISARD	Pouilles-Flussé

POMMARD

South of Beaune we come to the best red wines of the Côte de Beaune after the *grands crus* of Corton – Pommard and Volnay. The name Pommard is of malic origin (Pommarium, Pommone or Polmario) but there are few apple orchards today, every square metre being given over to the production of one of the most popular Burgundies.

There are 337 hectares of vineyards and just over a third (125 hectares) are *premiers crus*. The two best *premiers crus* (Épenots and Rugiens) are at opposite ends of the commune. At the northern Beaune end, largely behind a stone wall, lies Épenots, and above it Pézerolles; while Charmots and Arvelets, facing more to the south, are round the corner overlooking the river Dheune and the valley up to Meloissey in the Hautes-Côtes. On the southern side are Rugiens, Chanlins, Fremiers, Jarolières and Championnières.

Rugiens and Épenots – more particularly Les Grands Épenots and Les Rugiens Bas – produce the best Pommard wines, and would be contenders with one or two of the better Volnay *climats* for elevation to *grand cru* status. The soil structure of the Pommard *premiers crus* is complicated Burgundian limestone, stony in parts (dolomitic containing a high proportion of carbonate of magnesium), elsewhere comprising an iron-rich oolite. To the south of the village the land rises more steeply and the vineyards face due east. The soil here is red in colour – hence the name Rugiens – because of the iron it contains. On the Beaune side the vineyards face more to the south and the slope is more gentle. In general the soil is more clayey than in Volnay or Beaune and it is this which gives Pommard wine its full and sturdy character.

Pommard wines are closed, well-coloured and long-lasting compared with those of Volnay and Beaune. They can also be a bit solid, robust and alcoholic: four-square wines which lack grace. The wines are expensive, because of the demand from the American market but when they are good they are rich, fat and succulent. Sadly the name is often abused, and you can pay a high price for an indifferent wine.

The two leading domaines in Pommard are those of the Comte Armand, who has an enclave within Épenots called Clos des Epeneaux, and the Domaine de Courcel. Also recommended are Jean-Marc Boillot, Jean Garaudet, Michel Gaunoux, Aleth Girardin, Domaine Lejeune, André Mussy, Jacques Panut, who makes the wine of his wife's domaine (A.F. Gros), Daniel Rebourgeon-Mure and Joseph Voillot.

Pommard produced 15,149 hectolitres of wine 1996, all of it red.

VOLNAY

With Volnay we come to one of the most delightful wines and one of the most rewarding communes in the Côte d'Or. There are a large number of very fine and dedicated growers in the village, and the wine they produce is the epitome of elegance and delicacy, the most fragrant and seductively feminine expression of the Pinot Noir in Burgundy. Volnay is as far removed as it can possibly be, from the souped up, 'old fashioned' brews which were fraudulently bottled as non-*appellation* Burgundy in our parents' day.

Volnay is a small village tucked into the top of its slope above the vineyards and away from the main road. The name comes from a Celtic or early Gallic water god, de Volen.

The village appears in medieval times as Vollenay and was spelt Voulenay by Thomas Jefferson when he toured round France just prior to the French Revolution.

Hugues IV, one of the early Burgundian dukes, built a hunting lodge up in the hills in about 1250, and it is largely from the stones of this edifice, long since demolished, that the local houses are constructed. Much of the village dates from the seventeenth and eighteenth centuries. There are some fine mansions and imposing courtyards discreetly sheltered behind tall gates and thick walls.

Domaine-bottling in Burgundy can be said to have begun in Volnay. The present Marquis d'Angerville's father was a constant critic of the cynical fraud being perpetrated by the local merchants in the 1930s. As a result they refused to accept his wine, and so he was forced to bottle it himself and to look outside the local *négoce* for his markets. He was soon joined by other growers, including his friends Henri Gouges of Nuits-Saint-Georges and Armand Rousseau of Gevrey-Chambertin who were being similarly shunned. Encouraged by Raymond Baudoin, the French wine writer and consultant to many top restaurants, by the American Frank Schoonmaker and later by Alexis Lichine, these fine growers were eventually joined by more and more of the top estates, leading to the situation today where almost everyone who makes good wine bottles and sells at least some of it himself and one suspects that some of the Beaune *négociants* are increasingly hard-pressed to find good wine to mature and sell. The tables have well and truly been turned! D'Angerville was also a pioneer of clonal selection and has a particular low-yielding, high-quality strain, the Pinot d'Angerville, named in his honour.

There are twenty-six *premier cru* vineyards in Volnay, in whole or in part, and these overflow into the neighbouring commune of Meursault. The three vineyards of Santenots, Pitures and Cras can be planted with both Pinot Noir and Chardonnay and if red wine are labelled as Volnay. Any white wine goes under the Meursault name. Including these vineyards 144 of the 242 hectares under vine are *premier cru*.

Of these the best are generally regarded to be the Cailleret Dessous and the Clos des Chênes, the latter lying higher up above Cailleret Dessus at the southern end of the commune. Here you will find a poor but beautifully exposed, very stony, reddish soil of Bathonian origin on a rocky base, on quite a definite slope facing to the south-east. It is the lightness of the soil throughout the Volnay vineyards that largely contributes to the delicacy and finesse of this commune's wines.

Nearer to the village itself are the *premiers crus* of Taillepieds and the Clos de la Bousse d'Or – a name which has nothing to do with anything golden but derives from 'bousse terre' or good soil in the local *patois*. On the northern Pommard side are the *premiers crus* of Clos de Ducs, Pitures, Chanlins and Fremiets. Here the wines are generally just a shade sturdier than those from the southern side.

Among the many fine estates in Volnay – almost every house seems to have a placard on its front offering its owner's wine – Michel Lafarge and the Domaine de la Pousse d'Or, until recently run by the late Gérard Potel, must be particularly singled out. Those of the Marquis d'Angerville, Bitouzet-Prieur, Jean-Marc Boulay, Yves Clerget, Bernard Glantenay and Hubert de Montille are also very good. The Domaine des Comtes Lafon in Meursault additionally makes a fine Volnay Santenots du Milieu while the *négociant* Bouchard Père et Fils of Beaune produces Volnays under the label Ancienne Domaine Carnot.

Volnay produced 10,372 hectolitres of wine in 1996, all of it red wine.

MONTHÉLIE, AUXEY-DURESSES and SAINT-ROMAIN

South of Volnay the Autun road begins to ascend into the uplands of the Hautes-Côtes, but not before it has passed through the vineyards of Monthélie, Auxey and Saint-Romain, three rather neglected and consequently under-rated sources of good Burgundy.

Monthélie is the first commune after Volnay. It is an attractive village set back from the main road and fits snugly in between two slopes of vineyards. Those on the northern side are a continuation of the Volnay *côte*, though the slope is less steep and faces due south rather than south-east. On the other side of Monthélie the vineyards face more to the north-east and join those of Auxey-Duresses. There are ten *premiers crus* in Monthélie, all but one being on the Volnay side. These make up 31 of the 145 hectares under vine. The best *premiers crus* are Sur La Velle and Les Champs Fuillot and are the extension of Volnay, Clos de Chênes and Cailleret. The wines from these two *climats* is really very similar to Volnay, though a little lighter and with not quite so much definition. From the rest of its vineyards Monthélie can occasionally suffer from a lack of real ripeness and concentration, yet in good years can be excellent value at two-thirds the price of its more famous neighbour.

The Monthélie producers are headed by the de Suremain family, owners of the Château de Monthélie, an attractive, eighteenth-century building with a medieval tower. Madame Monthélie-Duhairet and various members of the Garaudet family also make good wine. Though both red and white wine can be produced under the Monthélie label, most of the wine is almost entirely red. The 1996 harvest produced 5130 hectolitres of red wine and 369 of white.

Auxey-Duresses – the first word is pronounced 'Aussey' – lies a little further along the D973 in a little valley between the Mont Melian and the Montagne du Bourdon. The latter is an extension of the Monthélie slope and faces east and then south. On it lie Auxey's nine *premiers crus* and the production is largely of red wine. Across the valley the vineyards face north, and here the Chardonnay is widely planted, as it is further round the hill above the village of Meursault. A total of 169 hectares are planted in Auxey-Duresses, 32 of which are *premiers crus*. The three best *premiers crus* are Les Duresses, La Chapelle and du Val. About two-thirds of the village wine is red, a lightish red similar to Monthélie's village wine; a little green in the poorer years but of value and consequence when the sun shines sufficiently to ripen the grapes. Less heat is required to mature the Chardonnay, and the white wines are, consequently, more consistent. This can be a good inexpensive substitute for Meursault. Auxey, an up-and-coming *appellation*, is perhaps most famous for the excellent *négociant* Maison Leroy whose headquarters are in the village. Leroy's owner Madame Lalou-Bize is additionally co-proprietor of the famous Domaine de La Romanée-Conti. The firm owns a few hectares of vineyards in Auxey. Jean-Pierre Diconne is an excellent source of good Auxey wine and there are a large number of members of the Prunier family in the village. In 1996 4915 hectolitres of red wine and 1836 of white were produced.

Saint-Romain is really part of the Hautes-Côtes, but has enjoyed full *appellation contrôlée* status in its own right since 1967. After Auxey-Duresses the road divides and the right-hand fork leads to the village of Saint-Romain, surrounded by cliffs and perched below the remains of an impressive fortified château. Below the village are the best sectors of the 135 hectares of vineyards which are entitled to the local *appellation*. The vineyards are largely planted with Chardonnay. There are no *premiers crus*, the only Côte de Beaune *appellation* without any.

Though roughly the same amount of red wine (2092 hectolitres in 1996) as white (2192 hectolitres) is produced, it is Chardonnay which has the greatest reputation, and in the best vintages this can be a useful and less expensive substitute for Meursault and Puligny. Roland Thévenin, poet and local grower-*négociant*, is the best-known name. Alain and René Gras, René Thévenin-Monthélie and Bernard Fèvre can also be recommended.

MEURSAULT

Choose selectively, and you will perceive a natural progression in the Côte de Beaune. First come the sturdy reds of Pommard; then the more elegant, softer red wines of Volnay; and finally the whites of Meursault. Meursault produces almost as much white wine as all the other communes of the Côte de Beaune put together. It is a large village — only Gevrey and Beaune have more land under vines in the Côte d'Or — and with a seemingly limitless number of individual growers. Since 1983 I have visited fifteen to twenty Meursault proprietors a year, usually eliminating three or four from the previous season in order to add on new names. I have still not got to the bottom of the list.

The name Meursault – Murrisault or Murassalt in old documents – is derived according to some authorities from the Latin for 'rat jump', *muris saltus*. Like the majority of the communes of the Côte d'Or, the history of Meursault is closely associated with the church. Even before there was a vine at Clos Vougeot, the new Cistercian abbey at Citeaux, founded by the ascetic Robert de Molesme in 1098 as a breakaway from the more comfortable order of the Benedictines at Cluny, had received a gift of land and vineyards in Meursault from the Duke of Burgundy. This was followed by further legacies in the next few centuries with the result that after Vougeot, Meursault was Citeaux's most important viticultural holding, a situation which continued until the French Revolution. Moreover, Meursault rather than Puligny is the heart of the Hospices de Beaune's white grape holdings. Though most of Meursault is equally as entitled to produce red wine as white, the commune seems always to have concentrated its production on white wines. Thomas Jefferson was told when he visited the area in 1787 that there was 'too much stone' in the soil for red wine production. No doubt the locals would have produced red wine if they could, for the former was much the more popular then. Volnay sold for 300 francs the cask but even the best Meursault (Jefferson refers specifically to Goutte d'Or) could fetch only 150.

The commune is divided into two distinct sections by the village itself. The smaller northern part is an extension of the Volnay-Monthélie slope as it falls gently towards the south-east. The soil is a similar reddish-brown limestone containing both pebbles and clay, and is more suitable for red wines than white. Here you will find the *premiers crus* of Santenots, Pitures and Cras. The red wine produced here is sold as Volnay.

South of the village the soil is lighter in colour, rocky rather than pebbly, and the aspect of the vineyards is more east or north-east. The vines lie sheltered under the forest of the Montagne du Châtelet de Montmélian, on the one side of which is the hamlet of Blagny and on the other the village of Auxey. The best vineyards are located below Blagny where the soil is at its lightest and stoniest. Perrières lies above Charmes on the boundary with Puligny, followed, as one moves north towards the village, by Genevrières, Poruzot, Bouchères and Goutte d'Or. All these are *premiers crus* for white wine only: this is the heart of white Meursault. In total there are 132 hectares of *premier cru* vineyards and 298 of village *appellation* land. Production of Meursault wine, not counting that sold as Volnay, reached 18,977 hectolitres in 1996, 4.5 per cent of which was Meursault red.

The large, sprawling village of Meursault lies between the two sections of the vineyards and contains a number of fine buildings, some dating back to the fifteenth and sixteenth centuries. Chief of these is the seventeenth-century Château de Meursault, now owned by André Boisseaux of the *négociant* Patriarche Père et Fils and housing an art gallery as well as a tasting centre. Across the N74, the main Beaune to Chagny road, is the village of L'Hôpital de Meursault where you can see the ecclesiastical remains of the old *leprosarium* and eat cheaply and well at the Relais de la Diligence. In the largest hall in the main village the third and least stuffy of the *Trois Glorieuses* banquets, the *Paulée*, is held at lunchtime on the Monday after the Hospices de Beaune auction. Everyone brings his own wine and shares it with his neighbours. The last time I attended, I counted afterwards no fewer than thirty-seven tasting notes in my notebook, from Aligoté to a pre-First World War Pommard, my descriptions becoming progressively more indecipherable and unintelligible as the afternoon progressed!

The best *premier cru* is Perrières, normally a beautifully elegant, sumptuous wine, followed closely by Genevrières. Charmes is a large vineyard with the result that the wine can vary, for part of the vineyard, the Charmes Dessous, is a little too far down the slope for really high-quality wine. Below it the land very soon becomes simple *appellation* Bourgogne. Poruzots and Goutte d'Or are more solid wines with less distinction and finesse but in good hands (and from the old vines and a restricted yield) can be equally fine. The best of the village *climats*, and you will often see these stated on the label – forming a sort of separate category between *premier cru* and anonymous village Meursault – are Le Limouzin, Les Grands Charrons, Le Tesson and Le Meix Charvaux, which continue the line of the *premier cru* vineyards. I often prefer the racier village wines from Narvaux and Tillets which come from higher up the slope.

In all, a Meursault should be an ample, round, ripe and fruity wine, with a rich, buttery flavour well supported but not overwhelmed by new oak; and with a good balancing acidity. There is a wide variation between the exciting and the bland and the wine can occasionally be a little too fat and heavy, the broadness of its style not matched with sufficient acidity. The plain village wines can be somewhat empty and anonymous.

The Hospices de Beaune produces seven Meursault wines, of which Baudot and Philippe Le Bon come from Les Genevrières and de Bahèzre de Lanlay and Albert Grivault from Les Charmes, the remaining three being blends of a number of *climats* and not AC *premier cru*. In total the Hospices owns 7 hectares in Meursault.

The largest single holding in the village belongs to the Ropiteau-Mignon family. This is leased to Nouson Bouchard Rèrcet Fils.

now owned by the Chantovent group, used to have the exclusivity of the wines of the family vineyard, Domaine Ropiteau-Mignon, until the 1985 vintage. This exclusivity has now passed to the Nuits-Saint-Georges merchant Chauvenet, but the Chablis firm of Laroche also have an interest, having purchased some of the vineyards from one member of the family, André Ropiteau. This has just been sold, along with the Château de Puligny which Laroche also used to own, to the Crédit Foncier bank.

Two other *négociants* with a particular interest in Meursault are Labouré-Roi of Nuits-

Another *négociants* with a particular interest in Meursalt is Labouré-Roi of Nuits-Saint Georges, who mature and sell the wines from the domaine of Réne Manuel. Louis Jadot, Joseph Drouhin, Louis Latour and other Beaunne merchants are obviously other important sources of Meursault, as are the Puligny-based white wine specialists, Olivier Leflaive and Chartron et Trébuchet.

The growers' wines, though, are of more interest than the merchants'; not that they are necessarily better, but in that they express the personality, expertise and philosophy of the domaine owners themselves. There are many growers in Meursault. Some are individualists, like Robert Ampeau, who is not interested in showing or selling you his wine until he considers it ready for drinking. He also likes to confuse you by giving you, blind, a really excellent wine from an off-vintage. Some growers are long established and aristocratic, such as the Domaine des Comtes Lafon. They bottle later than most, without filtering, and the wines lie in some of the deepest, coldest cellars in the village. Some growers have become super-stars relatively recently, such as the deservedly much sought-after Jean-François Coche-Dury. From my personal experience I would include in my first-division list as well as the above the domaines of Jean-Pierre Boillot, Bernard Boisson-Vadot, Hubert Bouzereau-Gruère, Joseph Matrot and Guy Roulot. I would also recommend the names of Ballot-Millot, Bitouzet-Prieur, Boyer-Martenot, Coche-Debord, Jean-Paul Gauffroy, Henri Germain, Patrick and Raymond Javillier, François Jobard, Michelot-Buisson, Jean Monnier, René Monnier, Pierre Morey, Madame Pitouzet-Urena (up to 1986 when the domaine was disbanded), Jacques Prieur, Marc Rougeot and Thévenot-Maréchal. There is plenty of choice. The local Syndicat Viticole lists well over 100 growers in the village as well as many owners based elsewhere. There is even one who lives in Great Britain.

BLAGNY

Up in the hills between Meursault and Puligny lies the hamlet of Blagny. Blagny is a curious *appellation*, existing solely for red wines. Most of the wine produced, though, is white and it is sold either as Meursault-Blagny *premier cru* or as Puligny-Montrachet, the boundary between Meursault and Puligny running right through the village.

The red wine is fairly sturdy, if not robust, a sort of cross between Chassagne and Pommard. It is certainly more interesting than red Meursault. In 1996 328 hectolitres were produced, from a surface area of about 8 hectares of Pinot Noir vines. Three vineyards on the Meursault side are classified as Blagny *premier cru*. One of the best-known Meursault-Blagny wines is made by the *négociant*, Maison Louis Latour, which has the exclusivity of the Château de Blagny estate, vinifying the crop themselves.

PULIGNY-MONTRACHET

Puligny-Montrachet is the greatest white wine commune on earth. Though with a mere 230 hectares of vineyards it is considerably smaller than either of its neighbours, Meursault and Chassagne, the village can boast two of Burgundy's six white wine *grands crus* in their entirety, Chevalier-Montrachet and Bienvenues-Bâtard-Montrachet, plus roughly half, and, so the authorities would have us believe, best sections of two of the others, Bâtard-Montrachet and Le Montrachet itself. Only Corton-Charlemagne and the diminutive Criots-Bâtard-Montrachet *grands crus* do not lie, at least partly, in Puligny.

Puligny's *grands crus* lie at the southern end of the commune, overlapping into neighbouring Chassagne, and this is where the Chardonnay grape realizes its most regal and supreme expression: this is wine to drink on bended knees and with heartfelt and humble thanks.

The origin of the village of Puligny-Montrachet is Gallo-Roman. In the first few centuries after the birth of Christ the vine was first commercially planted in the area and the village was known as Puliniacus. Subsequently, particularly during the Dark Ages, it was the local Cistercian monastery at the Abbey of Maizières which carried on the traditions of viticulture and viniculture. From time to time, the abbey would receive bequests of land.

At the time of the French Revolution the local *seigneur* was the Marquis d'Agrain, who emigrated to Austria to escape from the Terror. One aristocrat who remained behind was Charles de La Guiche who had married into the Clermont-Montoison family, the largest owners of Le Montrachet itself. His luck ran out, however, and he was guillotined in 1794. But perhaps because he had remained in France and not emigrated, his land was not seized. The Laguiche family remain the principal vineyard holders of Le Montrachet, with 2 hectares, one quarter of this remarkable vineyard. There are now sixteen other owners of Le Montrachet as well.

How do you begin to describe something as exquisite as Le Montrachet? It is, first, a wine of great reserve and, second, one not lacking in power. It can be misleadingly dumb when immature, and only after seven or eight years does it begin to open out to reveal the depth of character and complexity of flavour within. When mature it is a wine of astonishing richness and concentration, utterly disarming in its perfection.

Above Le Montrachet, solely in the commune of Puligny, lies Chevalier-Montrachet whose wine is second only in quality to Le Montrachet itself. Below is Bâtard-Montrachet, within whose boundaries is Bienvenues.

The *premiers crus* of Puligny, of which there are eleven, cover an area of 100 hectares and extend along the *côte* towards Meursault on the same level as the *grands crus*. Those nearest to the *grands crus*, Caillerets and Pucelles, have the highest reputation. Les Demoiselles and Clos de Meix are enclaves within these two *climats*, the latter solely owned by the Domaine Sauzet, the former only produced, as far as I know, by the Domaine Colin-Déléger of Chassagne. After these two vineyards come Clavaillon and Folatières, above which are Champ-Gain, Truffières and La Garenne. Nearer to the Meursault boundary you will find Perrières, Referts, Champ Canet and Combettes. Each of these *premiers crus* can produce wine of very fine quality. Combettes is the softest and roundest, an ample generous hazelnutty wine which is similar to its neighbour, the Perrières vineyards in

Meursault. The wines from vineyards higher up the slope such as Champ Canet, Truffières and Champ-Gain are lighter, more racy and mature sooner. There is something nervous, coltish, about their character. Folatières and Clavaillon are quite firm, rich and plump in character. They have plenty of finesse and keep well.

Of all these, Caillerets and Pucelles are the most exquisite; they are the nearest thing to a *grand cru* at half the price. And from a master vinifier they are much, much better value. Like the *grands crus*, they too need keeping for at least half a dozen years. Too many of the great wines of Puligny are drunk too young. It is tragic.

The village of Puligny is spread out and the houses seem less huddled together than in most other villages in Burgundy. It lies lower down the slope from the vineyards and because of a high water table the 'cellars' must be at ground level, yet still occasionally get flooded. There is a fine local restaurant, the Montrachet, a large shaded grassy square and a thirteenth-century church.

PULIGNY-MONTRACHET *GRANDS CRUS*

	Surface area in hectares		1996 harvest in hectolitres
BÂTARD MONTRACHET	5.7	in Puligny	521
	5.8	in Chassagne	
BIENVENUES-BÂTARD-MONTRACHET	3.7		176
CHEVALIER-MONTRACHET	7		340
	4	in Puligny	363
LE MONTRACHET	4	in Chassagne	

Domaine Leflaive is the leading Puligny producer. Though they have only a tiny holding in Le Montrachet this is indisputably the greatest estate for white wine in the whole world, producing wines that are the utmost in discretion and elegance; profound, long-lasting wines full of richly concentrated fruit which for me represent all that is best in white Burgundy, all that is glorious about the Chardonnay grape. Carillon, Chartron, Chavy, Clerc, Maroslavac, Pernot and Sauzet are also very fine producers indeed. The Domaine du Château de Puligny-Montrachet, formerly owned by Roland Thévenin of Saint-Romain, used to belong to the Domaine Laroche of Chablis but in 1989 it was sold to the Crédit Foncier bank. Olivier Leflaive and Chartron et Trébuchet, who vinify and distribute the Domaine Chartron wines, are local and respected *négociants,* the latter also selling as Dupard Aîné. From outside the village the Burgundian merchants of Drouhin make and sell the Montrachet and other wines of the Marquis de Laguiche and Remoissenet the Montrachet of Domaine Thénard. Jacques Prieur, Bouchard Père et Fils, Louis Jadot, Louis Latour, the Comtes Lafon of Meursault, André Ramonet and a number of estates based in Chassagne are also important vineyard owners.

The production of Puligny-Montrachet (village and *premier cru* wine together) in 1996 was a total of 11,266 hectolitres. It is nearly all white wine.

SAINT-AUBIN

The N6 main road cuts a great swathe through what is technically the commune of Chassagne – there are Chassagne vineyards on the northern side – but what feels like the border between Chassagne and Puligny. The Mont Rachet hill curves round to face south and up a little defile lies the hamlet of Gamay. The main road continues round to the left, and we come to the village of Saint-Aubin.

Saint-Aubin is another of those neglected lesser Burgundian communes, but in my view, it is the one which merits the most serious consideration, particularly for its white wine. Both the village and the communal land are quite extensive, though because of the sinuous layout of the hills not all the land faces in the right direction and is suitable for the vine. There are a number of separate parcels, one section extending along the Chassagne slope, another on the south and west side of the Mont Rachet while a third lies above the village of Saint-Aubin itself. The delimited area for the Saint-Aubin *appellation* is as much as 228 hectares, but only 100 of these are planted with vines.

Both red and white wine are produced but more white wine is produced than red. In 1996 the figures were 4254 and 3332 hectolitres respectively. The red is light and fragrant with a certain earthy quality, a sort of cross between Chassagne and Volnay but with less definition than either. Yet it is the white wine which is much the most interesting. The wine from the Charmois *climat*, an extension of the Chassagne slope, is much like a lesser Chassagne, as you might expect. The wines from the other well-known *premiers crus* – En Remilly, Les Murgers, Les Dents de Chien, La Chatenière – have much in common with those of Puligny. There are nineteen *premiers crus* in all but most of them are rarely seen. The white Saint-Aubin wines are excellent value and rather more interesting than those of Saint-Romain, Auxey and Monthélie, even than many a village Meursault. Leading domaines in the village include those of Jean Bachelet, Marc Colin, Hubert Lamy, Henri Prudhon, Roux, Gérard Thomas and the *négociant* and grower Raoul Clerget.

CHASSAGNE-MONTRACHET

Chassagne-Montrachet is the last-but-one important commune of the Côte d'Or before the hills peter out at Dézize, Cheilly and Sampigny-Lès-Maranges, and it is the third of the three great neighbouring white wine villages after Meursault and Puligny. Divided by the N6, the main highway between Chagny and Châlon to the south and Autun and Auxerre to the west and north-west, now to a large extent superseded by the A6 autoroute, Chassagne produces both red and white wine. Historically its vineyards have always been planted with Pinot Noir but today more and more Chardonnay can be found, and it is the white wines which have the greater renown and fetch the higher prices. This is not just because of the proximity of the white wine *grands crus* of Le Montrachet and Bâtard-Montrachet, both of which straddle the commune boundary between Puligny and Chassagne (indeed the smallest and most southern of the white wine *grands crus*, Criots-Bâtard-Montrachet, falls entirely within Chassagne), nor solely as a result of the current demand for fine white Burgundy. The white wines, simply, are better. The reds are good: full-bodied, stalwart, work-horse examples of the Pinot Noir, and occasionally rustic.

They are similar in a way to those of Pommard or even the less distinctive examples of the Côte d'Or. The white wines, too, are full and firm; less definitive perhaps than those of Puligny, but with a better grip than most Meursaults.

Like so many places in this part of France the village has had a turbulent history. It was known as Cassaneas in A D 886. Towards the end of the fifteenth century the local *seigneur* was Jean de Chalone, Prince of Orange. His castle at the top of the hill, surrounded by what was then the village of 'Chaissaigne', was besieged by the army of Louis XI, for the Prince had sided with Louis' rival, Margaret of Burgundy. After much fighting the locals had to capitulate, and as punishment their village was razed to the ground. Eventually a new village grew up halfway down the slope. This was largely monastic in its origins. The Abbot of Maizières, recognizing the value of the local terrain for vines, cleared much of the hillside, planted vines and built a local priory, the Abbaye de Morgeot, to house the brothers who worked on the vineyards. A sister establishment was established by the Abbess of Saint-Jean-Le-Grand. Morgeot and Clos Saint-Jean remain two of the largest and most important *premiers crus* in Chassagne.

Historically Chassagne was a red wine village like most in the Côte d'Or. Montrachet seems always to have been renowned for its white wines, but elsewhere, except in Meursault, the wine that was made was red.

Jullien in his *Topographie de Tous les Vignobles Connus* of 1816 makes no mention of white wines in the village apart from Le Montrachet and its satellites. This dearth of Chardonnay is confirmed by Dr Lavalle, who wrote one of the most interesting books on Burgundy in 1855: 'If one excepts the vineyards producing the white wine called Montrachet, one only finds a few *ouvrées* here and there in pinot blanc, as in Ruchotte, for example . . . everywhere the pinot noir is planted in the good sites and the gamay in the poorer soils.' However, he also mentions that Chassagne is the commune in Burgundy with the most Pinot Beurot or Pinot Gris (the so-called Tokay d'Alsace), also a white grape.

Old men with long memories of the village and its wines can remember when it was first decided to move from red wine to white. It was after the phylloxera epidemic when the vineyards were being replanted. Was this perhaps, I suggested, because the Chardonnay took to its graft better than the Pinot Noir? For this was one of the explanations why Sancerre, originally a red wine area, became a white wine one. No, they replied, merely a response to changing fashion. By the time of the introduction of the laws of *appellation contrôlée* in 1936 some 20 to 25 per cent of Chassagne's vineyards produced white wine. And, unlike every other village in the Côte d'Or (save Musigny and part of the *climat* of Corton and Corton Charlemagne), the top vineyards of Chassagne are allowed to produce *premier cru* wine of either colour. Since the Second World War the move to white wine has accelerated. The grower Albert Morey remembers that when he bought his plot of Caillerets in 1949 the entire *climat* was planted in Pinot Noir. Today it produces one of the best Chardonnays in the commune. During the 1980s 43 per cent of the village and *premier cru* wine was white, and the move to white wine is continuing. In 1996 more white wine than red was produced. The reason is self-evident. A village Chassagne can today (in 1998) command 90 francs a bottle if it is white but only 55 francs if it is red. For a *premier cru* wine the gap is wider still: red wine from Morgeot at 80 francs and white wine from Caillerets at 150 francs – almost double the price.

CHASSAGNE-MONTRACHET *GRANDS CRUS*

	Surface area in hectares	1996 harvest in hectolitres
CRIOTS-BÂTARD-MONTRACHET	1.6	73

(See also page 164 for Bâtard-Montrachet and Le Montrachet.)

Chassagne is one of the larger communes of the Côte d'Or with 331 hectares under vines of which 159 are *premiers crus*. This is similar to Santenay, Chassagne's neighbour to the south. It is smaller than Meursault but sizeably larger than Puligny. In 1988 the production of Chassange-Montrachet (both village and *premier cru* wine) was 7165 hectolitres of red wine and 9068 hectolitres of white wine.

The soil structure of the vineyards is complex. The rocky subsoil, like most of Burgundy, is basically an oolitic limestone. At Chassagne you can see a quarry half-way up the slope above the village, which produces polished slabs of pink, beige or grey marble-like stone used for local gravestones and fireplaces. The surface soil, essentially limestone debris, can have varying amounts of clay, chalk (Criot is a corruption of the French for chalk, *craie*), as well as changing colour; the heavier *terres rouges* being found lower down the slope at Morgeot, while higher up along the line from Embrazées through Ruchottes to Cailleret you will find the lighter *terres blanches*. In general it is here in the leaner, more chalky soils of the upper slopes south of the village that the best white wines have their origins. North of the village the slope from the top of Clos Saint-Jean down through Les Vergers and Les Chenevottes to the N6 is gentler, the soil contains both clay and gravel, and the Pinot Noir comes into its own, as it does at Morgeots, though much of this *climat* is now planted to Chardonnay. Finally, round towards the border with the commune of Saint-Aubin, across which is this village's best *climat*, Les Charmois, the higher slopes above Les Chaumées have recently been reclaimed from the scrub. Again this cooler, north-east-facing slope has been found to produce good racy white wines.

The only *grand cru* exclusively in Chassagne is Criots-Bâtard-Montrachet. It is the smallest *grand cru* in the Côte d'Or, apart from La Romanée, and the least well known. It is the most delicate of the local *grands crus*, I would suggest from my limited experience (those of Blain-Gagnard and his brother-in-law Fontaine Gagnard).

The best *premiers crus* for red wines are Clos Saint-Jean, Les Rebichots, Les Vergers, Les Chenevottes and Les Macharelles, plus La Maltroie, La Boudriotte and Morgeot. For white wines the best are Les Embrazées, La Romanée, Les Ruchottes, Les Caillerets and Les Champs Gain, plus Morgeot again.

In Chassagne it is the white wines that are the most distinctive. In general they are full and firm; more akin to Puligny than to the softer, rounder wines of Meursault. From the top of the slope on the Saint-Aubin side vineyards such as Les Chaumées produce lightish, racy wines with a touch of peach or crab apple, while lower down, for example, in Chenevottes, the wine is plumper and sometimes a touch four-square. For the best of the more masculine versions of white Chassagne you need to go to Morgeot; Caillerets is flowery, racy and feminine; Embrazées all in finesse and lighter still; while in Champs

Gain, halfway up the slope, you will get an elegant compromise; fullish, plump, succulent wines. My vote would go to the wines from Caillerets. But do I just prefer the *climat* because it is Albert Morey's best wine and I have known him longer than most other Chassagne growers? The village of Chassagne is rich in variations on the names of Gagnard, Delagrange, Bachelet and Ramonet. Domaines get divided as one generation succeeds another or unites by marriage, the husband tagging his wife's maiden name on to his when she has brought some vineyards with her as her dowry.

My favourite growers include the Morey family (Albert Morey and his sons Bernard and Jean-Marc), Michel Colin-Deléger, André Ramonet, Richard Fontaine-Gagnard, Jean-Marc Blain-Gagnard and Jacques Gagnard-Delagrange. Do not forget also Fernand Coffinet, Michel Niellon, Bachelet-Ramonet, Delagrange-Bachelet, Jean-Noel Gagnard, André Cornut at the Château de la Maltroye, René Lamy-Pillot, Fernand Pillot and Jean Pillot. Producers based elsewhere include Jean-Claude Bachelet, Hubert Lamy and Marc Colin in Saint-Aubin and Joseph Belland, Lequin-Roussot and the Mestre family in Santenay. The wine of the Duc de Magenta's domaine, based at the Abbeye de Morgeot, is now made by Louis Jadot in Beaune and the Marquis de Laguiche estate is run by the merchants, Joseph Drouhin. As well as their famous Le Montrachet they make a formidable Chassagne *premier cru* from the Laguiche vineyards.

SANTENAY

With Santenay we come to the last of the important villages of the Côte d'Or. In fact we come to two, because there is Santenay-Le-Haut and Santenay-Le-Bas, with a kilometre of vineyard between them. The upper part is a straggly hamlet of narrow winding streets and ancient patched-up houses. Santenay-Le-Bas is rather grander. It boasts the ruins of an old castle fortified by Philippe Le Hardi in the thirteenth century and the oldest plane tree in France, said to have been planted by Henri IV in 1599. The village has been a spa since Roman times. The spring water is extremely salty but is said to relieve the symptoms of gout and rheumatism.

The vineyards of Santenay continue the *côte* below Chassagne, the slope gradually shifting its orientation so that the exposure is more south than east. In the northern part of the vineyards the soil contains gravel over marly limestone – hence the name Les Gravières for one of the best-known *premiers crus*. This is the best sector. There is a local saying that the top wines of Santenay come from east of the belfry. West of the village the soil is richer and browner in colour: the wines have less finesse.

Santenay is a large commune with 394 hectares of vines. Of these 140 are *premier cru*, divided among eleven *climats* which are largely on the Chassagne side of the town. As well as Les Gravières, these include La Comme, Beauregard, Passetemps and the Clos de Tavannes. Behind the castle keep lies La Maladière.

While there is a litlle white wine, the village's production is almost entirely red. The red wine can range from being rather dense and burly to something with really quite a lot of finesse, rather less sturdy but rather more stylish than the red wine found in Chassagne. The production of Santernay in 1996 was 14,923 hectolitres of red wine and 1635 of white. The best domaines in the village are Roges Belland, Louis Lequin-Roussot, René Lequin-Colín, Louis Clair (Domaine de

L'Abbaye de Santenay), Vincent Girardin and Mestre Père et Fils. Adrien Belland and the Domaine Prieur-Brunet can also be recommended. The local firm of Prosper Maufoux has connections with other domaines in Santenay. Producers based elsewhere include the Domaine de la Pousse d' Or (their Clos de Tavannes) and the Morey family in Chassagne (their Clos Grand Rousseau).

MARANGES

Maranges is a new *appellation* (1989), combining the previous separate *appellations* for the villages of Dézize-Lès-Maranges, Cheilly-Lès-Maranges and Sampigny-Lès-Maranges. These three obscure villages, whose red wine has nearly always been bottled as Côte de Beaune-Villages rather than under their own village names, are where the golden slope of the Côte d'Or comes to an end. Administratively they lie in the *département* of Saône-et-Loire rather than Côte d'Or. They share a *premier cru*, Les Maranges, and there are five others. The wines are well-coloured and tannic. They share some of the earthy rustic character of the lesser, western Santernays. Some 226 hectares produce some 7250 hectolitres, almost all of it red wine.

Côte Chalonnaise

If I were to go back into the wine business and set up on my own I think I would like to specialize in the wines of a particular area of France. If I were to choose one part of the country whose wines were at the same time of good quality and reasonably priced, as well as being underrated and under-exploited, I would plump for the Côte Chalonnaise.

The Côte Chalonnaise, or Région de Mercurey, to give it its alternative name, has long been a well-known 'forgotten area', though this may seem paradoxical. Yet while everyone acknowledges that it is worth investigating, few merchants seem to bother to go prospecting. There are many well-known growers whose wines are hardly ever exported.

The Côte Chalonnaise begins at the southern tip of the Côte de Beaune but on a different ridge of hills slightly to the east. The vineyards lie on the most favoured parts of a series of hummocky hills, roughly following the line of the D981 road which runs due south from Chagny down to Cluny. The main wine villages are Bouzeron, Rully, Mercurey, Givry and Montagny. Total production is small, barely a seventh of that of the Côte d'Or.

Up to 1990, unlike the Mâconnais and Chablis, but like the Côte d'Or, there was no regional *appellation* for the generic wines of the Côte Chalonnaise: they were labelled anonymously as Bourgogne Rouge, Bourgogne Blanc and so on. Now a separate *appellation*, Bourgogne-Côte Chalonnaise has been authorized. The area covers land in forty-four communes in the Saône-et-Loire surrounding what has already been delimited as Rully, Mercurey, Givry and Montagny. This will cover red and rosé wines from Pinot Noir, and white wines from Chardonnay and Aligoté. If made from Aligoté, it must say so on the label.

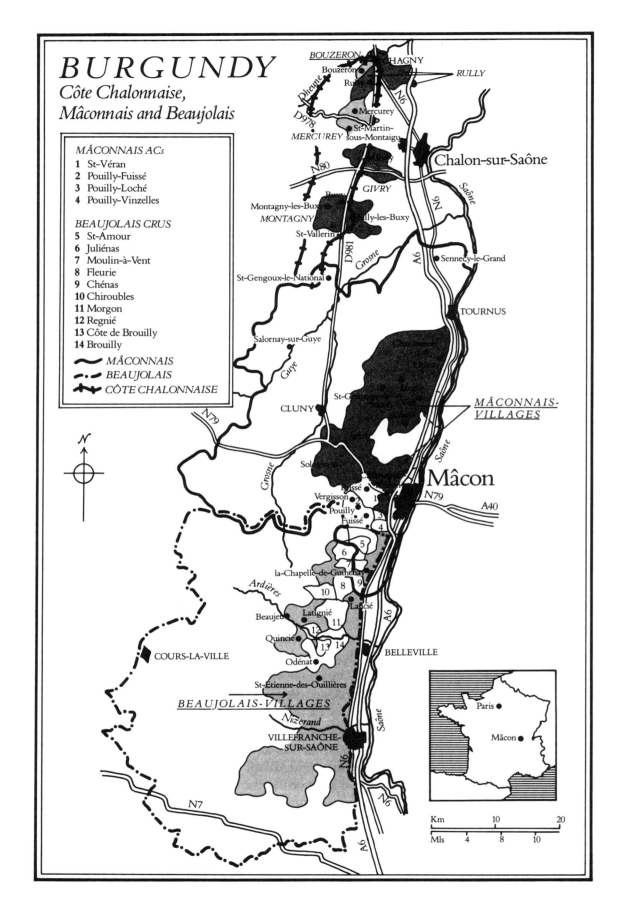

BURGUNDY
Côte Chalonnaise,
Mâconnais and Beaujolais

MÂCONNAIS ACs
1 St-Véran
2 Pouilly-Fuissé
3 Pouilly-Loché
4 Pouilly-Vinzelles

BEAUJOLAIS CRUS
5 St-Amour
6 Juliénas
7 Moulin-à-Vent
8 Fleurie
9 Chénas
10 Chiroubles
11 Morgon
12 Regnié
13 Côte de Brouilly
14 Brouilly

〜 MÂCONNAIS
-·-·- BEAUJOLAIS
✛ CÔTE CHALONNAISE

N

BOUZERON — CHAGNY
Bouzeron
Rully
RULLY

Dheune

D978

Mercurey

St-Martin-
MERCUREY sous-Montaigu

Givry

Saône

Chalon-sur-Saône

N6

N80

Buxy *GIVRY*

Montagny-les-Buxy
MONTAGNY Jully-les-Buxy
St-Vallerin

D981

Grosne

A6

Sennecy-le-Grand

St-Gengoux-le-National

TOURNUS

Salornay-sur-Guye

Guye

*MÂCONNAIS-
VILLAGES*

Grosne

CLUNY St-G

N79

Sol

Saône

Fuissé
Vergisson
Pouilly
Fuissé

Mâcon

N79 A40

3
4
5
6
7

la-Chapelle-de-Guinchay

Ardières

10 8 9
Lancié

Beaujeu
Latignié

11

Quincié
12
13 14
Odénat

A6

BELLEVILLE

COURS-LA-VILLE

St-Étienne-des-Ouillières

BEAUJOLAIS-VILLAGES

Nizerand

VILLEFRANCHE-
SUR-SAÔNE

Saône

N6

N6

N7

Paris
Mâcon

Km   10   20
Mls   4   8   10

CÔTE CHALONNAISE

	Surface area in hectares	*1996 harvest in hectolitres*		
		RED (69%)	WHITE (43%)	TOTAL
RULLY	297	4600	8200	12,800
MERCUREY	551	21,000	2700	23,7000
GIVRY	312	8800	1600	10,400
MONTAGNY	248	—	13,000	13,000
Total	1408	34,4000	25,500	59,900

In general there is little difference between the wines of the Côte Chalonnaise and the lighter wines of the Côte de Beaune. Broadly, the soils are the same, a mixture of different limestones and gravel and limestone mixed with clay. The grape varieties, Pinot Noir and Chardonnay, are used in both regions. The main difference is the microclimate of the vineyards. Lying at somewhere between 220 and 340 metres, their altitude is much the same as that of the Côte d'Or vineyards (though certain authorities would have you believe they are significantly higher) but they are less sheltered from the prevailing westerly wind, and, despite being further to the south, need more hours of sun to ripen fully and as a consequence are picked later.

The Côte Chalonnaise is not a monocultural vine-growing area. The surface under vine declined considerably after the phylloxera epidemic, and though it has increased in the last twenty years it is still but a shadow of what it was a century ago. For example, in 1860 there were 600 hectares under vine in Rully alone.

Instead, the vine occupies the particularly favoured sites – sheltered, well-exposed, gently sloping to the east or south-east, and on geologically correct, well-drained soil. This is the theory, at any rate. In practice, if a *vigneron* has so many hectares, absolutely every square metre will be planted, whether it is suitable or not, provided the law allows him to. At the same time the machinations of SAFER, a French bureaucratic body which authorizes transfers of land and changes in use, together with the chauvinistic attitude of the local left-wing political parties, means that it is difficult to increase the area under vine, much of which would be suitable, as well as for outsiders to come in and work the land. As a result, demand always exceeds supply.

BOUZERON

Travelling south the first village in the Côte Chalonnaise is Bouzeron. The area has long been renowned for its Aligoté wine, its reputation being acknowledged by the Abbé Courtepée in the eighteenth century; and in 1979 a special Bourgogne Aligoté de Bouzeron *appellation* was established, and in 1997 the village was elevated to a separate A.C. in its own right. In 1979 there were less than 20 hectares of

Aligoté in the commune, but this has now grown to 59 hectares, producing about 3000 hectolitres of wine a year.

According to Aubert de Villaine, the doyen of the village as well as co-proprietor of the Domaine de La Romanée-Conti, it is important to choose the right strain of Aligoté. The Aligoté Doré is much superior to the Aligoté Vert and gives a wine of greater perfume and elegance.

Monsieur Villaine makes a delightful Aligoté wine, as well as a fine Pinot Noir (Bourgogne Rouge La Digoine) and Chardonnay (Bourgogne Blanc Les Clous). Other local Aligoté enthusiasts are Pierre Cogny and Messieurs Chanzy (Domaine de L'Hermitage), Lechenault and Chemorin. The merchants Bouchard Père et Fils and Delorme have also made a speciality of this *appellation*. The Pinot Noir and Chardonnay wines of Bouzeron are now (as of 1990) *appellation* Bourgogne, Côte Chalonnaise.

RULLY

The vineyards of Rully begin in the suburbs of Chagny and continue south to the boundary with Mercurey. The Montagne de la Folie divides Rully from the commune of Bouzeron, and at the north end of this ridge, underneath a large water tower which you can see for miles, Xavier Noël-Bouton at the 18-hectare Domaine de La Folie produces some of the village's best wines. Though this small commune can boast no fewer than nineteen *premiers crus*, neither of Monsieur Noël-Bouton's Rully wines, the red Clos de Bellecroix made from Pinot Noir and the white Clos Saint-Jacques made from Chardonnay, is one.

The firm of Delorme, important proprietors throughout the Côte Chalonnaise, are perhaps the largest vineyard-owners in the commune. Their holdings include the 18-hectare *monopole* Rully Varots as well as other vineyards. These wines are sold under the name Domaine de La Renarde – somewhat confusingly as La Renarde is the name of one of Rully's *premiers crus*. Pierre Cogny of Bouzeron, Georges Duvernay, Eric de Suremain of the Château de Monthélie, and Armand Monassier are normally good sources, and I have had dependable wines from the Domaine Belleville, Raymond Bêtes, Michel Briday, Jean Daux, Henriette Niepce, René Ninot, André L'Héritier, Henri and Paul Jacquesson and Jean-Claude Brelière.

Rully produces roughly equal amounts of red and white wines. The white wines are lemony-crisp, not as fat as those of Montagny. Much of it goes to make the local sparkling wine, Crémant de Bourgogne. The reds are soft and less sturdy than those of Mercurey.

MERCUREY

Mercurey is a sizeable commune, larger than Gevrey-Chambertin which is the biggest on the Côte d'Or. It produces twice as much as either Nuits-Saint-Georges or Pommard and makes almost entirely red wine. The commune straddles the D978, the main road from Chalon to Autun, and includes the villages of Bourgneuf-Val d'Or and Saint-Martin-sous-Montaigu. As there is more wine to distribute, and as a number of well-known

Beaune *négociants* have vineyards in the commune, this is the Côte Chalonnaise's best-known red wine. It is also the most expensive. Whether the quality is worth the extra money is a moot point.

Five vineyards are currently entitled to call themselves *premiers crus*: Clos-du-Roi, Clos Voyen or Voyens, Clos-Marcilly, Clos-des-Fourneaux and Clos-des-Montaigus. Various others, including Les Champs Martins and Clos de Barraults, have in 1989 been proposed as additions to this list. The best known of these is Voyens which lies above Mercurey itself, on the south-facing slopes of a hill. Here there was once a Gallo-Roman temple dedicated to the god from which the village gets its name (Mercurey, the winged messenger, was also the god of commerce). There is now a windmill on the site.

The 23-hectare estate of Michel Juillot produces the best wines of Mercurey. His reds seem to achieve a depth and concentration, and also to have an elegance, which the others lack. Hugues de Suremain, a man whose personal finances must have taken quite some battering in recent years as, one by one, each of his nine daughters made her way to the altar, is another excellent local grower, with 12 hectares of vines. Émile Juillot, Paul de Launay and Jeannin-Naltet are also good producers. The wines of Luc Brinlet and Frédéric Charles, Delorme, Jean-Paul Granger, Paul Marceau, Jean Maréchal, Louis Menand, Jean-Pierre Meulien, Louis Modrin, Armand Monassier (Clos de la Vigne de Devant), Maurice Protheau, the Raquillet family, Fabien and Louis Saier and Émile Voarick are reliable. The *négociants* Bouchard Aîné et Fils and Maison Joseph Faiveley have sizeable holdings (Clos la Marche and the 65-hectare Domaine de la Croix Jacquelet respectively) while Antonin Rodet, who are based in the village, produce the wines of the Château de Chamirey as they do of the Château de Rully. The *négociant* François Protheau et Fils distributes the wines of the Domaine Maurice Protheau, but I cannot say that the wines have ever sung to me. The Domaine du Château de Santenay (Château Philippe Le Hardi) also has sizeable holdings in the commune. The best *négociant* wine from Mercurey after that of Faiveley is the Clos Fourtoul of Remoissenet which comes from Jacques Bordeaux-Montreiux, the proprietor of the Domaine Baron Thénard, who are the sole owners of this 4½-hectare vineyard.

Mercurey is the most structured of the Chalonnaise red wines, and this, in leaner years, can take the form of a rather stringy and skeletal character, lacking fruit and flesh. At its best it is rich and ample, though with a certain earthiness: the best of the Côte Chalonnaise reds.

GIVRY

The wines of Givry can be the most charming and the most stylish of the Côte Chalonnaise, though in structure more in the mould of Rully than of Mercurey. The commune lies to the south-east of Mercurey, across a gap of a few kilometres of woodlands and fields full of Charollais cattle. The best *climats* in Givry lie above the village, facing east towards the city of Chalon, and in the neighbouring villages of Jambles, Poncey and Russilly.

The soil here is just beginning to change from that of the marl and chalky limestone of the northern part of Burgundy to the richer, more sandy limestone of the Mâconnais. As in Mercurey, however, there is a little clay, and consequently the wines are predominantly red. Contrary to what is found elsewhere, according to the authoritative book *Terroirs et Vins de France*, it is the land which has the least clay which produces the best reds of Givry.

There is no official grading of the vineyards. Those generally regarded as the best include Clos Salomon, Clos Saint-Paul and Cellier-aux-Moines. Many of the labels will also inform you that Givry was *Le Préféré du Henri IV*. The Domaine Baron Thénard is the most important grower in the commune, with 18 hectares spread over three *climats*, including sole ownership of Clos-Saint-Pierre, which is bottled and sold by Remoissenet Père et Fils. I have enjoyed this wine for many years. Both Thénard and the Domaine Joblot have vines in the Cellier-aux-Moines and du Gardin is the sole owner of the 6-hectare Clos Salomon *climat*. These are all reliable producers. In addition there are the brothers Ragot, who also make white Givry, something of a rarity, René Bourgeon, Jean Chofflet, Thierry Lespinasse, the Lumpp frères, the Steinmayers of Buxy and Delorme (Clos du Cellier aux Moines).

MONTAGNY

Further south still, past the N80, the main road west from Chagny to Le Creusot, is Montagny, the last commune of the Côte Chalonnaise. Montagny's vineyards include those in the neighbouring villages of Buxy, Juilly and Saint-Vallerin. All Montagny wine is white, and, provided it reaches the necessary level of alcohol (11.5 degrees), it can be labelled *premier cru*.

This is potentially the best as well as the most substantial white wine of the region. It can be less crisp and flowery than Rully, fatter and more honeyed, sometimes nutty and sometimes broader. Under the label of a good merchant such as Louis Latour, who is prepared to age the wine in newish wood, a Montagny wine can be every bit as good as a lesser village wine from the Côte de Beaune – and excellent value.

The chief source of Montagny wine is the excellent Cave des Vignerons de Buxy, whose members own land amounting to 490 hectares in Montagny and the surrounding villages. The large co-operative also produces substantial quantities of Bourgogne Rouge and Blanc, and Aligoté and Passetoutgrains. Not surprisingly, this co-operative, under the able and enthusiastic direction of its director Roger Rajeot, is an impressively large concern. They are now vinifying and maturing more of their better Montagny wines in wood.

As you would expect, the non-oak-aged Montagny wines are best bottled and drunk young as if the wine were a Mâconnais. It is only recently that single-estate Montagny has begun to be seen abroad much. I am encouraged to find that more and more of these single-estate wines are also being fermented and aged in wood with the intention of producing a wine which can take bottle age. Among the best individual producers are Pierre Bernollin, Alain Roy (under the Château de la Saule label), Maxine Millet and Bernard Michel. The *négociant* Picard Père et Fils in Chagny distributes the wines of the Château de Davernay.

Mâconnais

The lush, rolling limestone hills of the Mâconnais form a natural interlude between the Côte d'Or and its satellite, the Côte Chalonnaise and the granite bedrock of the Beaujolais further south. As in the Côte d'Or, the white grape is the Chardonnay; as in the Beaujolais the red wines are predominantly produced from the Gamay. Climatically as well as geographically this is an area in transition between the North and South of France. It can be unexpectedly bitter in the winter, and spring frosts are an ever-present threat, but it is warm and balmy in high summer, and autumns are normally benign. I have picnicked in the shadows of the magnificent ruins of the Abbey of Cluny in late October. But I have had to scrape early-morning ice off my car windscreen in March.

This is a rich, polycultural region, extending from Sennecy-Le-Grand north of Tournus to the boundary between the Saône-et-Loire and Rhône departments south of Mâcon, reaching as far as Saint-Gengoux-Le-National and Salornay-sur-Guye in the hills to the west and confined by the river Saône to the east. The vine shares the countryside with Charollais cattle – Charolles itself is along the road from Mâcon to Paray-Le-Monial – and pasture alternates with fields of corn and maize and orchards of nuts and fruit; there are woods and meadows, sleepy villages each with its very own Romanesque church, or so it seems, and a large native population of goats.

Vinously this is a plentiful region; by no means as abundant as Beaujolais, but at least as generous as the Côte d'Or and the Côte Chalonnaise put together, for as well as a production of some 550,000 hectolitres under the various Mâconnais *appellations*, the bulk of the Saône-et-Loire department's yield of Bourgogne in its various forms comes from here. The wines are for the most part white, and largely produced by co-operatives, and they are increasingly well made. But they are wines for daily drinking in the year after the vintage. Only in the south, in Pouilly-Fuissé and its satellites, do the Mâconnais wines possess serious character. Only here will you find many individual domaines. Only here are there winemakers who vinify and mature their wines in new wood.

The landscape is at its most dramatic here in this southern part of the region. Aeons ago the undulating Jurassic limestone subsoil of the Mâconnais was forced up against the Hercynian granite bedrock of the Beaujolais. What is left after several millennia of erosion are two huge 500-metre cliffs looming above the villages of Vergisson and Solutré and the vineyards of Pouilly-Fuissé. On the lower slopes at the foot of these two rocks the vine is ideally exposed, bathed in sunshine from morning to night.

Pouilly-Fuissé itself is rich in pre-history. Solutré has given its name to a culture of the Stone Age, a period in the Upper Paleolithic between 15,000 and 12,000 BC. Solutréan man was one of the first to use flint arrowheads, and he formed needles out of reindeer bone. Hunting to him meant rounding up the local fauna – wild horses and deer – and he would then chase them to the top of the slope, create a hullabaloo by means of fire and loud noises and panic the animals into jumping over the cliff to their deaths. At the foot of Solutré there is an ossuary a metre thick and over a hectare in extent, a rather macabre memorial estimated at over 100,000 animal skeletons.

The vine arrived in Roman times but it was not until the founding of the abbey at Cluny in AD 910 that the Mâconnais became an important wine-producing region. It marked the start of an enormous expansion of the Benedictine movement, which at its height, with Cluny as its capital, held jurisdiction over 20,000 monks and 2000 dependent establishments stretching from Portugal to Poland.

Cluny and the other local churches – this area is a goldmine for anyone interested in Romanesque and early Gothic architecture – needed wine. The abbey itself housed 460 monks in 1155 and the abbot was said to be even more powerful than the Pope. The entertainment budget must have been colossal and most of the wine was consumed on the spot. It was only after the decline of Cluny's importance in the fifteenth and sixteenth centuries that it became necessary for the local growers to export their wines to other parts of France and elsewhere. Deprived of access to Franche-Comté and Alsace by the restrictive customs barriers so prevalent under the Ancien Régime, and obstructed from the nearby Pays Lyonnais, which was to all intents and purposes closed to wines made outside its jurisdiction, the Mâconnais wines were sent to Paris. Communications were almost impossible. To get to the Loire river, the gateway to the north, the casks would either have to be sent across country to Paray-Le-Monial and Digoin. Alternatively it was sent up the Saône to Chalon, thence to Dijon and over the hills to the Seine at Chatillon. The Canal du Centre which connects the Saône with the Loire was not opened until 1794. All three rivers were subject to flooding in the spring and drought in late summer. There were losses through accidents, faulty casks and robbery. Wine had to be set aside for consumption by the carriers *en route*, and the expense by way of local tolls and taxes or simply bribery was enormous. The journey would often take several months, by which time the wine was probably off.

One of the local heroes was Claude Brosse. Brosse, a giant of a man, had difficulty disposing of his harvest, and in 1660 decided to take it himself to the Court at Versailles. He yoked up his oxen, loaded his waggon with casks of his Mâcon and set off, braving the atrocious roads and the brigands who lay in wait for the unwary traveller. The journey took him a month. Once at Versailles he first met with little success, until his bulk attracted the attention of the Sun King. Louis XIV liked the wine, which he found better than those of the Loire currently fashionable in the capital, and gave him an order. His sycophantic courtiers followed suit. Brosse had ensured the commercial future of the Mâconnais wines.

The wine, though, was almost certainly red. White wines, until the time of the phylloxera epidemic, were of very secondary importance, fetching only half the price or less. Only in isolated pockets was the production of white wine a sensible proposition. André Jullien (*Topographie de Tous Les Vignobles Connus*, 1816) states that the local wine was generally red, and only mentions Pouilly, Fuissé and some of the adjoining communes as growths for white wine. Even by the end of the nineteenth century, eighty-odd years later, the position had little changed. As late as 1952 red wine made up 60 per cent of Mâconnais production.

Today the position is different. Mâcon Rouge finds few customers. If in Claude Brosse's day it was made from Pinot Noir it is now made from Gamay, and you only have to sneak a red Mâcon into a tasting of Beaujolais-Villages to see the difference. The Gamay simply produces a rather more interesting wine in the granite soil of Beaujolais than it does in a limestone Mâconnais vineyard. And the fashion for Chardonnay is today seemingly inexhaustible. Seventy per cent of the Mâconnais wine is now white and the percentage is increasing. The variety is exclusively Chardonnay for the superior wines with Pinot Blanc additionally permitted for the generic Mâcon *appellations*. Currently the Mâconnais is planted with 67 per cent Chardonnay (including a small proportion of Pinot Blanc), half a per cent of Aligoté, 25 per cent Gamay and 7.5 per cent Pinot Noir.

MÂCONNAIS

	Surface area in hectares	*Average production in hectolitres*	
		RED (15.1%)	WHITE (84.9%)
White wines			
POUILLY-FUISSÉ	741	—	44,000
POUILLY-VINZELLES	50	—	2900
POUILLY-LOCHE	522	—	1600
SAINT-VÉRAN	522	—	34,000
MÂCON BLANC VILLAGES	3110	—	215,000
MÂCON/MÂCON SUPÉRIEUR (BLANC)		—	
Red wines			
MÂCON SUPÉRIEUR (ROUGE)	835	53,000	—
Total	5287	53,000	297,500
		350,500	

There are in addition 3686 hectares producing Bourgogne (Rouge, Blanc, Aligoté), Bourgogne Passetoutgrains and Bourgogne Grand Ordinaire in the Saône-et-Loire. Most of this is in the Mâconnais rather than in the Côte Chalonnaise. The average annual production of these generic wines is a total of 220,00- hectolitres.

MÂCON and MÂCON SUPÉRIEUR

Red Mâcon can either be basic Mâcon Rouge or Macon Rouge Supérieur, the latter indicating a higher alcohol level and forming the vast bulk of this joint *appellation*. While in theory the wine can come from Pinot Noir, in practice it is made from Gamay, the wine made from Pinot Noir being sold as Bourgogne Rouge and attracting a higher price. Red Mâcon is a robust, earthy sort of wine, fuller than Beaujolais and without its class, certainly when compared with Beaujolais-Villages.

Mâcon Blanc and Mâcon Blanc Supérieur, the latter being higher in alcohol, are made from Chardonnay and come from that part of the region outside the delimited Mâcon-Blanc-Villages area. The wines are less fine, but then they are cheaper.

MÂCON-BLANC-VILLAGES

Well-made Mâcon-Blanc-Villages is in my view the ideal all-purpose wine, and is consumed in great quantities at Château Coates. This is Chardonnay at its most open and appealing: soft and crisp, reliable year in year out, never unduly acidic, invariably plump and fruity: a wine of quality and interest but a wine without pretension.

The best Mâcon-Blanc comes from a delimited region of forty-two villages which lie mainly in the southern section of Mâconnais, beginning at the village of Chardonnay, from which the grape variety itself might have been named, and continuing to the boundary with Beaujolais in the deep south. The wine can be labelled as Mâcon-Blanc-Villages, or as Mâcon followed by the name of the village itself. Forty-two is a large number and in practice the most commonly found names are Lugny, Viré, Prissé and Clessé, though I have seen both Macon-Fuissé and Mâcon-Vinzelles, *appellations* I would suggest are rather confusing. Some of the rest, like Romanèche-Thorins and Saint-Amour, are really part of the Beaujolais region and produce little white wine.

The wines vary from commune to commune as well as from winemaker to winemaker (though this is a region dominated by the co-operative movement). Those of Lugny are rich and nutty, fuller than the more fragrant delicate wines of Prissé, for instance; those of Viré are also quite full, occasionally a little four-square. The co-operatives in all three villages produce quality wines, as do those at Chardonnay, Azé and Igé.

Apart from selling wine directly under their own label, the co-operatives are also the chief source of supply to the local and Burgundian merchants. The following merchants can be recommended: Georges Duboeuf, Louis Tête and Dépagneux, among the local *négociants*, and Louis Latour (especially for Mâcon-Lugny, Les Genevrières), Louis Jadot and Joseph Drouhin (for Mâcon-Villages Laforet) in Beaune. Jean Thévenet and Jean Signoret at Clessé, André Bonhomme at Viré, Henri Goyard at the Domaine de Roally in the same village and the Château de Viré, distributed by Prosper Maufoux, are the leading independent estates. Also recommended are the Domaine Manciat-Poncet at Lévigny near Charnay, the Belgians Guffens-Heynen in Vergisson (expensive but excellent), Paul and Philibert Talmard in Uchizy and Henri Lafarge in Bray.

SAINT-VÉRAN

The *appellation* of Saint-Véran, created in 1971, was one of the first *appellations* whose wines had to be approved by a tasting panel, now compulsory everywhere else. The region was carved out of various villages in the southern Mâcon-Villages adjacent to the Pouilly-Fuissé area, many of which overlapped into the neighbouring Beaujolais. The white wines here had formerly been labelled Beaujolais Blanc, a wine which is now as a consequence much less common. The Saint-Véran villages are Chânes, Chasselas, Leynes, Saint-Amour, Saint-Vérand (with a 'd'), plus part of Solutré (those vineyards not entitled to produce Pouilly-Fuissé) and Davayé and Prissé north of the Pouilly-Fuissé area. Beaujolais Blanc now comes from the following four communes: Saint-Amour and Chânes (both also authorized for Saint-Véran), Crêches and Chaintré (part of whose vineyards are also allowed to make Pouilly-Fuissé).

As you might expect, the wines of Saint-Véran are a sort of halfway house between those of the Mâcon-Villages and those of Pouilly-Fuissé though prices are nearer to the former than the latter. Saint-Véran in my view is very good value. The *négociant* Georges Duboeuf produces some excellent wines, mainly coming from the *cave* at Prissé. Messieurs Corsin, Luquet, Pacquet, Tissier, Jean Bernard, the Lycée Agricole at Davayé, and Monsieur Vincent of Pouilly's Château Fuissé, all produce fine examples.

POUILLY-LOCHÉ and POUILLY-VINZELLES

Loché and Vinzelles are satellites of the four Pouilly-Fuissé communes. As they are separated from the hamlet of Pouilly itself by the commune of Fuissé one finds it hard not to accuse them of special pleading in their selection of this famous prefix. No doubt Fuissé-Loché or Vinzelles-Fuissé would not have worked quite such effective magic!

The magic, though, doesn't seem to be that potent. These are two very small *appellations*, and though one does see Pouilly-Vinzelles I have rarely encountered Pouilly-Loché. Even Vinzelles is hard to sell.

Most of the wine is supplied by the Cave des Grands Crus Blancs in Vinzelles, which serves both communes. Messieurs Martin and Mathias, the Berard family at the Domaine Saint Philibert, Georges Duboeuf and Loron are other important producers, the latter with the exclusivity of the Château de Vinzelles. In general you will pay higher prices for these wines than for Saint-Véran, but not necessarily get better wine. For some reason, the wine of Pouilly-Loché can be labelled as Pouilly-Vinzelles; but not vice versa.

POUILLY-FUISSÉ

Despite not being an easy name for English speakers to pronounce, Pouilly-Fuissé is a wine of enormous popularity on the export market, particularly in the United States. This is for two reasons: first it is made from the ever-popular Chardonnay, and second – normally, at any rate – it occupies the perfect psychological position on many a restaurant wine list. Pouilly-Fuissé is neither so cheap that it appears mean to select it, nor is it so expensive the businessman will have his expenses queried.

But it is not always so. Such is the demand, the growers have sometimes let the blood rush to their heads. Prices have regularly see-sawed between the normal and the ridiculous. The 1978s and the '85s were only two recent examples when prices hit the roof. At least these were good vintages. The 1972s were another story. There is usually some trigger to cause this high price: a small crop or a winter frost after the vintage. Whatever the excuse the effect is an over-reaction. As a result the bottom falls out of the market, sales evaporate to a dribble and one has to wait for a couple of vintages before reason once more rears its noble head. I wonder when the growers will ever learn.

The Pouilly-Fuissé vineyards extend over four communes. Running from north-west to south-east these are Vergisson, Solutré, Fuissé and Chaintré, the latter lying underneath Vinzelles. Pouilly itself is a small hamlet on the Solutré-Fuissé border.

Dominating the area are the twin cliffs of Vergisson and Solutré. On the lower slopes beneath these crags the vines are well protected and enjoy sunshine from morning to night. With the benefit of a warmer climate than in the Côte Chalonnaise or the Côte d'Or to add to this excellent exposure the Chardonnay grape often ripens to a potential 14 degrees of alcohol. This is a dangerous drawback as Pouilly-Fuissé wines can be too heavy – carthorses rather than thoroughbreds. This problem has been recognized for some time. Jullien in 1816 says that the wines are rich, elegant, full-bodied and attractive; they have a good bouquet, but 'they are accused, with reason, of being too *fumeux* [alcoholic]'. There have been vintages such as 1983 and '75 when the wines have even had an element of *pourriture noble*.

There are small differences between the wines of the four communes. Fuissé has the best reputation; Chaintré the least. Solutré produces the wines with the most body, but additionally has a tendency to coarseness; those of Vergisson have the most delicacy; in Fuissé there is some clay so the wines are structured; those of Pouilly are more *tendre*, they have more *finesse*. As always, the quality of the wine-making is as important as the specific geographical origin.

There are fundamental differences in wine-making techniques. Elsewhere in the Mâconnais the wines rarely see any wood. Stainless steel or concrete is the order of the day, and the wines are generally in bottle by May following the vintage. Some Pouilly-Fuissé is made in the same way. Others are made as in the Côte d'Or with vinification and *élevage* in oak. Elsewhere there is a mixture of methods, oak-fermented wine being later blended with wine which has not seen wood to produce a uniform blend.

The estate with the highest reputation is that of Jean-Jacques Vincent at Château Fuissé. The domaine occupies 24 hectares and produces three wines: Pouilly-Fuissé 'Cuvée Première', Château Fuissé and Château Fuissé Vieilles Vignes. Fermentation takes place in wood, 20 per cent of which is new. The wines are not bottled until they are a year old. As elsewhere in the region, the malolactic fermentation is not automatically sought after. In years of great ripeness, when the natural acidity level is low, it is avoided. The wines then spend a few months in wood, after which they are moved to tank to await bottling. These are subtle, ripe, balanced wines, with a honey and depth which could easily be mistaken for Meursault.

Other leading estates are those of Messieurs Besson (Domaine de Pouilly), Burrier (Château Beauregard), Cordier, Corsin, Curveux, Depardon, Ferret, Forest (both André and Michel), Leger-Plumet, Luquet, Mathias, Noblet and Paquet. The Belgian couple Jean-Marie and Germaine Guffens only arrived in the Mâconnais in 1980, but their extraordinary, almost paranoiac perfectionism produces excellent wines, albeit at a price.

Fine Pouilly-Fuissé can be found at the firm of Georges Duboeuf, who sells the wine of his brother's estate among others, at Louis Tête and the rest of the reputable local *négociants*, and from the leading Beaune merchants such as Louis Latour, Louis Jadot and Joseph Drouhin. The small grower/*négociant* Auvigne, Burrier et Revel produces several excellent examples.

Pouilly-Fuissé is rarely a wine which you would term elegant. The wine is larger than life: full bodied, fat, rich, exotic and often leaving the mouth with a burn of alcohol. It is an ample wine, but too often it will have a decided lack of acidity and will age badly. The 1986s, two years on, were already showing signs of falling apart in many cases.

Beaujolais

There are two places on the long journey from Paris to the Mediterranean coast where I always feel one moves from one climate zone to another. One is obvious, and will be recognized by anyone who has made this journey – somewhere between Valence and Montélimar in the Rhône Valley the countryside and the weather changes: you enter Provence. Further north there is another more subtle transition. Round about Mâcon the air becomes sweeter and warmer as you journey south. The countryside is lusher and riper. Small vineyards alternate with tiny villages, with copses of deciduous trees and meadows occupied by a few dozen Charollais cattle. Instead of the broad, treeless, windswept expanses of northern France, or the regimented, dry-stone-wall-divided vineyards of the Côte d'Or, the whole thing is more haphazard. The elements which make up the landscape come in smaller pieces and the countryside is noticeably more undulating. Even the buildings have changed. Roofs are flatter, the brick a softer shade of pink or dull brown changing as one travels further to a golden yellow; backdoors are open, the windows less firmly shuttered; chairs and tables under the refreshing shade of a venerable oak indicate that more life is spent outside in the open. There is an assumption of sun. This is the populous, hospitable, easy-going and now prosperous region of Beaujolais – home to one of the world's most popular wines.

It was not always thus. As we look back from the beginning of the 1990s it is difficult to realize that only since the Second World War has Beaujolais been widely drunk outside Lyon and the surrounding countryside. Only since then has the wine been regarded as more than just a relatively unimportant local *vin de pays*. Indeed it has been suggested that vines were first widely planted on a commercial scale only as recently as the early nineteenth century. Before the Revolution it was one of the most wretched and sparsely populated regions of France, comments Anthony Hanson in his book, *Burgundy*. Two things then happened. The large aristocratic estates were divided up and sold to the local peasantry, and with the elimination of internal customs barriers and improvements to the local roads it became easier to open up markets in Paris and elsewhere.

For some reason – a combination of ignorance, convenience, inertia and habit – Beaujolais is regarded as part of Burgundy. This is a misnomer. Geographically, yes, they are adjacent, but geologically and climatically they are vastly different. More importantly the wine is vastly different. It is made from a different grape and it is vinified in a different way. It need hardly be said that as a consequence the flavour of a true Beaujolais is totally unlike that of a true Burgundy even if the two bottles might hail from the same merchant in Beaune. Beaujolais is a separate entity, even if the custom has decreed that somehow it must be slipped in as a sort of Burgundian lesser relation.

Beaujolais is a large region. Vineyards total 22,400 hectares and produce about 13 million hectolitres annually: almost three times as much as red wine as in Burgundy proper, i.e. the Yonne, the Côte d'Or and the Saône-et-Loire put together, generics included. It is a prolific region. The above figures translate into over 60 hectolitres per hectare. It is a prosperous region. Fifty per cent of the harvest is exported and about this same proportion is annually sold as Beaujolais Nouveau, shipped in mid-November and drunk by Christmas: good cash-flow for one and all.

The area is bounded by the river Saône to the east (in practice the vines stop at the N6 between Mâcon and Lyon) and by the upper slopes of the Monts du Beaujolais to the west, where the vines are cultivated up to an altitude of about 500 metres. To the north there is no real dividing line. At some point roughly due west of Mâcon the Chardonnay of the Mâconnais gives way to the Gamay. To the south there is a somewhat arbitrary line along the N7 which runs between Lyon and Roanne. South of this the Monts du Beaujolais become the Monts du Lyonnais, and Beaujolais becomes Coteaux du Lyonnais, promoted from VDQS to AC in 1984.

Except for a minute amount of Chardonnay-based Beaujolais Blanc on the Mâconnais border, and an equally tiny portion of rosé, all Beaujolais is red, both rosé and red made from the Gamay Noir à Jus Blanc. Elsewhere this Gamay produces rather a dull wine. In the Loire it is light, often with rather more pronounced acidity than ripe fruit, one-dimensional; a carafe wine with little individuality. In the Ardèche or further south the grape may ripen more, but added sun does not bring additional character or elegance to the wine. Only in Beaujolais does the Gamay come into its own.

The reason is a particular vinification process, an adaptation of the classic system of carbonic maceration. In Beaujolais vinification takes place in a small closed vat, ideally no larger than 60 hectolitres. These are filled, but not filled to bursting, with whole, uncrushed, un-destalked bunches of grapes. The weight of the grapes releases some juice and this, warmed if necessary to get the fermentation going, is pumped over the mass of fruit. Carbon dioxide is formed by the fermentation which subsequently takes place, largely within the grapes themselves, and this blankets the top of the vats, enabling the process to take place in anaerobic conditions. The ideal temperature, controlled in the best establishments, is between 25°C and 28°C. Maceration takes place for five to six days, after which the free-run juice, now about 50 per cent of the eventual total, is racked off. The remaining pulp is pressed to extract further juice, this is added to the free-run juice, and the fermentation process continues normally.

Today, practically all Beaujolais is produced by this 'semi-maceration' method, as it is known, and few wines are matured in oak outside the top domaines of the firmer *crus*. One or two estates such as Jadot's Château des Jacques in Moulin-à-Vent remain faithful to the traditional vinification techniques as practised further north in the Côte Chalonnaise or in the Côte d'Or. These wines are quite different, having a size and, particularly, a tannin content and potential for development that 'modern' Beaujolais does not possess. I do not think, though, that they are any better for it. Good Beaujolais is a wine with a natural 11 to 11.5 degrees of alcohol which has probably been chaptalized up by another degree. It is a light red wine, not at all tannic, purple in colour, abundantly fruity and not a bit heavy or sweet. It is bottled early.

The bottling machines do not stand idle after the Nouveau rush but move straight into bottling the generic wines for consumption immediately after Christmas. By Easter even the solidest Moulin-à-Vent is usually in bottle. And it is a wine for drinking early. Beaujolais, whatever its designation, is a wine whose charm and character are in its youthful, perfumed, immediately appealing fruit. It is soft and should be utterly delicious and *gouleyant* (gulpable). Because Beaujolais is a wine without tannin, without structure, without real concentration and richness it will not age. It will not be transformed into something of depth and complexity by being imprisoned in bottle. It will merely get dreary. Some will tell you a fine Moulin-à-Vent will change into something resembling a Pinot Noir Burgundy if given age. It won't. This is not to say the wines won't keep; any wine of balance and fruit will last if stored correctly. But it won't improve. On the contrary it will merely become a rather strange brew of indeterminate character, of academic interest only. Most Beaujolais should be consumed within a year or at most two after the vintage.

BEAUJOLAIS and BEAUJOLAIS-VILLAGES

The most important distinction in Beaujolais is between plain Beaujolais (or Beaujolais Supérieur, an *appellation* rarely seen and indicating another degree of alcohol) and Beaujolais-Villages. This is not so much a question of alcoholic levels, though there are differences – half a degree more alcohol for Beaujolais-Villages than Beaujolais Supérieur at 10.5 degrees and a reduction in basic yield from 50 hectolitres per hectare to 40 hectolitres – as of location, geology and viticultural practices.

The northern part of the Beaujolais hills is formed of granite rock. The Mâconnais hills are limestone, the lower part of the Beaujolais region is sedimentary clay and more limestone. Between the two, roughly between latitudinal lines running west of Villefranche and Mâcon, lies the Beaujolais-Villages area. This is the true heartland of the Gamay. Here it is pruned to the *taille gobelet*, no more than five stumps each with two fruit-bearing buds.

In the south or Bas-Beaujolais, the *taille guyot* or long cane-pruning, is permitted. The wine is lighter. Most is sold if not as Nouveau in the winter and spring following the harvest, and is tired by the summer holidays. There is a lot of it – 670,915 hectolitres from 10,244 hectares in 1996, which means, of the surface area figures I have been given are correct, a yield of over 64 hectolitres per hectare. No wonder the wine is light! Drink a simple Beaujolais without pomp or ceremony. Do not look for majesty or complexity. Drink it cool and drink it soon.

Beaujolais-Villages is altogether different. It is Beaujolais' greatest bargain. For hardly one franc more you will get a wine of much greater consequence. For a start the soil north of the river Nizerand, which flows out of the Beaujolais hills into the Saône at Villefranche, is granite-based. This gives the wine an added individuality, an added bite. The wines are a little bit fuller and a lot more concentrated. More importantly they have a great deal more character. I don't understand why anyone bothers with straight Beaujolais instead of 'Villages'.

Beaujolais-Villages can come from any one of thirty-seven different communes, and you occasionally see it with the name of the commune hyphenated onto the word Beaujolais instead of 'Villages'.

In 1996 366,176 hectolitres were produced from 5900 hectares of Beaujolais-Villages vines, giving a yield of just on 60 hectolitres per hectare. There are many hundreds of individual producers of Beaujolais-Villages, many of whom also make *cru* Beaujolais. I list some of my favourites on page 185.

BEAUJOLAIS *CRUS*

There are ten *crus*. The villages run in a line from Saint-Amour in the north to Brouilly in the south, and occupy the best, north-eastern section of the Beaujolais-Villages.

BEAUJOLAIS *CRUS*

(in ascending order of weight and approximate price)

	Surface area in hectares	Average production in hectolitres
BROUILLY	1276	72,099
CÔTE DE BROUILLY	270	17,609
CHIROUBLES	363	21,100
RÉGNIÉ	629	31,409
MORGON	1125	64,119
FLEURIE	836	47,854
CHÉNAS	270	16,450
SAINT-AMOUR	292	18,213
JULIÉNAS	583	34,605
MOULIN-À-VENT	612	38,550
Total	6256	362,008

Brouilly is the largest and southernmost *cru*, extending through a number of neighbouring communes round the conical hill of Mont Brouilly. The wine is crisp and flowery, light in style, but not without zip. I find Côte de Brouilly, the wine from the slopes of Mont Brouilly itself, normally has more definition as well as power, and it is usually just a little more expensive. Régnié is a new *appellation* created in 1988, and lies between Brouilly and Morgon, but slightly to the west, overlapping into the commune of Durette. The wines are similar in style to those of Morgon. Moving north you next come to the large and well-known *cru* of Morgon itself. The Brouilly. Moving north you next come to the large and well-known *cru* of Morgon. The district is divided by the Mont du Py, south of which is the hamlet of Bas-Morgon. Here the wines tend to be lighter, more like Brouilly, than those made on the slopes of the hill or to the north round the more important village of Villié-Morgon. These denser Morgon wines can be quite hard when young and often are not at their best until the late summer or autumn after the vintage. The reason for this is said to be Morgon's own particular soil, a degenerated schist called *roche pourrie*. Prices of Morgon today no longer command the premium over Côte de Brouilly that they used to but I find the wines more interesting.

Chiroubles lies up in the hills north-west of Morgon and south-west of Fleurie. Very popular in France, and consequently expensive, it never seems to have really caught on abroad. In style the wines are like a soft, even more gently fruity version of Fleurie. They develop early. At their best they are wines of real delicacy and finesse.

Fleurie. Ah, what a success story! The easiest *cru* to pronounce; one of the easiest to enjoy; certainly the easiest to sell; and now more expensive than Moulin-à-Vent, hitherto the most expensive of all Beaujolais *crus*. The name suggests the wine to be flowery. I find it the epitome of gentle, velvety fruit. A good Fleurie is a wine of medium weight which has an ample flavour absolutely crammed full with this fruit and is overwhelmingly seductive. Some Fleurie wines can be already delicious in the spring after the vintage. Others need keeping for another six months.

Fleurie has a well-known co-operative, for many years presided over by Madame Marguerite Chabert, a lady of formidable force and personality. Overlooking the village is the Chapelle de la Madone perched on top of a little hill. This is an important *lieu-dit* and source of many of Fleurie's best wines.

Moulin-à-Vent and Chénas have become almost interchangeable; Chénas, from the French word for oak (*chêne*), comes from the higher ground above the village itself and Moulin-à-Vent from the flatter land running down towards Romanèche-Thorins. The surface soil at Moulin-à-Vent is a curious pink sand, the colour coming from a high incidence of manganese in the soil. There is no village of Moulin-à-Vent, merely the famous ruined windmill.

Moulin-à-Vent is the most structured, the most powerful, and up to now the most expensive of all the *crus*, while Chénas is a little lighter, as well as having less definition. Moulin-à-Vent has the deepest colour, the most body, the richest fruit, and normally needs a year before it shows itself at its best. Is it the best Beaujolais? For those to whom size is all-important, the answer is probably yes. I prefer to be caressed rather than bludgeoned and usually I'd rather cuddle up with a good Fleurie.

Juliénas is in my view the most underrated of the Beaujolais *crus*. Currently sold for the same level as Brouilly (indeed Brouilly, Côte de Brouilly, Morgon and Juliénas are all more or less the same price, while Chiroubles is 10 per cent more, Moulin-à-Vent 20 to 25 per cent more and Fleurie 25 to 30 per cent more) it is surely underpriced. The vineyards lie on high ground north and west of Chénas. Juliénas wines have a firm, full structure, not as rich or powerful as Moulin-à-Vent, nor as seductively fruity as Fleurie, but develop to wines of considerable depth, at their best by no means inferior to the best of these two communes. Like Chiroubles, and for the same reason – the vines being on higher ground – Juliénas often does better than its neighbours in years of great heat prior to the vintage and indeed in other years spoiled by rain. Even in well-nigh 'perfect' years, Juliénas can be the most successful *cru*.

With Saint-Amour we are at the northernmost limits of the granitic soil and the vineyards of the Beaujolais. Saint-Amour is a small commune and I find that the wines have something of the character of Gamays from the Mâconnais. They are fullish and more sturdy, less racy than the other Beaujolais *crus*.

BEAUJOLAIS PRODUCERS

Traditionally the chief source of good Beaujolais has been the *négociant*. While the Côte d'Or-based Burgundian merchant will invariably have a range of Beaujolais on his list it is my experience that most of these leave something to be desired. Like the *négociants'* Burgundies there is more of a common denominator – the house style – in their wines and less of the individuality that there should be from *cru* to *cru*.

Better are the local merchants, specialists as they should be in the wines of the region, and best still those who are able to offer a range of individual growers' wines. Among these I would particularly single out Louis Tête in Saint Didier-Sur-Beaujeu, Trenel in Charnay-Lès-Mâcons (who also make very good Crème de Cassis), Chanut Frères in Romanèche-Thorins, Jacques Dépagneux in Villefranche, Loron in Pontanévaux, Paul Beaudet, also in Pontanévaux, Pierre Ferraud and Sylvian Fessy in Belleville, Sarrau in Saint Jean d'Ardières and Gobet in Blaceret. Each of these, as well as offering their own blends, will be able to offer you their wines of individual growers with whom they have some sort of farming, bottling or marketing arrangement. Additionally, a small number of growers have formed their own bottling and marketing organization called Un Éventail de Vignerons Producteurs. Meanwhile, while the thriving local co-operative organizations – there are eighteen co-operative cellars in Beaujolais – are free to individually sell *cuvées* of wine to the merchants, they too now have a central bottling and marketing organization known as the Cellier des Samsons.

The king of Beaujolais, however, is Georges Duboeuf. The rise, expansion and success of the Duboeuf empire over the last twenty-five years has been remarkable and he now controls perhaps as much as 10 per cent of the entire annual Beaujolais business. His family are winemakers in Pouilly-Fuissé. Leaving his elder brother to manage the vineyard, Duboeuf set up as a broker in the 1960s. To broking he added contract bottling, moving round from property to property with a mobile machine in order to be able to offer his growers the marketing advantage of being able to print '*mise en bouteille au domaine*' on their labels. From then it was a small step to marketing their wines himself.

Duboeuf's genius is his ability to judge a wine, often before the fermentation is completed, and his unerring nose for the very best. An assiduous competition participant, his wines regularly win more gold medals in one season at the various fairs in Villefranche, Mâcon and elsewhere than others in a lifetime. Invariably Duboeuf wines win the Prix Bacchus (for the best Beaujolais *cru* of the year) and the Coupe Dailly (best Saint-Véran). Inevitably, the range of different wines Duboeuf can offer is wider than most. What is remarkable is that, despite the size of the operation today, there seems to be no deterioration in quality.

BEAUJOLAIS AND BEAUJOLAIS-VILLAGES

Among the many estates individually bottled and marketed by Georges Duboeuf are Château de Bluizard (who also make an excellent Brouilly), Domaine du Colombier and Château de Vierres. Members of the Éventail de Vignerons Producteurs include André Jaffre (Domaine de Chêne), Jean Verger, Francis Crot and Jean-Luc Tissier (Domaine des Esservies). Loron's Château de la Roche and Cuvée de Fondateur are normally reliable as are the best Villages *cuvées* of the co-operatives at Régnié and Juliénas (the latter known as Château du Bois de la Salle). Château Gaillard and Domaine Saint-Charles are also recommended. One of the best areas for Villages wines has always been Régnié and Durette and now promoted to *cru*.

BROUILLY AND CÔTE DE BROUILLY

Through Duboeuf you can buy the Château de Bluizard, though the Saint-Charles family now independently sell their Domaine de Conroy. Other Duboeuf wines include the

Domaines of Combillaty, Garange, Nervers, La Roche, Nazins, and Voujan in Brouilly, and Chavannes and Taillard in Côte de Brouilly. Another branch of the Geoffray family, proprietors of Chavannes, owns the Château Thivin in Brouilly, which, like many estates in the area, produces both *appellations*. Members of the Éventail include André Large, Lucien and Robert Verger and André Ronzières. A different style of wine – meatier, less *primeur* – is produced at Château des Tours.

MORGON

Jean Descombes (from Duboeuf) is recognized as having some of the best vines in the *appellation*. Duboeuf also supplies the Morgons of the Princesse de Lievin and Monsieur Marmonnier at the Domaine de Versands. The Lievin wines also appear independently under the label of Château de Bellevue. Paul Collonge at the Domaine de Ruyère, Noel Ancoeur at Le Rochaud and the Brisson family at the Domaine des Pillets are also good. Members of the Éventail include Louis Desvignes and Georges Brun. Loron produce Morgon 'Fontcraine' and Domaine des Vieux Cèdres. Finally the Domaine du Py of the Savoye family is a good source of Morgon.

CHIROUBLES

Among the top Duboeuf wines are the Château de Javernaud of Monsieur Fourneau, Domaine Desmures and those of René Méziat and Pierre Savoye. Pride of place should go to the Raousset family though. Their wine is sometimes sold as Château les Prés. Members of the Éventail include Georges Passot (Domaine de la Grosse Pierre) and René Savoye. Another Méziat is Gérard-Roger at the Domaine de la Combe au Loup.

FLEURIE

My favourite Fleurie is often Roger Darrose's Domaine des Quatre Vents, available from Duboeuf. This firm also bottles Fleurie from the Château de Raousset, Guy Depardon (Domaine du Point du Jour), and the Château de Déduits. Monsieur Manon's wine appears under the La Madone label, picturing the chapel at the top of the hill above the village. The *négociant* Loron sell the important Château de Fleurie of Madame Roclore. The Domaine de Montgenas is a member of the Éventail. Michel Chignard at les Moriers, Yvonne Couibes and Fernard Ferepoix at Clos de la Chapelle des Bois and Jean Matroy at Logis du Vivier are other good sources, as is the co-operative.

MOULIN-À-VENT AND CHÉNAS

The two most celebrated domaines in Moulin-à-Vent are the Château du Moulin-à-Vent, owned by the Bloud family, and the Domaine de la Tour de Bief, owned by the Comte de Sparre. Duboeuf sells some of the former and all of the latter, as he does of the Clos du Moulin-à-Vent owned by the Tagent family, Marius Laforet and Lucien Charvet. The local co-operative is misleadingly called the Château de Chênas (sold both through the Éventail and independently) and produce both *appellations*. Individual growers who sell their own wine include Jean Benon and Henri Lespinasse, who also have vines in Juliénas, while Devillane, Alphonse Mortet and Jean Brugne sell through the Éventail.

REGNIE

Promoted from Beaujolais Villages in 1989. Similar to Morgon.

JULIÉNAS

The Château de Juliénas, owned by François Condemine, is sold by Duboeuf, as is another Condemine domaine, La Seigneurie, and the Domaine des Vignes and the Domaine des

Mouilles. The *négociants* Loron sell the Domaine de la Vieille Église and Sarreau the Château des Capitans. Among the Éventail members are the excellent André Pelletier and René Monnet, two of the best growers in this organization. Monnet's wine comes from part of the Château de Juliénas' vineyard. The best of the independent growers is probably Ernest Aujas. The co-operative, Château du Bois de la Salle has a good reputation (and also produces Saint-Amour).

SAINT-AMOUR

Loron's Domaine de Billards is one of their best Beaujolais wines. From Duboeuf you can obtain the wines of the Domaines of Pins, Paradis and Sablons. It was Jackie Juillard who won the Prix Bacchus for the best Beaujolais *cru* in 1986. Jean Patissier's 'Côte de Besset' is sold through the Éventail. Elie Mongénie, an old boy who is a friend of Ernest Aujas, is well respected. André Poitevin sells some of his wine to Duboeuf and the rest independently. Monsieur Giraudin's Château de Saint-Amour is worth investigating, as is the wine of François Saillant.

COTEAUX DU LYONNAIS

South of Beaujolais, stretching round the western hills and suburbs of the vast city of Lyon, is the Coteaux du Lyonnais, promoted from VDQS to full *appellation contrôlée* in 1984. The wine is largely red, made from the Gamay grape and is similar in style to an ordinary Beaujolais, though it is normally lighter and more ephemeral. Since gaining its *appellation* the district has expanded and the quality has improved, though the wine is still rarely seen outside the region. The *appellation* covers 323 hectares and produced 14,262 hectolitres in 1996. Of this some 500 hectolitres was white wine, which can come from Chardonnay, Aligoté and Melon (or Gamay Blanc). The local co-operatives are the main source, and the wines are now being sold by some of the Beaujolais merchants such as Georges Duboeuf.

VIN DE PAYS

VIN DE PAYS DE L'YONNE

This is a white wine – a sort of young-vine Chablis – from the Chablis/Auxerre area, and usually in my experience comes from the Chardonnay grape. I have seen some interesting examples. William Fèvre, the Chablis grower, makes an oaky Vin de Pays de l'Yonne. The wine from Laroche is another good example.

VIN DE PAYS DE LA CÔTE D'OR

This is one of the more obscure *vins de pays*, an *appellation* I have rarely seen in Burgundy, let alone abroad. The wine comes from Pinot Noir and Gamay, and can also be made from Chardonnay and Aligoté, though I have only ever seen two versions. Most, if not all, comes from the co-operative at Sainte-Marie-La-Blanche in the plain east of Beaune. Their Pinot Noir is a little rustic but not too bad.

Chapter 3

THE LOIRE VALLEY

The urban centre of France is, of course, Paris; the spiritual heart is Reims where the French kings were crowned – or perhaps the Basilica of Saint-Denis outside Paris, where their mortal remains lay buried until desecrated during the Revolution. But for nine hundred years between the time that Charles Martel defeated the Moors at Poitiers in AD 732 and the ascent of the Sun King, Louis XIV to the throne the Loire Valley was the focus, the amphitheatre on which the history of France was enacted in peace and in war, in public and in private. In the castle of Chinon, Henry Plantagenet, having imprisoned his wife, the redoubtable Eleanor of Aquitaine, in England, died a solitary death, attended only by the faithful William Marshall. In Chinon 150 years later, Joan of Arc identified her dauphin cowering among his courtiers. At Blois the cavalier Salamander, François I, presided over a Renaissance court of quite spectacular and conspicuous expenditure, even attracting Leonardo da Vinci who spent the last years of his life in France and is buried at Amboise. At Nantes the famous Edict of 1598 was enacted by that cool and imaginative genius Henri IV, ensuring freedom of religious worship and expression and ensuring at least a respite in the internecine wars between Catholics and Protestants.

It was in the Loire Valley that the court collected and royalty received; where monarchs hunted, the company feasted and enemies intrigued. It was to châteaux in the Loire – thus far and no further, for it would have been uncharitable to isolate them entirely from civilization – that royal mistresses were banished when they fell out of favour, and dowager queens were relegated when a new king took over in case they should exert too much influence over the new order. Most important for French *cuisine*, it was Henri II's Italian wife, Catherine de Medici, who imported Italian chefs to teach the French how to cook meals fit for royalty, and thus laid the basis for what is still today the most creative and imaginative cooking in the world.

The heyday of the Loire was the period of the later Valois kings (from the accession of Charles VIII (1483) to the murder of Henri III (1589). The sixteenth century was the period of completion of the great Renaissance palaces of Azay-Le-Rideau, Chambord, Chenonceaux, Valençay, Villandry and many others. It was not until after the accession of Henri IV in 1589 that the Loire began to decline and the sphere of influence moved to the Île-de-France nearer Paris.

The development of Versailles under Louis XIV seventy years later was the most important factor in this decline. From then on the 'Garden of France' ceased to be the playground of its kings. The brilliant originality of the designs which flourished under François I (1515–1547) gave way to the spacious, elegant and classic, but essentially *bourgeois* architecture which marks the town planning of Saumur, Tours and Orléans: form without flair. From then on, particularly after Napoleonic times and as France became increasingly industrialized, the Loire remained a cultural backwater and its castles crumbled. The importance of its wines diminished as those of the rest of France found access to Paris easier; and as the era of great wine emerged in the pre-phylloxera years of the mid-nineteenth century, the Loire was forgotten. It was not until the 1960s that wines such as Sancerre and Savennières, even Muscadet and Vouvray, began to be widely exported outside the region. Yet the Loire Valley is a vast and rewarding area. Rich and varied in its beauty, historically fascinating in its echoes of the past, and with a vast array of wines, the Loire is indeed the 'Garden of France'.

The Wines

The Loire is the longest river in France. The river rises in the *département* of the Ardèche, on the slopes of the Gerbier de Jonc, a 1551-metre volcanic peak in the Massif Central a few dozen kilometres south-east of Le Puy. Here it is separated by merely a mountain ridge or two from the dusty wastes of the broad, industrialized Rhône, along the banks of which the motorway thunders its passage towards the beaches of the South. It flows first north, then west for some 600 kilometres before it debouches into the Bay of Biscay at Saint-Nazaire. It flows north for half this distance, until just before Orléans, where it is barely an hour's drive from Paris, then west through the château country of the Touraine and the Anjou, and finally through the Muscadet vineyards of the Pays Nantais.

The tributaries of the Loire are of great vinous importance, be they little more than streams, such as the Layon, or wide imposing rivers in their own right. The Loire and its contributory waters drain almost a quarter of the entire land mass of France, and hence wines from Clermont-Ferrand and Poitiers have as much right to be called *vins de Loire* as those of Tours and Angers. The most important tributaries of the Loire are the Allier, the Cher, the Indre, the Creuse, the Maine (itself only ten kilometres long, but formed by the junction of the Mayenne and the Sarthe) and the Sèvre Nantaise. All, except the Maine, flow in from the south.

The Loire basin, and therefore the territory of its wines, consists of all the land north of Limoges, west of Vézelay and south of Le Mans. It is a vast area, with some 300,000 growers and 180,000 hectares of vines, producing in a prolific year such as 1988 over 2½ million hectolitres of *appellation contrôlée* wine (14 per cent of the total AC production of France) and 400,000 hectolitres of VDQS wine. Additionally, there may be as much as 700,000 hectolitres of *vins de pays* wine and 1½ million hectolitres of *vin de table*.

The Loire Valley is commonly thought of as a white wine area, a sort of complement to the Rhône Valley, whose wines are almost entirely red. This is erroneous. Even allowing for the fact that French government statistics do not differentiate between red and rosé wine, and the enormous popularity of Anjou Rosé, there is much red wine produced in the Loire, and only 60 per cent of the total production is white.

The wines of the Loire can be divided into five main regions (though the positioning of some of the more outlying *appellations* within these regions is somewhat arbitrary). I have taken the logical order from the source of the Loire towards the coast. Within the sub-sections (except for the first), I have discussed the *appellations* in order of importance.

THE UPPER REACHES AND CÔTES D'AUVERGNE
VDQS: Côtes du Forez, Côtes Roannaises, Côtes d'Auvergne, Saint-Pourçain and Châteaumeillant.

THE CENTRE OR SANCERROIS
AC: Sancerre, Pouilly-Fumé, Blanc-Fumé de Pouilly or Pouilly-Blanc-Fumé, Pouilly-sur-Loire, Menetou-Salon, Quincy and Reuilly.

VDQS: Coteaux du Giennois or Côtes de Gien and Vin de l'Orléanais.

TOURAINE
AC: Bourgueil, Saint-Nicolas-de-Bourgueil, Chinon, Montlouis, Vouvray, Touraine, Touraine-Azay-le-Rideau, Touraine-Amboise, Touraine-Mesland, Coteaux du Loir and Jasnières. Plus *appellations* for *pétillant* and *mousseux* wines from Montlouis and Vouvray, as well as generic Touraine.

VDQS: Cheverny, Coteaux du Vendômois and Valençay.

ANJOU
AC: Coteaux du Layon, Coteaux du Layon-Villages, Bonnezeaux, Quarts de Chaume, Coteaux de l'Aubance, Saumur, Saumur-Champigny, Coteaux de Saumur, Cabernet de Saumur, Savennières, Anjou, Anjou-Villages, Anjou Coteaux de la Loire, Anjou-Gamay and Cabernet d'Anjou. Plus *appellations* for *pétillant* and *mousseux* wines from Saumur and generic Anjou.

VDQS: Haut Poitou, Coteaux d'Ancenis and Vins du Thouarsais.

MUSCADET
AC: Muscadet, Muscadet des Coteaux-de-la-Loire and Muscadet de Sèvre-et-Maine.

VDQS: Gros Plant du Pays Nantais, and Fiefs Vendéens.
Wines from both Anjou and Touraine can be blended to make the two *appellations contrôlées*: Crémant de Loire (sparkling) and Rosé-de-Loire. There is no generic Loire *appellation* as such for still white and red wines.

THE LOIRE

PRODUCTION AND SURFACE AREA (1996 HARVEST)

	Surface area in hectares	Production '000 hectolitres	
		RED & ROSÉ	WHITE
The Upper Reaches and Côtes d'Auvergne			
VDQS			
CÔTES DU FOREZ	193	7	—
CÔTES ROANNAISES	164	10	—
CÔTES D'AUVERGNE	460	18	(492 hl)
SAINT-POURÇAIN	542	22	7
CHÂTEAUMEILLANT	63	5	—
Cental Loire			
AC			
SANCERRE	2356	31	1210
POUILLY-FUMÉ	976	—	59
POUILLY-SUR-LOIRE	49	—	3
MENETOU-SALON	336	7	13
QUINCY	166	—	7
REUILLY	132	3	4
VDQS			
VINS DE L'ORLEÉANAIS	145	7	—
COTEAUX DU GIENNOIS	137	5	2
Touraine			
AC			
VOUVRAY	1049	—	54
MONTLOUIS	225	—	9
CHINON	2052	110	—
BOURGUEIL	1264	75	—
SAINT-NICOLAS-DE-BOURGUEIL	907	53	—
TOURAINE-AMBOISE	170	10	—
TOURAINE-AZAY-LE-RIDEAU	44	—	2
TOURAINE-MESLAND	153	6	—
TOURAINE	3243 red and rosé + 2194 white	181	103

	Surface area in hectares	Production '000 hectolitres	
		RED & ROSÉ	WHITE
COTEAUX DU LOIR	57	2	—
JASNIÈRES	41	—	2
TOURAINE MOUSSEUX	436	—	26
VOUVRAY MOUSSEUX	976	—	55
MONTLOUIS MOUSSEUX	140	—	8

VDQS

COUR-CHEVERNEY	42	—	2
CHEVERNEY	349	—	16
COTEAUX DU VENDÔMOIS	154	7	1
VALENÇAY	129	5	2

Touraine and Anjou

AC

CRÉMANT DE LOIRE	463	2	25
ROSÉ DE LOIRE	961	48	—

Anjou

Ac

SAVENNIÈRES	122	—	5
COTEAUX DU LAYON AND	1289	—	58
COTEAUX DU LAYON VILLAGES	350	—	8
QUARTS DE CHAUME	39	—	(866 hl)
BONNEZEAUX	102	—	3
COTEAUX DE L'AUBANCE	167	—	6
ANJOU COTEAUX DE LA LOIRE	50	—	1
SAUMUR	1043 red and rosé + 484 white	55	23
SAUMUR-CHAMPIGNY	1298	82	—
CABERNET DE SAUMUR	54	4	—
COTEAUX DE SAUMUR	30	—	(343 hl)
ANJOU-VILLAGES	438	22	—
ANJOU	2076 red and rosé + 1112 white	112	54
ANJOU-GAMAY	384	21	—
CABERNET D'ANJOU	2216	160	—
ROSÉ D'ANJOU	1998	141	—
ANJOU MOUSSEUX	72	(211 hl)	4
SAUMUR MOUSSEUX (SAUMUR D' ORIGINE)	1434	2	104
HAUT-POITON			

	Surface area in hectares	Production '000 hectolitres	
		RED & ROSÉ	WHITE
VDQS			
HAUT POITOU	419	16	13
COTEAUX D' ANCENIS	264	17	(122 hl)
VINS DU THOUARSAIS	21	(621 hl)	(384 hl)
Muscadet			
AC			
HAUT POITOU	419	16	13
MUSCADET DE SÈVRE-ET-MAINE	10,275	—	530
MUSCADET DES COTEAUX DE LA LOIRE	335	—	18
MUSCADET COTES DE GRANDLIEU	263	—	167
MUSCADET	2025	—	93
VDQS			
GROS PLANT DU PAYS NANTAIS	2713	—	187
FIEFS VENDÉENS	412	20	4
Total Loire AC	46145	1155	1419
Total Loite VDQS	5789	124	328
Total Loire	51,932	1279	1747
Total Red and White Wines		3026	

WHEN TO DRINK THE WINES

Most Loire wine is white, and made for early drinking; most of the rest is rosé or a simple red, and similarly produced for de-corking soon. The only ones made for keeping are the serious reds – Chinon, Bourgueil, Saint-Nicolas-de-Bourgueil, and Saumur-Champigny – and the medium-sweet or *doux* whites of Vouvray and the best parts of the Coteaux du Layon (such as Bonnezeaux and Quarts de Chaume) plus the dry white wines of Savennières and a few of the best dry Vouvrays.

With modern wine-making methods there is little fluctuation in quality between one year and the next when it comes to wine destined for quick consumption. One year's Cabernet Rosé d'Anjou or Touraine Sauvignon will taste much like the next. Rarely will the vintage be so abysmal that Sancerre or Muscadet cannot be enjoyed. Most of these wines are made one year for drinking the next, and by the time this vintage is put on the market, six months or so after the grapes have been picked, the previous year's wine should be finished up. It will already have begun to lose its freshness. Vintage charts for these sort of wines are therefore redundant.

There are a few dry white Loire wines which repay keeping. One or two Pouilly-Fumés are now vinified and/or aged in oak: the superior Ladoucette wine, 'Baron de L', and the 'Silex Cuvée' of Didier Dagueneau are examples. These will safely keep three or four years, sometimes longer. Some dry Vouvrays, those of André Foreau for instance, will keep even longer; so will the firmer Savennières.

The sweeter Loire wines will keep longer; in the case of those which are merely *moelleux* (medium-sweet) for five years, perhaps ten. Those which are truly *doux* (luscious) will keep for decades, particularly Vouvray, which tends to be fuller than Coteaux du Layon. The two great *doux* vintages of the century are 1921 and '47 though the first reports of the '89 vintage indicate that this year may be equally as fine. The wines of both are still fresh.

Fine red Loire vintages are few and far between. Serious red Loire, that is; not a light Anjou Cabernet, a Touraine Gamay or a Pinot-based Sancerre; all of which are destined for consumption, if not in the summer after the vintage then within a couple of years after that. The sun does not shine sufficiently this far north to fully concentrate the grapes, and if the grower attempts to produce a lasting, tannic wine from only moderately ripened fruit he will make something overbalanced and astringent. Only rarely are we fortunate enough to get red Loire wines which can be guaranteed a life-span longer than a Bordeaux *bourgeois* château wine, that is more than seven or eight years.

GOOD VINTAGES

Savennières and dry Vouvray: 1997, 1996, 1995, 1993, 1989, '88, '86, '85, '83, '82, '78 and '76.
Coteaux du Lanyon and the sweet wines of Vouvray: 1997, 1996, 1995, 1994, 1993, 1989, '88, '85, '83, '82, '76, '75, '71, '69, '64, '59, and '47.
Chinon, Bourgueil and other top red wines: 1997, 1996, 1995, 1994, 1993, 1989, '88, '86, '85, '83, '82, '78, and '76. Older vintages will be showing age.

The Wine Regions
The Upper Reaches and Côtes d'Auvergne

In contrast to the valley of the lower Rhône, only a few dozen kilometres to the east, the countryside of the source of the Loire is entirely different, a land of birch, ash and fir, rather than cypress, olive and pine: not in the least Mediterranean. Far off the beaten tourist track, this is a remote part of France. There are hills and valleys, freshly rushing streams abundant in fish and *écrevisses*, meadows and pasturelands with goats and sheep, but, as yet, no vines. It is cold and damp in winter, cool and fragrant even in the height of summer. There are few large towns and these are old, with fine Romanesque churches, touched with an element of the Byzantine brought back by returning Crusaders, and with the remains of crumbling castles, originally the fortresses of mountain brigand lords. There is little heavy industry to despoil the view or desecrate the beauty of the surroundings. It is a soft, romantic part of France, as far from the bustle of Paris as it is from the broad elegant acres of the château country of the Loire.

The Côtes d'Auvergne are the first important vineyards of the Upper Loire and lie in the valley of one of the Loire's largest tributaries, the Allier, in the *département* of Puy-de-Dôme around Clermont-Ferrand. Some fifty kilometres to the east, across the Monts de Forez near the town of Boën in the *département* of Loire, is the Côtes du Forez. North of the Côtes d'Auvergne lie the vineyards of Saint-Pourçain on the river Sioule, a tributary of the Allier south of Moulins. North of the Côtes du Forez is the Côtes Roannaises, west of Roanne, home of Les Frères Troisgros. A hundred kilometres west of Saint-Pourçain, almost where the four *départements* of Indre, Cher, Creuse and Allier meet, is the isolated district of Châteaumeillant. All these wines are VDQS. As yet, in our journey down the Loire, the wines are not prestigious enough nor expensive enough, nor the areas large enough, to merit *appellation contrôlée*. Indeed, many growers in the area are content to keep the VDQS – perhaps AC brings too much paperwork with it.

CÔTES DU FOREZ VDQS

North of Saint-Étienne the Loire Valley widens, dividing the Monts du Lyonnais on the east from the Monts du Forez on the west. On the south-eastern-facing slopes of the Monts du Forez hills, some fifteen kilometres or so as the crow flies from the river itself, lie the vineyards of the Côtes du Forez. The holdings are small, and scattered over twenty-one communes between Boën-sur-Lignon and Montbrison in the *département* of Loire on soil which is clayey limestone or clayey sand on a granitic base.

Forez is neither a very large nor very exciting region. There are some 400 hectares of vineyards in production, most of which is vinified by the local co-operative at Trelins, a suburb of Boën, as *vin de table* or Vin de Pays d'Urfé, with some 9000 hectolitres of VDQS wine. The co-operative was founded in 1962 and now has 260 members. Côtes du Forez is made from the Gamay Rouge à Jus Blanc, and can be either red or rosé.

I find Côtes du Forez one of the least inspiring of all France's VDQS wines. The wine from the co-operative is light, dull and an example of carbonic maceration at its worst, giving a flavour which is both rubbery and tasting of boiled sweets. The few growers' wines I have seen have been coarse and robust, inky and farmyardy. Their scruffy premises and rather cavalier attitude towards the possibility of bacterial contamination of wine do not engender much enthusiasm for the *appellation*'s future.

CÔTES ROANNAISES VDQS

After the Côtes du Forez, continuing north for some fifty kilometres, we come to the Côtes Roannaises which, as the name would suggest, is in the area of Roanne, still in the *département* of Loire. The alluvial flat land of the Loire Valley is several kilometres wide at this point, and the vineyards are planted in the granitic-based foothills of the Monts de la Madeleine some ten kilometres to the west in twenty-five communes between La Picaudière and Bully. The chief centre is Renaison.

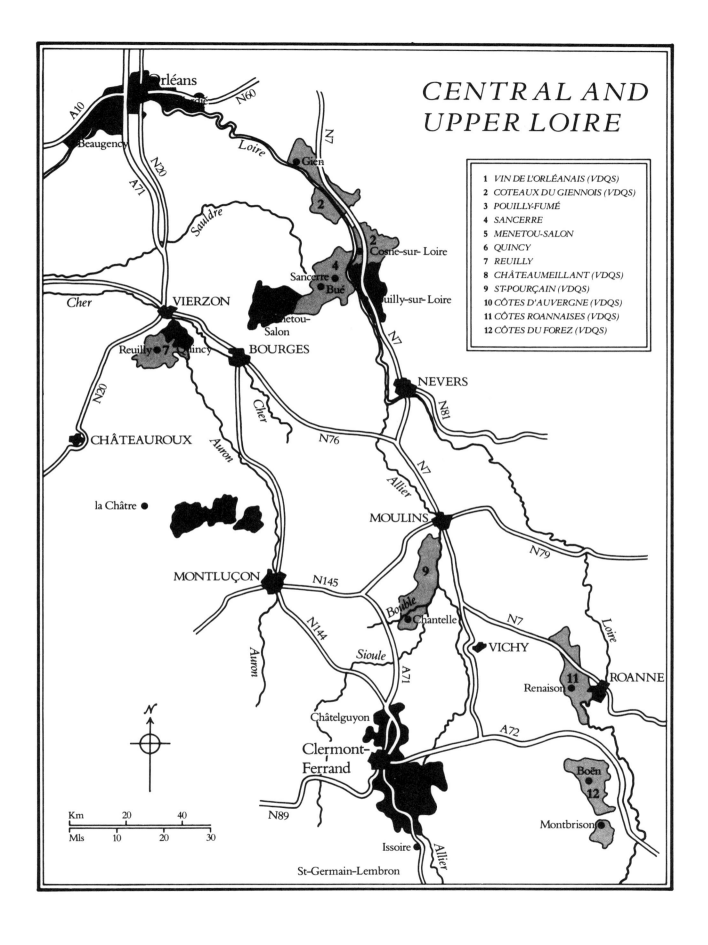

CENTRAL AND UPPER LOIRE

1 VIN DE L'ORLÉANAIS (VDQS)
2 COTEAUX DU GIENNOIS (VDQS)
3 POUILLY-FUMÉ
4 SANCERRE
5 MENETOU-SALON
6 QUINCY
7 REUILLY
8 CHÂTEAUMEILLANT (VDQS)
9 ST-POURÇAIN (VDQS)
10 CÔTES D'AUVERGNE (VDQS)
11 CÔTES ROANNAISES (VDQS)
12 CÔTES DU FOREZ (VDQS)

The area is small, with some hundred or so growers and 100 hectares of vineyards, planted with various forms of Gamay. The wines are red and rosé, and the best, from the Gamay Noir à Jus Blanc, the true Beaujolais grape, can be the nearest rival to the lighter Beaujolais *crus* such as Brouilly and Chiroubles. Much of the wine, however, is somewhat rustic in character, rough and farmyardy in taste, and not really worthy of its *appellation*. From my admittedly limited experience of the area, Robert Serol of Renaison, west of Roanne, is the best grower. Other important growers include Jean Vagneur-Tachon at Le Picatier, Saint Naon-le-Vieux, who is director of an agricultural college at Angers, and André and Maurice Villeneuve. Production of the Côtes Roannaises was 4823 hectolitres in 1988.

CÔTES D'AUVERGNE VDQS

Eighty kilometres to the west of the Côtes du Forez, in the shadow of the Puy-de-Dôme and overlooking the valley of the river Allier, is the noisy, unattractive, sprawling conglomeration of Clermont-Ferrand, birthplace of Blaise Pascal, and capital of the Auvergne. Now more famous as the base for the giant Michelin tyre empire, a century ago before the invasion of the phylloxera Clermont-Ferrand was the centre of a thriving wine region, the fifth largest in France. Today, at an average 20,000 hectolitres per annum, the production is a vestige of what it once was, and the reputation equally diminished. Rarely, if ever, will you find Auvergne wines for sale outside the bistros and hypermarkets of the immediate area. This is, I regret to report, no injustice. The majority of the wine produced is a rather dull rosé from the Gamay grape. Coarse reds are made from Gamay and the Pinot Noir; they are either rather heavy and robust from individual growers, or lighter and somewhat better made using carbonic maceration from the two co-operatives; and there is a minute amount of Chardonnay-based white.

The region is a sprawling one, covering some fifty-three communes in the *département* of Puy-de-Dôme, scattered between Châtelguyon in the north and Saint-Germain-Lembron, a distance of about sixty kilometres. The soil is varied: in parts granitic sand, elsewhere limestone or marl, or even volcanic debris. The land is dry and well drained, with the vineyards exposed to the south or south-east. Vineyards, perhaps, is an exaggeration, the average plot is tiny, the farming polycultural, and such wine that is made is mainly *ordinaire* for private consumption.

Within the broad *appellation* of Côtes d'Auvergne are five sub-areas, whose wines must achieve an alcohol level half a degree higher for red and rosé to gain this superior and more precise geographical designation. From north to south these are: Côtes d'Auvergne-Madargues (communes of Saint-Hippolyte and Châtelguyon near Riom); Côtes d'Auvergne-Châteaugay (communes of Ménétrol, Châteaugay and the north part of Cébazat, north of Clermont-Ferrand); Côtes d'Auvergne-Chanturgues (the slopes of the Puy de Chanturgue immediately north of Clermont-Ferrand); Côtes d'Auvergne-Corent (communes of Corent, Les Martres-de-Veyre, La Sauvetat and Veyre-Mouton, south of Clermont-Ferrand); and Côtes d'Auvergne-Boudes (communes of Boudes, Chalus and Saint-Hérent, west of Saint-Germain-Lembron). Chanturgues is said to be the best red, even being classed by Jullien in the early nineteenth century alongside the third class of Bordeaux. Corent is the best-known rosé. The tiny production of white is based at Sauvagnat-Sainte-Marthe north of Issoire. In total some 2000 hectares are planted with vineyards, almost entirely with Gamay, and only one-eighth of these produce VDQS wine. In my experience the best sources of Côtes d'Auvergne (not having found a grower like Robert Sérol in the Côtes Roannaises) are the two co-operatives: Le Clermontoise at Aubière, south of Clermont-Ferrand, founded in 1935, and the Cave Co-opérative des Coteaux d'Auvergne at Veyre-Mouton near Corent, founded in 1951. Between them they produce about two-fifths of the area's VDQS total, and a little Vin de Pays du Puy-de-Dôme. In all, however, this is not a very exciting wine-producing region, and I fear it will not become so until some eccentric (and rich) perfectionist arrives to take it by the scruff of its neck.

SAINT-POURÇAIN VDQS

About sixty kilometres north of Clermont-Ferrand, along the road to Moulins in the *département* of Allier, lies Saint-Pourçain on the Sioule, a tributary of the river Allier. Here we are in the Bourbonnais, the northern foothills of the Auvergne, a gently rolling, often densely wooded land (the forest of Tronçais producing some of the best oak for wine barrels lies to the north-west) and at first sight the countryside seems to be agricultural rather than viticultural. Cows graze, maize grows, other vegetables and cereals are cultivated. Where are the vineyards?

The vineyards are scattered over a region some forty-five kilometres long by eight wide, on the left bank of the rivers Sioule, Bouble and Allier, both north and south of Saint-Pourçain between Moulins and Chantelle. There is no obvious centre to the wine region and many of the vineyard holdings are little more than a few hundred square metres. Most of the vineyard owners grow other crops as well.

Saint-Pourçain, like the wines of the Auvergne, enjoyed a greater reputation in the past than it does today. The *vignoble* claims Gallo-Roman if not Phoenician origin, and the wine was for many centuries served at the table of kings of France. At the end of the eighteenth century the vines covered 8000 hectares, and could be compared, in the opinion of Jullien, or so local legend would have us believe, with the best of the Mâconnais in good years. Sadly both the size of the vineyards and their fame have declined since then.

Nineteen communes have land entitled to the Saint-Pourçain *appellation*, yet hardly 1000 hectares are planted with vines and only about half of this produces wine of VDQS standard. In 1996 production of VDQS wine totalled 21,590 hectolitres of red and rosé and 7491 of white. The co-operative (the Union des Vignerons), set up in 1952 when the area first acquired the status of VDQS, is by a long way the leading supplier of wine, but in recent years an increasing number of growers are beginning to vinify and bottle their own wine, and to sell direct, both to wholesalers and to private customers.

The soil is essentially clay and limestone, forming part of the Limagne, a zone which has subsided in the crystalline shelf of the Massif Central. To the north-west this soil is poor and infertile, and the land undulated, while closer to the Sioule the vineyards are more stony and steeply sloping, giving a sunny exposure to the south and east. Nearer to Saint-Pourçain the soil is richer and more fertile.

While the *appellation* produces red and rosé from Gamay and Pinot Noir, the white wine is the most interesting. Though several grapes are authorized, including Chardonnay, Aligoté and Saint-Pierre-Doré (maximum 10 per cent), the traditional grape for this white wine is the Tresallier (known as the Sacy in the Chablis area) which is mixed with Sauvignon Blanc to give the authentic taste of Saint-Pourçain. The maximum percentage authorized for Tresallier, a grape which gives a wine high in acidity but weak in alcohol, is fifty per cent.

Saint-Pourçain white has a pronounced racy acidity, and a delicate, if not weak, structure. Yet it can be interesting and individual in a good vintage, and if from a producer with up-to-date equipment and expertise in vinification. The taste is more fragrant and herbal than a wine from Sauvignon Blanc alone, though similar, and a suggestion of some alpine flower such as gentian can be perceived by those imaginative enough to notice it. It needs to be good though, for the growers' wines are more expensive than Touraine Sauvignons or the Sauvignon from Haut Poitou, and much of their produce is somewhat rough and ready, and would have been better if it had been vinified and bottled by the perfectly acceptable, if not inspiring co-operative. In a region which is relatively unimportant commercially, I dealt personally with a number of growers during the time I was a wine merchant. Largely this was due to an inability to find anyone with both the size of vineyards and the quantity of wine made to give me continuity of supply.

The wines of both Jean Ray and Gabriel Faure are on offer at the local Hôtel du Chêne Vert in Saint-Pourçain itself. Neither are large establishments, but the wines are good, and often gold medal prizewinners. There are two Cherillat families, Paul and Jean, whose wines I have enjoyed, and in Meillard is the sizeable, by the region's standards, 11-hectare vineyard of the Domaine de Bellevue owned by Gérard Pétillat. This is an excellent wine, but atypical, the vines being 50 per cent Chardonnay and 50 per cent Sauvignon Blanc with no Tresallier.

The Union des Vignerons vinifies the wine of 80 per cent of the region's 400-odd *vignerons*, and is responsible for two-thirds of the *appellation*'s production. They have taken the initiative in restructuring and regrouping the vineyards and preparing them for mechanical cultivation and harvesting. Vinification since 1983 has been entirely in stainless steel. The 'Grande Reserve', now exported widely, is a dependable wine.

CHÂTEAUMEILLANT VDQS

In the south-western corner of the *département* of Cher, near where it meets three others (Indre, Creuse and Allier) lies the rather obscure VDQS of Châteaumeillant. Four of the eight communes owning land entitled to the *appellation* are in the Cher, the other four across the border in the Indre, all either side of the D943 about halfway between Montluçon and Châteauroux. Vineyards total 62 hectares.

The wines are generally rosé, normally from the Gamay grape alone or from a Passetoutgrains mixture of two-thirds Gamay, one-third Pinot Noir. From my experience they are light, rather dull and a little coarse, and I am not surprised their reputation is small and their consumption is but local. Once again the local co-operative is the district's largest producer. In 1996 production was 4820 hectolites.

The Central Loire

On the left bank of the river Loire, some fifty kilometres north of Nevers in the *département* of Cher, lie the Sancerre vineyards; on the opposite bank in the *département* of Nièvre are the vineyards of Pouilly-Fumé. These are the first great wines of the river. Further to the south-west, on the road to Bourges, is Menetou-Salon. Yet further west still, across the new Bourges–Orléans motorway, lies Quincy on the banks of the river Cher and Reuilly on the river Arnon.

All these *appellations* produce white wine, either wholly or predominantly, and with the exception of a small amount at Pouilly the grape used is Sauvignon Blanc, locally known as the Blanc Fumé. It is commonly believed that the name refers to something smoky in the aroma of the wine. This is not so: the *fumé* refers to the grey-green bloom on the ripening Sauvignon grape. Sauvignon Blanc, perhaps the most important quality white wine grape of western France, is in its element on the limestone soils of these central vineyards. Away from the more alluvial, sandy, clayey soils of the Touraine, Poitou and Bordeaux, it can lose the greenness, the coarseness, the rasping acidity and the pong of cats that can frequently be encountered elsewhere. The acidity, of course, remains, but is coupled with a racy delicacy redolent of currants, gooseberries, even, say some, of rhubarb or asparagus. The wine is altogether more elegant; crisp and fresh but not mean, and light but not thin, and this comes together with the same gun-flint aroma one finds in Chablis. This last characteristic is no coincidence: the soils are very similar.

Of the five *appellations*, Sancerre and Pouilly-Fumé are the best known, produce the better wine, and are by far the largest. Menetou-Salon, Quincy and Reuilly, with only some few dozen growers apiece, are rarely seen outside the area, and only shipped by a few specialists. Their wines, by and large, lack the definition of their more important neighbours, and fetch prices about halfway between those of Sancerre and Pouilly-Fumé and the leading Sauvignon wines of the Touraine.

SANCERRE

Overlooking the Loire, at the centre of a series of undulating hills and valleys, lies the ancient town of Sancerre, strategically positioned on the highest hill of all, over 300 metres above sea level. The town is a maze of narrow, steep and winding streets with limestone buildings, rust-roofed, enclosing private, medieval courtyards and all the streets seem to lead to the shaded Esplanade de la Porte Cézar and the gardens of the ruined château of the tenth-century Count of Champagne, Thibault le Tricheur.

This is a magnificent spot to gaze over the Loire Valley and to appreciate the military importance of the site. At one's feet, the lazy river meanders between the reeds and the sandbanks, opposite lie the woods and vineyards of Tracy, the northernmost commune of Pouilly, topped by the spire of the church of Saint-Thibault.

Sancerre has had a violent history, particularly during the Wars of Religion in the sixteenth and seventeenth centuries, when it was a centre for the Reformed Church. In 1573, after having failed to take the town by force, the royal Catholic army under Charles

IX besieged Sancerre for seven months. Starvation eventually led to capitulation, but not before half the population were dead, sick or wounded, and the survivors, having exhausted their bread and eaten all their domestic animals, had had to resort to eating rats, mice and even voles. In 1621 Sancerre was again attacked, this time by the Prince de Condé, and the castle totally destroyed, except for the twelfth-century Tour des Fiefs. Many of the local Protestant families left for Switzerland and the Low Countries, despite the Edict of Nantes, and the town ceased to be a significant Protestant centre.

Though geographically part of western France, historically the region was part of the ancient Duchy of Burgundy, and in pre-phylloxera times vineyards continued intermittently across the hills of the Nièvre to Avallon and beyond. Hence, for the red wines, the Pinot Noir grape and, originally, for the whites, that dull, workhorse grape of Alsace and the Alps, the Chasselas. Historically, too, on the Sancerre side of the Loire at least, this was a red wine-producing area, but in the lean times at the beginning of the twentieth century it was found that white wine was easier to sell, and that the Sauvignon vine took to its graft (on to American rootstock) more successfully than either the Pinot Noir or the Chasselas. In immediate post-phylloxera times this grafting was done in the vineyard, rather than as today in the nursery or greenhouse. From 1900 Sauvignon Blanc began to take over as the dominant variety in Sancerre. Prior to this and to the enforcement of the *appellation contrôlée* laws, much of the white wine from either Chasselas or Sauvignon had been shipped to Champagne for blending.

In 1936 Sancerre achieved *appellation contrôlée* status for its white wine (exclusively from Sauvignon), but it was not until 1959 that AC for red and rosé from the Pinot Noir was granted. Such had been the swing of the pendulum, the red by then had gone almost entirely out of fashion; even when retained by a grower, the Pinot Noir was relegated to poor slopes with unsuitable soil and aspect, contrary to the normal practice which would, logically, put red grape varieties on the sunniest slopes as a red grape normally requires a higher quantity of sunshine to ripen it. The 1936 *appellation* regulations stipulated the best sites for the Sauvignon and, strangely, this law remained after 1959, and was not revoked until 1982. Now growers can choose which vine to plant where quite legally.

After phylloxera, the Sancerre vineyards declined, as did many elsewhere in France. From 1700 hectares in 1893, the area under vine declined to little more than 600 hectares in 1960, and the wine was rarely seen abroad. In the worldwide boom of the early 1960s, Sancerre and Pouilly-Fumé were in the vanguard; the wines enjoyed enormous popularity. It is hard to believe with Sancerre or Pouilly-Fumé, if not both, *de rigueur* on every wine list, that as late as 1959 only half a dozen growers exported their wine beyond Paris. Prices of Sancerre have also risen sharply, by as much as, if not more than, fine white wines in general. Sancerre is now quite an expensive bottle of wine, more than Mâcon-Villages, sometimes even more than Chablis. Producers should beware of killing the goose that lays the golden eggs.

In 1996 the Sancerre vineyards occupied 2356 hectares, and produced 120,491 hectolitres of white wine and 31,393 of red and rosé. The vineyard is expected to reach 2600 hectares within a few years. The red wines and rosé are making a comeback, and today more than 26 per cent of the production is red and rosé while twenty-five years ago it was less than 10 per cent. Today as much Pinot Noir as Sauvignon – and on well-favoured sites as well – is being planted, and the reds and rosés are increasingly fashionable.

The Sancerre vineyards cover fourteen communes: Bannay, Bué, Crézenay, Menetou-Ratel, Ménétréol, Montigny, Saint-Satur, Sainte-Gemme, Sancerre, Sury-en-Vaux, Thauveney, Veaugues, Verdigny and Vinon. Some of these villages (Montigny and Vinon, for example) are of minor importance, but Crézancy, Sancerre, Verdigny and Sury-en-Vaux each have over 100 hectares of vines, and Bué over 200 hectares.

The vines lie on undulating slopes, exposed to the east, south and west, and protected from the north and north-west by higher hills and trees. The soil is essentially limestone, mixed with clay; the higher up the slope the more pure limestone, the lower down the more clayey. The better wine, in the view of the locals, comes from the higher slopes and has more finesse, is more racy, and more delicate.

Within this limestone generalization, there are a number of sub-divisions. Roughly 40 per cent of the vineyards, particularly at Chavignol (a village, not a commune, and famous for its goat's cheese), Sury-en-Vaux and parts of Bué and Verdigny is *terres blanches*, a clayey marl sometimes mixed with gravel. These are the highest slopes, and the most westerly. Centrally, particularly at Bué, and also making up another 40 per cent of the vineyards, the soil is *caillottes*, small limestone pieces, often fossils, and normally stony soil, predominates. To the west, at Saint-Satur, Ménétréol, Thauveney, and part of Sancerre itself, the soil is flinty, very stony, and mixed with sand on a limestone base. Sainte-Gemme, to the north, is predominantly siliceous and, in contrast to the rest of the region, presents a red aspect, while the rest is grey. The soil here is less good from the quality point of view but easier to work than the more precipitous slopes round the town of Sancerre itself. Each of the three main soil types produces wine with a slightly different character. The *caillottes* soil gives a very perfumed wine, delicate in style, vigorously fruity and at its best young. The *terres blanches* make a firmer wine, sometimes a bit rustic, while the flinty soil gives a wine which is less perfumed but has more depth, and which keeps well. This is also the best soil for red wine.

Sancerre is an *appellation* of the *petit vigneron*. In 1979 the average holding of the 554 vineyards owners was 2.38 hectares, hardly enough to support one man, let alone one with a wife and family. The position has not materially changed in the last decade. Not only are the holdings small, but vineyard parcels are much dispersed. There are as many as 8000, despite efforts in recent years to rationalize by persuading growers to trade off and exchange pieces of land. Not surprisingly with so many small vineyards, the co-operative, the Cave des Vins de Sancerre, plays a major role. There are 166 members, owning 167 hectares of vines between them, though not all are contracted to give their entire harvest to the co-operative. It is a modern establishment, producing a good, standard, if not quite top-flight wine as well as Vin de Pays du Cher. It supplies Nicolas, the French retail and wholesale chain, among others.

Sancerre has many well-known *lieux-dits*, vineyard sites split up among a number of growers. The best known of these are Clos du Chêne Marchand and Le Grand Chemarin in Bué, Clos du Roy in Crézancy, Les Mont Damnés in Verdigny and Chavignol, Clos Beaujeu in Chavignol and Clos du Paradis in Sancerre.

RED AND ROSÉ WINES

Sancerre red and rosé wines are more variable in quality than the white wine. This, despite considerable replanting on better sites in the last decade, must owe as much to poor sites as to bad wine-making, though young vines must also, if only temporarily, come into it. The wines come from a cool climate – Sancerre, though on the same latitude as Dijon, suffers a significantly lower mean temperature during the summer months – and consequently lack 'flesh'. In poor years, in my view, they are best made into rosé.

Sancerre rosé can be one of the most agreeable and elegant rosés of France and a good example can certainly rival those of Marsannay in the Côte d'Or. Pinot Noir makes an attractive rosé, all flowers (violets) and summer fruits (cherry, strawberry and raspberry).

In years when there is enough sunshine and heat to ripen the grapes fully, fragrant, stylish, light red wine is made, similar in structure to a Côte Chalonnaise wine, or even, in the hands of a good domaine such as Vacheron, one of the few which persisted with the Pinot Noir and gave it right of place in the favoured slopes, perhaps with more of the elegance and clarity of definition of a Volnay. Nowadays, with modern vinification techniques such as *chauffage de la vendange* (must-warming) which extracts more of the colour, fruit and extract, but less tannin, the reds are more regularly successful. With better handling techniques and earlier bottling, the rather rustic, attenuated Sancerre reds of yesteryear are less common, and the wines can be recommended as an alternative to a lesser Burgundy. They come forward within a couple of years or so and can last up to ten. Good vintages since 1989 have included 1989, '90, '93, '95, '96 and 1997. Older vintages, for the most part, will be now a bit astringent.

WHITE WINES

But Sancerre is predominantly and justly best known as a white wine region. The wine is vinified at a low temperature – between 18°C and 20°C or so – to preserve as much of the volatile, aromatic compounds as possible. It is then matured in concrete vats, or, increasingly nowadays, in stainless steel, and bottled early for drinking young. In very ripe years like 1989 the malolactic fermentation is discouraged; in other years it is vital lest the wine become too lean and ungenerous. Similarly, in some years the wine is at its best in the summer after the vintage. In most years, though, a further two or three months in bottle will beneficially round off and soften the wines' dominant acidity. Few vintages should be kept more than a further year or two, not because they deteriorate, but because they lose their essential fresh, crisp, elegant, Sauvignon cut, which, to me, is the characteristic, the *raison d'être*, of the wine.

Is there any material difference between the wines of Sancerre and Pouilly-Fumé, its neighbour across the river? Some authorities would have us believe that 'Sancerre normally has more body and drive (and higher acidity) than Pouilly-Fumé' (Hugh Johnson's *Wine Companion*). In general I find Sancerres marginally softer and riper; Pouilly-Fumé steelier, and more racy. In vintages with a deficiency of acidity such as 1995 Pouilly-Fumé is often the better, in leaner years the opposite is sometimes true. But there is no hard and fast rule to differentiate between the two wines. Most of us, I fear, would be hard put to sort out a mixed blind tasting of samples into the two communes. Which is the better? Pouilly-Fumé is usually a franc or so cheaper, and perhaps, because it is more assertive and more angular, less easy to drink, and consequently less popular. In my view, however, there is more difference in quality between the peak wines and the run-of-the-mill ones in either region than between the peaks or even the averages themselves.

I have been enjoying the wines of the late Jean Vacheron and Maurice Bailly for more than twenty years and their wines remain for me the yardstick with which I judge all other wines of the area. The two were great friends, rivals perhaps, but not competitors, and quite different characters. Jean Vacheron, it could be said, used to take himself rather seriously. He was a reserved, undemonstrative man, and surprisingly erudite; traditionalist in outlook, if not in his wine-making. Bailly, on the other hand, is less sophisticated, and beneath the rugged peasant exterior beats the heart of a radical. Vacheron's wines are now made by his sons, Denis and Jean-Louis. Bailly is now in retirement and the wine-making has passed to the next generation and the land divided. Both domaines are prolific medal winners, Vacheron particularly for its red wines, which are matured in casks bought from the Domaine de La Romanée Conti. Vacheron's is easily the best red in Sancerre, primarily because the family has been making it longer than most, but also because its Pinot Noir vineyards are on good sites. 'People who like good wine make red, people who want to make money concentrate on white', Jean used to say. I regret his passing.

For red and rosé wines the following growers can be recommended: Jean-Balland Chapuis, André Dezat, Pierre and Alain Dezat, Serge Lalou, Bernard Noël-Reverdy, Pierre and Etienne Riffault, Michel Thomas and Jean Vatan. For white wines (as well as those mentioned above) the following can be recommended: Pierre Archambault, Philippe de Benoist, Henri Bourgeois (particularly his wood-fermented Cuvée Étienne Henri), Lucien Crochet, Maurice Gitton, Roland Tissier and the Domaines of Laporte, Alphonse Mellot, Thierry Merlin, Georges Millerioux, Paul Millerioux, Henri Natter, Lucien Picard, Pierre Prieur, Georges Roblin, Jean-Max Roger, Maurice Roger and Léon Vatan. The Bordeaux merchant Cordier has a large estate producing white Clos de la Poussie, red Guche Pigeon and Rosé Orme aux Loups. Without being outstanding these are good standard blends, the white being the most successful.

POUILLY-FUMÉ and POUILLY-SUR-LOIRE

Opposite Sancerre, on the eastern bank of the Loire, lie the communes which comprise the wine district of Pouilly-sur-Loire. Pouilly-sur-Loire − to differentiate it from countless other Pouillys, of which the best known from the wine point of view is Pouilly-Fuissé in the Mâconnais − is derived from the Latin *Pauliaca Villa*, but who this Roman Paul was, or whether it has any connection with Saint Paul, is not known. Nevertheless it is highly probable that vineyards were established here in Gallo-Roman times.

In the eleventh century Pouilly and the surrounding land was owned by a Baron Humbault, who perished in the First Crusade. His estates then passed into the hands of the Benedictine abbey at La Charité-sur-Loire, some thirty kilometres to the south, in whose control they remained until the French Revolution. Under the monks' careful auspices, the area under vine was extended and a reputation was established for the wine. Meanwhile to the north of the vineyard area, at Tracy, the Estutt d'Assay family, of Scottish antecedents, established themselves in the late sixteenth century, while in 1785 a Burgundian family, the Ladoucettes, arrived in the area at the Château du Nozet.

Despite the presence of these aristocratic landowners, Pouilly remains firmly a peasant wine-making area, and lives in friendly rivalry with its neighbour across the river: 'Water divides us, wine unites us', is a local saying. Until 1973, the town was a bustling noisy place on the N7, almost overwhelmed with its ceaseless traffic of *camions*, but it now seems practically deserted, the caravans and juggernauts storming past on the bypass and leaving it in an almost pre-industrial revolution tranquillity.

Pouilly appears to have always produced only white wine. Jullien in his *Topographie de Tous les Vignobles Connus* (1816) speaks of white wines with a light gun-flint flavour, and an annual production of 40,000 hectolitres, mostly exported to Paris, a mere 200 kilometres to the north. In the mid-nineteenth century, before the phylloxera invasion, the vineyards covered over 1000 hectares, nine-tenths planted with Chasselas.

As at Sancerre, the vineyards declined during the first half of the twentieth century, and Sauvignon Blanc gradually took over as the dominant variety. Unlike Sancerre, however, Chasselas has not entirely disappeared. There are today two *appellations* in the region: Pouilly-sur-Loire, from the Chasselas grape, and Pouilly (Blanc) Fumé, or Blanc Fumé de Pouilly, from the Sauvignon. The proportions, however, are the reverse of what they were a century ago, and little, if any, Chasselas is now being planted.

The area achieved *appellation contrôlée* status in 1937, and today some 640 hectares are planted, producing around 45,000 hectolitres of Pouilly-Fumé from Sauvignon and some 3300 hectolitres of Pouilly-sur-Loire from Chasselas. Rather more land was authorized for potential production than is under vine today, and there is consequently considerable scope for development.

Frost, however, is a great danger, more so than in Sancerre because the terrain is less protected from the elements. Almost every year there is some damage. Every now and then – the last time was in 1985 – the effect is catastrophic. This has been a deterrent against expanding the vineyards, despite the wines' increasing popularity and success.

Pouilly-sur-Loire is made from the Chasselas grape, with or without the addition of a small amount of Sauvignon Blanc. The wine is low in alcohol and acidity, and somewhat neutral in flavour. Nevertheless as a picnic wine, a wine for quaffing *en primeur*, it has its place. It is certainly, currently, better vinified than many alpine Chasselas wines, and is consequently fresher and more attractive than they are, with a similar gun-flint character to the Blanc Fumé wines. If it was as cheap as generic Muscadet – which it isn't, for the prices asked are comparable to single-vineyard Muscadet-sur-Loire wines – I am sure it could establish a place on the market. As it is, Pouilly-sur-Loire is rarely seen, and hardly ever exported. Growers have increasingly switched over to Sauvignon in recent years and Pouilly-sur-Loire will, I expect, soon be only a memory.

The vineyards of Pouilly-sur-Loire extend over seven communes: Pouilly itself, including the hamlet of Les Loges, Saint-Andelain, Tracy, Saint-Laurent, Saint-Martin-sur-Nohain, Garchy and Mesves-sur-Loire. Of these, the first three are the most important, with Saint-Andelain the largest of all; in Saint-Martin and Saint-Laurent the ground is flatter and largely falls to the north and east towards the river Nohain. The incidence of frost here is higher.

For the most part the ground is less hilly than at Sancerre, and the vineyards rise less steeply. They lie less on slopes facing the river than on the plateau above. Only at Les Loges and Les Berthiers, two of the leading Pouilly sites, does one get the feeling of exposed, *côtes* vineyards that is prevalent on the other side of the river.

As at Sancerre, the soil is essentially a limestone–clay mixture, predominantly marl, *caillottes* and Kimmeridgian clay, giving way to sandy clay soil in the commune of Tracy to the north. In general, the clay content is higher, the limestone content lower than at Sancerre, and the result is a wine which is normally fuller, perhaps richer in alcohol, but less delicate.

There are even fewer large estates in Pouilly than in Sancerre. Twenty-five years ago only the Ladoucettes at Château du Nozet possessed more than 10 hectares under vine. They have now been joined by the Château du Tracy, Michel Redde and Serge Dagueneau, while Maurice Bailly's holding has been divided between his sons and the Cave Saint Vincent, owned by the Saget family, has expanded into the *négociant* business, owning some 15 hectares in Pouilly as well as in Sancerre. The Cave Co-opérative 'Les Moulins à Vent' has a sound reputation. It was founded in 1948, and has 108 members who own 80 hectares between them. Not only does it produce Pouilly-sur-Loire and Pouilly-Fumé, but also the local VDQS wine, Coteaux du Giennois.

The development of the Ladoucette family business is one of post-war France's biggest wine success stories. The current head of the firm, Baron Patrick de Ladoucette, took over full control of the firm in 1972, at the age of twenty-one. At the time the estate had a fine reputation for Pouilly-Fumé, producing wine under the label of the Château du Nozet, but had largely been left in the hands of a resident manager, Patrick's father having emigrated to the Argentine in 1947 where he made a fortune breeding cattle.

On Patrick's succession he invested heavily in plant and machinery, installing thermostatically controlled stainless-steel fermentation tanks, glass-lined vats for storage and an automatic bottling line. He also set about expanding his sales with remorseless energy to the extent that he now claims an estimated two-thirds of the entire production of the *appellation*. Not surprisingly, though there are now 60 hectares under vine at the Château du Nozet, and this is still being expanded, the vast bulk of the wine is bought in (in the proportion of about 70 per cent must and 30 per cent wine). He has also diversified into Sancerre, under the Comte Lafond label (the name of an ancestor, once Governor of the French Bank, who ordered the demolition of the old château and the construction of the present imposing multi-turreted Château du Nozet); into the wines of the Touraine, under the Baron Briare brand name as well as in 1980 taking over the firm of Marc Brédif in Vouvray; into Chablis; and into the Napa Valley in California, where the wines are supervised by Robert Mondavi.

An oak-aged Pouilly-Fumé *tête de cuvée*, from the Nozet vineyards, is sold under the name of 'Baron de L' in an old-fashioned, embossed, dumpy bottle similar in shape to that of Dom Pérignon. Other leading estates in Pouilly include Guy Boudin, Paul Corneau, Serge Dagueneau, Paul Figeat, Georges Guyot, Jean-Claude Guyot, Masson-Blondelet, Raymond and Patrice Moreaux and Michel Redde. The best and most expensive, growers in the appellation is the *enfant terrible* Didier Dagueneau, who like Ladoucette produces an oak-vinified and -aged wine, this time under the name of Silex (flint). This is a Pouilly-Fumé which can age in bottle.

MENETOU-SALON

Menetou-Salon, Quincy and Reuilly suffer from being regarded as the poor country cousins of Sancerre. The wines are made from the same grapes and in the same way, on largely the same types of soil and in more or less the same climatic conditions. Not surprisingly, they are very similar. By comparison with Sancerre and Pouilly-Fumé the districts are much smaller, and, probably because they were situated further from the Loire, the wines have never attained the popularity of their famous neighbours. The general view is that, pleasant as they might be, none of these wines will ever quite have the class or definition of a Sancerre. As a result, understandably, prices are cheaper.

However, is there necessarily anything wrong in being a cheap substitute? The sword is double-edged. Without the fame of Sancerre, the wines of these three cousins would not be as well known as they are, or fetch the prices they now do. With it, dismissive comparisons are inescapable.

Closest to Sancerre geographically, and most like it in style, is Menetou-Salon. The vineyards lie some thirty kilometres to the south-west on the road to Bourges and cover a mere 100 hectares – one-seventeenth of Sancerre. At first sight, driving across the undulating hills on the D955, the vines are hard to spot. The heart of the *appellation*, at Morogues, lies off the road to the north, but even here the land is polycultural. The ground is somewhat flatter than at Sancerre, and the vineyards need neighbouring woods to protect them from the cold winds from the north and east. The countryside feels less open, more rural. The soil, though essentially calcareous, is darker and richer.

Menetou-Salon itself is a comfortable, sleepy French provincial town, with little to attract the tourist except for an impressive Renaissance château built by Jacques Coeur, Minister of Finance to Charles XII, and renovated in the nineteenth century by Prince Auguste d'Arenberg, President of the Suez Canal Company.

Menetou-Salon's vines are planted in the communes of Menetou-Salon itself, Morogues (the two most important), Aubignes, Humbligny (the closest parish to Sancerre), Parassy, Pigny, Quantilly, Saint-Céols, Soulangis and Vignoux-sous-les-Aix. AC was granted in 1959 and production, together with the overall surface area of the vineyards, has been increasing rapidly since. In 1988 13,213 hectolitres of white wine and 7182 hectolitres of red and rosé wine were produced.

One of the reasons for this expansion is that a number of the *négociants* in Sancerre have extended their range to include wines from Menetou-Salon. Jean-Max Roger of Bué and Alphonse Mellot produce good examples, as does Denis Père et Fils of Chavignol. Originally the wines were supplied under contract with growers in the area, but now the Sancerrois are increasingly planting their own vines in the Menetou-Salon *appellation*, while the growers there are extending their own vineyards.

The white Menetou-Salon is an attractive wine, sharing all the elegance and charm of Sancerre, while adding its own floral touch. I find it the most worthwhile, as well as the most consistent, of the cousins, and the closest to Sancerre in character as well as quality. It has less body and flesh than its famous neighbour, and the result is more *primeur* in style – often, as in a year with low acidity like 1995, a wine which can be drunk in January, only four months after the harvest. The reds and rosés can also be delicious, and are considered by some to be superior to those of the more famous Sancerre *appellation* up the road.

Leading growers in Menetou-Salon include Henri Pellé, the mayor of Morogues, Bernard Clément at the Domaine de Châtenoy, the Gilbert family, Jean Tellier, and Georges Chavet at Les Brangers. The local co-operative, 'Les Vignerons Jacques Coeur', makes about 10,000 cases of wine a year. The standard is variable.

QUINCY

Forty kilometres west of Menetou-Salon, south of Vierzon on the left bank of the river Cher, is the district of Quincy. Quincy is about the same size (108 hectares) as Menetou-Salon, but unlike it and Reuilly, its near neighbour, the *appellation* covers only white wine. Quincy's chief claim to fame is that it was the second wine-making area in France (after Châteauneuf-du-Pape) to achieve *appellation contrôlée* status, in 1936. The village has a long history of serious wine-making, stemming from the time it was an adjunct to the local Cistercian Abbey of Beauvoir in the Middle Ages, and the wines are said to have been exported to Paris and the royal court as early as the time of Henri IV.

This tradition continues today, with nearly every family in the village involved in wine-making in one form or another, numerous signs advertising *dégustation gratuite*, and *vente directe*, and even a scruffy street map bolted to the side of the *mairie*, surrounded by the names of local growers. Most seem to live in the village itself rather than in farmhouses out in the surrounding countryside.

Quincy is made within the single commune of Quincy itself, apart from a few plots in neighbouring Brinay, on soil less calcareous and with more sand and gravel than at Reuilly or the other vineyards of the Centre. Indeed much of the vineyard area lies in what was once the bed of the river Cher. Despite this I find Quincy the closest to Pouilly-Fumé of all the country cousins: the wine is light, racy and steely with a pronounced acidity and more than a hint of gun-flint; occasionally, in poorer years (and this is a fault of Reuilly too) there is a lack of ripeness. The vintage starts a week or so later than in Sancerre, but even this delay, in cold years, is not enough to ensure ripe grapes.

Quincy and its neighbour also suffer more from frost than do Sancerre and Pouilly, and at Quincy the danger is particularly prevalent as the vineyards are on flatter land and closer to the river. In 1977 the crop was literally decimated, and only 5000 cases were produced in total. In 1978 half the harvest was lost through hail. To compensate for this, perhaps, the yield is fixed at 45 hectolitres per hectare, while it is only 40 in Reuilly, Pouilly and Sancerre. In 1996 production totalled 6768 hectolitres.

Raymond Pipet used to be Quincy's best grower. He retired in 1988 and sold his domaine to Denis Jaumier. He was a man who in his rather guarded way was a fanatic after quality. Contrary to accepted custom, he de-stemmed his grapes and then subjected the pulp to a rather higher pressure than would normally be the case, in order, in his view, to extract the maximum flavour out of the pulp. The wines thereafter were only racked, not fined. The results were impressive and I trust will continue under the new management. I have also enjoyed the wines of Claude Houssier, Pierre Mardon and Bernard Pichard, while dependable wines are produced by the largest domaine in the *appellation*, the Domaine de Maison Blanche, a 25-hectare estate whose wines are vinified and sold by the *négociant* Albert Besombes of Saint-Hilaire Saint-Florent, near Saumur.

REUILLY

Reuilly lies a further ten kilometres to the south-west, on higher ground than Quincy above the river Arnon on the borders of the *départements* of Cher and Indre. It is the smallest *appellation* of Sancerre's three poor relations with only some 60 hectares producing *appellation* wine, though a further 100 are planted with Gamay and produce a *vin de pays*. Seven communes comprise the wine district: Reuilly and Diou in the Indre, Cerbois, Lury-sur-Arnon, Preuilly, Chery and Lazenay in the Cher. Vineyard holdings are small, with only two growers having more than six hectares, and production, naturally, is limited, particularly as the area is prone to frost damage in the spring. In 1996 3708 hectolitres of white and 2947 of red and rosé were produced. The area received *appellation contrôlée* status in 1937, a year after Quincy.

Most of the vineyards are around the village of Reuilly itself, broken up into minute smallholdings amid pasture and arable land, trees and orchards on the left bank of the river. This is rural France at its most typical; self-contained, self-sufficient, suspicious of change and foreigners – though with a few grudging overtures to the increasing importance of the tourist, be he only from Paris.

The Sauvignon Blanc grape on predominantly limestone soil of the *appellation* produces a vegetal, herby white wine which is lighter and leaner than Sancerre and Pouilly-Fumé, with its own *goût de terroir*. It is rarely more than a competent, attractive wine, lacking both the depth and length of its illustrious competitors and the charm of Menetou-Salon. The best it can aspire to, in my view, is a healthy austerity, crisp and fresh in the spring and early summer following the vintage, before the earthy, rather rustic flavours predominate. More interesting, for me, is the rosé (there is little red) which is produced, not from Pinot Noir, but from Pinot Gris. This grape, which also makes the so-called Tokay d'Alsace, has an orange–brown skin when ripe, and produces a wine with a delicate salmon pink colour and a refreshing slightly spicy fruit. It is both individual and full of character – an interesting wine which is well worth seeking out.

These are the only two domaines with more than 6 hectares of vineyards. Robert Cordier, a rotund avuncular figure, is the leading figure in Reuilly, and lives at La Ferté, a hamlet south of the village on the D918, the road to Issoudun. In contrast with his friend Pipet in Quincy, he is welcoming and his family generous in their hospitality. He is chairman of the local wine growers' syndicate and a representative on the Institut National des Appellations d'Origine (INAO). The Cordier wines are now made by his son Gilbert. The white wine is fresh and stylish and the rosé delicious. Henri Beurdin, at Preuilly, is the other major grower and also makes excellent white wine. Other growers include Claude Lafond and the quaintly named Oliver Cromwell, whose wine, I fear, does not live up to the promise of his name.

VIN DE L'ORLÉANAIS

The Orléanais region, so important in the days of the Ancien Régime, has, like many vineyards at the northern limits of cultivation, suffered from the twin blows of phylloxera and the easy access to northern France of the inevitably cheaper and more consistent wines of the Midi. Today production is barely 1 per cent (7000 hectolitres) of what it was a century or more ago.

The wine industry, however, is thriving, thanks to the tourists, and, no doubt, to the easily recognizable geographical name. It is a region of the *petit vigneron*, the *dégustation libre* and the *vente directe*. Reds, rosés and a small number of whites from a number of different grape varieties are found, along with the local asparagus and other market garden produce. And the wines are by no means beneath consideration.

The region stretches, on both sides of the river Loire, from Mardié, east of Orléans, to Tavers, a kilometre or two downstream from Beaugency, and covers some twenty-five communes in the *département* of Loiret. Most of the vineyards lie on plateaux of limestone, clay, gravel or sand mixtures, a small distance away from the Loire itself, and exposed to the south and south-east. While some 400 hectares are authorized for the *appellation*, only 100 are currently planted. Yet if the price of asparagus or *petits pois*, the main crops of the region, were to fall, I have no doubt we would see an abrupt change. In 1996 production totalled 6606 hectolitres.

Authorized grape varieties are many, and come under a number of different names. For the red wines, Pinot Noir (Auvernat Rouge), Pinot Meunier (Gris Meunier) and Cabernet Franc (Noir Dur); for the rosés the Gris Meunier and Cabernet, and for the white wines Chardonnay (Auvernat Blanc), Pinot Blanc and Pinot Gris (both called here the Auvernat Gris).

In good hands Orléanais wines can be clean, fresh and fruity, though perhaps a bit sour and thin if the summer has been unkind. Recent summers – 1995, 1996, 1997 – have been no means disagreeable, and interesting wines have resulted. The co-operative at Mareau-aux-Prés is a leading producer. Roger and Daniel Montigny in the same village is one of the few local growers to export his wines.

COTEAUX DU GIENNOIS VDQS

The Coteaux du Giennois or Côtes de Gien is a wine region which straddles the *départements* of Nièvre and Loiret, beginning at Cosne, where Pouilly-Fumé leaves off, and continuing north through sixteen communes until Gien. The best sector lies east of Cosne itself, in the commune of Saint-Père, where the land contains both clay and limestone; further downstream the soil is richer and more alluvial and the banks are of sand and gravel, giving a thinner, less distinctive wine.

This is not a large *appellation*, and is a shadow of what it was in pre-phylloxera days, when, like the Vin de l'Orléanais, close proximity to Paris ensured a ready market. Barely 100 hectares are commercially planted, largely with Gamay, but also with Pinot Noir, Sauvignon Blanc and Chenin Blanc. Most of the wine is vinified by the co-operative at Pouilly-sur-Loire.

Few growers individually 'commercialize' (a literal translation of the French) their own wine. I have only managed to unearth one grower who does so: Paul Paulat. His white wine, from Sauvignon Blanc, was light, pretty and unpretentious, his Gamay rosé similar and his Passetoutgrains thin. I was not enthused enough to return.

Production of Coteaux du Giennios in 1996 amounted to 4713 hectolitres of red and rosé and 2241 hectolitres of white.

Touraine

The Touraine, home of Vouvray, Montlouis and the great red wines of the Loire –
Chinon, Bourgueil and Saint-Nicolas-de-Bourgueil – broadly occupies the *départements*
of Indre-et-Loire and Loir-et-Cher, with the city of Tours as its geographical focus.

This is the region of most of the grand palaces, castles and stately homes of the Loire
Valley; of Chambord, a heavy, formal, Renaissance pile; Chenonceaux, the intimate,
unpretentious love-nest of Henry II and Diane de Poitiers; the classic symmetry of
Cheverney; the mysterious, fairytale atmosphere of Ussé; the elegant charm of Azay-le-
Rideau; the doom-laden fortresses of Sully, Loches and Montreuil-Bellay; the feudal
baronial keep of Chaumont; the abbey at Fontrevault, home of the tombs of the English
Henry II, Eleanor of Aquitaine and Richard the Lionheart, as well as the most
extraordinary Romanesque kitchen; and perhaps best of all, the castle at Chinon, now a
ruin but once the largest and finest fortification in medieval France.

The Touraine, *Jardin de la France*, as Rabelais called it, is suffused with history,
irradiated with flowers, particularly in the late spring, and fertile with vegetables and
fruit, not only of the vine. It is a beautiful countryside of fine forests, some rather formal to
English eyes and some particularly impressive gardens, such as that at Villandry.

Above all, the Touraine is a countryside of rivers, for the land is divided by the great
tributaries of the Loire such as the Vienne, the Indre and the Cher. Along the banks of
these fine waters lie the vineyards of the Touraine; from Candes-Saint-Martin in the west
as far as Chambord in the east; from Valençay, Saint-Hippolyte and Richelieu in the
south, to Neuillé-Pont-Pierre and Château-Renault in the north. Also included in the
Touraine are the small *appellations* of Coteaux du Loir, Jasnières and Coteaux du
Vendômois which lie further still to the north along the river Loir (le Loir), not to be
confused with the Loire (la Loire) itself.

To the west, on the borders of Anjou/Saumur, are the great red wine areas, Chinon,
Bourgueil and Saint-Nicolas-de-Bourgueil; in the centre the great white wine areas,
Vouvray and Montlouis; to the south-east, particularly along the banks of the river Cher,
are the vineyards which produce quantities of often excellent Sauvignon and Gamay de
Touraine.

In area, the Touraine *vignoble* measures 13,925 hectares. In 1988 the yield of AC wine
was some 697,000 hectolitres, roughly 37 per cent white and 63 per cent red and rosé,
with a further 32,000 hectolitres of VDQ. Through the Touraine, in extent, appears larger
than Anjou and Muscadet, in terms of wine production it is smaller than either – the vine
has to share its place with other crops, and with grazing cattle.

VOUVRAY

Vouvray is the leading white wine of the Touraine and the largest of its major *appellations*.
There are some 2025 hectares under vine and the total average production is some 109,000
hectolitres of still and sparkling wine. The village of Vouvray lies ten kilometres east of
the sprawling city of Tours on the north bank of the Loire. The vineyards are on a plateau

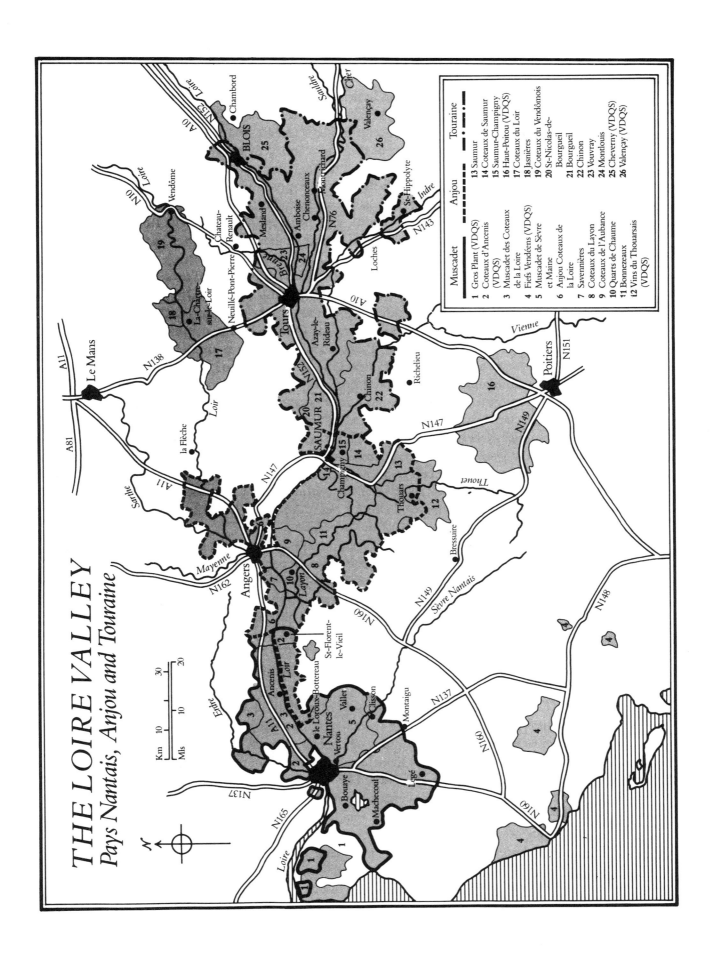

THE LOIRE VALLEY
Pays Nantais, Anjou and Touraine

Muscadet	Anjou	Touraine
1 Gros Plant (VDQS)	13 Saumur	
2 Coteaux d'Ancenis (VDQS)	14 Coteaux de Saumur	
3 Muscadet des Coteaux de la Loire	15 Saumur–Champigny	
4 Fiefs Vendéens (VDQS)	16 Haut-Poitou (VDQS)	
5 Muscadet de Sèvre et Maine	17 Coteaux du Loir	
6 Anjou Coteaux de la Loire	18 Jasnières	
7 Savennières	19 Coteaux du Vendômois	
8 Coteaux du Layon	20 St-Nicolas-de-Bourgueil	
9 Coteaux de l'Aubance	21 Bourgueil	
10 Quarts de Chaume	22 Chinon	
11 Bonnezeaux	23 Vouvray	
12 Vins du Thouarsais (VDQS)	24 Montlouis	
	25 Cheverny (VDQS)	
	26 Valençay (VDQS)	

above and behind the village itself, where many of its houses are wholly or partly built into the limestone rock-face. Underneath the plateau are a number of large and impressive cellars, originally hewn out to provide stone for the houses, and now providing ideal conditions for the maturing of the wine. Vouvray has its origins in the Abbey of Saint-Martin in Tours, founded in AD 372, to whom the hamlet of *Vobridius* was given by Charlemagne in 887. Vines, however, were probably first planted in the region in Roman times, again by the clergy, and, as elsewhere in France, it was they who were the dominant influence in the production of wine right up until the time of the Revolution. Legend has it that it was Saint Martin himself who planted the first vines on the *coteaux* above the village. Legend also has it that it was his donkey who, by eating many of the shoots of a particular row of vines, showed Saint Martin the benefits of pruning. Rabelais, born near Chinon and lover of all things sensual, wrote of Vouvray: 'Oh, gentle white wine. Upon my soul, this is a wine like taffeta.' Interestingly, he mentions elsewhere that the wine was made from Pineau, a local synonym for Chenin Blanc, the grape still used today.

Despite the proximity of Paris, and the presence of the aristocracy in their fine châteaux, much of the local production was exported to Holland shortly after the vintage, a state of affairs which persisted until the end of the nineteenth century. According to Jullien in 1816, most of the wine of the eastern Touraine was sold as Vouvray, whether it came from Vouvray itself or from further south along the banks of the Cher, a fraud still in practice over a hundred years later, according to Morton Shand.

As the Loire was a region almost entirely ignored by most of the nineteenth-century wine writers, it is difficult to decide precisely when and how the vinification of sweet wine evolved. Certainly by the end of the century the sweet wines were well known, and by this time, too, the area had already begun to make sparkling wines, a style which now makes up over 50 per cent of the *appellation*.

Appellation contrôlée was conferred on Vouvray in 1936, and the land was restricted then to eight communes: Vouvray itself, Rochecorbon, Vernou-sur-Brenne, Sainte-Rade-gonde (now part of the suburbs of Tours), Chançay, Noisay, Reugny and part of Parçay-Meslay. The vineyards lie on the plateau above the N152 which runs immediately along the north bank of the river. The plateau is broken up by a number of small valleys running south into the Loire, among which are the Vallée Coquette, the valley of the river Brenne, which runs down through Vernou, the Vallée Chartier, and the smaller valleys of the Vaugondy, the Raye, the Cousse and the Vaux, small streams which themselves flow into the Brenne.

The soil is largely siliceous clay or calcareous clay. The best terrains are known as the *perruches*, and consist of large amounts of flint, particularly at the surface. The second best sites, or *au buis*, are purer limestone. This is the *tuffe*, and it is from the subsoil under these that the marvellous cellars have been hewn. Both of these soils drain well and are excellent for producing quality Vouvray. The remaining vineyards, those with inferior aspect, or with a less-favoured soil containing more sand and gravel, are used to produce the wine destined to become *pétillant* or *mousseux*. In general, the best communes are those of Rochecorbon with a lot of *perruches* soil, Vouvray with *aubuis*, and Vernou whose soil is more varied. The terrain further inland does not have the concentration of limestone sufficient to produce still wines of quality.

Vouvray is a *vignoble* of *lieux-dits*, but most of these, unlike in Sancerre, are exclusive to a particular proprietor. The writer Brejoux in *Les Vins de la France* lists some forty-six, of which twenty-seven are in Vouvray and a further twelve in Rochecorbon. Those which are familiar, such as Clos Baudoin, Clos du Bourg and Clos le Mont, I only know as wines of a single estate.

Vouvray is a versatile wine; albeit white only, it comes in a range of sweetness, from bone dry to *doux*, and can be still, *pétillant* (2.5 kg/cm² pressure) or *mousseux* (4.5 kg/cm²). Moreover, within the still wines there are those which are ready for drinking almost as soon as they have been bottled and those more 'serious' wines which benefit from up to five or even ten years in bottle, even when made *sec*.

All Vouvray is made exclusively from the Chenin Blanc or, as it is known locally, the Pineau de Loire grape. This is a grape which normally produces a fairly firm, four-square wine, a bit hard in its youth and not taking kindly to the sulphuring essential in the *élevage* of a wine. Chenin appears to eat sulphur, and the taste lingers more than it does with other grapes, such as Muscadet or Chardonnay, for instance. Badly made, over-sulphured Vouvray has a smell and taste of wet wool or wet dogs. It is fortunate that a well-made Vouvray ages well, for it may take years to throw off the sulphury taste. Once this has occurred, or if the wine is tasted young, in cask, the true flavour of the Chenin can be discerned – full, ripe, Victoria plummy or greengage with a hint of quince, camomile or mint (in France they suggest *girofle* or wallflower), with, if the wine be sweeter, overtones of flowers, honey, fruit salad and lanolin.

There are two styles of still Vouvray. The more common, and the cheaper, can be found at the two local co-operatives or from Loire *négociants*. This is a soft, young wine, bottled early for drinking soon, and fermented and matured entirely in tank. It is normally *demi-sec*, with about 15 g to 25 g of residual sugar. The wine is light in alcohol, and sweet only because the fermentation has been arrested, not because the grapes were over-ripe.

Behind this 'commercial' Vouvray lie the wines of the better growers. Here the wine is sweet or not according to site and the weather prior to the harvest. In lesser years like 1987 the bulk will be *sec*; in others more wine will be *demi-sec*. In exceptional years such as 1989 and 1990/ or 1995 and 1996 these growers will have their patience rewarded. A proportion of the crop will be attacked by *Botrytis cinerea* or *pourriture noble*, and some enchanting honeyed, rich semi-sweet wines, *moelleux*, even *doux* (luscious), will result. Always, however, these Vouvrays are big, firm wines, austere when young, masculine in character, and long-lived. As different from the *négociant* wine as *cru classé* from a Bordeaux Rouge.

There are many good growers and *négociants* in Vouvray. Perhaps the best known, because it is one of the largest among the top flight producers, is the firm of Marc Brédif. Brédif used to be run by an enchanting man called Jacques Cartier, who had married a Brédif daughter. There was nothing Cartier would rather, it seemed, than have his work interrupted by a potential buyer and spend the afternoon opening old bottles, though he was a bit frosty on first acquaintance. I remember vividly a bottle of 1921 he opened in 1979. The year 1921 was an extraordinary one. Not a drop of rain fell between Easter and All Saints' Day. Every crop except the vine died that summer. The wine was *amontillado* in colour, velvet-textured, crammed with fruit, richly honeyed – and as fresh as a three-year-old one would have been – perfection. Cartier is now *en retraite* and the firm is owned by the Pouilly-Fumé producer, Patrick de Ladoucette.

André Foreau is perhaps the most 'serious' grower, in the sense that he produces the most long-lasting wine. He has 12 hectares of vines and is a great believer in making a wine for keeping, which he does by fermenting in cask at a low temperature and leaving the wine in the depths of his chilly cellars for a long time before bottling. Shy, diffident, reluctant to let one taste, let alone buy, anything he considers not yet ready to be put on the market, he appears withdrawn from the world, the perpetual outsider, viewing you and the rest of the hurly-burly with just the suggestion of a quizzical smile. Foreau's wines often take seven or even ten years to come round. When they do they are full, very aromatic, very distinguished.

Gaston Huet is generally reckoned to produce the best wine in Vouvray. I first came across his wines in the early 1970s when they were shipped to Britain. A few years later, I thought the quality slipped a little, in the 1980s the wines seemed back on top form. Huet owns three properties, Le Haut Lieu (mentioned in the preface to Sir Walter Scott's novel *Quentin Durward*), Clos du Bourg and Le Mont, totalling 32 hectares, which is large for Vouvray. Traditional methods (fermentation in wood and avoiding malolactic fermentation, like other top Vouvray growers) produce full, firm, long-lasting wines, though Huet bottles earlier than Foreau, in March or April after the vintage, and his wines are a little more supple when they are young.

Huet himself is largely occupied with his duties as Mayor of Vouvray (since 1947), Vice-President of the INAO for Loire wines, and President of the Comité Interprofessionel of the Touraine. For fifteen years or so, the day-to-day running of the Huet domaine has been in the hands of his son-in-law, Noël Pinguet.

Elsewhere in Vouvray, I have been impressed with the wines of David Allias, Prince Poniatowski at Clos Baudoin, André Treslier, Jacques Chevreau, Pierre-Jean Mathias at Domaine des Barquins and the Château de Moncontour – which also produces Blanc Foussy, a sparkling Touraine wine. Of the two co-operatives, the Cave Co-opérative des Producteurs des Vins Fins at La Vallée Coquette has a better reputation than that at the Château de Vaudenuits, and produces excellent, early-to-drink wines.

Production of still Vouvray in 1996 totalled 54,362 hectolitres, now overtaken by the amount of sparkling wine made (55,220 hectolitres). (*See also page 227.*)

MONTLOUIS

Opposite Vouvray, on a piece of land bounded by the Loire and Cher rivers, by the suburbs of Tours to the west and the Forêt d'Amboise to the east, is Montlouis, Vouvray's rather forgotten and smaller cousin.

There is little to differentiate the wines of Montlouis from the lesser, quicker-maturing wines of Vouvray. The soil is broadly the same, though sandier; the grape variety, the Chenin, is the same, and the microclimate can hardly be materially different. Indeed until *appellation contrôlée* was awarded in 1938, Montlouis wine was sold under the name of its illustrious neighbour, and fetched proportionately higher prices because of it. The imposition of AC, against the wishes of the local growers, suddenly leaving them with the problem of selling their wine under a totally unknown name, was a setback from which Montlouis has still not completely recovered. This disadvantage is compounded by the fact that the area is rather off the beaten track. If the tourist wants to visit Montlouis after Vouvray, he must go west to Tours to cross the river or continue on to Amboise and then double back. There is only a railway bridge across the Loire at Montlouis and I suspect most people leave Montlouis off their itinerary. Certainly the growers have seemed rather surprised to receive a British wine buyer!

Montlouis has three communes: Montlouis itself, which lies almost directly across the Loire from Vouvray, Lussault, upstream towards Amboise, and Saint Martin-Le-Beau, on the river Cher. These parish divisions are somewhat arbitrary. In essence, the vineyard area consists of a limestone-clay plateau which overlaps the three communes. This is some 60 to 90 metres in altitude and falls more sharply northwards towards the Loire, more gently towards the Cher. About a third of the wine is made into *mousseux* (*see also page 227*.) Production in 1996 was 9448 hectolitres of still wine and 7559 of *mousseux*, from a vineyard area of 365 hectares.

The leading grower in Montlouis is Dominique Moyer at Husseau, a small village equidistant between Montlouis and Lussault. Moyer has about 11 hectares of vines and is one of the few to produce a more *vin-de-garde* style of wine, fuller, firmer and avoiding any malolactic fermentation. Another property whose wines I have enjoyed is the 12-hectare Domaine de Liard in the village of Saint-Martin-Le-Beau which is owned by the Berger brothers.

Montlouis wine is some 10 per cent cheaper than Vouvray, and, as such, excellent value. Nearly all of it is dry or *demi-sec*. Few seek to risk all for the precarious and perhaps hard-to-sell possibility of making *moelleux* or *doux* wine.

THE GREAT RED WINES OF THE TOURAINE

The great red wines of the Touraine come from a number of districts at the western end of the region near where the river Vienne flows into the Loire. The two largest and most important are Bourgueil, on the north bank of the Loire, and Chinon, from either bank of the Vienne. Adjacent to Bourgueil is Saint-Nicolas-de-Bourgueil.

All these three increasingly popular and well-made red wines are made almost exclusively from the Cabernet Franc grape, locally known as the Breton. Cabernet Franc originates in Bordeaux, where in the Médoc it is a subsidiary to the Cabernet Sauvignon, and in Saint-Émilion, under the name of Bouchet, it is planted alongside the Merlot. Here in the Loire, the Breton is pruned to one long cane, with seven or eight buds (the *guyot simple*) and produces a wine which everyone from Rabelais onwards has compared to raspberries. The Breton is a hardy but relatively late-maturing plant. This might seem a disadvantage in a northerly red wine district such as this, but the variety is resistant to rot and so can take advantage of Indian summers, giving a must of good colour, alcohol and fruit, with a tannin content which is not too hard or unyielding. The result is a wine which does not take too long to mature. Cabernet Franc can even be made into a *vin de l'année*, for drinking cool in the summer following the vintage.

There are two hypotheses for Cabernet Franc's local name of Breton. The first story relates how Cardinal Richelieu sent his *intendant*, or local administrator, to Bordeaux in 1631 to bring back a better grape variety than the then widely planted Pineau d'Aunis and Cot (otherwise the Malbec of Bordeaux and Auxerrois of Cahors). The *intendant* was the Abbé Breton.

This story is flatly contradicted by references in Rabelais's *Gargantua*, written a century earlier in 1534 – 'This excellent Breton wine, which doesn't come from Brittany but from this fine countryside of Veron' (the Chinon area). The late Monsieur Ory, president of the Saint-Nicolas-de-Bourgueil viticultural syndicate as well as mayor of the village, considered that the name originated from Brittany, for the Bretons were Bourgueil's principal customers. There was also a vineyard on the Presqu'île de Rhins, in the Morbihan in south Brittany, whose fruity wine was said to resemble that of the Touraine and where the local monastery was of the same order, the Benedictines, as that of Bourgueil. What is still to be established is how the vine came to be transplanted from Aquitaine, but it is said to have been first planted in the Loire Valley by the Abbot of Bourgueil, Bauly, in about 1090.

The standard of the Touraine reds has increased immeasurably in recent years. A generation ago it was only in the best of years, in 1964, for example, which is still well-remembered as a classic, that good wine was made. In lesser years the wine was thin and astringent, lacking an essential element of fatness and richness, and so lacking charm. It aged badly, tending to attenuate and dry out. Vinification methods have improved. Nowadays the *cuvaison*, the time the wine macerates on its skins, is shorter, the temperature is better controlled, being warmed if necessary to extract a maximum of fruit as quickly as possible, and the wines are, as a result, more fruity, more supple, more attractive; above all, more consistent. Touraine reds can now be enjoyed in every vintage, and one can anticipate *vins de garde*, not merely *vins de l'année*, in most years.

CHINON

Wine has been made in the Chinon area since Gallo-Roman times, as the unearthing of a small Gaullish vase in the shape of a bunch of grapes has shown. The town of Chinon has been a strategic point since at least then, the existing castle being constructed on Roman fortifications, largely during the time of the Plantagenet king, Henry II in the twelfth century. Henry and his turbulent family based themselves in Chinon rather than in England, and both he and his son, the Lionheart, died in the castle and are buried in nearby Fontevraud. No doubt the regular presence of the English court ensured a ready market for the local wine, a taste which they took back with them to England when Chinon was lost, after an eight-month siege, to the French king, Philippe-Auguste in 1205.

Two centuries later, Chinon castle was again to become a focal point. At France's lowest ebb in the Hundred Years War, the dauphin Charles had brought his court to Chinon and summoned the Estates-General from the central and southern parts of the country still faithful to him to vote money for the relief of Orléans, besieged by the English and the Burgundians under Lord Salisbury.

With his confidence restored first by the faith and consequently by the successful exploits of Joan of Arc, Charles and his army were able to turn the course of the war, and eventually to drive the English out of most of France. The dauphin's revival began with the well-known story, set in Chinon castle, of how Joan recognized the king, though without his finery, and lurking among his courtiers. Later the castle was allowed to fall into ruins. Cardinal Richelieu had much of it demolished in order to build the town named after him forty kilometres to the south. For nearly three centuries the castle remained in the family of his descendants who neglected it. Today the castle is owned by the state and is slowly being restored.

The wine of Chinon is inseparable from the author Rabelais. He was born at La Devinière, a few kilometres to the south of the town, and spent his childhood in Chinon, interrupted only when he left to complete his studies in Angers and Montpellier. His books are liberally sprinkled with references to the wines, and by way of response the town has erected a statue of him, and the local wine promotional organization is called Les Entonneurs Rabelaisiens de Chinon. (An *entonneur* is someone who sings the praises of someone or something.)

Chinon lies on the river Vienne, some twelve kilometres before this river reaches the Loire at Candes, and is more of a Vienne wine than a Loire wine. The vineyards cover some 1640 hectares, double the area of twenty years ago, and run from the communes of Savigny, Avoine, Beaumont, Huismes and Saint-Benoit, north of Chinon, all the way along the north bank of the Vienne, through the villages of Cravant, Janzoult, Aron-les-Roches and Crouzilles. Crossing the river, the *appellation* returns along the south bank through Théneuil, l'Île-Bouchard, Tavant, Sazilly, Anché, Ligré, Marçay, Rivière and La Roche-Clermault. In all there are nineteen communes which produced 109,895 hectolitres in 1996. There is an infinitesimal amount of wine Chinon made from Chenin Blanc.

The Chinon vines are planted in a number of soils. Closest to the Vienne the terrain is sand mixed with gravel. From here come light wines, short-lived and for early drinking. Further up the slope the soil has more clay in it, mixed with sand, gravel and limestone: medium-weight wines, with depth and finesse. From the limestone *coteaux* come wines with the most weight and character, full-bodied wines which need five years to mature and will keep, in the best years, for twenty. These *vins de tuffe* are the great Chinons, but they are rare and expensive, and, dare I say it, only worth it in an exceptional autumn when it has been dry and sunny enough to concentrate fully the ripeness of the fruit. In most years, and with most growers, a judicious blend of the upper slopes and the plateau produces the best wine; from the lower slopes a delightful carafe wine for the local restaurants and the bistros of Paris is made, to be drunk in the year after the vintage.

A relatively large and increasingly prosperous wine-making area like Chinon will have many good producers to choose from, and it is impossible to write with personal experience of them all. The leading *négociant* in the area is the firm of Couly-Dutheil, whose cellars are in the Rue Diderot in Chinon, and reach deep into the rock underneath the castle itself. The firm was founded in the nineteenth century by Baptiste Dutheil and developed by René Couly, his son-in-law. Currently the management is in the hands of René's sons, Jacques and Pierre. The Coulys own or rent 40 hectares of vines, among which are the Clos de l'Écho, which is said to have belonged to Rabelais himself, and the Domaine René Couly, on the plateau above the town. They also have exclusive contracts on about 65 hectares of other vineyards. La Baronne Madelaine is one of their top wines. Couly's wines are always good, and their Clos d'Écho 1964 was still vigorous, rich and fruity in 1984, perhaps the best mature Chinon that has ever come my way. The best vintages since are 1976, '82, '85, '86, '88, '89, and 1990, with 1995, 1996 and 1997 waiting in the wings. This wine seems to be reserved for private customers and the top French restaurants.

Of the growers, one of the best I have come across is Jean-François Olek, who has 7 hectares of vines, mainly on the *coteaux*, at La Chapellière in Cravant-les-Côteaux, perhaps the best commune in the area. Monsieur Olek has Scandinavian ancestors and a healthy interest in wines from elsewhere, and, unlike many French winemakers, even from outside France. He is a great believer in the value of wood-ageing, rather than tanks which fail to give, in his view, depth and dimension as well as a capacity for longevity to the wine. A great character himself, he confesses to feeling that one must be a bit mad to be the sort of grower who insists on not compromising in the search for the best possible quality. His 1985 was enormously fat and rich but still very firm and closed in 1989; The '82 was still a giant, even the less auspicious '86 was big, full-flavoured and complex.

Along this northern section of the vineyards, east of Chinon to Panzoult, are many other good growers, including Serge Sourdais and Guy Lemaire for *vins de garde*, and the Chauveau brothers at the Domaine de Pallus Beauséjour, or Michel Fontaine at the Domaine de l'Abbaye for softer wines. Others include René Gouron, Raymond Desbourdes, Jean Baudry and Gaston Angelliaume. On the west side of Chinon is Olga Raffault and a number of other independent members of the Raffault family, including Jean-Maurice at La Croix and Raymond at the confusingly named Domaine de Raifault in Savigny-en-Véron, as well as Guy Jamet in Beaumont.

On the south bank the most interesting grower is Charles Joguet de la Dioterie in Sazilly. Joguet is a painter and sculptor as well as winemaker. His wine is fermented in stainless steel and in 1970 he started using oak barrels bought from Château Latour to mature his wines for eighteen months before bottling. His 'Vieilles Vignes' wine is particularly fine. Gallien Ferrand at the Château de Ligré makes a pleasantly fruity, forward wine, but elsewhere on this side of the river, where in general the soil contains more sand and less limestone than on the north bank, the wines are less noteworthy.

Apart from Rabelais and his raspberries, what does Chinon taste like, and how does it differ from Bourgueil? Chinon for me does have a taste of raspberries, but this is mixed with other fruit, strawberries and mulberries, blackcurrants and plums, overlaid with a slightly spurious perfumed quality I associate with violet cachous. When you get a very dense *vin de garde* Chinon other flavours and spices intrude, including chocolate and earth (which can be clean or rustic depending on the winemaker). Above all, Chinon is, or should be, a supple wine; essentially, however youthful and muscular, a wine with a soft centre. Bourgueil wines are more austere, more sinewy, normally fuller. I find Bourgueil wines less appealing, and also less successful in the lesser years. This might be my limited experience of growers; it might be the soil or microclimate; it may also be a failure of the Bourgueil growers to adapt their vinification to the production of a lighter, more supple wine when the condition of the fruit warrants it.

BOURGUEIL and SAINT-NICOLAS-DE-BOURGUEIL

North and west of Chinon, on the north bank of the Loire, lie the districts of Bourgueil and Saint-Nicolas-de-Bourgueil. Those who make wine in Saint-Nicolas will argue that their wine is superior, more elegant and delicate, to straight Bourgueil.

There is, in truth, no discernible difference between the two. The soils are the same and the *encépagement* identical – Cabernet Franc almost exclusively, though Cabernet Sauvignon is also authorized. Saint-Nicolas, though, has a more restricted *rendement*, 35 hectolitres per hectare as opposed to 40 hectolitres, and is marginally more expensive. According to the late Alexis Lichine the separate *appellation* for Saint-Nicolas is explained by the fact that when the INAO was codifying the Touraine, the mayor of Saint-Nicolas-de-Bourgueil, Monsieur Ory, was the largest vineyard holder and successfully lobbied for his own communal *appellation*.

Bourgueil is spread over the communes of Saint-Nicolas-de-Bourgueil, Bourgueil, Benais, Restigné, Ingrandes and Saint-Patrice, on a straight west-east line parallel to the Loire, plus the less important communes of Chouze and La Chapelle on the edge of the river. As in Chinon the soil varies between sand (*sables limoneux*), locally known as *varennes*, nearest to the Loire, gravels of various size in the centre, and limestone *tuffe*, over which is flinty clay on the higher slopes. Many growers have cellars underneath their vineyards in old quarries. The summit of the slope is densely covered with trees and shrub, giving the vineyards protection from the north.

If it is difficult to distinguish between Saint-Nicolas and the rest of Bourgueil, and indeed between both of these and Chinon, it is easier to tell the difference, as in Chinon, between the wines from different soils. As in Chinon, the differences are the same. Again, most growers have vineyards on two or more sites, and make a blend between them, or produce a *primeur* from the lighter soil, and a more substantial wine from the *tuffe*.

The leading local merchant, with cellars and offices in the middle of Bourgueil, is Audebert et Fils. The firm own 27 hectares of vines and their main wine, the Domaine du Grand Clos, also labelled as Les Marquises, is a soft, *primeur*-style wine, at its best after a year or two. A cousin, Marcel Audebert, has 10 hectares at Restigné. Another *négociant* is Lamé-Delille-Boucard in Ingrandes, whose 25 hectares are spread between Ingrandes, Saint-Patrice, Restigné and Benais. Their cellars are some of the most spectacularly mould-infested I have ever seen!

Among the Bourgueil growers Paul Maître at the Domaine Raguenières at Benais has 12 hectares and perhaps the leading reputation in the district. His wine finds its way on to the lists of the best local restaurants and the most prestigious importers abroad. Nearby, and of similar size, Caslot-Galbrun at La Hurolaïe produces a similarly sturdy wine, which in good years, such as 1989 and 1990 ages to produce a rich, round, meaty bottle, as does his kinsman Caslot-Jamet at the Domaine de la Chavalerie in Restigné.

Other growers in Bourgueil with a good reputation include: GAEC La Dîme (Jean-Baptiste Thouet and Michel Lorieux) which sells as Clos de l'Abbaye; Pierre Grégoire at the Domaine des Geslets whose vineyard is in fact in Saint-Nicolas but who sells his wine simply as Bourgueil; and Marc Mureau in Lossay and Raphael Galteau at Ingrandes.

In Saint-Nicolas, perhaps because the *tuffe* is less thick, the best growers, in my experience, produce wine which is no more than medium-weight, without the substance and power of wines from Maître and the Caslots. These Saint-Nicolas growers include Claude Ammeux at Clos de la Contrie, who manures his vines with seaweed; Claude Amirault at Clos des Quarterons, a big estate of 16 hectares, two families of Jamets, Pierre and Anselme, and Jean-Claude Mabilot, all of whom produce light, fruity *primeur* wines; plus Claude Moreau at La Taille and Joel Taluau at Chevrette. Production of Bourgueil amounted to 74,149 hectolitres in 1988 and Saint-Nicolas 53,194 hectolitres from a combined area of 2171 hectares. A wine similar in character and stature to Chinon and Bourgueil is made just across the Anjou boundary at Saumur-Champigny (*see page 236*).

TOURAINE-MESLAND

Between Amboise and Blois, on the north bank of the Loire, lies the first of three small vineyard areas which have been singled out from generic Touraine wine. These three communes can add their name to the Touraine AC provided they have one more degree of alcohol (10.5 degrees as opposed to 9.5 degrees). Touraine-Mesland (the others are Touraine-Amboise, its western neighbour, and Touraine-Azay-le-Rideau) is the second largest of the three, producing almost 16,265 hectolitres of wine in 1996. Why these three villages should have been so selected seems somewhat arbitrary, for there seems neither a significant increase in quality between these and 'ordinary' Touraines – there are poor and exciting growers on both sides – nor is there a particularly special or individual style of wine. No doubt political pressure and good relations with the powers in the INAO have played their part, and the reward to the growers of Mesland, Amboise and Azay is an extra franc or two per bottle.

The 153 hectares producing AC Touraine-Mesland lie in the communes of Mesland itself, Chambon, Chouzy, Molineuf, Monteaux and Onzain, on a soil which is predominantly clay mixed with sand or limestone. The main grape variety is the Gamay Noir à Jus Blanc but both Cabernets and the Malbec (known locally as the Cot) are also authorized. Chenin is authorized for white wine.

The *appellation* is dominated by the Onzain co-operative, an establishment whose wine has been variable in quality but which surely should be able to do good things. Onzain produces about a third of all Touraine-Mesland wine. Elsewhere the quality is equally variable. On a brief visit in the summer of 1984 the only grower out of half a dozen recommended to me, or noticed in lists of gold-medal winners that I could recommend, was the establishment of François Girault of the Domaine d'Artois and Château Gaillard. Even these, and I am speaking of wines of the successful 1988 and '86 vintages, were somewhat austere, even a little mean. The best of the wines are the Gamay-based rosés.

TOURAINE-AMBOISE

Michel Debré, mayor in 1954, is credited with the creation of the separate *appellation* of Touraine-Amboise halfway between Tours and Blois. This is a small but expanding region of some 180 hectares on both sides of the river, centred round the bustling town of Amboise which is dominated by its impressive castle overlooking the river.

Again, like Mesland, its neighbour slightly upstream, the region is more noticeable for other tourist attractions than its wine, for the castle at Amboise is truly *vaut le voyage*, and the Leonardo da Vinci museum – the great man was invited here by François I in 1515 and died at Amboise four years later – is equally worth a visit.

The *appellation* covers eight communes, and the same grapes, grown roughly in the same proportions and regulations, are authorized as in Mesland. In 1996 the yield totalled 9960 hectolitres.

The wine I have seen most regularly is that of the Château de Pocé, bottled and sold by the enterprising Amboise firm of Pierre Chainier. Château de Pocé lies on the north bank of the Loire and produces a white wine from Chenin Blanc, and both red and rosé from the Gamay. Elsewhere the Denay family at Le Breuil, near Amboise, produce a range of wines of dependable quality from a full range of grapes.

TOURAINE AZAY-LE-RIDEAU

Azay-le-Rideau's superb Renaissance château, built on the edge of the river Indre southwest of Tours, is justly one of the most popular in the Loire. Tourists flock by the charabanc-load to be conducted in the rather grudging French manner round its beautiful rooms, now somewhat denuded of furniture but still containing a few enviable examples as well as some fine tapestries and chimneypieces.

The wine, however, is less well known. The area is smaller then Mesland and Amboise, a mere 44 hectares of vines spread over eight communes. In 1996 1622 hectolitres of wine were produced. The *appellation* excludes red wine. It was the white wine which was authorized first. This comes from the Chenin Blanc grape and can vary in style from bone dry to appreciably sweet, depending on the weather and the inclination of the grower. The rosé received its *appellation* in 1976 and must be made primarily from the Groslot, not the classiest of varieties, together with Gamay, Cot and the two Cabernets.

The leading grower is Gaston Pavy who has only 3 hectares of vines. These are mostly planted with Chenin Blanc, from which he makes both dry and sweet wine. His vineyard in Saché, upstream from Azay, lies near the solid Château de Saché, frequent home to the author, Honoré de Balzac.

On the road from Azay to Tours lies the largest local vineyard, the Château de l'Aulée. The operation here is in complete contrast to the shy, modest perfectionism of Pavy. Owned by the champagne firm of Deutz and Geldermann, this is a factory, producing a competent but rather innocuous white wine as well as a Touraine Mousseux – which, I suspect, is what interests them most – from both their own vineyards and from grapes bought from local growers on a contract basis.

TOURAINE

Generic Touraine can be marvellous or dreary and can come from anywhere within the old province of Touraine, roughly bordered by Fontevraud and Blois to the west and east, and Château-Renault and Loches to the north and south. Production figures are impressive, more than 280,000 hectolitres in 1998 in roughly equal proportions of red and rosé and white. In 1988 red and rosé wine accounted for 180,874 hectolitres and white wine for 103,248 from a total of 5437 hectares.

White wines come from the Chenin Blanc and the Sauvignon Blanc, with Chardonnay also authorized but to a maximum of 20 per cent only. The reds and rosés can come from, in alphabetical order, Cabernet Franc, Cabernet Sauvignon, Gamay Noir à Jus Blanc, Groslot (rosé only), Pineau d'Aunis, Pinot Gris and Pinot Meunier, though it is Gamay which is the most widely planted.

In such a large area, with so many different grapes and soils – though the clay-limestone mixture the French call *argillo-calcaire* predominates – it is difficult to generalize about Touraine's run-of-the-mill wines. From the top *négociants*, such as Plouzeau in Chinon, Aimé Boucher in Huisseau, near Chambord, Pierre Chainier in Amboise, Bougrier in Saint-Georges-sur-Cher and Rabier in Menars, come a range of wines, from Vin de Pays du Jardin de la France to single-varietal wines which are more than equal in quality and value-for-money to those of higher *appellations*. These firms often farm the vineyard and vinify and sell the wines of single growers whom they have under contract. Firms from outside the immediate area, such as Patrick de Ladoucette of Pouilly and Moreau in Chablis, also produce excellent Touraine wines.

Good domaine wines include the Domaine de la Garrelière, south of Richelieu (owned by the Plouzeau family), Domaine des Roussières and Domaine du Grand Moulin from Pierre Chainier, Domaine de Châteauvieux, Domaine de la Charmoise (Henri Marionnet in Soigns) and Domaine des Corbillières (Maurice Barbon in Oisly). Joël Delaunay produces a lovely example from very flinty soil at Douillé near Vierson.

Co-operatives, when they are good, can be very good. The Confrèrie des Vignerons de Oisly-et-Thésée produce a range of generic wines at different prices. Their top Sauvignon wines are not cheap, but they can be excellent, with a light, crisp, grassy flavour which is characteristic of this grape in the eastern end of the area. There are other co-operatives at Civray and Francueil, near Bléré, at Onzain, at Limeray near Amboise, and at Saint-Georges and Saint-Romain on the Cher.

THE COTEAUX DU LOIR and JASNIÈRES

North of the Loire between La Flèche and Vendôme lies the valley of a river confusingly called the Loir (or le Loir as opposed to la Loire). This masculine tributary of a greater, feminine neighbour rises south of Chartres and for much of its distance runs roughly parallel to the Loire before joining the Sarthe north of Angers.

The Coteaux du Loir is a tiny *appellation* centred round the towns of Château-du-Loir and La Chartré about forty kilometres north of Tours. Though the district covers twenty-two communes only some 57 hectares are under production, and the yield totalled a mere 2497 hectolitres. The reds and rosés can be made from Pineau d'Aunis, Cabernet Franc, Gamay and Cot. The whites come from Chenin Blanc. Because of the northerly climate, the permitted yield is restricted to a maximum of 55 hectolitres per acre for white wine and 30 hectolitres per hectare for red wine. In my experience the wines are unexciting.

Jasnières is a sub-region of the Coteaux di Loir and is confined to white wines only, with the same reduced yield, 25 hectolitres per hectare. The *appellation* covers two communes, L'Homme and Ruillé. Some 41 hectares are under cultivation. The yield fluctuates widely. It amounted to 1672 hectolitres in 1996.

L'Homme and Ruillé lie on the north bank of the river Loir near La Chartré, on limestone *tuffe* soil similar to that at Vouvray. On a few sites, well-exposed to the south, protected from the north winds and in the best vintages, the Chenin Blanc grape can ripen satisfactorily to produce a light, acidic wine, raspingly dry when young, but attaining a certain fatness and plumpness if allowed a few years in bottle. It is somewhat of an acquired taste, but one or two local growers – Noël Gigou, whose wine I first met at the best local restaurant, André Paul in Coëment, and Jean-Baptiste Pinon in Montoire-sur-Loir – do produce wine with at least some merit. This is really, though, at the northern limits of wine-making, at least from native French grape varieties, and there has to be a magnificent autumn before the wines produced are anything but over-tart and impossibly austere.

CHEVERNY VDQS

South of Blois and the former royal parks of Russy and Chambord, at the eastern end of the Touraine, lies the fairly extensive VDQS of Cheverny and its much smaller subsiduary Cous-Cheverney. Through all the local Touraine Romorantin grape, said to have been introduced to the area from Burgundy by François I. I cannot say that I am a fan of this variety. It produces a rather sour white wine with a peculiar foxy taste, which is both green and acidic when young and tired and attenuated after a year or two more.

Since Cheverney received its VDQS in 1973 the combined area under cultivation has increased to 395 hectares in 1996. Production in 1996 totalled 150 of the Cous-Cheverney (white) and 16,613 hectolitres of Cheverney (red or rosé). The red or rosé is made from Gamy. The *appellation* communes twenty-three communes. Producers include the co-operative at Mont-près-Chambord and the Chai des Vignerons, a private co-operative at Chitenay. François Cazin is one of the few individual growers with any reputation.

VALENÇAY VDQS

Valençay lies at the extreme south-east of the Touraine, in the *département* of Indre, south of the river Cher. It comprises 129 hectares of vines spread over fourteen communes. In 1996 4874 hectolitres of red or rosé and 1914 of white were produced. The reds, mainly from the Gamay grape, are light and rustic, as are the whites, though these come from a potentially interesting blend of Sauvignon, Chardonnay and Arbois. Talleyrand, a noted gourmet, lived at the Château de Valençay in the early nineteenth century. I doubt that he thought much of the local wines either.

COTEAUX DU VENDÔMOIS VDQS

The Coteaux du Vendômois lies further upstream from Jasnières and the Coteaux du Loir, some thirty kilometers north-west of Blois. A total of 154 hectares produced 7201 hectolitres of mainly light red and rosé wine in 1996 and 1242 of white. The reds and rosés come largely from Gamay and Pineau d'Aunis. The whites are made from Chenin with up to 20 per cent Chardonnay. The quality is indifferent, no better than what one would expect from such a northerly region.

The Sparkling Wines of the Loire

Both Touraine and the Anjou produce excellent champagne-method sparkling wines. These can be found either under the regional *appellations* of Touraine and Anjou, or, as is more usual, under more specific district names such as Vouvray, Montlouis and Saumur. Names may vary but production methods, authorized grape varieties and other details are similar, as is the end product, so it seems logical to deal with these under one heading, and at this juncture, as we are about to traverse the boundaries between the Touraine and the Anjou.

The Loire sparkling wines are normally sold as *brut*, though in practice they are marginally sweeter than most *brut* champagnes. Those from Vouvray are a little lighter – more feminine perhaps – than those of Saumur, and in my view not as rich or complex. None are as fine as champagne, but they are, of course, considerably cheaper. What always surprises me is that production should be so tiny compared with champagne. Even if you take all the Loire sparkling wines combined, and then add the production of all the other *méthode champenoise* wines of France (the Crémants of Burgundy and Alsace, and Blanquette de Limoux) the total is barely a quarter that of champagne.

One of the explanations for the difference between the character of Vouvray *mousseux* and Saumur lies the mix of grape varieties authorized. Vouvray and Montlouis sparkling wines are made from Chenin Blanc only, and are solely white wines. Saumur and Anjou can also be rosé and red, though in practice production of the latter is very small indeed. Black grapes are permitted for all three colours of wine. These are Cabernet Sauvignon, Cabernet Franc, Cot, Gamay, Groslot, Pineau d'Aunis and even Pinot Noir (in Saumur only). The rosés and reds are made from any mixture of these. For white sparkling Saumur Chenin plus a maximum of 20 per cent each Sauvignon Blanc and Chardonnay is allowed, plus the black varieties already listed, to a maximum of 60 per cent of the *cuvéee*. Anjou is slightly different, Chardonnay and Sauvignon not being permitted, and Chenin has to make up a minimum of 60 per cent of the blend.

Méthode champenoise can be translated as the way sparkling wines are made in Champagne, and defined as the production of carbon dioxide (which vaporizes once the cork and pressure within the bottle is released) by means of inducing a second fermentation in a bottle. Thereafter the wine never leaves this particular receptacle until the cork is drawn prior to drinking. This process is discussed in greater detail in the chapter on Champagne (*see page 303*).

The technique was brought from the Champagne region to the Loire in Napoleonic times by a Belgian, Jean Ackerman, who married a girl named Laurance from Saumur. He produced his first sparkling wine in Saumur in 1811. For thirty-seven years his was the only local firm to make sparkling wine, and today Ackerman-Laurance, now largely owned by the Rémy family of Rémy-Pannier, is still the largest sparkling wine firm in the Loire, though now, naturally, there is considerable competition from other producers. Originally, until the name of champagne was protected early in the twentieth century in a series of decrees, the wine was sold as champagne, with the Loire element played down to a minimum. Among the Loire regional sparkling *appellations* Saumur has until recently been the dominant one. In 1996 106,497 hectolitres were produced.

CRÉMANT DE LOIRE

In 1975 a new *appellation* for a quality white sparkling wine was authorized, Crémant de Loire. The yield was restricted to 50 hectolitres per hectare, as against 60 hectolitres for Saumur Mousseux (or as the locals prefer to call it, Saumur d'Origine) and the weight of grapes required for one hectolitre of must was fixed at 150 kilograms as opposed to 130. A longer period of bottle-ageing was also required. A Crémant has to remain on its lees before disgorging for a year while Saumur d'Origine needs only nine months.

The *appellation* excludes the inferior Cot and restricts the amount of Groslot to 30 per cent. The grapes can come from either Anjou or Touraine, though in practice Crémant seems to have become sort of superior Saumur. As yet production is small (26,989 hectolitres in 1996 of which 25,401 was white wine) but the advance in quality, even over the best Saumur d'Origine, is considerable. Ackerman-Laurance (Cuvée Privée and Cuvée Privilège), Bouvet-Ladubay and Gratien, Meyer and Seydoux all have excellent examples.

VOUVRAY MOUSSEUX and MONTLOUIS MOUSSEUX

Sparkling-wine production in Vouvray and Montlouis is a relatively recent development. According to Monsieur Cuvier, the now retired director of the Cave Co-opérative des Producteurs de Vins Fins at La Vallée Coquette, the idea was dreamed up by the Mayor of Vouvray, Monsieur Vavasseur, during the First World War, when there was a shortage of champagne. Production has boomed since 1950, and now stands at nearly 63,000 hectolitres per annum. This is less than that of Saumur, but it comes at a time of increasing demand for the still wines. Nevertheless, the *mousseux* wines now make up an important part of most Vouvray producers' portfolios.

One of the best sparkling Vouvrays comes from Château Montcontour, a handsome fifteenth-century château just outside the town on the road to Tours. Since being taken over by the firm of Foltz, the estate has expanded to some 65 hectares of vines, the largest holding in the Vouvray *appellation*. Their still wines, impeccably vinified by the most up-to-date methods, are also recommended.

Both the co-operatives, Château de Vandenuits and La Vallée Coquette, produce good examples of Vouvray Mousseux, and also make the sparkling wines for several of the other local firms.

TOURAINE MOUSSEUX

The *appellation* Touraine Mousseux is relatively new, being created in 1974. Production in 1996 totalled 25,829 hectolitres. This is very small compared with sparkling Vouvray, let alone Saumur. Two firms dominate the appellation. The first is the Société Foltz at Rochecorbon who, as well as owning Ch‚teau Montcontour, own the brand Blanc Foussy. Like sparkling Vouvray, Blanc Foussy is made only from Chenin Blanc. I find the wine easy to drink without being particularly elegant.

On the Cher at Montrichard, is the firm of J.M. Monmousseau with some 60 hectares of vines. The Monmousseaus are and old Touraine family and have been *négciants* since 1886. Their best-known sparkling wine is the Brut de Mosny, which, like Blanc Foussy, is a Blanc de Blancs.

SAUMUR D'ORIGINE

Sparkling Saumur – the name of the *appellation* was changed from Saumur Mousseux to Saumur d'Origine a few years ago – is perhaps the best-known champagne-method wine (excluding Champagne itself) produced in France. At present a dozen or so firms produce about eleven million bottles of Saumur d'Origine, (104,497 hectolitres in 1996), a figure which has grown considerably since the Second World War.

Some champagne houses have had the foresight to diversify into the sparkling Saumur field. Taittinger own Bouvet-Ladubay (and Monmousseau who make other Loire sparkling wines in Montrichard) and Bollinger own Langlois-Château.

Most of the leading Saumur houses were founded in the second half of the nineteenth century – Bouvet-Ladubay in 1851, De Neuville in 1856, Veuve Amiot in 1882, Gratien, Meyer in 1884, and Langlois-Château in 1885. The exception is the Compagnie Française de Grand Vins who own the brand Cadre Noir. Together with Ackerman-Laurance, these six houses have formed the Comité du Vin de Saumur, with the objective of maintaining and promoting the quality of sparkling Saumur. This association possesses a joint harvest reception centre on the outskirts of Saumur, for most of these producers prefer to buy grapes, not wine. Each has its own extensive cellars, cut out of the limestone *tuffe* cliffs on the left bank of the Loire, on either side of the town of Saumur. These cellars, often stretching back into the hillsides for several hundred metres, and comprising many kilometres of galleries, are great tourist attractions during the summer months. Gratien, Meyer even has an underground spring, and can arrange banquets deep inside their *caves*.

Between them, these seven *grandes maisons* plus the co-operative at Saint-Cyr-en-Bourg produce practically all the sparkling Saumur. The wine will vary quite considerably in style depending on the balance of the grape varieties in the base wine. Most of the firms have a number of grades of quality, and as elsewhere you get what you pay for. At the lowest level the blend will normally be fairly four-square and uncomplicated, and ascending upwards in value as well as in finesse and delicacy of fruit until one reaches Crémant de Loire, the highest level. The top wines of Bouvet-Ladubay and Gratien, Meyer and the co-operative can be strongly recommended.

ANJOU MOUSSEUX

The regulations governing Anjou Mousseux are the same as those for Saumur. It is not a common *appellation*. Indeed the only examples I have come across are those made from base wine produced at the Union Agricole du Pays de Loire at Brissac by the co-operative at Saint-Cyr-en-Bourg.

Anjou

The large province of Anjou lies between Touraine and the Pays Nantais or the Muscadet region, between Fontevraud Abbey in the east and the dungeon of Champtoceaux in the west, a distance of more than 100 kilometres. It includes the sweet wines of the Coteaux du Layon, the excellent dry whites of Savennières and the reds of Saumur-Champigny as well as a great deal of generic AC wine of no great presumption, red, white and rosé, under the regional names of Anjou and Saumur.

The vineyards for AC wines occupy 14,413 hectares. They lie almost entirely in the Maine-et-Loire dÈpartement and produce on average some 850,000 hectolitres of wine a year. Thirty-seven per cent of this is rosé wine, with roughly 33 per cent red and 30 per cent white. This makes it the largest of the four main Loire regions, and even if most of this is fairly ordinary wine – or, at least, from a fairly basic *appellation* (Anjou) – there is much wine that is good, if not excellent, from an increasing number of enthusiastic, dedicated growers or from larger concerns with modern installations and all the latest wine-making techniques.

Anjou is much like Touraine, a countryside of sleepy villages and old country mansions, gently undulating away from the wide, slowly meandering Loire. It is lush and fertile, gentle in its colours and with its climate. The soil is a heterogeneous mixture, generally more sandy than the Touraine to the east, less clayey than the Muscadet area to the west: a combination of shale, marl, sand, limestone and gravel. As well as vineyards there are fields of arable crops, cherry orchards and market gardens, and pasture for cattle. Here and there are greenhouses full of orchids and other exotic flowers, or quarries for the slate roofs of Angers and Saumur.

The capital of the province is Angers, a more elegant town than Tours. It possesses an impressive early medieval fortified castle, built under the direction of Saint Louis in the thirteenth century. The castle has seventeen squat round towers within whose wide battlements can be found a small vineyard.

Henry II of England was also Count of Anjou. His ascent to the throne of England in 1154 gave a great boost to the wines of the region, so much so that two centuries later a law was passed prohibiting the import into Anjou of wines from outside the region, in order to protect the local produce from adulteration with 'inferior' wines.

Some centuries later while the French court was concentrating its attention on the Touraine and Orléans wines, and the English had diverted theirs to Bordeaux, the Angevins were cultivating the Dutch. The Dutch traders, who would in the seventeenth century come in search of base wine for brandy as well as for table wine, could sail their shallow boats up to the Pont de Cé, just south of Angers, and the Low Countries became an influential export market. The Dutch traders would arrive as soon as the winter weather had ameliorated, and swiftly departed with the pick of the new wine. This relationship was fostered by a strong Protestant presence in the area – Saumur is still one of France's most important Protestant centres – and it lasted, despite interruptions of war, until the French Revolution in 1789.

Traditionally, Anjou was a white wine-producing area, and for the most part this wine was sweet or semi-sweet. Red grapes for rosé, and, more recently, for red wine, is a twentieth-century innovation. It is only since the Second World War that the popularity of the soft, fruity, off-dry Anjou Rosé has become so important. But if rosé is the first thing we associate with the Anjou, there is much else which is worth investigating.

SAVENNIÈRES

If most of the dry white wines of the Loire are wines made one year for drinking the next, one small area, at least, aspires to produce something a little more substantial, a little more serious: a white wine which, like Bordeaux or Burgundy, needs time to develop. This is Savennières. Savennières lies on the north bank of the Loire, some thirteen kilometres downstream from Angers. At this point the river is flowing roughly south-west, so the vineyards, in steep little side valleys whose streams debouch into the Loire itself, have an exposure which is practically due south. The vines are protected from the wind, and enjoy full sun from dawn to dusk.

The soil is volcanic in origin, and consists of a thin layer of loess, mixed with a peculiarly coloured, blue-violet schist, with veins of sandstone and granite. This sits on a more solid schistous base which, even in the hottest summers, retains enough humidity to succour the vines. The colour of the stones is, as far as I know, unique to Savennières: certainly I have not met their like in any other vineyard area.

Savennières is small, with only 122 hectares under vine, though this figure has increased by 50 hectares since the mid 1980s. This is only just larger than one reasonably sized Médoc classed growth. Production is even smaller: 4512 hectolitres in 1996. Currently there are fifteen local growers.

The most important part of Savennières is the 2-hectare *lieu-dit* known as La Roche-aux-Moines. This site, as the name suggests, is a rocky promontory which dominates the Loire, roughly opposite where the Layon river enters it from the south near Rochefort. It is said to have been donated to the Abbey of Saint Nicolas at Angers by one Buhard, a Breton squire in the service of Geoffrey Martell, Count of Anjou, in 1063. However, this legend has been disputed by modern historians who have shown that all the poor Buhard ever possessed in the way of land were two islands in the middle of the river, one of which still preserves his name, now corrupted into Béhuard.

At the beginning of the thirteenth century, during the wars between King John of England and King Philippe Auguste of France, a fortress was built on the site, which successfully withstood several sieges by the hapless John. Both at La Roche-aux-Moines, and later at Bouvines, the English troops were defeated, as John fulfilled his destiny – to be Jean Sans Terre, or Lackland. At the end of the fourteenth century the land passed from a local *seigneur*, Guillaume de Craon, to Louis II, Duke of Anjou, and it was probably about this time that the site was first planted with vines on a large scale. A document from the mid-fifteenth century refers to the despair of local monks at the damage to the vineyard caused by a particularly bad storm. By this time the fortress and its dependencies had passed to Jean de Brie, Seigneur de Serrant, and it was one of his descendants, Pontus du Brie, who was authorized by Louis XI in 1481 to call the property La Roche du Serrant. At the end of the sixteenth century, during the religious wars between the Huguenots and the Catholics, the old fortress fell into disrepair and was largely dismantled. Only a few ruins remain to this day, notably a round tower which today stands guard over part of the vineyard known as the Clos du Château.

That the site was certainly a flourishing vineyard is shown by a story Hubrecht Duijker repeats in his admirable book on the Loire, Champagne and Alsace. Louis XIV is said to have proposed a journey to Savennières after having been much impressed by the quality of the wine when it had been presented to him at court. News of this project soon passed back to the region, and the local proprietors set about plans to receive the royal entourage. The owner of the Château de la Roche-aux-Moines actually went as far as building another storey on his mansion, and constructing new wings and towers to it. Unfortunately the king never arrived. His coach got stuck in the mud, and the king, thwarted, frustrated and angry, was forced to turn back. Later still, at the time of the Revolution, the site was known as the Roche Vineuse. Once again, under Napoleon, the wine was enjoyed at court, for one of the Empress Josephine's ladies-in-waiting was the Comtesse de Serrant.

La Roche-aux-Moines still exists, as does the tiny neighbouring 3-hectare vineyard of Coulée-de-Serrant, exclusively owned by the Joly family who are the current owners of the Château de la Roche-aux-Moines itself. They are both sub-*appellations* of Savennières itself and lie at the north-eastern end of the *appellation* between the villages of Savennières and Epiré. Epiré is next to the commune of Bouchemaine, nearest to Angers; further downstream is the commune of La Possonière. Only the most favourable, best-exposed, protected sites within these three communes are suitable for the vine, and to all intents and purposes these are all in Savennières and Epiré.

When *appellation contrôlée* was bestowed on Savennières in 1952 the yield was fixed at 25 hectolitres per hectare, and a minimum alcohol level of 12 degrees. This may seem parsimonious on the one hand, and presumptuous on the other. The explanation is that up until this time, most of the wine of Savennières, like that of its neighbours in the Layon Valley, was sweet or semi-sweet, depending on the climate. It was not dry, though some, such as Coulée de Serrant, had been vinified dry for much longer. In the last thirty years most of Savennières has been made as a dry wine, but even now in some vintages some producers make a wine which is off-dry or *tendre*, or even one which is sweeter still. Despite this change in style, the minimum yield is still only 30 hectolitres per hectare, while in the rest of Anjou 40 hectolitres for dry and medium-dry white wine is allowed.

To produce a wine with a minimum alcoholic content of 12 degrees in a northern climate such as the Loire at the very limits of successful cultivation is no mean thing. It means risking all to pick as late as possible, or, alternatively, ruining the balance and breed of the wine by excessive chaptalization. It is no wonder that making wine in Savennières is a precarious procedure. Indeed the Joly family did not make any Coulée de Serrant in

1963, '65 and '72: the grapes were just not good enough. Frost also is a problem. Inevitably, in all but the luckiest years, some vineyards are damaged.

Savennières is made exclusively from the Chenin Blanc grape. When young the wine is very austere, bone-dry, and the acidity is dominant. The 'old style' of Savennières, as practised by Nicolas Joly at the Château de la Roche-aux-Moines, is a wine which carries this austerity to an extreme. Because the wine is deliberately made as a *vin de garde*, it is bottled with a high degree of sulphur, and this combines with the Chenin Blanc grape to produce a rather solid, four-square wine with a clumsy wet-wool flavour – or so it seems for at least five years. However, in the best years patience is eventually rewarded, and the wine opens out to show a firm, full, ripe, complex character with a flowery, greengage, Victoria plum aroma and with nuances of honey and lime trees.

Elsewhere in Savennières, the trend has been to produce something a little more supple. Baron Brincard, a well-known name ten years ago, at the Domaine de la Bizolière used to have vineyards in La Roche-aux-Moines sub-*appellation* and shared another *lieu-dit*, the Clos du Papillon, with Jean Baumard, a leading grower who has cellars in Rochefort. The Bizard family at the Château d'Epiré make their wine in the crypt of a small, deconsecrated, eleventh-century church. The brothers Yves and Michel Soulez run the 11-hectare domaine of the Château de Chamboureau, and now rent the vineyard formerly owned by Baron Brincard. Madame de Jessey at the Domaine de Closel has cellars in the Château de Savennières itself. All these five properties produce excellent, somewhat softer wine than Nicolas Joly, both fruitier and more supple: also quite a bit less expensive and arguably better value. They all additionally produce well-made red wines from the Cabernet Franc grape under the Cabernet d'Anjou *appellation*.

COTEAUX DU LAYON and COTEAUX DU LAYON-VILLAGES

If Savennières produces the best dry Loire white wine, so the Layon provides the best sweet wines. In Vouvray the grapes which produce sweet wines are only very rarely, in exceptional years, attacked by the *pourriture noble* but this noble rot arrives more frequently in the Layon Valley, as a result of its microclimate. Moreover, the Layon wines can only be sweet: not for these growers the alternative of making a dry or merely *tendre* wine in lesser years though they are allowed to produce simple Anjou.

The Layon is more of a stream than a river. It rises just over the border in the *département* of Deux-Sèvres, and flows north-westwards through some of the most beautiful Loire countryside for some forty kilometres, as the crow flies, before reaching the Loire downstream of Rochefort. On the map this looks like a relatively large area; much bigger than Chinon, or even Saumur. Yet not all the area is suitable for Coteaux du Layon wine; only the best-exposed vineyards, conditioned by the microclimate of the valley itself and on precisely the correct soil, can produce, in so northerly a vineyard, the correct combination of morning mists and hot, sunny afternoons late into October, which is necessary for an attack of the noble rot. Out of a total of some 3000 hectares of vines, only about half produce Coteaux du Layon or the superior commune *appellations* of Quarts de Chaume or Bonnezeaux. The rest produce *appellation contrôlée* Anjou.

As in Sauternes, when the noble rot arrives the grapes shrivel up and dry out, both the sugar and acidity contents increase and the action of the fungus imparts a particular spicy, luscious, honeyed, herbal flavour. These wines never have the weight or richness of their Bordeaux rivals and are unsuitable for any but the most delicate desserts. But, of course, they are marvellous as dessert wines on their own, and also as an aperitif.

In order to pick each bunch of grapes at its peak of ripeness and noble rot, it is necessary to harvest through each row of vines several times – but in order to afford to do this, the growers need to be able to command a high enough price for their wine. Unfortunately the base price for a Layon wine is low. Usually there is only one picking, though this is made as late as possible. Only the top domaines have the resources to make more than one *passage* through the vineyards.

The Layon vineyards stretch over twenty-five communes between Les Verchers, south of Doué-La-Fontaine, and Chalonnes, on the Loire. The best vineyards are on the north side of the valley between Thouarcé and Rochefort on the slopes of hills which rise up to 100 metres above the river itself. The soil consists of various clay–sand–limestone mixtures such as loess and marl over a subsoil of schist. Only the Chenin Blanc is authorized, and the yield must not exceed 30 hectolitres per hectare. 1996 production totalled 57,518 hectolitres including Coteaux du Layon-Villages.

In 1955, five years after Coteaux du Layon became a separate *appellation*, the INAO decreed that seven communes could be designated Coteaux du Layon-Villages. These communes are Rochefort-sur-Loire, Chaume, Saint-Aubin-de-Luigné, Saint-Lambert-du-Lattay, Beaulieu-sur-Layon, Rablay-sur-Layon and Faye-d'Anjou. The wine from these communes must reach 12 degrees of alcohol plus another one of unconverted sugar, as against 11 degrees plus one for straight Coteaux du Layon. Moreover in Chaume itself the maximum yield was reduced to 25 hectolitres per hectare, the same as in Sauternes. Elsewhere the maximum is 30 hectolitres. Rather than sell their wine as Coteaux du Layon-Villages, it is more usual for the local growers to suffix the name of the commune; for example, Coteaux du Layon-Rablay, and so on.

Despite the limited enthusiasm and demand for sweet wines, the Layon Valley abounds in dedicated and hospitable growers. At Rochefort-sur-Loire Jean Baumard has the head growers of his excellent domaine. He also has an important holding in Quarts de Chume (*see page 234*) and a small vineyard in Rochefort called Clos de Sainte-Cathérine. Also in Rochefort are Michel Doucet at the 17-hectare Château de la Gaumonière, the Gaschet brothers, Jean and André, at the Domaine Les Martereaux and André Sorin at the 16-hectare Domaine de la Motte. Sorin recently founded the Club des Layon-Villages, a group of the best local growers. Aimé Boucher, the *négociant* at Huisseau near Chambord, have the exclusive rights to sell Jean-Paul Tijou's Domaine de Bellevue. In Saint-Aubin-de-Luigné the Gousset family own the Clos de l'Aiglerio.

One of the best estates in Saint-Lambert-du-Lattay is the 13-hectare Domaine des Hardières, owned by the Aubert brothers who are important *négociants* at La Varenne in Muscadet. I have also enjoyed the wines of Albert Morin of the Domaine de la Grande Chauvière and Fernand Moron of the Domaine des Maurières. Beaulieu-sur-Layon boasts the 50-hectare Château du Breuil run by Marc Morgat (Château la Roche is another family property in the *appellation*), and in Chaume lives Pierre-Yves Tijou, brother of Jean-Paul Tijou above, who has the excellent 40-hectare Domaine de la Soucherie. The Fermaine family of Château de Fesles (*see below*) own two properties in Chaume: Chaleau de la Fuimoniereand Châlean de Le Roulerie. Another good property is the Domaine d'Ambinos, who sell thier wines under the Château des Rochettes, owned by Louis Douet. I remember buying a very luscious 1976, labelled Sélection des Grains Nobles.

QUARTS DE CHAUME and BONNEZEAUX

Quarts de Chaume is a *lieu-dit* lying in the commune of Rochefort five kilometres inland from the river. The name derives from the medieval practice of share-cropping. The local *seigneurs* were the Guerche family – whose ruined castle can still be seen nearby – who demanded a quarter of the crop each year, exercising the right to choose the best from their local tenants, the monks from the Abbaye du Ronceray.

Quarts de Chaume is a tiny appellation. The vineyards occupy only 39 hectares, on land which contains more clay than the rest of the Layon Valley, and is magnificently situated. The vines undulate gently down towards the river, away from the hamlet of Chaume, and face due south. On the other three sides the horseshoe-shaped hill of Chaume protects the vineyards from cold and wind.

The maximum yield is the lowest prescribed for the entire Loire Valley – 22 hectolitres per hectare, and the wine must attain 12 degrees of alcohol plus a further one of unconverted sugar, as in the Layon-Villages *appellation*. Understandably the yield is small, for here several *passages* through the vines are normal, and only grapes affected by *pourriture noble* are used. Frequently the yield fails to reach even 18 hectolitres per hectare, and total production rarely exceeds 1000 hectolitres. In 1996 it was 866 hectolitres.

The three most important owners in the Quarts de Chaume *appellation* are Jacques Lalanne at the Château de Belle Rive whose quality of wine belies the dullness of its label; Jean Beaumard; and the Laffourcade family who own two estates, Château de l'Echarderie and Château de Suronde.

Bonnezeaux is altogether larger (in 1996 it was some 102 hectares) and lies fifteen kilometres inland from the Loire, north-east of Thouarcé. Here 25 hectolitres per hectare is the maximum yield, but the wine must reach an extra half degree of alcohol higher than the ordinary Coteaux du Layon.

The vineyards occupy the south-eastern-facing slope of a hill broken up by several tiny valleys, roughly two and a half kilometres long by half a kilometre wide. Not all the land is suitable for the production of top quality wine, and moreover the terrain is split between a large number of proprietors. The best of these, such as the Fermain family at the Château de Fesles or the Fourlinnies at the Château des Gauliers, have a policy of only declaring Bonnezeaux in the best vintages, demoting the rest to plain Coteaux du Layon. Others produce a less reliable wine, no better than their neighbours outside Bonnezeaux. The production of Bonnezeaux in 1996 was 2629 hectolitres, over three times that of Quarts de Chaume.

The sweet Layon wines vary from communal Coteaux du Layon, as offered by one of the Loire *négociants* or local co-operatives such as UAPL at Brissac, to the more substantial wines of the Coteaux du Layon-Villages, Bonnezeaux or Quarts de Chaume, from a single domaine and a good vintage, made from fruit affected by the noble rot. The lesser wines are made for early drinking: light, fruity and, one hopes, not overlaid with sulphur. The better wines are made to last, and in their youth, until the sulphur has been absorbed, may be ungainly. A venerable old bottle, a 1964, '59, even a '47 if you are really fortunate, is a great delight, with a soft, almost flowery fragrance, a high-toned, racy, delicate, peachy or greengagy fruit, and a pronounced freshness maintained by the wine's high acidity.

There are said to be pronounced – or at least discernible – nuances between the wines of the different communes in the Layon Valley. In my experience the styles vary as much from grower to grower as from village to village. Baumard's Quarts de Chaume, for instance, is quite a different wine, being less rich, more lemony, than that of the Domaine de Belle Rive. Which is your yardstick? In general I must admit to finding Bonnezeaux more pedestrian – slightly earthier, less elegant – than Quarts de Chaume, and indeed than the best single-domaine Coteaux du Layon-Villages wines. This, however, may be my bad luck. Perhaps I have had the misfortune to meet too many pedestrian Bonnezeaux growers.

COTEAUX DE L'AUBANCE

Parallel with the Layon, a few kilometres upstream, runs the Aubance river. The *appellation*, created in 1950, covers ten communes on the opposite bank of the Loire to Angers, and is for a medium-sweet wine from the Chenin Blanc grape. Though the area is of a reasonable size (167 hectares in 1996), many growers now concentrate on the production of the more popular red, rosé or dry white wine, selling them as Anjou or Anjou-Villages. 6003 hectolitres of Coteaux de líAubance were produced in 1996 and this was a splendid vintage for sweet wines. One source, with an impressive aray of old vintages still tucked away in the cellars, is The Daviau brothers at the Domaine de Bablut at Bussac. They also have old vintages of sweet Cabernet rosé.

ANJOU COTEAUX DE LA LOIRE

Similar wine to the Coteaux de l'Aubance comes under the label of Anjou Coteaux de la Loire from 50 hectares of vines in ten communes on the north bank of the Loire west of Angers behind Savennières. Production is even smaller than Coteaux de l'Aubance and in 1996 amounted to 1281 hectolitres. The main communes for this somewhat rare *appellation* are Montjeau-sur-Loire, La Pommeraye and Chalonnes.

Neither of these *appellations* is particularly common – indeed it could be argued that a medium-sweet wine is neither one thing nor another, too sweet to be drunk with food, but not luscious enough to be a pudding wine. Moreover, being wines containing residual sugar, it is necessary to bottle them with a higher than normal level of sulphur, and this sulphur may often obtrude. The Boré-Blouin family at La Pommeraye is the leading name in the area.

SAUMUR

Saumur, dominated by its castle, which is so magnificently illustrated in the prayer book, the *Très Riches Heures*, painted for Jean, Duc de Berry by Pol Limbourg and his brothers in 1416, is an attractive market town. It is host to the famous Cadre Noir Cavalry School, founded in 1814, now equally involved with modern tanks and mobile guns. The area is a centre for mushroom cultivation which is carried out in the multitude of caves dug out of cliffs on the left bank of the Loire. And the town is the home of all the important Saumur d'Origine producers.

Because of the importance of these sparkling wines (*see page 228*), Saumur is the largest centre of wine production in the Loire. About half of the grapes from the twenty-eight communes which run down from the river towards Montreuil-Bellay and beyond are used for Mousseux and the remainder is used for still wine. In 1996 there were 59,411 hectolitres of Saumur Rouge (including rosé Cabernet de Saumur) and 23,604 of Saumur Blanc (including Coteaux de Saumur). In addition to this there is the *appellation* of Saumur-Champigny for Saumur's best red wine.

The regulations for Saumur are somewhat stricter than for generic Anjou. Red wines are made from Cabernet Franc, Cabernet Sauvignon and Pineau d'Aunis; and the whites from at least 80 per cent Chenin Blanc together with Chardonnay and Sauvignon Blanc. Unlike generic Anjou the Gamay is not authorized and neither are the Cot or Groslot. Saumur Blanc denotes a dry wine and Coteaux de Saumur a semi-sweet wine. Cabernet de Saumur is a superior rosé made, as you would expect from its name, solely from the two Cabernet varieties, Cabernet Sauvignon and Cabernet Franc.

Most of the local production of still wine is sold by the reliable Cave-Co-opérative des Vignerons de Saumur at Saint-Cyr-en-Bourg and much of the rest by the sparkling-wine merchants themselves (Bouvet-Ladubay have attractive examples). One of the few independent growers I have come across is Giles Collé who works from the cellars of the Château du Parnay a few kilometres upstream from Saumur itself. His 12½-hectare estate produces both white and red wine, and I remember having a considerable success with a fresh, well-handled Saumur Blanc 1978, the only time I ever bought his wine.

SAUMUR-CHAMPIGNY

In the Maine-et-Loire *département*, excellent red wines are made in the small but rapidly expanding district of Saumur-Champigny. Like the wines of Chinon and Bourgueil, these are also produced from the Cabernet Franc.

Within the much larger general region of Saumur lie ten communes roughly bounded by the forest of Fontevraud, the Loire and the river Thouet. Here the soil is not *tuffe* but another, much harder limestone, which is more heat-retentive, and thus able to produce a riper grape from a given amount of sunshine than the surrounding area.

From the river the land rises very steeply, giving the appearance of a cliff in places, at the base of which are a number of troglodyte houses. On the plateau lie the vineyards, in the communes of Champigny, Souzay, Chacé, Dampierre, Montsoreau, Parnay, Saint-Cyr-en-Bourg, Saumur, Turquan and Verrains. Cabernet Franc is the main grape, though both Cabernet Sauvignon and Pineau d'Aunis are authorized.

Saumur-Champigny is a thriving area whose production has tripled in a generation and now stands at about 82,259 hectolitres per year (1996 harvest), now almost outstripping that of Chinon and Bourgueil. Leading the advance has been the excellent co-operative at Saint-Cyr, presided over by the genial Marcel Neau, a familiar face at wine trade exhibitions in England. The Saint-Cyr cellars are so vast that as well as descending by lift through fifty metres or so of rock beneath the offices, one can also drive in by car. The combined efforts of the co-operative's 220 members produce about 35 per cent of the *appellation*, as well as grapes for generic and sparkling Saumur.

There must be something in the Saumur air which attracts attractive foreigners, or perhaps the local girls leave something to be desired, for two of the best growers have foreign wives. Bernard de Tigny's wife is American, and his property is the 20-hectare Château de Chaintres. I remember his excellent 1976, as well as a refreshing white of the same vintage, the first time I went to visit him. Another producer, Paul Filliatreau, with a Swedish wife, is also in the hamlet of Chaintres, and his 'Vieilles Vignes' is perhaps the best wine of the area. This is a full-bodied but inherently round, ample, rich wine, which ages well. The 1976 still had bags of life when I last tasted it in 1988 and the '82 was a delight. in 1990. Later fine vintages such as 1985 will also keep well. Filliatreau is young, gentle and easy-going, but his friendly, well-built frame conceals a fierce dedication as well as a well-deserved pride in the produce of his cellar. His 27 hectares consist of a number of plots, of vines of different ages. The grapes of each are vinified separately, in thermostatically controlled stainless steel, and from them a number of blends are made, from a *nouveau-*style *primeur*, sold in the local restaurants by Christmas, to the 'Vieilles Vignes'.

Claude Daheuiller and his wife, Marie-Françoise farm 18 hectares in Varrains, on the Chaintres side, while on the other side of this sleepy little village lies the Les Poyeux vineyard, owned by Alain Sanzay.

Saumur-Champigny is normally fresher than Chinon, both looking more purple and somehow even after a year in cask tasting more *primeur*. It is less sturdy than Bourgueil. The best wines – and the co-operative produces an excellent, cheap example – are full of fruit and by no means inferior to their more famous neighbours. And they are cheaper.

ANJOU

Basic red, rosé and white Anjou wine are at the bottom of the Angevin vinous pyramid. The vineyards lie entirely south of the Loire and extend round behind the regions of Coteaux du Layon and Saumur towards Thouars to the east and Somloire in the west. In all there are nearly 200 communes with some 6200 hectares of vines which in 1996 produced 155,626 of Cabernet Rosé d'Anjou red and rosé, 160,433 of Cabernet Rosé d'Anjou and 54,449 of white wine.

As in Saumur, the red wines must come from Cabernet Franc, Cabernet Sauvignon and Pineau d'Aunis, or if from Gamay, it must be from Gamay exclusively and the wine labelled as such. (In 1996 21,143 hectolitres of Anjou-Gamay were produced.) The whites are made from at least 80 per cent Chenin Blanc together with Chardonnay and Sauvignon Blanc.

Anjou Rosé, which can be *tendre* or even medium-sweet, can be made from the same black grapes used for the red wine, but normally comes from mainly Cot and Groslot, particularly the latter. Gamay is also authorized. There is also a Rosé de Loire which can come from either Anjou or Touraine. The *appellation* was created in 1974 to meet the increasing demand for drier wines. Rosé de Loire is bone-dry as opposed to Anjou Rosé which is off-dry and must have a minimum of 30 per cent of Cabernet grapes in the blend. Cabernet d'Anjou is another rosé wine and must be made exclusively from the two Cabernet grapes. It cannot be bone dry and must contain at least 10 grammes of residual sugar per litre. Well-made, chilled Cabernet d'Anjou can be a delicious, abundantly fruity wine, to be drunk in a deckchair on a hot summer's day, or, alternatively, with cold salmon at a smart picnic. Reliable producers include the Co-opérative Union Agricole du Pays de Loire at Brissac, and the *négociants* of Rabier in Menars, near Blois, and Aubert Frères at La Varenne. Rather more superior Cabernet rosés are made at the Château de Beaulieu on the Layon, by Henri Verdier at the Domaine de Chanteloup at Brigné-sur-Layon, and by Gérard Chauvin of the Domaine des Rochettes at Mosé-sur-Louet. Much generic Anjou Rosé, jumping on the Californian bandwagon, is now sold as 'blush' wine.

To make good red wine from the Cabernet grapes requires more than the usual amount of fine weather in September and October. In the hot summer of 1976 the UAPL produced a prodigiously good, ripe wine, at a bargain price, and there were other good vintages in 1982, '85, '86, '89 and '90; more in 1995, 1996 and 1997. I must admit that I find most of the attempts, even at much higher prices, to be far less exciting. Modern methods are raising the standards, however, and growers are learning to shorten the maceration, warming it in cool years in order speedily to extract the fruit before too much tannin is released. Thereafter the wine must be kept in tank and bottled early, not left to dry out in a dirty old cask. Those who follow these procedures are increasingly making better wine, but yet I fear, in all but best years, a concentration on rosé would make a more interesting wine.

ANJOU-VILLAGES

Just as Cabernet de Saumur or Saumur-Champigny denote superior red wines in their part of the world, so Anjou-Villages indicates a better Anjou Rouge. The *appellation* was created in 1987 and covers the villages of the Aubance and Layon valleys south of the Loire. The wines must be made only from Cabernet Franc and Cabernet Sauvignon. From my initial experience of the vintages from 1986 onwards (backdating was permitted) it would seem that Anjou-Villages is destined to eclipse plain Anjou Rouge. It is certainly worth paying the little extra. Production in 1996 totalled 22,012 hectolitres.

COTEAUX D'ANCENIS VDQS

Though officially the Coteaux d'Ancenis is an Anjou wine, it would be more logical to consider it under the heading of Pays Nantais or Muscadet. Most of the land is also authorized for making Muscadet des Coteaux de la Loire, and much of it also for Gros Plant du Pays Nantais. Though half the area, that on the south bank of the Loire, lies in the *département* of Maine-et-Loire, the rest, on the north side, is in Loire-Atlantique. There are a total of 264 hectares under vine.

Why it is included with the other Anjou wines is because it is mainly a red or rosé wine, which no Nantais wine, whether *appellation contrôlée* or VDQS (except for Fiefs Vendéens), can be. The grapes authorized are those used for other Anjou wines. Gamay is the main red wine grape, but both Cabernets and Pinot Beurot are also permitted. Chenin Blanc and the little-known Malvoisie are the white wine grapes. The grape name must always follow the Coteaux d'Ancenis name on the label.

Malvoisie, in the hands of the best-regarded local grower, Jacques Guindon, is the most interesting Ancenis wine. This Malvoisie said by the locals to be the same as the Malmsey grape of Madeira, and to other similar varieties grown round the Mediterranean is, in fact, none other than the Pinot Gris. In Ancenis, and elsewhere in the Loire where I have occasionally seen it (the Saumur *négociant* Verdier used to make a wine from it) it produces a wine of medium sweetness, soft, aromatic and slightly spicy; a curiosity, but well worth sampling. In 1988 there were 173,45 hectolitres of red and rosé and only 112 hectolitres of white wine.

HAUT POITOU

The Poitou wines are interesting. An excellent co-operative at Neuville, sixteen kilometers north-west of Poitiers in the *département* of Vienne is now owned by Feorges Duboeuf of Beaugolais and produces 97 per cent of the wine under *appellation* which in 1991 was elevated from VDQS to AC. The co-operative's wines are now deservedly widely distributed, and the Sauvignon is more than the equal of most AC Touraine. Since 1988 the co-operative has also made single-estate wines from Châteaux de Brizay, Le Logis and La Fuye.

Both red and white wines are found. Though it is the red which is produced in the highest proportion it is the white which is most often exported. This comes mainly from Sauvignon Blanc and Chardonnay though Chenin Blanc and Pinot Blanc are also permitted; the reds come largely from the Gamay, but also from both Cabernets, Merlot, Cot, Groslot, and even Pinot Noir. In 1996 15,618 hectolitres of red and 13,178 of white wines were produced from a total of 419 hectares of vines.

VINS DU THOUARSAIS VDQS

Barely 1000 hectolitres per annum (in 1996 there were 384 hectolitres of white, from the Chenin Blanc, and 621 hectolitres of red and rosé from Cabernet Franc and Cabernet Sauvignon) of rather modest wine is made near the rather anonymous town of Bressuire in the *département* of Deux-Sèvres. It is rarely found outside the locality, and does not deserve more renown. Michel Gigon's wines are the exception, though.

Pays Nantais

More white wine – over 800,00 hectolitres a year – is made in the Pays Nantais or Muscadet than in Anjou and Touraine put together. The production of Muscadet wine is a quarter of the entire Loire harvest, including VDQS. Muscadet, then, is a prolific vineyard area; and Muscadet wine is one of the cheapest *appellation contrôlées* and one of the most popular wines, both in France and on the export market.

The Muscadet area is the Pays Nantais, the last of the five main regions of the Loire. Here we are in the ancient Duchy of Brittany – the border was the old fortified town of Ancenis – long independent of the kings of France, and before them of the kings of England, to whom it was more closely allied. At Ancenis a treaty was finally agreed in 1468 between Duke François II of Brittany and King Louis XI, and the Bretons lost, if in legality only, their fierce independence. The castle ruins can still be seen and it is worth paying a nostalgic visit.

The capital of Muscadet and the Pays Nantais is the sprawling, impossible, frustrating city of Nantes. Until only a few years ago here were the first bridges across the Loire going upstream, and round this connection has grown up one of the least charming conurbations in France. There is still no by-pass, and if you arrive from England by means of a night boat to Cherbourg and have an appointment in Vallet to see your Muscadet supplier, you need to allow an extra three-quarters of an hour just to traverse the city.

Visually, the Pays Nantais is the least interesting part of the Loire Valley. The countryside has no forests and grand landscaped parks. There are few historic houses and monuments – though there is a charming cottage museum to Abélard and Heloïse in Le Pallet, and the Château de Goulaine is worth a visit – and in the main area, the Sèvre-et-Maine, the villages are hemmed in by vines, with hardly a tree to break the landscape.

As elsewhere in the lower Atlantic end of the Loire Valley, the Dutch have had a strong influence. The vine was brought here by the Romans, but the original varieties produced only black grapes, which in the harsh local climate could not be said to have prospered, and whose produce gave rise to appropriately acidic comments in medieval texts. In the seventeenth century the Dutch, brandy drinkers, were forced to seek an alternative source of supply for their base wine, for the taxes in the Charente, now the home of Cognac, were becoming too prohibitive. The city of Nantes levied no duties on the export of wine, and the Dutch, already trading in the wines of the Anjou, persuaded the Nantais growers to switch to producing white wine.

Fortuitously a variety had recently arrived from Burgundy, where it was called the Melon. The story goes that following a catastrophic frost in the winter of 1709, which wiped out the unpopular red varieties, Louis XIV ordered that a new white grape should be planted instead. The Nantais christened it the Muscadet because it was said to have a musky flavour. It has no connection with any of the Muscat varieties nor the Muscadelle of Bordeaux. Muscadet or the Melon de Bourgogne is actually a white cousin of the Gamay. The Muscadet grape prospered in the Pays Nantais. It suffered little from frost, and ripened early, essential for successful cultivation in the Breton climate. It thrives on the predominantly clayey soil of the Pays Nantais and despite the region having the least summer sun of any wine area in France outside Champagne, it produces a wine which is by no means acid.

Until the early 1950s, Muscadet was a pleasant regional wine. It was drunk as a *vin d'année*, but could only be found locally. It was seldom exported, even to metropolitan France. Then came the boom. As a sort of white equivalent of Beaujolais, light, refreshing, uncomplicated and, above all, cheap, Muscadet has conquered the world.

Muscadet, then, is not only the name of an area and a wine, but the name of the grape from which the wine comes. The grape is a fairly prolific variety, and the maximum yield per hectare for Muscadet wine is as high as 50 hectolitres.

Mainly in the *département* of Loire-Atlantique, but also overlapping into Maine-et-Loire and Vendée, the entire area covers some 11,000 hectares and extends from the river Erdre in the north-east round three sides of a circle clockwise with Nantes as its centre to Legé in the south and Machecoul in the west. The bulk of the vineyards and the best wine comes from the Sèvre-et-Maine district south-east of Nantes.

MUSCADET DE SÈVRE-ET-MAINE

Muscadet de Sèvre-et-Maine is named after the two small rivers, La Sèvre Nantaise and La Petite Maine, and consists of the four cantons Clisson, Loreaux-Bottereau, Vallet and Vertou. The district is roughly bounded by the N137 road to Montaigu, the river Loire and the border of the Loire-Atlantique *département*. This is the source of some 75 per cent (529,891 hectolitres in 1996) of all Muscadet.

The Sèvre-et-Maine is a compact, undulating district, with a soil that is predominantly clay, particularly away from the Sèvre and Maine rivers, mixed with sand and gravel. At its centre, at La Haie-Fouassière on the right bank of the river Sèvre, it is worth climbing up the little hill of the Moulin du Breil. From its rocky summit, some 65 metres above sea-level, there is an excellent panorama over the entire area.

Though seemingly 100 per cent cultivated, if not by the vine then with vegetables and fruit, there is still further potential for growth in this increasingly thriving part of the world, as every little patch of land, not only the south-facing slopes, is planted, and as the inferior Gros Plant vine is replaced with Muscadet. The current surface area is 10,275 hectaresof vines (1996 figures).

MUSCADET DES COTEAUX DE LA LOIRE

The Muscadet des Coteaux de la Loire occupies much the same region as that of the Coteaux d'Ancenis (*see page 238.*) Some 335 hectares are cultivated on both banks of the Loire between Mauves in the west and Saint-Florent-Le-Vieil in the east, with Ancenis as its centre. The soil here contains less clay and more limestone and the wine is consequently lighter and more *primeur* in style. Production was 180,52 hectolitres in 1996.

MUSCADET CÔTES DE GRAND-LIEU

The Côtes de Grand-Lieu is a recently introduced surface-area surrounding the lake of the same name south of Nances. The surface area under vines is 263 hectares and production in 1996 amounted to 15,800 hectolitres.

MUSCADET

South and south-west of Nantes, in what is predominantly Gros Plant country, the Muscadet vine is also found. Here, and from one or two isolated pockets elsewhere, comes the wine labelled simply as Muscadet. In 1996 production totalled 92,694 hectolitres from 2055 hectares of vines. All three Muscadet *appellations* stipulate 12 degrees as the maximum level of alcohol, as well as a minimum (9.5 degrees for simple Muscadet, 10 degrees for the other two wines). All three wines have the same regulations for the production of Muscadet *sur lie*.

Sur lie, literally 'on the lees', denotes a wine that has been left on its lees throughout the winter before being bottled, usually early in the spring – by law this has to be done before 1 July. Normally a white wine must is left to settle before the fermentation is allowed to commence (*débourbage*) and then, after fermentation is complete, decanted off its lees – the sediment being predominantly dead yeast cells – into a new tank or vat. The malolactic fermentation then takes place, if the winemaker so wishes. Before bottling fining will take place to ensure that the wine is completely bright.

The rationale behind the principle of bottling *sur lie* is twofold. Muscadet is a fairly light, relatively anonymous wine. If this wine is allowed to feed on the dead yeast cells it will gain an extra element of richness and character. Also if the wine is left undisturbed in its original fermentation tank, some of the carbon dioxide released by both the original and by the malolactic fermentations will be retained within the wine in the form of carbonic acid. Thus the bottle will have a slight sparkle, and this will give an extra crispness and freshness to a wine which is sometimes slightly deficient in acidity. Genuine Muscadet *sur lie* cannot be fined, and in some cases is not filtered either. The production of Muscadet *sur lie* presupposes modern fermenting and storage equipment, as well as a high standard of cleanliness in the winery. If the lees are not themselves 'clean', the wine will be ruined. Within the last twenty years most growers, particularly in the Sèvre-et-Maine, have changed to making their Muscadet *sur lie*. The result is a more interesting wine.

Muscadet wine at its best should be dry without being lean, should have a reasonable fullness without being fat or oily, and, if made *sur lie*, a suggestion of a yeasty richness. The character is neither herby nor fruity, and difficult to describe. Some suggest wild roses. Others detect a hint of vanilla. I can find neither of these, though I do occasionally (but this is probably auto-suggestion) detect a faint crisp ozone whiff in some Muscadets. Above all the wine must be fresh – after as little as a year in bottle it begins to get tired.

Muscadet is a large area of intensive production. Though there are a number of big *négociant* companies, the majority of the best Muscadet wines are the products of single domaines, selling direct to the consumer in France or importer abroad. Among the many hundreds – if not thousands – it is impossible to speak with personal authority about more than a few dozen, so the following list must not be considered exhaustive.

The two leading quality *négociants* in the Muscadet area are the firms of Sauvion and Métaireau. Both are run by personalities who are great individuals – and individualists – often rather arrogant about their own wines and suitably disparaging about the rest. Louis Métaireau is one of the few who does not filter his *sur lie* wines. Both *négociants* make classic Muscadet, which, unlike many, can take a little bottle age. Both produce a range of Muscadets at different price levels and presentations. The Métaireau firm is in fact an association of nine independent growers who also jointly own the Grand Mouton Estate at Saint-Fiacre-sur-Maine. The best wine is labelled as the Coupe Louis Métaireau. The Sauvion business is based at the Château du Cléray at Vallet. Their top wine is called Cardinal Richard.

A number of other Muscadet firms started off as growers and then, as their business increased, began to buy in wine from their neighbours and enter into farming and marketing arrangements, and so evolved into *négociants*. These include Marcel Sautejeau at the Domaine de l'Hyvernière at Vallet; Donatien-Bahaud at the Château de la Cassemichère, also in Vallet; and Chereau-Carré at Chasseloir, who distribute a number of estates, including the Domaines of Chasseloir, Bois-Bruley, Grand Fré de la Cormeraie, Moulin de la Graves and the Châteaux de l'Oiselinière and du Coing de Saint-Fiacre.

The Marquis de Goulaine at his château at Haute-Goulaine produces an excellent series of Muscadets, the best wine being the Cuvée du Millénaire. The firms of Martin-Jarry at La Chapelle-Basse-Mère and Aubert Frères at La Varenne can also be recommended. Among the individual growers Pierre Lusseaud owns two fine estates in Vallet, the Châteaux de la Galissonière and Jannière; the Comte de Malestroit de Bruc at the Château la Noé also produces very good wine in Vallet; the Comte de Camiran's Château de la Bidière at Maisdon-sur-Sèvre is also widely distributed.

Not all the Muscadet growers, of course, are aristocrats, although it may appear so from the above paragraph. Elsewhere I have enjoyed the wines of Guilbaud Frères de la Ragotière; Auguste Bonhomme; Gilbert Bassard; Henri and Vincent Chereau; the Domaine Drouet; Monsieur Braud of the Château de Fromenteau; Yves Huchet at the Domaine de la Chauvinière; Joseph Landron; Joseph Hallereau (who claims to have invented the *sur lie* process in 1947) and the Domaine de la Tourmaline of the Gadais family at Saint-Fiacre.

GROS PLANT DU PAYS NANTAIS VDQS

Until 1984 the *département* of Loire-Atlantique possessed only one other *appellation* besides the Muscadet, the VDQS Gros Plant du Pays Nantais. The wine can come from throughout the Muscadet area, as well as from certain other areas to the south and west. Gros Plant is normally an undistinguished wine with a pronounced, even savage acidity and a rather coarse flavour. It is produced from the Gros Plant grape, imported from the Charente, where it is known as the Folle Blanche (it is also the same as the Picpoul in the South of France), by the Dutch in the seventeenth century. In 1996 some 2713 hectares were planted, giving a yield of 187,220 hectolitres. The VDQS dates from 1254.

In the hands of some growers and *négociants*, Gros Plant in a good year such as 1988 or '89 can be an agreeable wine. It is noticeably 'greener' than Muscadet, and this can make a pleasant change, particularly if one is on holiday in the area. I shipped a very good 1978 Gros Plant from Pierre Lusseaud in 1979 and have also enjoyed those of Aubert Frères and the Marquis de Goulaine. Nowadays, however, the difference in price between Muscadet and Gros Plant is marginal, and I suspect the consumers would prefer the former.

FIEFS VENDÉENS VDQS

South of the Pays Nantais is the Vendée. Fiefs Vendéens is a recently elevated Vin de Pays, having enjoyed the status of VDQS since 1984. Most of the wine is red (19,679 hectolitres in 1996), largely from the Gamay grape, though both Cabernets, Pinot Noir and Pineau d'Aunis are also authorized. There is a small amount of wine (4072 hectolitres in 1996) from Chenin Blanc, Sauvignon Blanc, Gros Plant and Chardonnay. These are simple, somewhat rustic country wines for local drinking.

VINS DE PAYS

VIN DE PAYS DU BOURBONNAIS
This is a white *vin de pays* from the Saint-Pourçain area of the Upper Loire in the Allier *département*. It is produced from the local grapes, Tresallier, Sauvignon Blanc, Chardonnay, Aligoté and Saint-Pierre-Doré.

VIN DE PAYS DU CHER
This is a departmental *vin de pays* from the *département* of Cher around Bourges. Reds and rosés come from Gamay and whites from Sauvignon.

VIN DE PAYS DES COTEAUX CHARITOIS
These are Sauvignon-based whites from Pouilly-sur-Loire in the Nièvre *département*.

VIN DE PAYS DES COTEAUX DU CHER ET DE L'ARNON
A zonal *vin de pays* from the Reuilly-Quincy area in the Cher and Indre *départements*. The grapes used are Gamay for red and rosé wines and Sauvignon for white wines.

VIN DE PAYS DES DEUX-SÈVRES
The Deux-Sèvres *département* lies south of Angers and west of Poitiers. These are mainly white wines, from Chenin, Muscadet, Gros Plant and Sauvignon grapes.

VIN DE PAYS DU JARDIN DE LA FRANCE
This is the regional *vin de pays* of the Loire Valley and the most commonly seen Loire *vin de pays* outside France. The wines are mainly white, and made from Chenin Blanc and/or Sauvignon Blanc. There are also some interesting Chardonnay-based wines.

VIN DE PAYS DE L'INDRE
A departmental wine from the southern part of the Touraine round Châteauroux. All three colours of wine are made, mainly from Gamay, Sauvignon and Chenin.

VIN DE PAYS DE L'INDRE ET LOIRE
A departmental wine from the heart of the Touraine. Red, rosé and white wines are made, mainly from Gamay, Sauvignon and Chenin.

VIN DE PAYS DE LA LOIRE-ATLANTIQUE
A departmental wine from the Pays Nantais, the Muscadet region. Red and rosé wines are made from Gamay and Groslot and whites from Muscadet and Folle Blanche (Gros Plant). Some interesting Chardonnays.

VIN DE PAYS DU LOIR-ET-CHER
A departmental wine from the eastern end of Touraine. All three colours of wine are made, mainly from Gamay, Sauvignon and Chenin.

VIN DE PAYS DU LOIRET
A departmental wine from the far eastern end of the Loire basin, south of Paris around Orléans. Red and rosé wines come from Gamay and the whites from Sauvignon.

VIN DE PAYS DE LA MAINE-ET-LOIRE
A departmental *vin de pays* from the Anjou. Red and rosé wines come from Gamay, Groslot and Cabernet Franc and the whites from Chenin Blanc, though Chardonnay is also found.

VIN DE PAYS DES MARCHES DE BRETAGNE
A zonal *vin de pays* from the Pays Nantais. Mainly red and rosé wine, from Gamay and Cabernet Franc.

VIN DE PAYS DE LA NIÈVRE
A departmental *vin de pays* from the Côteaux du Giennois/Pouilly-sur-Loire area. Red, rosé and white wines, mainly from Gamay and Sauvignon Blanc.

VIN DE PAYS DU PUY-DE-DÔME
The departmental *vin de pays* of the Auvergne. Mainly red and rosé wine, mainly from Gamay.

VIN DE PAYS DE RETZ
A zonal wine from the southern part of the Pays Nantais. Mainly red and rosé wine from Groslot and Cabernet Franc.

VIN DE PAYS DE LA SARTHE
A departmental wine from north of Anjou and Touraine. All three colours of wine are authorized, and a wide range of local varieties. I have never seen it.

VIN DE PAYS D'URFÉ
A zonal *vin de pays* for the Forez/Roannaises area. Red and rosé wines from Gamay.

VIN DE PAYS DE LA VENDÉE
A departmental *vin de pays* from south of the Muscadet area. Red and rosé wines from Gamay. I have not seen this wine since the VDQS of Fiefs Vendéens was created in 1984.

VIN DE PAYS DE LA VIENNE
A departmental *vin de pays* from the Haut Poitou area. Mainly Gamay is used for the reds and rosés and Chenin and Sauvignon for the whites.

Chapter 4

THE RHÔNE VALLEY

The river Rhône rises in the Valais canton of Switzerland, enters France at Lake
Geneva and travels at first in a generally south-westerly direction until it is joined
by the river Saône at Lyon. Diverted by the Montagnes du Lyonnais it is then
forced south, flowing initially through a narrow, steep-sided valley past the towns of
Vienne, Tain, Tournon, Valence and Montélimar, while being joined by several major
tributaries, among them the Isère and the Drôme. South of Montélimar the valley begins
to widen out, particularly on the Alpine side, and the Rhône begins to slow and meander.
At Avignon it is joined by the Durance, and we soon reach the wild, sandy flatlands of the
Bouches-du-Rhône and the Parc Régionale de la Camargue. At Arles the river splits into
two; the smaller section, the Petit Rhône, reaches the Mediterranean at the old gypsy
rendezvous of Saintes-Maries-de-la-Mer; the Grand Rhône at Port Saint-Louis, 800
kilometres from its source.

Viticulturally speaking, the Rhône Valley is that part between Lyon in the north and
Avignon in the south, a distance as the crow flies of some 200 kilometres. The upper
Rhône is dealt with under its more usual title of the Savoie (*see page 336*), the wines of the
Rhône delta under Provence and Languedoc (*see pages 348 and 361*).

For most of its course – particularly between Lyon and Avignon – the immediate
surroundings by the river are dull, unattractive, even despoiled. The Rhône is a major
industrial and commercial artery. Large sections are canalized; hydro-electric dams,
atomic centres, quarries, cement works, metallurgical industries and other factories
pollute the river and send columns of smog into the atmosphere. It is noisy, dirty, arid and
dusty – thoroughly unpeaceful, decidedly uncongenial.

Away from the river the picture is a total contrast. Even a five-minute drive up the
winding roads into the hills above the northern Rhône Valley will bring one into an

entirely different land. This is a countryside of meadows and pasture full of herds of cattle, walnut trees and orchards of peaches, apricots and cherries; of small hamlets apparently deserted except for the odd tethered goat and free-range chicken; a pre-industrial countryside, a land of private smallholdings, tranquillity and agricultural plenty.

In the south the valley undulates its way between the Cévennes in the west and Mont Ventoux and the Dentelles de Montmirail in the east. Here the landscape is provençal: the terrain of the olive and the cypress as well as the vine. The light is vivid and penetrating. The sky is more violet than blue. The smells are of lavender and wild thyme, rosemary and oregano. The well-irrigated fields on the flatter, more alluvial soils yield artichokes and melons, cucumbers, peppers and courgettes, asparagus, lettuce and tomatoes. The vines lie on the stonier, higher slopes, where the land has been prised away from its rightful owners, the heather, broom and scrub of the *garrigues*. Further inland and uphill, the countryside is spectacular, deserted and beautiful. Dense forests of pine, aspen and birch alternate with jagged outcrops of bare rock, or the rounded bald expanse of ancient hills. This is France at its most dramatic, both savage and glorious.

History

The earliest historical roots in the Rhône Valley go back to the Ligurians, a savage, nomadic hunting people, originally from Asia, who arrived in the Rhône and Provence about 1600 BC. They were followed by the Celts, a more settled people who practised farming. The first cultivated vines together with the art of wine-making were probably introduced by Phocaean Greeks from the west coast of Asia Minor about 600 BC. Their chief trading post and settlement was Massilia (Marseille) which can probably claim to be the oldest city in France. According to Herodotus, these Phocaeans were the first to undertake distant sea journeys, and introduced the vine to mainland Greece, Italy and the Dalmatian coast, as well as to northern Africa and Mediterranean Spain.

At this time the Lydian empire, which bordered on Phoenecaea, was a rich vine-growing country. After the defeat of the Lydian Croesus by Cyrus I of Persia in 546 BC, the Phocaeans came under Persian domination, and many of the itinerant traders settled permanently in southern France, and began opening up trade routes to the north. Massalian coins from 500 to 450 BC have been found all the way up the Rhône Valley, and early Greek amphorae of the same period both in Marseille and in Tain l'Hermitage.

The Phocaean colony prospered, but as time went on came under heavy pressure from the local inhabitants and sea pirates. About 150 BC the Massalians had to appeal to the Romans to come to their aid. Within a generation they had returned with an army to conquer the country for themselves. The Roman era lasted some 600 years, and its legacy has been both striking and long lived. Many of the Roman ruins, at Vienne, Nîmes, the Pont du Gard, Vaison-La-Romaine and Orange, are the most extensive outside Italy. Most of the important towns, roads, and, most importantly, the vineyards which exist today, were established in the Roman era.

By the early Christian era, Vienne was the capital of mid-Gaul, and its pitched wine *vinium picatum* was exported to Rome, where it became a fashionable drink of the time. The fall of Rome and the decline of civilization in the fifth and sixth centuries AD was accompanied by a decline in wine-making and a reduction in communications and trade. France was colonized by the Germanic tribe, the Franks, and invaded from the south by Moors and Saracens, and even Vikings who sailed through the Straits of Gibraltar and are said to have reached almost as far north as the Hermitage vineyards.

Around the ninth century civilization began to return with the Church emerging as the driving force behind the sophistication of agricultural techniques and the focus for stability and learning. In 1309, Bertrand the Goth, Archbishop of Bordeaux, was elected Pope Clement V. With relations badly strained between the king of France and the papacy in Rome, and Italy in a state of chaotic religious warfare, he elected to stay in France, and established his court at Avignon. His successor, John XXII, was able to improve the papal finances and set about enlarging the modest official residence in Avignon. He also built a summer palace on the foundations of an old castle at Châteauneuf. This 'new château' was a huge construction and took fifteen years to build, and, of course, the surrounding vineyards went with the property.

The papal stay in Avignon lasted through seven popes until 1378, after which there were two anti-popes until the differences were healed with Rome in 1410, and during this time the city enjoyed an expanding and prosperous period. The Avignon area, together with a small parcel to the north around Valréas, which was purchased by the popes during their stay – and remains, curiously, as part of the *département* of Vaucluse completely isolated from the rest – continued as part of the Papal states until 1791.

Rhône wines were exported to Italy in the sixteenth and seventeenth centuries, but exports to the north of France and to England were more difficult, and virtually unknown until the opening of the Midi canal in 1681 gave access to the great sea route from Bordeaux (when the Bordelais chose to revive some of their ancient rights and reimpose quotas and duties on these 'up-country' wines). Later they used Rhône wine, particularly Hermitage, to add body and alcohol to their own.

Soon other trade routes opened. In 1710 work on the upper Loire made it navigable from Saint-Étienne, and canals provided a direct route to Paris; later came further canals and finally the railways. In the early eighteenth century the first Rhône names began to appear in England: Vin de Mure (a *négociant* in Tain), Vin de la Nerte, an estate in Châteauneuf-du-Pape, and Vin d'Avignon.

In the 1730s the first grouping of villages under the generic name of Côtes du Rhône made its first appearance, and casks began to be marked 'CdR' with the vintage date. The phylloxera bug first appeared in France in the *département* of Gard in 1863, and the Rhône vineyards were among the first to be devastated. One of the major research stations into combating the pest was at Montpellier, further down the Languedoc coast.

In 1923 the first quality controls, the origins of what were later to become the laws of *appellation contrôlée*, were self-imposed by the Châteauneuf *vignerons*, led by Baron le Roy of Château Fortia (who even had a statue erected to him during his lifetime). By 1936 the French had made the Châteauneuf quality controls broadly applicable to the whole country. Since the Second World War, and particularly since the early 1970s, modern viticultural and wine-making methods have arrived in the Rhône Valley and, as a result, there has been a well-deserved export success. Côtes du Rhône exports have climbed from under 100,000 hectolitres in 1964 to approaching 750,000 hectolitres today. The area has overtaken both Burgundy and Beaujolais in popularity in recent years and though it still exports less than Bordeaux, it is rapidly catching up. The main reason for this surge has been the remarkable value-for-money of Rhône wines compared with those of elsewhere. At all levels, whether at generic Côtes du Rhône (versus Bordeaux Rouge or Beaujolais) or at the summit of quality (a good grower's Hermitage or Côte-Rôtie versus a super-second claret or *premier cru* Burgundy) Rhône wines are singularly attractively priced, though regrettably less so today than a decade ago.

The Wines

The Rhône Valley is largely a red wine region, and the reds befit their setting, being bold, solid and weighty, powerful and uncompromising. In the south, particularly at Tavel, a dry, masculine rosé is found; in the north there is a little white, some of which, that from Condrieu and Château-Grillet, is among the most delicious of the entire country. But mainly the production is of red wine: of Châteauneuf-du-Pape, Gigondas and the Côtes du Rhône-Villages in the south; of Hermitage, Côte-Rôtie, Cornas and Saint Joseph in the north. The northern Rhône grows one red grape variety, the Syrah (if we exclude some Gamay cultivated for *vin de pays*), and three white varieties: Roussanne and Marsanne – normally blended together – and Viognier (only in Côte-Rôtie, Condrieu and Château Grillet). In the southern sector the varieties used are many. There are no fewer than thirteen authorized for Châteauneuf-du-Pape. Chief of these are Grenache, Cinsault, Mourvèdre and again Syrah. There is also the Muscat, used to provide the *vin doux naturel* of Beaumes-de-Venise, and some minor white varieties for the small proportion of southern Rhône white wine. All these southern Rhône varieties are planted throughout the South of France.

For reasons of differences in climate and soil, grape variety and styles of wine, it is customary, indeed logical, to treat the Rhône Valley as two separate sections, divided by a vineless no-man's-land between Valence and Montélimar. The northern section, or Rhône *septentrionale*, begins at Vienne and continues south for some seventy kilometres. It is a long, narrow region, the vines themselves clinging precariously to the steep sides of the valley itself. South of Donzère the southern section or Rhône *méridionale* continues on to Avignon, a distance of fifty kilometres, and the vines lie on mounds and slopes upon the valley floor as well as its hillsides, a distance from east to west of fifty kilometres again.

In total, not including the peripheral areas, the Drôme and the VDQS areas, some 60,000 hectares are under vine, producing some three million hectolitres of AC wine annually. Of this, only 1713 hectares lie in the northern section. The Rhône is dominated by its south. The whole of Hermitage produces no more than one of the largest Bordeaux estates. In terms of production, more wine is made in Châteauneuf-du-Pape alone than in all the northern section combined, and twenty times as much wine is declared as simple, generic Côtes du Rhône as is declared as Châteauneuf-du-Pape. And they are now increasingly well made. A generation ago the cheaper reds were fiery, rustic and over-alcoholic; the more expensive very firm and dense – more often than not too solid for their own good. The rosés were hard and unstylish; the few whites heavy, oily and spirity. Today the picture is different. The cheaper wines are largely made using carbonic maceration and have fruit and colour without being too robust. The better wines are rich and elegant, without having lost their essential sturdiness; the rosés are supple and fruity and the whites crisp and aromatic.

The Rhône is a good hunting ground for the adventurous wine buyer. His enthusiasm for the new generation of well-made, sensibly-priced wines will find many kindred spirits; dedicated, individual growers who have travelled and tasted widely and who understand that the public taste has changed and is more demanding, seeking wines of style rather than mere size, and fruit rather than alcohol.

The wines of the Rhône Valley can be divided into the following sections. They are all *appellation contrôlée* unless indicated otherwise.

NORTHERN RHÔNE
Right (west) bank: Côte-Rôtie, Condrieu, Château Grillet, Saint-Joseph, Cornas, Saint-Péray.

Left (east) bank: Hermitage, Crozes-Hermitage.

Valley of the river Drûme: Clairette de Die, Coteaux de Die, Cremand de Die, Châtillon-en-Diois.

SOUTHERN RHÔNE
Right (west) bank: Lirac, Tavel, Côtes du Rhône-Villages.

Left (east) bank: Châteauneuf-du-Pape, Gigondas, Côtes du Rhône-Villages, Coteaux du Tricastin, Côtes du Ventoux, racgueyras, Rasteau (VDN), Muscat de Beaumes de Venise (VDN).

Valley of the river Ardèche: Côtes du Vivarais (VDQS).

Valley of the river Durance: Côtes du Lubéron, Coteaux de Pierrevert (VDQS).

Côtes du Rhône can come from both the northern and southern sections of the Rhône Valley. In practice it comes almost entirely from the south.

To put a bit of life into the figures in the table on the facing page one could point out the following facts. Over 95 per cent of the Rhône Valley's vines are in the southern half of the region (if one includes the vineyards in the Drôme Valley in the centre) and over 95 per cent of the harvest comes from the south. Just over 5 per cent of the Rhône Valley harvest is white wine. Two-thirds of the entire harvest of the Rhône Valley is simple Côtes du Rhône red or rosé. In practice it is overwhelmingly red wine. Apart from Champagne this is the most important single *appellation* in France, being almost twice as large as Bordeaux Rouge and four times as large as Beaujolais. While French agricultural statistics do not separate red and rosé wine, it is estimated that 15 per cent of the grand total for red and rosé wine given above is rosé.

THE RHÔNE

PRODUCTION AND SURFACE AREA (1996 HARVEST)

	Surface area in hectares	Production '000 hectolitres	
		RED & ROSÉ	WHITE
Regional wines			
AC			
CÔTES DU RHÔNE	43556	2111	44
CÔTE-RÔTIE	196	8	—
CONDRIEU	108	—	4
CHÂTEAU GRILLET	3	—	(124 hl)
HERMITAGE	132	4	1
CROZES-HERMITAGE	1236	47	5
SAINT-JOSEPH	819	30	3
CORNAS	89	3	—
SAINT-PÉRAY	60	—	2
Drôme Valley			
AC			
CREMANT DE DIE	157	—	5
COTEAUX DE DIE	3	—	(221 hl)
CLAIRETTE DE DIE	1089	—	65
CHÂTILLON-EN-DIOSIS	73	2	1
Southern Rhône			
AC			
CÔTES DU RHÔNE-VILLAGES	4986	224	4
CHÂTEAUNEUF-DU-PAPE	3134	91	6
GIGONDAS	1171	48	—
MCQUEYRAS	872	26	(153 hl)
LIRAC	429	16	1
TAVEL	942	43	—
COTEAUX DU TRICASTIN	2493	104	2
CÔTES DU VENTOUX	7335	295	6
CÔTES DU LUBÉRON	3165	122	27
MUSCAT DE BEAUMES DE VENISE (VDN)	443	—	16
RASTEAU (VDN)	97	2	—

	Surface area in hectares	Production '000 hectolitres	
		RED & ROSÉ	WHITE
VDQS			
CÔTES DU VIVARAIS	644	29	I
COTEAUX DE PIERREVERT	310	13	I
Total Rhône AC	72,588	3176	190
Total Rhône VDQS	954	42	2
Total Rhône Valley	73,542	3218	192
Total Red and White Wines		3410	

WHEN TO DRINK THE WINES

Rhône wines are not for the faint-hearted. They are full and assertive, rich and powerful, firm and muscular. In total contrast to Burgundy they are wines of heat and alcohol rather than fragrance and finesse. They show their origins; whether from the baked granite cliffs of the north or the *mistral*-swept, boulder-strewn plateaux of the south.

The wines are almost entirely red. If from the north they are based almost exclusively on Syrah. If from Châteauneuf-du-Pape and its surrounding vineyards they are based on Grenache and other varieties. This produces two wines of quite distinctive styles. The Syrah makes a purple, tannic, austere wine: full-bodied and closed in its youth; but with a good level of acidity. Young Syrah smells of blackcurrant leaves. As much as ten years or more is required before the leafy denseness – almost brutal at first – is replaced by warm fruit. And the wines will last for decades, as they mature taking up more and more of a complexity and character similar to that of a fine Bordeaux; though always a claret with the voluptuousness of Mouton Rothschild or Cheval Blanc rather than the restrained Cabernet Sauvignon of Château Latour.

The most precocious of the northern Rhône *appellations* is Crozes-Hermitage. A minor Crozes will be mature after four years. Saint-Josephs will begin to be ready a year or so after that, and Côte-Rôties after six or seven years. The most backward are those of Cornas and Hermitage itself. These need a minimum of eight years' ageing.

Grenache-based wines mature quicker and have an altogether different character. The wines are rich, warm, spicy, peppery and alcoholic, but the acidity level is lower and development is faster. Even today when the best wines have quite significant proportions of Syrah or the yet more brutally firm Mourvèdre blended in with Grenache and Cinsault a top Châteauneuf-du-Pape will usually be mature after half a dozen years, while a minor Côtes du Rhône will be drinkable after a year. There is even some Côtes du Rhône Nouveau.

The majority of the white wines, like white wines everywhere, are for early drinking. This applies to most Condrieu, to Crozes-Hermitage Blanc, to Saint-Péray and to all the white wines of the Rhône *méridionale*, except one or two white Châteauneufs. It also applies to Tavel Rosé. Only top, oak-aged, white Hermitage can last in bottle. I find these delicious when I taste them out of cask, then ungainly for the first three or four years in bottle, and totally different – subtle, scented and aromatic, after six or so years. They have an individual taste. It makes quite a change, almost a culture-shock, after Chardonnay!

RHÔNE VINTAGES

1989: A good to very good year in the north, similar in quality to 1988, say first reports. Equally, if not more encouraging noises – because recent vintages have been more uneven – are emerging from the south as this book goes to press.

1988: A very good vintage in the northern Rhône and a large vintage. Best in Côte-Rôtie, where the harvest was less prolific; least good in Cornas. Some fine Hermitage. Also successful for the white wines. The Condrieu are delicious. The quality is more patchy in the south as there was rain towards the end of the harvest. Those who picked early – and this means most of the Châteauneuf-du-Pape owners – have made big fruity wines which compare well with 1985. All the top red wines will keep well. The vintage will not be cheap.

1987: A medium-quality year in the northern Rhône, best in Côte-Rôtie. As a result of rain the Cornas, Saint-Josephs and Hermitages lack depth and strength, richness and definition. Acidity levels are also dilute, so that the wines will evolve soon. It was a large crop. Rain also affected the vintage in the south, though not as much as in 1986.

1986: Another large vintage in the northern Rhône and another medium-quality year. In the Cornas-Hermitage sector the quality is better than in 1987; in Côte-Rôtie less exciting. Torrential rain caused a lot of mildew and rot in the southern Rhône. Here the vintage should be approached with caution.

1985: A highly successful year throughout the Rhône Valley, though not quite as magnificent as 1983 in the northern sector. Nevertheless big, ripely-concentrated, long-lasting wines. This was the vintage when the cost of Rhône wines began to climb. Many northern Rhône proprietors almost doubled their 1983 prices.

1984: Not as bad as elsewhere in France, but nevertheless a modest vintage. The southern Rhône wines will now show age. In the north the vintage was better than that of 1981. But best avoided.

1983: Magnificent wines in the north; the best will still improve and it would be infanticide to open them yet. The prices in retrospect seem absurdly cheap. Good wines in Châteauneuf-du-Pape, though in general 1981 and '85 are to be preferred. These '83s are now ready.

1982: A big hot vintage. Very good quality in the north. Uneven in the south. All but the best Châteauneufs will now be showing a little age. The best Côte-Rôties and Hermitages will still keep well.

1981: Disappointing in the north and to be avoided. Very good in Châteauneuf-du-Pape where it is the best vintage of the early 1980s. These are now ready.

EARLIER VINTAGES

Northern Rhône: 1978 (magnificent), '76, '71, '70, '69, '66, '64, '62, and '61 (magnificent).

Southern Rhône: 1978. Older vintages will show age.

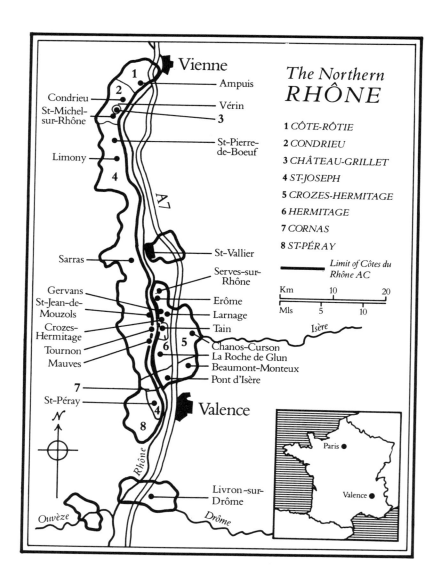

The Wine Regions

CÔTE-RÔTIE

The most northerly vineyard in the Rhône Valley is one of its most neglected and one of the most difficult to work. Yet it produces one of the finest wines not only of the Rhône but of the whole of France. Côte-Rôtie, or the Roasted Slope is centred round the village of Ampuis on the west bank of the river a few kilometres south of Vienne, itself twenty-five kilometres south of Lyon. Côte-Rôtie produces a limited quantity of excellent, Syrah-based red wine, full-bodied but elegant; a wine which needs ageing in bottle. Côte-Rôtie is rarely seen and almost impossible to secure when mature. It deserves more recognition. The vines occupy small terraces which have been hacked out of the wall of the hillsides which rise abruptly away from the valley floor. This is the most precipitous vineyard in the Rhône Valley and probably the steepest in France. In places the incline is as much as 55 degrees.

Nevertheless, this is one of the oldest vineyards in the area. The city of Vienne was one of the first staging posts established by Phocaean traders based at Marseille in the south five centuries or so B C. Wine was originally brought to the upper Rhône from the Mediterranean vineyards. Later, certainly well before the Romans, the vine was cultivated in the Vienne region, and Vienne became the thriving capital of mid-Gaul and a place of great importance in the early days of the Roman Empire, its wine being exported back to the capital, laced with pitch to preserve it. The *vinum picatum* of Vienne is mentioned by Lucius Columella, Pliny and Martial in the first century A D.

Vienne began to decline in eminence as Lyon rose to fame, and the wine, equally, sank into obscurity, re-emerging as Côte-Rôtie in Jullien's *Topographie de Tous Les Vignobles Connus* (1816) when he classified it among his *Deuxième Classe* along with the best of Châteauneuf-du-Pape, the Third Growths of Bordeaux and what today we would term the *premiers crus* of Burgundy. Only the best wines of Hermitage were deemed superior among local wines.

Phylloxera and the economic difficulties of the first half of the twentieth century hit Côte-Rôtie particularly hard. Rather than reconstitute the vineyard terraces with American rootstocks and wait five years for the first crop many local growers turned to fruit-growing. This trend was further accelerated, first by the ease of communication between Paris and the South, opening up the competition of the wines of the Midi, and then by the lack of labour after the First World War. The price of Côte-Rôtie sank to uneconomic levels and the terraces fell into disuse.

Since the 1950s, cautiously, slowly but surely, Côte-Rôtie has made a comeback. Production has increased from 1000 hectolitres to 8463 in 1996 and equally, though not so dramatically, the area under vine has been enlarged. At first this was on the ancient hillsides; terraces perhaps several hundred years old being cleared of bramble and scrub, the walls rebuilt and eventually the sites replanted. In the last few years, however, a disturbing new development has taken place: vines have been planted on the plateau above the slopes. Apparently the land, though unsuitable for quality wine, is, nevertheless, authorized for Côte-Rôtie, and, of course, it is easier to work. (The same problem has erupted further south in Saint-Joseph where, in addition, vines have been planted in the more alluvial soil of the valley floor.) The wine resulting from these as yet immature plateau vineyards is thin, weedy, pale and attenuated. At the stage where top Côte-Rôtie can at last fetch prices which make production a profitable proposition, it would be tragic if the reputation of the wine were to suffer as a result of being debased with this inferior coinage. It is time the INAO stepped in.

Côte-Rôtie today comprises some 196 hectares in the communes of Ampuis, Saint-Cyr-sur-le-Rhône and Tupins-et-Semons, and doubled in the last twenty years. The best vineyards are those immediately above Ampuis itself, the Côte Brune and those adjacent to the south, the Côte Blonde. As the name suggests, the soil in the Côte Blonde is lighter in colour. The bedrock of both is granite or gneiss, a hard metamorphic rock, but in the Côte Brune the soil is sand mixed with clay while in the Côte Blonde it is lighter and has more limestone.

The origins of these two names is Côte-Rôtie's best-loved legend. Many centuries ago the local *seigneur*, named Maugiron, had two daughters, as perfectly beautiful as they always are in fairy-tales. One was blond, vivacious and gay, the other a brunette, quiet and reserved but passionate when aroused. Maugiron gave as a dowry his two best vineyards for his heiresses, and henceforth they were named after the daughters, particularly as the wines they produced were somewhat in character as well, that from the Côte Blonde being then and today, a more delicate, lighter wine which did not last as well as the fuller, more austere Côte Brune.

Côte-Rôtie is made principally from the Syrah grape, locally known as the Serine, a name which would be unfamiliar even in nearby Hermitage. In Côte-Rôtie the Syrah can be blended with up to 20 per cent of the Viognier grape, a rare and wonderful white variety. In practice many growers have abandoned growing Viognier, for the yield is small and inconsistent, and it is now only found in isolated pockets, primarily on the Côte Blonde, and to the extent of perhaps 5 per cent of the *appellation*.

The steep, small terraces of the Côte-Rôtie also make it impossible to train the Syrah in the usual (Gobelet) way. This is impractical in the Côte-Rôtie and the vines are trained up and around a framework of four poles tied together at the top, making a shape somewhat like that of a steep wigwam. Two or three plants may be trained up the same structure, and there will be perhaps half a dozen such 'wigwams' per terrace.

Though some of the leading growers such as Guigal and Gentaz do produce separate Côte Blonde and Côte Brune wines, Côte-Rôtie today is normally a wine blended from the yields of several small parcels scattered over the *appellation*. The 196 hectares are divided between fifty or so families and holdings are small, barely economic for most, who need to supplement their activities as winemakers with other jobs.

The wine is made by traditional methods, often being fermented with the stalks and macerated for two or even three weeks. Ageing can be in *barrique* or in *foudre* and for three or more years before bottling. In the *barrique* the wine has more contact with the air and it develops quicker. In the *foudre* which more often than not will be considerably encrusted with tartrate crystals, the wine ages more slowly; indeed it can often remain dumb, drying out in fruit without softening in tannin and so deteriorate, if the winemaker is sloppy with his *élevage*.

The leading grower-*négociant* in Côte-Rôtie is Établissements Guigal. Étienne Guigal, a relaxed, sprightly but shy man who sadly died in the autumn of 1988, used to work for the local *négociant* Vidal-Fleury, but set up on his own at the end of the Second World War. In 1984 he bought the company of his former employers. The family have 10 hectares of vineyards of their own, and contracts with a wide number of even smaller local growers. Maison Guigal is now run by Étienne's son Marcel who is a fund of information on the area. The top Guigal wines are La Mouline, a wine entirely made from the Côte Blonde, La Ladonne, exclusively from the Côte Brune, the Château DíArmaris and La Turque. All three wines are spectacular; La Mouline, which was first launched in 1966, is a wine of great complexity and delicacy when mature, with a totally individual flavour as a result of the tiny percentage of Viognier in the blend and has a character which bears no relation to Hermitage at all. La Landonne, which was only produced from the 1978 vintage onwards, is altogether different, a wine of substance, richness and power, and a worthy rival in intensity of flavour and 'manliness' to a Hermitage La Chapelle. Recent vintages – 1996, '95, '91, '90, '89, '88, '85, '83, and '82 were all very fine years in Côte-Rôtie – have been excellent. The 1985 La Turque, the first vintage, is unbelievably good.

Robert Jasmin is another grower with a very high reputation and I have enjoyed many mature vintages of his wines at the hospitable table of Robin and Judith Yapp, his British agents. The Jasmin holding is small (4 hectares) and the average age of the vines a venerable half century or so. As a result production is limited to only 300 cases or so per year. Jasmin's wine is soft, ample, plummy and voluptuous, less hard than Guigal's when young, but, I would suggest, equally long-lived for all that. The age of the vines, producing in the better vintages a very exhilarating concentration of ripe fruit, gives Jasmin's wine an extra richness and depth not often found elsewhere.

Other leading growers in Côte-Rôtie include Pierre Barge, Bernard Bourgaud, Émile Champet, Joel Champert, Didier Chol, Gilbert Cluzel, Edmond Duclaux, Jean-Michel Gereu, Jean-Paul and Jean-Luc Jamet.

Ampuis, is the local driving force behind a consortium of French and American businessmen which has been responsible for much of the new plantations on the plateau. These wines should be watched with care.

Among the *négociants* Vidal-Fleury (now owned by Guigal but still operated independently) and Chapoutier both own vineyards in the area, the former with 8 hectares and the latter with 3. Both companies' Côte-Rôties are dependable without being very exciting, though recent Vidal-Fleury wines are now showing a distinct improvement. Paul Jaboulet Aíné of Tain do not actually own any vineyards but produce a wine called Les Jumelles. As with all Jaboulet's wines their Côte-Rôtie Les Jumelles is bottled earlier than that of the local growers but is nonetheless full, rich, sturdy and long-living. But it misses the individuality and concentration of the best growers' wines.

CONDRIEU and CHÂTEAU GRILLET

Condrieu, home to one of the most rare and mysterious, intriguing, individual and delicious white wines of France, lies on the right or west bank of the Rhône adjacent to the vineyards of Côte Rôtie, just where the river makes an S-bend after passing the town of Vienne. The name Condrieu comes from *coin de ruisseau*, or corner of the stream – though one would be hard put, these days, to describe the wide, grey, muddy, polluted Rhône as a *ruisseau*.

As with many of the vineyards in this part of the Rhône, the precipitous hillsides topped with deciduous woods have had, until recently, a somewhat sorry, decayed aspect. A hundred years ago this was a flourishing vineyard. The difficulties of working the land and the lure of an easier "nine-to-five" life in the factories and offices of Vienne and Lyon, together with the temptation of high prices offered by real estate speculators intent on developing the land for holiday homes, led to the abandonment of the slopes. Scrub and bramble cover the ancient terraces, the walls of which have crumbled away. Here and there the vines are planted but most is once again nature's domaine.

Until recently, then, Condrieu and its even smaller neighbour Château Grillet were names in books rather than wines we had actually tasted. Outside the local restaurants the wines were hardly obtainable. They were wines of myth and fable. Those who had enjoyed them, of course, at the restaurant La Pyramide in Vienne, at the Beau Rivage in Condrieu itself, pronounced them fabulous. When I first began to encounter them, in the early 1960s, I could only agree.

The last 15 years have seen a renaissance in this part of the world. First it was the neighbouring Côte-Rôtie which was "discovered." Prices rose and rose again. Once more it became economical to plant vines on what are some of the steepest vineyard hills in Europe. A new generation of young, dedicated men and women could be seen gradually reconstructing the old terraces, increasing the land under vinous cultivation.

Then it was the turn of Condrieu. The same thing happened. From a couple of dozen hectares under vine the *appellation* has increased eight-fold, and is still expanding. Many growers combine wine production with that of soft fruit: apricots being a particular local success story. But at present the vast majority of the harvest comes from young vines.

Currently there are 108 hectares under vine within a delimited area of 200 hectares scattered over the communes of Vérin, Saint-Michel-sur-Rhône, Saint-Pierre-de-Boeuf and Chavanay in the *département* of Loire, Condrieu to the north in Rhône and Limony to the south in Ardèche. The southern two communes, Limony and Saint-Pierre, are also authorized for Saint-Joseph, and were added to the Condrieu *appellation* in 1953 in an effort to expand the production.

The Viognier is not an easy vine to grow, nor is it productive; and though it is authorized for cultivation in parts of the southern Rhône, and even in Provence and Languedoc, it is rarely found outside Condrieu and Château Grillet. According to local legend it is said to have been imported from Dalmatia in AD 281 at the behest of the Emperor Probus, perhaps as a compensation for the total destruction of the Condrieu vineyards by his predecessor the Emperor Vespasian. The Viognier is susceptible to both *coulure* (failure of the flower to set into fruit) and *millerandage* (shot berry); the latter more than the former for even after a successful flowering the grapes may remain shrivelled and undeveloped. It is, however, long-lived. Once established, the vine may last for fifty or even seventy years, and its best fruit will be provided between the ages of twenty-five and fifty. Yields are low, though. While the *appellation* laws permit a maximum yield of 30 hectolitres per hectare, the average yield over the last twenty years has been barely half that, and even in 1994, the most abundant year anybody can remember, Georges Vernay only produced 28 hectolitres per hectare, the most he has ever made in his long career.

The vines are mainly planted in isolated pockets, facing south or south-east, and on slopes which run back perpendicularly from the river and so are protected from the wind. Viognier is trained along wires and pruned to a single cane with six buds (*guyot simple*). The soil is granite based, and carries a fine topsoil containing decomposed mica, known locally as *arzelle*. It is sandy-grey in appearance, and washes away easily. Livingstone-Learmonth (*The Wines of The Rhône*) quotes the late André Dézormeaux, a grower who had 1.25 hectares in Saint-Michel. Some years ago he had to retrieve 100 cubic metres of soil from the bottom of his vineyard after the winter rains. "I had to carry it all up on my back, and it makes me wonder what I did wrong to deserve such a penance," he said ruefully.

CHÂTEAU GRILLET

Within the delimited area of Condrieu lies a single estate with its own *appellation contrôlée*. In this respect, so they claim, Château Grillet is unique in France, though as each of the *grands crus* of Burgundy have their own separate *appellation*, the Domaine de la Romanée-Conti could argue that they, too, have this exclusive right, and for two vineyards, Romanée-Conti and La Tâche, while Mommessin can boast the same for the Clos du Tart. Château Grillet is often said to be the smallest *appellation* in France but this is not so. Fifteen years ago there were 1.75 hectares under vine at Château Grillet but since then the vineyard has been expanded to 3.08 hectares. Meanwhile Romanée-Conti has remained at 1.6 hectares; and the adjacent La Romanée at 0.85 hectares. It is the latter which is the smallest *appellation* in France.

Grillet has for long had a particular eminence, separate from the rest of Condrieu. Jullien (1816) rates it a wine of his *première classe*. The wines can be made *liquoreux*, he says, but more often than not they are dry rather than sweet. Today, Château Grillet is a dry wine, and seems to have been so since the first decades of the twentieth century.

Château Grillet's pre-eminence seems to have been consolidated by the arrival of the Neyret-Gachet family in 1820. Prior to this there are few records of the wine being held in any particular esteem though the estate and its wine must have been well established – Livingstone-Learmonth (Op. Cit.) says that prior to 1820 it was always shipped in cask and adds that the château records date back to the time of Louis XIII (1610-1643) – nor, it seems, do we know who or what the original Grillet was. Perhaps like Côte-Rôtie ("roasted slope") the word Grillet is a corruption of *grillé* ("grilled"). Indeed it has often been mis-spelled as such. Yet by 1830 the wine was already being exported to Moscow and to the court of Saint James in London, an order for 12 dozen bottles being placed on behalf of King George IV. Ninety years later, with an arrogance only the French could adopt when talking about food and wine, the self-styled Prince of Gastronomes, Curnonsky, wrote that Château Grillet was "quite simply the third (after Montrachet and Yquem) of the five best wines of France and *therefore of the world*" (my italics) – the other two being Coulée de Serrant and Château Chalon.

The château of Grillet rests in the middle of its vineyard above the village of Saint-Michel-sur-Rhône. The soil, poorer than in Condrieu, is a decomposed, almost powdery granite rich in mica. The vineyard itself could not be more ideally situated. It is a natural amphitheatre, facing due south, steep, terraced, sheltered, a veritable sun-trap. With such a perfect setting, coveted jealously, so it is said, by the neighbouring Condrieu growers, it was natural that something out of the ordinary could be produced.

The building itself is a rather engaging architectural hotch-potch. Built on medieval foundations, the facade is Renaissance and, as Livingstone-Learmonth writes, "subsequent owners built on as the fancy took them, their main criterion being size rather than charm"; and one might add, defence against local marauders, for the sides are heavily fortified.

The Neyret-Gachet family is still the proud owner of Château Grillet, and the current incumbent, 70-plus André Canet, who married Hélène Neyret-Gachet, has been gradually extending the area under vine by restoring ancient terraces on his domaine. From an average of 44 hectolitres per annum in the 1960s he can now make over 100 in a good year. In 1996 production was 124 hectolitres.

The grapes are collected in three days in late September (earlier than in Condrieu, so producing a wine with a higher acidity) by a team of some two dozen local harvesters who supplement the three full-time employees on the estate. The fruit is crushed in a modern pneumatic press and vinified in epoxy-resin-lined steel vats, where the wine remains on its lees until the spring and when the malolactic fermentation has finished. It is then racked into small, old, oak barrels, and not bottled until after the second winter. Unlike Condrieu, Grillet uses a special 70cl brown, flute-shape bottle, not the normal *feuilles-mortes*, 75cl, Burgundy-shaped bottle.

It is this longer ageing which gives Grillet its distinctive character, different from Condrieu. The maturation in wood produces a darker colour and a richer and fuller flavour, at the expense, it could be argued, of the more racy and delicate fragrance of a Condrieu. Monsieur Canet would reply that at Château Grillet the *bouquet* and character becomes more aromatic and more complex, the wine has more weight and more depth, and it keeps better, though his own preference is to drink the wine young, generally before its fifth birthday, and never after eight years of age.

I have drunk some splendid Châteaux Grillets: the 1969 and 1971, the 1978, for example. Since then, I felt, and was it a coincidence that this coincided both with the expansion of the vineyard and an increase in yield per hectare, standards slipped somewhat. I think M. Canet's policy of early-harvesting is a mistake: the wines simply lacked substance; the grapes were not ripe enough. The 1985 was harvested later, however. The 1988 and 1989 were better than average, and the vintages of the 1990s I have seen so far – M. Canet is reluctant to receive visitors and so my notes are mainly on wines in bottle – have been generally complimentary. But at twice the price of Condrieu? The answer is: not worth it.

* * * * * *

At the outset both Condrieu and Château Grillet are made in the same way. It is after the first fermentation that the processes diverge. Firstly, most, but not all Condrieu goes through malo-lactic (those that do not preserve a higher natural acidity, which may well be an advantage). Secondly, Condrieu is bottled earlier, and most never see wood.

As the growers will normally have sold their previous year's harvest, part of the crop will be bottled as soon as possible. These lighter wines are crisp and enticing in the spring and summer after the vintage, but will appear tired as little as a year after that. The rest of the wines will be bottled later in the summer and will last better, but even then are at their best almost as young as possible, though the locals would aver that the optimum is between two and four years old. Condrieu is both oak- and tank-aged, and it is difficult to be hard and fast about which method is better. Vernay's young wines do not "see oak" in the sense of being matured in small barrels. Other growers' wines are both fermented and stored in large wooden *foudres*, but these are normally so encrusted with tartrates that the influence of the oak is negligible. Some *négociants'* wines such as those of Guigal and Delas have a definite oaky taste, and are all the better for it, but other sources, while oaky, lack style. Vernay's young Condrieu can be enticing, but his special *cuvée*, the Coteau de Vernon, which is left for a year in cask, is one of the best Condrieux you can get.

I adore the wine. Young Condrieu is delicious. Difficult to describe but delicious nevertheless. The wine is paradoxical: quite high in alcohol, rather low in acidity; but instead of being heavy, as this might indicate, it is in fact rather delicate. Some talk about a combination of Vouvray and the Moselle with an added element of alpine flowers thrown in for good measure. Jonathan Livingstone-Learmonth *(Op. Cit.)* says "Young Condrieu gives the impression of slightly unripe pears or of eating the fruit near the pear skin." When the wine is old, he adds, "honey and apricots are sometimes mentioned by the growers."

Personally, what characterises Condrieu for me is an aspect of candied peel, of citrus, even of marmalade. In my view it is best young. I don't think the wine ages well, though the oaky examples last longer than others. But a lot of this may well be a consequence of the young vines. When these come of age, and consequently produce a more concentrated balanced wine, they may age better.

Georges Vernay, now in his 70s, suffering somewhat from cataracts and about to be succeeded by his son Luc, is the guru of the *appellation*, with 12 hectares of vines, 7 of which are old Condrieu. He used to produce half the entire crop under the Condrieu label in the old days, and he remains ever ready to lend equipment and offer encouragement and advice to the new generation. As well as Condrieu, of which his best *cuvées* are the Coteau du Vernon and the Chaillées d'Enfer, he offers Côte du Rhône, Saint-Joseph and Côte-Rôtie. Vernay's Condrieux vary from light, *primeur*, tank-fermented examples to wines of structure with just a hint of wood.

Other good growers include: Christophe and Patrick Bonnefond; Louis Chèze; Cluzel-Roch; Yves Cuilleron; Pierre Dumazet; Pierre Gaillard; Jean-Michel Gerin; Ets Etienne Guigal; Jean-Yves Multier, Château du Rozay; Robert Niéro; Alain Paret; André Perret; Robert Jurie des Camiers; Philippe and Christian Pichon; René Rostaing; and François Villard.

In addition to these local growers and merchants, reliable Condrieux can be found *chez* the leading Rhône *négociants* Chapoutier, Délas, Jaboulet, de Vallouit and Vidal-Fleury.

VINTAGES

As has been made clear, Condrieu is a wine best drunk young. The oaky *cuvées* will last, but hardly more than three years after bottling. The non-oaked wines are best drunk as soon as they are released.

1997: First reports indicate a very good vintage for Condrieu. The harvest season was fine, without interruption by rain.

1996: A very good vintage, especially for those with the courage to wait until their fruit was properly ripe, for together with maturity came a satisfactorily high acidity. Those who picked earlier made correspondingly thin and characterless wine which has evolved quickly.

1995: Very much a similar pattern to 1996, benefiting the later harvesters. Neither of these vintages was as good as 1994. Most wines now getting tired.

1994: A fine vintage, but except for superior oak-aged *cuvées*, now getting towards its end.

1993 and 1992: Mediocre vintages: now passed their best.

1991: A fine vintage. A few oaky *cuvées* may still be enjoyable.

1990: and earlier. Too old.

HERMITAGE

The apogee of the Syrah is reached in Hermitage. Great Hermitage is truly great, by any standards; in its own way as fine as a First Growth claret, a top *grand cru* Burgundy and anything any other country or region might have to offer.

According to Livingstone-Learmonth and Master in *The Wines of the Rhône* Tain l'Hermitage was already a thriving vineyard in Roman times, and the wine, then known as Tegna, is mentioned not only by Pliny, who wrote about agricultural matters in his *Natural History* in AD 77, but in Martial's *Epigrams*, which seem to indicate that it enjoyed more than a local fame. This is a part of France which is rich in Roman ruins. From Arles and Nîmes in the south to Vienne and even Lyon in the north, the Rhône Valley abounds in antiquities, and in Tain there is an ancient altar, known as the Taurobole, that was used for the sacrifice of bulls to the god Mithras. It may have been the Phocaeans who introduced the cultivated vine to the South of France in about the sixth century BC, but it was the arrival of the Romans which gave the impetus to organized viticulture.

Looming above the bustling town of Tain, rugged and bleak in the winter, and the colour of rhinoceros hide, is the granite hill of Hermitage. There are many legends accounting for the origin of this name. Without a scrap of evidence to support their claims, James Joyce and Maurice Healy, both Irish, each aver that the site was a resting place for Saint Patrick, on his way to convert the Irish to Christianity. Another story is of a Christian priest who, fleeing from the Romans, took refuge on the hill and was supplied with food by the wild animals around him. There was nothing to drink, however, and he was in danger of dying from thirst, when the good Lord intervened and sent down a band of angelic growers with vines which produced wine overnight. The best-known story is of the holy knight Gaspard de Stérimberg. Stérimberg was wounded in a crusade against the Albigensian heretics in 1224, and, disgusted with the follies of his fellow mortals, chose the hill of Hermitage as a place to build a small chapel of retreat, wherein he would pray for the souls of his fellow men. In due course he decided to plant vines on the steep slopes surrounding him. The reputation of the excellence of this wine soon spread, and the local peasants began to cultivate the remaining sections of the hill.

The modern era for the wines of Hermitage seems to date from 1642, when, a year before his death, Louis XIII stopped at Tain. As might be expected the local wine was offered as part of the royal refreshment. It was enthusiastically appreciated and orders were given for Hermitage to be included in the royal cellar. The reputation of the wine never looked back. Shipments were being exported as far as Russia only a couple of decades later and by the end of the seventeenth century Hermitage was established as one of the greatest red wines of France.

By the end of the eighteenth century the wine of Hermitage had found its way to Bordeaux. From 1780 until the time of phylloxera, the wine was used extensively to give a bit of muscle to the sometimes insipid wines of the Gironde. This blending was quite legal – it was well before the introduction of the INAO laws – and quite open. Wines, even estate wines such as Château Lafite, were offered either pure or Hermitagé, and often the latter was the most appreciated.

The mid-nineteenth century saw a series of great vintages. Professor Saintsbury (*Notes on a Cellar Book*, 1920) described an 1846 (the year before he was born) as 'really a wonderful wine . . . the *manliest* wine I ever drank; and age (the bottle was forty years old) has softened and polished all that might have been rough in the manliness of its youth'. Red wines then were made bigger than they are today. The grapes were picked somewhat earlier, and so had a higher acidity; and the *cuvaison* was longer, so the wines were burlier and more tannic. Bottles of the best years, therefore, would last well into their third or even fourth decade. Hermitage, however, must have been one of the most indestructible of all wines. In 1981, at a pre-auction tasting which I presented in Chicago on behalf of Heublein Inc., an anonymous 1825 Hermitage was offered. The most badly ullaged bottle in the lot – a cache discovered in the back of a cellar near Lyon – was opened for tasting. Even that was still well-coloured, vigorous, recognizably Syrah, and still had fruit. And yet the wine was over 150 years old!

By a quirk of geography the hill of Hermitage is comprised of a granite base over which lies a thin layer of decomposed flint and chalk and odd because the surrounding countryside is a mixture of limestone and clay. The explanation for this is that originally the river Rhône ran its course to the east of Hermitage. Geologically the hill is part of the right bank of the valley, and, indeed, shares the same soil structure as Saint-Joseph and Côte-Rôtie. At some stage, however, the river changed its direction, leaving Hermitage isolated on the left, eastern bank. The hill dominates a bend in the river. North of Tain, the river is flowing due south and once past the town, it flows east for a kilometre or so before correcting itself. This leaves the prime vineyards of the granite hills of Hermitage with an exposure which is due south, and bathed in sunlight from dawn to dusk.

The 130 hectares of vines are sub-divided into a number of *climats* or individual vineyards, and most of these are split between a number of owners. Each site produces wine which varies subtly from the others, and most growers and *négociants* make a wine which is a careful blend originating from a number of different plots. In *Topographie de Tous les Vignobles Connus* (1816), Jullien listed the three best *climats*; les Bessards, at the western end of the hill, producing a full, sturdy wine; le Méal, next door, with a deeper layer of flint and chalk, producing a wine of fine perfume; and les Greffieux, below le Méal, making generous, supple wine. The ideal is said to be a blend of these three.

Cultivation on the steep hill is a problem. While spraying these days is done by helicopter, Gérard Jaboulet of Paul Jaboulet Aîné still reckons on one labourer per hectare on the hill rather than one per ten hectares on the flatter Crozes vineyards. Though not as precipitous as Côte-Rôtie the terrain is steep and the fragile layer of topsoil has to be protected within terraces, or too much would be washed away every time there was a thunderstorm. The first machines which can work the soil efficiently are just beginning to be developed, and some of these have been invented by Gérard Jaboulet himself. But much of the ploughing is still done using horses and mules.

The Syrah vine is pruned by the Gobelet (spur) method and, on the steepest parts of Hermitage, trained up a single stake to help protect it against the strong mistral winds. On the flatter land the vines can be trained along wires by the Cordon de Royat method to form the traditional hedge aspect somewhat similar to that in Bordeaux or Burgundy.

The hill of Hermitage makes both red and white wine. Just under 25 per cent of the total output is white, produced from a mixture of Roussanne and Marsanne grapes grown where the topsoil is rich in clay. The Marsanne is today the predominant variety. It produces a wine which is richer and has more structure if having less finesse than the delicate, alpine-flowery Roussanne and is less prone to disease. Traditionally, white Hermitage was a full-bodied wine, high in alcohol; a wine of muscle rather than finesse. Often it was aged too long before bottling, and as a result was heavy and flat, with a rather oily aspect to add to the nutty, herby peach-kernel flavour. Maturation was in oak, but in large oak *foudres* rather than in new barrels.

Led by Paul Jaboulet Aîné, the leading *négociant*, production methods in the last twenty years have somewhat changed. Fermentation is now at a low temperature, storage is in vat or tank, malolactic fermentation is discouraged, and bottling is early. This is fine for a Crozes-Hermitage Blanc, whose aspiration is to Mâconnais rather than Meursault and which is destined for drinking young, but I feel that for a top white Hermitage itself, a leaf out of the book of Vincent Leflaive of Puligny, say, would not be amiss and maturation in new or newish oak barrels would be an advantage. White Hermitage today is a puzzling wine. Only a few producers have currently got it right. Jaboulet now ferments his white Hermitage in oak.

Another puzzling factor is the evolution of white wines for keeping. When young the white wines can be delicious, crisp and fruity and youthful. After three years or so they seem to go through a prolonged awkward adolescence. White Hermitage becomes lumpy, hard, even resinny. Patience, however, provided the wine has been well made in the first place, will be rewarded. After four or five more years, i.e. after seven in bottle, the ugly duckling becomes a swan – once more clean and fruity, but now rich, mellow and profound. This curious process, which I put down to the side effects of an oxidation/reduction in bottle, does not occur in Burgundy, though I have noticed it in some dry Bordeaux and in white Châteauneuf-du-Pape.

Theoretically, a maximum of 15 per cent of white grapes can be included in the vats for red Hermitage – a curious decree which does not pertain for any other red wine *appellation* except for Côte-Rôtie and Crozes in the northern Rhône. In practice few growers ever use more than 5 per cent and I suspect that all the top wines such as Jaboulet's La Chapelle and those from Gérard Chave are made exclusively from Syrah.

Vinification methods for the red wines are still largely what might be termed 'old-fashioned', with a long *cuvaison* in glass-lined concrete vats or large oak *foudres*, together with most of the stalks, the object being to produce a big, full-bodied, tannic wine – a wine of power and strength which will need a decade or more to mature. The result is one of the fullest, densest and richest wines in the world. When young the colour is immense; a solid, viscous, almost black purple that continues to the very rim of the glass. The nose is leafy, with an undercurrent of unripe blackcurrants. The wine is full-bodied and very tannic, strong, powerful and alcoholic. The best examples are also oaky, and despite their 'size' not the least fiery, robust or spicy. When mature, these retain their vastness of structure, but the flavour is now rich, ample, profound and aromatic with a depth of flavour and a concentration of character which has few rivals. The fruit is now a ripe and subtle combination of blackcurrants and blackberries with a hint of raspberry, all underpinned by a slightly baked smell, as if the wine could remember its origins as the sun slowly heated up the granite bed rock day after day as the grapes ripened. What I find particularly memorable about top Hermitage of a good vintage is the way the wines manage to achieve an extraordinary retention of fresh, ripe fruit, even after fifteen or even twenty-five years in bottle.

The leading producer, both grower and *négociant*, is Paul Jaboulet Aîné. Little is known about the origins of the Jaboulet family. The only information we have is that they were already owners of vineyards in Hermitage before 1834, the date the firm was formed, and that the family is local, or at least from no further away than Vienne. Now, of course, it is one of the most prestigious *négociants* in the Rhône Valley and sells to almost every wine-drinking country in the world. Gérard Jaboulet, its P.D.G. or *Président-Directeur-Général*, until his sad death in 1997, was constantly jetting to and from Tokyo, New York and more exotic places, promoting the Jaboulet image and selling their wine. The wines of the Jaboulet firm are indeed excellent, yardstick examples of their kind, and I do not begrudge the firm its success. I just wish, selfishly, that there was a little more La Chapelle to go round, and that it were possible to pick up a twenty-year-old bottle as easily as a 1970 claret.

Jaboulet own 24 hectares out of the 132 hectares of vines on the hill of Hermitage, including the land on which lies the tiny, dilapidated chapel of Saint-Christophe near the top of the hill, and from which they take the name of their most famous wine. Nineteen of these hectares are planted with the red-wine-producing Syrah grape and those which traditionally produce the La Chapelle lie in the le Méal and les Bessards *climats*. The remaining 5 hectares grow the Marsanne and Roussanne varieties from which they make their celebrated white Hermitage, Le Chevalier de Stérimberg.

The harvest of the Syrah grape normally commences about two-thirds of the way through September, after the white wine varieties have been picked, and takes a fortnight. I asked Gérard Jaboulet once if the La Chapelle vineyards were picked earlier or later than the family vineyards in Crozes, or if his date was different to, say, that of Gérard Chave, whose Hermitage is also a magnificent wine. Apparently not, though the firm of Chapoutier are traditionally always the last to start picking.

The vinification of La Chapelle takes place in glass-lined concrete vats, and only 25 per cent of the bunches are de-stalked in a normal vintage. For two or three days the temperature is allowed to rise – as it will, naturally, for fermentation is an exo-thermic reaction – to between 28°C and 29°C, in order to extract the maximum amount of colour. Thereafter the vats are cooled to between 22°C and 20°C and the *cuvaison*, during which the juice is in contact with the skins, continues for three weeks. By this time the fermentation has finished. The wine is racked off into a clean vat, and the remaining pulp is pressed. Only the wine from the first press, which is very slow and gentle, hardly more than a nudge, is returned to the free-flow wine.

As soon as the malolactic fermentation is complete the wine is racked a second time, filtered with kieselguhr, and put into oak barrels. Thereafter, apart from occasional rackings to separate the wine from the lees of dead yeast cells and tartrates which naturally separate out, what has now become Hermitage La Chapelle is interfered with as little as possible. There is no further filtering. The wine remains in wood for between nine and eighteen months before bottling, normally a year after the vintage. Exceptional years, such as the 1990 which was not bottled until June 1992, are bottled later.

The Jaboulets are very specific about the oak they use for maturing, not only for La Chapelle, but for all their red wines. They abhor new oak. One-year-old casks are acquired from leading white Burgundy growers, such as Sauzet and Leflaive. These casks have therefore been broken in, so to speak, but are as young as second-year casks can be. A barrel which had previously held new claret or another new red Rhône wine would be significantly more 'used'. A quarter of the Jaboulet crop goes into these one-year-old casks, another quarter into those bought the previous year and the rest into older wood.

When mature Jaboulet's Hermitage La Chapelle is not just an impressive glass of wine, it is nectar. It has all the body and 'manliness' of Hermitage, but in addition a concentration and a sheer aristocracy which is truly exhilarating. This is not just the best wine of the Rhône Valley but one of the top dozen wines of the whole of France.

La Chapelle, though the greatest wine in their portfolio, is, of course, not all that Jaboulet produces. The white Stérimberg is one of the best of the new-style whites. Their Crozes, particularly the *tête de cuvée* Domaine de Thalabert, is very fine, as is their Cornas and to a lesser extent their Côte-Rôtie 'Les Jumelles'. The portfolio, obviously, covers the southern Rhône as well, and includes an excellent Châteauneuf-du-Pape, Les Cèdres.

Equally high in the Hermitage hierarchy of producers is Gérard Chave. The Chave family have been cultivating vineyards on the granite hill since as far back as 1481 and this probably makes them the longest established *vignerons* in France. Twelve hectares of old vines in Hermitage are farmed as well as a small parcel in Saint-Joseph and the wine is made in the cellars underneath the family house at Mauves south of Tournon in Saint-Joseph.

A visit to Chave, particularly before he has blended his red wine *cuvée*, and therefore when one can taste the different *lots* each from a separate *climat*, soil and microclimate, is a fascinating experience. I learned more on a single visit to Chave in 1986 about the wine-making of the Syrah grape and the differences between the varying *lieux-dits* on the Hermitage hill, than in a decade of visits to the Rhône Valley. His hospitable table and a splendid array of old bottles waited afterwards. *Merci!*

Chave's Hermitage is different from that of Jaboulet. It is oaky, but in a less obviously 'new-oak' way; equally big, rich, amply fruity, concentrated and long-lasting; but somehow leaning more to Burgundy, as well as to Châteauneuf, rather than to Bordeaux. His white, apricot and peach-flavoured, full and profound, is clearly the best white Hermitage there is.

Until recently, the best of the rest of Hermitage was only made by the other leading *négociants* of the northern Rhône: Chapoutier in Tain, Delas in Tournon, Léon Revol and de Vallouit. Now they have been joined by one or two other growers. The Cave Co-opérative used to be a good source but in the 1980s I have found their wines less interesting.

The Sorrel family own 3½ hectares on the Hermitage hill, and since 1970 have been making their own wine rather than selling their grapes to the co-operative. Their best wine, aged in casks bought from the Domaine de la Romanée-Conti, and called Le Gréal, is excellent. Other growers include Jean-Louis Grippat of Tournon, Jules Fayolle et Fils, Michel Ferraton, and Alphonse Desmeure Père et Fils. Terence Gray was another Hermitage name which appeared from time to time. The 2-hectare Gray vineyard was run on a share-cropping basis by Gérard Chave until 1985. He has now bought the land from Mr Gray, a retired Irish archeologist, and incorporated it into his own holdings. The Desmeure family recently acquired a parcel of vines beneath the 'Chapelle' on the best part of the hill. I have admired their recent vintages.

Until recently Hermitage was a remarkably inexpensive wine. Despite the low production – 5000 hectolitres from 132 hectares – and despite the quality, it did not have the fame of the top Bordeaux and Burgundy estates. The last decade has seen prices climb somewhat, and the better vintages reach premium prices on the rare occasions that they actually turn up at auction. Yet the wines are still marvellous value. All you need is a good cellar to store them in, and the patience to wait the dozen years or more until they are fully mature.

CROZES-HERMITAGE

Surrounding the hill of Hermitage itself is the expanding *appellation* of Crozes – the largest *appellation* in the northern Rhône. The *appellation* covers eleven communes and takes its name from one of them, that nearest to the hill itself. To the north of Hermitage lies Crozes, Larnage, Gervans, Erôme and Serves-sur-Rhône; Mercurol and Chanos-Curson are to the east; Beaumont-Monteux, Pont de l'Isère and La Roche de Glun to the south. The vines occupy undulating gentle slopes situated on a mixture of soils, some of which, like that at Gervans, are of a similar granite to that of Hermitage itself, while in other parts – at Mercurol, for instance – sand can be found, making it a suitable commune for white wines. Elsewhere, in parts of Mercurol again, at Beaumont and at Les Chassis on the way to Pont de l'Isère, the soil contains a large amount of smooth pudding stones, these *galets* showing evidence of the Rhône's old route to the east of the Hermitage hill. Generally the soil is much less granitic than at Hermitage itself, and this, plus a less ideal exposure, helps explain the difference in the wines. The best reds are said to come from Gervans and Larnage, where the ground is heavier and contains more clay, while the best wine of the *appellation*, Jaboulet's Domaine de Thalabert, comes from their own domaine of the same name at Les Chassis.

The same grapes are used as at Hermitage: Syrah (with 15 per cent white grapes allowed) for the red wine and Marsanne and Roussanne (almost entirely the former) for the white. The area now covers some 1236 hectares and in 1996 produced 51,747 hectolitres of wine, of which just under 10 per cent was white. This is about 60 per cent of the total northern Rhône production.

Crozes-Hermitage, together with Saint-Joseph, is the lightest and the cheapest of the northern Rhône red wines. Prices compare to that of a lesser *cru* Beaujolais and some of the wine, too, is made by carbonic maceration. In my view, however, this is a mistake as the syrah grape does not take kindly to this vinification technique. It loses not only the character of its fruit but also any individuality deriving from the soil. The result is anaemic, anonymous, and compared with some of the Syrahs from the South of France, very poor value for money.

The best wines are made by traditional methods, and along the lines of that of Hermitage, though Crozes, being less structured, needs to be bottled after a maximum of a year in cask, lest the fruit dries out. In good hands Crozes can be a very interesting wine, somehow less spicy and peppery, more refined than Saint-Joseph, and it is then excellent value. This sort of red is at its best after five or seven years. The best whites are those made by low-temperature fermentation, with no malolactic fermentation and with early bottling. These are similar in body, cost price and aspiration to a Mâcon-Blanc-Villages. The difference lies in the grape varieties used, and in a soil which has less limestone and more sand. I find the flavour of white Crozes-Hermitage difficult to describe, particularly as one grower's wine may be quite different to that of his neighbour. At a stab, a mixture of hay and vegetables, plus a whiff of peaches and apricots, as well as their kernels. Jaboulet's Mule Blanche is an excellent example of white Crozes-Hermitage, and it is at its best within a couple of years after the vintage.

As well as Jaboulet, all the local *négociants* produce Crozes, as do the co-operatives at Tain and Beaumont-Monteux. There are an increasing number of local growers who have left the co-operative in the last decade and who now bottle their own wine. Two such are Charles Tardy and Bernard Ange who operate under the name of GAEC de la Syrah and have combined their vineyards, one part of which is on the slopes of Chanos-Curson and the other at Beaumont. The blend of the wines of the two is better than the sum of their respective parts. The wine is amply fruity and excellently made. Alain Graillot, who arrived as recently as 1985, is another excellent grower, and other good Crozes, both red and white, are produced by Jules Fayolle et Fils at Gervans, Desmeure et Fils and the Collonge family (both in Mercurol), and the Domaine Pradelle in Chanos-Curson.

SAINT-JOSEPH

Saint-Joseph, an *appellation* which has only existed since 1956, lies on the west bank of the Rhône, centred round Tournon, but running sporadically from south of Condrieu as far as Cornas, a distance of some fifty kilometres as the crow flies. In all there are twenty-three communes covering 819 hectares which produced in 1996 32,334 hectolitres of wine, of which 2788 were white. This is the second largest *appellation* in the northern Rhône, after Crozes-Hermitage, and the grape varieties and regulations are the same.

Saint-Joseph, like Crozes, is an expanding *appellation*, the increase having been largely, and regrettably, in land not entirely suitable for fine wine, being predominantly on the flatter, more alluvial soils of the valley floor, rather than on the slopes themselves. As a result the wine of Saint-Joseph varies enormously, ranging from substantial wines for ageing from the steep slopes above Tournon itself, Mauves and Saint-Jean-de-Muzols, where the soil is essentially granite, to weaker wines made by carbonic maceration methods from the Cave Co-opérative at Saint-Désirat-Champagne and others. There are those who think highly of the better wines from the Saint-Désirat co-operative (indeed they are prolific gold medal winners at the annual *Concours Agricole* in Paris) but for me they lack the truly masculine character and depth of a northern Rhône wine.

At their best, however, after five years or so, Saint-Joseph can be very good, and, like Crozes, the wine is inexpensive. At the *négociant* level, prices are marginally more than for a simple Crozes, but cheaper than a better Crozes, let alone Cornas.

A few growers produce a really fine Saint-Joseph, a wine which in years like 1988, '85 and '83 will need seven years to soften and show its real quality. Among these I would rate Jean-Louis Grippat, whose vineyards lie above Tournon, the most highly. Grippat should not be confused with his distant cousin Bernard Gripa a couple of kilometres further south at Mauves, where Gérard Chave also makes an excellent Saint-Joseph. Raymond Trollat, Pierre Coursodon and Maurice Courbis can also be cited.

Saint-Joseph in general is a rugged wine, more open than Hermitage or Cornas, yet chewy and sometimes peppery. It lacks, for me, a certain finesse. Finesse may be a strange word to apply to the northern Rhône; yet the best wines of all the other *appellations*, underneath their sturdy character, seem to have it, and this is apparent when the wines are mature. Saint-Joseph has power without grace, size without, ultimately, class. There is a small amount of white Saint-Joseph, produced from Marsanne. In character it is very similar to a white Crozes-Hermitage.

CORNAS

Cornas lies south of Saint-Joseph on the west bank of the Rhône, twelve kilometres south of Tournon, and almost opposite Valence. It is a small *appellation*, producing about half that of Hermitage, and half that of Côte-Rôtie. The wines are exclusively red, and come from the Syrah grape. Eighty-nine hectares are under vine and in 1996 production totalled 3398 hectolitres. In the last few years the area under vines has begun to expand – but, like Côte-Rôtie, not always in the right place.

The wines are considerably superior to Crozes and Saint-Joseph, and at their best can match those of Hermitage. The main reason for this is the amount of granite on the hillsides behind the village, though, as these cannot be worked mechanically, the flatter stretch at the foot of the slopes, with more clay, limestone and sand, has now been planted. It gives inferior wine, but a better yield. The second factor is the aspect; the Rhône Valley is very broad here and the vines above the village are set back and sheltered from the prevailing mistral. As a result the general level of heat here is often the greatest in the northern Rhône.

Cornas is much fuller and richer than Crozes and Saint-Joseph. It is normally vinified in the traditional manner and given a good two years in cask. When young the wine is dense and black, with a baked quality missing in most Saint-Joseph wines, and a muscle which makes it difficult to divine the real quality of the wine within. This density takes a long time to disappear – eight years at least – and, as a result, in the less successful vintages I have found Cornas can begin to dry out before its inherent hardness has softened up. In the best vintages, however, Cornas can be tremendous. The size and power of the wine can be awe-inspiring. This is a real austere, uncompromising, manly wine, if anything is.

The best grower in Cornas is Auguste Clape. Clape has enlarged his vineyard since first I began to call on him, and now has 6 hectares – which may not sound much, but still makes him one of the major growers of the *appellation*. He produces about 20,000 bottles a year. Clape is, above all, a stylist, with an open, enquiring mind, and a quiet conviction of what Cornas should be. His wines are remarkably consistent and as well as being extremely long-lasting, they are impressively good.

Jaboulet, in my experience, produce the best *négociant* Cornas and its price demonstrates the neglect of this *appellation*. It is excellent value for money though it is not up to the standard of the best growers' wines. Of these growers the most noteworthy are Guy de Barjac, Jean-Luc Colombo, Marcel Juge, Jean Lionnat, Robert Michel, Noël Versey and Alain Voge. Judging by their vintages since 1982 Auguste Clape at last has some worthy competition at the grower level.

SAINT-PÉRAY

Saint-Péray lies immediately south of Cornas on the west bank of the Rhône opposite Valence. It is a small *appellation*, with only 60 hectares of vines, like Cornas, but this time the *appellation* is for white wine only, both still and sparkling, from the traditional northern Rhône varieties of Marsanne and Roussanne. Saint-Péray is a rare wine, little seen outside the immediate area. Yet it was not always as obscure as it is today. There is a well-known story of Richard Wagner ordering 100 bottles to be sent to Bayreuth in 1877, where he was occupied in completing *Parsifal*. Napoleon was stationed as a cadet at Valence, and later spoke of Saint-Péray with affection as his first vinous discovery. Perhaps deliberately taking a contrary view, Wellington is said to have despised it. All these references are to the sparkling wine, made by the champagne method, which makes up about 80 per cent of the production. Some 250,000 bottles of this are made each year, always *brut*, and nearly always sold as non-vintage. According to legend the champagne-method technique was brought to the area by Dom Pérignon himself.

Why is it that Saint-Péray, in a predominantly red wine area, is exclusively a white wine? One reason may be a change of soil. At Saint-Péray, whose vineyards also lie in the adjoining commune of Toulaud, the slope is more gentle than it is further north, and the soil less granitic. The *terroir* is made up from clay, sand, flint and stones, without any chalk or much limestone. This is similar to the sections in Hermitage and Crozes given over to white grapes. Another reason, I would suggest, is a question of the local competition. As a red wine, the quality could not compete with neighbouring Cornas. As a sparkling white, it has the field to itself. Saint-Péray has a round, herby, nutty flavour with a certain *goût de terroir* and a southern fullness. It reminds me a little of the Cava wines from Penedés in northern Spain.

Jean-François Chaboud has the highest reputation among the local growers. He makes a full wine with an assertive character and a pronounced Marsanne flavour. A wine with less personality is made by the local co-operative, who are the largest producers in the area. Production in 1996 totalled 1908 hectolitres.

CLAIRETTE DE DIE and CHÂTILLON-EN-DIOIS

Half-way between Valence and Montélimar the river Drôme, flowing in from the Alps, reaches the Rhône near Livron. This marks the boundary between the Rhône *septentrionale* and the Rhône *méridionale*, and, if travelling south, this is where the Midi effectively begins. Within the space of a few dozen kilometres the countryside changes completely. Walnut and cherry are exchanged for cypress and olive; the light becomes brighter and the sky bluer, even with a touch of violet at times; the soil exudes heat and crickets begin incessantly to chirrup: we are in Provence. Before however we reach the southern Rhône we must make a little detour up into the Alps to survey the wines of a small region which belongs neither in the North nor in the South: the wines of Die.

The town of Die lies on the river Drôme some fifty kilometres up into the hills, just about at the point where deciduous forest – beech, birch, poplar and aspen – give way to larch and pine. Here the countryside is distinctly alpine, with houses built in the chalet style, meadows where goats or cattle graze in the lush grass, and jagged, snow-covered peaks standing quietly imposing in the distance while nearer crags loom close by.

Until the mid-1920s Clairette de Die was a still white wine, made, as the name suggests, from the Clairette grape, a variety more associated with the South of France where it produces a soft, slightly anonymous but nevertheless fruity wine rather deficient in acidity, and so for early drinking.

In 1926 the first sparkling wines were made, and from this date a second grape, the Muscat à Petits Grains, began increasingly to be used. A large and up-to-date co-operative was inaugurated in 1951, and this now produces three-quarters of the *appellation* which is now entirely sparkling wine. Two types of sparkling wine are made. The Brut, using at least 75 per cent Clairette, is made by the Champagne method and is a crisp, clean, but rather neutral drink. Cremant de Die is a superior version. The Tradition is made using both Clairette and Muscat à Petits Grains, which can vary in proportions from three of Clairette to one of Muscat, to one of Clairette to three of Muscat. The Cave Co-opérative de Die uses half and half. The only a quarter of Muscat in the blend will have the very positive grapy character typical of Muscat, and the Tradition is always made *demi-sec*, or even sweeter. Those who prefer a mildly grapy wine should go for a blend with less Muscat. Those who really enjoy its pronounced flavour should seek a wine like that of Monsieur Vincent of Sainte-Croix which is made with 70 per cent Muscat and 30 per cent Clairette. Today, however, Tradition is less in favour, and the Brut, which started in 1960, now makes up 40 per cent of the total production of around six million bottles.

The Tradition method involves cooling the newly extracted must in isothermal vats at a temperature of minus 3°C for 48 hours, then centrifuging and lightly filtering to remove loose particles, and then allowing the wine to ferment very slowly. The wine is bottled in January before all the original sugar has been transformed into alcohol. During the nine months' bottle-ageing the remaining sugar ferments and the malolactic fermentation occurs, thus producing carbon dioxide. Finally the deposits produced by this further fermentation are removed by filtration under pressure, before rebottling.

The grapes themselves come from an area of 1246 hectares within the confines of thirty-two communes stretching between Aouste, in the west near Crest, and Luc-en-Diois, nineteen kilometres south-east of Die along the Drôme Valley. The soil is predominantly limestone and clay on a hard rock base and becomes more meagre and the rock harder as the altitude increases.

South and east of Die, round the town of Châtillon itself, alternative grapes for the manufacture of still wines have been planted. These wines, under the *appellation* of Châtillon-en-Diois, were promoted from VDQS status to full AC in 1974. The reds and rosés are made from 75 per cent Gamay, with Pinot Noir or Syrah making up the remainder. The whites come from Aligoté and Chardonnay.

All this sounds rather promising, and some fifteen years ago I made a special journey up the beautiful Drôme Valley to visit the Die co-operative, main producer, then and now, of Châtillon-en-Diois. They seemed rather surprised when I expressed interest in the still wines rather than the *mousseux*, and when I came to taste them I could see why. Not only were the wines weak, thin and unripe but they were also surprisingly rustic. The ripeness of the grapes, perhaps, was something over which the co-operative had little control. The cleanliness of the wine-making, or in this case the lack of it, was their responsibility. I regret to report that recent tastings of Châtillon-en-Diois have shown that there has been little improvement. There is, however, only a tiny amount produced. Only some 50 hectares are under vine, and these are spread out into tiny artisanal parcels among eleven communes. Production in 1996 reached 1852 hectolitres or red and rosé and 1260 hectolitres of white.

CHÂTEAUNEUF-DU-PAPE

Châteauneuf-du-Pape, twenty kilometres north of Avignon, is both the geographic centre of the southern Rhône and also its leading quality *appellation*. It is a large *appellation*, its 3136 hectares producing over a million cases of wine a year (97,733 hectolitres in 1996). It is also, like Bordeaux, a region of large estates which are self-sufficient and individual in wine terms. The styles of the top Châteauneuf-du-Pape domaines contrast interestingly with one another, as do individual châteaux in Bordeaux, and for the same reason. Each reflects its own particular soil, mixture of grape varieties, microclimate, and, perhaps most important, differences in vinification techniques. Each, obviously, is a mirror of the personality and skill of the man who makes the wine.

While it was Bertrand de Goth, former Archbishop of Bordeaux – and owner of Château Pape-Clément in the Graves – who on taking up the papacy in 1309 decided to reside in Avignon rather than in Rome, it was his successor who built the summer palace and gave the impetus that went with papal patronage to the area. Pope John XXII first started to enlarge what was a relatively modest set of buildings in Avignon itself. The result, now being extensively renovated, is the magnificent papal palace we know today. With this complete, his thoughts turned to strengthening his defences in the surrounding countryside, and, *inter alia*, to building himself a residence wherein he could escape from the oppressive summer heat and stench of busy medieval Avignon and the duties of his office. A castle at Châteauneuf already existed but was in ruins. Between 1318 and 1333 a 'new castle' was constructed. For a summer palace it was huge, but it also formed part of a defensive circle of fortifications surrounding Avignon.

Châteauneuf was already an important wine area. It has been estimated that 1000 hectares were under vine in the early part of the fourteenth century. The church, however, was the only important proprietor and most of the land was in tiny plots and under peasant ownership. There was a ready outlet for their wine, however, for the papal holdings, originally only 10 hectares, were totally insufficient for the papacy's needs.

The official papal stay at Avignon lasted until 1378, after which anti-popes resided until the schism was healed in 1410. Thereafter the area sank back into being a backwater and the wine into obscurity. The modern era for Châteauneuf-du-Pape begins in the eighteenth century with the rise of a number of individual estates. La Nerthe or La Neste was the first, and is said to have commenced 'château-bottling' in 1785. That Thomas Jefferson passed close by in May 1787, without stopping to taste the wines, would indicate that any reputation was but local. Jullien in 1816 rated de la Nerthe in the 'Comtat d'Avignon' as a *vin de deuxième classe* and names the *crus* of Saint-Patrice, Bocoup, Coteau-Pierreux at Châteauneuf-du-Pape plus Coteau-Brulé at Sorgues as wines of the third class. 'The wines of this area, coming from long-established local varieties and new ones from Spain, though warm are delicate, *fin* and show a pretty bouquet . . . the moment to drink them is when they are three or four years old and in their prime.' The recent Spanish arrival is obviously the Grenache or Garnacha, today the dominant grape not only of Châteauneuf but of the entire Midi, as far as quality wines are concerned. The strange reference to Châteauneuf as being delicate would seem to indicate both that this Grenache was not yet fully established as well as perhaps the absence of grapes which would give solidity such as Syrah or Mourvèdre.

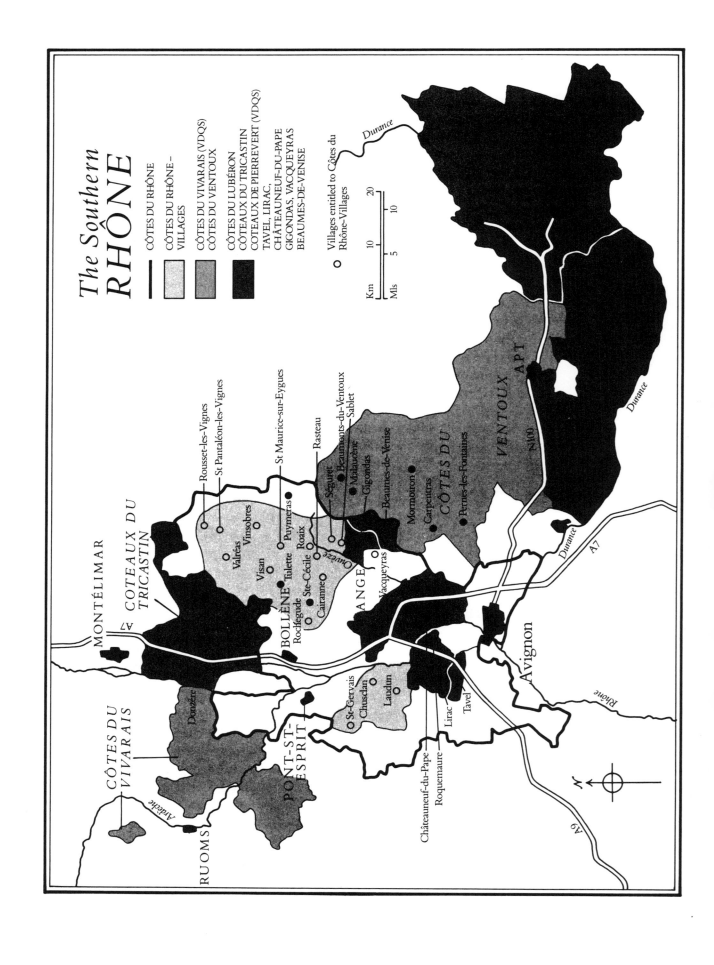

The Southern RHÔNE

— CÔTES DU RHÔNE

CÔTES DU RHÔNE–
VILLAGES

CÔTES DU VIVARAIS (VDQS)
CÔTES DU VENTOUX

CÔTES DU LUBÉRON
COTEAUX DU TRICASTIN
COTEAUX DE PIERREVERT (VDQS)
TAVEL, LIRAC,
CHÂTEAUNEUF-DU-PAPE
GIGONDAS, VACQUEYRAS
BEAUMES-DE-VENISE

○ Villages entitled to Côtes du
Rhône-Villages

Km   10   20
     5   10
Mls

Durance

CÔTES DU VIVARAIS

Ardèche

RUOMS

Donzère

MONTÉLIMAR

COTEAUX DU
TRICASTIN

PONT-ST-
ESPRIT

Rousset-les-Vignes
St Pantaléon-les-Vignes

Valréas
Vinsobres

Visan

BOLLÈNE
Rochegude
Ste-Cécile
Tulette
Cairanne
Puyméras
Roaix

St Maurice-sur-Eygues

Rasteau

Séguret
Sablet
Malaucène
Gigondas
Beaumes-de-Venise

Beaumonts-du-Ventoux

Mormoiron
Carpentras
Pernes-les-Fontaines

CÔTES DU
VENTOUX

APT

N100

Durance

A7

Ouvèze
ORANGE

Vacqueyras

St-Gervais
Chusclan
Laudun

Lirac
Tavel

Châteauneuf-du-Pape
Roquemaure

Avignon

Rhône

Durance

A9

N

At the time Jullien was writing there were some 2000 hectares of vineyards at Châteauneuf-du-Pape, a figure which was to remain constant until the onset of phylloxera, which struck the vineyards very soon after it was first noticed in the neighbouring *département* of Gard in 1863. Pre-phylloxera levels were not attained once more until the 1950s, since when the area has reached almost saturation point.

Meanwhile, the local producers led by Baron Le Roy of Château Fortia imposed on themselves a system of voluntary *appellation contrôlée* in 1923, complete with the necessity for the wines to pass a tasting test (not a universal requirement elsewhere until recently). These were to become the basis of all French AC laws. Châteauneuf-du-Pape can be made from a large number of different grape varieties. There are as many as thirteen authorized for the *appellation*, though several of these are now rarely encountered. Some of these are white varieties, added to the red wine to give it a bit of zip and freshness. The most important grape is the Grenache, widely grown throughout the South of France, in Provence as well as the Languedoc, and also in Spain. Next comes Syrah, the staple red wine grape of the northern Rhône – responsible for the undervalued but increasingly popular wines of Hermitage and Cornas – and then Cinsault and Mourvèdre. The other varieties are: Counoise, Vaccarèse, Terret Noir and Muscardin (all red grapes) and Clairette, Bourboulenc, Roussanne, Picpoul and Picardin (all white). Grenache Blanc and Terret Blanc additionally are authorized for the production of white Châteauneuf.

At the end of the nineteenth century a Commandant Duclos published a voluminous paper on the area, and recommended the following blends as likely to produce the optimum wine:

20 per cent Grenache and Cinsault, 'giving warmth, liqueur and mellowness'.
30 per cent Mourvèdre, Syrah, Muscardin and Vaccarèse, 'giving solidity, durability, colour and a pure refreshing flavour'.
40 per cent Cournoise and Picpoul, 'giving vinosity, charm, freshness and bouquet'.
10 per cent Clairette and Bourboulenc, 'giving fire and brilliance'.

This was the 'ideal' *encépagement*. However, because much Châteauneuf was constantly shipped up to Burgundy (to be used as 'a bolster wine' and blended in with the wines of the area), the Grenache percentage was more habitually 80 per cent if not 90 per cent. The Grenache gives a wine of high alcohol and plenty of body, if low in acidity, ideal for making 'old-style' Burgundy – if you like that sort of thing.

Nowadays, the normal blend is usually the following: 50 to 70 per cent Grenache; 10 to 30 per cent Syrah; up to 20 per cent Cinsault, Mourvèdre, Cournoise and Vaccarèse (the latter two in very small proportions); and up to 10 per cent Clairette, Picpoul and Bourboulenc (all white grapes).

The soil in Châteauneuf is very varied. The Rhône Valley is some fifty kilometres wide at this point, and the vines are planted on undulating mounds rather than on the valley hillsides themselves. The Rhône river has changed its course many times over recent millennia, and the glaciers of succeeding ice ages have deposited stones over the alluvial debris left on the valley floor. Châteauneuf is a geological hotch-potch: there is gravel, clay, sand and limestone. South of the village in the direction of Avignon, gravel predominates; north, towards Orange, the soil is *argillo-calcaire* (clay and limestone); west of Châteauneuf is limestone and east is sand. Overall, especially to the north and north-east, the soil is covered by large quarzite boulders, the size of large baked potatoes, and beige or terracotta in colour. These stones or *galets* aid the maturity of the grapes, for they absorb the heat of the sun during the day and reflect it back onto the vines at night (like storage radiators). They also help to retain moisture in the soil, which would otherwise quickly evaporate in the heat of the day. On the other hand, these stones are an understandable hindrance in the mechanical working of the soil – the sharpened end of a plough-share hardly lasting 24 hours before being blunted to a stump during the weeding season.

One of the most original regulations of the *appellation contrôlée* code, self-imposed in Châteauneuf-du-Pape long before similar regulations elsewhere, was the stipulation of *triage*. A minimum of 5 per cent of the grapes, the least ripe and the rotten, must be discarded before fermentation, to ensure that the wine is made only of healthy, well-ripened fruit. Châteauneuf is also distinguished by having the highest minimum alcoholic strength (12.5 degrees) of all *appellation contrôlée* wines in France.

With such a multiplicity of grapes, soils, and now, vinification methods – for there are some estates which seek to produce a more *primeur*, early-drinking style of wine – it is not surprising that there is no such thing as a typical Châteauneuf-du-Pape. All wines, however, will be full in colour and full in body; somewhat fiery and peppery, robust with a warm rich southern flavour and a broad, spicy, slightly farmyardy aroma and character. Those estates with a high proportion of Grenache, and who keep the wine long in wood (large oak *foudres* rather than the *barriques* traditional in Bordeaux and Burgundy), make a wine with a pronounced, somewhat attenuated earthy character, full of guts but lacking in finesse, and not able to age gracefully. Others, adopting modern methods but not discarding the concept of Châteauneuf as it is known and appreciated, produce excellent wine, which, price for price, is undoubtedly one of the best value of the top reds in France.

There is, additionally, a very small amount of white wine (6476 hectolitres in 1996). This can be made from a number of grapes: Bourboulenc, Clairette, Roussanne, Picardin, Picpoul, Grenache Blanc and Terret Blanc, and can, like the red, vary enormously in character. Only lately has white Châteauneuf been anything other than heavy, hard and alcoholic. The best is now made by modern methods: the grapes are pressed immediately after picking and fermented at 18°C for a month and the malolactic fermentation needs to be prevented, though it seldom seems to occur. The result can be a decidedly fragrant wine, with a mountain herb flavour, a touch of spice and a crisp character reminiscent of peaches and nectarines, particularly if drunk young. White Châteauneuf is, nevertheless, an assertive, full, uncompromising wine. It is also highly alcoholic. It is not the wine to drink as an aperitif in a deckchair on a warm summer's evening but rather as a good accompaniment to *bouillabaisse*. Like white Hermitage it needs to be drunk either young, or, provided it is not solely a *primeur* wine, after seven years or so. Between three and seven years the white wines often do not show well, they seem very oily and resinny but this is a phase that passes.

All estate-bottled Châteauneuf-du-Pape – that is wine from estates who themselves bottle all the wine appearing under their labels – appears in a special bottle, which is a Burgundy shape (i.e. low, sloping shoulders) with the papal emblem, mitre and crossed keys, embossed on the shoulder.

Château de Beaucastel

Château de Beaucastel leads the hierarchy of the eighty-odd domaines in Châteauneuf-du-Pape, and is also one of the largest with 70 hectares of vines up in the north-east corner of the *appellation*. The family also own another thirty or so across the motorway making an excellent Côtes du Rhône called Cru du Coudoulet. It is owned by the Perrin family, whose ancestors arrived in the area in 1880, and is managed by one of two brothers, François, while Jean-Pierre runs a *négociant* business in nearby Jonquières. François, the brother who 'runs Beaucastel from A to Z' as he puts it, is handsome, young and bespectacled with a catholic taste in wine and winemakers, and a constantly enquiring mind. This is a dedicated and perfectionist domaine. The vineyard contains all the thirteen authorized varieties, the usual blend for the red consisting of 30 per cent Mourvèdre, 30 per cent Grenache, and 10 per cent Syrah, with the balance being made up with the remaining varieties. A superior Curée is named Mommefe à Jacques Femin (the brothers' fathers). This is predominantly Mourvèdre.

A feature of the wine-making at Beaucastel is that the bunches are entirely de-stemmed and then, before crushing, they are heated to 80°C for about two minutes as they are pumped towards the vats before rapidly being cooled to room temperature. This flash-heating process only affects the skins of the grapes, and it is said to aid the extraction of colour and fruit as well as milking off the phenol-oxidase enzymes which cause wine to oxidize quickly. This process was introduced by Jacques Perrin, the father of François and Jean-Pierre, shortly after the Second World War.

The Perrins have invested heavily but wisely in Beaucastel. Unlike most other producers, they have the storage facility which enables them to bottle an entire harvest in one go, at the optimum time rather than as and when orders are received. Equally, and this time uniquely, in my experience, they will at any one moment have the equivalent of five vintages maturing in their cellars, an investment others are not prepared to make.

About 25,000 cases of red wine are produced annually. The wine normally takes five or six years to come into its own. Like most Châteauneuf, Beaucastel is full, sturdy and meaty, with a robust hardness – even fieriness – when immature, a solid, warm richness when ready for drinking. What distinguishes Beaucastel from the run of the mill is its inherent elegance – a word not often used for the wines of this area – albeit in a rather opulent, even aggressive, spicy and aromatic manner. It also ages very well indeed in bottle. While many Châteauneufs are already beginning to tire after eight years, Beaucastel is still vigorous at fifteen.

An excellent white Châteauneuf -du-Pape, made 80 per cent from Roussanne and 20 per cent from Grenache Blanc and other varieties, is also produced. This wine is unexpectedly fresh and racy, and is more like a Hermitage than a normal Châteauneuf white. There is also an impressively seniors only Roussanne Vieilles Vignes. This also keeps well.

Domaine du Vieux Télégraphe

Close behind Beaucastel is Vieux Télégraphe, a 55-hectare estate on the eastern side of Châteauneuf-du-Pape at Bédarides. The curious name comes from a tower in the vineyard which the inventor of the optical telegraph system, Monsieur Chappe, built to help him with his experiments. I think I can fairly claim to have 'discovered' Vieux Télégraphe as far as the British market was concerned. This was in 1976, when I spent a week in the area, and took the opportunity to visit most of the top estates in Châteauneuf-du-Pape. Shortly afterwards I shipped the first Vieux Télégraphe wines.

The man I met in 1976 was Henri Brunier, now retired and succeeded by his sons Daniel and Frédéric. Henri is a genial, if initially a little suspicious, hospitable man with a quiet confidence in his wines. and absolutely no 'side'. In 1979 he began installing an ultra-modern vinification hall complete with eighteen very large stainless-steel vats. The grapes are never de-stalked, and about 30 per cent enter the *cuves* uncrushed; the rest are only 'bruised', as he puts it.

Brunier has modified his wine-making in two ways since he completed his new *cuverie*. He now macerates the grapes for only 12 to 15 days, and he ages in oak for only a year, the rest of the time in enamel-lined vats. (Hitherto it would have been two years in wood.) The result is a fresher wine which keeps better.

Vieux Télégraphe is made from 75 per cent Grenache, 15 per cent Syrah and 5 per cent each Cinsault and Mourvèdre. It is full-bodied, less rich but more peppery and cigar-boxy than Beaucastel, yet full of fruit and concentration. It is neither burly, nor aggressively solid. I find it an excellent wine, improving year by year even from what was in 1976 a very high level. It also keeps well. There is also a fine white, from 40 per cent Clairette and 20 per cent Bourboulenc, Grenache Blanc and Roussanne.

CHÂTEAU RAYAS

Rayas is a controversial estate. The wine is very expensive, it used to be magnificent, but there are those who aver that what comes out of Rayas today is not just mediocre but ruined by sloppy *élevage*, even indeed that the wine is '*now* [my italics] made solely from Grenache'. (Livingstone-Learmonth/Master, *The Wines of the Rhône*, 2nd Edition, 1983). Château Rayas used to be owned by a real charmer, the eccentric old Louis Reynaud. If anyone was the epitome of the absent-minded professor it was he. He was scruffy and unkempt, unpredictable (he once hid in a ditch to avoid a wine merchant friend of mine) but – to put it simply – a genius. His red wine was quite incredible. From a yield deliberately restricted to 15 hectolitres per hectare, less than half the authorized maximum yield, and normally, from at least as far back as the early 1950s, from 100 per cent Grenache (usually a quick-maturing variety) he would make a densely coloured, solid wine which seemed to have more in common with Hermitage than Châteauneuf and which would need at least a decade before it even reached its prime.

He also produced an excellent white wine which, rumour had it, benefited from the addition of a little Chardonnay and Sauvignon into the Clairette and Grenache Blanc. Despite the cellars always being indescribably chaotic, dirty and unhygienic, the wine was magnificent.

Rumour also had it that when he first planted the vineyard in 1922 Louis Reynaud removed every single one of the pudding stones from his vineyard. There may be some truth in this. It must be pointed out, though, that the land on which Rayas lies, halfway between Châteauneuf and Courthézon, happens to be a relatively unstony part of the *vignoble*. Louis Reynaud died in 1978, and the domaine was then run, until his untimely death in 1997, by his son, Jacques, who was said not to be up to it. I can only go by the finished wine – there have always been good and bad casks and *cuvées* at Rayas. It seems to me to be as good as ever. Sister domaines of Rayas are the Châteauneuf 'Pignon' and an excellent single-domaine Côtes du Rhône, Château de la Fonsalette.

Other leading Châteauneuf estates include the following: Château Fortia is now run by the son of Baron Le Roy who 'invented' the AC rules. Near Châteauneuf on the road to Bédarrides the estate produces a full, sturdy, spicy wine from 80 per cent Grenache; it is a good example of traditional Châteauneuf-du-Pape. Domaine de Mont-Redon, run by the cousins Didier Fabre and Jean Abeille, and situated north-west of the village, in an area which is almost totally stony, is the largest estate with more than 90 hectares of vines. The wine is made with great care and attention, deliberately avoiding what the cousins consider to be 'the faults of yesteryear – wines which are too heavy, robust and alcoholic'. The results are very good, particularly in the lesser years, if not quite in the Beaucastel class.

Among the traditional Châteauneuf properties I would also include in my 'best of the rest' Château de la Nerthe: Reserve des Céleslins (Henri Bonneau), Domaine Chante Cigale (Christian Favier and Noël Sabon), Clos du Mont Olivet Frères – nephews of Henri Brunier), Le Vieux Donjon (Lucien Michel), Clos des Papes (Paul Avril) and Domaine des Cailloux (Lucien and André Brunel). There are a very large number of individual domaines so this list is not exhaustive. The two leading *négociants* of the northern Rhône also have a Châteauneuf-du-Pape in their portfolio. Jaboulet have 'Les Cèdres', a wine that I know well and have long admired. It keeps well. Chapoutier have their own Domaine de la Bernadine.

There are also the new-style Châteauneuf-du-Papes: wines made partly if not exclusively by carbonic maceration methods, producing round, fruity wines for early drinking. The results can be good, but are not my idea of the *appellation*, and to avoid consumer confusion it would seem to me sensible if they were not allowed to use the name Châteauneuf-du-Pape. The domaines of Nalys and Solitude are pioneers of this method, and the Château des Fines Roches with a huge ultra-modern vinification centre next to a ludicrous Victorian-Gothic mock castle (now a hotel) used to be another but has since changed its method of vinification back to traditional methods. I see no merit in these wines, though Nalys at least produces a good clean *primeur*-style white Châteauneuf.

TAVEL

The second best well-known wine of the southern Rhône is Tavel. Tavel is one of the few *appellations* in France which exists solely for *vin rosé* and its rosé lays claim to being the country's best. It is certainly the fullest and the firmest; the most 'masculine' perhaps.

Tavel lies south of Lirac on the western side of the Rhône in the *département* of Gard, some fifteen kilometres north-west of Avignon. In contrast to the more market garden aspect of the countryside in the Vaucluse the appearance here is much more that of the Languedoc: arid, sparse, rocky *garrigues* within which certain parcels of land have been laboriously hacked out, flattened and planted with vines. Constant vigilance and attention are required to prevent these plots from being reclaimed again by nature.

Tavel has been a well-known and prosperous vineyard area for many centuries, and considerable quantities of the wine were exported outside the immediate area to the Versailles Court and beyond as early as the eighteenth century. After phylloxera the Tavel vineyards, like so many other areas in France, largely fell into disuse, and the *vignoble* declined from 750 hectares in the heyday of the nineteenth century to a mere 100 hectares in 1930. The formation of the local co-operative in 1937, which now makes 55 per cent of all Tavel, and the growth of the wine's popularity in the United States in the 1950s, encouraged the opening-up of new tracts of land in the hillsides, first north of the village on a well-exposed plateau known as the Vallongue and then to the south and west. The area under vine totalled 942 hectares in 1996.

The Tavel soil is lighter than on the other side of the Rhône Valley. It consists predominantly of chalk, mixed with sand on the flatter land nearer to the village itself, clay north of the village and covered in parts with white, flat, crumbling stones. Grenache (maximum 60 per cent) and Cinsault (minimum 15 per cent) are the mainstays of the recipe for Tavel, though seven other grapes (Carignan to a maximum of 10 per cent, Syrah and Mourvèdre, the white Bourboulenc, Clairette and Picpoul, and the fast-disappearing Calitor) are also permitted. The use of Syrah and Mourvèdre, authorized since 1969, is somewhat controversial. They certainly add colour and backbone to the wine, but is this not somewhat of a contradiction in terms, particularly as there has been a move away from the old-style, hard Tavel to a more supple, fruity, forward wine?

One of the myths that has done much disservice to Tavel is the notion that Tavel Rosé is a *vin de garde*. No rosé is, or should be, for keeping, certainly for more than two or three years after the vintage. The idea that Tavel is somehow better after five years in bottle is nonsense; the wine will have dried out, the fruit will have disappeared, and all the fresh attraction will have gone. Equally, a rosé, like a white wine, must be vinified at a cool temperature, aged in vat rather than oak *foudre*, and bottled early in order to retain the maximum amount of aromas and personality from the fruit. Armand Maby at the Domaine de la Forcadière, and one-time mayor of Tavel, is one of the leading exponents of this 'modern-style' Tavel. I find his wines delicious: supple, racy and full of fruit. Paul de Bez at the Château d'Aquéria, Georges Bernard at the Domaine de la Genestière and Gabriel Roudil at Le Vieux Moulin produce equally excellent examples, the former perhaps a little fuller than the rest. The co-operative and the Demoulin family at Château de Trinquevedel are other good sources. Production in 1996 totalled 43,107 hectolitres.

LIRAC

Lirac, north of Tavel, covers four communes west of the Rhône and makes red, rosé and white wines. I suspect that some red wine is made on Tavel soil and bottled as Lirac and perhaps vice versa for rosé. Certainly many Tavel growers have land in Lirac and so offer a range of colours. The Lirac *appellation* extends over the communes of Lirac itself, Saint-Laurent-des-Arbres, Roquemaure and Saint-Géniès-de-Comolas, opposite Château-neuf-du-Pape, and is definitely an up-and-coming and expanding area. Some 620 hectares of vineyard are authorized, though only 429 are currently planted, and production has increased from 4500 hectolitres per annum in the early 1960s to 16,935 in 1996 (of which 1231 was white wine). The main thrust behind this expansion has been the influx of ex-Algerian *pieds noirs* in the early 1960s after independence. Why there should be this enclave of North African expatriates here rather than elsewhere I do not know for sure but one can conjecture that the attraction of a ready-made if not widely known *appellation*, a dependable climate and a soil not dissimilar to what they had been used to, plus, above all, land that was cheap, proved irresistible.

Château de Clary at Lirac is said to have had the dubious honour of being the site in France where the phylloxera louse was first detected in 1863. The owner at the time was possessed of 'insatiable curtiosity' and planted all sorts of different varieties and species of vines, American as well as *vinifera*, thus letting the bug loose to devastate the non-resistant vines of France, and ultimately the whole of Europe.

The soil at Lirac is similar to that at Tavel but more sandy, and near the Rhône at Roquemaure, densely covered in the large pudding stones or *galets* so familiar in Châteauneuf on the opposite bank. The *encépagement* is the usual southern Rhône mixture; Grenache, chiefly, which with Cinsault, Mourvèdre and Syrah makes up the bulk of the blend, white grapes such as Clairette, Ugni Blanc, Bourboulenc and Picpoul making up most of the remainder, and the inferior Carignan restricted to a maximum of 10 per cent.

Livingstone-Learmonth and Master in *The Wines of the Rhône* describe Lirac wines as lighter-styled, softer and easier to drink than the wines on the opposite side of the valley from Cairanne or Vacqueyras. They put this down to a large proportion of Cinsault vines dating from the expansion of the *vignoble* in the early 1960s in the blend. I cannot agree with this. In my experience Liracs are somehow more baked and have a more pronounced *goût de terroir* than the wines of Vacqueyras, and they can be harder too. I can see in Lirac similarities with the Costières du Gard, if at a superior level. Far from being easy to drink, I would suggest Lirac is a meaty and sturdy wine, less generous than a Vaucluse Côtes du Rhône-Villages, and it is more of an acquired taste.

Armand Maby of Tavel produces two red Liracs, as well as a supple rosé and a delicious white wine. One of his red Lirac wines has Mourvèdre but no Syrah as the variety to give backbone to the wine, the other has Syrah but no Mourvèdre. In Maby's view – and he is quick to assert that this may be peculiar to Lirac – the two varieties do not blend well. It is interesting to compare the two wines and I prefer the Mourvèdre *cuvée*.

Georges Bernard at the Domaine de la Genestière, also in Tavel, produces excellent Lirac, ageing his wine in wood for twelve to eighteen months. Other good growers include Antoine Verda at the Château Saint-Roch, François de Regis at the Château de Ségriès, Jean-Claude Assémat at Les Garriques at Roquemaure and the Pons-Mure family, one of the first of the ex-Algerian settlers, with their Domaines de la Tour and Castel Oualou. (Assémat is a Pons-Mure son-in-law, and Louis Rousseau, who lives in nearby Laudan, Madame Pons-Mure's brother.) Philippe Testut, who combines a domaine in Chablis with one in Lirac, also produces reliable wines, if not with the individuality of the estates mentioned above.

French statistics do not differentiate between red and rosé wine so it is difficult to be exact about the breakdown in production between these two colours. One grower estimated the amount of Lirac rosé to be no more than 8 per cent, which is about the same as the amount of white wine produced. Both of these can be – should be – fresh and crisp and full of fruit: the rosé is similar to that of Tavel, the white is like a modern, *primeur*-style Châteauneuf-du-Pape Blanc. Both are for drinking within a couple of years after bottling.

GIGONDAS

After Châteauneuf-du-Pape, the most prestigious and the most expensive southern Rhône red wines come from the commune of Gigondas. The village of Gigondas lies in the shadow of the jagged peaks of the Dentelles de Montmirail some sixteen kilometres due east of Orange at the end of a no-through road. The vineyards lie beneath the village, on slopes which run down in a westerly direction towards the river Ouvèze, and border those of Vacqueyras and Sablet. The soil structure is varied, ranging from rich, yellowish clay in the highest vineyards, which can go up to 550 metres, to stony and sandy areas on the lower slopes and flatter ground.

Until 1971, Gigondas, like Sablet and other neighbouring hillside villages, was one of the villages entitled to the Côtes du Rhône-Villages *appellation*, but then it was elevated to *appellation contrôlée* in its own right. Why this should have been so, and why, with the precedent set, it was not joined by others, no one seems to be able to explain. In 1989 it was announced that Vacqueyras would be elevated also but no final date has been announced. This singling out has certainly done the local growers good, for they obtain a substantially higher price for their wines over those enjoyed by their neighbours.

Some 1171 hectares are under vine and in 1996 48,354 hectolitres of wine were produced. The *appellation contrôlée* regulations (the AC applies to red and rosé only) stipulate an *encépagement* of Grenache (maximum 80 per cent) plus at least 15 per cent Syrah and/or Mourvèdre for the red wine and Grenache (maximum 80 per cent) for the rosé, plus all the other Côtes du Rhône varieties except Carignan (maximum 10 per cent for the red, 25 per cent for the rosé) to make up the residue. A *triage*, as in Châteauneuf, must be carried out.

It is this high amount of Syrah and Mourvèdre and the elimination of the rather harsh, insipid Carignan which makes Gigondas stand out, though not all Gigondas is necessarily worth the extra money, and elsewhere in this part of the Rhône there are numerous fine domaines and dedicated proprietors making wine from the same mixture of grapes. The intrepid seeker after excellence can find as good a Côtes du Rhône-Villages as he can a Gigondas, and at 30 per cent less or so. The consumer, however, can rely on the fact that there are many good growers in Gigondas to choose from.

Most Gigondas wine is red, for the rosé is hardly a commercial proposition with a price which if based on the level of the red would greatly exceed that of Tavel. This red wine is well-coloured, similar to a lesser Châteauneuf, but without the intensity and structure of the best domaines. It is in general at its best between three and eight years old, though some individual vintages will keep for ten years or more. Like Châteauneuf, it often used to be kept two or more years – far too long – in wood. Today most growers bottle after a year. Gigondas is a cheerfully prosperous, thriving, expanding and improving *appellation*.

The best wines of Gigondas include the Domaine de Cayron of Michel Farand, the Domaine Saint-Gayan of Roger Meffre (not to be confused with the giant *négociant* also in the commune, Gabriel Meffre), Roger Combe at L'Oustaou Fauquet, Jean-Pierre Curlier at the Domain Les Souberts, Henri Barriol at the Domaine Saint-Cosme, Denis Cheron, owner of the local *négociant* Pascal, at the Domainedu Grand Montmirail, and Pascal at Vacqueyras are also good sources of Gigondas as is the local co-operative, the Cave des Vignerons.

CÔTES DU RHÔNE-VILLAGES

The *appellation* Côtes du Rhône-Villages was first set up in 1953 and comprised the wines of only four communes: Gigondas and its near neighbour Cairanne in the Vaucluse and Chusclan and Laudun on the other side of the Rhône valley in the Gard. The *appellation* applies to red and rosé wines only, and its aim was to bridge the quality gap between Châteauneuf-du-Pape and basic Côtes du Rhône. The wines would need to reach 12.5 degrees of alcohol rather than 11 degrees, while the yield was restricted to 35 hectolitres per hectare as opposed to 50 hectolitres for straight Côtes du Rhône. The *encépagement* was made stricter than for Côtes du Rhône. For simple Côtes du Rhône there are fourteen recommended grape varieties plus a further ten accessory varieties – some like Pinot Noir and Gamay admittedly hardly ever used. A Villages wine must be made with Grenache (maximum 65 per cent) and Syrah, Mourvèdre and Cinsault (minimum 25 per cent in total). The lesser varieties can only make up 10 per cent of the total.

Gradually more communes were admitted to the fold, while Gigondas became AC in its own right in 1971 and Vacqueyras in 1990. There are now sixteen villages in the group, mostly on the higher slopes overlooking the valleys of the rivers Ouvèze and Aigues (or Eygues), which run down into the Rhône from the Alps. In *département* order these are as follows:

Drôme: Rochegude, Saint-Maurice-sur-Eygues, Vinsobres, Rousset-Les-Vignes, Saint-Pantaléon-Les-Vignes.
Vaucluse: Cairanne, Rasteau, Roaix, Séguret, Valréas, Visan, Sablet, Beaumes-de-Venise.
Gard: Chusclan (including land in Orsan, Codolet, Bagnos-sur-Cèze and Saint-Etienne-des-Sorts), Laudun (including parts of Saint-Victor-Lacoste and Tresques) and Saint-Gervais.

The wines can either be described as Côtes du Rhône-Villages, indicating that the wine is a blend from any or all of these villages, or as Côtes du Rhône-Cairanne and so forth.

Just as a Beaujolais-Villages wine is decidedly superior to a simple Beaujolais, so a Côtes du Rhône-Villages is a much better example than a simple Côtes du Rhône. The soil is better, and better exposed, the wines are in practice made almost entirely from 'noble' grapes, often with a substantial proportion of Syrah, and the result is something which is well-coloured, well-structured, rich, ripe, warm, meaty and generous. While most Côtes du Rhônes, certainly at the cheapest level, are carbonic maceration blends, soft and fruity, and for drinking soon, a Villages wine is a *vin de garde*, if only for a matter of two or three years.

I have had many a happy time driving round in the rolling southern Rhône countryside visiting grower after grower in order to find good Villages wines. There are many. Prices are very reasonable and the quality is very exciting.

As by no means all of the wines of the sixteen Villages communes are declared as Villages wine, it is not possible to determine precisely the area of Côtes du Rhône-Villages which could be under vine. Annual production is in the region od 228,000 hectolitres, 7 per cent that of generic Côtes du Rhône, and this comes from a declared aka of 4986 hectares.

If you add up the totals of the sixteen villages however, you arrive at a figure more than two-and-and-a-half times that sum. The explanation for the difference is not so much that only 40 per cent of the land is suitable for Villages wine as that for most growers the attraction of a higher price for a Villages wine is counteracted by the inconvenience of having to restrict the yield to a basic 35 hectolitres per hectare (plus 20 per cent subject to annual permission and tasting approval) and the fact that, sadly, the demand for Côtes du Rhône, whether generic or Villages, falls off abruptly once the price moves above 25 francs (at 1996 levels). Most growers have a range of styles and only the top wine will be classified as Côtes du Rhône-Villages.

The two leading Villages, in my experience, are Vacqueyreyas and Cairanne. Vacqueyreyas lies between Beaumes-de-Venise and Gigondas, underneath the Dentelles de Montmiral, and abounds in good growers. It was promoted to AC in its own right in 1990. Leading the field is the Château des Rocques owned by Édouard Dusser but run by André Fregire. This is a 35-hectare property planted with 30 per cent Syrah and 60 per cent Grenache. The wine is no longer matured in large oak *foudres* but in a mixture of small *barriques* and stainless steel. Each *cuvée* is named after a Greek god. The wines are full but not too robust, fresh, elegant, rich and round: the epitome of good Midi wine-making. Equally highly regarded is Roger Combe at the Domaine la Fourmone and Danielle Paille at the Domaine des Amdariers. Combe has 27 hectares in Vacqueyras to add to his 9 hectares in Gigondas. His Gigondas wine is fuller, sturdier and longer-lived, but his cheaper Vacqueyras, in its looser-knit way, is equally good.

Elsewhere in Vacqueyras I can recommend the Alazard family, trading under the name of GAEC 'Le Parc' at the Domaine de la Colline Saint-Jean. The better wines (there is a little Gigondas too) are bottled after six months in cement vats and a year in *foudre*. The Domaine des Lambertins owned by two brothers, is another good estate and the *négociant* Pascal is another good source. The local co-operative, named La Cave du Troubadour after the poet Rimbaud, Vacqueyras' most famous son, was established in 1957. Much of its wine is made by carbonic maceration, which may be fitting for a simple *vin de pays* or a Côtes du Rhône but is not suitable for Vacqueyras. The more traditional Villages wines from the co-operative are worth investigating also.

Some ten kilometres to the north, across the flat stony plain of the river Ouvèze, lies the village of Cairanne. Here any list of good domaines and sources would include at its head the name of Fréderic and Francois Alary at L'Oratoire Saint-Martin. The Alary's produce a very fine wine from a 35-hectare vineyard on the higher, clayey *garrigues* on the east side of the village and I used to have a considerable success selling both his better generic blend and his Villages wine, the Clos de L'Oratoire Saint-Martin. The white wine is also good as is that of their cousins Denis and Daniel Alary elsewhere in the village, and that of Marcel Richmond.

While in Cairanne I must also mention the local co-operative, the Caves des Coteaux, though I never, in fact, shipped their top Villages, their 'Réserve des Voconces', preferring their cheaper but fresher Caves des Coteaux or Grande Réserve. Monsieur Lacrotte, the managing director, and Monsieur Coulouvrat, the technical director, run a quality-conscious, highly able team, and produce excellent wines, from Vin de Pays de Principauté d'Orange upwards. This is in my view the best co-operative in the southern Côtes du Rhône area.

My principal experience of the remaining villages in the *appellation* is also with their co-operatives. There are at least six co-operatives on the west side of the Rhône serving the growers in Chusclan and Laudun, many of whom make a particular speciality of rosé. A Chusclan Rosé from the Cave de Vignerons at Chusclan or a Laudun Rosé from either of the two co-operatives in Laudun can be a delightful wine – as good as all but the very best that you can find in Tavel. The rosés produced in the Vaucluse or Drôme villages are less exciting, but good red wines can be obtained from the co-operatives at Visan, Valréas, Saint-Maurice, Sablet, Beaumes-de-Venise and Rochegude. It is important, though, to select wines which have not been kept too long in wood or tank, and often I prefer, as I do at the Cairanne co-operative, the second or third best *cuvées* to the 'Grande Réserve', normally the biggest and most alcoholic wine, but the last to be bottled.

CÔTES DU RHONE

While all the villages mentioned in the previous section lie in the southern half of the Rhône Valley, generic Côtes du Rhône can come from both parts, indeed from anywhere between Vienne and Avignon. In practice most comes from the Rhône *méridionale*, south of Bollène and Pont d'Esprit, and from the flatter, less highly prized soils which lie between the Villages and the other more serious *appellations*. Côtes du Rhône is an enormous *appellation*. Some 43,556 hectares are under vine, and some 2 million hectolitres are produced each year. This is two thirds of the entire Rhône Valley – even if one includes such productive but peripheral areas like the Ventoux and the Lubéron in the grand statistics.

The *appellation* covers red, rosé and white wine, though barely $1\frac{1}{2}$ per cent is white. The maximum yield per hectare and the register of authorized grape varieties, both 'recommended' and 'accessory', are generous. The maximum yield is 50 hectolitres per hectare (plus 20 per cent *plafond limité de classement*) and the list of varieties includes all the varieties discussed, the sole restrictions being that the maximum amount of Carignan permitted is 30 per cent and that the 'recommended' varieties must make up at least 70 per cent. In practice, Grenache, Carignan and Cinsault are the basic varieties used for Côtes du Rhône.

Not surprisingly in such a vast area, with almost every type and combination of soil, styles and aspirations, styles, qualities and prices can vary enormously. At the top level are wines which are as good as the best Gigondas, and will cost accordingly. Elsewhere, there are quantities of cheap generic wines, which can range in style from the traditional to the carbonic maceration and in character from the agreeable to the undrinkable.

For good basic wines, the co-operatives are the best source. There are some sixty-five in the Rhône Valley, the best of which, like that at Cairanne, have been already mentioned, and produce a whole range of wines from *vin ordinaire* and *vin de pays* upwards. Among those not so far listed I recommend those at Puymeras, Sainte-Cécile and Tulette. The Cellier des Dauphins in Tulette acts as a bottling and marketing centre for some ten of its co-operative neighbours.

More interesting, but more expensive, are wines from individual domaines. No one could possibly speak with experience of all of them. Those which have come my way that

I can safely recommend include the following: Château du Grand Moulas (Les Frères Ryckwaert) at Mornas; Château de la Fonsalette (Jacques Reynaud) at Lagarde-Paréol; Cru du Coudoulet (Les Frères Perrin) at Château de Beaucastel, Courthézon; Château de Saint-Estève (Gérard François-Monier) at Uchaux; Château Malijay (Jean-Louis Nativelle) at Jonquières; Domaine de Renjarde (Alain Dugas) at Serignan-du-Comptat; Château de L'Estagnol at Suze-La-Rousse; and Château La Borie (Émile Borie) at Suze-La-Rousse.

HAUT-COMTAT VDQS

The north-east corner of the Rhône *méridionale* near the town of Nyons in the *département* of Drôme is allowed to produce a red or rosé VDQS as well as Côtes du Rhône. In practice this obscure *appellation* seems to have disappeared. No production was declared in 1988. Some of the growers who do not produce *appellation contrôlée* wine are now experimenting under the label of Vin de Pays des Coteaux des Baronnies. There is the Liotaud family at Saint-Jalle, for example, who produce an excellent barrel-aged Chardonnay and a 100 per cent Syrah wine.

BEAUMES-DE-VENISE

Beaumes-de-Venise lies some seventeen kilometres east of Orange at the southern end of the Dentelles de Montmirail, and produces what most people regard as the best of France's *vins doux naturels* or fortified sweet wines. As my translation shows, there is nothing 'natural' about a *vin doux naturel*; indeed the wine is made on essentially the same lines as Port, the object being to retain the natural sugar of the ripe fruit by arresting the fermentation of the must with the addition of pure grape alcohol.

The Muscat grape, which is only grown here in the southern Rhône, though found elsewhere in the South of France, at Lunel and Frontignan for instance, is a relative newcomer to the area, planting having commenced at the beginning of the nineteenth century. The vineyards were then destroyed by phylloxera and despite the efforts of a few growers and the granting of the *appellation* in 1945, the situation was at almost rock bottom until 1956, when the co-opérative was founded. The area under Muscat vines has since increased to 443 hectares, and 1996 production totalled 15, 923 hectolitres.

The Muscat variety used is the most elegant one, the Muscat à Petits Grains, of which there are two sub-varieties, the Grain Blanc and the Grain Noir. The difference in flavour between these two is slight. The Grain Noir produces more prolifically but by itself is considered to produce a wine of too pronounced a colour, so most growers prefer to have a combination of the two. These vines are planted in a variety of soils around the village ranging from pure sand in the south, sand and stones in the east and heavy clay in the north. The Muscat is prone to disease particularly oidium and red spider.

The grapes are harvested late, not until mid-October, by which time the sugar is well concentrated, giving a potential natural alcohol level of 15 degrees. The must is vinified slowly, being cooled if necessary, and then comes the *mutage*, or addition of 5 to 10 per cent neutral alcohol at a strength of about 96 degrees volume. This will raise the potential alcohol level to 21.5 degrees (the actual level is normally just over 15 degrees) and must leave 125 grams of sugar per litre in the finished wine. Sometimes the *mutage* is done all in one go, but some growers prefer to do it in stages, to avoid the spirit becoming too obtrusive. Thereafter the wine is racked as little as possible to avoid both the evaporation of alcohol and the dilution and coarsening of the Muscat flavour by oxidation. Some growers age their wines in vats – for the above reason wood is never used – for a year, others bottle after six or nine months.

Muscat de Beaumes-de-Venise is a mini-success story of the 1980s. In 1972 the co-operative shipped its first export order (twenty-five cases) to the wine merchant, Robin Yapp in Britain. Today the co-operative exports by the pallet if not container load, and the wine is stocked by supermarkets the world over. The flavour of the Muscat grape is instantly recognizable, opulent and aromatic and it is the most 'grapy' of all grape varieties. A good *vin doux naturel* retains a fresh acidity, a ripe, welcoming fruit and it is softly, generously sweet. It is delicious both as an aperitif and with desserts and puddings. Muscat de Beaumes-de-Venise is at its best while young and fresh, but once the bottle is open, the wine will keep for up to a fortnight, especially if stored in a cool place such as a refrigerator.

The co-operative now produces 90 per cent of the commune's Muscat de Beaumes-de-Venise, which it sells in a rather unattractive screwtop bottle, more resembling cheap bath essence rather than anything vinous. The wine, however, is excellent, perhaps lighter and marginally less sweet than that of the leading growers, but fresh, balanced and full of fruit. And it is cheaper. The co-operative is also a good source of Côtes du Rhône, Côtes du Rhône-Villages and Côtes du Ventoux. A number of *négociants* from elsewhere in the Rhône, notably Paul Jaboulet Aîné and Vidal-Fleury, also sell Muscat de Beaumes-de-Venise.

There are only – as far as I am aware – four individual growers in Beaumes-de-Venise who make Muscat, all of whom have perceptibly changed their wine to a more *vin de l'année* style in recent years. Bernard Leydier at Domaine Durban and Yves Nativelle at Domaine de Coyeux are the best known. Monsieur et Madame Castaud Maurin at Domaine des Bernardins. and Guy Rey at Domaine Saint-Saveur complete this list of private *vignerons* in Beaumes-de-Venise.

RASTEAU

Rasteau, between Cairanne and Vaison-la-Romaine some fifteen kilometres to the north is also one of the sixteen villages in the Côtes du Rhône-Villages *appellation*. It too makes a *vin doux naturel*. Unlike Beaumes-de-Venise which uses Muscat, the base for Rasteau is the Grenache grape and the wine can be either white or red. The result, I regret to say, is not nearly as appealing as Muscat de Beaumes-de-Venise, particularly when the wine is deliberately aged and oxidized so that it becomes *rancio*. The *vin doux naturel* makes up a very small propotion of Rasteau's production. There are 97 hectares of vines. In 1996 production amounted 1875 hectolitres.

COTEAUX DU TRICASTIN

Between Bollène and Montélimar lies a wine area which has been entirely created since 1950. It now covers some 2493 hectares of vines. In 1996 the appellation produced 104,148 hectolitres of red and rosé wine and a token 1207 hectolitres of white. Tricastin takes its name from the Trois Châteaux of Saint-Paul. There had been vines here and further north near Donzère and Grignan in pre-phylloxera times but the vineyards had been allowed to decline, and when Côtes du Rhône was delimited in 1937, as there was nothing in the Tricastin area worth limiting, the area was excluded.

The nucleus of the area lies now in the communes of Les Granges Gontardes and Roussas, both of which lie a few kilometres east of Donzère. It was here in the early 1960s that a number of families who had been forced to leave Algeria after independence decided to settle. They found a soil which is very similar to Châteauneuf-du-Pape and in parts similarly completely covered in large pudding stones or *galets*, so much so that it is impossible to see the earth underneath.

The usual Côtes du Rhône varieties were planted: Grenache, Cinsault, a little Mourvèdre and Carignan, plus a relatively high percentage of Syrah. Most Tricastin is made in the soft *vin de l'année* style, and is similar in style and price to Côtes du Ventoux or lesser Côtes du Rhône. Only the better wines, those with a large proportion of Syrah, are matured in wood and need more than a few months in bottle before being ready for consumption. While there is a little rosé Tricastin's reputation rests on its red wine.

The most widely seen Tricastin wine used to be the Domaine de la Tour d'Elyssas of Pierre Labeye who died in 1987. Wine is still made on the estate by the current owners, however, and the Cru de Devoy, with 30 per cent Syrah in the blend, and the 100 per cent Syrah are the wines of the greatest interest.

The other well-known Tricastin estates are the two belonging to Madame Odette Bour, the Domaine de Grangeneuve and the Domaine des Lones. Both of these make wines with a good proportion of Syrah in the mix, and need to be kept in bottle for a year or so after they have first been released. Wines like these are worth paying a premium for. Coteaux du Tricastin, like the Ventoux, was elevated from VDQS to AC in 1974.

CÔTES DU VENTOUX

The Côtes du Ventoux is a large area of 7335 hectares of vines – three times the entire surface of the northern Rhône. It begins to the north-west of Mont Ventoux at Beaumont-du-Ventoux and Malaucène and continues south past Carpentras and Pernes-les-Fontaines as far as Apt, covering some fifty-two communes. Most of the wine, however, comes from either the south side of Mont Ventoux itself, in a line between Beaumes-de-Venise and Flassan, or on the north side of the Plateau de Ventoux around Montmoiron. The lower land in the valley between is used for table grapes, grapes for *vin ordinaire* and fruit trees.

Côtes du Ventoux is made from the same grape varieties and with similar criteria as Côtes du Rhône, and these vines are planted in soils which range between gravel, sand, clay, limestone and chalk. With a few exceptions Ventoux is an undemanding, easy-to-drink, light wine of *vin de l'année* style, a wine for which one can see little justification for the accolade of *appellation contrôlée* as far back as 1974. The bulk of the production is in the hands of the local co-operatives.

There are a few local growers, and at least one excellent *négociant* wine. Jean-Pierre Perrin of Châteauneuf's Château de Beaucastel owns no vineyards himself but he produces an excellent Côtes du Ventoux called La Vieille Ferme from contracted growers. This red wine, richly fruity and medium to full-bodied, is made from 60 per cent Grenache and 30 per cent Syrah, and would not disgrace itself if served alongside a good Gigondas, but it is quite atypical of the *appellation*. Perrin also makes a white Côtes du Lubéron. Among the growers must be included the English exile, Malcolm Swan, who has 10 hectares of vines at the Domaine des Anges at Montmoiron, and the Domaine de Marotte.

In 1996 production of Ventoux totalled 294,610 hectolitres for red and rosé wine and 8174 hectolitres of white. The area also produces Vin de Pays de Vaucluse, as does the Côtes du Lubéron.

CÔTES DU LUBÉRON

Is the Côtes du Lubéron a Rhône wine or a Provence wine? Livingstone-Learmonth and Master do not include it in their book, *The Wines of the Rhône*, as likewise they do not include the wines of the Coteaux de Pierrevert. But if these are not Rhône wines, what are they? The Montagne de Lubéron and the Durance valley, on the northern slopes of which lie the vineyards, may be deemed Haute-Provence, and on the other side of the valley lies the Coteaux d'Aix-en-Provence. The *département*, however, is Vaucluse, and the area covered by the Lubéron *appellation* shares the Vin de Pays de Vaucluse with Côtes du Ventoux. Moreover, French governmental statistics list Côtes du Lubéron under the Rhône. For me, therefore, the logical place to discuss Lubéron wines is here.

The area covers some thirty communes stretching east of Cavaillon on the north or right bank of the river Durace towards Manosque. In 1996 there were 3165 hectares of land under vine. Eighty-two per cent of the region's 149,502 hectolitre production in 1996 was for red wine or rosé, from boadly the same grape varieties and under the same other regulations as that of Ventoux or generic Côtes du Rhône.

While the red and rosé are very similar wines, if a little leaner and fresher, to those of the Ventoux, it is the whites that attract interest. According to the latest INAO regulations these whites, as elsewhere in the southern Rhône, must come from Clairette and Bourboulenc, as principal varieties, with Grenache Blanc, Pascal Blanc, Roussette and Ugni Blanc as tolerated 'accessory' varieties. In practice, more and more Chardonnay is being planted. It flourishes on the chalky, limestone hills of the upper Lubéron, particularly away from the more alluvial soils of the valley floor and on higher ground east of Cadenet where the temperature does not rise to quite such high levels during the long summer afternoons. Yet this grape is not, unless I have missed a recent decree, authorized.

An example of a Chardonnay-based Côtes du Lubéron white is La Vieille Ferme of Jean-Pierre Perrin. Jean-Pierre Margan at the Château de Canorgue is perhaps the leading local grower while excellent wines are produced by Jean-Louis and Cécile Chancel at Château Val-Joanis near Pertuis and at Conrad Pinatel's Château de Millé. Most of the rest of the production is in the hands of the local co-operatives. That at La Tour d'Aigues, the Cellier du Marrenon, is an excellent, up-to-date establishment.

Côtes du Lubéron was promoted from VDQS to *appellation contrôlée* in 1988 while Côtes du Ventoux has been AC since 1974. There seems little to choose between them.

COTEAUX DE PIERREVERT VDQS

Further upstream, across the boundary into the *département* of Alpes de Haute-Provence, scattered over some forty-two communes round the city of Manosque, lie th 310 hectares authorized for thr VDQS Coteaux de Pierrevert. Most of the area's 13781 hectolitres litres of wine are rosé, and this is the most successful wine. So far I have found the wines dull at best, but some of the local growers, such as Claude Dieudonné at the Domaine de Regusse, are now planting Cabernet Sauvignon and Chardonnay to add to the indigenous Rhône varieties, and one hopes for something more interesting in the future.

CÔTES DU VIVARAIS VDQS and the ARDÈCHE

A drive up the Ardèche Valley from Pont Saint-Esprit is one of the most breathtaking journeys in France. The Gorges de l'Ardèche vie with the canyons of the Tarn as the deepest and most spectacular in the country. Up beyond the famous Pont d'Arc, where the Ardèche has ploughed its way through the side of a hill, forming a large natural bridge, the countryside becomes less dramatic. Here there is a series of large fertile valleys, some 100 to 250 metres above sea level. This is the wine land of the Ardèche.

Twelve communes in the *département* of the Ardèche and two more south of the river itself in the *département* of Gard are entitled to the VDQS of Côtes du Vivarais. Some 644 hectares are planted with the general Côtes du Rhône varieties such as Grenache, Cinsault and Carignan. In 1996 29,419 hectolitres of red and rosé wine were produced, and 1378 hectolitres of white. This is good, holiday quaffing *vin de l'année* stuff, similar to that made in the Ventoux or the Lubéron. Frankly the Vin de Pays de l'Ardèche is just as good, and marginally cheaper.

Vin de Pays de l'Ardèche can come from other varieties, and the most successful, in my view, are those from Chardonnay and Gamay. The network of upper Ardèche co-operatives around the town of Ruoms are a good source of wine. Another is the Saint-Désirat-Champagne co-operative, further north in the Rhône Valley. An exciting developement in the 1980's was a joint venture between the Beaune *négociant* Louis Latour and the local Ardèche co-operatives and their members. Latour was looking for a source of inexpensive Chardonnay and the growers have been encouraged to provide it. The wine has now been on the market for several years and is improving steadily as the vines mature. It sells for about the same price as a Mâcon Blanc-Villages. The Beaujolais merchant Feorges Duboeuf followed suit, but with vioguses, in the 1990s.

VINS DE PAYS

VIN DE PAYS DES ALPES DE HAUTE-PROVENCE
This is a departmental wine from the upper Durance near Manosque. The wines are mainly red, with some white and a little rosé. From Grenache, Cinsault, Carignan and Ugni Blanc, plus a number of other varieties.

VIN DE PAYS DE L'ARDÈCHE
A departmental *vin de pays* covering both the northern and southern Rhône. The wines are mainly red from Gamay and South of France varieties. There are interesting recent developments with Chardonnay (*see page 290*).

VIN DE PAYS DES COLLINES RHODANIENNES
This zonal *vin de pays* covers all the northern Rhône. The wines are mainly red from Gamay and Syrah. The small proportion of white comes from the Marsanne.

VIN DE PAYS DU COMTÉ DE GRIGNAN
This is a zonal *vin de pays* from the Tricastin area. The wines are mainly Grenache-based reds, with a little rosé and a little white from traditional South of France varieties.

VIN DE PAYS DES COTEAUX DES BARONNIES
This zonal *vin de pays* comes from the area around Nyons in the southern Rhône Valley. The wines are mainly Grenache-based reds.

VIN DE PAYS DE LA DRÔME
This departmental *vin de pays* covers the eastern side of the Rhône Valley between Tricastin and Valence. The wines are mainly Grenache-based reds.

VIN DE PAYS DE LA PRINCIPAUTÉ D'ORANGE
A zonal *vin de pays* covering two parts of the Vaucluse *département* formerly part of the Papal states, including Châteauneuf-du-Pape. The wines are mainly Grenache-based reds.

VIN DE PAYS DE LA VAUCLUSE
A departmental *vin de pays* covering the eastern part of the Rhône *méridionale* and the Côtes du Ventoux area. The wines are mainly Grenache-based reds.

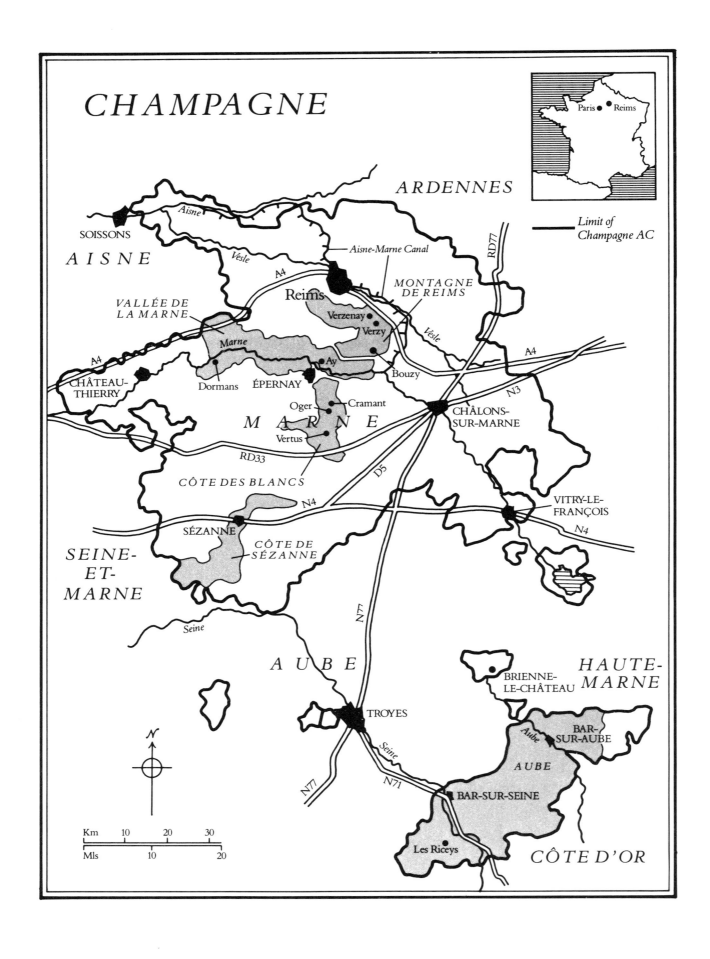

CHAMPAGNE

ARDENNES

Paris • Reims

Limit of
Champagne AC

SOISSONS

AISNE

Aisne

Vesle

A4

Aisne-Marne Canal

Reims

MONTAGNE
DE REIMS

Verzenay •
Verzy •

Vesle

VALLÉE DE
LA MARNE

Marne

Ay •

Bouzy

A4

Dormans •

ÉPERNAY

N3

CHÂTEAU-
THIERRY

A4

M   A   R   N   E

Oger •
Vertus •

• Cramant

CHÂLONS-
SUR-MARNE

RD33

CÔTE DES BLANCS

D5

VITRY-LE-
FRANÇOIS

N4

SÉZANNE

N4

SEINE-
ET-
MARNE

CÔTE DE
SÉZANNE

N77

Seine

N
N
N

AUBE

BRIENNE-
LE-CHÂTEAU •

HAUTE-
MARNE

TROYES

Aube

BAR-
SUR-AUBE

Seine

AUBE

N77

N71

BAR-SUR-SEINE

Km   10   20   30

Mls   10   20

Les Riceys •

CÔTE D'OR

Chapter 5

CHAMPAGNE

There is something special about champagne, and this something – which is unique to champagne, not just to sparkling wines in general – has, I suspect, always been there, ever since champagne as we know it today first began to be produced in the later half of the seventeenth century.

Champagne is *the* celebration wine. It launches ships; it commemorates anniversaries; it toasts weddings. As Talleyrand said, it is a civilizing wine; an elevating wine, as Jorrocks neatly put it ('champagne certainly gives one very gentlemanly ideas'). It can even change principles: 'I'm only a beer teetotaller, not a champagne teetotaller' (*Candida*). And it can lead to flights of fancy which no other wine can match. John Arlott in his book on Krug quotes a schoolgirl's first experience of champagne: 'It's like icicles of rainbow in my mouth.' What a marvellous expression! I wish I'd thought of it!

Above all, champagne is a joyful and luxurious wine – and by that I do not mean one has to live in the lap of luxury to be able to afford it. It is not pricy; indeed it is less expensive by comparison with other top wines than it was ten or twenty years ago. By luxurious I mean that it induces a feeling of luxury, of well-being and gracious living, in the same way as dressing-up for dinner does. André Simon, champagne promoter and connoisseur *par excellence*, coined the phrase 'The Art of Good Living'. No wine is more an example and a celebration of this art than champagne.

Champagne is both a province and a wine. *La Champagne* is the region; *le champagne* is what is produced. The reason for the change of gender is that *le champagne* is really short for *le vin de la Champagne*. The name is derived from the Latin *campania*, meaning plain, and the region is one of the historic provinces of France, bounded by Belgium and

Luxembourg on the north, Lorraine on the east, Burgundy to the south and Picardy and the Île de France to the west. At the Revolution France was divided into *départements* and the province of Champagne was divided into the *départements* of Ardennes, Marne, Aube, Haute-Marne and parts of Aisne. La Champagne *viticole* is almost entirely centred on the Marne with about 75 percent of the total vineyard of 30,717 hectares (1996). The Aube has 17 percent and the rest are scattered between Aisne, Seine-et-Marne and Haute-Marne.

Theoretically, the total production of champagne could reach 350 million bottles a year. In practice, in a region at the extreme northern limits of grape-ripening, frost and other weather hazards bite into the potential crop. Harvests in recent years have been as low as 152 million bottles (1985), and even in super-abundant vintages such as 1982 and '83, only the equivalent of some 300 million bottles were produced. The annual average for the years 1993 to 1997 was 258 million bottles, and that is before allowing for the inevitable loss and evaporation between harvest and bottling. Meanwhile consumption climbed from 188 to 250 million bottles between 1984 and 1995. Another short crop will be a disaster. The 1997 harvest, though of good quality, only produced 235 million bottles, not enough to keep pace with demand.

History

While it is possible that the odd vine-cutting might have found its way up the Rhône, through Burgundy and into Champagne in pre-Roman times, it is highly unlikely that there was any large-scale vineyard cultivation before AD 50, and in a new vineyard, with forests to be cleared and the correct match of variety and site to be established, initial progress must have been slow, exacerbated by the edict of Emperor Domitian in AD 92 that all colonial vines must be uprooted. Appropriately this law was rescinded by a gardener's son, the Emperor Probus, in AD 202. In Reims, in celebration, a temple to Bacchus was erected, and on one of the columns of the Porte Mars, constructed about the same time but now destroyed, there is known to have been a vineyard scene. The years following were the first heyday of the *champenois*. The wine, then red, but light and fruity, was exported to Rome where no doubt it was appreciated as a contrast to the heavy, alcoholic Italian brews, which were often spiced with resin and herbs, or laced with sea-water.

Already, however, even in Probus's time, Champagne, so vulnerable to attack from the east, was subject to raids from Alamans and Franks. One wonders if the search for wine – for it was forbidden to sell wine to the barbarians – was a spur to these incursions. At first these invasions were easily repelled, but as the Roman Empire decayed, communications evaporated and requests for help and reinforcements became increasingly ignored, so the pressure, the numbers and the frequency of this aggression mounted. Reims was burnt to the ground in AD 355 and sacked again in 406. The European tribes had already made some permanent settlements throughout Gaul and Iberia. It was further waves of invaders from Asia forcing the first barbarian settlements westwards which was to become the real threat to the Roman Empire, and it was in the Champagne district that a decisive battle was fought between Attila and his Asiatic Huns and the Gallo-Romans and their European barbarian allies, commanded by the Roman general Aetius. This battle – with perhaps as many as a million men in the field, and it is estimated that 200,000 never left it alive – was of a size and savagery probably unparalleled before, and not equalled thereafter until the senseless brutality of the First World War was fought on the same soil.

Though Attila was defeated, the tide irretrievably turned for the Romans. In the ensuing interregnum Clovis, king of the Franks, emerged as the master of northern Gaul. His conversion to Christianity at the hands of Saint-Rémi, Bishop of Reims, in AD 496 – his baptism is said to have taken place roughly where the cathedral now stands – was as important and far-reaching as that of Constantine a century and a half earlier. It ensured for the Champagne country a continuing prosperity, for Reims the prestige of being the spiritual centre of France, and for the French vineyards as a whole the continuity of the Church, for it was through the monastic orders that the techniques of vine-tending and wine-making were preserved, refined and transferred through the succeeding generations. The barbarian domination was not then in the end as hostile or unpropitious to viticulture as is generally supposed. With the monastic movement gaining force throughout the seventh century, Champagne became a centre of new orders, and hardly had the first stone of a new monastery been laid than the monks would snap up the best land for their vines. Had it not been for them the story would have been entirely different. In the middle of the ninth century, on the death of Charlemagne, the Frankish Empire was divided. Champagne was ruled by its local counts, and because of its geographical position gradually but inevitably was sucked into the kingdom of France. In 1285 Jeanne, heiress of Champagne and Navarre, married Philip the Fair, heir to the French throne, and the absorption was complete.

Dom Pérignon, of course, did not 'invent' champagne. What he had, however, was an undoubted genius for knowing where the vine would flourish best, which soils would produce the best vines, the vinification, handling and maturation of wine, and, above all, for the blending of different wines to make up a whole which was infinitely more than the sum of its constituent parts.

Pierre Pérignon was born, it is thought, in the late autumn of 1638, into a family of lawyers and local government officers. He entered the Saint-Vanne monastery at Verdun at the age of nineteen and some ten years later was appointed to the post of cellarmaster at the Abbey of Hautvillers, near Épernay, where he remained until his death in 1715. The position of cellarmaster was second only in importance to that of the abbot himself. Pérignon was responsible not only for the vineyards and the wine, but for all procurement – food, clothing and implements – for maintenance of the abbey and even for the abbey finances. He must have been highly thought-of to have been given that position at the young age of thirty or so.

Under Dom Pérignon's aegis the wines of the Hautvillers Abbey soon became the most sought-after in the area, fetching prices up to four times that of its neighbours. Until his arrival the local wine, though made from red grapes, was not exactly red in colour. It must have been a sort of rosé, for only in exceptional years would the fruit have been ripe enough, the skins pigmented enough, to give the resulting must a really ruby colour. What Pérignon developed was, first, the technique of making white wine from red grapes; second, that of mixing young wines from different provenances and even ages to make a quality blend; and, third, the importance of maturing this wine so that instead of a harsh, rough, youthful brew, one would get a mellow, richly flavoured, mature wine. He was helped in his experiments by three factors: the considerable stock at his disposal, for the abbey's own holdings were sizeable, and this would be increased by the donations of wine they received in tithes; that in 1673 a very large underground cellar, called the Biscomettes *cellier*, was constructed beneath the abbey in the chalk subsoil; and because, early in his life, Dom Pérignon gradually went blind. He was obviously blessed with an exceedingly fine palate and, as can happen, this sense developed unusual powers to compensate for the other loss.

Additionally, the period of office of Dom Pérignon coincided with two important new developments. There was the arrival of a new technique of glass-blowing developed in England, which resulted for the first time not only in a container which can be properly called a bottle, as we know it today – rather than a carafe or decanter – but one of a thickness and strength much tougher and more consistent than hitherto. And then there was the cork, a stopper certainly known to the Romans, but out of fashion and memory since the Dark Ages. Corks once again began to be used at the same time. The stage was set for the initiation of the wine we call champagne; for the bottling of a carefully vinified and blended wine – a white wine from black grapes – which would at first be bottled before the first fermentation had entirely been completed, easy enough in Champagne's cold climate where the initial chemical reaction and certainly the malolactic fermentation would be temporarily halted by the winter snows, and then, increasingly be bottled with a little extra yeast and sugar, so that the amount of carbonic acid created would produce the fizz we expect today.

Whether Dom Pérignon actually was the first to bottle effervescent wine we can never establish. What we can certainly credit him for is the turning of champagne's greatest weakness, the insipidity of its wine – and whose popularity would come under increasing threat as communications developed and the wines of Burgundy and further south could easily reach Paris – into its greatest strength.

The success of champagne was not exactly instant, but once the sober régime of the elderly Louis XIV and his purse-lipped mistress, Madame de Maintenon, had given place to the debauched Regency of Louis d'Orléans, champagne rapidly became the beverage of fashion. The ladies, in particular, liked the wine. It made them drunk without bringing too much of a flush to their cheeks. Champagne, said Madame de Pompadour, is the only wine that leaves a woman beautiful after drinking it. Once Voltaire had given the wine a splendid notice after visiting Épernay in 1737, and the Champenois had geared themselves up to meeting the demand from all corners of France, the prosperity of the wine was well and truly established.

The eighteenth and nineteenth centuries – for the Revolution and its consequences hardly affected the market for the wine – saw the consolidation of this early fame, the establishment of most of the firms we know today and the creation of an export market. Ruinart was founded in 1729, Moët in 1743 and the origins of Roederer and Lanson (the latter originally Delamotte Père et Fils) date from the 1760s; while Taittinger stems from Forest, Fournaux et Cie which began as Jacques Fourneaux in 1734, and Philippe Clicquot, a banker and textile merchant, started a champagne business in 1772. The original Heidsieck concern was founded in 1785, while Bollinger, Mumm, Krug and others followed after the Restoration in the early decades of the nineteenth century.

The early shippers were gentlemen (and ladies) of great personality, initiative and drive. They thought nothing of travelling enormous distances by stagecoach (in those days it would take three days to reach Orléans from Reims, and a fortnight to make the trip to Vienna) and journeyed to Russia, the United States and, later, to South America to promote their wares, always with great panache and extravagance. Böhne, the traveller for the widow Clicquot, went to Moscow to impress the Tsar and pick up his business only months after the retreat of Napoleon. Charles-Henri Heidsieck also cultivated the Russian market, on a white horse. Later the shippers of Moët & Chandon sent a trainload of the house brand to the survivors of the San Francisco earthquake in 1906. By this time no *soirée*, party or nightclub extravaganza was complete without fizz, as the Victorians called it, bubbly as it was christened by the Edwardians, or champers as the gay young things of the 1920s named the wine. George Leybourne, as Champagne Charlie, sang the praises of Moët (or indeed any other *marque* you cared to name, for a shilling). A rival, the Great Vance, extolled Clicquot, and Edward VII was followed on shooting parties by the 'boy' with a basket of bottles.

Meanwhile in Champagne itself, there was unrest. Champagne was Big Business, and big business meant big profits. Yet the growers, then, as now, mainly small peasant landowners, with holdings of barely a hectare each on average, were being paid derisory amounts for their grapes. Not only this, but as demand continued to grow, as well as the area under vine expanding, some unscrupulous firms began to bring in wine from outside the Champagne area and incorporate it into *cuvées* destined to be made into champagne. Unrest turned to fury, and fury to riot. Despite the creation, with the blessing of the honest champagne houses, of a *Syndicat Général des Vignerons*, and government legislation – the first attempts at a definition of a delineated Champagne area – in 1908 and 1911, the tocsin began to beat. A fearful night of arson and looting took place in Aÿ, though the house of Bollinger (as they had been fair) was spared. Suddenly the normally temperate *vigneron* had become anarchist. The threat of continuing insurrection was swiftly dealt with. Accounts differ as to how many troops were drafted in (20,000 to 40,000), but the Champagne district became an armed camp. Additionally, further legislation, more satisfactory to the Marne growers, was proposed.

Enough has already been written about the First World War. I merely need to remind the reader that the Battle of the Marne, the first decisive event in the war, took place in the middle of the Champagne vineyards, with the grapes already having turned colour and almost ready to be picked. For the next three years the front line ran along the Reims to Châlons road, round Reims and along the Aisne-Marne canal. By the end of the war half the houses in the city were in ruins and it is a wonder that the cathedral, started in 1211 and finally completed in the fifteenth century, managed to survive.

The 1930s saw Prohibition in the United States and the slump on the one hand, but the establishment of the rules and regulations of *appellation contrôlée* on the other. It also saw the start of attempts to prohibit the use of the word 'champagne', even with a qualifying prefix, by wines from outside the district. This culminated in the celebrated Spanish Champagne Case in London in 1958, which the Champenois originally lost, but won two years later on appeal.

In 1941, in the dark days of the Second World War, a new organization, the *Comité Interprofessional du Vin de Champagne* (CIVC), was established. The responsibilities of this body include organizing and controlling both the production and the sales of champagne 'with the constant aim of ensuring that honest and traditional practices are adhered to and quality is maintained', organizing and disciplining the relations between grower and shipper, taking action in years of plenty or meagre yield to stabilize prices, and deciding the price to be paid to the grower each year for the grapes he has produced. The Council of the CIVC consists of five representatives from each side, from the vineyard owners on the one hand and the champagne producers on the other. Since the war production has increased sixfold, and so have sales. Exports have increased even more, though while in 1900 they represented two-thirds of total sales, now they make up only 40 per cent.

Meanwhile, some of the well-known champagne houses, the *Grandes Marques*, have lost the family character they had possessed since their inauguration. There have been amalgamations and take-overs, mergers and public flotations. The giant Moët–Hennessey group owns Mercier and Ruinart, as well as Christian Dior, and is itself associated with the Louis Vuitton group which owns Veuve Clicquot. Seagrams, the North American spirit conglomerate, owns Mumm, Heidsieck and Co. Monopole and Perrier-Jouët. Rémy Martin have a controlling interest in Krug and in 1985 bought Charles Heidsieck; Taittinger owns Irroy just as Lanson owns Massé; Laurent-Perrier owns shares in Castellane. Six firms are quoted on the Paris *bourse* and a number of champagne houses have interests in the Loire Valley and further afield, in the Napa Valley of California, for example. The changes have become necessary as a result of the considerable sums of money involved. Most firms have a stock-holding of some three or four times their annual sales. Money is required for investment in increasingly sophisticated plant and machinery. It is needed for the ever more ruthless and expensive costs of maintaining and improving the brand image. Champagne is not a wine which can be successfully made, if quality is to be the keynote, on an artisanal scale.

The Champagne Districts

The three most important districts within the Champagne area are the Montagne de Reims, the Vallée de la Marne and the Côte des Blancs. The Montagne de Reims begins at Montchenot, south of Reims on the Épernay road, and runs clockwise round the side of the *montagne* itself until Bouzy and Ambonnay. Here it meets the Vallée de la Marne district, which runs west along the banks of the Marne and the Marne-Rhin Canal towards Dormans. South and east of Épernay a range of hills runs south perpendicular to the river valley. The vineyards on these south-eastern-facing slopes make up the Côtes de Blancs. There are several smaller areas. South-west of Reims round the village of Ville-Dommange is the Petite Montagne; south-west of Épernay are the Cubry and Grauves valleys. Beyond Dormans lie the Aisne vineyards. Finally, some 100 kilometres to the south, half the way to Dijon, is the district of the Aube round the two Bar townships: Bar-sur-Aube and Bar-sur-Seine.

CHAMPAGNE DISTRICTS

	Surface area in hectares (1996 harvest)
MONTAGNE DE REIMES	8796
VALLÉE DE LA MARNE	4967
CÔTE DE BLANCS	3275
AISNE VINEYARDS	2811
AUBE VINEYARDS	6580
COTE DE SEZANNE	1325
ISOLATED VINEYARDS	2993
Total	30,717

Département	*Surface area in hectares (1996 harvest)*
MARNE	22,781
AUBE	5854
AISNE	2045
HAUTE-MARNE	18
SEINE-ET-MARNE	19
Total	30,717

THE MONTAGNE DE REIMS

The mountain of Reims is a hill some twenty kilometres wide from east to west and ten kilometres long from north to south. Though it is a flat plateau on its thickly wooded top where there is a wild boar sanctuary, the sides of the Montagne rise steeply away from the surrounding countryside, from the valleys of the river Vesle on the north and Marne on the south. Near Verzy, on the eastern side, the forest is very curious. Strange, stunted, withered parasol beeches of considerable age, known as the Faux de Verzy, are to be found. A viral infection has produced this deformed growth, and I originally assumed the word *faux* (false) was a statement of description. I now find (from Patrick Forbes' excellent book *Champagne, The Wine, The Land and The People* (1967)) that the word is the plural of the old French for beech: *fay*. On the western side of Verzenay stands a disused windmill, now owned by Heidsieck Monopole & Co. This is an excellent place to stop and regard the vineyards, which stretch before and to the side in an unbroken succession. In the distance, through the smoke of Reims, one can see the cathedral.

The vines begin hard by the Épernay to Reims road, in the village of Montchenot, and continue through Villiers-Allerand, Rilly, Chigny-Les-Roses, Ludes, Mailly, Verzenay, Verzy, Villiers-Marmery, Trépail, Louvois, Tauxières, Bouzy and Ambonnay; lower down lie Sillery, Puisieulx and Beaumont-sur-Vesle. The Montagne de Reims is a region of predominantly black grapes – Pinot Noir and Pinot Meunier. Indeed, Bouzy produces the best-known still red wine of the Champagne area. The champagnes are powerful, rich and full of depth.

THE VALLÉE DE LA MARNE

Beyond Bouzy and Ambonnay, whose vineyards already have a southerly as opposed to easterly aspect, the Vallée de la Marne begins. This stretches between Tours and Dormans, a distance of some thirty-five kilometres. The Vallée de la Marne district can be divided into two sections. The more easterly, and better section, known as the Vins de la Rivière, lasts until Cumières. From Damery westwards, the soil and aspect is poorer. Vineyards continue on both sides of the river bank until Dormans, where they become the Aisne district, and stretch intermittently onwards for nearly another twenty-five kilometres, past Château-Thierry until Nanteuil which lies just within the border of the Seine-et-Marne *département*. Here we are only fifty-odd kilometres, as the crow flies, from Notre-Dame in Paris.

The important Vallée de la Marne communes are Tours-sur-Marne, Bisseuil, Avenay, Mareuil-sur-Aÿ, Aÿ, Mutigny, Dizy, Champillon, Hautvillers, and Cumières. Like the Montagne de Reims this is a black-grape district. Though the resulting white wine is less powerfully bodied than that from the Montagne de Reims, it is nevertheless full, and is finely perfumed and of great, elegant character.

THE CÔTE DES BLANCS

As the name suggests, the Côte des Blancs is the white grape section. While there are some Chardonnay vineyards among the Pinot ones of the Montagne and Vallée, in the Côte des Blancs you will hardly find a single red grape. The vines cling to the eastern side of a hill approximately twenty kilometres long and form a strip no more than a couple of kilometres wide, not unlike the Côte d'Or. The main villages, running north to south, are Chouilly, Cramant, Avize, Oger, Le Mesnil-sur-Oger and Vertus.

SOIL AND CLIMATE

What distinguishes the Champagne area from the surrounding countryside, and what gives its wines their special character, is the nature of the soil, the subsoil, and its climate. Much of northern France – and indeed southern England – has a chalky or limestone soil dating from the Upper Cretaceous era, roughly 65 million years ago. It is also fairly flat. At the end of the Tertiary period (30 million years ago) earthquakes of considerable violence struck at the eastern side of the Paris basin, forcing the land to buckle and rise up above the surrounding countryside. This chain of hills – the Falaises de Champagne – consists of a particular type of chalk, *Gonio Teuthis Quadrata*, not found in the outlying areas. The Montagne de Reims, the Côte des Blancs and the other Champagne hills are also the only important hills between Normandy and the Vosges. The tops of these hills are thickly wooded which helps protect the vines on the slopes below.

The chalk subsoil, rich in minerals and trace elements, is covered by a very thin layer of surface soil, nowhere more than a metre thick and in places hardly 15 centimetres. This often washes away in the heavy winter rains and laboriously has to be replaced.

The soil varies marginally between the three main regions described above. In the Côte des Blancs there is clay, in the valley of the Marne sand, on the Montagne de Reims *cendres noirs*, a sort of impure lignite. These nuances, as well as the dissimilarities in microclimate, help explain the differences between the wines.

Chalk is a soil which is excellent for a vine-growing area, particularly one at the northern limits of successful cultivation. It drains well, yet does not dry out; it is loose and friable, enabling the vines' roots to penetrate deep; and it is heat-retentive, radiating the heat of the day back on to the vines in the cool of the night. The climate in Champagne is what you would expect in an area only a few degrees south of the 50 degrees latitude line generally agreed as the northern limit for successful vine cultivation. It is wet, it is cold and grey for much of the year, and it is prone to frost. Yet the mean average temperature on the vineyard slopes is a good half a degree centigrade above the minimum required for the cultivation of the vine, and the vines are for the most part sheltered from the prevailing westerly winds. Rain, however, is a problem, as is late spring frost. It rains for 160 days a year on average, with July being the wettest month of all. This makes hail an additional hazard, and renders spraying of the vines against mildew and other diseases a constant necessity. Frost damage is something the Champenois, like their colleagues in Chablis, just have to accept. Hardly a year goes by without some devastation just as the buds are beginning to shoot in the spring (it is less of a problem while the vine is dormant).

THE GRAPE VARIETIES

The three great grape varieties of the Champagne area are the black Pinot Noir and Pinot Meunier and the white Chardonnay. Overall the black varieties predominate, with about 80 per cent of the vineyard region, the Pinot Noir found particularly in the Montagne de Reims and both in the Vallée de la Marne. The Chardonnay is king in the more clayey soil of the Côte des Blancs. In champagne it is the Pinot Noir which gives backbone, richness of flavour and depth of character, as anyone who has tasted a really good Blanc de Noirs will know.

The advantage of the Pinot Meunier is that it will grow on land which the more fussy Pinot Noir would disdain. It is hardy, and it buds late. The wine from it is very scented but has less breed, and it ages more rapidly than the Pinot Noir. Nevertheless some houses, Krug and Deutz, for instance, would not be without it. It is the most widely planted variety in Champagne, accounting for 44 per cent of the surface area (Pinot Noir covers 30 per cent and Chardonnay 26 per cent).

The Chardonnay buds earlier than the other two, making it the most susceptible to frost, but takes longest of all to complete its cycle from shoot to ripeness, hence its higher acidity, so necessary for quality sparkling wine. Normally the Côte des Blancs is not picked until a week after the Montagne de Reims. Chardonnay produces wine of less alcohol but great delicacy, finesse and freshness. Wine made solely from the Chardonnay, Blanc de Blancs, is noted for its light, almost ethereal, filigree character, and a subtle, unmuscular complexity of fruit.

CHAMPAGNE GROWERS

Champagne is a region of the small husbandman. There are some 19,000 growers in an area of 30,717 hectares, an average of just over 1 1/2 hectares each. Take away the roughly 3500 hectares, one-eighth of the area, which is owned by the champagne houses themselves, and the average holding falls even more. It has been estimated that in the Champagne district a family needs $2\frac{1}{2}$ to 3 hectares of vines in order to survive without other means of remuneration. Only some 200 families have this sort of holding. Most can only work part-time in their vineyards, and have jobs in Reims, Épernay or Châlons during the day. Few, obviously, can be self-sufficient in wine terms, and though an increasing number now sell their own champagne, one suspects that the majority of these may be own-label but are co-operatively produced.

Of the 140 or so champagne firms, some 60 have vineyard holdings, and these are concentrated more in the best areas. In the Montagne de Reims and Côte des Blancs, for instance, the *négociants* own one-fifth of the *vignoble* as against one-eighth over the whole region. The size of their holdings, naturally, is very much larger. The champagne houses who have extensive holdings of their own, will, of course, assure you of the wisdom and good fortune of this fact. They are able to control the entire process from start to finish. They are less reliant on the vagaries of the open market and the increasing competition for the best grapes of the best growers. Those who have no vineyards will be equally adamant that theirs is the best policy: total freedom and flexibility to purchase only the best and in whatever quantities they wish depending on the quality of the vintage and the state of the market.

Most of the large champagne houses do have vineyard holdings. The amount these provide, relative to production, can be as much as 80 per cent in the case of Louis Roederer and 70 per cent in the case of Bollinger, though the figure is more usually far less. Some – Alfred Gratien, Charles Heidsieck, Piper Heidsieck, for instance – possess no vineyards at all. I don't think it can be suggested that the presence or lack of a large in-house landholding has any bearing on the quality of the *marque*.

A decade ago the champagne houses, or *négociants-manipulants* (N.M. in small letters on the label), produced 74 per cent of all champagne. Today the figure has diminished somewhat, to 64 per cent, as a result of the increase in the numbers of independent growers (*récoltants-manipulants* or R.M.). On the export market, however, the shippers are supreme, only the co-operative at Mailly on the Montagne de Reims is any rival to the *négociants* in the sense that it sells under its own name rather than supplying B.O.B. (*See page 308* for full details of the code numbers you will see on champagne bottles.)

The communes in the Champagne area were first classified in 1911, originally into Hors Classé, Première Catégorie and Deuxième Catégorie. Later this was refined into percentages, with the Hors Classé communes being given 100 per cent, those in the first category, the *premiers crus*, between 90 and 99 per cent, and so on. It is on this basis that the *négociant* and grower agree a price for the grapes which are produced. Each year just before the vintage commences, the CIVC fixes a price for a kilo of grapes from a 100 per cent *cru* – in 1996 it was 24 francs – taking into account the current world and champagne's economic and stock position, and the potential size and quality of the harvest. The price of grapes in the rest of the area follows according to the rating of each vineyard.

There are now seventeen *grands crus* or 100 per cent communes: Avize, Cramant, Chouilly, Oiry, Oger and Le Mesnil-sur-Oger (for white grapes only) in the Côte des Blancs, Aÿ and Tours (black grapes only) in the Vallée de la Marne, and Ambonnay, Beaumont-sur-Vesle, Bouzy, Louvois, Mailly, Sillery, Tauxières, Verzy and Verzenay on the Montagne de Reims. Those above 95 per cent include Vertus (for white grapes only) in the Côte des Blancs, Grauves and Cuis (again white only) in the Cubry/Grauves valleys, Mareuil-sur-Aÿ and Dizy in the Vallée de la Marne, and Trépail and Villers-Marmery on the Montagne de Reims.

How Champagne is Made

The key to the making of champagne, indeed of any non-carbonated sparkling wine, is the induction of a second sugar-alcohol fermentation, producing carbon dioxide, and the retention of this carbon dioxide within the wine, in the form of carbonic acid, until the cork of the bottle is released. Once that pressure is off, the carbonic acid can revert back to water and carbon dioxide and the carbon dioxide escapes in the form of tiny bubbles which well up mainly from the bottom of the glass. This is the fizz.

What is special about the champagne method is that the second fermentation takes place in a bottle and that the wine remains in the same receptacle from the moment the bottling takes place until the moment of consumption. The problem, and one of the causes of the expense of a *méthode champenoise* wine, multiplied in the case of champagne by the high price of the base fruit, is that this second fermentation produces a sediment which has to be eliminated without losing the carbon dioxide.

Champagne is first made like any other white wine, the difference again between most other sparkling white wines – whether *méthode champenoise* or not – being that the main ingredient is usually black grapes, not white. Most varieties of grapes, however, all that are white and most that are black, whatever the colour of their skins, have white juice. The pigmentation causing the red colour in red wines comes from these skins, and so the first task is to ensure a quick and uncomplicated pressing to extract juice without allowing the skins to colour the must.

The traditional *pressoir cocquart* or champagne press consists of a round or square base, loose planks which can be inserted on their sides to enclose the platform, and a vertical screw press which descends once this receptacle has been filled with fruit to press the grapes. Nowadays these presses are being replaced by horizontal machines. The champagne regulations stipulate that 4000 kilograms of grapes are required in order to produce 2666 litres of must. This is equivalent to thirteen of the traditional champagne 205-litre *pièces* or casks. The first pressing yields 2050 litres (ten *pièces*) of the best quality, and is termed the *cuvée*. The second pressing will give two further casks (the *première taille*) and the last a further 205 litres (the *deuxième taille*). The best champagnes are only made from the *cuvée* and *première taille* wine.

The next step, after the must, or grape juice, has been allowed to settle so that some of the gross lees can be racked off, is the fermentation. This takes place in concrete or stainless-steel tanks at 15°C to 20°C and usually with the aid of special yeasts – of the houses only Krug and Alfred Gratien, to my knowledge, still vinify their entire harvest in oak – and is followed, if the winemakers desire, by a malolactic fermentation. So far, apart from the separation of the pressings, the process has been similar to white wine-making all over the world. But now comes the first important divergence, the *assemblage*.

Nowhere is the wine-maker's expertise more of an art than in the blending of champagne. Champagne is an area of three grape varieties, many different subtle soil variations, and a multitude of microclimates. Most houses will have contracts with growers from all over the region, as well as grapes from their own vineyards. Their aim, with this variety of base ingredients, and despite the difference in the weather pattern from year to year, is to produce a standard, consistent and quality blend which typifies the style and personality of their house; and they have to make this assembly with young wine, harsh, raw, acid and unpalatable. It is a skill unparalleled in modern wine-making.

Once the blend has been prepared – in the case of non-vintage wine this may, probably will, require the use of older reserves of wine especially kept back for the purpose – the wine is bottled, and at the same time a carefully calculated amount of *liqueur de tirage*, sugar and yeast dissolved in wine, is added. This will produce the second fermentation, and because of the build-up of pressure of carbon dioxide, the by-product, the bottle will need to be tougher than usual, and the closure firmly attached. Most closures these days are a sort of crown cork, as found on a Coca-Cola bottle, but in the past, only today for some de luxe *cuvées*, a cork, secured by a metal clip (*agrafe*), was used. The bottles are then binned away, the second fermentation takes place, and the wines are allowed to mature, feeding on the lees or sediment of dead yeast cells left over after this fermentation process.

The next process is the elimination of the sediment. It has first to be collected into a compact little cup, on the underside of the closure, and then removed without allowing the gas to escape. In order to shake down the sediment, an operation known as *remuage*, the bottles are put into *pupitres*. These consist of two rectangular planks of wood a little smaller than a door, into which have been cut a number of angled holes, fastened together at the long ends, and stood upright in an A-shape. The bottles are inserted into the holes, which are wide enough to trap them by the neck, and at the beginning lie horizontally. The task of the *remueur* is to give each bottle a series of turns, shakes and tilts so that over a period of two or three months the bottles are lifted from horizontal to vertical, neck downwards, and the sediment shaken down so that it rests on the underside of the closure.

By passing the bottles, still upside down, through a freezing solution, the *dégorgement*, or removal, of the original closure and sediment, can be simply accomplished as the bottom inch or so of the wine, including the sediment, forms a little block of icy slush. The bottles are then topped up, normally with a little sugar solution (the *liqueur d'expédition* or dosage), corked and then given a rest for several months before labelling and shipping.

This is the process in a nutshell, and, as can be seen, it takes time, it requires space – for the hundreds of *pupitres* – and it is expensive. An experienced *remueur* is said to be able to handle 30,000 bottles a day, but in terms of the millions of bottles exported each year this is negligible, particularly if the *remuage* process is to last for the full three months. Today, *remuage* is speeded up, in many houses, to five or six weeks, or is being done mechanically. The mechanical systems, using *gyropalettes* or *champanex*, are increasingly widely adopted, and consist of metal bins, holding 500-odd bottles, which rotate and oscillate mechanically every few hours, day in and day out, and reduce the process of shaking down the sediment to a week. Another new technique, still experimental, is to introduce the yeast for the second fermentation encapsulated in a small ball. The membrane of these balls or *pilles* allows the yeasts to do their work in the wine without allowing the deposit to escape, and it is hoped that this will make the work of *remuage* easier still.

The penultimate process before the final resting and labelling is the introduction of the *liqueur d'expédition*. This will determine how sweet the champagne is to be. Champagne, even though it undergoes two fermentations, is a fully fermented wine, so it will be bone-dry. As a wine from such a northern area it would also normally be unduly austere. A little sweetening will round the wine off and accentuate the fruit.

This is the appropriate place to mention that nearly all France's *appellation contrôlée* sparkling wines are made by the champagne method (though there are moves afoot to confine the use of the phrase *méthode champenoise* or a translation thereof solely to champagne itself). Lesser wines are made by the *cuve close* or Charmat method, the second fermentation taking place in bulk, in tank rather than in bottle, prior to filtration and bottling under pressure.

Champagne Styles

The driest champagnes are termed 'Brut', with less than 15 grams of sugar per litre. Then comes 'Extra Dry' (12 to 20 grams), 'Sec' (17 to 35 grams), 'Demi-sec' (33 to 50 grams) and 'Doux' (50 grams or more). A new trend is to produce wines with less sugar, even none at all. These have various names such as Brut Sauvage, Brut de Brut, Brut Zero, Brut 100 per cent, and so on. They will have less than six grams of sugar and will need to have several years' ageing before they are mellow enough to be palatable.

CRÉMANT

Normally champagne has a gas pressure of five or six atmospheres, as it must by law. Crémant champagne is produced by adding less *liqueur de tirage* at the bottling stage and will have a pressure of about 3.6 atmospheres. It can be both vintage and non-vintage. (Crémant sparkling wines from elsewhere such as Loire, Alsace and Burgundy have the normal amount of pressure.)

PINK CHAMPAGNE

There is an increasing vogue for both champagne rosé and champagne produced exclusively from white grapes, Blanc de Blancs. The rosé is produced by adding a little red wine at the time of bottling (champagne is the only wine where this is allowed), although it can be produced by making a rosé and then applying the champagne method to that. In my view, though this is not stipulated in the legislation, it should also be produced entirely from the Pinot Noir grape, and those which are do stand out as more elegant and interesting examples. For some reason which I do not fully understand, rosé champagnes are more expensive than the normal wines. It can be both vintage and non-vintage. Recommended wines: Billecart-Salmon, Bollinger, Lanson, Perrier-Jouët, Pol Roger, Pommery's Cuvée Louise Pommery, Roederer, Taittinger's Comtes de Champagne and Veuve Clicquot.

BLANC DE BLANCS

Blanc de Blancs, made exclusively from the Chardonnay grape, is, or should be, lighter, slimmer, delicate as well as elegant. There are some delicious Blanc de Blancs, which fully justify the extra price, for if they come from the Côte des Blancs exclusively they are bound to be expensive. Other examples, though, seem rather thin and pale in character when drunk alongside a good non-Blanc de Blancs wine. It can be both vintage and non-vintage. Recommended wines: Billecart-Salmon, Krug's Clos de Mesnil, Mumm's Crémant de Cramant (now relabelled Mumm de Mumm), Bruno Paillard, Pol Roger, Salon and Taittinger's Comtes de Champagne.

BLANC DE NOIRS

Blanc de Noirs, literally 'white of blacks', is a champagne made entirely from either or both of the two black grapes, Pinot Noir and Pinot Meunier. There are very few of these. Bollinger produces a delicious but very, very expensive wine from a small plot of *vieilles vignes françaises* (ungrafted vines); and I have seen fine examples from Bruno Paillard. The colour is golden, rather than straw-yellow and the wine is full-bodied, intensely flavoured, and very rich (though without being sweet): certainly a champagne for food rather than for drinking as an aperitif.

NON-VINTAGE

Champagne can be sold with or without a vintage date, though if it is to have a vintage date 100 per cent of the blend needs to come from the stated vintage. If it is a non-vintage wine, it cannot be put on the market until one year after bottling. If a vintage wine, the stipulation is a minimum of three years' age after the vintage. All houses will produce a range from a basic non-vintage wine upwards. It is the non-vintage wine which is the mass-produced brand, and therefore in this sense the flagship wine of the champagne house. Non-vintage champagne probably makes up 85 per cent or more of the market.

VINTAGE

Vintage champagne, like vintage port, is something special. It is, or should be, only declared in exceptional years, say, three or four times a decade, and it should be a wine of high quality, left to mature until it is round, complex, richly textured and full-flavoured. It should not be drunk as an apéritif, before the taste buds are ready to appreciate it, but with food. It should be consumed with due deference, as behoves any fine wine, and perhaps *after* a splendid meal when it can receive the full attention it deserves.

DE-LUXE

The same applies to the increasing number of prestige brands or de-luxe wines. Led by Dom Pérignon, the brand of Moët & Chandon, nearly all houses now produce a superior vintage, often in a fancy bottle, usually with a fancy name. All are expensive, some are delicious. In my view, sadly, rather too many, and that applies also to ordinary vintage champagne, are put on to the market too young. All vintage and de-luxe champagnes should have at least five years on their lees and further age thereafter.

LARGER BOTTLE SIZES FOR CHAMPAGNE

MAGNUM	2 bottles
JEROBOAM	4 bottles
REHOBOAM	6 bottles
METHUSELAH	8 bottles
SALMANAZAR	12 bottles
BALTHAZAR	16 bottles ⎫ rarely commercially produced
NEBUCHADNEZZAR	20 bottles ⎭

A Jeroboam of champagne is a different size from a Jeroboam of Bordeaux, which used to be 6 bottles (4.5 litres) but is now 5 litres.

REGISTRATION CODE NUMBERS

The CIVC has apportioned initials and a code number for each producer and all brand names used by that producer. The code can be found at the bottom of the label.

If the producer owns the brand name, the initials to be used are:

NM   indicating a *négociant-manipulant*: champagne house.
CM   indicating a *co-opérative de manipulation*: champagne made by a co-operative.
RM   indicating a *récoltant-manipulant*: grower producing champagne from his own grapes.
RC   indicating a *récoltant-co-opérateur*: a new designation, for a grower selling champagne produced by a co-operative.
SR   indicating a *société de récoltant*: a new designation, for a company created by winegrowers who are members of the same family.

In all other cases, labels will carry the code:

MA   indicating *marque d'acheteur*: Buyer's Own Brand (B.O.B.).

COTEAUX CHAMPENOIS

Until 1974 the still wines of Champagne were called Vin Nature de la Champagne. This was changed, at the insistence of the EC, to Coteaux Champenois. To some extent, Coteaux Champenois may be deemed the surplus wine from the Champagne area, for in order to keep supply and demand for the sparkling wine in equilibrium, the CIVC decides annually how many kilograms of grapes per hectare may be made into champagne. Production, therefore, varies widely from one vintage to another. Sometimes it can be several thousand hectolitres. In 1996 it was a mere 159 hectolitres.

Most Coteaux Champenois is white, and produced as a generic wine by the champagne houses themselves, Laurent Perrier and Moët & Chandon (under the Saran label) being the best known. One or two village red wines, particularly Bouzy (from George Vesselle, the local mayor) can be found. There are one or two Coteaux Champenois rosés. Coteaux Champenois Blanc has to be compared with a white Burgundy, and I regret does not stand up. It seems austere, as well as a little thin. Sadly it is also considerably more expensive.

ROSÉ DES RICEYS

Rosé des Riceys is a separate *appellation*, centred on the village of Riceys in the Aube *département*. It is a still wine, and in my view undistinguished. Production in 1996 totalled 482 hectolitres.

WHEN TO DRINK CHAMPAGNE

Though it is said that fifteen years is the maximum lifespan for champagne, I have found that to be unduly pessimistic. I have had champagnes of almost 100 years old – admittedly only in the region itself – which have shown no sign of decay or lack of *mousse*, and I have had many wonderful champagnes with twenty years or more bottle age. Old champagne is delicious, and a year or two's landed age given to a raw non-vintage champagne can work wonders.

CHAMPAGNE VINTAGES

1997: A small harvest (about 235 million bottles). After a poor summer fine September weather produced very good wines high in both alcohol and acidity. Very good quality at best: but variable.

1996: A good-sized harvest (about 270 million bottles). Excellent weather during the run up to the vintage produced very healthy ripe fruit. Never before has there been musts with such high sugar readings and such high acidities. Fine quality. Almost certainly to be declared as vintage.

1995: A large harvest (about 286 million bottles). After a shaky start - frost in April and again in May – the flowering was successful and the summer warm and dry. After a rainy start to September the harvesting weather was benign. Very good quality.

1994: A small harvest (about 244 million bottles). The summer was largely fine, but the weather deteriorated in September but improved at the end of the picking period. Nevertheless rot was widespread and a severe sorting out of the fruit was vital. Average quality only.

1993: An average harvest (about 257 million bottles). The summer was uneven, oidium and mildew prevalent, and heavy rain set in just as the harvest was about to commence, causing widespread rot, and lowering the acidity of the wine. Not great, but a stop-gap vintage for some houses.

1992: A large harvest (about 288 million bottles). An early harvest after a generous good summer was a little interupted by rain but nevertheless produced a satisfactory if not outstanding crop, best in the Chardonnays of the Côte des Blancs. Already declared by some houses as vintage.

1991: A large harvest (about 278 million bottles), despite frost in late April. After a good summer the harvest, which began late, was spoilt by rain. Quality is only fair.

1990: A large harvest (about 288 million bottles). After a poor spring, including frost in early April, the summer weather was excellent. The harvest was early, the fruit ripe, the level of potential alcohol high, as were the acidities. A splendid vintage of very high quality: firm, beautifully balanced, elegant wines which will keep for a long time.

1989: A large harvest (about 275 million bottles). After a fine summer the harvest was early and took place in warm weather. Another fine vintage. The wines are rich and concentrated, full bodied, exotically spicy. They will last well.

1988: A small harvest (about 224 million bottles). The spring was wet and the flowering unsuccessful. It was a cool summer at first, but the vintage weather was better. These are very well balanced, medium bodied, slightly aloof wines, in total contrast to 1989, but very classy.

Earlier Vintages: 1986, 1985, 1983, 1982, 1979, 1976, 1975, 1973, 1971, 1970, 1969, 1966 and 1964.

Leading Champagne Houses

Champagne can vary widely in style. Not only will there be differences according to the quality – vintage, non-vintage, de luxe and the rest – and according to the *encépagement* – whether it is a Blanc de Blancs, or the percentage of Pinot Meunier in the blend, for instance; and not only will a champagne change its character as it ages. Additionally each house has its own particular style, and just as the discerning ear and eye can recognize, say, Mozart, and differentiate between Monet and Renoir, so can – though I must personally confess with rather more difficulty – the discerning palate distinguish between, say, Bollinger and Pol Roger, and identify Krug without seeing the label.

Which style you will prefer – which vintages you will prefer – will be as much a question of personal taste as inherent quality. In the profiles of the leading champagne houses which follow I attempt to give an indication of the house style as well as denoting which are my particular favourites. In fact my taste for champagne is extremely catholic. I love all good champagne. It is the supreme wine to drink alone or in company, at any time of the day or night, with or without food. It is the wine I would take, above all others, to a desert island.

This is a personal selection of the leading champagne houses, in alphabetical order.

BOLLINGER

Annual production is about 2 million bottles and they own 142 hectares of vineyards. The original Bollinger, Joseph (later changed to Jacques when he took French nationality), was a young German from Württemburg who was engaged by Admiral Count Athanase de Villemont to supplement the family fortunes by making wine on his estates. In 1829 Jacques Bollinger set up in business on his own, and later married the Admiral's daughter. One of Champagne's best-loved characters was the wife of Jacques' grandson, Lily, who ran Bollinger from the death of her husband in 1941 until her own death at the age of seventy-eight in 1977.

Bollinger's own vineyards have an average quality rating of 97 per cent, and produce two-thirds of their own requirements. They include two small plots of ungrafted Pinot Noir, the wines being reproduced by layering, or *provinage*. This produces the Vieilles Vignes Françaises, a champagne of great breed and immense depth of character. Bollinger's vintage champagne is called Grande Année, a reference to the fact that vintage champagne is, or should be, only declared in the finest years. Bollinger R.D. is one of my all-time favourite champagnes. The initials stand for *récemment dégorgé* (recently disgorged) and indicate a wine which has been kept longer than normal – up to as much as ten years – between bottling and disgorging. All this time it has been feeding off the lees, and the result is a wine of great complexity, concentration and richness. Bollinger were the first to publicize the idea and have in fact registered the words R.D. as a trademark. Année Rare is a wine kept even longer on its lees. Bollinger do not use the second and third pressings, even in their non-vintage Special Cuvée; 80 per cent of their production is vinified in wood, and the firm has a stockholding equivalent to five years' sales. A subsidiary company is the sparkling Loire firm Langlois-Château.

Bollinger is one of the great champagne houses, producing firm, full, meaty wines which last well. Even the special Cuvée needs keeping, and it has occasionally been put onto the market a little early. The vintage and de-luxe wines are truly classic, especially in masculine vintages such as 1990, 1985, 1982, '75 and '70.

VEUVE CLICQUOT-PONSARDIN

Annual production is about 8.4 million bottles and vineyard ownership 280 hectares. The famous widow Clicquot was left on her own with a three-year-old daughter in 1805 at the age of twenty-seven. Thanks to the ingenuity of her salesman, Monsieur Böhne, 20,000 bottles reached Saint Petersburg during the autumn of 1814 (having set off in defiance of a Russian embargo on French imports), where they sold for 12 roubles apiece, and Clicquot soon dominated the Russian market, though at the time it hardly sold at all within France. Madame Clicquot is also credited with the development of the *pupitres* in order to facilitate *remuage*. The whole range of Clicquot champagnes are impeccably made wines, from the non-vintage to the prestige *marque*, La Grande Dame. Subsidiaries are Canard Duchêne and Henriot. Veuve Clicquot now belongs to the Louis Vuitton group.

The house style of Veuve Clicquot is for wines which are full and rich and firm but not as austere as, say, Bollinger. The non-vintage is consistent and one of the very best.

ALFRED GRATIEN

Alfred Gratien is by no means a large champagne house, with an annual production of some 200,000 bottles, and neither do they own any vineyards, but it is one of the very best and one of my favourites. Wine-making is traditional: vinification is in oak; a proper cork, not a crown cork, is used for the second fermentation; and the champagne is not put on the market until fully mature, some not until ten years after the vintage, which virtually allows them (if they were permitted so to do) to call every vintage bottle R.D.!

The composition of the vintage wine varies with every year. Gratien was founded in 1864 and is a subsidiary of Gratien, Meyer and Seydoux of Saumur. The Gratien style is rich, full, firm wines, always fully mature.

HEIDSIECK & CO MONOPOLE, CHARLES HEIDSIECK, PIPER-HEIDSIECK

Florens-Ludwig Heidsieck, a German wool merchant, set up Heidsieck and Company in the years just before the Revolution, and the firm passed to three nephews in the 1830s, each of whom went their separate ways. Piper is now the largest of the three, with an annual production of 6.5 million bottles. Its de-luxe wine is called Florens-Louis. Heidsieck and Co Monopole was taken over by Mumm in 1972 and now belongs to Seagrams. Unlike the other two it owns 110 hectares of vineyards. The prestige *marque* is called Diamant Bleu. It produces two million bottles a year, as does Charles Heidsieck, who merged with Henriot in 1976; only to split from them when they were taken over by Rémy Martin at the end of 1985. Their top wine is called Champagne Charlie.

Charles Heidsieck is my favourite of the three – though none would be in my super-star league – and the wines are fresh, generous, fruity and medium-bodied. Heidsieck and Co Monopole makes standard, dependable wines. Piper-Heidsieck I find a bit green, and I have not found it ageing as gracefully as the others.

KRUG

Krug has an annual production of about half a million bottles, 20 per cent of which can be provided by their own vineyards, or from vineyards rented, most of which are in the Côte des Blancs. Quality is the keynote in this small but prestigious house. Fermentation is in oak, no malolactic fermentation is allowed to occur, and no wines are put onto the market until they have had considerable bottle age. Only vintage and de-luxe champagnes are produced. The de-luxe *marque*, which used to be called Private Cuvée but was redesigned and relaunched as Grande Cuvée a few years ago, is an elegant, refined, complex wine which makes an excellent aperitif. I prefer the more masculine, fuller and firmer richness and depth of the vintage wine, always held back six to eight years before being sold. Recent additions to the range are a rosé and an elegant, harmonious single-vineyard Blanc de Blancs, Clos de Mesnil. Krug is not a cheap champagne – which is why I refer to their non-vintage as a de-luxe *marque*. Personally, good as it is, I can think of a number of vintage champagnes I would rather spend my money on. The vintage wine, despite its even higher price, *is* worth it, and it lasts and lasts.

LANSON

Annual production is about 10 million bottles and they own 210 hectares of vineyards. The house of Lanson was originally that of François Delamotte, founded in 1760. One of their employees, Jean-Baptiste Lanson, took over on the death of the last of the Delamottes, and began trading under his own name in 1838. Originally almost the entire production went to England but under the chairmanship of Victor Lanson – reputed to have drunk over 70,000 bottles of champagne during his lifetime – sales expanded worldwide. After his death in 1970 Ricard, the *pastis* firm, acquired a 48 per cent interest, and in 1980 the Gardiner brothers, manufacturers of artificial fertilizers, and relations by marriage, bought out Ricard. Lanson also has a majority interest in Pommery et Greno, and since 1969 has owned 30 per cent of Laurent Perrier. In 1984 the group was acquired by the French food group, BSN. At Lanson, as at Piper-Heidsieck and Krug, the base wine does not undergo a malolactic fermentation. The firm was one of the last to produce a de-luxe *marque*, Noble Cuvée being launched in 1982.

The Lanson style is for light, flowery, quite forward wines – feminine, if you wish. The non-vintage is standard, but not one I would number in my first division.

LAURENT-PERRIER

Annual production is about 8 million bottles and they own 80 hectares of vineyards. Laurent-Perrier is one of Champagne's recent successes. The house, though founded in 1812, was small, and business was moribund when Bertrand de Nononcourt took over in 1939. Even in 1959 annual production was only 400,000 bottles. Since then the growth has been spectacular yet without losing the family atmosphere of the business or the personality of the wines. Laurent-Perrier's rosé is one of the few to be made from an original genuine still rosé. Their prestige *cuvée*, Grande Siècle, also unusually, is a blend of several vintages, though it sells under a vintage in the United States.

The Laurent-Perrier non-vintage is a good dependable wine, marginally sweeter than some. It is soft and fresh, medium-bodied and fruity, without perhaps the depth and *élan* of the very best. I love the Cuvée Grand Siècle, however. This is an excellent, multifaceted wine, rich and profound.

MARNE & CHAMPAGNE

This house has a production of over 10 million bottles, selling them under over 100 different labels as Buyer's Own Brands (B.O.B.) champagnes. Names include Pol Albert, Eugène Chequot, Denis Père et Fils, Gauthier, Pol Gessner, Giesler, Giesmann and Georges Martel. Qualities and styles vary, as you might expect. The buyer can dictate what he requires and prices are keen.

MOËT & CHANDON

Moët, even without its associate companies Mercier and Ruinart – not to mention its association with the Louis Vuitton group which owns Veuve Clicquot and others – is by far the largest at champagne house with a production of over 27 million bottles. The

group as a whole owns 485 hectares of vineyards, and Moët's share of this supplies about 20 per cent of its needs. Pierre-Gabriel Chandon, son-in-law of Jean-Rémy Moët, himself the grandson of the founder of the firm, bought the Abbey of Hautevillers in 1823 – the monks had previously supplied his father-in-law with wine. Jean-Rémy was a personal friend of Napoleon who decorated him with the Légion d'Honneur. Another famous customer was Wagner, who consoled himself with Moët & Chandon after the disastrous flop of *Tannhaüser* in Paris in 1861. At the suggestion of Lawrence Fenn, an English journalist, the firm launched Dom Pérignon in 1935 to celebrate the centenary of its agency in Britain. This wine, from a blend of roughly half Pinot Noir and half Chardonnay and only from their own 100 per cent rated vineyards, is one of the best, as well as the best known, of the de-luxe brands.

Despite the quantity produced, the standard and consistency of the non-vintage Moët is high: a medium-bodied, fruity wine, not absolutely bone-dry, which I would put at the top of my second division. It is estimated that the quantity of Dom Pérignon sold equals more than the combined total of all the other de-luxe brands put together. Despite this it really is a top-notch wine, worth every penny of its sadly inflated price.

MUMM

Annual production is about 7 million bottles and they own 219 hectares of vineyards. Mumm was founded in 1827 by a German from Endelheim in the Rheingau. After the launch of Cordon Rouge in 1873 the firm prospered only to find itself confiscated as enemy property in the First World War as none of the Mumm family had taken up French citizenship. The new director, René Lalou, after whom the firm's prestige brand is named, gradually acquired a majority holding but sold this in 1973 to the Canadian distillers Seagram who also own Perrier-Jouët and Heidsieck & Co Monopole. Mumm also produce a Crémant de Cramant (now relaunched as Mumm de Mumm), an excellent Blanc de Blancs.

The style of Mumm's champagne is for something mild and soft, fruity and on the sweeter side, as far as their non-vintage Cordon Rouge Brut is concerned. I do not find it very stylish. Nor have I ever been particularly struck by the vintage, though the René Lalou is better. This makes the finesse of the Crémant de Cramant/Mumm de Mumm all that more surprising.

PERRIER-JOUËT

Annual production is about 3 million bottles and they own 108 hectares of vineyards. Founded in 1811, Perrier-Jouët, like Heidsieck & Co Monopole and Mumm, now belongs to the Seagram Group. The house has two de-luxe brands: the Belle Époque, also produced in rosé, sold in a delightful bottle with an embossed Art Nouveau flower motif; and the Blason de France.

The Perrier-Jouët house style is for elegant, fragrant wines on the delicate side. Fine quality throughout the range.

POL ROGER

Annual production is about 1.2 million bottles and they own 70 hectares of vineyards. Pol Roger's most famous customer was Sir Winston Churchill, and on his death a permanent black band was added to the label of their non-vintage White Foil, when shipped to England. Churchill did much to promote the brand, even naming one of his racehorses Pol Roger. Not unnaturally one of the house's prestige *cuvées* is named after him. The other, rarely seen for obvious reasons in Britain, is PR.

All the Pol Roger wines have great finesse, a beautiful mousse and a fine depth. This house belongs indisputably in the first division. Their non-vintage is excellent, the vintage Blanc de Blancs called Chardonnay one of the very best examples, and the Cuvée Sir Winston Churchill truly excellent.

POMMERY & GRENO

Annual production is about 6.5 million bottles and they own 307 hectares of vineyards. Pommery & Greno, like Clicquot, is another firm whose fortunes were in the hands of a young widow in its early years, and it was one of the first to sell a really dry wine. The firm was in the hands of the de Polignac family until it was acquired by the Gardiner-Lanson group in 1979. Their headquarters in Reims, built in 1878, was largely based on two Scottish castles, Inverary and Mellerstain. André Simon was the Pommery agent in Great Britain between 1902 and 1932.

Pommery is another first-division house. The wines are dry and austere, though not as firm and masculine as, say, Bollinger. The non-vintage is full and rich and the prestige wine, Cuvée Louise Pommery, which also comes in a delicious rosé, is ample, elegant and with real depth and complexity.

LOUIS ROEDERER

Annual production is about 2.5 million bottles and they own 185 hectares of vineyards. Roederer's history goes back to 1765 when a champagne firm called Dubois et Fils was founded. In 1827 Louis Roederer joined his uncle in the business and from then on it prospered greatly. It is now in the fortunate position of being able to produce 80 per cent of its requirements from its own vineyards, which have an average quality rating of 98 per cent. Louis Roederer's most famous wine is its excellent Cristal, a de-luxe champagne sold in a clear bottle.

Roederer is indisputably one of the great champagne houses, and its non-vintage, recently relaunched as Brut Premier, is in my view currently the best of the *grandes marques'* non-vintage wines on the market. This is a firm wine of depth and maturity. Cristal, a lighter wine, is produced in almost every vintage, a practice of which I disapprove, as it seems to make a nonsense of the idea of 'vintage' or 'de luxe' being only the most successful years. Curiously, and to spite my argument, the lesser vintages have produced excellent Cristal, while in vintages when it can be compared with others it scores well but fails to number in the top two or three.

RUINART

Annual production is about 1.1 million bottles. Ruinart is the oldest champagne firm of the leading *marques*, and was founded in 1729. In 1963 Moët & Chandon bought 80 per cent of the equity and took over completely ten years later. The prestige brand is Dom Ruinart, a Blanc de Blancs. Like Taittinger, Ruinart wines are Chardonnay-based, light, fruity and elegant.

TAITTINGER

Annual production is about 5 million bottles and they own 250 hectares of vineyards. Pierre Taittinger took over the business of Fourneaux Forest in 1932 and the group, now run by his son Claude, has since bought the champagne house of Irroy and the Loire businesses of Monmousseau and Bouvet-Ladubay. Taittinger is one of the houses which is better known for its prestige *marque* – in this case, the excellent Blanc de Blancs, Comtes de Champagne – than for its non-vintage. Taittinger also produce Brut Absolu, a wine with a nil dosage.

All Taittinger wines, like those of Ruinart, contain a large proportion of Chardonnay in the blend. I find the non-vintage elegant, fruity and reliable. The Comtes de Champagne is very full and rich, not obviously a Blanc de Blancs: a very fine example which lasts well.

OTHER CHAMPAGNE HOUSES

Ayala, who own Château la Lagune in the Médoc; Besserat de Bellefon, owned by the Pernod-Ricard group; Billecart-Salmon; Boizel, who also produce wine under the labels of Louis Kremer and Camuset; Champagne de Castellane; Deutz & Geldermann, who own the firm of Delas in the Rhône valley, a *Sekt* plant in Germany and Château de l'Aulée in the Loire; Gosset; Henriot, owners of De Venoge and Trouillard and producers of champagne under the Reserve Baron Philippe de Rothschild name; Abel Lepitre, owners of Saint-Marceaux and George Goulet; the Mailly co-operative; Mercier, subsidiary of Moët & Chandon; Bruno Paillard, a new and rising star; Joseph Perrier; Philipponat; and Salon de Mesnil, now owned by Laurent-Perrier, who only produce a Blanc de Blancs vintage wine, aged in wood and with no malolactic fermentation.

Chapter 6

ALSACE

Alsace is one of the loveliest parts of France. Its plains are covered in orchards of walnut, cherry and plum, its lower hillsides with vines and the higher slopes with pine and beech, larch and ash, spruce, maple and fir. In the uplands of the Vosges, the mountains which protect Alsace from the west, there are deep, lonely lakes beside alpine meadows, bestrewn in the spring with flowers, on which graze the cattle which give the milk for Munster cheese, one of the most powerful as well as the most delicious in France. Sheltered by the mountains of the Vosges, the Alsace region enjoys an exceptional climate. This gives the countryside a feeling of richness and plenty, an abundance which extends to the people of Alsace, who are generous and welcoming and who know how to have a good time.

The foothills and side valleys are dotted with attractive villages, some in a mixture of architectural styles, others almost pure Renaissance with gables, half-timbered houses and cobbled courtyards, as at Riquewihr. Throughout, Alsace is festooned with flowers, from windowboxes, hanging baskets, on balconies and in parks, squares and gardens.

Alsace has been fought over for centuries. The Vosges and the Rhine form natural boundaries, and it is the Vosges rather than the Rhine which is the natural barrier between the French language, culture and cuisine and that of Germany. Be that as it may, the region is loyally French, despite remaining staunchly independent, and the wine, like the local cooking – and this is one of the great gastronomic centres of the world – is a subtle combination of German ingredients and French flair. It is this flair, with German grape varieties, which makes Alsace one of Europe's finest wine regions.

You can divide Alsace, longitudinally, into three parts. The plain is that of the Rhine Valley, together with its tributaries, chief of which is the river Ill. This is fertile land, but unsuitable for the vine. The Vosges, whose summits mark the frontier with neighbouring

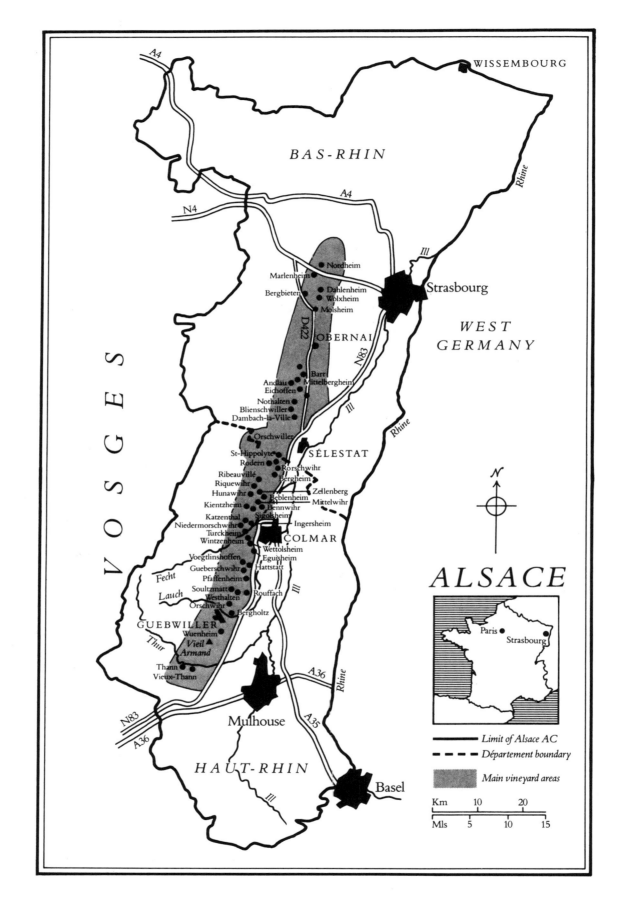

A4

WISSEMBOURG

BAS-RHIN

N4

A4

Rhine

Ill

Nordheim

Marlenheim

Dahlenheim

Bergbieten

Wolxheim

Molsheim

Strasbourg

*WEST
GERMANY*

D422

OBERNAI

N83

Ill

Bart

Andlau

Mittelbergheim

Eichoffen

Nothalten

Blienschwiller

Dambach-la-Ville

Rhine

Orschwiller

SÉLESTAT

St-Hippolyte

Rodern

Rorschwihr

Ribeauvillé

Bergheim

Riquewihr

Zellenberg

Hunawihr

Beblenheim

Mittelwihr

Kientzheim

Bennwihr

Katzenthal

Sigolsheim

Niedermorschwihr

Ingersheim

Turckheim

Wintzenheim

COLMAR

Wettolsheim

N

Voegtlinshoffen

Eguisheim

Gueberschwihr

Hattstatt

Fecht

ALSACE

Pfaffenheim

Lauch

Soultzmatt

Westhalten

Rouffach

Orschwihr

Ill

Bergholtz

GUEBWILLER

Wuenheim

*Vieil
Armand*

Thur

Paris

Strasbourg

Thann

Vieux-Thann

A36

Rhine

Mulhouse

A35

N83

A36

HAUT-RHIN

Basel

Ill

—— *Limit of Alsace AC*

- - - *Département boundary*

Main vineyard areas

Km   10   20

Mls   5   10   15

Lorraine, are gently rounded, well weathered and much eroded. They rise to not much more than 1000 metres, and stretch from the Saar border to the Belfort gap. Between this chain of hills – for they can hardly be called mountains – and the plain, at altitudes of between 200 and 400 metres, are the vineyards, in a continuous line some 100 kilometres long by 3 or 4 kilometres wide. The vineyards lie on south-eastern-facing slopes.

Alsace, although one of France's smaller provinces, is a major wine-producing region. Now divided into the *départements* of Haut-Rhin and Bas-Rhin, the region occupies 14,256 hectares of vines, yielding on average a million hectolitres of wine per annum. This is 4.8 per cent of the total AC production of France (13.4 per cent of the total white wine figure). The wines are almost entirely *appellation contrôlée* white; they are dry, fruity and aromatic; they are all bottled in the region itself, and they are largely named after the grapes from which they are made. There is one simple *appellation*, that of AC Alsace itself, though better wines are deemed Alsace Grand Cru, a new *appellation* introduced in 1981.

History

The history of Alsace is violent and bloody, and in parts tragic. The wine it has produced has suffered along with its people, who have been forced to change nationality almost as often as another frontier people, the Poles, and have consequently frequently had to adjust their wine-making to the decrees of foreign oppressors. The first mention of a form of the name Alsace occurs in the time of the Frankish and Merovingian kings when it was termed Alesia. This is thought either to derive from Alisa, or from a combination of 'Ill' from the river, and *Säss*, old German for 'resident'. In medieval times the wine was known in England and the Low Countries as Aussey.

Clovis, having defeated the Alamans near Wissembourg in A D 496, established Alsace for the Franks at the same time as Christianity was beginning to become a force in the area. The next few centuries, particularly after his successor Charlemagne became Holy Roman Emperor in 800, saw the establishment of numerous monasteries and other religious institutions, all of which required the produce of the grape both for religious use and for the diet of the clergy and their guests – for the many abbeys were the chief hostelries for travellers – as well as for wine's use in medicine.

In 843, the Treaty of Verdun divided the empire of Charlemagne, and Alsace was ceded to Louis the German 'in order that he might have wine in his new kingdom', and for the next seven hundred years was nominally under teutonic rule, though in practice local dukes and other feudal lords held the sway. Both bishops and nobles owned land and encouraged the cultivation of the vine. Export markets developed, for the wine could be shipped via the Rhine as far as England and Denmark, perhaps even into the Baltic. By 1400 according to the historian Monsignor Médard Barth, there were 430 communes producing wine in the Alsace region. At this time the wines of Mainz and Worms were of little importance and probably most of what was 'Rhenish' came from Alsace. It was a prosperous time, and not only the clergy and the nobility, but the merchants and smallholders were also able to benefit. But it was not to last.

First there were invasions by bands of marauding Armagnacs, then there were a series of natural disasters, a great freeze followed by a terrible flooding when the thaw came in 1480, a six-month-long frost in 1487/88 and a peasants' revolt in 1525, when 20,000 were killed. Finally the local nobility grew too greedy. Customs duties were raised and raised again – at one period between Strasbourg and Cologne there were sixty-two points along the route when dues had to be paid. Then Strasbourg decreed that all Alsace wine had to pass through its gates, in order to collect a levy, and in addition decided that a proportion of each shipment had to be sold to the inhabitants at a knock-down price. Alsace had killed the golden goose, and north Germany began to develop its own vineyards.

Worse was to follow. Alsace was one of the battlefields of the Thirty Years War (1618–1648), devastated, pillaged, looted and burned. The vineyard owners deserted the countryside for the safety of the towns, production fell to negligible totals and the misery was increased by outbreaks of plague.

Peace was restored by the Treaty of Westphalia, and Alsace passed into the French kingdom. There was a concerted move to encourage people, especially catholics, to settle in the area – for the population had declined to barely a quarter of a million – and this seems to have been successful, settlers arriving from Austria, Lorraine and particularly from Switzerland, which as the northern market had evaporated was to become an important export target. On a visit to Alsace, Louis XIV was to exclaim: '*Ah, l'Alsace . . . quel beau jardin*', echoing Montaigne, who in 1584 had noted: 'the beautiful and extensive plain, bordered on the left by slopes covered in vines'.

It was about this time that a number of well-known, present-day wine firms first set up in business (Hugel in 1639, Kuehn in 1675, Dopff around the turn of the century) and specific grape varieties begin to be first mentioned. Muscat had been recorded in 1523, Traminer in the seventeenth century, Riesling and Tokay about 1750. In 1766 a decree defined the viticultural area of Alsace, discouraged the planting of inferior, high-yielding varieties and promoted vineyard expansion on the slopes. The area under vines began to expand, and this expansion accelerated after the French Revolution, when the property of the nobility and the church was sequestered and sold off, and when the trade associations and guilds were abolished, leaving 'each person to carry on such business or pursue such profession, art or craft as he thinks fit'. Unfortunately a by-product of the fragmentation of these large domaines and the introduction of the Code Napoléon, regulating that an equal share of an estate must pass to all heirs on the death of the owner, was a division and sub-division of the Alsace vineyard into ever-smaller and inefficient units, a problem which persists today.

In 1870, as a result of the Franco-Prussian war, Alsace was annexed by Germany. This was a sad time for the province. The Germans imposed their language, their restrictions and their culture in a particularly harsh and unpleasant manner. One in every eight inhabitants fled the country. For the vine-grower the situation was even worse. Though most of the expansion during the previous half-century had been on the plain, and with inferior grapes, there had at least been some move towards the planting of noble varieties. This was discouraged. And then, to exacerbate the situation further, came phylloxera. In the 'Land of Unshed Tears', as an American put it, the *vignoble* declined to 18,700 hectares by 1900, and what it produced, for the most part, was fairly ordinary wine, largely from Burger (Ebling), with some Chasselas and Sylvaner.

After the First World War Alsace returned to France, and the growers found themselves in a difficult position. Under German rule they had been the dominant wine-producing area, providing 40 per cent of the total crop of what was then Germany. Now they were once again part of the most prolific wine-producing country in the world, and had to compete on an equal basis with the cheap wines of the Midi and French North Africa – and with wines which were unknown, as well as very different from those provided by the rest of the country.

In 1925 the decision was taken to go for quality rather than quantity, with the encouragement of the Station de Récherches Oenologiques and the Institut Vinicole de Colmar. The growers' association opted to concentrate on planting the noble grape varieties and condemned the planting of hybrids. The vineyard area continued to fall, but the standard of the wine produced considerably improved.

The regime imposed by the Nazi occupation forces in the Second World War was harsher still than it had been during the 1870–1918 period. Everything French, even the language, was prohibited. The Alsatian dialect, incomprehensible to an outsider, was banned and young men were sent to serve on the Russian front, where many perished and others ended up in labour camps. In the last winter of the war, as the Germans retreated across the Rhine, many villages, including Ammerschwihr, Bennwihr, Sigolsheim and Mittelwihr, were almost totally destroyed, as was much of Colmar. When the allied troops arrived in Strasbourg they were reminded by a poster put up by the Mayor, 'Soldiers, do not forget you are in a French town, though you may hear a German language'.

Since 1945 the policy of quality has been continued. Regulations were drawn up in that year prohibiting the Burger (Ebling) – a large number of prolific German varieties had already been banned in 1932 – and draft proposals on the definition and delimitation of the area, rules and regulations for the planting of the vine and the making of the wine, were established. This was eventually codified into the INAO statutes, and Alsace became *appellation contrôlée* in 1962, the last of the great French vineyard areas to be so covered.

In 1972 the decision was taken to make bottling of Alsace wines in the region mandatory – in order to keep control of the entire process in local hands. More recently certain sites have been designated *grand cru* and the necessary criteria for the use of the words Vendange Tardive and Sélection de Grains Nobles have been established.

The Wine Region

An east to west cross-section across the Alsace region – or a glance at a map – will show that the Rhine basin is confined on the one side by the Vosges and on the other by the hills of the Black Forest. Both these ridges are comprised of either granite or *grès rouge*, a very compact red sandstone, much used in the local buildings. In the Tertiary period about 60 million years ago, as the Alps were suddenly forced above the surrounding waters, the Black Forest and Vosges chains rose as well, but leaving a fault between them. This remained flooded, and was later further eroded and deposited as glaciers came and went.

The result of these geological movements is a soil structure which is varied and complex. Somewhere in Alsace is almost every type of soil composition, clay and limestone, sand and gravel, chalk, marl and loess. There is granite at Turckheim and Wintzenheim, adjoining soil which is largely limestone; at Riquewihr there is more limestone as well as marly clay-limestone mixtures; there are zones of loess, a greyish–yellow loam at Guebwiller and to the north of Molsheim; more limestone, rich in fossils, at Eguisheim and Barr; and *grès rouge* as well as schistous soil can be found in the region of Andlau. One commune can have several types of soil, making the choice of variety and rootstock complicated, but this gives the local growers the chance of having a wide range of grapes to play with. Each variety is suited to a particular soil and site: Gewürztraminer to the richer, more alluvial clayey soil nearer to the valley floor, the Riesling to the chalk and limestone of the upper slopes, the Sylvaner to a heavy loam, and so on. The soil determines the grape variety, as well as the yield, quality and style of the wine produced.

What this means is that the character and flavour of an Alsace wine will vary considerably as one journeys through the region, and that, for instance, a Gewürztraminer from Ribeauvillé or Riquewihr, whoever makes it, will be markedly less perfumed – what the French call *pommadé* – than one from land to the south. As there are a number of different styles, particularly for this grape, and some may be more to your taste than others, it makes sense to have an idea of where one's source lies along the ladder from Thann, west of Mulhouse, northwards to Nordheim, west of Strasbourg. Though the *négociants* obviously buy in grapes, must or wine, most do so from within a confined area, and, for obvious reasons, individual growers and co-operatives are even more restricted.

The climate of the Alsace vineyard is largely determined by the protection it is given by the Vosges from the prevailing westerly winds. Alsace enjoys a propitious climate, and a weather pattern which is far drier and sunnier than other regions of France on the same latitude. After Perpignan, Colmar is the driest city in France. Precipitation measures 500 mm per annum in Alsace while it is 2000 mm on the western side of the Vosges.

Though Alsace is on the same latitude as Paris – and the northernmost vineyard region in France after Champagne – the climate is continental, with long, hard winters, warm, sunny summers and often exceptionally fine autumns. While the mean average temperature in Colmar is not exceptionally warm – at 10.8°C it is at the same level as Dijon but a whole degree less than Angers – it is the weather between April and October which is crucial to the production of quality wine, and particularly the weather after the grapes have changed colour at the beginning of September. Here Alsace is favoured, with on average fifty more days of sunshine during the entire summer season than in the Rheingau, and better ripening conditions than Dijon, the Loire and even Hermitage in the Rhône.

Frost, hail and poor weather during the flowering can be more of a problem. Though the incidence of a really hard winter's frost is slight, and has occurred only three times since 1918 to the extent of damaging the vines, frost in the spring can be a problem. By planting the vines on the slopes above the valley the danger is reduced, and as an added precaution the vines are trained high, one to two metres above the ground. Many of the Alsace grape varieties, particularly the Muscat, are extremely susceptible to both *coulure*, failure of the flowers to set into fruit, and *millerandage*, failure of the fruit to develop, and this problem is made worse if the weather is wet and humid during the flowering season in June. Hail is unpredictable and can cause one vineyard to be completely devastated, while leaving a neighbour's untouched. In Alsace there are two means of insurance against this: first, most growers have plots of vineyards in several areas, so they are unlikely to experience a total destruction of their crop. Second, some combine forces with neighbours to hire small aeroplanes to seed the hail-bearing clouds.

In Alsace the grape variety is of even more crucial importance than in the rest of France. In Bordeaux and Burgundy the variety is taken for granted, the site is all-important, and the wine is sold under a vineyard or château name. In Alsace the wines are sold under the names of the grapes from which they are made, together with some indication of a level of quality such as *grand cru*, Réserve, and so on. The site is of subsidiary interest.

There are either eight grape names or there are eleven varieties, depending on which way you look at it, for AC Alsace wine. The eight names are Gewürztraminer, Riesling, Tokay d'Alsace, Muscat, Pinot Blanc, Sylvaner, Chasselas and Pinot Noir. Tokay d'Alsace is made from Pinot Gris and Muscat can be made from either Muscat Ottonel or Muscat d'Alsace à Petit Grains, or from both. Chasselas comes from either the white or rosé version, while Pinot Blanc can come from Pinot Noir vinified as a white wine, or from Pinot Auxerrois or even from Pinot Gris, as well as from Pinot Blanc itself.

ALSACE AND EASTERN FRANCE

PRODUCTION AND SURFACE AREA (1996 HARVEST)

	Surface area in hectares	Percentage 1996	Production '000 hectolitres	
			RED & ROSÉ	WHITE
Alsace				
By grape variety				
MIXED CULITVATION	345	3.2	—	38
CHASSELAS	155	1.2	—	14
SYLVANER	2187	18.7	—	192
PINOT BLANC	2967	22.5	—	263
TOKAY D' ALSACE (PINOT GRIS)	1305	8.8	—	103
MUSCAT	340	2.6	—	30
GEWÜRZTRAMINER	2526	10.7	—	126
RIESLING	3294	25.3	—	297
PINOT NOIR	1225	9.3	109	—
Total	14,344		109	1063
Total Red and White Wines			1172	

	Surface area in hectares	*Production '000 hectolitres*	
		RED & ROSÉ	WHITE
By category			
AC ALSACE	12,008	91	901
AC ALSACE GRAND CRU	644	—	37
AC CRÉMANT D'ALSACE	1692	17	126
Wines of Eastern France			
VDQS			
CÔTES DE TOUL	92	3	(299 hl)
VIN DE LA MOSELLE	22	(340 hl)	(799 hl)
Total	14,458	111	1065
Total Red and White Wines		1176	

The *vignoble* has grown by 35.6 per cent in the last 20 years, and the proportions of the lesser, 'ignoble' varieties such as Sylvaner and Chasselas have diminished considerably, being replaced with Pinot Blanc and Riesling and, to a limited extent, Pinot Noir. The superior *appellation*, Alsace Grand Cru can only be made from the last five noble varieties. It is estimated that 80 per cent of the total production is from unblended varieties. If bottled under a varietal name, the wine must be 100 per cent of that stated grape.

The Alsace vineyard begins at Thann, west of Mulhouse, and runs north for some 100 kilometres to Nordheim, west of Strasbourg, with a further isolated pocket in the extreme north near Wissembourg on the German frontier. Most of the vineyards, the southern and better section, is in the *département* of Haut-Rhin (8000 hectares). North of Sélestat and the castle at Haut-Koenigsbourg lies the Bas-Rhin (5000 hectares). Here there is less protection from the Vosges and so the climate is marginally less warm and less dry, and a lower proportion of the best varieties such as Riesling and Gewürztraminer are planted. The heart of the Alsace vineyards lies just above and below Colmar, in the geographical centre of the region. Ribeauvillé, Hunawihr, Riquewihr, Kaysersberg, Ammerschwihr, Turckheim, Wintzenheim and Eguisheim follow each other along the wine route and produce many of the finest wines in Alsace.

When the *appellation contrôlée* decrees became law in 1962, they established a single *appellation* for the whole of Alsace – Alsace, or Vin d'Alsace. The wines need to achieve 8.5 degrees of alcohol. The maximum yield per hectare is fixed at 100 hectolitres per hectare, whatever the grape variety, but, unlike elsewhere in France, this can be averaged out over the total holding of any one grower, whatever the grape variety, so that if, for instance, one of his Riesling vineyards only produces 50 hectolitres per hectare, theoretically, another of Gewürztraminer can legally yield 150 hectolitres per hectare. If the name of a variety is stated on the label, then the wine has to consist of 100 per cent of that variety, and if a vintage year is stated, then the wine must come solely from that vintage.

GRANDS CRUS

A decree of 30 June 1981, which, like the 1962 *appellation* regulations, largely followed the original order drawn up in 1945, set out the definition of *grand cru*. To be called *grand cru* a wine would have to attain a minimum natural strength of 10 degrees for Riesling and Muscat, and 11 degrees for other varieties, but could only be made from Pinot Gris, Muscat, Gewürztraminer, Riesling and Pinot Noir. The maximum yield was reduced to 70 hectolitres per hectare.

In 1975 the first moves were made towards redefining *grand cru* and restricting it to the produce of certain specific well-favoured sites. A list of some ninety-four vineyards thought suitable for classification was drawn up, and the new proposals were originally intended to come into force from the 1978 vintage. As a result of considerable opposition, largely from the merchants who would be then deprived of the opportunity of making their own, large-scale, *grand cru* blends, this initiative floundered somewhat. A decree of 23 November 1983 defined twenty-five *lieux-dits*. This was expanded by a further twenty-five in November 1985.

Vineyard	Commune	Surface area in hectares (where delimitation is complete)	1988 harvest in hectolitres
Bas-Rhin département			
KASTELBERG	Andlau	6	252
MOENCHBERG	Andlau/Eichhoffen	12	266
WIBELSBERG	Andlau	12	499
KIRCHBERG	Barr	40	769
ALTENBERG	Bergbieten	29	897
WINZENBERG	Blienschwiller	—	291
ENGELBERG	Dahlenheim	—	106
FRANKSTEIN	Dambach-la-Ville	—	1291
STEINHOTZ	Marlenheim	—	600
BRUDERTHAL	Molsheim	—	171
ZOTZENBERG	Mittelbergheim	—	575
MUENCHBERG	Nothalten	—	307
PRAELATENBERG	Orschwiller	—	234
ALTENBERG	Wolxheim	—	648
Haut-Rhin département			
SONNENGLANZ	Beblenheim	33	535
MARCKRAIN	Bennwihr	—	498
ALTENBERG	Bergheim	35	1013
KANTZLERBERG	Bergheim	3	139
EICHBERG	Eguisheim	57	1260
PFERSIGBERG	Eguisheim	—	1520
GOLDERT	Gueberschwihr	45	897
KESSLER	Guebwiller	28	491
KITTERLÉ	Guebwiller	26	718

Vineyard	Commune	Surface area in hectares)	1988 harvest in hectolitres
SAERING	Guebwiller	27	459
SPIEGEL	Guebwiller	18	343
HATSCHBOURG	Hattstatt/Voegtlinshoffen	47	1000
ROSACKER	Hunawihr	26	855
FLORIMONT	Ingersheim	—	604
WINECK-SCHLOSSBERG	Katzenthal	—	478
SOMMERBERG	Katzenthal/ Niedermorschwihr	28	612
SCHLOSSBERG	Kaysersberg/Kientzheim	80	1758
FURSTENTUM	Kientzheim/Sigolsheim	—	353
MANDELBERG	Mittelwihr	—	469
PFINGSTBERG	Orschwihr	—	554
STEINERT	Pfaffenheim	—	379
GEISBERG	Ribeauvillé	8	89
KIRCHBERG	Ribeauvillé	11	295
OSTERBERG	Ribeauvillé	—	360
SCHOENENBOURG	Riquewihr	—	1439
SPOREN	Riquewihr	—	809
GLOECKELBERG	Rodern/Saint-Hippolyte	23	156
VORBOURG	Rouffach/Westhalten	—	1207
MAMBOURG	Sigolsheim	—	1048
RANGEN	Thann/Vieux Thann	19	141
BRAND	Turckheim	58	1676
ZINNKOEPFLÉ	Westhalten-Soultzmatt	—	1919
STEINGRUBLER	Wettolsheim	—	470
HENGST	Wintzenheim	76	1358
OLLWILLER	Wintzenheim	36	884
FROEHN	Zellenberg	—	100
Total		(when established) 1600 approx.	32,873

Wine Styles

VENDANGE TARDIVE and SÉLECTION DE GRAINS NOBLES

The culmination of long years of lobbying by a number of producers, pioneered by the late Jean Hugel, resulted in a framework which became law in 1984, defining the necessary criteria for the production of Vendange Tardive or late-harvested Alsace wines and Sélection de Grains Nobles (individually selected noble-rotted grapes). These can only be produced from Gewürztraminer, Tokay d'Alsace, Riesling and Muscat. In the case of the first two, the grape juice must achieve a ripeness equivalent to 14.3 degrees of potential alcohol in order to be labelled Vendange Tardive, and 16.4 degrees for Grains Nobles. For Riesling and Muscat the levels are 12.9 degrees and 15.1 degrees.

These are the top Alsace wines, the very epitome of excellence. Vendange Tardive wines will occur in most good years, and are roughly the equivalent of German Auslese wines, though the requirements are for much riper grapes, and as Alsace wines are fermented out to dryness, the wines will be rich rather than sweet. Sélection de Grains Nobles, made from botrytized grapes, will only occur in exceptional years such as 1976, '83 and '89. Here the wines certainly will be sweet, and with the power, intensity of character and 'size' more of a Sauternes than a German Beerenäuslese wine.

RÉSERVE, CUVÉE SPÉCIALE

Most producers, whether merchants or co-operatives, will produce a wide range of wines of different qualities and they will have most, if not all, the grape varieties for sale. Designations such as Réserve or Cuvée this and that are used to differentiate between the qualities, but they have no legal definition. Many of these fancy titles are long established, and will no doubt continue to be used, even for Vendange Tardive wines.

CRÉMANT D'ALSACE

The pioneer of Alsace sparkling wines was Julien Dopff of Dopff au Moulin. He was a lifelong friend of the Heidsieck family of Reims and, having seen the champagne method demonstrated at the Paris Exhibition in 1900, started to make his own sparkling wines in Alsace. The wine has had its own AC since 1976, since when production has expanded enormously. In 1983 sales topped 5 million bottles for the first time, over five times what it had been in 1977. Today the figure approaching is 20 million.

Crémant d'Alsace is a wine that is fully sparkling, that is the pressure would be in the region of five to six atmospheres, not between 3.5 and 4.5 as a Crémant de Champagne would be. It is normally made largely if not exclusively from Pinot Blanc and this base wine must conform to the standards required by a still Alsace wine. Other permitted varieties are Riesling, Pinot Gris and Pinot Noir, and Pinot Noir exclusively for the rosé version. All Crémant d'Alsace must be made by the champagne method.

EDELZWICKER

Edelzwicker is an Alsace wine made from a blend of the better grape varieties, most commonly from Pinot Blanc and Sylvaner but perhaps also from the lesser *cuvées* (young vines, etc.) of the grander grapes such as Riesling and Pinot Gris. It is often sold under a brand name such as Hugel's Flambeau d'Alsace or Beyer's Spécial Fruits de Mer.

KLEVNER DE HEILIGENSTEIN

In and around Heiligenstein in the Bas-Rhin some 13 hectares are planted with the Savignin Rosé, a variety related to the Gewürztraminer and used further south in Jura to make Vin Jaune. In Heiligenstein the wine is dry, white and fairly spicy, though without any great definition or distinction. The firm of Charles Wantz in Barr is the only source of Klevner I know.

WHEN TO DRINK THE WINES

For the majority of Alsace wines the variation in style and quality from one vintage to the next is negligible. As with inexpensive white wine produced elsewhere – in Muscadet, Bergerac or the Mâconnais – modern techniques of vinification and early bottling ensure crisp, fruity Edelzwickers and basic qualities of Pinot Blanc, Sylvaner and Riesling year in, year out and these are produced for drinking within a couple of years. Gewürztraminer, though, does need a good *fin de saison* to fully ripen, otherwise it will be somewhat hard and lacking charm. Few vintages in Alsace, luckily, are really disastrous.

ALSACE VINTAGES

The following vintage notes, therefore, apply to the better grades of quality; to Réserve, Vendange Tardive and so on. These are the sort of Alsace wines which can be kept – indeed should be – to mature in bottle.

1997: A large harvest and a very good one indeed, the third in a row. The harvest was early. An Indian summer continued well into November, allowing plenty of wine of *vendange tardive* quality to be made.

1996: A large vintage and a fine one, saved by a splendid autumn after a largely indifferent summer. High degrees of ripeness coupled with high acidities but little botrytis have produced very pure wines which will keep well. Only the Gewurztraminers are a bit of a disappointment.

1995: An uneven flowering reduced the crop. A fine autumn created significant botrytis, and this has detracted from the finesse of some of the lesser wines. A year of fine quality, nevertheless, except in Gewurztraminer, but certainly in Riesling.

1994: Poor lesser wines, cropped in the rain. Adequate wines in the better grades, collected in better weather during the first three weeks of October.

1993: Everything indicated an exceptionally fine vintage until the rains began on the 23rd September. Much was salvaged, but the weather did not clear for three weeks. Good results among the *vendanges tardives*. But, like 1994, not the greatest.

1992: Unlike in the rest of France, it was dry during the harvest, and this is the best vintage of the 1991-1994 years, inclusive. The quantity was good.

1991: A late harvest, and one with irregularly ripened fruit as a result of spring frost and a prolonged flowering. Good wines though despite only a modicum of richness.

1990: A great vintage. One of high sugar weight, hence alcohol, a high degree of acidity and a very high concentration of fine fruit. Delicious pure wines which will keep well.

1989: Another successful vintage. Very high sugar levels plus widespread botrytis meant a huge quantity of *vendange tardive* and *sélection de grains nobles* wines.

EARLIER VINTAGES:
The best years are 1988, '85, '83, '81, '79, '76, '75 and '71.

The Wine Trade

Like most of France, the dissolution of the large ecclesiastical and lay estates after the Revolution and the effects of the Code Napoléon have led to a region of smallholdings. Since 1969 concerted efforts have been made to reduce the number of tiny individual plots by encouraging amalgamation, and at the same time the vineyard area has been expanded. In 1969 12,000 growers shared 9500 hectares of vineyards, producing 700,000 hectolitres. In 1988 8500 growers shared 13,000 hectares of vineyards and production now averages a million hectolitres. Yet, still today 65 per cent of growers have less than 1 hectare each, and only a few hundred own more than 5 hectares. Few proprietors therefore can make a living solely out of wine. Most will need to have other jobs, leaving the vineyard as a weekend 'hobby' or to be worked in their spare time. Some 1870 growers sell their own wine, accounting for about 30 per cent of the total production (though 80 per cent of this growers' total is accounted for by only 175 proprietors). The *négociants* buy both wine and grapes and sell 40 per cent of the harvest, leaving 30 per cent to the co-operatives, who have some 2500 members.

The co-operative movement started at the beginning of the twentieth century, during the period of German occupation, but has really only come to the fore since the Second World War. The first two co-operatives were in Eguisheim and Dambach-la-Ville, and originally they were merely central, collective storage units for the surplus production over and above what the *négociants* were immediately prepared to buy. After 1945 growers of Bennwihr and Sigolsheim, two villages which had been completely devastated in the last six months of the war, grouped together to create a couple of vinification units, primarily with the aim of selling in bulk to their traditional customers, the merchants. Faced with a reluctance on the part of the latter, they began to bottle and sell the wines themselves. There are now seventeen in the Alsace region, and many of these have justifiably high reputations – one could single out those of Eguisheim, Beblenheim, Pfaffenheim, Westhalten and Bennwihr. Recently, two *négociants*, Kuehn of Ammerschwihr (by the Ingersheim co-operative) and Heim of Westhalten, have been absorbed by their local co-operatives.

Leading Alsace Producers

Alsace, like Champagne, is a region where the producer's name on the bottle is all-important. We leave it to him to decide where the wine is to come from and how the blend is to be made up, and once having chosen a grape variety, merely have to decide which of his categories of quality, from basic to Réserve Exceptionelle, we wish to have. Though the co-operatives and one or two of the larger growers like Zind-Humbrecht, Domaine Weinbach and Schlumberger now export widely, it is the merchants who have traditionally dominated the export market. And it is they who have created the reputation of Alsace wine. The following personal selection is listed in alphabetical order.

LÉON BEYER, EGUISHEIM

The Beyer family have been growers in Eguisheim since 1580 and *négociants* since 1867, and possess 50 hectares of their own, mainly planted in Gewürztraminer and Riesling. The style of Beyer wines is full-bodied, fairly alcoholic, rich and dry. The Rieslings are firm and austere and the Gewürztraminers more open and scented than some. Their superior Riesling sells under the Cuvée des Écaillers label and the best Gewürztraminer is the Cuvée des Comtes d'Eguisheim. These two keep well in bottle. Production is about 65,000 cases a year.

DOPFF ET IRION, RIQUEWIHR

Dopff et Irion is one of the largest wine companies in Alsace. They own some 130 hectares of vineyard, about two-thirds of which came from the Charles Jux estate near Colmar which it took over in the early 1970s. Their wines are dry, on the light side, soft and fruity in style and appear to be for early drinking. Sometimes they appear a little slight, but this does not seem to prevent them taking bottle age, for I have been lucky enough to taste a number of twenty-year-old examples, thanks to the generous hospitality of Guy Dopff, which have shown no signs of fade. Their top wines are Les Amandiers (Muscat), Les Murailles (Riesling) and Les Sorcières (Gewürztraminer), once single-vineyard wines, but now brands but produced from their own vineyards. Dopff et Irion's Vendange Tardive wines are drier than most.

DOPFF 'AU MOULIN', RIQUEWIHR

Dopff 'au moulin' – the firm has the same origins as Dopff et Irion, though they have been separate companies for some considerable time – is another large concern, with a production of some 200,000 cases per annum. It owns 75 hectares of vineyard, most importantly in the Schoenenbourg above the town where Riesling is planted and on the Eichberg at Turckheim for Gewürztraminer. It is also an important producer of Crémant d'Alsace. The wines are firmer and fuller than those of Dopff et Irion, and the malolactic fermentation is discouraged. Sometimes I have found the wines lacking a little fruit, though the top wines are an exception.

HUGEL ET FILS, RIQUEWIHR

If Hugel is the first Alsace name that comes to mind it is not without reason, for their wines until recently have almost outsold all the others put together on the British and American markets. There have been Hugels in Riquewihr since 1637 and the late Jean Hugel was an indefatigable traveller and ambassador for Alsace wines. One of his sons, 'Johnnie', now continues his father's noble work. The Hugels have 25 hectares in Riquewihr, notably in the Schoenenbourg and Sporen vineyards, and the firm produces about 100,000 cases a year.

The Hugel methods combine the best of the old with the best of the new. Their Sainte-Cathérine cask, made in 1715, and richly carved, has been in constant use ever since – the oldest in the world, they proudly claim. After pressing the must is centrifuged in order to clarify it, vinified slowly at a low temperature (20°C to 22°C), and in lesser years like 1984 and '80 the malolactic fermentation is allowed to proceed. As Johnnie Hugel puts it: 'Customers don't like sweet wines; but they don't like acid wines either.' Thereafter there is no cold treatment, which in their view is harmful to the aromas of the wine, and only a light filtration before bottling. The quality range is from standard, to Cuvée Tradition, Réserve Personnelle, Vendange Tardive and finally, in the best vintages, Sélection de Grains Nobles, of which they have made a speciality.

Hugel wines are softer and richer than some, fullish and easy to appreciate. This suppleness may come from the wines having partly undergone their malolactic fermentation, yet it does not preclude the ability to sustain bottle age. Recent vintages of Hugel's Pinot Noir have also been most impressive.

KUENTZ-BAS, HUSSEREN-LES-CHÂTEAUX

Husseren lies above Eguisheim, and claims to be the highest wine village in Alsace. It is home to one of the best of the smaller *négociants* in the region, formed in 1919 after the marriage of André Bas to a girl named Kuentz. The domaine possess about 12½ hectares which provide about 30 per cent of their requirements. I have repeatedly been impressed by the Kuentz-Bas wines which have a firm, upright, well-made character with plenty of breed. In ascending order of quality, the firm's better wines are Cuvée Tradition, Réserve Personnelle (exclusively from their own vineyards) and Vendange Tardive.

DOMAINES VITICOLES SCHLUMBERGER, GUEBWILLER

The Schlumbergers are growers rather than merchants, but growers on a fairly massive scale. Above the rather drab town of Guebwiller at the southern end of the vineyard route looms a huge steep hill. Vineyards were first bought on this site by a local mill owner, Nicolas Schlumberger, in Napoleonic times, when the estates belonging to the Abbey of Murbach were put up for sale. Successive generations gradually built up the domaine, particularly between the First and Second World Wars, when as a result of the phylloxera epidemic a lot of land had been allowed to go to waste and could be picked up cheaply. The result is the largest single-vineyard property on slopes in the whole of France, as well as the largest domaine in Alsace, some 140 hectares in all, and all in one piece.

The slopes above Guebwiller are too steep to be worked mechanically, even with the latest developments in tractors, and still have to be worked by horses. More than one writer has remarked on the resemblance to the Hermitage hill above Tain. Similarly the vines are in terraces, and range in aspect from east to south-west. There are a number of different site names, including Kitterlé, perhaps the best, Kessler, Spiegel and Saering, all now *grand cru* vineyards. Though the hill consists mainly of sandstone and has little clay, Schlumberger is best known for its Gewürztraminers. Cuvée Christine and Cuvée Anne are the top wines and only produced in exceptional years. While the latter, in 1976, was an exceptionally fine, fat, aromatic concentrated wine, full of depth and fruit, the former in that vintage was unbelievable. It was made from must with an Oeschlé rating of 156 degrees, an Alsatian record, and is amber in colour: in Germanic terms not so much a Beerenauslese as a Trockenbeerenauslese! There is a *tête de cuvée* Riesling called Cuvée Ernest but this has not been produced since 1971. Schlumbergers' annual output is about 80,000 cases.

F.E. TRIMBACH, RIBEAUVILLÉ

The magnificent, austere wines of Trimbach are in complete contrast to those of Hugel, and are almost equally well known. The firm was founded as long ago as 1626, and is now run by Bernard, who makes the wine, and his younger brother Hubert, as tireless a salesman as Johnnie Hugel. Trimbach have 12.5 hectares of their own and a further 16 hectares which they have on lease in Ribeauvillé, Hunawihr, Mittelwihr and Bergheim. Bernard Trimbach's wine-making is impeccable, and the result – firm, masculine, bone-dry and richly fruity wines of enormous breeding – are for me the yardsticks by which I judge all others in the region.

Trimbach wines are vinified in stainless steel, not allowed to undergo their malolactic fermentation, and the better Cuvées matured in large oak casks. Bottling is early to preserve freshness. Quality categories range from standard, Réserve and Réserve Personnelle to their top wines, Gewürztraminer Cuvée des Seigneurs de Ribeaupierre, from the Trottsacher vineyard in Ribeauvillé (a small part of the Oesterberg vineyard which slopes down directly above their cellars), Gewürztraminer Vendange Tardive,

Riesling Cuvée Frédéric Émile, also from the Oesterberg vineyard, and, the finest of them all, probably the finest wine in Alsace, Riesling Clos Sainte-Hune, from a 1½-hectare vineyard below the church and its graveyard at Hunawihr. A Clos Sainte-Hune is always a wine of great style and faultless finesse. In lesser vintages it is surprisingly good. In years such as 1996, '90, '88, '85, '83 and '76 it is glorious. Total production at Trimbach is around 63,000 cases a year.

DOMAINE WEINBACH, THÉO FALLER, KAYSERSBERG

This is a family of growers rather than *négociants*, and their wines are some of the greatest in all Alsace, selling under the name Domaine Weinbach. The Faller brothers bought the estate in 1885 and it is now run by Madame Colette Faller, widow of Théo, who died in 1979 and did much to bring up the domaine to its present very high level. Faller wines are firm, austere and aristocratic, made for maturing in bottle over a long period of time. This 24-hectare domaine produces about 13,000 cases a year. Cuvées Théo (Riesling and Tokay), Sainte Cathérine (Riesling) and Laurence (Gewürztraminer), and in the very best years a Cuvée d'Or, represent the pick of the selection.

DOMAINE ZIND-HUMBRECHT, WINTZENHEIM

Though the origins of this family firm, again growers rather than merchants, go back to the seventeenth century, it is really only since the 1960s that it has become a major force. In 1959 Léonard Humbrecht, twelfth in his line, married Geneviève Zind, and an 18-hectare domaine was established. This has since been increased to 29 hectares by the purchase of land on the Rangen vineyard in Thann. Humbrecht is a passionate believer in the importance of the soil structure in the character of the resultant wine, as a tasting of his wines will demonstrate, as well as the need to maintain a low-temperature fermentation for as long as possible in order to preserve all the aromas. His wines are usually fairly full and firm, dry and masculine, and need bottle age, but they are of high quality. Their Rieslings are excellent, the Gewürztraminers less exciting. Production is some 17,000 cases a year.

OTHER ALSACE PRODUCERS

Alsace is fortunate in having a large number of excellent producers for the standard of wine-making is high. In an unknown restaurant, faced with an anonymous wine list, it is often the safest bet to plump for an Alsace wine. I have rarely been disappointed.

Kaysersberg, Beghen Say prop', a grower of whom I had never heard, and neither, it appears, has Liz Berry in her comprehensive book, *Wines of Alsace*. The wine was firm, fresh, full of fruit and thoroughly delicious.

OTHER LEADING GROWERS AND MERCHANTS IN ALSACE

These are listed in geographical order, running from north to south. Those marked with an asterisk are particularly recommended.

Producer	*Commune*
LAUGEL	Marlenheim
KLIPFEL	Barr
WILLM	Barr
MARC KREYDENWEISS*	Andlau
DOMAINE OESTERTAG	Epfig
BOECKEL (also sells as ANDRÉ SCHMIDT)	Mittelbergheim
W. GISSELBRECHT	Dambach-la-Ville
L. GISSELBRECHT	Dambach-la-Ville
ROLLY-GASSMANN	Rorschwihr
GUSTAVE LORENTZ	Bergheim
MARCEL DEISS	Bergheim
LOUIS SIPP	Ribeauvillé
ROBERT FALLER	Ribeauvillé
ANDRÉ KIENTZLER*	Ribeauvillé
BOTT FRÈRES	Ribeauvillé
PREISS ZIMMER	Riquewihr
ROBERT SCHMIDT	Riquewihr
PREISS HENNY (associated with LÉON BEYER)	Mittelwihr
PIERRE SPARR	Sigolsheim
BLANCK	Kientzheim
KUEHN	Ammerschwihr
SICK-DREYER	Ammerschwihr
ALBERT BOXLER	Niedermorschwihr
CHARLES SCHLERET	Turckheim
JOS. MEYER	Wintzenheim
A. GASCHY (also sells as F. BRUCKER)	Wettolsheim
THÉO CATTIN	Voegtlinshoffen
A & O MURE	Rouffach
HEIM	Westhalten
LUCIEN ALBRECHT	Orschwihr

There are co-operatives at Andlau-Barr, Beblenheim, Bennwihr, Dambach-la-Ville, Eguisheim, Ingersheim, Kientzheim, Kaysersberg, Orschwiller, Pfaffenheim, Gueberschwihr, Ribeauvillé, Sigolsheim, Traenheim, Turckheim, Vieil-Armand and Westhalten.

Additionally there is the Union Vinicole Divinal at Obernai, a union of seven other co-operatives from all over the Alsace region. Of these the best are at Beblenheim, Eguisheim, Pfaffenheim and Westhalten.

VIN DE LA MOSELLE VDQS

Before we leave the extreme north-east of France a few lines must be given to one of the rarest wines of France, the VDQS wines of the French Moselle. The *vignoble* here is a brief echo of that of Luxembourg. The wines are of little consequence, and even the locals do not take them seriously, only one local restaurant, to my knowledge, bothering to stock them. Three small sectors near Sierck, Metz and Vic-sur-Seille in the *département* of Moselle are authorized for the wine, which can be red or white; if red made from Gamay or Pinot Noir; if white from Pinot Gris, Auxerrois, Meunier Blanc, Sylvaner, Riesling or Gewürztraminer. With a great deal of difficulty, I managed to track down a sample of each colour on a recent visit on my way to Alsace. I was not impressed. Production averages 1000 hectolitres per annum from 22 hectares of vines.

CÔTES DE TOUL VDQS

Another obscure wine is the Côtes de Toul, made in some nine communes near the town of Toul, equidistant between Bar-le-Duc and Nancy in the *département* of Meuse. Once upon a time these Toulois or Lorraine wines were of some importance, and they certainly can boast a long history. Phylloxera and then the railway have dealt a body blow, and the *vignoble* is a shadow of what it was even as recently as Napoleonic times. The wine is mainly rosé or gris, though red and white are also authorized. The red wines come from Gamay, Pinot Meunier and Pinot Noir (the grapes of champagne), the rosé from Gamay only and the white can be made from Chardonnay, Aligoté and Auxerrois. The Vin Gris des Côtes de Toul is an agreeable, light, fruity, Gamay-flavoured wine, neither remarkably exciting nor beneath contempt. I have only met it in the local restaurants, where I have also seen a *perlé* version. Production averages 4000 hectolitres per annum.

VINS DE PAYS

VIN DE PAYS DE LA MEUSE

This obscure departmental *vin de pays* hails from the valley of the river Meuse west of Metz and Nancy. The varieties are the same as for Côtes de Toul. I have never sampled it: nor seen it, even in the region itself.

Chapter 7

JURA AND SAVOIE

E ast of Burgundy and Beaujolais lie the Alpine foothills of the Jura and the more
mountainous slopes of the Savoie, a region of impressive beauty, mysterious rock
formations and deep silent lakes. This is one of the forgotten corners of France, and
only recently have I seen the wines exported widely. The Jura is famous for its *vin jaune*, a
unique wine everyone seems to have heard of but few to have sampled. The Savoie wines
are even more obscure. Best known, perhaps, are the sparkling wines of Seyssel. Between
the two regions north of where the Rhône is joined by the river Ain is the area of Bugey.
This combined region comprises a number of *appellations*:

JURA
AC: Côtes du Jura, Arbois, Arbois Mousseux, Château Chalon and L'Étoile.

SAVOIE
AC: Vin de Savoie, Roussette de Savoie, Crépy, Seyssel and Seyssel Mousseux.

VDQS: Vin du Bugey, Roussette du Bugey.

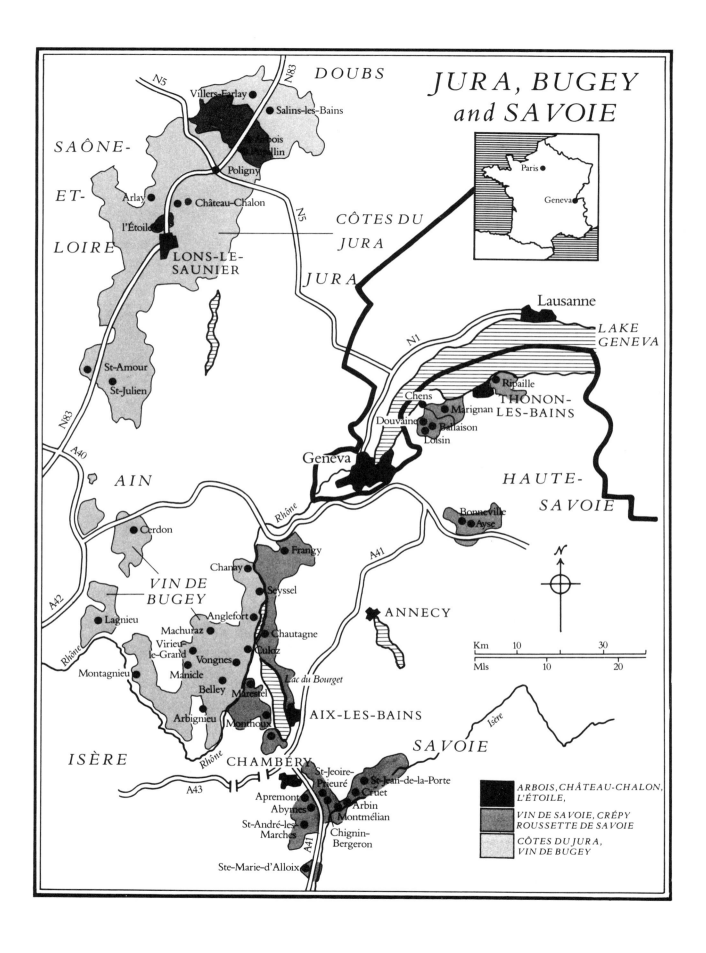

JURA, BUGEY
and SAVOIE

DOUBS

SAÔNE-
ET-
LOIRE

Villers-Farlay
Salins-les-Bains
Arbois
Pupillin
Poligny
Arlay
Château-Chalon
l'Étoile
LONS-LE-
SAUNIER

CÔTES DU
JURA
JURA

Paris
Geneva

Lausanne
LAKE
GENEVA

St-Amour
St-Julien

AIN

Ripaille
Chens
Marignan
Douvaine
Ballaison
Loisin
THONON-
LES-BAINS

Geneva

HAUTE-
SAVOIE

Bonneville
Ayse

Cerdon

Frangy
Chanay
Seyssel

VIN DE
BUGEY

Lagnieu
Machuraz
Anglefort
Chautagne
Virieu-
le-Grand
Vongnes
Culoz
Montagnieu
Manicle
Belley
Marestel
Arbignieu
Monthoux

ANNECY

Lac du Bourget

AIX-LES-BAINS

ISÈRE

CHAMBÉRY

SAVOIE

Isère

St-Jeoire-
Prieuré
St-Jean-de-la-Porte
Cruet
Apremont
Abymes
Arbin
Montmélian
St-André-les-
Marches
Chignin-
Bergeron
Ste-Marie-d'Alloix

Km   10   30
Mls   10   20

ARBOIS, CHÂTEAU-CHALON,
L'ÉTOILE,

VIN DE SAVOIE, CRÉPY
ROUSSETTE DE SAVOIE

CÔTES DU JURA,
VIN DE BUGEY

JURA AND SAVOIE

PRODUCTION AND SURFACE AREA (1996 HARVEST)

	Surface area in hectares	Production '000 hectolitres	
		RED & ROSÉ	WHITE
Jura			
AC			
ARBOIS	733	25	23
CHÂTEAU CHALON	39	—	1
CÔTES DU JURA	660	9	27
CREBANT DU JURA	96	1	10
ÉTOILE	78	—	4
Total Jura AC	1606	36	55
Savoie			
AC			
CRÉPY	63	—	4
ROUSSETTE DE SAVOIE	116	—	9
SEYSSEL	60	—	4
SEYSSEL MOUSSEUX	16	—	1
VIN DE SAVOIE	1730	38	82
Total Savoie AC	1985	38	100
Savoie			
VDQS			
VIN DU BUGEY ROUSSETTE DU BUGEY	456	12	14
Total Savoie	2441	50	114
Total Jura and Savoie	4047	86	169
Total Red and White Wines		255	

WHEN TO DRINK THE WINES

Most of the wines of the Jura and the Savoie – certainly the best wines – are the whites. The Savoie wines are light, crisp, herbal, and flowery. Their essence is their youthful fragrance. The summer after the vintage is the optimum moment to drink them as they will not keep. Nearly all of the Chardonnay-based Jura wines, in my experience, do not see oak. The parallel is Mâcon, and they should be treated likewise, consumed within a year or two after the bottling which will take place in the spring after the vintage.

Vins jaunes are another matter. These are kept in cask for a minimum of six years. They are delicious then, but have a splendid capacity for ageing. I have had wonderfully complex twenty-year-old examples. They even last, for a week or two at least, after the bottle has been opened.

The Jura

Mention Jura and most wine-lovers will think of Henri Maire, or alternatively of *vin jaune*; geologists will be reminded of a particular epoch when dinosaurs roamed the earth, the Jurassic; chemists will recall Pasteur, he who penetrated the complexities behind the fermentation of beer, provided the explanation of why milk turned sour, and, incidentally, discovered the antidote to rabies. The traveller will remember one of the most dramatically beautiful and private corners of France, a land of gentle alpine uplands, sudden limestone cliffs descending hundreds of feet into the valleys below; a lush region of pasture, vineyards and rushing rivers lying between the flat plains and sleepy lakes and lagoons of the Plaine de Bresse and the mountains which form the barrier between France and north-west Switzerland.

Historically and geographically the Jura was part of the Middle Kingdom: France to the west, Germany to the east, and a line which ran from the Low Countries, through Alsace, to Switzerland and the Savoy in the middle. When Charlemagne's empire was divided among his children in AD 843 this Middle Kingdom was born and the seeds were sown for a millennium of strife between east and west. The Jura became part of Burgundy, itself soon to be divided between the Duchy – Burgundy proper – and the Comté, the 'Franche-Montagnes', fiercely independent of their liberty, be it from the suzerainty of the Holy Roman Emperor or of the French king. It was not until the Peace of Nijmegen in 1678 that Louis XIV's dominance over the Jura was finally assured.

Until phylloxera in the late nineteenth century this was an important *vignoble*. In 1836 the Jura possessed over 18,000 hectares under vine. In 1988 the figure was 900 hectares. Phylloxera, followed by the increasing availability of more inexpensive wines owing to the railway and other means of cheap transport between the Midi and the north, dealt an almost mortal blow. As the vineyards between Dijon and Chablis declined to a few straggly rows of vines used for *vin ordinaire* for local consumption, so the vineyards of the Jura declined. Today, chiefly at the hands of Henri Maire, there has been a renaissance, but the wines of the Jura are still little exported, and rarely seen on wine lists and restaurants outside the region.

The Wine Region

The Jura vineyards extend in a thin line from north of Salins-Les-Bains to south of Saint-Amour (no relation to the Beaujolais *cru* of this name), a distance of eighty kilometres. The important section lies in the upper half between Arbois and Lons-Le-Saunier. Lons is halfway between Beaune and Geneva. As you approach the Jura from the west, and cross into the *département* of the same name, the countryside changes, the land begins to rise. In the distance are the Jura mountains, protecting the land from incursions from the east. These are precursors of the Alps, a ridge of hills – few rise above 1000 metres – which runs from the valley of the upper Rhône east of Lyon to Basle in roughly a north-easterly direction. On the western slopes of these hills lies the *vignoble* of the Jura.

The soil in the lowlands is almost pure clay. As the altitude increases it becomes progressively more calcareous, on a bedrock of oolitic limestone. This marl is mixed with sand and clay to the north, gravel and other pebbles in the south of the area. The vineyards face the setting sun at an altitude of 300 to 450 metres, not in a continuous line, as in Burgundy, but much interrupted by sudden valleys, above which a limestone cliff might rise a hundred metres into the sun, or by isolated village enclaves, copses of mixed deciduous and coniferous woodland and tumbling streams issuing from underground springs deep in the undiscovered hills.

THE GRAPES

The grape varieties in the Jura are the same as those commonly found in Burgundy – Chardonnay and Pinot Noir – with several indigenous and, dare I say it, for the red wines at least, inferior varieties. As well as Pinot Noir, locally known as Gros Noiren, there are Trousseau and Poulsard for the red wines. The Trousseau would not inspire any newly married man with great delight. It makes a lumpy, well-coloured, tannic wine, full-bodied perhaps, but without style, nor the quality to age gracefully. It oxidizes fast and loses its colour quickly; the fruit, always rustic in character, soon dries out. While September and October are generally sunny in the Jura, the region otherwise suffers an abundance of rain, particularly compared with Alsace which though further north is sheltered from the west by the Vosges. Trousseau wines, like those reds from the middle Loire, are frequently stringy in their tannins, and have an absence of fat. Poulsard makes a lighter wine with higher acidity. Never highly coloured, even in the best years, it resembles rosé rather than red, and is normally labelled as such. When fresh it can have merit, but with age it makes a dispiriting bottle. The locals will aver that a Poulsard rosé has the merit of a Tavel. I must demur. Both the red and rosé wines are often kept far too long in wood.

The whites are much more interesting. Now largely from Chardonnay (locally known as the Melon d'Arbois) with an admixture of Savignin added at the time of the *écoulage* (descent from the fermentation vat into barrel or tank) or by means of *ouillage* or topping up, these whites are rather like a full and spicy Mâconnais – the more Savignin, the more individual, the less quasi-Burgundian. Pinot Blanc is also used. Jura whites are either 100 per cent Chardonnay or a mixture. If the first, they should be bottled early and consumed reasonably soon. If the latter, they will take age both in barrel and in bottle, and can mature to something with real character and merit. These keep remarkably well.

The Savignin grape, however, is the Jura's own special variety. Savignin Blanc is said by ampelographical experts to be the Traminer of Alsace (the Savignin Rosé makes a particular, rather uncommon wine in Alsace (*see* Klevner de Heiligenstein, *page 328*), but is said not to be a true relation). It is sometimes known locally as Naturé. Legend has it that it was brought from Hungary to France by Benedictine monks in the tenth century. It is a late developer and a poor cropper but produces a wine powerful in both alcohol and flavour. I find it has little in common with the Traminer, but that is not to say that it does not have either quality or individuality. You will rarely see it on its own as a table wine. As the 'onlie begetter' of the Jura speciality, *vin jaune*, however, it is incomparable.

The Wines

VIN JAUNE

Vin jaune is peculiar to the Jura and, in its own way, great. The wine is made exclusively from Savignin and the grapes are picked late, though without *pourriture noble*. The wine is then vinified slowly after which it is racked off into old oak barrels which are sealed up and left in a cool cellar for a legal minimum of six years. Topping up is disallowed. A film of yeasts – a *flor* similar to that in a Jerez *fino* – forms on the top of the wine. This imparts a particular flavour of oxidation to the wine but otherwise protects it from turning into vinegar. The result is something which is dry but fat and rich in extract, with a green walnut flavour akin to a dry sherry, though in this case the wine is not fortified; nor does a *vin jaune* have sherry's pronounced acidity.

I find *vin jaune* simply delicious. The wine is a deep yellow in colour; it is mellow but pungent in flavour, powerful, subtle and complex. When young – recently bottled at the age of six, that is – it has a ripe, alpine-flower fragrance and a certain racy crispness. As it ages it becomes rounder and softer, the nutty elements are joined by flavours of crab-apple, camomile and elderflower and it becomes more and more multi-dimensional. *Vins jaunes* are bottled in a special dumpy 62-cl bottle known as a *clavelin*. *Vin jaune* is expensive and hard to come by, but it is worth the effort. It is one of the world's great drinks.

VIN DE PAILLE

Vin de paille is another wine which, if not unique to the Jura, is something of a speciality there as well as being uncommon elsewhere. They make a little *vin de paille* – more as a curiosity than a commercial proposition – in the northern Rhône.

After harvesting the ripe but not botrytized grapes the bunches are left to dry out before pressing, for a minimum of two months by law. This was originally on straw mats – hence the name *vin de paille* (straw) – but now as often they are dried hanging from the rafters or alternatively in shallow trays in a well-ventilated room. This drying has the effect of concentrating the sugars and other elements in the fruit. Pressing and fermentation then takes place; because of the concentration of sugar the latter often taking months if not years.

The resulting wine has a deep gold or even amber colour, is full and rich; not just very sweet but possessing a nutty, raisiny quality with good balancing acidity. While it doesn't have the complexity of a Sauternes, it certainly in its own way has merit as well as character. Again, quite naturally, it is expensive. Production, sadly, is in decline.

CÔTES DU JURA

The generic *appellation* of the Jura is the Côtes du Jura, a delimited area of twelve cantons from Villers-Farlay and Salins in the north-east to Saint-Julien and Saint-Amour in the south-west by way of Arbois and Lons-Le-Saunier. 660 hectares are under vine, producing red, rosé, white, sparkling wine by the champagne method (Crémando du Jura), *vin jaune* and *vin de paille*. Eighty per cent of the 45,885 hectolitre production (1996) is white wine.

While much of the production within this catch-all *appellation* is fairly mundane, if not downright artisanal, there are nuggets to be unearthed. Two of Jura's most respected quality growers, Jean Bourdy and the Comte de Laguiche, are based at Arlay which lies outside the more specific districts listed below.

ARBOIS

The canton of Arbois is entitled to its own *appellation*, and is the nucleus of the Jura wine-making area. Arbois itself is a charming, bustling, picturesque town with plenty of medieval features and it lies near the foot of one of the most spectacular of Jura's many *cirques*, the curious horseshoe-shaped cliffs which suddenly jut out of the surrounding countryside like the step of some giant staircase. Louis Pasteur is the local hero. He was born at Dôle but brought to Arbois at the age of five in 1827. His statue, showing him seated, gazing rather quizzically at what looks to be an onion, is worth a nostalgic visit. His research provided the basis for the understanding of what wine was and how it became. This was the start of making wine by modern methods.

The vignoble covers thirteen communes and some 733 hectares. As with Côtes du Jura (though generally with a marginally more strict degree of ripeness of the fruit) the *appellation* covers red, rosé, white, sparkling, *vin jaune* and *vin de paille*. Unlike the generic *appellation,* about 60 percent of the 48,086-hectolitre production (1996) is red of Rosé. Some of this appears as Arbois Pupillin, the name of one of the communes.

L'ÉTOILE

A few kilometres north of Lons-Le-Saunier lie the three communes which make up the small 78-hectare *appellation* of L'Étoile. Only white wine is authorized, though as well as Chardonnay and Savignin it is permitted to vinify the red Poulsard grape *en blanc*. *Vin jaune, vin de paille* and sparkling wines are also produced. In 1996 production totaled 4010 hectolitres.

CHÂTEAU CHALON

Some fifteen kilometres north-west of Lons-Le-Saunier lies Château Chalon, an *appellation* and a village rather than a single property, producing *vin jaune* only. The name derives from an old castle which overlooked the area from the vantage of a limestone crag and which was built to protect a Benedictine abbey to which the local nobles would send their children to be educated.

The vines are found on the sheltered slopes below the castle, and cover 39 hectares. *Vin jaune* is only produced in the best years, and necessarily in limited quantity. One thousand hectolitres per annum is the average (1372 hectolitres in 1996). In bad vintages the entire production is declassified to Côtes du Jura.

THE PRODUCERS

According to official figures there are some 1000 growers in the Jura of whom a quarter belong to the five main co-operatives at Arbois, Pupillin, Voiteur, Puligny and L'Étoile. Most of the rest, one imagines, are contracted to Henri Maire. Only about a dozen growers have more than a dozen hectares under vine. Very much the biggest producer of Jura wines (and of other non-*appellation*, branded wines such as the sparkling Vin Fou) is Henri Maire at Château-Monfort at Arbois. The Henri Maire enterprise can be measured in millions rather than thousands of bottles, and the bulk of this is sold by mail-order direct to the private customer in France. Production is based on Maire's own domaines which cover some 300 hectares. These names are now used as brands for the top *cuvées*: Domaine de Grange Grillard for white wine, Croix d'Argis, Domaine de Sorbief for a Poulsard/ Trousseau red and Monfort for a Pinot Noir.

I find Henri Maire's wines, frankly, dull; and frequently rather tired as well. They are pasteurized and therefore do not keep well in bottle. The reds are suspiciously sweet. Their success demonstrates not so much a public awakening of the excellence of Jura wines, than the efficacy of aggressive marketing. Paradoxically, in the long term, the presence of Henri Maire may be counter-productive to the growth of a quality Jura wine business.

An estate with an aristocratic background and connections with some of the best wines and vineyards elsewhere in France, is Château d'Arlay, perhaps the best property in the Jura. The domaine has been in the hands of the same family since the twelfth century and at one time was owned by William the Silent, Prince of Orange, and at another by the

Spanish royal family. The present owners, the charming Count and Countess Renaud de Laguiche, are not only descended, if at times indirectly, from both these royal houses as well as from the original twelfth-century owner, but are related to the Marquis de Laguiche of Le Montrachet, the De Vogüé of Champagne and Chambolle-Musigny and the Ladoucette family of Pouilly-sur-Loire. The vineyard has recently been enlarged, regaining some areas not under the vine since pre-phylloxera days, and now comprises some 70 hectares.

The Bourdy family are also based in Arlay. This is a business which has been handed down from father to son since the sixteenth century, and it is now in the hands of Christian and his son, Jean-François; Jean himself, Christian's father, having retired in 1979 after fifty-two years at the helm.

Other growers include the Rolet brothers and André and Mireille Tissot at Montigny-les-Assures near Arbois; Sylvie and Luc Boilley at Chissey-sur-Loire; Jacques Forêt and the Cave Fruitière Vinicole at Arbois and the Compagnie des Grands Vins du Jura at Crancoit. On visits to the area I have enjoyed the wines of Hubert Clavelin at Voiteur, Château Gréa owned by Monsieur de Boissier at Rotalier near Beaufort, and Joseph Vendelle at L'Étoile.

VINS DE PAYS

VIN DE PAYS DE FRANCHE-COMTÉ

Franche-Comté, comprising the *départements* of Jura and Haute-Saône, is one of France's most obscure wine-growing regions, a no-man's-land north of the Jura proper, equidistant between Dijon and Mulhouse. Yet there are vines, if you look hard, as there are in almost every part of France, and this zonal *vin de pays* has at least one reputable grower, Pierre-Marie Guillaume at Charcenne on the marly slopes of the Coteaux de Gy. Monsieur Guillaume and his father possess 10 scattered hectares in what was formerly part of the estate and summer palace of the Archbishops of Besançon. I have enjoyed recent vintages of their Chardonnay and Pinot Noir. The former can fairly be compared with a light Mâcon; the latter is more in the style of a red wine from Alsace than a Burgundy. There is also a Gamay and a sparkling wine.

Savoie and Bugey

The wines of the French Alps and their foothills, of the upper Rhône and the river Ain, of Chambéry and Aix-Les-Bains, and of the shores of Lake Geneva (or Lac Léman) are little seen outside their region of production, the *départements* of Savoie and Haute-Savoie, Isère and Ain. The *vignoble* is small and fragmented and the *appellations* unnecessarily complicated. There are a number of different grape varieties and an even larger number of local grape names. Yet for all its obscurity and eccentricity of nomenclature this is an area well worth pursuing. There are signs recently that the outside world is beginning to take the area seriously and local producers are becoming less insular in their attitude to the idea of export.

The Wine Regions

Let us first of all make it clear where Savoie and Bugey are. Immediately north-east of Lyon lie the southern extremities of the plains and wild duckponds of the Doubs. If you sit in one of the best restaurants in France, that of Alain Chapel at Mionnay, as I did once, and order a bottle of the local wine, you will be offered something called Montagnieu. Where is Montagnieu you may well ask. You will be asked to look behind you; across the marshy flatlands, dimly in the distance, you will discern the first foothills of the Alps. At the foot of these slopes is the river Ain, and round the corner out of sight is the town of Belley in the *département* of Ain. All this is the terrain of the wines of Bugey.

Over into Savoie and deeper into the mountains, north of Aix-Les-Bains on the shores of France's largest lake, the Lac du Bourget, is the town of Seyssel on the Rhône and one of the many areas for Vin de Savoie. South of Chambéry in the upper valley of the river Isère is another. Other areas are near Bonneville on the road from Geneva to Chamonix, and on the southern French shores of Lake Geneva either side of Thonon-Les-Bains.

The wines of all these separate *vignobles* are largely white and they have a certain resemblance despite coming from a number of different grape varieties. They are mountain wines: light, floral, evanescent, often better out of cask than in the bottle, frequently with a slight *pétillance*.

Savoie and Bugey wines are made from a number of grape varieties. The whites are made from Roussette (also known as the Altesse), Jacquère (otherwise called the Cugnette or Abymes), Chardonnay, Aligoté, Molette, Roussanne (known as the Bergeron), Pinot Gris, Savignin (known also as the Grignet), Chasselas, Mondeuse Blanche and Verdesse, a variety so obscure it is not even listed in Jancis Robinson's book, *Vines, Grapes and Wines*. The reds and rosés come mainly from Gamay, but Mondeuse Rouge, Pinot Noir and even Cabernet Sauvignon and Cabernet Franc are also found. There are three further arcane grapes authorized in the Isère: Etraine de La Dui, Serène and Joubertin.

SAVOIE

The basic Savoie *appellation* is Vin de Savoie which can be red, rosé or white. The reds and rosés are light, thin and of little consequence. The whites are rather better. They deserve our interest. Additionally there is a separate more interesting *appellation* of Roussette de Savoie for whites only which can come not only from Roussette but also from Mondeuse and Chardonnay. There are fifteen *cru* villages for Vin de Savoie: Abymes, Apremont, Arbin, Ayse, Charpignat, Chautagne, Chignin, Chignin-Bergeron (Roussanne only), Cruet, Marignan (Chasselas only), Montmélian, Ripaille (Chasselas only), Saint Jean-de-la-Porte, Saint Jeoire-Prieuré and Sainte-Marie d'Alloix. Roussette de Savoie has four *cru* villages: Frangy, Marestel, Monteminod and Monthoux. These *cru* wines must be 100 per cent Roussette with no Mondeuse or Chardonnay.

Those producers near Lake Geneva, where you will also find the separate *appellation* of Crépy, concentrate on the Chasselas grape. Chasselas is known as the Fendant over the border in Switzerland. Not surprisingly the wines are very similar: light, dry, rather anonymously herbal, with a slight *pétillance*. In my view they are over-priced. Local estates include the Château de Ripaille (made by the firm of Fichard at Chens), Mercier et Fils at Douvaine, Monsieur Goy at Ballaison and the Métras family at Loisin.

Of more interest are the wines of Seyssel, itself a separate *appellation* for wines from Roussette only, and the other Roussette de Savoie wines from Frangy and the slopes overlooking the Lac du Bourget. Roussette is an individual and intriguing grape variety, and at its best when used for mountain wines. The flavour is a delicate but quite intense combination of mountain herbs and flowers with a touch of citrus, not as alcoholically powerful as Condrieu but with something of the same elusive, hard-to-pinpoint fragrance. The *négociant* Mollex at Corbonod near Seyssel has some good estate wines, as do the celebrated sparkling-wine producers, Varichon et Clerc in Seyssel itself. I spent a rather frustrating day in Frangy once, failing to find a good source, but I live in hope.

South of Aix-Les-Bains and Chambéry, famous for its delicate vermouth, is the best-known part of vinous Savoie and the villages of Aprémont, Abymes, Chignin and Saint André-Les-Marches. The best whites come from the Jacquère or the Roussanne. In Aprémont there is Gilbert Tardy at Challes-Les-Eaux; in Tormey, near Chignin, André and Michel Quenard produce a Chignin from Jacquère and a Chignin-Bergeron from Roussanne, both of which are very fine; and at the Domaine de Rocailles at Saint-André-Les-Marches you will find the engagingly enthusiastic, able Pierre Boniface, a *négociant* as well as a grower. Jean-Pierre Mercier at Chapareillan near Saint-André is another impressive source.

In all Savoie there are some 1985 hectares of vines which produced 133,042 hectolitres of wine in 1996, of which 37,646 were red and rosé wine. The figure also includes a little *mousseux* (though the Varichon et Clerc wine is no longer AC Seyssel).

VIN DU BUGEY, ROUSSETTE DU BUGEY VDQS

As in Savoie there are two *appellations* for the wines of Bugey: Vin du Bugey, red, rosé or white, from the same varieties as for Vin de Savoie, and Roussette du Bugey, which is made from Roussette and Chardonnay. Once again the bulk of the harvest, and the main interest, is in the white wines. The area covers some 456 hectares scattered over sixty-five communes in the *département* of Ain. The best communes are allowed to add their name to the generic title on the label. For Vin du Bugey these are Cerdon, Machuraz, Manicle, Montagnieu and Virieu-Le-Grand and for Roussette du Bugey they are Anglefort, Arbignieu, Chanay, Lagnieu, Montagnieu and Virieu-Le-Grand.

I find there is little difference either in quality or in style between the Bugey wines and the non-Chasselas wines of the Savoie. While I would not allow the dignity of AC for the reds and the rosés of either region I can see no reason not to bestow this accolade on the Roussettes and Chardonnays of Bugey.

Bugey produced 12,254 hectolitres of red and rosé in 1996 and 14,378 hectolitres of white wine. Jean Peillot at Montagnieu, Antoine Riboud at the Domaine de Bel Air near Culoz and Eugene Monin at Vognes are the most important local growers.

VINS DE PAYS

VIN DE PAYS D'AIN
This is the departmental *vin de pays* of the Bugey area. A light white wine is made in small quantities from the local grape varieties.

VIN DE PAYS D'ALLOBROGIE
This zonal *vin de pays* is the main one of the Savoie area from the *départements* of Ain, Savoie and Haute-Savoie. The wine can come in all three colours – the reds and rosés from Gamay, Mondeuse and the other Savoie grapes; the white, which makes up 95 per cent of the wines produced, mainly from the Jacquère grape. I have had some well-made whites, if rather ephemeral and acidic. The reds and rosés are weak, thin and rustic.

VIN DE PAYS DES BALMES DAUPHINOISES
This is a zonal *vin de pays*. The Balmes Dauphinoises is in the Isère *département* south-east of Lyon. I have seen – and rejected – some thin, Gamay-based reds and rosés, but enjoyed crisp, dry, flowery whites made from Jacquère, Chardonnay and other varieties.

VIN DE PAYS DES COTEAUX DU GRÉSIVAUDAN
This zonal *vin de pays* comes from the Isère and Savoie *départements* around Grenoble itself. The reds and rosés based on Gamay are thin. The whites are Jacquère-based. I have not sampled many wines.

Chapter 8

PROVENCE AND CORSICA

From a wine point of view, Provence is that part of south-eastern France bounded on the east and west by Italy and the Rhône delta and on the north and south by the Alps and the Mediterranean. It includes the Riviera and the Côte d'Azur as well as Cézanne's Montagne-Sainte-Victoire. It is Marseille and Nice as well as Aix and Draguignan. It is Bandol and Cassis, the tiny *appellations* of Bellet and Palette and the large ones of Côtes de Provence and Coteaux d'Aix-en-Provence. Away from the bustling seaside resorts, this is a wild and rugged countryside; blazing hot in summer, bleak in winter; a land of olive groves and *garrigues* – a scrub land of bramble and broom, of stunted oaks and pine, of rocky outcrops with wild thyme, oregano and rosemary; at its prettiest in May and June when the land is still green and not yet parched, when butterflies dally and flowers bloom. It is a countryside of contrast. Here an ultra-modern development by Le Courbusier out of *Clockwork Orange*; a few miles away, a crumbling brigand castle, a beat-up Romanesque church or a secluded monastery.

Yet it is also a fertile country. Between the coast and the mountains, near where the motorway thunders between Avignon and Marseille or Menton, the land is lush and the soil abundant. This is ideal country for the vine, the sort of land and climate the plant found in Kurdistan when it was first cultivated by neolithic man. The vine can withstand the long periods of drought it often encounters in Provence. Its roots dig deep for the moisture it needs to see it through the arid summers. The wines, like the climate, have tended to be larger than life – full and robust, fiery and alcoholic. Today, tamed by man and vinified by modern methods, often with the use of *cépages améliorateurs* such as Cabernet Sauvignon to supplement the indigenous Grenache, Mourvèdre and other varieties, the standard is rising. Wines of elegance and depth are being made.

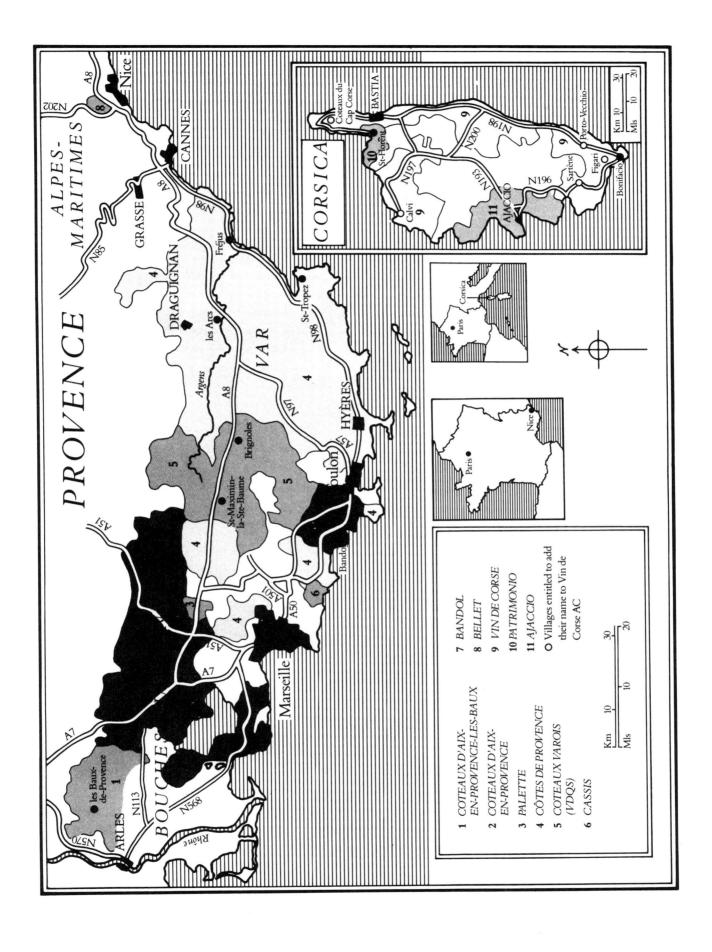

PROVENCE

ALPES-MARITIMES

Nice

Cannes

Grasse

Draguignan

les Arcs

Fréjus

St-Tropez

VAR

Hyères

St-Maximin-la-Ste-Baume

Brignoles

Toulon

Bandol

Marseille

Arles

BOUCHES

Rhône

les Baux-de-Provence

CORSICA

Bastia

Coteaux du Cap Corse

St-Florent

Calvi

AJACCIO

Sartène

Figari

Bonifacio

Porto-Vecchio

Paris

Corsica

Paris

Nice

1 COTEAUX D'AIX-
  EN-PROVENCE-LES-BAUX
2 COTEAUX D'AIX-
  EN-PROVENCE
3 PALETTE
4 CÔTES DE PROVENCE
5 COTEAUX VAROIS
  (VDQS)
6 CASSIS

7 BANDOL
8 BELLET
9 VIN DE CORSE
10 PATRIMONIO
11 AJACCIO
○ Villages entitled to add
  their name to Vin de
  Corse AC

Km 10   30
Mls   10   20

PROVENCE AND CORSICA

PRODUCTION AND SURFACE AREA (1996 HARVEST)

	Surface area in hectares	Production '000 hectolitres	
		RED & ROSÉ	WHITE
Provence			
AC			
BANDOL	1451	40	2
CASSIS	172	2	4
PALETTE	28	(1 hl)	(154 hl)
BELLET	32	(495 hl)	(283 hl)
CÔTES DE PROVENCE	18,916	833	29
COTEAUX D'AIX-EN-PROVENCE	3261	157	6
LES BAUX-DE-PROVENCE	148	7	—
Provence			
VDQS			
COTEAUX VAROIS	1737	61	2
Corsica			
AC			
AJACCIO	244	7	(1 hl)
PATRIMONIO	425	11	2
VIN DE CORSE	1779	60	8
MUSCAT DE CAD CORSE	65	—	2
Total AC	26,456	1148	54
Total VDQS	1737	61	2
Total Provence and Corsica	28,193	1209	56
Total Red and White Wines		1265	

APPELLATIONS IN PROVENCE

AC: Côtes de Provence, Coteaux d'Aix-en-Provence, Coteaux d'Aix-en-Provence-les-Baux, Bandol, Cassis, Palette, and Bellet.

VDQS: Coteaux Varois.

Bandol, Cassis, Palette and Bellet are quality *appellations*, confined to small areas, and the rest are more general. All produce predominantly red wine, a certain amount of rosé but little white. The one exception is Cassis, a curious *appellation* for a South of France wine in that its fame, and the bulk of its production, is its dry white.

APPELLATIONS IN CORSICA
AC: Ajaccio, Patrimonio, Vin de Corse, Vin de Corse Calvi, Vin de Corse Coteaux du Cap Corse, Vin de Corse Figari, Vin de Corse Porto Vecchio, and Vin de Corse Sartène.

WHEN TO DRINK THE WINES

Modern methods of vinification and *élevage* have largely tamed the undue robustness and fiery solidity of Provence wines. The wines are better balanced. They have a better acidity which preserves the freshness of the fruit. And this fruit is not submerged under the 'size' of the wine. This means both that the wines are ready for drinking earlier and that they will keep better. With such a variation in style across the region – from the lightish wines of some of the producers in Coteaux d'Aix, such as Château Fonscolombe, to the serious examples made at the top levels in Bandol – it is unwise to generalize. The rosés and the few whites should be consumed early. Many reds are equally delicious in the summer or the following winter, early after the vintage. The best reds, obviously, are made for keeping. In principle, unless the wine, like those in Bandol, is largely Mourvèdre-based or unless it is essentially a Syrah or Cabernet Sauvignon wine, I would drink them earlier rather than later, as soon as they have softened up, and this means at the age of five years or so for a good Côtes de Provence.

There are, of course, exceptions. Bandol wines can require a decade or more to soften up and here the particular vintage is more important. Fine vintages in Bandol include 1996, '95, '93, '90, '89, '88, '85, '82, '78, '75, '71 and '70.

The Wine Regions

BANDOL

About two-thirds of the way between Marseille and Toulon, just across the boundary between the *département* of Bouches-du-Rhône and that of Var, lies the Mediterranean town of Bandol, holiday resort and fishing village combined into one. Bandol, like Bordeaux, has given its name to the wines which hitherto were despatched through its port, and these wines can justly lay claim to being not only the best of Provence but the most interesting of the whole of southern France. Based on the Mourvèdre grape, Bandol reds are full, rich, firm and long-lasting, and as such have more in common with the Syrah wines of the northern Rhône than the Grenache-based wines of Châteauneuf-du-Pape. That they are cheaper is an added advantage. Strangely, however, the wines of Bandol have not yet received the recognition they deserve. In my view they are serious wines that age and I am sure that anyone who has experienced a ten-year-old bottle will enthusiastically echo this view. The difficulty is being able to lay your hands on the ten-year-old bottle!

I have had a particular fondness for the wines of Bandol for many years. In 1964, in possession of a travelling scholarship for doing well in my final exams at hotel school, I spent a few days in Bandol after a holiday further up the coast *en route* towards Bordeaux, where I was to spend several months. I can't remember who I saw or what I tasted, as I didn't keep notes then in the methodical way I do today, but I still remember the flavour of one old bottle a grower opened for me. The aroma was a combination of a fine cigar and the cooked fruit of an old tawny port; the colour was more like hot chocolate sauce than wine; and the aftertaste was both ethereal – nuances wafted around the back of one's throat like a swirl of silk ribbon – and powerful, in that one was enveloped in a warm cloud of alcohol on the finish.

The vine is generally considered to have been first cultivated in France around 600 BC when Phoenician traders established an outpost at Marseille, bringing with them the techniques of tending the vine and fermenting the juice to make wine. Phoenicians were succeeded by Greeks and the Greeks by the Romans. By this time Bandol had already been colonized, Julius Caesar mentions Tauroentum, the Latin version of the Phoenician Taurois. This is present-day Bandol, and evidence of considerable activity in wine-production is found in the quantity of amphorae brought up from the sea-bed and two dolia stone fermenting-vats, dating from the Roman epoch, discovered in the hinterland. The French historian Abbé Magloire Giraud has suggested that the famous wine of Marseille, well-known throughout the empire, might have been at least in part the wine of Bandol. In the aftermath of the collapse of the Gallo-Roman civilization, the Mediterranean coast was prey to barbaric invasion, Saracen occupation and spasmodic, more entrepreneurial harassment from pirates. The inhabitants retreated into their *vieilles villes perchés* so familiar throughout Provence – the one at Le Castellet is of Roman origin – to sit it out. Eventually life grew easier, and under local war-lord or ecclesiastical settlement, peace, at least for most of the time, returned to the vineyard. Documents throughout the Middle Ages attest to commercial and proprietorial vinous transactions and reveal not only that what was produced enjoyed a high reputation, but that wine dominated the economy of the whole of this area.

Bandol always seems to have been a full and sturdy wine. The local *seigneur*, Monsieur de Boyer-Bandol, in a petition he addressed to the king at the beginning of the seventeenth century remarks that 'these wines keep well, and even improve during long journeys'. He adds that he 'exports them in large quantities to the French Antilles'. We do not know the success of Monsieur de Boyer-Bandol's petition but about a century and a half later there are accounts of Bandol being consumed at Versailles. Louis XV and the royal family according to 'reliable sources' usually drank *only* (my italics) carefully prepared wine from the Rouve district (a *lieu-dit* in the commune of Le Beausset).

When a sycophantic courtier asked the king where he obtained his 'everlasting youth', the 'much-loved' monarch is supposed to have replied: 'Why, from Rouve wine. It gives me all the vital sap and wits I need.' According to culinary documents the amount of Bandol consumed at Versailles continued to increase throughout Louis XV's reign. For a wine which not only would have had to have been shipped the long way round via the Straits of Gibraltar to northern ports such as Rouen or Le Havre, but also would have been facing forceful competition from Burgundy, Bordeaux and Champagne, this is no mean achievement.

Following the Napoleonic wars, an average of 1200 ships called at the port of Bandol each year, shipping 60,000 to 65,000 hectolitres of wine annually (this is double the current AC production). The casks were branded with the letter B which is still the symbol of Bandol wines.

The first serious reference to the wine of Bandol appeared at the end of the eighteenth century. In a book entitled *The Geography of Provence, the County of Avignon, the Principality of Orange and the County of Nice*, written by a Monsieur Achard and published in 1787, we find: 'The soil of Bandol is very dry and stony. Its main product is first quality red wine, the most highly prized (in the area) . . .' Another writer of the time states: 'The climate of Bandol and its vicinity, particularly mild and sheltered, its limestone soil containing a high proportion of carbonate of lime, the intensity of sunshine on its slopes (which the immediate proximity of the sea protects from winter frosts), the salt and the iodine present in the air, all contribute to make the wines of this locality that famous product which the Provençal poets called 'bottled sunshine'. 'These wines have the consistency, bouquet and finesse appreciated by connoisseurs who look for true quality rather than the name on the label. They sum up quite simply the real virtues of the Provençal soil and its products: honesty, finesse and ardour.' You could echo this sentiment two centuries on today.

In 1816 André Jullien placed the wines of Bandol among his *deuxième classe*: '. . . very deep colour, plenty of alcohol . . . full-flavoured, they keep well and acquire quality on ageing or being sent on a long sea-voyage'.

Thereafter the wines of Bandol seem to have gone into decline as far as the world at large was concerned. Most early nineteenth-century writers such as Henderson and Redding remorselessly plagiarize Jullien without acknowledgment. The later writers don't even seem to have visited Provence! Oidium in the late 1860s followed by phylloxera in the early 1870s totally destroyed the Bandol vineyards and the area only recovered slowly in the difficult economic climate which followed. According to P. Morton Shand in *A Book of Wine* (1926), the best that could be said of Bandol (and a few other Provence wines mentioned) was that they were 'the best of a bad lot'.

Nevertheless, a few pioneering spirits soldiered on, led by Monsieur Peyraud of Domaine Tempier and Monsieur Estienne of La Laidière. When the Comité National des Appellations d'Origine was set up in 1935, these Bandol growers were quick to respond. They established their own Syndicat de Producteurs des Vins Appellation d'Origine Contrôlée Bandol and between them set up laws which came into effect on 11 November 1941. With Cassis and the tiny vineyard areas of Palette and Bellet these were Provence's first AC wines.

The Bandol vineyards lie a few kilometres inland from the coast and run round in a sort of natural amphitheatre formed by a semi-circle of hills, the slopes of which overlook the motorway in the valley floor. Only these slopes are authorized for AC Bandol; the valley is merely *vin de pays,* and the 1451 hectares currently in production (getting on for half as much again what it was ten years ago) extend over eight communes. La Cadière d'Azur and Le Castellet are the principal centres; the communes of Bandol and Sanary and in part Le Beausset, Saint-Cyr-sur-Mer, Ollioules and Evenos are also authorized. Starting from the Golfe des Lecques in the west, rising to the Plateau du Camp and then curving towards Le Beausset, the boundary of the production area follows the N8, crosses the Gorges d'Ollioules and runs back to the sea along the river Reppe, ending to the east of Sanary.

Almost the whole of this area consists of silioco-calcareous soil, a complex mixture of flints, calcareous sandstone and sandy marl, lying on a harder rock of the same composition. The land is arid and well drained, and the vines, enclosed and protected by the hills behind them which rise up to a height of 400 metres, face towards the south and enjoy sunshine from morning to night. They receive more sunshine than any other locality on the French Riviera (3000 hours per annum). The views from some of the hill-top wineries or *bastides* (Provençal manor houses) are breathtaking. The chief grape variety is the Mourvèdre, and it is on the characteristics of this grape – not exactly unique to Bandol but nowhere else planted in such profusion – that the wine of Bandol is based. Red and rosé wines must be made from a minimum of 50 per cent Mourvèdre. In practice the percentage for the rosé is (unofficially of course) often less and that for the red is between 60 per cent and 70 per cent, in some cases 95 per cent. Even in the most prolific years its production rarely surpasses the maximum permitted yield of 40 hectolitres per hectare.

Red Bandol when young is well coloured, moderately high in alcohol and rather dense and unforthcoming. Frankly, it is rather aggressively solid, and seems to lack both richness and generosity. It must be kept for a minimum of eighteen months in wood before bottling. With time, in a successful vintage, it will mellow, acquire complexity, warmth, flesh and concentration. But it does need time. Mature Mourvèdre and therefore mature Bandol – a wine of ten plus years of age – has black fruit flavour: black cherries, blackberries and bilberries mixed with truffles, liquorice, cinnamon and a hint of peonies. Even when fully evolved and fully ripe there is an element of austerity though, a hint of masculinity. But so there is, in a different way, in a fine Paulliac.

Grenache and Cinsault are the other varieties for the red and rosé wines, the former adding a bit of warmth and alcohol in its robust and rather boorish way and the latter a touch of acidity and freshness. For the white wines Clairette and Ugni Blanc are the standard varieties and Bourboulenc and Sauvignon Blanc are also authorized. In practice it is the increasing use of Sauvignon which is helping to produce something less oily, heavy and 'southern' than the wines of yesteryear. Today Bandol produces nearly 40,000 hectolitres per annum of which perhaps 60 per cent is red and most of the rest rosé. In 1996 2043 hectolitres of white wine were made, just over half of that of nearby Cassis.

The Peyraud family of Domaine Tempier have been the driving force behind Bandol for so long that it is hard to imagine Bandol without them. Theirs is the leading reputation and to them are paid the highest prices. This attracts a little jealous commentary from some neighbours who are not so fortunate but it seems to wash over the Peyrauds' heads and they are some of the most openly welcoming and charming people in the area. The family possesses 25 hectares of vines spread over three *lieux-dits* which are vinified separately. These plots contain a goodly proportion of old Mourvèdre, for the Peyrauds can be certainly numbered among the pioneers of the *appellation*. Tourtine, a hillside facing due south, contains most; Le Plan near the Tempier *manoir* is also high in Mourvèdre; Migoua on top of the hill near the old church of Le Beausset has least but perhaps produced the most elegant wine in 1985. One or other of these, in the best years, used to be bottled as the Cuvée Spéciale. In recent years the best of the Tourtine and Migoua *cuvées* have been bottled separately. The wines will need a decade before they are mature. There are a number of other good growers in Bandol. I can firmly recommend the Bunans at Moulin des Costes and Mas de La Rouvière, Domaine Ray-Jeanne, Domaine de Pibarnon, Domaine de La Bastide Blanche, Château Vannières, Château Pradeaux and the Domaine de La Laidière.

CASSIS

Fifteen kilometres west of Bandol is the smaller and prettier fishing village of Cassis. Cassis, like much of the Mediterranean coast, is in danger of losing its charm. A generation or two ago artists could afford to live and work there. Today it is a very self-conscious, mini-Saint-Tropez, full of expensive yachts with sugar daddies and their bimbos. East of Cassis overhangs the 360-metre Cap Canaille, the tallest cliff in France. Above and behind, up in the hills, precariously surviving in the midst of the continual expansion of holiday homes, a few brave souls continue to produce the wine of Cassis.

Wines are said to have been introduced to Cassis by a refugee Florentine family named Albrizzi in 1520, and from the start it seems to have been the white wine that caught on. This is doubly odd: it is hard to imagine that a Tuscan white grape (surely not the ubiquitous Trebbiano or Ugni Blanc) could have excited the Cassis farmers and their customers; and why a white wine? Ninety-nine per cent of the produce of the Midi is red or rosé. What isn't is usually a *vin doux naturel*.

Yet it was the white wine which made Cassis famous. André Jullien (*Topographie de Tous Les Vignobles Connus*, 1816) is ignorant of any red wine. The Cassis whites, he states, are the best of the region and are three times as expensive as the local reds. He describes them as *liquoreux*; while a contemporary document quoted by Philippe Muguier in his *Vins de Provence* says, '*Les Vins Blancs de Cassis jouissent d'une certaine reputation; ils sont secs et tres spiritueux*.' (The white wines of Cassis enjoy a certain reputation; they are dry and very alcoholic.) Perhaps they were both right. The writer, M.A. Saurel, surveying the devastation at the height of the phylloxera epidemic sixty years later, writes of the highly regarded dry, white wine and the Muscat Noir, an amber-coloured sweet wine.

The best place to find Cassis, even today, is in the locality itself. Naturally it is the wine for the local *bouillabaisse* and *bourride*, as well as other seafood and shellfish dishes. Only recently has the wine begun to find its way abroad.

The *vignoble* occupies an area of some 150 hectares planted on a calcareous soil, often on steeply sloping terraces protected by dry stone walls. Grape varieties are similar to Bandol: Ugni Blanc, Sauvignon Blanc, Doucillon (Grenache Blanc), Clairette, Marsanne and Pascal Blanc for the white, and Grenache, Carignan, Mourvèdre, Cinsault and Barbaroux for red and rosé. In 1980 5749 hectolitres were produced, of which two-thirds was white wine. While the reds and rosés are almost indistinguishable from lighter and lesser Bandols, the whites have more personality, particularly if Marsanne, Doucillon and Sauvignon are planted in sufficient quantity to bring a little character to the wine, and vinification has been controlled at a low temperature. The wine then is light and racy, not too alcoholic and somewhat herby and spicy. It should be bottled young and consumed within a year or two after the vintage. I have to say, though, that I find the white wines of Cassis expensive for what they are. Among the best are François Sack's Clos Sainte-Magdelaine and the Domaine du Paternel. François Paret's Domaine de La Ferme Blanche and the Château de Fontcreuze can also be recommended. (It is worth pointing out that Cassis the wine has nothing to do with the Burgundian blackcurrant liqueur, Crème de Cassis.)

PALETTE

Palette, situated in calcareous soil in the eastern suburbs of Aix-en-Provence, is the smallest vineyard area in Provence and consists of two estates only: Château Simone with 15 hectares and Domaine Crémade with 5 hectares. While Crémade produces only red wine, René Rougier at Simone makes all three colours; the red and rosé from Grenache, Mourvèdre, Cinsault and several obscure Provençal varieties; the white from 80 per cent Ugni Blanc plus Clairette, Muscat and Grenache Blanc. Like a good Bandol but with a flavour that reminds one more of Châteauneuf-du-Pape (or perhaps a cross between the two), Simone wines keep well. Indeed, they spend three years in *tonneau* and *barrique* before being bottled, and need a decade after that to throw off the burliness of their youth. Of equal interest, despite the *encépagement*, is the white wine. After five years or so the flavours come to remind one somewhat of a white Hermitage. It is worth trying. The wines of Château Simone are not cheap, however.

BELLET

Bellet is found up in the hills of the Var Valley above Nice. Like Palette, the 50-hectare (officially – it's probably more like 25 hectares in reality) *vignoble* has been almost engulfed by the encroaching city suburbs and by a glistening hillside eruption of huge greenhouses growing carnations and other plants for the flower markets of France and the local perfume distilleries.

The best wine is the white, a curious, fragrant and, in my view, very high-class mixture of Rolle, Roussanne, Clairette and Chardonnay. The red and rosé are a cross between France and Italy in flavour, being made primarily from Braquet and Folle Noir, intriguing and individual but in my view not as special as the white. The Château de Crémat and the Château de Bellet are the only producers I have ever come across though I understand there are four others including Clos Saint-Vincent.

CÔTES DE PROVENCE, COTEAUX D'AIX-EN-PROVENCE and COTEAUX D'AIX-EN-PROVENCE-LES-BAUX

These are the three generic *appellations* of the area covering a distance, as the crow flies, of some 200 kilometres between the Rhône delta and Saint-Raphael. Some 19,000 hectares are under vine producing 800,000 hectolitres of wine. Quite why Côtes de Provence should have been elevated to AC in 1974 while the other two remained VDQS until 1985 is beyond me. There is good, bad and indifferent wine in each of the three areas. The best wine is the red, and the prices of the best Coteaux d'Aix reds are no less than the best Côtes de Provence wines.

The Baux area from the region of Saint-Rémy-de-Provence is the smallest of the three *appellations* but contains perhaps the most prestigious wine, Eloi Durrbach's Domaine de Trévallon, a wine made from 40 per cent Syrah and 60 per cent Cabernet Sauvignon. Other leading estates in the Baux sub-region include Noel Michelin's 'Terres Blanches', Nicolas Cartier's Mas de Gourgonnier, Mas de la Dame, Mas Sainte Berthe and Paul Cavallier's Domaine de la Vallongue.

In the Aix area is Château Vignelaure, a wine largely made from Cabernet Sauvignon and an estate owned until recently by Georges Brunet, once owner of Château La Lagune in the Médoc. Both this and Trévallon are as expensive as anything in Provence. Less pretentiously priced, indeed well-made wines of very good value, are produced at Château Fonscolombe by the Marquis de Saporta, at the Château de la Gaude by the Baron de Vitrolles, at Chateau Pigoudet, Château de Seuil, Domaine des Bastides and at Château La Coste. There are several other up-to-date modern establishments.

Officially, the Côtes de Provence begins south and east of Aix and covers a vast area, 15,660 hectares in 1988. In practice, the three best areas surround the Massif des Maures and are found near Toulon, along the coast near Saint-Tropez and in the valley of the Argens near Les Arcs. There is a self-appointed group of 21 *crus classés* in the Côtes de Provence, some of which, but by no means all, produce very good wines. These are long-established properties which survived the post-phylloxera, 1960s slump. Since then, a large number of new estates have surfaced. The best of these produce red wines which are at their best between five and ten years after the vintage.

Of the many dozen, if not several hundred, serious producers, here is a personal selection. It does not attempt to be exhaustive. Domaine de la Bernard at Le Luc, Domaine de Bertaud and Château Minuty at Gassin, Domaine de La Croix at Croix Valmer, Domaine des Feraud and Domaine Peissonel at Vidauban, Commanderie de Peyrassol at Flassans, Domaine Richeaume at Puyloubier, Domaine de Rimauresq at Pignans, Château Sainte Rosaline at Les Arcs-sur-Argens and Domaine de la Source Sainte Marguérite at La Londe des Maures. In addition, Domaines Ott of Bandol possess several different Côtes de Provence domaines or *crus*; there is the Château La Gordonne which belongs to the Domaines Viticoles des Salins du Midi and Les Maîtres Vignerons de la Presqu'île de Saint-Tropez produce a number of interesting wines.

COTEAUX VAROIS VDQS

In the middle of viticultural Provence the land is not AC but VDQS. North and south of Saint-Maximin de la Sainte-Beaume and Brignoles you will find the Coteaux Varois, elevated in 1984 from a *vin de pays*. Here, you should look out for the Cabernet Sauvignon and other wines of the Domaine de Saint-Jean at Villecroze (until recently the property of Alain Hirsch). I shall never forget a visit in a rare winter blizzard, driving gingerly up (and even more gingerly down after a delicious lunch of *oeufs brouillés aux truffes* and salad) to the Hirsch domaine up in the hills near Tourtour. The wines are stylish and neat. All the better, in Monsieur Hirsch's view, for not having to comply with AC legislation, meaning that he can produce wines from 100 per cent Cabernet or 100 per cent Syrah rather than having to dilute them with the less positive Grenache or Cinsault. These special *cuvées* may very well remain *vin de pays*, however. The VDQS regulations stipulate a maximum of 30 per cent Cabernet Sauvignon in the blend.

CORSICA

As with so many wine regions, said the late Alexis Lichine in his *Guide to the Wines and Vineyards of France*, the more beautiful the countryside, the more ordinary the wine. This holds as true in Corsica as it does on the mainland of France. Corsica is indeed an island of outstanding visual attraction. Stretching roughly 200 kilometres from north to south, and at its widest point almost 100 kilometres from east to west, Corsica is a mountainous land of wild and wooded beauty. Away from the holiday resorts along the coast – and there are still many secluded coves and beaches – the interior is lonely and spectacular. In parts it is rocky and arid, covered with a herby scrub known as *maquis*, like the *garrigues* of southern France; elsewhere densely forested, like Madeira. It was probably the Phoenicians who first brought wine to Corsica, as they did to so much of the western Mediterranean. They named the island Korai, meaning 'covered in forests'. It became part of the expanding Genoese empire in 1347 and was to remain under Italian hegemony for four centuries. In 1768 the Genoese, having failed to subdue island unrest, sold Corsica to the French. Yet the island is still fiercely independent: neither Italian nor French; just Corsican.

The Italian influence persisted. It was not until well into the nineteenth century that Midi varieties, Grenache, Cinsault and Carignan, began to be planted alongside the Italian grape, Aleatico, which Jullien described in the early nineteenth century as being from Florence, but today is only found further south in Puglia, and other Italian varieties. In Jullien's day some 13,500 hectares were under vine on the island, forming the backbone of its economy. Decimated by the phylloxera some sixty years later prosperity suffered, and it was not until the arrival of hundreds of Algerian expatriates after the colony received its independence in 1960 that a revival began. These *pieds noirs* were only interested in making *vin ordinaire*, however, and it was not until the institution of *appellation contrôlée* in 1976 that the production of quality wine began to be encouraged. Yet still today the amount of *appellation* wine made in Corsica is miniscule. There are perhaps 1600 hectares of *appellation contrôlée* vineyards out of a total of 29,000, producing some 10,000 hectolitres of wine, five per cent of the grand total.

The vine is grown throughout the island on the lower, less mountainous slopes and coastal areas. There are two individual *appellations*, Ajaccio and Patrimonio, and five superior sub-areas of the generic Vin de Corse: Calvi, Cap de Corse, Figari, Porto Vecchio and Sartène. Grape varieties are a mixture of Italian and French. For red wines the Italian varieties are primarily Sciacarello and Nielluccio. The former produces a wine which the French wine writer Woutaz describes as well-coloured, distinguished and fruity and Jancis Robinson as naturally lean and astringent; scented, light but interesting. Nielluccio is said to be related to Tuscany's Sangiovese and produces quite alcoholic wines which lack colour and can lack guts, says Jancis Robinson again. These, plus a variety called Barbarossa, are blended with the French varieties, Cinsault, Mourvèdre, Syrah and Carignan and the Italian white grape, Vermentino.

Authorities are divided as to whether the Vermentino is the same as the Malvoisie or a distant cousin. Throughout the island it is the mainstay of the *appellation contrôlée* white wines, forming 75 per cent to 80 per cent of the blend, into which is added Ugni Blanc. The result is a full and sometimes rather deeply coloured wine with plenty of fruit, opulent but dry. Well vinified, and with enough Ugni to maintain the acidity, it can be pleasantly fragrant but often the result is coarse and blowsy.

Ajaccio, the region surrounding Corsica's capital of the same name on the west side of the island, produces medium-bodied red wines and a certain amount of rosé, predominantly from the Sciacarello grape. Patrimonio, west of Bastia on the north coast, on the other hand, concentrates on the Nielluccio to make fuller, richer red wines, and some interesting rosés. Further north, the peninsula of Cap Corse is a source of the best white wine on the island, Clos Nicrosi. Here Luigi Toussaint makes a 100 per cent Vermentino wine. In the north-west, the gravelly soils near Calvi yield fruity, medium-bodied reds and one or two fresh, flowery (if occasionally somewhat neutral) whites. This is one of Corsica's largest wine-making areas. Sartène, Figari and Porto Vecchio are at the southern end of Corsica and produce more structured wines; at times somewhat rustic, with a strong smell of tobacco, almost as if someone had dunked their dogend in the glass. Christian Imbert at the Domaine de Torraccia near Porto Vecchio is the leading grower.

Other important producers include Dominique Gentile at Saint-Florent near Patrimonio, the Discala brothers at the Domaine de Cantone at Calenzana near Calvi and the Couvent d'Alzipratu in the same area. At the basic level the wine-making is dominated by a number of local co-operatives, some, particularly that at Calenzana, producing a number of *cuvées* of interest.

It is difficult to describe the general character of Corsican wine. The flavour is neither that of the South of France, nor that of any easily recognized sector of Italy, and I can't say that I have ever been enthused enough by the value for money of a Corsican wine to buy any, either for myself or commercially. The most elegant red wines tend to be the most neutral: soft and fruity and more Italian than French, but without anything special or individual about them. For those on holiday on the island there are some perfectly drinkable rosés and white wines, but these are – if clean – also somewhat anonymous.

VINS DE PAYS

VIN DE PAYS DES ALPES-MARITIMES
This is the departmental *vin de pays* from the area around Nice. All three colours are authorized. I have only seen it in red and rosé, made from the local Provençal/Niçois varieties. This is a simple, slightly rustic South of France brew. Little is produced.

VIN DE PAYS D'ARGENS
This zonal *vin de pays* comes from the heart of the Var around the towns of Les Arcs and Vidauban along the valley of the river Argens. Mainly red and rosé are produced, from

the usual varieties. I have seen one or two interesting examples which have additionally incorporated Cabernet Sauvignon.

VIN DE PAYS DES BOUCHES-DU-RHÔNE

A departmental *vin de pays* that appears mainly as red, with a little rosé. These are made from the usual local varieties.

VIN DE PAYS DE L'ÎLE DE BEAUTÉ

This is an appropriate name for the Corsican *vin de pays*. It appears both as red and as rosé (there is also a little white but I have never encountered it) and can be made from a large number of grape varieties. In my experience it is either rather light and neutral, or fuller but somewhat rustic.

VIN DE PAYS DES MAURES

This zonal *vin de pays* comes from the eastern, coastal side of the Var, mainly from the area around Saint-Tropez. The wines are largely red, with some rosé, and made from Carignan, Cinsault and Grenache. Again I have seen some good examples which have benefited from the addition of Cabernet Sauvignon.

VIN DE PAYS DU MONT CAUME

This is the zonal *vin de pays* of the Bandol area and the wines are similar in style to Vin de Pays des Maures. The Bunan family of Moulin des Costes produce an attractive pure Cabernet Sauvignon example.

VIN DE PAYS DE LA PETITE CRAU

This zonal *vin de pays* comes from the area around Les Baux. The wines are mainly red, with some rosé and some white, and from the local varieties. I have seen few examples.

VIN DE PAYS DU VAR

This departmental *vin de pays* is by far the largest – in quantity terms – of the Provençal *vins de pays*. The wines are mainly red, with some rosé, from Carignan, Cinsault and Grenache. There are some interesting wines made from 100 per cent Cabernet Sauvignon and Syrah.

Chapter 9

LANGUEDOC-
ROUSSILLON

While what the French call the Midi is what we roughly translate as the South of France, from a wine point of view the Midi is that part west of the Rhône and its delta, that half of the South which is not Provence. This is where the bulk of French *vin ordinaire* is produced. In an arc bounded by the southern slopes of the Massif Central – the Cévennes and the Montagne Noir – by the Pyrenees and by the Rhône, the Mediterranean coast and the Spanish border, a total of 25 million hectolitres of non-AC wine is produced a year from the four *départements* of Gard, Hérault, Aude and Pyrénées-Orientales.

Vines here can produce ten times the quantity of a Pinot Noir in Gevrey-Chambertin or a Cabernet Sauvignon in Pauillac without raising a sweat. Prodigious quantities of wine are produced, most of it very ordinary indeed, and much of it destined for the EC Common Agricultural Policy's distilleries rather than even the most undiscriminating Frenchman's throat. Hitherto this liquid, weak, acidic and barely within the legal alcoholic limit of the word wine, was bolstered up with highly coloured, heavily alcoholic blends from Algeria and other sources in North Africa.

After Algerian independence in 1962 this trade was officially barred, and the new Moslem governments of these countries pursued a policy of neglect if not of destruction of their vineyards in favour of cereals and other crops. A large number of *pied noir* growers, taking advantage of their French nationality while they still had time, upped sticks and moved to France. The *vin ordinaire* bottling factories of the Midi looked for an alternative source of blending wine within the EC and found it in the similarly rustic wines of southern Italy.

It soon became apparent, however, that as standards improved, this Italian wine was perfectly palatable in its own right – if one's standards were no higher than 11 degrees or

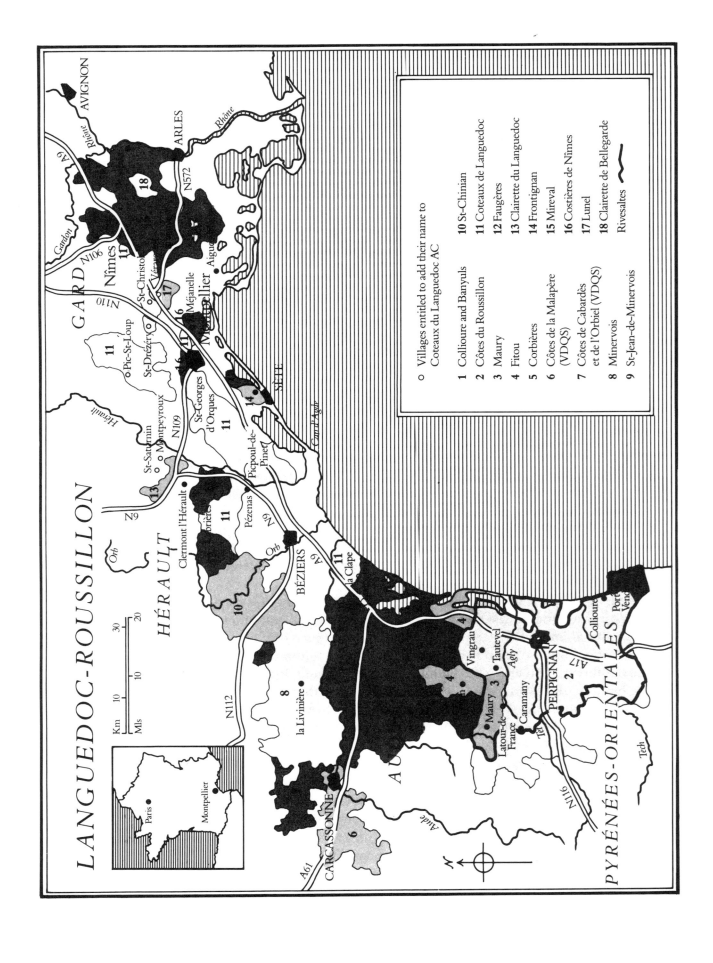

LANGUEDOC-ROUSSILLON

Villages entitled to add their name to
Coteaux du Languedoc AC

10 St-Chinian
11 Coteaux de Languedoc
12 Faugères
13 Clairette du Languedoc
14 Frontignan
15 Mireval
16 Costières de Nîmes
17 Lunel
18 Clairette de Bellegarde
Rivesaltes

1 Collioure and Banyuls
2 Côtes du Roussillon
3 Maury
4 Fitou
5 Corbières
6 Côtes de la Malapère (VDQS)
7 Côtes de Cabardès et de l'Orbiel (VDQS)
8 Minervois
9 St-Jean-de-Minervois

Km 10   20   30
Mls 10   20

12 degrees 'plonk' – and the Italian brews were substantially cheaper than the thin rubbish produced in the Languedoc. The result eventually was that what looked like domestic *vin ordinaire* was made increasingly with almost entirely non-French wine, leaving the local brew and its producers quite superfluous. The consequence was confusion, occasionally erupting to riot as tankers of Italian wine *en route* from the ports of Sète and Marseille to nearby bottling factories were overturned by furious locals. The French government found themselves with a political hot potato which a European Common Agricultural Policy for all its earlier machinations was powerless to solve.

Belatedly, and still inadequately, the French bureaucratic machine began to edge towards an answer to the problem. Encouragement was given to the local growers to plant better qualities of grapes and to reduce the size of their harvests. Loans at favourable rates were made available to facilitate the installation of modern equipment. The establishment of up-to-date co-operatives, viticultural and vinicultural research institutes and oenological departments in local universities was encouraged and a new and higher grading for *vin ordinaire*, the *vins de pays* was introduced. This process has continued with the gradual but now accelerating elevation of local VDQS regions to full *appellation contrôlée*, and, one hopes, eventually to the situation where it will be truly economically viable for every local grower to go for quality rather than to continue to make enormous quantities of indifferent wine which nobody wants and for which he will have to be subsidized, only for it to be distilled into industrial alcohol or further swell the bulging storage vats of the European wine lake.

The result, as much I feel in spite of as because of the efforts of successive French governments, has been a positive, encouraging and sometimes exhilarating improvement in the quality of Midi wines in the last generation. Perhaps the single most exciting thing that I have experienced in my wine trade career has been the enormous improvement in the standard of wine-making, *élevage* and bottling that has taken place in the South of France and elsewhere since the early 1970s. This means that the days are now firmly past when a venture off the beaten track was a gamble, when it was a risk to approve a wine on a mere cask sample and take the successful handling of the wine from then on for granted. There is now plenty of well-made wine of character in these lesser areas of France.

One of the positive hindrances to the improvement of quality has been the continued intransigence of the INAO. When the original laws were set up for *appellation contrôlée* in 1936 and for VDQS in 1949 the object primarily was to determine and codify existing practices, to limit growing areas to the soils and areas known to be the best, to establish a list of the proven suitable fine grape varieties, to legislate minimum levels of alcohol and maximum levels of production, and so on. By and large, for the mainstream quality wine regions of Bordeaux, Burgundy and elsewhere the laws are fine, though in my view they were slow to react to the consequence of the increases in quantity which could be obtained with better husbandry in the vineyard, more effective methods for controlling pests and diseases, and the development of more productive clones of vines. Where the AC and VDQS laws were at fault – or perhaps I should say too rigid – was in their insistence that Midi wines should continue until time immemorial to be made with indigenous Midi grape varieties – Grenache, Carignan, Cinsault, Terret Noir and the rest for red and rosé wines, Clairette, Ugni Blanc, Picpoul, Maccabeo and others for whites. It was only belatedly that recognition was given to what the addition of a quality variety not historically planted in the area, like Cabernet Sauvignon, could do to the standard of quality. Still now, varieties such as these are not officially permitted or encouraged in certain *appellations*.

Yet it is with the use of these *cépages améliorateurs* such as Cabernet Sauvignon and Merlot, Syrah and Mourvèdre (the latter two always allowed but only recently positively encouraged for reds) and Chardonnay, Chenin Blanc and Sauvignon Blanc for whites, that the more enterprising growers have started to produce the most interesting local wines. Often these are not AC or VDQS but *vin de pays*, just as many of the 'new style' Italian wines remain *vini da tavola*. All the INAO seems to be able to do is to recommend the decreasing use of rather boring grapes such as the Carignan when promoting a region such as Corbières from VDQS to AC.

The result is something which currently is a mess. More and more areas – the Côtes du Roussillon in 1977, Faugères and Saint-Chinian in 1982, Minervois, and the whole of the rest of Coteaux du Languedoc (in which are found the *appellations* of Faugères and Saint-Chinian) plus Corbières in 1985 and Costières du Gard (now Costières de Nîmes) in 1986 – have been elevated from VDQS to *appellation contrôlée*. Yet the wines are not better, and no more expensive, than the best of the *vins de pays*. There is a bewildering array of *vins de pays* in the Midi: twenty-one in the Aude, fifteen in the Gard and no fewer than twenty-nine in Hérault. *Appellation* means nothing in the Midi and the consequence is confusion to the consumer.

Across the expanse of the Languedoc-Roussillon there are broadly speaking five major *appellations*. These are the Costières de Nîmes in the *département* of Gard, the Coteaux du Languedoc in the Hérault, Minervois and Corbières on opposite sides of the river Aude, and the Côtes du Roussillon. These *appellations* together with the smaller ones are summarized below. Each of these main areas, however, prescribes broadly the same menu of grapes and is subject to the same regulations and restrictions of minimum alcohol level and maximum yield. Soils are also similar, being largely limestone based, and all areas are subject to a climate which is open, sunny, warm and Mediterranean. Not surprisingly there is a strong resemblance between the wines, the nuances deriving more from the character of the winemaker and his wine-making than from any other material difference. The exceptions are the wines of Limoux which have formerly been regarded as part of the Languedoc-Roussillon, but are now included by the French authorities in their statistics on the South-West (*see page 399*).

In the summary below of the Languedoc-Roussillon *appellations* the dates in brackets after the *appellation* refer to when the wine was elevated from VDQS to AC. Dates have only been given for elevations in the 1980s.

GARD
AC: Costières de Nîmes (AC 1986); Clairette de Bellegarde.

HÉRAULT
AC: Coteaux du Languedoc (AC 1985); Coteaux du Languedoc *crus* (AC 1985): Cabrières, Coteaux de Saint Christol, Pic Saint-Loup, Saint-Drézéry, Saint-Saturnin, Coteaux de la Méjanelle, Coteaux de Véragues, Montpeyroux, Saint-Georges d'Orques and Picpoul de Pinet; Faugères (AC 1982); Saint-Chinian (AC 1982).

HÉRAULT/AUDE
AC: Clairette de Languedoc (AC 1985); Minervois (AC 1985); Corbières (AC 1985); two Coteaux du Languedoc *crus*, Quatorze and La Clape (AC 1985).

AUDE
AC: Fitou
VDQS: Côtes de la Malepère; Côtes de Cabardès et de l'Orbiel.

PYRÉNÉES-ORIENTALES
AC: Côtes du Roussillon; Côtes du Roussillon-Villages; Collioure.

VINS DOUX NATURELS (VDN)
Muscat-based: Muscat de Lunel; Muscat de Mireval; Muscat de Frontignan; Muscat de Saint-Jean-de-Minervois; Muscat de Rivesaltes.
Grenache-based: Rivesaltes; Banyuls; Maury.

LANGUEDOC-ROUSSILLON
PRODUCTION AND SURFACE AREA (1996 HARVEST)

	Surface area in hectares	*Production '000 hectolitres* RED & ROSÉ	WHITE
Languedoc			
AC			
COSTIÈRES DE NIMES	3060	196	9
CLAIRETTE DE BELLEGARDE	88	—	2
COTEAUX DU LANGUEDOC	8255	333	55
COTEAUX DE LANGUEDOC	88	—	4
SAINT-CHINIAN	28886	119	—
	FAUGÈRES	1693	73
	MINERVOIS	5128	
—			
214	3		
CORBIÈRES	14,158	656	10
VDQS			
CÔTES DE LA MALEPÈRE	550	25	—
CÔTES DU CABARDÈS ET DE L'ORBIEL	331	16	—
COTES DE MILLAU	34	2	(89 hl)

	Surface area in hectares	Production '000 hectolitres	
		RED & ROSÉ	WHITE

Roussillon

AC

FITOU	2499	100	—
CÔTES DU ROUSSILLON	4940	220	12
CÔTES DU ROUSSILLON-VILLAGES	1842	78	—
COLLIOURE	320	8	—

AC Vins Doux Naturels (VDN)

MUSCAT DE FRONTIGNAN	806	—	28
MUSCAT DE LUNEL	307	—	11
MUSCAT DE MIREVAL	268	—	9
SAINT-JEAN-DE-MINERVOIS	153	—	5
BANYULS	1468	29	—
MAURY	1712	48	—
MUSCAT DE RIVESALTES	4468	—	147
RIVESALTES	14,653	—	238
Total AC table wine	44,947	1997	93
Total AC vins doux naturels	23,855	77	438
Total VDQS	915	43	—
Total Languedoc-Roussillon	69,717	2117	531
Total Red and White Wines		2648	

Grape Varieties

When the Coteaux du Languedoc and the other Languedoc-Roussillon areas were VDQS, the rules governing the *encépagement* stipulated the following main grape varieties: for red and rosé, Carignan, Cinsault, Mourvèdre and Syrah plus various auxiliary varieties such as Terret Noir, Aspiran Noir, Oeillade and Counoise. The white wines were principally made from Clairette, Grenache Blanc and Ugni Blanc, plus Maccabeo, Terret Blanc, Malvoisie, Marsanne, Muscat Blanc, Picpoul and Roussanne (Maccabeo solely in the Côtes du Roussillon).

With the promotion to *appellation contrôlée*, it is proposed to phase out a number of the auxiliary varieties, the proportion of Carignan and Cinsault has been pegged (at 50 per cent maximum each in the Coteaux du Languedoc, for instance), and the quantity of Grenache, Syrah, and Mourvèdre is being increased. From 1990 in the Coteaux du Languedoc, for instance, Grenache must be at a minimum of 20 per cent, and the proportion of Syrah and Mourvèdre combined must be at least 10 per cent. In Faugères the minimum of these last two varieties must be 25 per cent by 1990. We can therefore anticipate a typical Midi red wine mix as being 50 per cent Carignan, 20 to 30 per cent Grenache Noir, 10 to 20 per cent Mourvèdre or Syrah and 10 to 20 per cent Cinsault.

To avoid tedious repetition in the pages that follow the specific regulations affecting grape varieties in the Midi *appellations* are summarized here.

COSTIÈRES DE NÎMES
Red: 50 per cent maximum Carignan, plus Aspiran Noir, Cinsault, Counoise, Grenache, Mourvedre, Oeillade, Syrah and Terret Noir.
White: Clairette, Grenache Blanc, Maccabeo, Malvoisie, Marsanne, Muscat Blanc, Picpoul, Roussanne, Terret Blanc and Ugni Blanc.

COTEAUX DU LANGUEDOC
Red: 50 per cent maximum each Carignan and Cinsault, 10 per cent minimum in total of Syrah and Mourvèdre, 20 per cent minimum Grenache and Lladoner Pelut, plus up to 10 per cent maximum Counoise, Grenache Gris, Terret Noir and Picpoul Noir.

FAUGÈRES
Red: 50 per cent maximum each Carignan and Cinsault, 10 per cent minimum in total Grenache and Lladoner Pelut, 5 per cent minimum in total Syrah and Mourvèdre.

SAINT-CHINIAN
Red: 50 per cent maximum each Carignan and Cinsault, 20 per cent minimum in total Grenache and Lladoner Pelut, and Mourvèdre and Syrah. The last four combined must represent a minimum of 35 per cent.

MINERVOIS
Red: Carignon (60 per cent maximum), Cinsault, Picpoul Noir, Terret Noir, plus a minimum of 30 per cent combined Grenache, Lladoner Pelut, Syrah and Mourvèdre. The last two must represent a minimum of 10 per cent.

CORBIÈRES
Red: Carignan (70 per cent maximum), Grenache, Lladoner Pelut, Mouvèdre, Picpoul, Terret Noir, Syrah, Cinsault, Grenache Gris, plus white grapes Maccabeo and Bourboulenc.
White: Bourboulenc, Clairette, Grenache Blanc, Maccabeo, Muscat, Picpoul and Terret Blanc.

FITOU
Red: Carignan (maximum 75 per cent), Grenache, Lladoner Pelut, plus at least 10 per cent in total combined of Cinsault, Maccabeo, Mourvèdre, Syrah and Terret Noir.

Côtes du Roussillon, Côtes du Roussillon-Villages

Red: Carignan (maximum 70 per cent), at least 10 per cent in total Syrah and Mourvèdre, maximum 10 per cent Maccabeo, plus Cinsault, Grenache and Lladoner Pelut. No two varieties may exceed 90 per cent.
White: Maccabeo.

Côte du Cabardès et de l'Orbiel vdqs

Red: At least 60 per cent in total Carignan, Cinsault, Grenache, Mourvèdre and Syrah, plus a maximum 30 per cent Carignan and maximum 30 per cent each and 40 per cent in total Aubun, Cabernet Sauvignon, Malbec, Fer, Merlot, Negrette, Picpoul Noir and Terret Noir.

Côtes de la Malepère vdqs

Red: Maximum 60 per cent each Merlot, Malbec and Cinsault, plus maximum 30 per cent in total of Cabernet Sauvignon, Cabernet Franc, Grenache, Lladoner Pelut and Syrah.

Vins Doux Naturels

Red: Minimum 50 per cent Grenache.

The Wine Regions
THE COSTIÈRES DE NÎMES

The Costières du Gard – which from 1989 onwards was renamed Costières de Nîmes in order to avoid confusion with the Vin de Pays de Gard – lies on a low range of hills southeast of Nîmes between Beaucaire and Vauvert, and is bounded by the river Gard, the Rhône-Sète canal and the motorway. This encloses an area roughly rectangular in shape, measuring forty kilometres by sixteen kilometres and covering 2500 hectares of vines. On the more exposed and better-drained slopes you will find the vine; on the richer, more alluvial land between is a mixture of pasture, market gardening and fruit trees.

Most Costières de Nîmes wine is red (in 1988 the AC produced 196,576 hectolitres of red and rosé and only 6751 of white). Today the red is a lightish *primeur*-style wine which can vary from the rather coarse, robust and peppery to something with reasonable fruit and elegance. In my experience there is a certain baked hardness, not necessarily disagreeable, about the wine which I do not find elsewhere in the Languedoc. Like elsewhere in the Midi most of the wine comes from the many local co-operatives, and there has been a discernible improvement in standards in the 1980s as a result of new wine-making techniques: carbonic maceration, for instance, or thermo-vinification (warming the must to extract fruit and colour but not too much tannin). Additionally an increasing use of Grenache and Syrah and *cépages améliorateurs* such as Cabernet Sauvignon are playing their parts.

The Costières de Nîmes seemed to have lost out in the 1985 wholesale elevation of the

Languedoc from VDQS to *appellation contrôlée*, having to wait until 1986. It has always been to some extent the poor relation, fetching inferior prices to Corbières and Minervois. The Costières de Nîmes comprises a wide range of different soils. There is sand and chalk in the north-east, chalk and clay in the south-west, sandstone, quartz pebbles, even gravel elsewhere. With all this mixture you would think that some really exciting wine must be made somewhere. I have yet to find it. Yet the best is very competent. Leading growers and co-operatives include: Château Roubaud at Gallician near Vauvert; Domaine de L'Amarine at Bellegarde; Château Saint-Vincent at Jonquières; Mas Carlot and Domaine Saint-Louis La Perdrix at Bellegarde; Mas des Tourelles at Beauclaire; Mas Aupellière at Vauvert and Domaine de Rosier at Manduel. Madame Chantal Comte at Château de la Tuilerie at Nîmes is perhaps the best of the lot. The Cave Co-opérative de Bellegarde and the Société Vinicole de la Costière de Gallician at Vauvert are also good sources.

CLAIRETTE DE BELLEGARDE

Bellegarde is halfway between Nîmes and Arles on the Rhône-Sète canal. The main road, in fact, by-passes this rather attractive town lying beneath a small hill – as does the newly constructed motorway between Nîmes and Arles. This small *appellation* of 50 hectares lies within the Costières de Nîmes AC and is for white wines only, made from the Clairette grape. Clairette is a late-ripening variety with a thin skin, making it prone to rot. The result is a wine of high alcohol and low acidity and with a tendency to oxidize rapidly. It needs to be very carefully vinified if it is to be at all decent, and the wine certainly needs to be consumed within a few months of bottling. It normally tastes much better from tank in January than it ever does in bottle later in the year.

Sadly at Bellegarde, apart from the Domaine Saint-Louis La Perdrix and the Domaine de L'Amarine, both of which produce a pleasantly soft, aromatic wine, the local producers have not yet found the key to success, either qualitatively or financially. This local Clairette is on the decline – and one is inclined to say a good thing too. Only 1960 hectolitres were produced in 1996.

SAINT-CHINIAN, FAUGÈRES and COTEAUX DU LANGUEDOC

The Coteaux du Languedoc are essentially the *appellation contrôlée* wines of the *département* of Hérault and lie in the hills in a line behind Montpellier and Béziers; overlapping on either side into the Gard and the Aude *départements*. Grape varieties are similar to those used in the Gard. The Hérault is a large *département*. What the tourist will see as he whizzes his way along the motorway is a sea of vines; vast, undulating tracts of vineyard which are mechanically harvested and whose rich, alluvial soils will yield vast quantities of indifferent *vin ordinaire*. Turn off the motorway and drive inland and you will arrive in a different world. Though not as attractive as Provence, the Languedoc hills can be enchanting. The landscape is the typical Midi mixture of rocky scrub (*garrigues*), looming limestone outcrops, secluded valleys and farmsteads, and sleepy, cramped little towns enlivened only by the occasional early medieval church or a modern factory or co-operative. Vineyards share the hillsides with fields of sunflower or lavender; the vine yields only a third or a quarter of what it does down in the plain; and some increasingly interesting wines are being made.

The Coteaux du Languedoc stretches over 121 different communes between Narbonne and Nîmes and covered 8255 hectares of vines in 1996. Of these the largest and best villages of Saint-Chinian and Faugères, adjacent to one another north of Béziers, were elevated separately to *appellation contrôlée* status in 1982. These *appellations* apply to red and rosé wines only. The noble grapes of Grenache, Syrah, Mourvèdre and Lladoner Pelut (a variant of the Grenache) are encouraged, slowly being phased in as the maximum allowable percentage of Carignan is decreased. Good sources include the two main co-operatives, those at Berlou and Faugères respectively, Château Cazals-Viel and the Domaine des Jougla in Saint-Chinian, Jean Vidal at the Château de la Liquière, the Luvac family at Château de Grezan, the Domaine de Saint-Aimé and Bernard and Claudine Vidal, all making Faugères, and the co-operatives at Laurens (for Faugères) and Roquebrun (for Saint-Chinian). The estates marketed by Dominique Rivière under the label of Delta Domaines are also exemplary examples of the Coteaux du Languedoc and other local wines. Les Vignerons du Val d'Orbieu is another quality-conscious producer (Domaine des Albières for Saint-Chinian and Château de Moujan at La Clape in the Coteaux du Languedoc) and the firm of Georges Bonfils in Sète has some interesting estates under its belt.

Twelve villages in this area are called Coteaux du Languedoc *crus* and can add their names to the generic *appellation*. La Clape and Quatourze lie between Narbonne and the coast in the *département* of Aude; Pic Saint-Loup, Saint Drézery, Saint Christol and Véragues are in the north of the region; La Méjanelle and Saint-Georges d'Orques lie to the east and west of Montpellier, as does Saint-Saturnin, which is most renowned for a deep rosé known as Vin d'Une Nuit; Montpeyroux and Cabrières are up in the hills near Clermont l'Hérault. The Coteaux du Languedoc wines vary greatly. Saint-Chinian and Faugères wines can be quite full, and certainly have personality. Coteaux du Languedoc wines tend to be lighter, less hot and muscular than Costières de Nîmes. Modern techniques such as carbonic maceration are much in evidence, as they are throughout the Midi. The twelfth Coteaux du Languedoc *cru* is Pinet which is chiefly known for its single-grape white wine, the Picpoul de Pinet. Picpoul produces a fresh, crisp but evanescent wine. It needs to be drunk young. The late Jean Demolombe's Château du Pech Redon and the Comte de Saint-Exupéry's Château Pech-Céleyran are both in La Clape. Jacques Boscery at Château Rouquette-sur-Mer in nearby Grussan and the Domaine du Temple at Cabrières can be recommended. The chief sources of wine, though, are the local co-operatives.

CLAIRETTE DE LANGUEDOC

Between Pézenas and Clermont L'Hérault, a rather more serious white wine is produced from the Clairette grape than that at Bellegarde. There are three basic styles of wine: as well as a dry wine, a sweeter fortified and a *rancio* version are produced, though I must confess I have sampled neither. The dry Clairette, particularly from Monsieur Jany at Château de la Condemine-Bertrand, is fuller and richer than the Clairette de Bellegarde, ripe and supple with a touch of apricot jam on the finish. It needs drinking young, within the year of the vintage. There are 88 hectares of vines which produced 4061 hectolitres of wine in 1988.

MINERVOIS

West of Saint-Chinian, in the hills above the Aude valley and straddling the *départements* of Hérault and Aude, lies the Minervois. The area contains 18,000 hectares of vine stretching across an area of roughly forty kilometres from east to west, as the crow flies. Of these 18,000 hectares, some 5128 produce Minervois AC wine, the rest are used for *vins de table* and *vins de pays*. The AC vineyards are concentrated in the eastern part of the region near La Livinière, Minerve and Saint-Jean-de-Minervois. The countryside in the Minervois tends to be rougher and more arid than in the Coteaux du Languedoc or on the slopes of neighbouring Corbières to the south across the river Aude. The light seems more vivid, life to be more primitive, the uplands more jagged and the roads more twisted.

The wines can be red, rosé or white and, like the countryside, have their own individual character. In general they are a little lighter than those of neighbouring Saint-Chinian and Faugères. But they have a cool, refreshing acidity about them, and often a more fruity personality than either a Corbières or a Coteaux du Languedoc. In the days when I was a wine buyer I often found myself preferring Minervois to all my Midi wines save for the Côtes du Roussillon-Villages. And it was the cheapest. The wines are mostly red and rosé (in 1996 214,156 hectolitres were produced, only 2830 of white).

The grape varieties are similar to those of Costières de Nîmes; and are echoed but modified in the VDQS *appellation* of Côtes du Cabardès et de L'Orbiel which lies at the western edge of the Minervois, north of Carcassonne.

There are many enterprising estates in the region, a number of outsiders having arrived with the intention of making wines of interest in this up-and-coming area. The Domaine de Gourgazaud is owned by Roger Piquet of Chantovent, one of France's leading producers of *vin de table* and other inexpensive wines. The Château de Paraza, the Domaine Sainte-Eulalie, the two Châteaux de Villerambert (Julien and Marcel) and the Domaine of Jacques Meyzonnier can all be recommended. There are a number of good co-operatives, especially that at La Livinière. Delta Domaines in Béziers and Les Vignerons du Val d'Orbieu in Lézignan are the best of the local *négociants*.

CÔTES DU CABARDÈS ET DE L'ORBIEL VDQS

The Côtes du Cabardès lies at the western edge of the Minervois, north of Carcassonne. Two good properties in the Cabardès are Château Ventenac and the Domaine Saint-Roch. A new estate is that of the Count and Countesse Medas de Loregal: Château de Pannauties and Bastide. Here the grape varieties used are a mixture of those of the Languedoc and the South-West: Syrah, Grenache and Cinsault, but Cabernet Sauvignon, Merlot and Malbec as well. The climate here is somewhat cooler than it is further to the east, and potentially this area could show promise. It is early days still.

CORBIÈRES

Corbières is the largest appellation in the Midi (14158 hectares under AC in 1996) and lies south of the river Aude. It is divided into four different regions: Corbières-Maritimes, Haut-Corbières, Alaric-Corbières and Central-Corbières. It is a quiet, gently undulating countryside, peaceful almost to the point of desertion. The hills are lower and more rounded than in the Minervois. Somehow the effect is more lush. Despite the size of the production, the vine does not occupy every single corner of the region. There is pasture and woodland, the uplands are bare and bleak, and the landscape is perfumed with wild herbs and cultivated lavender. Once again this is an area of red wine production, with a little rosé and only a token proportion of wine (in 1996 65,612 hectolitres of red and rosé and 9900 of white were produced). Grape varieties are the usual Midi mixture. While I find Corbières generally duller than Minervois – the wines are more sturdy, with at times a rather baked, aromatic, Provençal wild-herbs flavour – there are a number of good domaines, and because of the large quantity produced this is the Midi wine you will most regularly see in the shops.

Recommended sources include Château Le Palais, Château Surbery Cartier (formerly Château Les Ollieux), Château La Tour Fabrezan, Château Le Bouis and Domaine de Villemajou. From the Val d'Orbieu group come the oak-aged Domaine de Serre Mazard and Domaine de Fontsainte, plus Château La Voulte Gasparets, Château de Ribaute and the oak-aged Château Saint-Auriol. The co-operatives at Embrès-Castelmaure, Camplory and at Paziols are also of note. Interesting *vins de pays* are produced at Domaine d'Ormesson at Lézignan.

CÔTES DE LA MALEPÈRE VDQS

Inland, between Carcassonne and Limoux, lies the VDQS of Côtes de la Malepère. Here we are approaching the watershed between the influence of the Mediterranean and the Atlantic, and this is reflected in the list of the permitted grape varieties. The red wines can be made from Merlot, Malbec and Cinsault, with smaller amounts of Cabernet Sauvignon, Cabernet Franc, Grenache, Lladoner Pelut and Syrah. The Carignan and other ignoble southern varieties are not permitted. This is a new area, since 1983, and I am sure we will hear more of it. Strangely, despite the proximity of Limoux and its sparkling wines, white wines are not authorized. The leading estate is Château de Malvies-Guilhem at Malvies.

FITOU

Two distinct zones within Corbières, one near the coast around Fitou itself and the other inland between Villeneuve and Tuchan, produce the wine of Fitou. Fitou is the oldest

appellation contrôlée in the Midi, dating from 1948. For almost thirty years it was the sole table wine AC amid a sea of VDQS and *vin ordinaire* wines. It is a curious *appellation*. The five communes near the coast are low-lying and gently undulating and contain soil which is largely alluvial and clay, not, on the face of it, suitable for the production of quality wine. The more precipitous limestone hills inland form a quite different aspect. The four communes here produce distinctly better wine. Fitou is more expensive than most of the rest of the Midi wines. In essence the wines (red only) are a sort of superior Corbières in character. They are strong and rich and often quite high in alcohol. They normally need longer in bottle before they are ready. The best Fitous are made by Robert Daurat-Fort at the Château de Nouvelles and by Les Producteurs Réunis at Narbonne (Cuvée Madame Claude Parmentier). The Cave Co-opérative de Mont-Tauch at Tuchan is another good source with a fine *tête de cuvée*, Château de Ségure, as is the Cave Pilote at Villeneuve and the best of the rest of the region's leading *négociants* such as Les Vignerons du Val d'Orbieu. In 1996 10,086 hectolitres of wine were produced from 2499 hectares of vines.

CÔTES DU ROUSSILLON and CÔTES DU ROUSSILLON-VILLAGES

Across the departmental border in the Pyrénées-Orientales the Spanish proximity becomes more and more noticeable. Roussillon was part of the kingdom of Majorca until 1642. Catalan is still spoken, as it is across the frontier, and the local cuisine, rich in garlic, red peppers and tomatoes, is as much Spanish as French. Around Perpignan, the departmental capital, there is a large fertile plain, largely given over to orchards and market gardens, through which a number of rivers, the Agly, the Tet and the Tech, flow out of the Pyrenees into the Mediterranean. It is in the hinterland that the *appellation contrôlée* wines are produced, particularly in the northern Roussillon along the shores of the Agly and its tributaries. This is the best part, the Côtes du Roussillon-Villages. Both Côtes du Roussillon and Côtes du Roussillon-Villages were elevated to *appellation contrôlée* status in 1977. Between them in 1996 they occupied some 6782 hectares of vines and produced nearly 300,000 hectolitres of wine, mostly red. The Villages section extends over twenty-five communes, of which two, Caramany and Latour de France, are entitled to add their name to the name of the *appellation*. The soil is complex: there is limestone, schist and granite. The climate is dry, the surrounding mountains cutting off rain from most directions. But up in the hills it can be refreshingly cool, in contrast to the plain below which is reputedly the hottest spot in France.

Soil and climate combine to create a wine of a style superior to the rest of the Midi, even though it is based on the usual grapes of Grenache, Cinsault, Carignan, Syrah and so on. I find the wines have richness and balance. They lack the hot peppery character of the Languedoc wines and are full, fleshy, and keep well in bottle. They are in general cheaper than Fitou and offer good value.

Among the best domaines are the Domiane des Chenes (Atlain Razugles), Gerard and Ghislaine Goveby at Calce, Château de Jau at Cases de Pene and the Château de Rey Latour de France, Vingrau and Tautavel. The Vignerons Catalans, an association of growers and co-operatives set up in 1965, can be relied on. This is an exciting area.

COLLIOURE

One of France's least well-known ACs is Collioure, named after the old fishing village and artists' colony on the Côte Vermeille south of Perpignan. This is where the mountains of the Pyrenees finally fall into the sea, and up in the hills behind the town, a small quantity (7523 hectolitres in 1996) of full, sturdy, spicy red wine is produced from 310 hectares of vines. Compared with Côtes du Roussillon-Villages it is quite expensive, but those few I have seen I have enjoyed. Good producers include Thierry Parcé at Domaine de La Rictorie; Dr Parcé at Domaine du Mas Blanc; Jules Campadieu at Domaine de la Villa Rosa; Monsieur Daurès of Château de Jau in the Roussillon; Alain Soufflet and Laurent Escapa of Banyuls; and Rémi Herre of Cave Tambour.

VINS DOUX NATURELS

As at Beaumes-de-Venise and Rasteau in the Rhône, *vins doux naturels* or VDN are made also in Languedoc-Roussillon. These are sweet, dessert wines and the sweetness is produced by stopping the fermentation with the addition of grape spirit. They can be made either from the Muscat grape, in which case the colour of the wine is light golden, or from the Grenache grape, producing something which looks like a dry red wine when young. Production details vary, but essentially the principle is the same. The must, which needs to have a minimum sugar content equivalent to a potential of at least 14.5 degrees of alcohol, is partially fermented. At approximately 5 per cent volume of alcohol the fermentation is stopped (*mutage*) by the addition of between 5 and 10 per cent neutral grape alcohol (minimum strength 96 per cent). This will produce wine with an alcoholic strength of 15 per cent volume minimum and sufficient residual sugar for a potential of 21.5 degrees volume. The resulting wine is rich, sweet, aromatic and very fruity but it retains the natural grape acidity, so, like good, sweet wines anywhere is not cloying.

The Muscat versions, like that of Beaumes-de-Venise, are best drunk as young as possible: freshness is the essence of its delicacy. The Grenache-based *vins doux naturels* can be kept, and are often blended together in a *solera*-type system. They can also be deliberately left to stew and oxidize by leaving the casks exposed to direct sunlight. This produces a *rancio* version, not to my taste. Ageing for the Grenache-based *vins doux naturels* is obligatory. The minimum age is one year. Ninety-five per cent of the Midi VDNs come from the Roussillon, from Banyuls, Maury and Rivesaltes. Rivesaltes is the generic *appellation* and can be Grenache- or Muscat-based (in which case it is called Muscat de Rivesaltes), while Banyuls and Maury are more precisely delimited areas, on the Spanish border and north-west of Perpignan respectively. Banyuls and Maury must be made from 50 per cent Grenache, and 75 per cent for Banyuls *grand cru*, with a minimum ageing of two and a half years.

As well as Rivesaltes there are four other districts for Muscat *vins doux naturels*. Frontignan and the smaller *appellation* of Mireval are on the Hérault coast between Sète and Montpellier; Lunel lies on the other side of Montpellier along the road to Nîmes; and Saint-Jean-de-Minervois is up in the hills on the Minervois and Saint-Chinian borders.

I find none of these Muscats as fine as of Beaumes-de-Venise, for they seem to be heavier and richer, to the detriment of their finesse. Nevertheless, they have the advantage of a more competitive price, and I prefer them to other Mediterranean Muscats. The Grenache versions become tawny as they get older, and can be an alternative to port. Production is dominated by the local co-operatives. The following are recommended producers: (Frontignan) Co-opérative Muscat de Frontignan and Château La Peyrade; (Mireval) Cave Co-opérative Rabelais; (Lunel) Cave Co-opérative de Lunel; (Rivesaltes) Château de Jau, Cazes Frères, Domaine de Canterrane and Domaine Saint-Luc; (Saint-Jean de Minervois) Co-opérative de Saint-Jean de Minervois and Le Pardeillan; (Banyuls) Domaine du Mas Blanc and Château La Rictorie; and (Maury) Mas Amiel.

VINS DE PAYS

There are a very large – too large, I would suggest — number of *vins de pays* in the Languedoc-Roussillon. The vast majority of these are very similar lightish reds (there is some rosé and a very small amount of white wine) made from local varieties such as Carignan, Cinsault and Grenache. They are largely clean and well made, though somewhat anonymous, and more reliable than even more basic *vin de table*.

Regional vins de pays	Vin de Pays d'Oc
Departmental vins de pays	Bouches-du-Rhône, Gard, Hérault, Aude, Pyrénées-Orientales
Zonal vins de pays BOUCHES-DU-RHÔNE, AND GARD	Sables du Golfe du Lion, Coteaux Cévenots, Coteaux de Cèze, Coteaux du Pont de Gard, Coteaux du Salavès, Coteaux Flaviens, Côtes du Vidourle, Mont Bouquet, Serre de Coiran (renamed in 1989 as Côtes de Libac), Uzège, Val de Montferrand (part Hérault), Vaunage, Vistrenque
HÉRAULT	Ardailhou, Bénovie, Bessan, Bérange, Cassan, Caux, Cessenon, Collines de la Moure, Coteaux d'Ensérune, Coteaux de Bessilles, Coteaux de Fontcaude, Coteaux de Laurens, Coteaux de Murviel, Coteaux de Peyriac (part Aude), Coteaux du Libron, Coteaux du Salagou, Côtes de Thau, Côtes de Thongue, Côtes du Brian, Côtes du Ceressou, Gorges de l'Hérault, Haute-Vallée de l'Orb, Mont Baudile, Monts de la Grage, Pézenas, Val de Montferrand (part Gard), Vicomte d'Aumelas
AUDE	Cucugnan, Coteaux de la Cabrerisse, Coteaux de la Cité de Carcassonne, Coteaux de Miramont, Coteaux de Narbonne, Coteaux de Peyriac (part Hérault), Coteaux du Littoral Audois, Coteaux du Lézignanais, Coteaux du Termenes, Côtes de Lastours, Côtes de Perignan, Côtes de Prouille, Hauterive en Pays d'Aude, Hauts de Badens, Haute-Vallée de l'Aude, Torgan, Val d'Orbieu, Val de Cesse, Val de Dagne, Vallée du Paradis
PYRÉNÉES-ORIENTALES	Catalan, Coteaux des Fenouillèdes, Côtes Catalanes, Côte Vermeille, Vals d'Agly

Here and there in the Languedoc-Roussillon imaginative and energetic proprietors have eschewed the indigenous varieties and set their aspirations higher. Some of these are discussed below.

DOMAINES VITICOLES DES SALINS DU MIDI (VIN DE PAYS DES SABLES DU GOLFE DE LION)

If anything proves that with attention to controlled vinification and the selection of the better grape varieties one can make good wine almost anywhere in the world it is the Domaines Viticoles des Salins du Midi. As the name suggests, the main business of the parent company, the Compagnie des Salins du Midi, is the manufacture of salt, which is produced literally on the edge of the land in the extensive sand-flats of the Camargue, by making very shallow reservoirs of sea water which then evaporate, leaving behind salt.

Under the direction of one of the most engaging wine geniuses I have ever met, the now-retired Pierre Jullien, the Salins du Midi decided after the Second World War to turn its attention to making quality rather than quantity. The company had moved into wine production at the time of the phylloxera epidemic, when the remainder of France's vineyards were under threat, as it was found that vines planted in sand were immune from the devastation of the phylloxera louse. But with the re-establishment of the usual Midi vineyards, now under grafted vines, they found they could not compete at the basic level.

The operation is vast. The vineyards total more than 1700 hectares and it is the largest wine estate in France. There are two enormous vinification, storage and bottling factories, one at Aigues-Mortes and the other at Sète, and almost exclusive production of the Vin de Pays des Sables du Golfe du Lion. Particular attention has been given to *cépages améliorateurs*: Cabernet Sauvignon, Sauvignon Blanc, Chardonnay, and even Riesling. The wines are inexpensive and impeccably made and are sold under the name of Listel.

MAS DE DAUMAS GASSAC (VIN DE PAYS DE L'HÉRAULT)

Daumas Gassac has achieved such fame in the last ten years that one might be forgiven for imagining that the owner was some sort of media super-star. It simply produces one of the best wines, not just of the Languedoc, not just of the Midi, but of the whole of France, and this has been widely recognized. Naturally when something new and fantastic comes on the scene we all wax enthusiastic and want to tell everybody about it.

The domaine is located at Aniane in the Hérault, thirty kilometres west of Montpellier, up into the mountains. The guru behind Daumas Gassac is Aimé Guibert who bought the property in 1970. Originally he and his wife Véronique had no thought of becoming *vignerons*. They had just wanted a place where their children could grow up in the country. A friend was the late Henri Enjalbert, Professor of Geography at the University of Bordeaux. Soon after they moved in, Enjalbert came to visit, and noticed with astonishment that a cut Guibert had made when building a road showed that the soil consisted of a very thick deposit of porous glacial debris, soil which reminded him of the best parts of the Côte d'Or and the Médoc, and which would be superb for the vine. 'Guibert, listen,' he said. 'You are sitting on top of a geological miracle. If you turn this land into vineyard I believe you could have a *grand cru* in three generations.' And when Enjalbert talked about *grands crus* he meant Lafite and Latour, Cheval and Pétrus, nothing less. Guibert planted 12 hectares with 70 per cent Cabernet Sauvignon plus Malbec,

Merlot, Cabernet Franc and other red grapes, and, interestingly, a little of the Condrieu grape, Viognier, and produced his first vintage in 1978. The wine is macerated for fifteen to twenty days at a temperature of 28°C or less and before bottling matured in new Allier oak casks for eighteen months.

The result is startling. Though the red wine has little Syrah and no Grenache in its make-up, somehow the effect is of a fine, firm Châteauneuf-du-Pape with a good dollop of Cabernet Sauvignon in it, rather than, as one might expect, a Médoc with the addition of something from Château de Beaucastel or Hermitage. It is unbelievably good. It needs a good six or seven years before it comes round. It is not inexpensive though. The white wine, from 40 per cent Viognier, 40 per cent Chardonnay, plus a number of other varieties, and first produced in 1986, is also very fine.

DOMAINE DU BOSQ – CANTE CIGALE (VIN DE PAYS DE L'HÉRAULT)

Pierre Bezinet's enterprise at Vias near the Cap d'Agde on the coast of Hérault is a tribute not only to imaginative wine-making but also as in Mas de Daumas Gassac to a very particular soil, one highly suitable for growing vines. This soil is of volcanic origin, black or grey in colour, deficient in nutrient, and exceedingly well drained. The produce from a wide range of varieties – Cabernet Sauvignon, Merlot, Cinsault, Syrah and Grenache, as well as whites such as Grenache Blanc (excellent!) and others – is vinified carefully, by both carbonic maceration or whole grape vinification and by traditional methods, and a wide range of *cuvées* is available. Not only does Bezinet produce the Domaine du Bosc range from his own vineyards, but now, increasingly, he vinifies the wines of several of his neighbours. This is imaginative wine-making at its best, and the prices are startlingly cheap. Cellier du Pioch is one of the alternative labels.

OTHER *VINS DE PAYS* PRODUCERS

Every time I visit Languedoc-Roussillon, every time I open a new wine list of some enterprising wine merchant, my attention is drawn to another new domaine producing wine of quality and individuality. The following list does not therefore pretend to be exhaustive: Guy and Marc Benin at Domaine de Ravannes, Thézan-les-Béziers; Alain Roux at Prieuré de Saint Jean de Bebian, Pézanas; Comte d'Ormesson at Domaine d'Ormesson, Lézignan; Domaine du Prieuré d'Amilhac, Servian; Domaine de La Fadèze, Marseillan; Guy Bascon at Domaine de La Condemine L'Eveque, Lézignan; Henri Boukandoura at Domaine de Limbardie, Murveil; Domaine Tusserenc, Pouzolles; Marcel Granier at Domaine Mas de Montel, Aspères; and Domaine de La Grange (Pourthié Père et Fils).

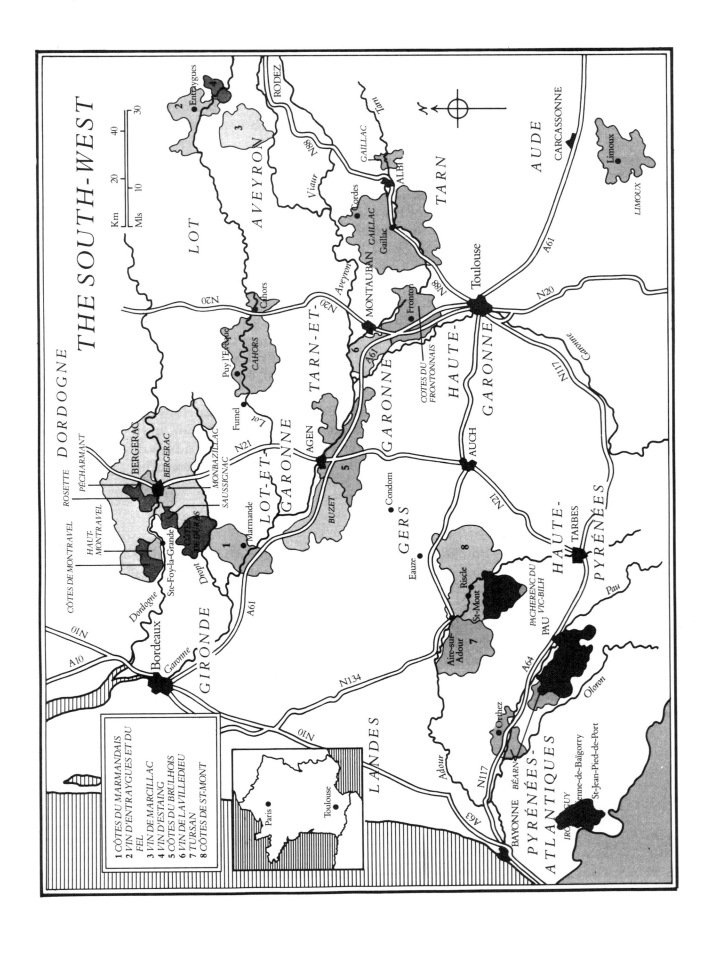

THE SOUTH-WEST

Km
Mls
10
20
30
40

N

DORDOGNE

LOT

AVEYRON

RODEZ

Entraygues

2

4

3

GAILLAC

Tarn

ALBI

TARN

Cordes

Gaillac

MONTAUBAN GAILLAC

Viaur

N88

AUDE

CARCASSONNE

Limoux

LIMOUX

A61

CÔTES DE MONTRAVEL

ROSETTE

PÉCHARMANT

BERGERAC

BERGERAC

HAUT-
MONTRAVEL

CÔTES DE DURAS

MONBAZILLAC

SAUSSIGNAC

N21

Ste-Foy-la-Grande

Dropt

Dordogne

Marmande

1

LOT-ET-GARONNE

AGEN

Fumel

Lot

Puy l'Évêque

CAHORS

Cahors

N20

N20

Aveyron

TARN-ET-GARONNE

6

A61

Fronton

CÔTES DU
FRONTONNAIS

Toulouse

N20

HAUTE-GARONNE

N88

Garonne

N117

GARONNE

BUZET

5

GERS

Condom

Eauze

AUCH

N21

HAUTE-PYRÉNÉES

TARBES

PYRÉNÉES

Riscle

St-Mont

8

PACHERENC DU
PAU VIC-BILH

Air-sur-
Adour

7

A64

Oloron

Pau

GIRONDE

Bordeaux

Garonne

N10

A10

LANDES

N134

N10

Adour

N117

A63

BAYONNE

Béarn

Orthez

**PYRÉNÉES-
ATLANTIQUES**

IROULÉGUY

St-Étienne-de-Baïgorry

St-Jean-Pied-de-Port

1 CÔTES DU MARMANDAIS
2 VIN D'ENTRAYGUES ET DU FEL
3 VIN DE MARCILLAC
4 VIN D'ESTAING
5 CÔTES DU BRULHOIS
6 VIN DE LAVILLEDIEU
7 TURSAN
8 CÔTES DE ST-MONT

Paris

Toulouse

Chapter 10

THE SOUTH-WEST

Time was – and it wasn't that long ago either – when the majority of regional French wines, the *petits vins* from areas outside the mainstream ones of Bordeaux, Burgundy, the Rhône and Alsace, were rustic, insipid and were said 'Not to Travel'. For the most part these wines were produced by artisanal methods, their balance was imperfect and they oxidized quickly. On holiday on the banks of the Loire, accompanying a picnic in the leafy uplands of the Auvergne or on a beach in the South of France, these unpretentious, inexpensive bottles may have tasted delicious. Intoxicated by the relaxed atmosphere and seduced by the cheap prices, we pronounced these wines amazing finds, stashed away a dozen or so in the boot, only to face inevitable disappointment when we returned home and tried to recapture the romance of the sunny circumstances when we first sampled them. Happily, at the same time as escalating prices in the more traditional parts of France have pushed all but their basic *appellations* out of the reach of what most of us can afford for regular drinking, increased prosperity and up-to-date vinification methods have ensured that the standard of quality of the minor regional wines has increased out of all recognition.

These wines now *can* be transported and *will* live up to their original holiday attraction. Moreover, they can be found today with increasing regularity, and at attractive prices, on the shelves of the more enterprising wine merchants. France has always been one of the most fruitful hunting grounds for the enterprising wine buyer but today the search for quality is easier than it used to be. No longer are there only one or two worthwhile growers per minor *appellation*. Armed with a list from the local Syndicat d'Initiative, even the newcomer can soon build up a portfolio of interesting sources and if his customers have faith in his judgement and can be encouraged to be a little more imaginative in their wine buying, the wines will sell without difficulty.

The South-West of France is a region rich in interesting 'little' wines. The area can be defined as everything south of Cognac and the Massif Central, excluding Bordeaux, and west of the imaginary watershed somewhere between Toulouse and Carcassonne where the climatic influence becomes Atlantic rather than Mediterranean. The South-West offers a wide range of wines, each with its own individual characteristics based on local grapes, often varieties hardly seen elsewhere. There is Gaillac, based on the Duras and Braucol grapes; Fronton from the Negrette; Cahors largely produced from the Auxerrois or Malbec. The Bergerac wines are made from the traditional Bordeaux varieties, as are those found in the other *appellations* which surround the Gironde *département* such as Buzet, Duras and the Marmandais. Less commonly found are the wines of Irouléguy and Tursan, Lavilledieu, Marcillac, Estaing and Entraygues.

While the majority of these are red wines there are also white wines. The white Gaillac comes largely from the Mauzac grape; Jurançon from the Gros and Petit Manseng; Pacherenc du Vic-Bilh from the Ruffiac or Arrufiat variety. There are some inexpensive but remarkably stylish Vins de Pays des Côtes de Gascogne from the Ugni Blanc and Colombard.

THE SOUTH-WEST

Production and Surface Area (1996 harvest)

	Surface area in hectares	Production 'ooo hectolitres	
		RED & ROSÉ	WHITE
AC			
MADIRAN	1266	72	—
JURANÇON	814	—	38
IROULÉGUY	170	5	(273 hl)
PACHERENC DU VIC-BILH	180	—	8
BÉARN	216	9	(239 hl)
BERGERAC	10,056	208	377
CÔTES DE DURAS	1705	61	42
BUZET	1805	110	6
CAHORS	4216	244	—
CÔTES DU FRONTONNAIS	1752	104	—
GAILLAC	2407	95	30
BLANQUETTE DE LIMOUX	1153	—	47
CREMANT DE LIMOUX	41	—	13
MONBAZILLAC	2121	—	
VDQS			
CÔTES DE SAINT-MONT	862	38	6
TURSAN	—	6	2

	Surface area in hectares	Production '000 hectolitres	
		RED & ROSÉ	WHITE
CÔTES DU MARMANDAIS	1369	86	3
CÔTES DU BRULHOIS	204	12	—
VIN DE LAVILLEDIEU	70	2	—
MARCILLAC	109	6	—
ENTRAYGUES ET DU FEL	17	(650 hl)	(205 hl)
ESTAING	9	(384 hl)	(55 hl)
Total AC	27,902	908	515
Total VDQS	2640	151	11
Total South-West	30542	1059	526
Total Red and White Wines		1582	

WHEN TO DRINK THE WINES

As there is such a wide variety of different styles of wine in the South-West – indeed even within different *appellations* – it is difficult to generalize about when they will be ready for drinking. The sturdiest reds are those of Cahors and Madiran, followed by the better wines of Bergerac and Buzet. These certainly need two or three years bottle age at the very least. Some may even continue to improve until they reach their second decade. The minor wines of Bergerac, those of Côtes de Duras and Côtes du Marmandais will be ready rather sooner, as will those of Fronton and Gaillac. A year in bottle (less still for the Fronton) is probably enough. With one exception the white wines, like most across the French vineyard area, are made one year for drinking the next. They will not repay keeping. Only the sweeter Jurançons need time and will keep.

The Extreme South-West

MADIRAN

North of Pau and Tarbes you will find the best Béarnais red wine: Madiran. Madiran owes its character and individuality to yet another obscure grape variety, the Tannat. The *appellation* only applies to red wine and, like Cahors but unlike Fronton and Gaillac, this is a *vin de garde*. The Madiran area is near the junction of four *départements*: Landes, Gers, Pyrénées-Atlantiques and Hautes-Pyrénées. Through it flows the river Adour and its tributaries, dividing this green and unspoilt region into numerous gentle valleys. Mixed woodland alternates with pasture, cornfields and vineyards. Ancient homesteads, small Romanesque churches and the occasional fortified manor house decorate the landscape and show evidence of an unhurried, self-sufficient way of life which seems to have hardly changed for centuries.

The name Madiran is derived from the Latin, *Mariae Donarium*, the 'gift of the mayor'. Vines have been grown here since Gallo-Roman times. There is evidence of commercial wine-making in the eleventh century and when a Benedictine abbey was established in the town in 1030 the Tannat grape makes its first recorded appearance. The author Hubrecht Duijker suggests that this might have been transported from a brother establishment at Burgundy. Others say it came from Bordeaux where it was certainly cultivated in the nineteenth century.

Communications were good and the reputation of the wine was propagated by pilgrims who encountered it on their journey through the South-West to Santiago de Compostella. The wine could be taken overland to the river Garonne for shipment down to Bordeaux as one of the many *Haut Pays* wines, which were often used to bolster up the lighter wines of the Gironde, or sent directly down the river Adour to Bayonne. It was exported to the Low Countries and Germany, particularly to Hamburg and Bremen, to Britain and even as far afield as Finland and Russia as early as the sixteenth century. In 1816 Jullien judged Madiran the most important of the Béarnais wines. According to him they were rich in colour, *âpres et pâteux* (tart and inky) but would keep for eight or ten years in cask or bottle and eventually soften, comparing to advantage with wines which enjoyed a higher reputation. Often they were softened up by blending in a little white wine. They are much in demand in Bayonne to give colour and body to some of the weaker wines of the South-West.

Despite the creation of a Syndicat de Défense of the wine in 1906 and, indeed, the award of *appellation contrôlée* in 1948, phylloxera and its aftermath almost wiped out the vineyards of Madiran. The first half of the twentieth century was a depressing time. The Tannat grape, in particular, was on the point of extinction. By 1953 the *vignoble* was down to 6 hectares. It has only been in the last twenty years that horticulturalists have mastered the technique of reproducing the Tannat on a commercial scale in the greenhouse.

For many years the co-operative at Crouseilles was the sole source of the wine, and even when I first started visiting the area in 1974 or 1975, there were few private estates apart from the Laplace family at Château d'Aydie. As in Cahors and elsewhere in the South-West, there has been a resurgence of the *appellation* since 1970. Then there were 100 hectares under vine, a decade later the figure was 700 and in 1996 it was 1266. The Crouseilles co-operative now has 380 members farming 400 hectares of Madiran and has been joined by similar organizations at Plaimont and at Castelnau-Rivière-Basse, the latter under contract for its Madiran wine to the local *négociants* Menjucq. There are now many individual domaines bottling and selling their own wine, though few are on a really large scale.

This part of South-West France enjoys a mild winter and a long, dry summer, though it suffers from a wet spring. The valleys are prone to frost so are left as grazing for cattle or planted with wheat and maize. Most of the vineyards are on the *coteaux* which are limestone of various types, mixed with clay and sand, very stony in parts. Thirty-seven communes, forming the shape of a rough shield beginning just below Saint-Mont and Riscle and extending southwards to Lembeys, are entitled to produce Madiran. The harvest in 1996 was 72,546 hectolitres.

The chief and, until recently, dominant grape variety is the Tannat, the classic red wine variety of the extreme South-West. Tannat on its own produces a very full, solid, astringent wine. Today, the *appellation* laws decree a maximum of 60 per cent in the blend and a minimum of 40 per cent. This, however, is in the vineyard. Some growers, particularly those who use a lot of new wood, make superior blends with quite a bit more Tannat in the *encépagement*. The Cuvée Prestige of Alain Brumont's Château Montus, contains 90 per cent Tannat, for example. Traditionally the other grape used has been Cabernet Franc, known locally as the Bouchy. This softens the burly Tannat and adds to the bouquet. Recently, more and more Cabernet Sauvignon has been planted. Up to 1975, Madiran had to spend eighteen months in wood or vat before bottle, but this has since been reduced to one year. New wood and careful vinification have immeasurably increased the quality of today's Madiran. Fifteen years ago the wine was solid and inky. Today, while firm and masculine, full and sturdy, it is solid without being robust. The elements of denseness and bitterness are still there in the young wine – a cross between Saint-Estèphe and Châeauneuf-du-Pape in flavour – but the wines are richer and more concentrated, the fruit classier and more positive. A good Madiran still needs a decade to mature but will now produce an unexpectedly fine bottle. When the best 1985s and 1990s are ready for drinking. They will also keep extremely well. The three co-operatives mentioned above all produce *têtes de cuvées* matured at least partly in new wood, as well as some single domaines and their standard blends. The Crouseilles establishment has its Rot de Roy; the Union de Producteurs at Plaimont its 'Collection', and the Castelnau enterprise makes a Domaine de la Fitère, exclusively sold by Menjucq.

Leading individual domaines include August Vigneau's Domaine Pichard; Denis de Robillard at Château Peyros; the Terradot brothers at Château d'Arricau-Bordès; Domaine Barrejat and Domaine du Crampilh. But best of all are the Laplace family at Château d'Aydie and Alain Brumont who owns Domaine Bouscasse and Château Montus. Good vintages include 1995, 1990, 1989, 1988, 1985, and 1992. Madrian is a good buy well worth investigating.

JURANÇON

Pau, capital of Béarn and the birthplace of Henri IV, lies in the deep South-West in the *département* of Pyrénées-Atlantiques. It was to the ancient château, once a proper *donjon* or fortified castle but extensively reconstructed both in the Renaissance and again by Louis-Philippe and Louis Napoléon in the nineteenth century, that Jeanne d'Albret, wife of Antoine de Bourbon and daughter of Marguérite d'Angoulême, retired to have her important child. On 13 December 1553, after nineteen days travelling in a carriage from the battlefields of Picardy to Pau in the foothills of the Pyrenees, she was safely delivered of the future king, whose lips, as was the custom, were duly rubbed with garlic and moistened with the local wine. Grandfather d'Albret then held up the child before the waiting crowds: '*Voici le lion enfanté par le brebis de Navarre*' (Here is the lion which has been borne by the ewe of Navarre)', he cried. This was in response to the crowd's insolent reaction on the birth of Jeanne: 'A miracle, a cow (the heraldic motif of the Bearn) has given birth to a ewe!' Thirty-six years later Henry proclaimed himself King of France and Navarre. Henri remained in Béarn throughout his childhood and retained fond memories of his *jeunesse paysanne* all his life.

From the Boulevard de Pyrénées in Pau you can exult in one of the most impressive views in the whole of France. You look south, and almost immediately the land falls steeply away into a gulley through which flows the Gave de Pau. Beyond, across the river, is the town of Jurançon itself, a suburb of Pau. Behind this is a gently rolling landscape, rather too densely wooded at first sight to be an important vineyard. In the background, encased in sunlight if you are lucky, are the mountains: the Pic du Midi d'Osseau in the middle is the most spectacular but the panorama stretches from the Pic de Bigorre to the left to the Pic d'Anie on the right. These are the real Pyrenees (the Pic du Midi d'Osseau is almost 3000 metres high, and snow-capped even in the height of summer).

The vines on the Jurançon hills are planted a mere 300 or 400 metres high, about the same altitude as the vineyards of the Hautes-Côtes in Burgundy, and yet these are truly mountain wines. The proximity of the Pyrenees produces frosts in the spring and a first half of the year which is wetter than most. Happily the autumn is mild and dry, influenced both by the Atlantic and warm winds which float across the mountains from the plains of Spain. The vineyard area extends over twenty-eight communes south and west of Pau between two rivers, the Gave de Pau and Gave d'Oloron, a lush countryside of mountain foothills, discreet valleys and swiftly running streams, with the vineyards being exposed towards the mountains, to the south and south-east.

There are some 814 hectares of vines, producing 38,388 hectolitres of wine in 1996 and planted on soils which are a mixture of marl and loam, mixed together with glacial debris and large *galets* similar to the pudding stones found at Châteauneuf-du-Pape. As a result of the risk of frost there is a particular form of training the vine which applies throughout the extreme South-West, known as *en hautain*. The vines are grown up metal or wooden stakes supporting a cross piece some 1.70 metres from the ground. Once the danger of spring frosts has passed the vine shoots are trained along wires connecting these cross-pieces. In winter the vineyards have a rather macabre aspect of a field of crosses.

Jurançon is produced from Petit Manseng, Gros Manseng and Corbu. The smaller of the Mansengs is the more noble of the two: a short cropper which produces wine rich in aromas of exotic fruit and which is prone to the *pourriture noble*. Its larger cousin produces a less concentrated wine, but one which has good levels of both acidity and alcohol; and it is rather more productive. Gros Manseng is on the increase where the producer's intention is to concentrate on dry wine. Corbu I have never tasted on its own. It is said to make a soft round wine and is susceptible to *coulure*.

Until recently, Jurançon was exclusively a sweet wine. Its reputation was built on wines made from late-harvested and occasionally botrytized grapes. They are more luscious than a sweet wine from the Loire but less rich than a Sauternes, having an individual tang all of their own which has something of pineapple, something of nutmeg, plus in the very best vintages the marmalade flavour common to a lot of botrytized wines. There is something intriguingly 'off' about it. It can be a bit hard when young, needing four years or so to develop.

Sadly these wines went out of fashion, and indeed the *vignoble* as a whole declined abruptly after phylloxera and the economic difficulties of the first half of the twentieth century. Almost when it was too late the region's fortunes were revived by the creation of a co-operative, appropriately in the Avenue Henri IV in Gan in 1950. It has some 350 members, and has been responsible for the launching of a Jurançon dry wine which is now very much the main wine for Jurançon. The wine is medium-bodied, occasionally very slightly *pétillant*, with a good acidity and some of the curious floral aroma of the sweeter version. I find it somewhat four-square in the basic co-operative or local *négociant* version (though the new Grain Sauvage from the Cave des Producteurs has an attractive *primeur* style); rather more individual at a higher price from one of the better local estates. Many of these have only come into existence in the last few years, the co-operative continuing to sell several individual estate wines such as Château Les Astons, Château Conte and Domaine Lasserre. Among the best are Henri Ramonteu's Domaine Cauhapé, the Clos Cancaillaü (Alfred Barrère) and the Clos Lapreyre, Jean Chigé's Cru Lamouroux, the Domaine Vincent Labasse, the Domaine Bellegarde, the Domaine Bru-Baché, Madame Maunce Migné's Clos Joliette, Pierre-Yves Latville's Château Jolys, a very large property, and Charles Hours at the Clos Uroulat. A number of these such as Messieurs Ramonteu and Hours are now maturing their sweet wines in new oak, an interesting development. I predict an exciting future for the Jurançon wines.

IROULÉGUY

In 1982 I fulfilled a life-time's ambition. In October of that year I finally arrived at Saint-Jean-Pied-de-Port in the Basque Pyrenees south-east of Biarritz, the chief town of Irouléguy, the most obscure *appellation contrôlée* in France. I had now visited and tasted in every single *appellation contrôlée* and VDQS in the country. I was ready to contemplate writing this book. Sadly what I found at Irouléguy was not very impressive. I began to understand why I had had to come down within spitting distance of the Spanish border to sample the wine; why it was not exported. The district is tiny – 170 hectares produced 4551 hectolitres of red and rosé wine and 273 hectolitres of white in 1996 – and the wine was confined to the production of the local co-operative at Saint-Étienne-de-Baïgorry whose aspirations were modest. There was a rather watery red, made largely from the Tannat and other varieties grown elsewhere in the Béarn, an insipid rosé, and a small quantity of rather anonymous white *vin de pays* made from the Mansengs and Corbu, as in the Jurançon.

Subsequent visits have shown me reds which are rather more sturdy than those I saw in 1982 but still not wines I could get enthusiastic about. The local *négociant* Étienne Brana has now planted his own estate. His first vintage was in 1990. This is a good source.

PACHERENC DU VIC-BILH

Pacherenc du Vic-Bilh is the white wine of the Madiran area, produced in small quantities – in 1996 production was 8149 hectolitres – largely from the Ruffiac or Arrufiat grape, together with Corbu and Petit and Gros Manseng, Sémillon and Sauvignon Blanc. The name comes from the local dialect for '*picquets en rangs*', posts in rows, the Béarnais way of training the vines high to protect them from frost. Vic-Bilh is the old name for the Madiran district. Pacherenc is normally a dry wine, rich and aromatic, somewhat in the style of Jurançon but lighter and more scented. In the hottest vintages a semi-sweet version is produced. In the hands of good growers such as Lucien Oulie at the Domaine du Crampilh, who vinifies at a low temperature in stainless steel and bottles *sur lie*, it can have a flowery aroma which makes one fleetingly think of Condrieu.

BÉARN

In theory the wines of Béarn can come from any one of seventy-four communes in the Pyrénées-Atlantiques, six in the Hautes-Pyrénées and three in the Gers. In practice production is centred round Orthez, downstream from Pau, and the local co-operative at Bellocq. Most of the Béarn's production is red and rosé, from the usual South-West France varieties. The Bellocq co-operative produces a quaffable Cabernet Franc rosé. The Jurançon grower Jean Chigé (Cru Lamouroux) also makes a light, elegant Béarn rouge. In 1996 8909 hectolitres of red and rosé were produced and only 239 hectolitres of white.

CÔTES DE SAINT-MONT VDQS, TURSAN VDQS

North and north-west, respectively, of Madiran lie the VDQS *appellations* of Côtes de Saint-Mont and Tursan. Saint-Mont is by far the larger of the two districts and runs on either bank of the river Adour from Aire l'Adour to Marciac in the south of the *département* of Gers, a distance of some forty-five kilometres. Some 30,000 hectolitres, mainly of red wine, is annually produced, from a vineyard area of some 850 hectares. The red wine is made from a similar *encépagement* to that in Madiran: at least 70 per cent Tannat and the rest made up with Cabernet Franc, Cabernet Sauvignon and Merlot, though with more emphasis on the Fer, which makes up one-third of the non-Tannat element from 1989 onwards. A small amount of white wine is produced, from 50 per cent Ruffiac, also known as Arrufiat, together with Clairette and Corbu; the two Mansengs are also permitted.

Saint-Mont comes largely from ancient alluvial soils mixed with gravel and marl, and this gives the wines a lighter, leaner character to Madiran. Most of the wine is made by the Union de Producteurs Plaimont whose headquarters is at the co-operative at Saint-Mont. This up-to-date organization, formed in 1976 by uniting the marketing efforts of the co-operatives of Saint-Mont, Aignan and Plaisance, now produces an oak-aged Saint-Mont Rouge, as well as a standard blend.

The wines of the small *appellation* of Tursan come from the rolling hills and lush valleys of the southern Landes south-west of Aire-sur-L'Adour: Eugénie-Les-Bains country. Indeed Michel Guérard, the genius behind the famous three-star hotel, Les Prés d'Eugénie, has his own vineyard, the Domaine du Meunier, though his wine is produced by the Cave at Plaimont rather than by that at Gaune, which processes almost the entire *appellation.* The only individual grower I have come across is Alain Dulucq at the Domaine de Perchade-Pourruchot. He produces two red wines; one from a blend of 60 per cent Tannat and 40 per cent Cabernet Franc, the other from 90 per cent Cabernet Franc and 10 per cent Tannat. In general the Tursan red wines are made from the same varieties as those of Saint-Mont and the white from 90 per cent Baroque, a variety which produces rather a heavy wine unless vinified with care. Ten per cent of Sauvignon Blanc improves the blend immeasurably. Some 8488 hectolitres of Tursan were produced in 1988, a quarter of which was white.

Bergerac

East of Bordeaux, across the *département* border from Gironde into Dordogne, lies Bergerac. Of all the *vignobles* of south-west France, outside Bordeaux, Bergerac is the most prolific, as well as producing wines the closest in character to Bordeaux itself. This is the southern and western part of the ancient province of Périgord, a land that grows progressively more unspoiled and more dramatic journeying upstream towards the Massif Central. It is a country rich in pre-history for it was here rather than nearer the Atlantic coast of today that the land ended and the sea began in the time of Cro-Magnon man and his relations a million or more years ago. The world-famous caves with their wall-paintings at Lascaux near Montignac (you now visit a replica), and those at Les Eyzies de Tayac (where you should not fail to eat at the celebrated restaurant Centenaire), lie upstream from the town of Bergerac in a land of impressive beauty. This is one of the most attractive and hospitable parts of France and despite its popularity not too crowded with tourists even in the height of summer. The locals know how to eat well. There are *cèpes* and truffles, walnuts, plums and home-made local cheeses, river trout, goose and duck, the fish steamed *au bleu*, the fowl often served as a confit, not forgetting *foie gras*. Along the winding, gushing, wooded valley of the river Dordogne and its tributaries lies many a feudal stronghold – old walled villages perched on a rock or a *château-fort*. Elsewhere, there are medieval ruins, grand Renaissance palaces which rival those of the Loire and solitary peaceful hamlets a century away from the bustling civilization of the cities of Bordeaux or Toulouse. West of the confluence of the rivers Vezère and the Dordogne, beyond the impressive meander of the Cingle de Tremolat, the hills subside into a gently flowing, undulating countryside of orchards, wheat and maize fields and vineyards. Here, the land is less wooded, the views are wider-ranging, the atmosphere is bucolic rather than raptorial. Dordogne, the prehistoric and picturesque, has given way to Bergerac the *vignoble*.

Bergerac, like Cahors and other wines of the Aquitaine hinterland, was part of the *Haut Pays*. In medieval times, there was much rivalry between Bergerac and Bordeaux. Sometimes there was a great need for the Bergerac wines to beef up the rather lighter wines of the Gironde. At other times, in order to protect themselves against the competition, the Bordelais imposed taxes on the border between French and English territory and these taxes continued even after the departure of the English. The only port out of which the wines could be shipped was Bordeaux whose merchants jealously guarded their privileges, imposing all sorts of restrictions on the unfortunate producers.

The Dordogne wines, for instance, were prohibited from being sent down river until after Christmas, long after the annual fleet, carrying the Gironde harvest, had departed for the northern markets. Taxation was by the hogshead rather than volume, and it was decreed that the Haut-Pays container should be smaller than that used in Bordeaux. Despite this, wine was a profitable commodity and business flourished. The area under vine in the sixteenth century and even later in the nineteenth century was vastly more extensive than it is today and the chief markets – the British disdaining anything other than 'quality wines' – were Holland, Scandinavia, Hamburg and the Baltic Ports.

The Bergerac wine area extends on both sides of the river Dordogne downstream from Lalinde past Bergerac and Sainte-Foy until the *département* boundary at Castillon-la-Bataille, scene of the famous 1453 defeat which brought about the end of English hegemony in Aquitaine. South of the river from Sainte-Foy onwards is the wine area of the Côtes de Duras, not part of Bergerac.

MONTRAVEL

North of Sainte-Foy are the three areas of Montravel: Montravel itself on the flatter land between the river and the main road to Bordeaux, and Haut-Montravel and Côtes de Montravel up on the hills behind. Altogether, there are some 487 hectares under vine. These are mainly medium-sweet white wines, similar to Premières Côtes de Bordeaux or Cérons and are produced from the same varieties: Sémillon, Sauvignon Blanc and Muscadelle. With the lack of demand for these styles of wines – justifiable neglect, it should be said, when one considers the rustic, sulphury brews of yesteryear – there has been a move to drier examples. These will be sold as simple Montravel, which now represents 80 per cent of Montravel's annual harvest (1996) of 19,113 hectolitres.

SAUSSIGNAC

Travelling upstream from Montravel, the next *appellation* is Côtes de Saussignac. This is a small area producing some 1340 hectolitres per annum (1996) of a mildly sweet wine similar to Montravel. The leading estate is Monsieur Sadoux's Château Court-les-Mûts, which produces red and dry white wines under various Bergerac *appellations* as well as Côtes de Saussignac.

ROSETTE AND PÉCHARMANT

North of the busy market town of Bergerac itself is another sweet wine *appellation*, Rosette. Production has now all but disappeared. Next to it lies Pécharmant, said to produce the best reds in Bergerac. Pécharmant is made from Merlot, Cabernet Sauvignon, Cabernet Franc and Malbec and is akin to a lesser Saint-Émilion in style. The land is a chalky gravel plateau exposed to the south and west and the *vignoble* extends over some 352 hectares, yielding about 18,346 hectolitres of wine. Good estates include the Château de Tiregand, Domaine de Grand Jaure and the Domaine du Haut-Pércharmant.

MONBAZILLAC

To the south, across the river, lies the now thriving area of Monbazillac. The name is a corruption of the Gascon name 'Mont Bazailhac' which is said to mean 'mountain of fire' or 'mountain of gold'. This is an ancient *vignoble*, renowned for centuries and the wine was widely exported. Two pilgrims from the area, at an audience with the Pope in the sixteenth century, found he was already acquainted with the wine and Talleyrand is said to have served it as a 'wine of peace' at the Congress of Vienna. At this time, according to Jullien (*Topographie de Tous les Vignobles Connus*, 1816), it was already better than a mere sweet white wine, for Jullien describes the grapes being left on the vine until they turned brown and the fruit was almost rotten. He also mentions that during the harvest each section of the vineyard is picked over a number of times, just as happens today in Sauternes and Barsac.

Despite this reputation, which some have dubbed the poor man's Sauternes, the quality and demand declined abruptly after the phylloxera epidemic and the First World War, and by the 1960s production was a mere echo of its heyday. The establishment of the Cave Co-opérative de Monbazillac in 1940 and perhaps, more important, its amalgamation with a number of other local establishments under the umbrella of Unidor (*Union des Co-opératives Vinicoles de la Dordogne*) in 1965 did much to promote a revival of the fortunes of Monbazillac. The co-operative produces much of the best wine of the area, including the wines of the Château de Monbazillac itself – a handsome sixteenth-century château which now houses a restaurant and a museum – and Châteaux La Brie, Pion and Septy. Armand Vidal-Hurmic's Château de Treuil de Nailhac is another good source. The same family also own Château Le Borderie.

Monbazillac is a sweet wine, produced by the Sauternes method from identical grapes: Sémillion, Sauvignon Blancand Muscadelle. There are 2121 hectares of vines in the communes of Rouffignac-de-Sigoules, Colombier, Pomport, Saint-Laurent-des-Vignes and Monbazillac itself. Annual production varies between 11,000 and 70,000 hectolitres depending on the vintage. In 1996 it was 50,595 hectolitres.

BERGERAC

There are three Bergerac *appellations*: Bergerac, Côtes de Bergerac and Côtes de Bergerac Moelleux. The *appellation* of Bergerac is for red, rosé and dry white wines. The reds and the semi-sweet whites which reach 11 degrees of alcohol instead of 10 degrees are called Côtes de Bergerac (for the reds) and Côtes de Bergerac Moelleux (for the whites). The styles of wine vary a great deal as a result of *encépagement*, soil structure and the competence and aspiration of the winemaker. The vineyards extend northwards from the border with the Lot-et-Garonne *département* through Monbazillac and Saussignac, over the river Dordogne; beyond Pécharmant up to Villamblard to the north-east as well as running west to Saint-Martin-de-Gurçon and Villefranche-de-Lonchat.

Bergerac is a large *appellation*. Some 75 per cent – as much as 186,586 hectolitres in 1996 – of the total wine production of the Dordogne comes under one of the 'Bergerac' *appellations*, in one form or another. Historically, the wine was *moelleux* (sweet), today over half is red and most of the rest is dry white. Bergerac can range from serious, oak-aged wines from the specialist estates to an insipid *rouge* which is little different from *vin ordinaire*. The whites, too, can be similar to a Sauvignon-based Entre-Deux-Mers and often as dreary as these so often are; or they can be delightful. Bordeaux grapes are used, Cabernet Sauvignon increasingly being planted, superseding Malbec and replacing Merlot. Sauvignon Blanc is the dominant white grape, though Ugni Blanc and Chenin Blanc are also authorized as well as Sémillon and Muscadelle.

The most interesting wines are the whites. Bergerac is an area which has seen the arrival of a number of enterprising *vignerons* who have been quick to seize on the latest techniques of mechanical harvesting (so that the entire harvest can be gathered in at the optimum moment), cold fermentation in wood with selected yeasts, skin contact (*macération préfermentaire*) and even *élevage* in new oak.

It is a happy hunting ground for the enterprising wine buyer. Among the leading estates is the Count de Boisredon's Château de Belingard – similar wines are produced under the Château du Chayne and Château Boudigand labels. Others include the Château de Pannisseau and Château Thenac. Many of the estates mentioned already such as Château Court-les-Mûts and Château du Treuil de Nailhac also produce white Bergerac. Without a doubt the best wine though is that of Château La Jaubertie at Colombier. Jaubertie is owned by an Englishman, Nick Ryman who bought the property in 1973 and sold on to his son and various partners in 1995. As well as a standard Merlot-based red, and two white wines, one more Sauvignon-dominated than the other, Jaubertie produces a number of *têtes de cuvée*, chief of which are the two Réserves de Mirabelle, a Cabernet Sauvignon, oak-aged red which would not be out of place in a line-up of the best *crus bourgeois* of Bordeaux, and an oaky, succulent white. These two are excellent wines.

Central South-West

CÔTES DE DURAS

The Duras region lies east of the Entre-Deux-Mers, south of Sainte-Foy, west of Bergerac and north of the Côtes du Marmandais and the river Dropt. It is a secluded, peaceful land of gentle hills and mixed farming which only failed to be part of mainstream Bordeaux as a result of being placed in the *département* of Lot-et-Garonne rather than Gironde when the *département* boundaries were drawn up after the Revolution. As far as reputation and the export market is concerned, this is largely dry white wine country. Sémillon, Sauvignon Blanc, Muscadelle, Mauzac, Chenin, Ondenc and Ugni Blanc are all authorized and contribute roughly 60 per cent of the production (in 1996 this totalled 103,290 hectolitres). Cabernet Sauvignon, Cabernet Franc, Merlot and Malbec are used for the red wines. A total of some 1705 hectares of essentially limestone soil are planted with vines.

Though there are a number of individual domaines the reputation of the *appellation* rests largely on the Duras co-operative, a pioneer of modern methods and the driving force behind the trend towards crisp, fragrant, dry wines produced mainly from

Sauvignon Blanc. The co-operative also produces attractive reds made by carbonic maceration for early drinking. Lucien Salesse at the Domaine de Ferrant produces an attractive Sauvignon white wine and a more traditional red.

BUZET

Midway between Agen and Casteljaloux a small tributary approaches the Garonne from the woodlands of the Gers and reaches the river near a town called Buzet. Some twenty-seven communes on the south or left bank of the Garonne are entitled to produce wine. In practice, for this is a land of mixed farming; the vines are confined to well-exposed sites in the gentle valleys that ripple away from the Garonne. Some 1805 hectares are under vines. The soil is mixed: gravel, clay and limestone mixed with alluvial soil and stony parts and becoming more sandy to the west where the vineyard area meets the eastern edges of the Landes forest. It is marly to the south where it overlaps into Armagnac country. This is the centre for the thriving and value-for-money *appellation* of Buzet.

Like Duras, the wines of Buzet suffered from being outside the Gironde *département*. As *Haut Pays* wines they had to pay a forfeit to be sent down the river or were even excluded from the Bordeaux commerce altogether. Unlike Duras this is an area of almost exclusively red wines. Buzet is dominated by its co-operative, located at Damazan, which is responsible for over 90 per cent of the local production. It was set up in 1955, two years after Buzet was promoted to VDQS, and from the start adopted a policy of quality, using the best modern methods, including oak-ageing for the best wines and a severe selection for the *appellation* wine. *Appellation contrôlée* was awarded in 1973.

The *encépagement* is typically Bordeaux: Merlot, Cabernet Sauvignon, Cabernet Franc and a little Malbec for the reds; Sauvignon Blanc, Sémillon and Muscadelle for the small quantity of white. The *tête de cuvée* of the co-operative used to be called Cuvée Napoléon but is now sold as Cuvée Baron d'Ardeuil. Bourbon feeling or more realistically perhaps petty legislation restricting the use of the name Napoleon has obviously got the better of marketing commonsense. This is made from one-third each of the three major red varieties, and one third is aged in new oak: this is a classy bottle which can compete with a good Bordeaux *cru bourgeois*. The co-operative also vinifies and sells the wines of Château de Gueyze, Château du Bouchet and Domaine Roc de Cailloux. Château de Padère, Château Sauvagnères and Château des Jonquilles (100 per cent Merlot), both the latter two produced by the Belgian Jacques Thérasse and his son Bernard, are the other leading wines. Production of Buzet totalled 115,871 hectolitres in 1996 of which only 6007 hectolitres were white.

CÔTES DU MARMANDAIS VDQS

Between Duras and Buzet, marching with the Entre-Deux-Mers but at the eastern limit of the Lot-et-Garonne *département*, lies the VDQS of Côtes du Marmandais, another district excluded from mainstream Bordeaux merely by the whim of a Parisian bureaucrat in 1790. The district straddles both banks of the Garonne, and takes its name from Marmande, an active market town and the centre for the area's main activity, which is tomato-growing. In the gently rolling countryside of the Marmandais, the vine has to share the predominantly marly soil with a number of other fruits, and though the delimited area looks large on the map and covers some twenty-seven communes only about 800 hectares are under vine. The grape varieties are chiefly the Bordeaux ones, though interlopers such as Abouriou, Fer-Servadou, Gamay and even Syrah are allowed in small quantities.

Production is almost exclusively in the hands of two co-operatives. The one at Cocumont on the left bank, where the soil contains more gravel on a sandstone base, enjoys a higher reputation than the one at Beaupuy. The red wines are lighter and not as interesting as those of Buzet, the small amount of white is less definitive than those of the Duras. Production in 1996 totalled 89,134 hectolitres of which just under 4 per cent was white.

CÔTES DE BRULHOIS VDQS

Côtes de Brulhois is a recent addition to the ranks of VDQS, having been elevated from *vin de pays* in 1984. The area adjoins Buzet, and continues south of the Garonne, past Agen, as far as the boundary between Lot-et-Garonne and Tarn-et-Garonne. Production is mainly in the hands of the Goulens-en-Brulhois co-operative a few kilometres south of Agen in the valley of the Gers. Agen is a centre for plums – and indeed for peaches and table grapes – rather than for wine, which is nothing to get excited about. The wines are somewhat unstylish reds or rosés and made from the three Bordeaux grapes plus Fer, Malbec and Tannat. Production in 1996 totalled 11,741 hectolitres.

CAHORS

A number of the Garonne's tributaries flow due westwards out of the Massif Central. After the river Dordogne the two most important are the Tarn, with its own main addition, the Aveyron, and the Lot. The Lot has its source near the town of Mende in the *département* of Lozère, not far from that of the river Allier, a major tributary of the Loire. It flows through spectacularly wild, empty and beautiful country – there is a Gorges du Lot, not as impressive perhaps as the Gorges du Tarn, but nevertheless worth visiting, and less tourist-infested during the summer months – before reaching the old fortified town of Cahors, capital of the *département* which takes its name from the river. Cahors, in the old French region of Quercy – from *quercus*, the Latin for oak – is the Lot's major wine region whose wine (red only) lays claim to be the best and most interesting of all the South-West.

The *vignoble* of Cahors, comprising 4216 hectares in forty-five communes in the cantons of Cahors itself, Catus, Lalbenque, Luzech, Montcuq, and Puy l'Evêque, is equidistant (200 kilometres), as the crow flies, from the Atlantic Ocean, the Pyrenees and the Mediterranean. The vineyard area lies mainly to the west of Cahors itself, on either bank of the weaving, meandering river for about fifty kilometres, the western boundary being near Fumel where the Lot *département* meets the Lot-et-Garonne.

The Cahors climate, though governed by the Atlantic Ocean, and in many respects similar to that of Bordeaux, nevertheless differs in some important respects. Chiefly, and crucial to the quality of the wine, is the incidence of warm, dry wind from the south-east during September and October. While no hotter than Bordeaux – on average Cahors is marginally cooler throughout the year, probably because of the higher altitude – September and October are considerably drier, not only by comparison with Bordeaux but also with Montpellier in the Languedoc. The prevailing westerly rain-bearing clouds appear to pass to the north of the region and the annual precipitation in Aurillac, Brive or Figeac can be as much as three times the 500 or 600 mm that of Puy l'Evêque, further south in the middle of the Cahors region. Frost is always a threat, though the region is protected for most of the year from the cold winds issuing from the Massif Central and the river itself often swathes the valley in an insulating blanket of fog. As Bordeaux, the 1991 and 1977 vintage were reduced by frost damage, the '75 was also affected, and also the '71, though to a lesser extent.

Just as the more exposed *causse* or limestone plateau is more susceptible to frost than the valley, so it is to hail. Hail appears to be more frequent in the south-east corner of the vineyard region and steps are in hand for united action by means of helicopters, despatched to seed hail-bearing clouds before they devastate the vineyards.

The Lot has carved a narrow, steep-sided, fertile valley into the dusty, more arid, limestone bedrock of the Quercy region, and the vineyards lie both on the flatter, more alluvial soil of the serpentine valley floor and on the hillsides and plateaux overlooking the river. The soil structure is complex; gravel and quartz mixed with sand and limestone in the valley, limestone debris on the hillsides, and Kimmeridgian soil comprised of limestone rubble, clay and marl on the plateau. Nowhere is the top soil more than a few metres deep at most. Everywhere the base is limestone rock. Parts of the valley are too alluvial for the cultivation of quality wine and have never been included in the *appellation*. The local Comité Interprofessional, now that the Cahors *vignoble* has been re-established, wants more vineyards in the richer soil of the valley to be declassified.

Historically Cahors has for long been an important vineyard area. Indeed it was flourishing in Gallo-Roman times, even before Bordeaux became established as a major wine-making region, and the wines of the *Haut Pays* were shipped through the port of Bordeaux. The region was producing the equivalent of 1.4 million hectolitres in the Middle Ages, and in 1816, according to Jullien, there were more vineyards in the Lot (40,000 hectares) than in the Pyrénées-Orientales, the Aude or the Bouches-des-Rhône. This was the era of the fabled 'black wine' of Cahors. It was made by concentrating part of the must, lightly fortified with grape spirit, and able to last, according to the author Cyrus Redding, up to thirty years in wood, or fifty in bottle. It was not a wine for drinking though but for blending with in order to bolster up the thinner wines of Bordeaux.

From the phylloxera epidemic onwards, however, Cahors went into decline. 'Direct producers' (hybrids between *Vitis vinifera* and a phylloxera-resistant species of vine) replaced the noble vines, and the area under plantation disappeared almost completely. What could have been the final straw was the terrible February frost of 1956. In 1958 the whole of Cahors produced barely 650 hogsheads of wine.

The renaissance of the Cahors vineyard since then has been impressive. The area under vine has risen from 200 hectares in 1960 to over 4000 today and is currently increasing by an average of 150 hectares per annum. Production now comfortably tops 200,000 hectolitres (in 1996 it was 243,995 hectolitres) – a pittance perhaps compared with the Middle Ages but we are talking now about AC wine, analysed, blind-tasted and approved by the local office of the INAO. Currently the region produces 4 per cent of France's total of *appellation contrôlée* wine. The resurgence of Cahors was double pronged. On the one hand there were the co-operatives, on the other the indomitable spirit of one of the few growers who had soldiered on through the depression such as Jean Jouffreau at the Clos de Gamot. Jouffreau is a traditionalist and a perfectionist. Clos de Gamot had been in his family possession since 1610; and when he saw the area beginning to revive he set out to encourage other growers to remain independent of the co-operative movement and to aspire to the quality end of the market.

The co-operative 'Les Côtes d'Olt' ('Olt' is an old form of 'Lot') at Parnac was established in 1947. Approximately half the region's 500-plus growers are members of the co-operative. It has a research station and experimental vineyards, and has been in the forefront of developing disease-resistant and more prolific strains of the vine by clonal selection, establishing the most suitable rootstocks for each variety and soil type, and introducing and promoting *cépages améliorateurs* – Merlot and Tannat – to complement the *appellation*'s indigenous quality variety, Auxerrois.

As the vineyards have expanded, so has the quality of the wine and the aspirations of those who make it. It was one of the original VDQS *appellations* created in 1949, and was then elevated to *appellation contrôlée* in 1971.

The principal grape in Cahors is locally known in the Quercy as Auxerrois. This is the Cot of the Loire Valley and the same as the Malbec, Pressac or 'Cahors' of the Gironde. Why it should be so called – for as far as I can find out it has no connection with Auxerre near Chablis – history or legend does not relate, though the latter insists on derivation or even direct descent from the Latin vine Aminee from which was made the famous Falernian wines of the ancients. The Malbec forms a loose cluster of sizeable berries, is prone to downy mildew and rot – and particularly *coulure* – and produces a satisfactory quantity of sturdy, well-coloured, quite tannic wine. Auxerrois must make up to 70 per cent of the Cahors blend. It is planted particularly on the *coteaux* where *coulure* is less prevalent as the humidity is lower, and where there is less danger, as the soil is more meagre, of too vigorous a yield.

The secondary varieties in the original AC legislation included a number which have since been banned, Valdiguié or Gros Auxerrois, Abouriou or Gamay du Rhône, Syrah and Negrette (the Côtes du Frontonnais grapes). Since a decree in 1979 there are now only three subsidiary grapes. Jurançon Rouge (also known as the Folle Noire, and here in the Quercy as the Dame Noire) is a variety which has nothing to do with the wine called Jurançon, which is white and made from Gros and Petit Manseng. Jurançon Rouge forms a tight cluster, and for this reason, and because of its thin skin, it tends to rot in wet and humid weather, so it is little grown on the valley floor. It is better on the stony slopes away from the river. It produces well and regularly but the wine is light and forward and tends to attenuate rapidly. Acreage is decreasing and is estimated by 1990 to be no more than 10 per cent of the *appellation*.

Merlot is a relative newcomer to Cahors. As in Bordeaux the wine it produces is rich and alcoholic, soft and aromatic in character and matures quickly, though by no means as fast as the Dame Noire. It is planted on the richer soils. The third variety is Tannat, the main grape of the Madiran and other reds of the Béarn and Pays Basque. Though a distant cousin, from the ampelographical point of view, of Auxerrois, the bunch is more compact and the wine it produces is less alcoholic than wine from Auxerrois and Merlot. The wine is tough, tannic and astringent and when young gives the muscle and stuffing, and, because of a good level of acidity, the longevity to the wine of Cahors. Tannat ripens last of all, often not entirely successfully.

All these vines are trained and pruned to the *taille guyot*, both single and double, though here and there in the vineyards some *gobelet* (bush-shaped) old vines can be seen. There is increasing use of machine-harvesting (in some vineyards 4 hectares a day can be covered) and for this the vines must be specifically planted further apart and trained higher off the ground. First of all, the vines are pruned to eight or ten buds per cane, i.e. up to a maximum of twenty per vine, but this number, particularly rigorously in the best properties, is pruned back once the danger of frost has passed.

Cahors no longer produces the fabled black wine of yesteryear (must concentration is now forbidden), and is sometimes – from a vineyard in the valley and at the basic level of the *appellation* – rather on the weak and feeble side. This is a result of the extensive vineyard enlargement since the early 1960s – much originally in the valley rather than on the hillsides. Moreover, a lot of the generic Cahors sold in the 1970s – and still today – was never matured in wood so lacked density and staying power. In good years such as 1990, 1985 and 1992 the wine was acceptable, but in other years when there was not enough sunshine during the late summer, or rain during the vintage, such as in the vintages of the early 1990s it was thin and insipid. It did the reputation of the *appellation* an injustice.

Better, indeed a totally different animal, is the sort of Cahors obtainable as a *négociant*'s 'Réserve', one that has been matured using new oak, provided it is not kept in wood excessively long. Traditionally Cahors was matured in large wooden *foudres* or vats and, somewhat in the Italian or Spanish manner, was left in wood until mature. A few growers such as Jouffreau still use this method, believing that more Bordeaux methods using new *barriques* are foreign to the true character of Cahors. In the early 1970s, a range of old Clos de Gamot vintages was auctioned at Christie's (Jouffreau wanted to raise enough money to buy the Château de Cayrou) and I remember tasting them. They were certainly very impressive, and gave the lie to the generally accepted idea that a wine kept too long in wood dries out and loses all its fruit. Today, inevitably, the trend has changed towards barrel-ageing and to bottling in advance of maturity, though growers are still shy of using too much new wood. Most of the best properties use a combination of *barrique* and *foudre*, secondhand casks from Bordeaux being preferred to new wood.

The best Cahors are the single-vineyard or domaine wines, often from long-established estates, and from the hillsides or the *causse*, though the wines from the *causse* tend to lose in style what they gain in robustness. These wines give one an idea of the 'manly' wines – to borrow Professor Saintsbury's expression about Hermitage, but perfectly appropriate in the Cahors context – produced in pre-phylloxera times.

The wine is quite distinctive, and fully worthy of the rating 'fine wine' in its individual right, even if, in some cases, one is tempted to give it the benefit of the doubt until the vineyard is mature, or indeed until the winemaker has really learned how to produce the best out of his vines.

Just because Auxerrois is one of the grape varieties used in the lesser, eastern regions of Bordeaux does not mean to say that there is any resemblance with the loose-knit wines of the Saint-Émilion satellites. Cahors is, or should be, a solid wine: and a Cahors from the *causse* is as solid by comparison with a valley wine as Bandol is to the Coteaux d'Aix-en-Provence, or a good Cornas is to a lesser Saint-Joseph wine.

A solid Cahors wine is strong, baked, full-bodied, rich and sturdy, yet not without warmth and even elegance if allowed to mature and to round off the muscle and density of the wine in its youth. It lasts well, often being not at its best before seven or ten years, and will keep another decade thereafter. This is the sort of Cahors which is worth pursuing and cellaring.

The Union Interprofessionelle du Vin de Cahors' list of producers in the area lists some sixty names, of which thirteen, including the co-operative – who represent 45 per cent of the production – are said to be *négociants* rather than *viticulteurs*. Some of these *viticulteurs* are growers and winemakers on quite a large scale, such as the Rigal brothers, owners of Château Saint-Didier in Parnac, a *premier cru* of Cahors, if there could be said to be such a thing, who are also 'farmers' or winemakers or distributors for at least five other estates, including the Domaines de Meriguet and Castellasse, and responsible for at least 60 hectares of vineyard. The Les Côtes d'Olt co-operative, unlike Rigal, keeps little wine in wood, and I have found their generic wine disappointing in recent years. Nevertheless their superior blend 'Count André de Monpézat' is reliable and they make the wine for a number of single properties, including Châteaux Clos, Bouysses, Cayrou d'Albas and Cénac.

Among the other growers and *négociants* perhaps the best is Victor Bernède's Clos la Coutale at Viré near Puy l'Evêque. He has 25 hectares of vineyards and seems to win most of the gold medals at the Mâcon and Paris wine fairs. He produces a remarkably elegant wine with great balance and therefore potential for ageing. Robert Decas' establishment up on the *causse* at Trespoux-Rasseils is more primitive, and the wine can be a bit on the rustic side. Yet the wines are old, and a ten-year-old wine I once had in his kitchen, to the accompaniment of one of the oldest and most noisy washing-machines I have ever encountered, was a revelation.

George Vigouroux of the Château de Haut-Serre took Cahors by storm a few years ago when he replanted 40 hectares of vines at Cieurac to the south-east of Cahors, and was perhaps the first to give Cahors wine a bit of modern 'hype'. He produces good wine, and it has become even better as the vines have matured.

Another excellent property is the Clos Triguedina of Baldès et Fils to the south of Puy l'Evêque. This is a wine you will often find in local restaurants in the Lot and further north in the upper Dordogne. I have seen most of the vintages of the 1970s and 1980s and have rarely been disappointed. The superior *cuvée* 'Prince Probus' is matured in new oak. The wines of the impressive estate of the Château de Chambert, at Floressas, again near Puy l'Evêque, have I'm sure the potential to be very fine indeed. So far they are competent but have never really sung to me. Other good estates include Jean Jouffreau's Château de Cayrou and Clos de Gamot, already mentioned, Domaine de Gaudon (owned by Durole et Fils), Charles Burc at the Domaine de Courberac, his cousin René at the Domaines des Leygues and Pineraie and Philippe Heilbronner at the Domaine de Quattre.

CÔTES DU FRONTONNAIS

Halfway between Montauban and Toulouse, lying on a predominantly gravel plateau between the rivers Tarn and Garonne, is the up-and-coming *appellation* of the Côtes du Frontonnais, created out of two local VDQS *appellations* in 1975. The *appellation* covers the wines of both Fronton and neighbouring Villaudric and the label will denote one or the other in a suffix. The fourteen communes producing Fronton lie to the north and west of the six parishes which make Villaudric. There are 1752 hectares under vine, and in 1996 103,505 hectolitres of light red or rosé wine were produced.

There was a time when the towns of Fronton and Villaudric were deadly enemies. During the Wars of Religion in the sixteenth century Fronton was destroyed, though Villaudric spared. During the siege of Montauban, Louis XIII had his headquarters in one, and his minister Richelieu in the other and they used to send each other complimentary hogsheads of wine. With the expansion of Toulouse in the nineteenth century the wines of neighbouring Fronton enjoyed a boom, and after the restrictions imposed by the Bordelais on *Haut Pays* wines were lifted, they began to be exported abroad. The arrival of phylloxera, though, dealt a deadly blow. The traditional local grape, the Negrette, took badly to its grafted rootstocks, and the region went into decline.

Revival began after the Second World War. A Fronton co-operative was started up in 1947, followed by one at Villaudric two years later – this has since been shut down and its activities transferred to the Fronton co-operative. It is really only since the arrival of *appellation contrôlée* that anyone outside the region has begun to take notice of these wines.

Fronton is based on the Negrette grape, a variety little seen elsewhere. Negrette gives a wine which is abundant in aroma but meagre in tannin and low in acidity. It has a tendency to attenuation and a susceptibility, only overcome recently, to oxidation if harvested by machine. The Negrette accounts for 50 to 70 per cent of the blend. Malbec, Cabernet Sauvignon, Cabernet Franc, Syrah, Gamay, Fer Servadou and others, none of which must individually provide more than 15 to 20 per cent, make up the remainder. At Château Bellevue La Forêt, for example, the blend in principle is made from 57 per cent Negrette, 25 per cent Cabernet Franc and Cabernet Sauvignon and 18 per cent Gamay and Syrah. At Château Flotis, another leading estate, the basic *encépagement* is 50 per cent Negrette, 25 per cent Cabernets and 25 per cent Syrah, while the 'Cuvée Spéciale' is pure Negrette. Château Cahuzac (Ferran Père et Fils) is another good source. Here there is Syrah in the blend. I have also enjoyed the wines of Château Montauriol. Correctly vinified, the wine is an abundantly fruity, supple, aromatic wine without a great deal of tannin. It is bottled early and is intended for drinking cool within eighteen months of bottling. Fronton does not age gracefully: there are other wines for that.

VIN DE LAVILLEDIEU VDQS

The Vins de Lavilledieu come from the extension of the Fronton plateau near the confluence of the rivers Tarn and Garonne. The name of this VDQS comes from La Ville Dieu du Temple, an old centre of the Knights Templar. Production of this Negrette-based wine is tiny (1841 hectolitres in 1988), and is made only by the local co-operative

GAILLAC

Until the time of the phylloxera epidemic at the end of the nineteenth century Gaillac was one of the largest vineyard areas in France. It is also one of the oldest. From the Roman settlements on the coast near Narbonne, only some 120 kilometres away, the vine made its way up the valley of the Aude and across the mountains to the Tarn valley, and found near the ancient city of Albi a rich agricultural land suitable for its cultivation.

Geographically, despite the proximity to the Mediterranean, this is the extreme south-east of the Aquitaine basin. The land is protected from the north, east and south by the *causses* and the Montagne Noir, but open to the west, in the direction of the flow of the river, and the climate is more Atlantic than Mediterranean. Like in Cahors winters and springs can be cool and wet, with an ever-present danger of frost. Come the summer one can sense the nearby presence of the Midi. It is hot and dry, and autumns are long and sweet. The airy, rose-brick city of Albi is one of the loveliest in France. Religious capital and birthplace of Toulouse-Lautrec, Albi is the western gateway to the spectacular Gorges du Tarn. By the time the river Tarn has reached Albi, however, it has thrown off the wildness of its adolescence. It is sedate and expansive and flows through a soft, undulating mixed landscape of cereals, fruit and vegetables. Other crops such as saffron, anis, madder and hemp are also cultivated. Above all, of course, there is the vine.

In 1852 the Gaillac region produced 12,500 hectolitres of white wine and no less than 4.48 million hectolitres of red. There must have been 150,000 hectares under vine at the very least. Today the AC production can hit 120,000 hectolitres in a good year (of which 75 per cent approximately is red), denoting a surface area of perhaps 2400 hectares, though there is additional land given over to a very acceptable Vin de Pays des Côtes du Tarn, which produces approximately 125,000 hectolitres of wine. The vineyard extends over seventy-eight communes west of Albi, a roughly circular area which reaches as far north as Cordes and downstream to beyond Rabastens.

Gaillac comes in a mixture of styles as well as colours and from a wide palette of grape varieties. The red wines are made from Duras and Braucol (the local name for Fer Servadou). These produce wines of body and substance, if on the rustic side. Gamay, Syrah and Negrette are also authorized, and together or singly these five must make up 60 per cent of the blend. Among the subsidiary varieties are Cabernet Sauvignon, Cabernet Franc, Merlot, Jurançon Rouge and others. The white wines are produced from Mauzac (the Blanquette of Limoux), the quaintly named Len de L'El (Lanque d'Oc for 'out of sight'), Muscadelle, Sauvignon Blanc, Sémillon and Ondenc. The Len de L'El must make up 15 per cent of the blend. In practice Mauzac makes up most of the rest and Muscadelle tends to be more important than Sauvignon or Sémillon.

There are both *primeur*-style reds, largely based on Gamay and produced by carbonic maceration, and sturdier wines. The whites range from fairly dry to *moelleux* (Gaillac Premières Côtes is a superior version) and can be still, *perlé* or fully sparkling. These sparkling versions are produced either by the champagne method or by the *méthode gaillaçoise*, a more artisanal technique which involves bottling the wine when it has only partially finished its first fermentation, without the addition of extra sugar. This results in a semi-sweet wine.

There are so many different versions of Gaillac it is hard to come to a view of what exactly it is, or should be, and where it stands within the galaxy of the wines of France. Most popular on the export market is the gently *pétillant* dry white *perlé*, of which one is most likely to see the examples of the co-operatives at Labastide de Levis or Rabastens. Based on the Mauzac grape, and bottled early before all the malolactic fermentation is complete, or with the addition of a jet of carbon dioxide, this is a somewhat anonymous but clean, slightly herbal wine without excessive acidity. It should be drunk within the year.

In the better domaines such as that of Alan Sedder at Château de Mayragues, Jean Cros at Château Larroze, Jacques Auque at Mas Pignou or Jean Albert at the Domaine de Labarthe the wines have rather more personality. The Labarthe still white (they make a *perlé* as well) comes from Sauvignon and Len de L'El. At the Domaine Roucau-Cantemerle, Robert Plageoles produces a wine from 100 per cent Sauvignon and the wine is racy and aromatic. I find these wines, in general, more interesting than the reds.

LIMOUX

Until it makes a right turn at the old walled city of Carcassonne, the river Aude flows north out of the foothills of the Pyrenees. Near the town of Limoux in this upper part of the valley a very curious wine is made. Despite its proximity to the Mediterranean it is regarded as a South-West wine, not one of the Languedoc-Roussillon. Unlike most of the local wines it is white. It is also sparkling. And the locals even claim to have 'invented' the champagne method before Dom Pérignon. The sparkling wine is known as Blanquette de Limoux. Blanquette is the local name for the Mauzac grape, planted also in Gaillac and elsewhere in the South-West. It is thought that the nickname derives from the downy white dust on the underside of the leaves. On its own the Mauzac produces a four-square, somewhat malic wine. Up to 20 per cent Chardonnay and Chenin Blanc are permitted (as Clairette was up to 1978) and these serve to round the wine off and give it more fruit. Nevertheless Vin Nature de Limoux, as this still wine is called, strikes me as rather heavy and acid. The sparkling version is much better.

Some 80 per cent of the local sparkling wine is made by the Limoux co-operative, and very good it can be, especially the superior vintage wines. With a turnover of some eight and a half million bottles this is a very up-to-date establishment, with sixteen Vaslin presses, *giropalettes* for the automatic *remuage* and the wine-making is computer controlled throughout.

The wine has to have a minimum of nine months' ageing before *dégorgement*. Most of the wine is *brut*. It has a distinctive, flowery, herby character all of its own, quite 'un-southern' and surprisingly elegant compared with the still wine. I prefer it to most of the non-champagne-method sparklers of France.

There are a few private domaines or individual merchants. Maison Guinot, founded in 1875, is one of the oldest, as well as one of the most serious. Their Crémant Impérial is a five-year-old wine, made from 80 per cent Mauzac and 20 per cent Chardonnay. Domaine Robert at Preusse and Domaine Les Terres Blanches (Eric and Christine Vialade) can also be recommended. The region produced 54,404 hectolitres plus 2092 hectolitres of still wine in 1996 from 1194 hectares.

MARCILLAC VDQS, ESTAING VDQS and ENTRAYGUES ET DU FEL VDQS

Three of the most isolated and obscure French country wines are to be found north of Rodez, capital of the *département* of Aveyron. Further north still lies the Auvergne, but there are no vines here until Clermont-Ferrand and the wines of the Upper Loire (*see page 195*). Gaillac and Cahors are equally far away to the south and west. Why has wine-making persisted here? Indeed why is the local wine honoured with VDQS? This is a wild and rugged countryside of gorges and ravines, of thickly wooded hillsides and exposed limestone *causses*. It is not a promising terrain for the vine.

Marcillac lies in a sheltered, enclosed amphitheatre called Le Vallon. The wine is mainly red (there is a little rosé) and largely made from Fer Servadou (locally known as the Mansoi). The grapes are vinified with the stalks and the wine is rough and tannic. There are about 109 hectares of vines scattered over eleven communes with red sandstone and marly soil. In 1996 it produced 6490 hectolitres of wine. The co-operative at Valady is the principal source. Monsieur Laurens-Teulier at the Cros de Cassagnes is one of the few local growers to sell his wine in bottle. As this book goes to press (January 1990) the INAO has proposed the elevation of Marcillac from VDQS to AC. The official legislation has not yet been passed.

The production of Estaing is even smaller, less than one-tenth of Marcillac. The red wine is a mixture of Fer Servadou and Gamay, the white comes primarily from Chenin. The only grower I have ever come across in Pierre Rieu at Le Viala. In 1996 production of red and rosé wine amounted to 384 hectolitres and 55 of white.

Nearby, also in the valley of the upper Lot, is the attractive little town of Entraygues. Production is similarly tiny. I have again only encountered the wine of one grower, Jean-Marc Viguier. From his 3 hectares of vineyards he produces a white made exclusively from Chenin, a rosé from Cabernet and Negrette and a red from one-third each Gamay, Fer Servadou (Mansoi) and Cabernet. In 1996 only 650 hectolitres of red and rosé were produced and 205 of white.

VINS DE PAYS

Here is a full list of the *vins de pays* in the South-West.

Regional *vin de pays*	Vin de Pays du Comté Tolosan
Departmental *vin de pays*	Dordogne, Haute-Garonne, Landes, Pyrénées-Atlantiques and Tarn-et-Garonne.
Zonal vins de pays AVEYRON	Gorges et Côtes de Millau.
GERS	Côtes de Gascogne, Côtes de Montestruc, Côtes du Condomois.

Zonal vins de pays (continued)

HAUTE-GARONNE	Saint-Sardos (part Tarn-et-Garonne)
HAUTES-PYRÉNÉES	Bigorre
LANDES	Terroirs Landais
LOT	Coteaux de Glanes, Coteaux du Quercy (part Tarn-et-Garonne)
LOT-ET-GARONNE	Agenais
TARN	Côtes du Condomois (part Gers), Côtes du Tarn, Thézac-Perricard
TARN-ET-GARONNE	Coteaux du Quercy (part Lot), Saint-Sardos (part Haute-Garonne), Coteaux et Terrasses de Montauban

With the exception of Côtes de Gascogne these wines are mainly red. All the wines are based on the local *appellation contrôlée* and VDQS grape varieties. These are simple wines, best consumed soon after bottling. I have seen few – again with the exception of Côtes de Gascogne – on the export market.

VIN DE PAYS DES CÔTES DE GASCOGNE

There are a large number of *vins de pays* in the South-West but of these the one which is the most widely seen is Côtes de Gascogne, which can be roughly translated as the Armagnac country. This is the undistilled base white wine of the region, largely produced from Ugni Blanc and Colombard and it is one of the best of the lesser, inexpensive wines of France. The wine is light, dry, crisp and fruity and fairly high in acidity, especially if made solely from Ugni. Colombard softens the Ugni and brings out the fruit. The Union des Producteurs de Plaimont is an important source and Alain Lalanne at Ramonzans is another reputable grower, but in my view better still is the wine of Yves Grassa at Eauze. His *vins de pays* appear under a large number of individual domaine names (Tariquet, Rieux, Escombes, Planterieu, Pouy, Pajot, Cap de Bosc, Jalousie and Prada, for instance) and some 150,000 cases are produced a year. It's all the same wine. Five years ago he started vinifying and maturing some of the wine in new wood. This 'Cuvée Bois' is a wine of great interest, with a depth of character and an oaky underpinning which give it an unexpected amount of class. It is well worth seeking out.

APPENDIX ONE

FRENCH WINE PRODUCTION AND SURFACE AREA (1996 HARVEST)

	Production '000 hectolitres	Hectares
Appellation contrôlee	20,346	376,904
VDQS	680	12,701
Total	21,036	3,009,605

APPENDIX TWO

SURFACE AREA UNDER VINE (1996 HARVEST)

	AC	VDQS	Total hectares
ALSACE AND EASTERN FRANCE	14,256	114	14,370
BORDEAUX	112,217	—	112,217
BURGUNDY	47,118	99	48,117
CHAMPAGNE	30,717	—	30,717
JURA, SAVOIE	3591	456	4047
LANGUEDOC-ROUSSILLON	68,802	915	69,717
LOIRE VALLEY	46,145	5789	51,932
PROVENCE/CORSICA	26,456	1737	28,193
RHÔNE VALLEY	72,588	954	73,542
SOUTH-WEST	27,902	2640	30,542
Total			
Surface area 1988	376,904	12,701	387,605

1996 HARVEST REGIONAL BREAKDOWN

APPELLATION CONTRÔLÉE AND VDQS		Production '000 hectolitres			Percentage
		RED & ROSÉ	WHITE	TOTAL	of total
ALSACE AND EASTERN FRANCE	AC	108	1064	1172	
	VDQS	(340 hl)	1	1	
	Total	108	1065	1173	4.4
BORDEAUX	AC	5434	980	6414	26.1
BURGUNDY	AC	2020	777	2797	
	VDQS	—	6	6	
	Total	2020	783	2013	8.2
CHAMPAGNE	AC	(618 hl)	2006	2007	8.2
JURA, SAVOIE	AC	74	155	229	
	VDQS	12	14 26		
	Total	86	169	255	0.1
LANGUEDOC-ROUSSILLON	AC and VDN	2074	531	2605	
	VDQS	43	—	43	
	Total	2117	531	2648	10.8
LOIRE VALLEY	AC	1115	1439	2594	
	VDQS	124	328	452	
	Total	1279	1747	3026	12.3
PROVENCE/CORSICA	AC	1148	54	1202	
	VDQS	61	2	63	
	Total	1209	56	1263	8.8
RHÔNE VALLEY	AC	3176	190	3366	
	VDQS	42	2	44	
	Total	3218	192	3410	13.7
SOUTH-WEST	AC	908	515	1423	
	VDQS	151	11	162	
	Total	1059	526	1585	6.4
Total		16,098	7771	2809	
Total		433	364	797	
Grand Total		16,531	8075	2606	
		66%	33%	100%	

APPENDIX FOUR

1988 Harvest Regional Breakdown

Vins de Pays	RED & ROSÉ '000 hectolitres (%)	WHITE '000 hectolitres (%)	TOTAL '000 hectolitres (%)
LANGUEDOC-ROUSSILLON	8222 (80.7)	580 (49.8)	8802 (77.5)
PROVENCE, SOUTHERN RHÔNE	869 (8.5)	105 (9.0)	973 (8.6)
LOIRE VALLEY	328 (3.2)	169 (14.5)	497 (4.4)
SOUTH-WEST	11 (2.1)	223 (10.1)	434 (3.8)
ALPES, PAYS RHODANIENS	328 (3.2)	23 (1.9)	350 (3.1)
CORSICA	203 (2.0)	13 (1.1)	216 (1.9)
AQUITAINE, CHARENTES	25 (0.2)	50 (4.3)	75 (0.6)
RÉGIONS DE L'EST	2 (0.1)	3 (0.3)	5 (0.1)
Total	10,187 (100%)	1164 (100%)	11,351 (100%)

1988 Vins de Pays Production Summary

	'000 hectolitres (%)
RED & ROSÉ WINES	10,187 (89.7)
WHITE WINES	1164 (10.3)
Total	11,351 (100%)

APPENDIX FIVE

VINS DE PAYS

Regional vins de pays
Languedoc :   Vin de Pays d'Oc
South-West :   Vin de Pays du Comté Tolosan
Loire Valley: Vin de Pays du Jardin de la France

Departmental vins de pays
Vins de Pays followed by the name of the *département*: Ain, Alpes-de-Haute-Provence, Alpes-Maritimes, Ardèche, Aude, Bouches-du-Rhône, Cher, Côtes d'Or, Deux-Sèvres, Dordogne, Drôme, Gard, Gironde, Haute-Garonne, Hérault, Indre, Indre-et-Loire, Landes, Loire-Atlantique, Loir-et-Cher, Loiret, Maine-et-Loire, Meuse, Nièvre, Puy-de-Dôme, Pyrénées-Atlantiques, Pyrénées-Orientales, Sarthe, Tarn-et-Garonne, Vaucluse, Var, Vendée, Vienne, Yonne.

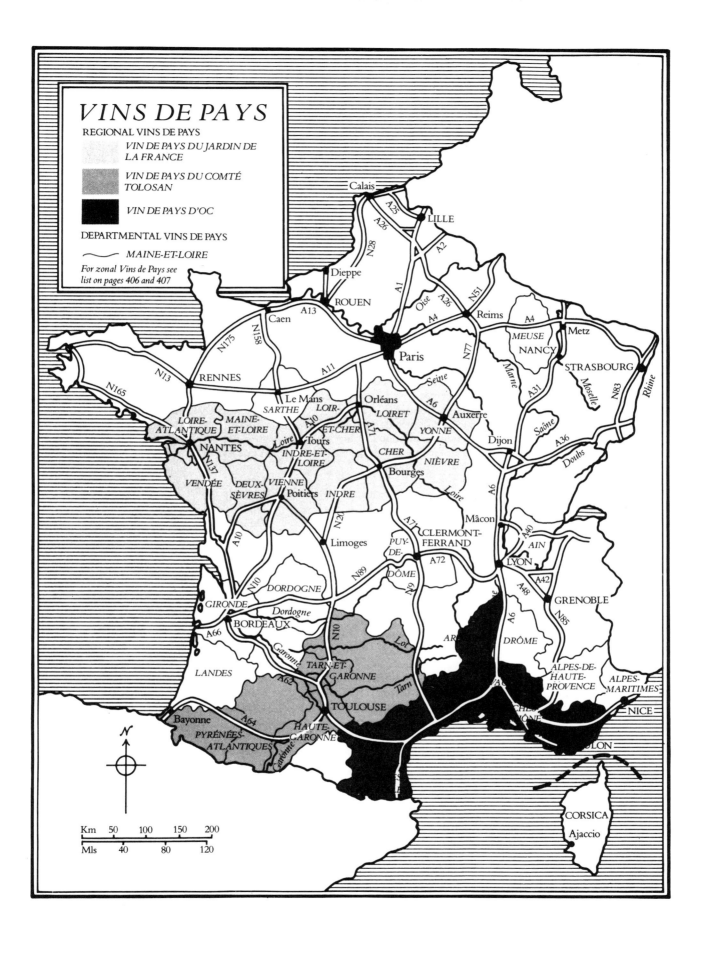

VINS DE PAYS

REGIONAL VINS DE PAYS

VIN DE PAYS DU JARDIN DE LA FRANCE

VIN DE PAYS DU COMTÉ TOLOSAN

VIN DE PAYS D'OC

DEPARTMENTAL VINS DE PAYS

MAINE-ET-LOIRE

For zonal Vins de Pays see list on pages 406 and 407

Calais

LILLE

Dieppe

ROUEN

Caen

Reims

Metz

MEUSE

NANCY

Paris

STRASBOURG

RENNES

Le Mans

Orléans

SARTHE

LOIR-ET-CHER

LOIRET

Auxerre

LOIRE-ATLANTIQUE

MAINE-ET-LOIRE

Tours

YONNE

Dijon

NANTES

INDRE-ET-LOIRE

CHER

NIÈVRE

VENDÉE

DEUX-SÈVRES

VIENNE

Poitiers

INDRE

Bourges

Mâcon

Limoges

PUY-DE-DÔME

CLERMONT-FERRAND

LYON

AIN

DORDOGNE

GRENOBLE

GIRONDE

Dordogne

DRÔME

BORDEAUX

ALPES-DE-HAUTE-PROVENCE

ALPES-MARITIMES

LANDES

TARN-ET-GARONNE

Garonne

TOULOUSE

NICE

Bayonne

HAUTE-GARONNE

PYRÉNÉES-ATLANTIQUES

N

CORSICA

Ajaccio

Km 50 100 150 200

Mls 40 80 120

Zonal vins de pays

Name	Département
Vins de Pays Catalan	Pyrénées-Orientales
Vins de Pays Charentais	Charente et Charente-Maritime
Vins de Pays d'Argens	Var
Vins de Pays d'Urfé	Loire
Vins de Pays d'Allobrogie	Ain, Savoie, Haute-Savoie
Vins de Pays de Bessan	Hérault
Vins de Pays de Bigorre	Hautes-Pyrénées
Vins de Pays de Cassan	Hérault
Vins de Pays de Caux	Hérault
Vins de Pays de Cessenon	Hérault
Vins de Pays de Cucugnan	Aude
Vins de Pays de Franche Comté	Haute-Saône, Jura
Vins de Pays de Hauterive en Pays d'Aude	Aude
Vins de Pays de l'Agenais	Lot-et-Garonne
Vins de Pays de l'Ardailhou	Hérault
Vins de Pays de l'Île de Beauté	Corse
Vins de Pays de l'Uzège	Gard
Vins de Pays de la Bénovie	Hérault
Vins de Pays de la Côte Vermeille	Pyrénées-Orientales
Vins de Pays de la Haute-Vallée de l'Aude	Aude
Vins de Pays de la Haute-Vallée de l'Orb	Hérault
Vins de Pays de la Principauté d'Orange	Vaucluse
Vins de Pays de la Vallée du Paradis	Aude
Vins de Pays de la Vaunage	Gard
Vins de Pays de la Vicomté d'Aumelas	Hérault
Vins de Pays de la Vistrenque	Gard
Vins de Pays de Petite Crau	Bouches-du-Rhône
Vins de Pays de Pézenas	Hérault
Vins de Pays de Retz	Loire-Atlantique, Vendée
Vins de Pays de Saint-Sardos	Haute-Garonne, Tarn-et-Garonne
Vins de Pays de Thézac-Perricard	Lot-et-Garonne
Vins de Pays des Balmes Dauphinoises	Isère
Vins de Pays des Collines de la Moure	Hérault
Vins de Pays des Collines Rhodaniennes	Ardèche, Drôme, Isère, Loire, Rhône
Vins de Pays des Coteaux Charitois	Nièvre
Vins de Pays des Coteaux Cévenols	Gard
Vins de Pays des Coteaux d'Ensérune	Hérault
Vins de Pays des Coteaux de Bessilles	Hérault
Vins de Pays des Coteaux de Cèze	Gard
Vins de Pays des Coteaux de Fontcaude	Hérault
Vins de Pays des Coteaux de Glanes	Lot
Vins de Pays des Coteaux de l'Ardèche	Ardèche
Vins de Pays des Coteaux de la Cabrerisse	Aude
Vins de Pays des Coteaux de la Cité de Carcassonne	Aude
Vins de Pays des Coteaux de Laurens	Hérault
Vins de Pays des Coteaux de Miramont	Aude
Vins de Pays des Coteaux de Murviel	Hérault
Vins de Pays des Coteaux de Narbonne	Aude
Vins de Pays des Coteaux de Peyriac	Aude, Hérault
Vins de Pays des Coteaux de Baronnies	Drôme
Vins de Pays des Coteaux des Fenouillèdes	Pyrénées-Orientales
Vins de Pays des Coteaux du Cher et de l'Arnon	Cher, Indre

Zonal vins de pays

Name	*Département*
Vins de Pays des Coteaux du Grésivaudan	Isère, Savoie
Vins de Pays des Coteaux du Libron	Hérault
Vins de Pays des Coteaux du Littoral Audois	Aude
Vins de Pays des Coteaux du Lézignanais	Aude
Vins de Pays des Coteaux du Pont du Gard	Gard
Vins de Pays des Coteaux du Quercy	Lot, Tarn-et-Garonne
Vins de Pays des Coteaux du Salagou	Hérault
Vins de Pays des Coteaux du Salavès	Gard
Vins de Pays des Coteaux du Termenes	Aude
Vins de Pays des Coteaux et Terrasses de Montauban	Tarn-et-Garonne
Vins de Pays des Coteaux Flaviens	Gard
Vins de Pays des Côtes Catalanes	Pyrénées-Orientales
Vins de Pays des Côtes de Gascogne	Gers
Vins de Pays des Côtes de Lastours	Aude
Vins de Pays des Côtes de Montestruc	Gers
Vins de Pays des Côtes de Perignan	Aude
Vins de Pays des Côtes de Prouille	Aude
Vins de Pays des Côtes de Thau	Hérault
Vins de Pays des Côtes de Thongue	Hérault
Vins de Pays des Côtes du Brian	Hérault
Vins de Pays des Côtes du Ceressou	Hérault
Vins de Pays des Côtes du Condomois	Gers, Lot-et-Garonne
Vins de Pays des Côtes du Tarn	Tarn
Vins de Pays des Côtes du Vidourle	Gard
Vins de Pays des Gorges de l'Hérault	Hérault
Vins de Pays des Gorges et Côtes de Millau	Aveyron
Vins de Pays des Hauts de Badens	Aude
Vins de Pays des Marches de Bretagne	Loire-Atlantique, Maine-et-Loire, Vendée
Vins de Pays des Maures	Var
Vins de Pays des Monts de la Grage	Hérault
Vins de Pays des Sables du Golfe du Lion	Hérault, Gard, Bouches-du-Rhône
Vins de Pays des Terroirs Landais	Landes
Vins de Pays des Vals d'Agly	Pyrénées-Orientales
Vins de Pays du Bourbonnais	Allier
Vins de Pays du Bérange	Hérault
Vins de Pays du Comté de Grignan	Drôme
Vins de Pays du Mont Baudile	Hérault
Vins de Pays du Mont Bouquet	Gard
Vins de Pays du Mont Caume	Var
Vins de Pays du Serre de Coiran (changed in 1989 to Vin de Pays des Côtes de Libac)	Gard
Vins de Pays du Torgan	Aude
Vins de Pays du Val d'Orbieu	Aude
Vins de Pays du Val de Cesse	Aude
Vins de Pays du Val de Dagne	Aude
Vins de Pays du Val de Montferrand	Hérault, Gard

GLOSSARY

Acid, acidity Essential constituent of a wine (though not in excess!). Gives zip and freshness and contributes to the balance and length on the palate.

Appellation d'origine contrôlée Often abbreviated to AOC or AC. French legislative term referring to the top category of quality wines and the controls surrounding their production.

Aroma The smell or 'nose' of a wine.

Aromatic Flavours/constituents of smell: more than just the grape variety.

Astringent Dry taste and finish of a wine which has lost some of its fruit.

Backbone Structure, implying body and grip.

Baked Slightly burned flavour resulting from a very hot dry vintage.

Balance The harmony of a wine; its balance between body, fruit, alcohol and acidity.

Bien national Term given to the estates sequestered and then sold by the state at the time of the French Revolution.

Bitter Self-explanatory, but if not in excess, not necessarily a bad thing in an immature claret.

Blackcurrants Said to be the characteristic fruit taste of Cabernet Sauvignon.

Blanc de Blancs White wine made from white grapes only.

Body The 'stuffing' or weight of a wine.

Botrytis cinerea A fungus which attacks grapes and which can cause 'noble rot' in certain climatic conditions. Noble rot is responsible for the wines of Sauternes and elsewhere.

Bouquet The smell or 'nose' of a wine. A term used for mature wine.

Brut Very dry.

Calcaire French for limestone.

Canton 'County', an administrative district within a *département*.

Cépage French for vine variety. *Cépage améliorateur* refers to a 'noble' or better grape variety.

Chapeau The 'cap' of accumulation of grape skins etc. which tends to rise to the top of the must during fermentation.

Chaptalization Addition of sugar to the must with a view to increasing the eventual alcoholic content of the wine.

Charater The depth or complexity of a wine.

Château The country house or villa of a wine estate.

Climat A vineyard in Burgundy.

Clos Originally an enclosed vineyard within a wall.

Coarse A wine lacking finesse and possibly not very well made.

Comité Interprofessionnel Professional organization, representing wine growers or promoting the wines of a region.

Code Napoléon French law of succession abolishing primogeniture.

Commune French for parish.

Côte and *coteau* French for slope.

Coulure Failure of a vine's flowers to set into grapes. Results from poor, humid weather during the flowering.

Creamy A richness and concentration in a wine's character and flavour as a result of old vines.

Cru French term for 'growth', or vineyard or the vines thereof.

Cru classé Officially classed growth.

Cuvasion The length of time a red wine must macerates with the skins.

Cuve French term for wine vat.

Cuvée The contents of a wine vat; used to denote a blend or particular parcel of wine.

Département French administrative area, equivalent to an English county.

Deuxième marque or *second wine* The produce of less mature vines or less good vines.

Domaine A wine property or estate.

Doux Sweet.

Dry Opposite of sweet. Sometimes, when used of wine, indicates a lack of fruit.

Dumb Used for an immature wine which has character but which is still undeveloped.

Earthy Character deriving from the nature of the soil. Not always a pejorative expression.

Élevage Literally the 'rearing'. In wine used to denote the length of time and processes undergone between vinification and bottling.

Encépagement Proportion of grape varieties.

En primeur Sale of the young wine within the first few months of the harvest.

Fat Full in the sense of high in glycerine, ripeness and extract.

Finish The 'conclusion' of the taste of a wine.

First growth or *premier cru* In Bordeaux the top wines in a classification. In Burgundy, however, it refers to the second category of wines after great growth or *grand cru*.

Flat Dull, lacking in zip of acidity.

Floraison Flowering of the vine.

Foudre Large oak vat.

Full-bodied Ample body. High in extract and probably alcohol and tannin.

Goût de terroir Earthy, though not necessarily in a pejorative sense. Denoting literally a 'taste of soil'.

Grand cru 'Great Growth'; without the qualification *classé* it need not necessarily mean anything.

Grand cru classé 'Classed great growth'; a term used in the official classifications of Graves and Saint-Émilion. Also used for the top vineyards in Burgundy.

Grand vin The first wine, i.e. product or wine which will eventually be bottled under the château or domaine name. Can also be used, of course, in its literal, complimentary sense.

Gris Literally 'grey', but in a wine sense means a rosé.

Guyot A system of long-cane pruning.

Hard Firmness of an immature wine normally denoting plenty of body, tannin and acidity as yet unmellowed.

Harsh Similar to hard but in a fiery way, and perhaps to excess.

Heavy Denoting a full, alcoholic wine; could be used where it is rather too full-bodied, perhaps out of balance and 'stewed'.

Hectare International measure of area; equivalent to 2.471 acres.

Hectolitre International measure of capacity; 100 litres equivalent to 11 cases of wine or 22 Imperial gallons.

Hogshead English name for the traditional Bordeaux barrel or *barrique*, holding 49.5 Imperial gallons or 225 litres.

Institut National des Appellations d'Origine or *INAO* French government body which legislates vine-growing and wine-making controls.

Lees Sediment or deposit of dead yeast cells, tartrate crystals, etc. which settles out of a wine.

Lieu-dit A place-name.

Liquoreux Luscious, very sweet indeed.

Meaty Full, rich, fat wine, normally used of a wine still young, with a tannic grip – almost a chewable quality.

Mellow Round, soft, mature – used for a wine no longer hard, firm or harsh.

Mildew A cryptogamic or fungus disease of the vine. Also known as 'downy' mildew. Counteracted by the application of copper sulphate solution.

Millerandage Shot berries; as a result of poor flowering some of the berries fail to develop.

Millésime Vintage year.

Moelleux Medium-sweet, literally 'mellow'.

Must Grape juice which has not yet fully fermented out and become wine.

Négoce A collective term for the wine trade or merchants.

Négociant A wine merchant.

Noble rot See *Botrytis cinerea.*

Oenology The science of wine and wine-making.

Oidium 'Powdery' mildew. A cryptogamic or fungus disease of the vine. Counteracted by the application of sulphur.

Oxidized Flat, tired taint in a wine which has at some time had excessive exposure to air.

Pétillant Slightly sparkling.

Phylloxera A parasitic disease of the vine caused by a member of the aphid family. The problem is held at bay by grafting European vines onto phylloxera-resistant American rootstocks.

Pourriture grise 'Grey rot' caused by the same fungus responsible for 'noble rot' in Sauternes and elsewhere, but occurring in wet, humid weather.

Pourriture noble French for 'noble rot'. See *Botrytis cinerea.*

Premier cru (classé) First (classed) growth. See *First growth.*

Rancio A fortified wine that has been deliberately allowed to oxidize.

Récolte Harvest.

Remuage The shaking down of the deposit formed by the second fermentation in the champagne method of producing sparkling wines.

Réserve Specially selected superior *cuvée* created by some properties. It has no legal meaning.

Rich For red wines, not an indication of sweetness but rather a combination of fullness of body, abundance of ripe fruit, extract and probably alcohol.

Ripe The result and confirmation of healthy fruit picked in a ripe condition, giving richness and fullness of flavour to a wine.

Rootstock The American base vine on to which European vines have been grafted since the phylloxera epidemic.

Stalky A 'green', rather raw, possibly stewed flavour particularly noticeable in young wine. Can derive from over-long maceration with the stalks.

Tannin An essential constituent of young red wine. An acid deriving from the skins of the grape which leaves an astringent, chewy taste in the mouth. Adds to the weight of the wine. Broken down and mellowed by ageing.

Tartaric acid Natural acid in grapes and the base by which the acidity is measured.

Tête de cuvée Literally the juice of the first pressing, and therefore the best, and used as such in champagne. Elsewhere it indicates the grower's best wine.

Tonneau A larger wooden barrel or vat which can be used for both vinification and storage. Also the measure of production of a Bordeaux estate.

Ullage The gap of air between the cork and the wine in a bottle. On ullage means the wine left in a partially consumed bottle.

Vendange Harvest.

Vignoble Vineyard area.

Vin de garde A wine made for keeping, which is capable of improving in bottle.

Vin délimité de qualité supérieure or *VDQS* The second category of quality wines after *appellation contrôlée.*

Vin de pays French country wine. A superior *vin de table.*

Vin de table Table wine. The lowest category of French wine.

Viniculture Everything to do with the production of wine.

Vinification The process of wine-making.

Vintage The year of the harvest.

Viticulture Everything to do with the growing of vines.

BIBLIOGRAPHY

The following is a short list of recommended titles published recently on the wines of France.

GENERAL

Johnson, Hugh and Duijker, Hubrecht *The Wine Atlas of France and Traveller's Guide to the Vineyards*, Mitchell Beazley, London 1987.

Lichine, Alexis *Guide to the Wines and Vineyards of France*, Papermac, London 1986.

Spurrier, Steven *The Académie du Vin Guide to French Wines*, Willow Books, London 1986.

Stevenson, Tom *Sotheby's World Wine Encyclopedia*, Dorling Kindersley, London 1988.

Sutcliffe MW, Serena *The Wines of France*, Futura, London 1985.

BORDEAUX

Bolter, William *The White Wines of Bordeaux*, Octopus, London 1988.

Coates MW, Clive *Claret*, Century, London 1982.

Duijker, Hubrecht *The Great Wine Châteaux of Bordeaux*, Mitchell Beazley, London 1988; *The Good Wines of Bordeaux*, Mitchell Beazley, London 1983.

Penning-Rowsell, Edmund *The Wines of Bordeaux*, Penguin, London 1989.

Peppercorn MW, David *The Pocket Guide to the Wines of Bordeaux*, Mitchell Beazley, London. 1986; *Bordeaux*, Faber, London 1990.

Vandyke Price, Pamela *The Wines of the Graves*, Sotheby's Publications, London 1988.

BURGUNDY

Arlott, John and Fielden, Christopher *Burgundy, Vines and Wines*, Davis-Poynter, London 1976.

Duijker, Hubrecht *The Wines of Burgundy*, Mitchell Beazley, London 1983.

Fielden, Christopher *White Burgundy*, Helm, Bromley 1988.

George MW, Rosemary *The Wines of Chablis*, Sotheby's Publications, London 1984.

Ginestet, Bernard *Chablis*, Nathan, Paris 1986.

Hanson MW, Anthony *Burgundy*, Faber, London 1982.

Sutcliffe MW, Serena *The Pocket Guide to the Wines of Burgundy*, Mitchell Beazley, London 1986.

THE RHÔNE VALLEY AND PROVENCE

Hallgarten, Peter *Century Companion to the Wines of the Rhône*, Century, London 1980.

Livingstone-Learmonth, John and Master, Melvyn *The Wines of the Rhône*, Faber, London 1983.

Parker, Robert *The Wines of the Rhône Valley and Provence*, Dorling Kindersley, London 1988

THE LOIRE VALLEY, CHAMPAGNE AND ALSACE

Berry, Liz *The Wines of Alsace*, Bodley Head, London 1989

Duijker, Hubrecht *The Wines of the Loire, Champagne and Alsace*, Mitchell Beazley, London 1983.

Forbes, Patrick *Champagne*, Gollancz, London 1967. (Despite being published over twenty years ago this is still indispensable.)

Stevenson, Tom *Champagne*, Sotheby's Publications, London 1986.

Sutcliffe MW, Serena *A Celebration of Champagne*, Mitchell Beazley, London 1988.

Vandyke Price, Pamela with Christopher Fielden *Alsace Wines*, Sotheby's Publications, London, 1984.

THE REST OF FRANCE

George MW, Rosemary *French Country Wines*, Faber, London 1990.

INDEX